NORTH EAST INDIA

About the Editor

Dr. Manis Kumar Raha, M.Sc., Ph.D. (b.1937) got his degrees from the University of Calcutta. He joined Cultural Research Institute, Government of West Bengal and served it till 1970. He joined Anthropological Survey of India, Government of India in 1970 and served this organization in different capacities till January 1995. In 1981 he completed a course on Management Development Programme from Indian Institute of Management, Joka, Kolkata. In January 1995, he retired from Anthropological Survey of India as Joint Director. During his service tenure he undertook anthropological research among both tribal and non-tribal people of West Bengal, Jammu and Kashmir, Himachal Pradesh, Uttarakhand, Andaman and Nicobar Islands, Madhya Pradesh and Sikkim. He is still continuing his research work. He was elected as the President, Anthropology and Archaeology Section of 83rd Indian Science Congress in 1996. He was the paper setter, examiner and moderator of P.G. and M.Phil. Classes of different universities and also Ph.D. Guide and examiner. He was editor and also in editorial board of different scientific journals and also Visiting Fellow of Dibrugarh University, Assam and Rajib Gandhi University, Itanagar, Arunachal Pradesh. He is the Life Member of different academic organizations and served many of these in different capacities. He has already written or edited 30 books, written over 200 articles and over 140 book reviews.

NORTH EAST INDIA

The Human Landscape

Edited by

MANIS KUMAR RAHA

CONCEPT PUBLISHING COMPANY PVT. LTD.
NEW DELHI-110059

ISBN-13 : 978-93-5125-047-0

First Published 2014

Published and Printed by

Concept
Since 1974

Concept Publishing Company Pvt. Ltd.
A/15-16, Commercial Block, Mohan Garden
New Delhi-110059 (India)
T: 25351460, 25351794, *F*: 091-11-25357109
E: publishing@conceptpub.com, W: www.conceptpub.com
Editorial Office: H-13, Bali Nagar, New Delhi-110 015, India.

Cataloging in Publication Data—*Courtesy:* D.K. Agencies (P) Ltd. <docinfo@dkagencies.com>

North East India : the human landscape / edited by Manis Kumar Raha.
p. cm.
Contributed articles.
Includes bibliographical references and index.
ISBN 9789351250470

1. India, Northeastern—Economic conditions. 2. India, Northeastern—Social conditions. 3. Ethnology—India, Northeastern. I. Raha, Manis Kumar.

DDC 330.9541 23

To my friends
Dipak, Parimal, Asit, Pijus, Rupen
and
Viswanathan (Rambabu)
and
In memory of my friends
Aloke, Kishor, Sunil, Kamal, Arun and Mukul
who are no longer on this beautiful Earth.

Preface

My first book on North East India entitled, ***North-East India: The Human Interface*** which I edited along with my friend, Late Prof. Aloke Kumar Ghosh, was published in 1997 and its new edition was published in 2008. Since then I kept myself busy with other publications, research work and some other jobs. In the beginning of the second quarters of 2011 I started thinking to edit another book on North-East India, the region which is ethnicwise and culturally one of the most interesting and attractive places in India. On finalizing the theme I started requesting eminent academicians and scholars for their contribution. Most of these learned and experienced academicians and scholars are either staying for a long period in this region or belong to one of the states of this region. They have long research experience on the people of this region and are also keeping good relation with the people there. Others, who live outside North-East India, also have good research experience and knowledge about the land and people of different states of North-East India. In response to my request I got an overwhelming response from most of those academicians and scholars. They belong to different disciplines like Anthropology, Sociology, Tribal Studies, Geography, History, and Economics. At first I thought of editing a book on livelihood pattern, resource utilization and survival strategy of the people of North East India, but the response of the contributors compelled me to broaden the theme of my book. I am really highly impressed of the response I got from them, and for which I am truly grateful to all of them. And this book is the out come of this exercise.

North-East India with its rich natural diversities and resources attracted and still attracts people from different parts of India, and other places even across the border. They settled on the virgin soil of this region alongside the indigenous people there. This helped in the formation of greater diversities of socio-cultural and bio-genetical aspects of life of the people there. Naturally these ethnic, socio-cultural and bio-genetical diversities have attracted the attention of social scientists including social anthropologists, bio-geneticists, physical anthropologists and others since long. Many of them studied and are still studying the people there, both tribal as well as non-tribal. Even then many of the ethnic groups have not been studied yet, and so, very little is known about them. Therefore, more and more studies among different people of this part of India are essential as these will definitely help in understanding these people and also understanding the problems these people there are facing. And the knowledge about them and their problems at the same time, will surely help the planners to formulate the development plans properly and the administrators to put these in action.

Apart from many academicians and scholars of both Indian and foreign, who have keen interest on the land, people and the environment of North-East India, even the common people, also show interest to have some general idea about the region and its people. So this publication on North-East India will surely help all of them who want to know something more about North-East India and its inhabitants and the environment, and therefore, their knowledge will definitely be enriched.

Manis Kumar Raha

Acknowedgements

From the beginning to the finalization of this book, I got much encouragement from my friend, Sri Sarajit Kumar Chatterjee, IPS (Retd.). He is a great scholar and has vast knowledge about North East India. I am really grateful to him. I am also thankful to Dr. Satyabrata Chakraborty, Sri Kanchan Mukhopadhyay, Dr. Debashis Basu, Dr. Goutam Kumar Bera and Prof. Sarit Kumar Chowdhury. They have given me name of different academicians and scholars who could contribute papers in this book. I requested many of them, and many of them have contributed papers in this book. I would never forget the response I got from the contributors of this book who on my request, contributed articles in this book. Without their help and cooperation I could not have published this edited volume. I gratefully acknowledge their kind help and cooperation. Sri Mantu Ram Das and Sri Khudiram Bag have helped me immensely from the very beginning in typing some of the articles and correcting the edited articles through their computers. They did the same in case of my earlier books also. I am grateful to them. I must express my gratitude to Mr. Ashok Kumar Mittal and all the staff members of Concept Publishing Company (P) Ltd.), New Delhi for publishing this book on North-East India. Mr. Ashok Kumar Mittal has always come forward to help me with books and also encouraged me to continue my writing habit. I am really grateful to him. My elder sister, Hashi De has always cleared the burdens those could cause hindrance against my academic exercise. I express my deep sense of gratitude to her. Finally, I have no hesitation to express my gratefulness to all the people of North-East India because their help and cooperation only have enabled the contributors of my book to write articles for my book, and I have been able to publish this volume.

Contents

PART TWO
SOCIAL LANDSCAPE

Contributors

Akhuan Gangmei, Research Scholar, Department of Anthropology, Manipur University, Manipur.

Prof. Amitava Mitra, Professor, Department of Economics, Rajib Gandhi University , Itanagar, Arunachal Pradesh.

Arundhati Phukan Gogoi, Scholar, Department of Anthropology, Dibrugarh University, Dibrugarh, Assam.

Dr. Debashis Basu, Research Associate, Anthropological Survey of India, Govt. of India, Kolkata.

Deblina Biswas, Research Scholar, Department of Anthropology, Dibrugarh University, Dibrugarh, Assam.

Dr. Deepanajana Dutta Das, Associate Professor, Department of Anthropology, Dibrugarh University, Dibrugarh, Assam.

Dr. Dilip Kumar Bhuyan, Assistant Professor, Kherajkhat College, Lakhimpur, Assam.

Dipa Patir, PhD. Student, Department of Anthropology, Dibrugarh University, Dibrugarh, Assam.

Dr. Gadadhara Mohapatra, Assistant Professor, Department of Sociology, Tripura University, Tripura.

Dr. Goutam Bera, Assistant Director, Census Operation Office of the Registrar General, Govt. of India, Kolkata. Earlier in Anthropological Survey of India, Kolkata.

Prof. Indira Barua, Former Professor, Department of Anthropology, and at present UGC Emeritus Fellow, Dibrugarh University, Dibrugarh, Assam.

Prof. J. J. Roy Burman, Professor, Centre for Social Exclusion and Inclusive Policies, Tata Institute of Social Science, Mumbai.

Father K. Jose, Director, Sanskriti, North Eastern Institute of Culture and Religion, Guwahati, Assam.

Kaju Nath, Research Scholar, Department of Economics, Rajib Gandhi University, Itanagar, Arunachal Pradesh.

Prof. Lipi Ghosh, Professor, Department of South and South East Asian Studies, University of Calcutta and Director, Centre for South and South East Asian Studies, Kolkata.

Prof. Lucy Zehal, Associate Professor, Department of Anthropology, North-East Hill University (NEHU), Shillong, Meghalaya.

Dr. M. C. Arunkumar, Associate Professor, Department of Anthropology, Manipur University, Manipur.

Dr. M. K. Raha, Former Joint Director, Anthropological Survey of India, Govt. of India, Kolkata.

Dr. Manoj Kumar Singh, Assistant Professor, Department of Economics, Nagaland University, Nagaland.

Dr. Mita Sarkar, Research Associate, Indira Gandhi Centre for National Integration, Viswa Bharati, West Bengal.

Dr. Mithilesh Kumar Sinha, Associate Professor, Department of Economics, Nagaland University, Nagaland.

Molly Kaniampadickal, Deputy Director, Don Bosco Institute, Jaipur, Guwahati, Assam.

Prof. Nitul Gogoi, Professor, Department of Anthropology, Dibrugarh University, Dibrugarh, Assam.

Dr. P. K. Guha, Research Associate (Cartography), Anthropological Survey of India, Govt. of India, Kolkata.

Dr. Pranjal Boruah, Assistant Professor, Department of Anthropology Dibru College, Dibrugarh, Assam.

Prof. R. K. Kar, Former Professor of Anthropology, Dibrugarh University, Dibrugarh, Assam.

Dr. R. P. Atpariah, Former Superintending Anthropologist in Anthropological Survey of India and at present Research Advisor, North Eastern Institute of Culture and Religion, Guwahati, Assam.

Prof. Ranjana Ray, Former Professor, Department of Anthropology and at present Emeritus Professor, Calcutta University, Kolkata.

S. K. Chatterjee, Former DIG, Catcutta Police, Kolkata, Author of a number of books including a book on North East India (in 2 Vols).

Prof. Sarit Kr. Choudhury, Professor, Department of Anthropology Rajib Gandhi University, Itanagar, Arunachal Pradesh.

Prof. Sarthak Sengupta, Professor, Department of Anthropology, Dibrugarh University, Dibrugarh, Assam.

Dr. Sudhansu Gangopadhyay, Research Associate (Cartography) Anthropological Survey of India, Govt. of India, Kolkata.

Dr. Surajit Sen Gupta, Assistant Professor, Department of Sociology, Maharaja Bir Bikram College, Agartala, Tripura.

Tama Ramya, Research Scholar, Department of Anthropology, Rajiv Gandhi University, Itanagar, Arunachal Pradesh.

Prof. Tamo Mibang, Vice-Chancellor, Rajib Gandhi University, Itanagar, Arunachal Pradesh.

Introduction

In that Golden Age, when Man was young
When the whole race was vigorous and strong;
When nature did her wondrous dictate give,
And Taught the Noble Savage how to live…
When every sense to innocent delight,
Th' agreeing elements unforced invite.
Mrs. Aphra Behn

(from Elwin 1960:37)

The Northeastern part of India, where eight states, namely Arunachal Pradesh, Assam, Manipur, Meghalaya, Mizoram, Nagaland, Sikkim and Tripura, are situated, 'is the sentinel of the Indian continent' (Chatterjee, 2010:1) and the habitat of a large number of tribes, castes and other groups. While many of them are the indigenous people, others are immigrants who came and settled in this part of India in different period of time. 'It is the meeting place of various ethnic and linguistic groups, i.e. Austric, Indo-Mongoloid, Tibeto-Burman and Aryan, who entered into this area during different historic and pre-historic periods from all directions' (*ibid*). Das is also of the opinion that 'a series of immigration brought the Mongoloids to North-East India from the North, Northeast and Southeast' (2004:8-9). In fact from the earliest times India has received successive waves of foreign peoples with diverse languages, culture and racial affiliation' (Chatterjee *ibid*:31). With the opening of tea estates in this region, a large number of people, mostly the tribal people, were inducted in this region as labourers from West Bengal, Bihar, Madhya Pradesh and some other areas. The past history of the region also gives proof of the incoming of several waves of people in this region. As a result the North-East India 'has witnessed the synthesis of cultures right from the prehistoric times' and 'The culture of North-East India has evolved through several centuries of fusion' (Chatterjee *ibid* :31).

During the colonial rule the whole of North-East India, barring Tripura, Sikkim and Manipur was under the Province of Assam. 'Indeed, Nagaland, Mizoram and Meghalaya were very much its constituent parts then, while the administrated portions of Arunachal Pradesh were its affiliates' (Chatterjee *ibid*:37). But during post-independence period the undivided Assam was reorganized. In 1969 the Autonomous State of Meghalaya was formed of the parts of the State of Assam. Ultimately in 1972 Meghalaya became 'a full-fledged state comprising three hill districts of Khasi, Jaintia and Garo' (*ibid*:563). Nagaland became full-fledged state in 1963 and Mizoram in 1987. In 1987 Arunachal Pradesh (earlier NEFA) as a State, was formed. So North-East India was then formed of seven states, namely Assam, Arunachal Pradesh, Manipur, Meghalaya, Mizoram, Nagaland and Tripura. In 2002 Sikkim became a member of the North-Eastern Council. So, now we get all those eight states in North-East region of India.

Surrounded by different foreign countries like Myanmar, Nepal, Bhutan and Bangladesh, North-East India is strategically very important. In spite of this importance this region remained secluded and isolated for a long time. The colonial rulers in the pre-independence period did not do much for the development of this region. They adopted the policy of keeping this region isolated so that the waves of independence movement could not enter this region and stir the hearts of the people here and so they would never join the said movement. Even then the British Rulers were not successful in preventing the movements and agitations of different groups of people here against the British policy and British rule.

But after independence, particularly after Chinese aggression in 1962, the Government of India turned its attention towards this region and sanctioned and implemented a number of development projects for the improvement of this region and its people. But the region is so much ecologically divided and partly inaccessible and also inhabited by so many ethnic groups with varied economy, social structure, religion and political ideologies, that it became a hot spot of different burning problems of varied intensity. The governments were also facing great difficulty in implementing the development schemes properly. Chatterjee has rightly said:

> The mulli-racial, multi-linguistic, even multi-religious character of the region brings in its train a plethora of problems. The

> problems of the region are indeed intriguing, ranging from social, cultural, political and economic to ethnic, religious and linguistic. The increasing magnitude of such problems has made North-East India a sensitive area where a spark is enough to put the entire area to flame (2012:18).

No doubt several attempts have been made to dilute the problems of socio-political tensions and several prescriptions have been placed to solve the same. But the results of these attempts were not as satisfactory as was expected. 'The raising problems of poverty, unemployment and privatization of land ownership...' are keeping the burning issues alive. The ethnicity and identity problem is another very important issue that is also keeping the socio-political crisis active.

The people of North-East India can be grouped into two major categories, tribal and non-tribal. While most of the tribal people are distributed in the hilly region, the non-tribal populations, mostly Hindus, inhabit in the plains and valleys

> Thus North-East India may be regarded as a miniature India, an epitome of the subcontinent. The region provides shelter to varied people having divergent socio-cultural traditions, speaking different languages and exhibiting different physical features and biological make-up (Das, 2004:4).

At present a large number of ethnic groups live in North-East India. They belong to the Scheduled Castes, Scheduled Tribes and other ethnic groups (Raha & Ghosh, 2008:20).

All these ethnic groups differ from one another

> in their socio-political structure, as well as economic activities. Their activities are conditioned by traditions, customs, norms, values, etc. and their economic activities are inseparably linked with certain social systems... (Buragohain 1990:8).

Each of these groups of people has its own characteristic features, and each of them differs from the other by one or more distinguishing features.

> Different ecological conditions present in different parts of this region, have added environmental diversities to this region. Deep forests, difficult hills and mountains, large rivers, plateaus, plains, high rainfall, high altitude regions, etc. all have increased the attraction for this region (Raha & Ghosh, *ibid*:20).

In such diverse ecological set up and weather conditions, the people who live here, have basic characteristics of heterogeneity and different biological make-up. It is the meeting place of two major races of man kind, viz. Caucasoid and Mongoloid (Das, 2004:14).These people have settled in different types of settlements. Their material culture is distinct by varieties and shows 'clear impression of their culture.' They also have diverse economic activities. They practice different types of cultivation-shifting, terrace and also settled. While in the hilly region many of them practice shifting and/or terrace cultivation, in the plains they are settled cultivators. Though agriculture is the main livelihood of the people of North-East India, still in the present day many of them are found to remain engaged in different other occupations like labour, service, business, weaving, household industry, etc. Many of them are also tea garden labourers. While most of them are living in the societies with patriarchal form, some of them still prefer matriarchal form of societies. Like many other societies, people here have different social sub-divisions, moity, phratry, clan, family, marriage, kinship, etc. They have different systems of social control and practice different religions like Buddhism, Christianity, Hinduism, Islam and even animism (Raha & Ghosh, 2008:20-21).

In this book entitled **North-East India: The Human Landscape,** I have included thirty articles written by distinguished academicians and scholars, and these articles have highlighted various problems imbedded in the economic, social and bio-demographic aspects of the people there. I have divided all these articles into three parts. Part-One includes fifteen articles on occupational pattern and economic situation of the people. Part-Two covers eleven articles dealing with the socio-cultural aspects and lastly, Part-Three has accommodated four articles three of which are on demographic issues and the last one on the effects of tuberculosis on the people.

As said above I have included in this book, a total of thirty articles, and I am fortunate to get articles from all the eight states of North-East India. Apart from five articles on North-East India in general, I have included five articles on Arunachal Pradesh, nine articles on Assam, one article on Manipur, two articles on Meghalaya, one article on Mizoram, five articles on Nagaland, one article on Sikkim and one article on Tripura. Partwise, I have included three articles on Arunachal Pradesh, four articles on Assam, one article on Mizoram, four articles on Nagaland and one article on Sikkim in Part-One. In addition there are two articles on North-East India in general in this part. In Part-Two I have included two general articles on North-East India, two articles on Arunachal Pradesh, two articles on Assam, one article on Manipur, two articles on Meghalaya, one article on Nagaland, and one article on Tripura. Lastly in Part-Three I have include one general article on North-East India and three articles on Assam.

Further in this book I have arranged the articles of each part statewise. Each part starts with the general articles covering the whole of North-East India. Then in order come articles on Arunachal Pradesh, Assam, Manipur, Meghalaya, Mizoram, Nagaland, Sikkim and finally Tripura. Following this order, Part-One begins with the article by Shri S.K. Chatterjee, I.P.S. who has shown different aspects of economy of North-East India. He has covered the text of his paper through a discussion on the points like funding pattern, communication, power generation, rural economy, urban development, minerals, oil and gas, industry, handicrafts, trade and commerce, service sectors, poverty and its elimination, etc.

The next article is by Mr. Mithilesh Kumar Sinha who has in his paper, analyzed the perspective of socio-economic growth and examined the level of inter-state regional disparities in North-East India. He has also noted the causes of inter-state disparities and hindering factors to development.

Prof. Amitava Mitra and Mr. Kaju Nath have examined the challenges of development, economic condition and livelihood linkages of the people of some villages of Arunachal Pradesh.

Arunachal Pradesh has a large number of tribes and the Noctes is one of these. Through his article Dr. R.P. Athparia has tried to show the occupational pattern of the Noctes, a tribe of Arunachal Pradesh.

Mr. Tame Ramya's paper is on the role of forest in the life of the tribal people of Kurung Kumey district of Arunachal Pradesh. To these tribal people, forest is a very important source of livelihood as it supplies many forest products, very vital for these people.

The article by Prof. Lipi Ghosh was on the 'predominance of alien moneylenders' in the late 19th century Assam who had a motive to expand their trading interest and not for acquisition of the peasant's holding.

One of the very important resources of Assam is tea gardens. Prof. R.K. Kar and Sr. Molly Kaniampadickal have jointly attempted to show, in their article, the nature and extent of the gainful employment of the women in the tea estates of Upper Assam and their engagement in household work also.

The Rabhas are an important tribe of Assam who are mainly found in Goalpara,Kamrup and Darrang districts. Fr. K. Jose SVD, in his paper, has dealt with the resource utilization of the Rabhas and changes in their socio-economic life.

The paper of Dr. P.K. Guha deals with the population structure and occupational diversification of the Moria Muslims of the Brahmaputra valley of Assam.

Not much research works are done on the people of Mizoram and their social and economic life. However, Dr. Mita Sarkar (Das) has attempted to analyse the economic activities of the people of Mizoram.

Dr. Lucy Zehol has examined the experience of the rural Naga women as resource managers and how their experience raises some gender issues in resource management.

Livelihood and health care are very important for the survival of any group of people. Lack of sufficient resources and health care system may cause fatal. Dr. Pranjal Boruah has tried to show through his article the livelihood pattern and healthcare of the Ao Naga of three villages of Mokokchung District of Nagaland.

Dr. Manoj Kumar Singh has also written article on the Naga of the Nagaland. He has discussed about the nature and extent growth and development of agriculture in Nagaland.

Another article on the Naga is by Dr. Mita Sarkar (Das) who has highlighted the land use pattern among the Naga of the Nagaland and importance of land use pattern on their social and economic life.

The article on the Lepcha of Sikkim is written by Dr. Sudhansu Gangopadhyay who has highlighted the variation in the management of the land resources among the Lepcha, and has shown the way they use their traditional wisdom in the management of the resources.

The first article of Part-Two is of Dr. Manis Kumar Raha. He has written his article on the life and activities of the tribal people in North-East India. North-East India is inhabited by a large number of tribal groups. In many states of this region they are numerically dominant. They belong to different ethnic groups and have different economy, different social organization, different system of social control and religious beliefs and practices. Through his article Dr. Raha has tried to show the way of life of these tribal groups of North-East India.

Dr. Gadadhara Mohapatra through his article has shown the impact of globalization and the changing nature of the tribal identity in North-East India.

Prof. Tamo Mibang in his paper has lucidly discussed about the societal development with reference to Arunachal Pradesh. His view is that every product is the result of co-operative efforts of many people 'beyond the boundary of caste, creed, sex and religion'. And the development should be done peacefully, harmoniously and with co-operative efforts.

The landscape in Arunachal Pradesh is variable and similarly the people living here, belong to different ethnic groups. So obviously their cultural life particularly their economic pursuits are also variable. Prof. Ranjana Ray has tried to show this.

The water is essential for the survival of human life as also millions of other organisms like vegetations and animals. But the same water when comes through floods, causes havoc to the human, animal and vegetation life. While hundreds of people die every year in India due to flood, which also damages crops and causes death of domestic and wild animals. Dipa Patir and Prof. N.K. Gogoi have discussed in their paper, how the Mishing have formulated adaptive strategies during flood for their survival.

Dr. Dilip Kumar Bhuyan has in his paper discussed about the role of education in the adoption of scientific method of agriculture by the Mishings of Assam and how education has brought social change among the Mishing.

The ethnic identity is very important in the life of any group of people. A group or a section of it may revolt if the members feel that their ethnic identity is at stake. Through their paper Dr. M.C. Arunkumar and Akhuan Gangmei have highlighted the problem of identity among the Kabui of Manipur.

The Maan is a little known Scheduled Tribe of Meghalaya with about thousand population living in six villages of West Garo Hills. The author, Prof. Sarit Kumar Chaudhuri, has tried to focus the social formation along with the historicity of the tribe 'to relocate their position with reference to time and space'.

Dr. Surojit Sen Gupta's paper is based on socio-economic and cultural relation among the people who live in the neighbourhood of Laban in the city of Shillong, Meghalaya.

The Nagar are a very important and numerically very large tribe of Nagaland and also of North East India. Prof J.J. Roy Burman's paper is an ethnographic study on the Ao Naga of Nagaland.Through his article Prof. Roy Burman has briefly touched upon different aspects of the life of the Ao Naga of Nagaland.

The Reang is the second largest tribal group inhabiting in different parts of Tripura. Dr. Goutam Kumar Bera's paper is the last paper of Part-Two of this book where Dr. Bera has given the ethnographic details on this tribe.

In Part-Three we have four articles and the first article is by Dr. Debashis Basu who has attempted to assess the status of population of North-East India and 'its dimension with reference to the national demographic perspective'.

The paper by Prof. Indira Barua and Dr. Deepanjana Dutta Das discusses about the socio-demographic aspects of the Sema Naga of the village Lalpahar of Tinsukia district, Assam.

Arundhati Phukan Gogoi and Prof. Sarthak Sengupta have highlighted the effects of migration on the demographic pattern of some tea garden labourers (the Munda, the Oraon and the Savar) of Assam in their paper, and also examined the variation that is present in their reproductive characteristics.

The last paper of this book and also of this part has been written by Debolina Biswas and Prof. Sarthak Sengupta. The authors have discussed in their paper factors which might help tuberculosis to remain alive and active in some population groups of two districts of Upper Assam.

With the above thirty articles written by eminent academicians and scholars I have embellished this book. The intention, I have, is to provide our learned readers some more information about different aspects of life and activities of some of the population groups of different states under North-East India. No doubt there are a good number of publications (articles, books, reports, etc.) on North-East India already in the market, and through these one can get some information about the people of North-East India and their life and activities. But in comparison to the vastness and variations of the area and variations in the biological and cultural life of the large number of ethnic groups living there, the number of publications present in the market, could provide not much of information. So more number of studies and publications on North-East India are required so that interested people can come to know more about this region and the people living there. In a similar way I feel that this edited book of mine will be able to part with some fresh information to the people of all walks of life who are interested in North-East India and its people. In fact what I feel is that no information whatever may be its nature and depth, will go waste. Someway it will be useful to certain sections of people, people of certain disciples, if not for all the people.

REFERENCES

Buragohain, S.N. (1990), Institutional factors affecting economic development in the hill regions of North-East India. In J.K. Sarkar & B. Dutta Ray (Eds) *Social and Political Institutions of the Hill People of North-East India*. Calcutta, Anthropological Survey of India.

Chatterjee, Sarajit Kumar (2010), *North-East India: Dispersion and Discontent.* Delhi, Abhijeet Publications (in 2 vols).

Chatterjee, Sarajit Kumar (2012), *SCs, STs and OBCs in the Indian Polity.* New Delhi, Abhijeet Publications.

Das, B.M. (2004), North-East India and its People. In *Anthropology for North-East India.* (Eds) Arabinda Basu and others. Calcutta, INCAA, IAS, N MM.

Raha, M.K (2008), North-East India and Nehru. In *North-East India: The Human Interface* (Eds) M.K. Raha & Aloke Kumar Ghosh, New Delhi, Gyan Publishing House.

M.K. Raha & Aloke Kumar Ghosh (2008), *Introduction of North-East India: The Human Interface*. New Delhi, Gyan Publishing House.

PART ONE

ECONOMIC LANDSCAPE

1

Down to Earth—Economy and Resources of North East India

S.K. Chatterjee

Till 2002, North East India was a cluster of seven States of Arunachal Pradesh, Assam, Manipur, Meghalaya, Mizoram, Nagaland, and Tripura, popularly known as seven sisters. Only in 2002 Sikkim was added to it. At present the North East of India constitutes these eight States. The term

'North-East' may uphold an image of a homogeneous state, but is practically a region of intense disparity and distinctness and a politically sensitive one as well. The states of this region are as different from each other as chalk is from cheese. The eight states that comprise the region, reflect ecological and cultural contrasts between the hills and the plains; there are also significant elements of continuity. Available medieval and modern records indicate interdependence and interaction between the hills and plains.

The entire hill and mountain sector forming about 70 per cent of the region, is dissected by a large number of major rivers with deep gorges flowing into the main river system. The remaining part of this region is plains area and is formed by the Brahmaputra and Barak Valleys of Assam and the Imphal Valley of Manipur. Flanked by hills and with the mighty Brahmaputra slashing a central path between its north and south, the North East is bounded by the States of Manipur, Meghalaya, Mizoram, Nagaland, Tripura with Assam comprising the heart. Arunachal Pradesh lies to its north and Sikkim a little away in the North West. The North-East India encompasses the vast verdant plains of the Brahmaputra Valley and the several chains of wooded hills and mountains. It embraces the whole of the hill ranges north, east and south of the Brahmaputra Valley as well as the western slope of the great mountain system lying between West Bengal and Myanmar. It covers an area of 2,62,179 sq. km. bounded by Bhutan and Tibet on the north, Myanmar on the east and south and Bangladesh on the south and west. The region is almost isolated from the rest of India except for a narrow strip of land connecting it with the rest of India through West Bengal, popularly known as the Siliguri Corridor or "Chicken's Neck".

The North-East India possesses a very marked individuality. Some writers often describe it as a miniature India—an epitome of the sub-continent. Anthropologists consider it as a paradise for their research, an anthropological museum. The lovers of nature describe it as the Switzerland of the East. The botanists and zoologists find in the region all the pleasure of rare discoveries among the varied fauna and flora of the land. The vegetation of this region is the richest in India and probably in Asia. The region favours luxuriant growth of a variety of forests in the form of tropical moist evergreen, semi-deciduous and wet temperate conifer forests. The region is considered to be the original home of many citrus, cereals and orchid species. More than 50 per cent of the total mammalian fauna of the Indian subcontinent is represented in this region; all kinds of cats from Royal Bengal Tiger to Clouded Leopard, Leopard

Cat, Wild cat, etc., inhabit this region. It is the home of Binturong (*Arcticitis binturong),* so also the hoolock (*Hylobats hoolock*), the only true ape found in India. Meghalaya has the highest concentration of elephants per sq. km. of forests. For the philologists and ethnologists, North-East offers a fertile field for research, a melting pot of two diverse traditions—the East and the West, the Mongoloids and the Caucasoids. Zoologically this tract stands at the junction of Indo-China, Indo-Malayan and Indian sub-regions of the Oriental regions of naturalists (Chatterjee, 2010: 26-27).

North-East India, which is the sentinel of the Indian continent, is the homeland of a number of social and ethnic groups. The ethnic history of the region is extremely complicated. It is the meeting place of various ethnic and linguistic groups, i.e. Austric, Indo-Mongoloid, Tibeto-Burman and Aryan, who entered into this area during different historic and pre-historic periods from all directions. The population of the North-East is characterized by an enormous diversity, which this region acquired along with the inflow of varied groups of immigrants over several millenniums.

This land-locked region covers an area of 2,62,179 sq. km. of uneven surface. It accounts for 7.9 per cent of total geographical area of the country. It supports a population of 45,387,982 which accounts for 3.75 per cent of total population of 12,10,193,422 of India, according to the 2011 Census.

Arunachal Pradesh (83,743 sq.km.) happens to be the largest, and Sikkim (7,098 sq. km.) to be smallest State in terms of area whereas the heaviest concentration of population is in the State of Assam (3,11,69,272) and the smallest number is in the State of Sikkim (6,07,688). The density of population in the region is very much uneven. The hills are sparsely populated mostly by the tribal people. The density of populated areas is in the plains inhabited mostly by the non-tribal people. The density of population is the highest in Assam with 397 persons per square kilometre, closely followed by Tripura with 350, while it is the lowest in Arunachal Pradesh where it is 17 persons per square kilometre.

The largest number of tribal communities lives in this part of the country, most of them have been designated as Scheduled Tribes in Independent India. The tribal population of the hills and plains of North-East India can be divided into the following five broad groups: (1) Arunachal tribes; (2) Nagas; (3) Lushai (Mizo)-Kukis; (4) Bodos; and (5) Khasis. According to the Constitution (Scheduled Tribes) Order, 1950, as amended till 2010, 138 tribes/groups of tribes have been enlisted as Scheduled tribes in the eight States of North East India. If the tribes/

sub-tribes included under the same serial number, are counted as separate tribes then the number would be 310, which will further increase if all the tribes/sub-tribes coming under the generic term 'Any Naga tribe', 'Any Mizo tribe" or 'Any Kuki tribe" are mentioned individually. There are ongoing movements for recognition of some other communities as Scheduled Tribes. Taking all these facts into consideration, the number of tribal communities living in this region, will be more than 400.

However, all these tribal communities are not homogeneous one, but a medley of different races divided into numerous tribes, sub-tribes, and clans, different in origin, myths and traditions, distinct in language/ dialect, diverse in physique, character, culture, manners and customs, dress, eating habits and traditional socio-political organizations depending upon the peripheral geographical locality, although basically they are more or less the same having much in common affiliations, common heritage, religion, values, norms, common idea of liberty and decencies. But they were, as we find even today, sometimes in conflict with one another and with the outsiders as well.

The States of Mizoram (94.46%), Nagaland (89.15%), Meghalaya (85.99%) and Arunachal Pradesh (64.22%) are the tribal majority States and about half of the population of Tripura (48.54%) belong to the ST/ SC category. The followers of Christianity are in majority in the three States of Nagaland (90%), Mizoram (87%) and Meghalaya (70.3%) while those of Hinduism are in majority in Tripura (85.6%), Assam (64.9%) and Sikkim (60.09%). In Arunachal Pradesh and Manipur no religious community can claim majority though the Hindus remain a major force in both the States. Buddhists have a sizeable following in Sikkim (28.1%), Arunachal Pradesh (13.0%) and Mizoram (7.9%).

The multi-racial, multi-linguistic, even multi-religious character of the region brings in its train a plethora of problems, ranging from social, cultural, political and economic to ethnic, religious and linguistic. Divisive forces are very much active in this region which is embroiled in armed insurgency in one part or another since the emergence of Independent India. Some basic data about the North East States are given in Table 1.1

Economy

India adopted the policies of globalization, liberalization, privatization and market economy in the wake of economic crisis of 1991.The New Economic Policy (NEP) launched by the Government in 1991, had the clear objective of integrating the Indian economy with the rest of the

Table 1.1: NER States: Various Indicators.

State	Area	Population lakh persons	Literacy rate (%)	Infant mortality rate (per '000)	Poverty ratio based on MRP consum-ption	Per capita GSDP(Rs.)	Forest coveage (%)	Per capita electricity consum-ption (kwh)	Road length km/1000 sq. km area
	2001	2011	2011	2005-06	2004-05	2004-05	2003	2004-05	2002
1	2	3	4	5	6	7	8	9	10
Arunachal Pradesh	83,743	13.83	66.95	61	13.4	21,919	61.55	144.8	219.38
Assam	78,438	311.69	73.18	66	15.0	15,661	34.45	85.3	1140.9
Manipur	22,327	27.22	79.85	30	32.4	16,299	78.01	70.05	512.1
Meghalaya	22,429	29.64	75.48	45	25.2	20,775	42.34	352.2	426.5
Mizoram	22,081	10.91	91.58	34	13.2	30,357+	75.71	133.7	229.8
Nagaland	16,579	19.81	80.11	38	14.1	26,129+	52.05	87.2	1267.9
Sikkim	7,098	6.08	82.20	34	5.2	26,215	82.29	397.7	284.4
Tripura	10,486	36.71	8.75	52	15.2	24,984++	60.01	113.1	1554.1
NER States	262179	453.88		45#		18,032	54.52	110.4	660.9
India	3287240	12101.93	74.04	57	25.50	25,944*	23.57	411.1	755.4

Note: # Simple averages used for NER; + Refers to estimated per capita GSDP for 2003-04 and 2004-05;
++ refers to its estimated value for 2004-05;
* Per capita GDP at factor cost (RE) from RBI, Handbook of Statistics on the Indian Economy, 2005-06.

Sources:
1. Indiafacts.in/India-census 2011/census 2011 population percentage for Col.1.
2. Statistical Abstract of India (2006), used for Col. 2, 6, 7, 8, 9, downloaded from www.mospi.nic.in
3. Table 14 for Col. 3.
4. Table 7.20 of North Eastern Region Vision 2020 used for Col. 4.
5. Table 17 for Col. 5.

World. The policy instruments consist mainly providing all faculties to the private sector for starting new industrial ventures by removing all kinds of government restrictions which had been a characteristic feature of the Indian economy from 1950. The NEP has marginal impact on the people of North East India. This is due to economic backwardness of the region with its semi-feudal anarchy in land relations which is the basic anchor of the economy of the region. The possibility of foreign and domestic investment in a big way for North East India's economic development is not so bright. The investment if any, is likely to be limited to the service sector (Datta Ray, 2008:1-4).

The Centre announced the North East Industrial and Investment Promotion Policy (NEIIPP) on December 24, 1997 for attracting investment in the areas of industry and infrastructure and removal of regional disparity through sustainable economic development for raising per capita income of people and better standard of living.

The policy ensures continuance of 100 per cent excise duty exemption in respect of finished products made in the North East. Capital subsidy would be enhanced from 15 per cent of the investment in plant and machinery to 30 per cent. Further, the limit of automatic approval for capital subsidy has been announced to Rupees 1.4 crore from Rupees 15 lakh. Again, for grant of capital investment subsidy higher than Rupees 1.5 crore but up to a maximum of Rupees 30 crore, the decision would be taken by an Empowered Committee. What is noteworthy is the eligibility of new as well as existing units to enjoy incentives for a period of 10 years. The industrial units could be located anywhere in the region and there would be no distinction between thrust and non-thrust industries as it existed earlier. Besides 100 per cent income tax exemption, there is provision of eligibility for reimbursement of 100 per cent insurance premium. The inclusion of service sector, bio-technology and power generating industries within the policy framework is likely to bring about a qualitative change in the pace of industrialization. But the extension of similar benefits to other special category States later has robbed the NER of whatever benefit it could enjoy from this Policy. Better law and order situation, better infrastructural facilities like power and transport system and nearness to mainstream market, domestic investors have shown their preference for these states for investment. This is true in the case of foreign investment also. Unfortunately, not a single large scale industry came up in the region, rather during the period from 2001 to 2005 as many as 19,940 small industries were closed down due to the various reasons including lack of governmental help (Alam, 2008: 71) .The policy having proved to be a damp squib for the NER, the States of this region are now engaged in an all out offensive in favour of an alternative package with additional incentives for the region.

Funding Pattern

All the North-eastern States are listed in the Special Category States and their funding pattern is different. Till 2008, the funding of any central social sector projects was shared between the Centre and the States in the ratio of 75:25. As a special dispensation, in September 2008, the Centre decided to increase its share in the funding for various flagship programmes like the Indira Awas Yojana (IAY), the Swarnajayanti Gram Swarozgar Yojana (SGSY), the District Rural Development Agency (DRDA) administration, the Jawaharlal Nehru National Urban Renewal Mission (JNNURM), and the Sarva Siksha Abhiyan (SSA) from 75 per cent to 90 per cent for the North-eastern States. So long only the National Rural Employment Guarantee Scheme (NREGS) followed the 90:10 funding pattern for the North-eastern States (Chatterjee 2010:881-882).

As the benefits of economic development have yet to steadily accrue to the Region, efforts have been initiated in this direction in the recent past through various supportive measures. In October 1996, the then Prime Minister announced "New Initiatives for North Eastern Region" and stipulated that at least 10 per cent of the Budget(s) of the Central Ministries/Departments would be earmarked for the development of North Eastern States. With the approval of Parliament the Non-lapsable Central Pool of Resources was constituted from the financial year 1998-99. The broad objective of the Non-lapsable Central Pool of Resources (NLCPR) scheme is to ensure speedy development of infrastructure in the North Eastern Region by increasing the flow of budgetary financing for new infrastructure projects/schemes in the region. Both physical and social infrastructure sectors such as Irrigation and Flood Control, Power, Roads and Bridges, Education, Health, Water Supply and Sanitation — are considered for providing support under the Central Pool, with projects in physical infrastructure sector receiving priority.

In 2000 the institutional arrangements for administering the Non-lapsable Central Pool had been streamlined. The guidelines to administer the Pool were revised. The Committee to administer the Non-Lapsable Central Pool of Resources was also reconstituted. The reconstituted Committee is headed by Secretary, Ministry of Development of North Eastern Region and has representation from Ministries of Finance, Home Affairs and Planning Commission. Financial Adviser to the Ministry of Development of North Eastern Region has been included as a member. Representatives of Union Ministry/Departments, whose proposals are to be considered in a particular sitting for funding under NLCPR, are also invited.

For identification of projects under Non-Lapsable Central Pool of Resources, States are asked to submit, before the beginning of the financial year, a prioritized list of projects with a short write-up on each project. The earlier practice of receiving projects throughout the year directly from the various state departments concerned has been stopped. Now the Planning and Development Department of the state concerned is the nodal department for NLCPR and that department is DoNER's interface with all other departments of the state. The Committee scrutinizes the projects in the lists in order to identify and finally retain the suitable projects for detailed examination. Detailed Project Report (s) for such retained projects are then prepared by the state concerned. These project proposals are thereafter examined in consultation with the concerned Central Ministry/Department. The recommendations/views, thus received are placed before the Committee to administer the Non-Lapsable Central Pool, which considers the proposal and accords approval. After approval of the Committee, funds are sanctioned and released by the Ministry of Development of North Eastern Region on submission of an implementation schedule. Subsequent releases are made only after receipt of Utilisation Certificate of earlier releases.

Infrastructure Development

The biggest constraint in the NER has been the poor state of infrastructure in regard to roads, railways, waterways and power. At 66 km/100 sq. km area, the road length in the region is lower than that the average of the country (75 km/sq. km) and the quality of roads in the region is extremely poor. The total railway track length in the entire region is 2,592 km, with broad gauge track confined to Assam. Inland waterways in the Brahmaputra and smaller rivers, such as the Kolodyne in Mizoram and Barak in Assam, have become virtually non-functional after the partition of the country and at best, they can be used for the transportation of goods and not people. Air connectivity to the region is poor: three of the state capitals do not have airports, and feeder services from Delhi/Kolkata/Guwahati to the state capitals where airports exist are scarce. Most intra-regional connection is routed through Kolkata, which is expensive in terms of both time and money.

Infrastructure deficiency in the region remained a major concern. So infrastructure projects in the NER were given the status of "national projects" with a special funding pattern. "An ambitious programme of road building has been taken up under the Special Accelerated Road Development Programme and Rupees 31,000 crore are being invested in roads in the 11th Five Year Plan period (2007-12)." the Prime Minister said while releasing the Northern Eastern Region Vision 2020 document on July 2, 2008 (*The Hindu*, July 3 ,2008). The ambitious East-West Road Corridor project that will provide road connectivity with Southeast Asian countries will open up the land-locked North-East for public and private investments. The proposed Moreh-Tamu-Kalewa-Mandalaya-Bangkok Road and the Ledo-Moegaung-Kunming Road are much-hyped symbols of economic integration. Of vital relevance to this trans-national corridor is the internal road connection between commercial hubs and cities of the region. There are, however, relaxed guidelines for rural roads under the Pradhan Mantri Gram Sadak Yojana so that even the farthest hamlets on the border are linked by road. Performance of this rural development programme in the region is quite encouraging with 99.74 per cent performance in Arunachal Pradesh followed by 92.85 per cent performance in Nagaland, and by 62.95 per cent in Tripura during 2005-06 (Singh, 2008: 322-323).

Port

The recent visit of the Indian Prime Minster to Myanmar on May 27-29, 2012 is likely to open new doors for the North-east. The Kaladan project which India is helping to develop, would benefit the NE the most. It will bring more volumes to Kolkata Port, opening up a new transit route to the NE from the mainland. The project includes developing the Sittwe port in Arakan state and a multi-modal transport system from there to Mizoram. The distance between Kolkata and Sittwe is about 540 km. From Sittwe, the Kaladan river would be made navigable up to Kaletwa, a distance of 225 km. From there, a 62 km highway would take the traffic to Mizoram border. A road from the border would link the project to National Highway 54 to Assam (*The Times of India*, May 4, 2012)

Airports

Fifty airports and airstrips spread across the North East and with 600 flights a week were the target to be achieved in the 11th Plan. Of them only Baljek airport, 30 km from the district headquarters of Tura in Meghalaya was inaugurated in October 2008 by President Prativa Patil. It is yet to be made operational. Moreover, in the wake of the persistent threat from China, the army is giving top priority towards easy connectivity with the remote border areas by development of the unused small airfields and construction of all-seasons good metalled roads.

Railway Network

Geographically isolated, the main hurdle to development and progress in North-East is the poor state of transport and communication infrastructure. The Railways has an ambitious plan to link all North-East state capitals by rail by 2016, provided the State Governments ensure early handover of land. As of now, Assam (Guwahati) and Tripura (Agartala) are connected, and Nagaland (main railhead Dimapur) and Manipur (Jiribam) are on the railway map. But Arunachaal Pradesh, Mizoram and Meghalaya have no railheads of their own. Very recently Union Minister of State for Railways Bharat Singh Solanki informed Parliament that the Centre has a Rs 17,495-crore outlay for 13 projects in the North-East. He also said a dedicated North East Railway Development Fund had been created to finance the execution of national projects (Lama, *Statesman*, May 28, 2012).

After much delay, work on the 84-km Jiribam-Tupul-Imphal railway line is progressing smoothly after the Centre sent security forces to the work site. The first locomotive engine traversed a distance of 12 km from Jiribam to Dholakhal on March 22, 2012 (*The Times of India*, March 24, 2012). Hopefully the project will be completed by 2016, as promised by the Prime Minster.

The 40-km Dimapur-Zubra (16 km from Kohima) railway link has run into trouble because the owners are demanding exorbitant prices for the land. Nagaland Chief Minster Neiphiu Rio recently said that if the owners' demands were to be met then the entire cost of the project—Rs. 850 crore—would have to be spent on compensation for land acquisition alone! (Lama, *Statesman*, January 9, 2012).

A 15-km rail line is under construction between Agartala and Akhaura, a Bangladesh railway town along the border in order to link Agartala with Bangladesh's railway network. Dhaka has already allowed the north-east access to Bangladesh's river and seaports, including Ashuganj, Mongla and Chittagong. Dhaka has already approved India's proposal to construct a bridge across the 110-metre wide Feni River that flows along

Tripura's fringe line to link the state's southernmost border town of Sabrum with the seaport in Chittagong, just 70 km from the international border. The project will be taken up soon at an estimated cost of Rs. 14 crore. The extension of the railway line to Sabroom would improve connectivity to the Chittagong port. Access to the Chittagong port and opening up of the inland water route could lead to economic resurgence of the region.

Meghalaya is the only state which is not connected by rail. The railway line to Byrnihat from Guwahati (25 km) was first mooted by P.A. Sangma when he was state chief minister in 1988-89. At that time, the Khasi Students' Union opposed the railhead vehemently, arguing that it would merely encourage the influx of outsiders. Many agitations shook the state. But the discontent on railways continues even today. The KSU is as defiant on this issue as it was then, and without enough arguments to back up its chagrin, except to say that railways would create influx. Hopefully in course of time the KSU will see ground realities and change its mind.

Mizoram, Manipur, Tripura and Barak Valley will open up only after the completion of the metre gauge conversion of the 208-km Lumding-Badarpur-Silchar hill section. The foundation of broad gauge conversion project in this section was laid in 1996 by the then Prime Minister Deve Gowda and it was to have been commissioned by 2005. Originally estimated at Rs. 640 crore, the cost had already shot up to Rs. 3,990 crore. It is doubtful if the project will be completed by December 2013, as indicated by a senior Railway Board Member.

Another project, the Bogibeel road-cum-railway bridge, the fourth and the longest over the Brahmaputra is behind schedule. Work started in 2002 at an estimated cost of Rs. 1,767 crore was to have been ready in 2008-09. Progress is reportedly slow and no one can say for certain when it will be ready. The construction of this bridge finds mention in the Assam Accord of 1985 (Lama, *Statesman* May 28, 2012).

If the Railway projects are executed within a stipulated timeframe it will, no doubt, do away with the landlocked North-East's transport and communication bottlenecks.

Power Generation

Power is the basic infrastructure requirement for the growth of industries as well as economy of any State. The degree of economic growth is correlated with the generation and consumption of electricity. Table 1.2 will indicate State-wise generation of Thermal/Nuclear/Hydro power in the North-eastern States as on December 31, 2011.

Table 1.2: State-wise Generation (Thermal/Nuclear and Hydro)

(In MW) (As on 31.12.2011)

States	*Thermal*				*Nuclear*	*Hydro (Renewable)*	*RES (MNRE)*	*Total*
	Coal	*Gas*	*Diesel*	*Total*				
Arunachal Pradesh	0.00	0.00	15.88	15.88	0.00	0.00	78.83	94.71
Assam	60.00	239.00	20.69	319.69	0.00	100.00	27.11	446.80
Manipur	0.00	0.00	45.41	45.41	0.00	0.00	5.45	50.86
Meghalaya	0.00	0.00	2.05	2.05	0.00	198.00	31.03	231.08
Mizoram	0.00	0.00	51.86	51.86	0.00	0.00	36.47	88.33
Nagaland	0.00	0.00	2.00	2.00	0.00	0.00	28.67	30.67
Sikkim	0.00	0.00	5.00	5.00	0.00	0.00	52.11	57.11
Tripura	0.00	148.50	4.85	153.35	0.00	0.00	16.01	169.36
All India	104021.38	17742.85	1199.75	122963.98	4780.00	38748.40	20162.24	186654.62

Source : Ministry of Power, Govt. of India. Quoted in North Eastern Development Finance Corporation Ltd. (NEFDi) Databank downloaded from db.nedfi.com

The Union Government is pushing for 157 hydro power schemes with an installed capacity of 57672 MW in the North-East including Sikkim for meeting the shortfall in the country's power generation. Of the 133 projects already allotted to the States, 125 projects, with an installed capacity of 32,883.40 MW, have been given to private developers. The Central public sector undertakings have got eight power projects with an installed capacity of 8,735 MW. Of the total 133 projects, 36 are mega ones, with each having an installed capacity of 350 MW and above. The rest (25 MW and above) involve construction of large dams. So far only four projects have got the final clearance and are in various stages of construction. The Ministry of Environment and Forests has granted pre-construction (scoping) clearances to over 50 projects under the EIA notification 2006. Final environmental clearance has been given to 13 projects.

The Centre has identified the ecologically fragile Arunachal Pradesh as the powerhouse of the country. According to an estimate of the Central Electricity Authority (CEA) and private power developers, this State bordering China has the potential to generate over 57,000 MW of hydropower. Arunachal will get 12 per cent free power from each project. The State Government collected revenue in terms of processing fee and upfront premium to the tune of Rs. 1320 crore (as on September 30, 2010) from the allottee owner-developers (*The Hindu*, June 2, 2012).

Work for the construction of a mega dam over the river Barak at Tipaimukh in Manipur's Churachandpur district for the 1500-MW Tipaimukh Multipurpose Hydel Project was started on 16 December, 2006, when its foundation was laid. The Rs. 8,138-crore project is being executed by the state-owned National Hydroelectric Project Corporation and Satluj Jal Vidyut Nigam. The Tipaimukh Dam controversy has been raised at various Indo-Bangladesh meetings.

The Tamanthi Dam on the Chindwin river in Myanmar is being built by the National Hydroelectric Project Corporation of India and Colenco Power Engineering Ltd. Switzerland at an estimated cost of $ 3 billion. The dam will be 80 meter high and, when completed, will have an installed capacity of 1,200 MW. The project will supply power to Myanmar and also India's North-East States.

The foundation of a 52-MW power plant at Ramchandranagar near Agartala was laid by the Union Power Minster in February 2011. It will be run by water and the heat emitted from the existing thermal power project. This is the second combined cycle power unit in the region after Kathalguri in eastern Assam. This Rs. 290 crore project of the NEEPCO will be commissioned within the next 30 months.

The Rs. 2,000-crore 726-MW gas-based project in south Tripura's Platana is being set up jointly by the ONGC and the Tripura Power Company Limited. Four North-eastern States—Assam, Mizoram, Meghalaya and Manipur would buy power from this plant.

When these projects are completed, North-East not only will be a power-surplus region but will also be instrumental in changing the industrial face of India.

Table 1.3 will indicate the State-wise number of villages electrified and un-electrified in the North-East. It will appear therefrom that apart

Table 1.3: State-wise Number of Villages Electrified and Un-electrified in NER

(As on 31.03.2011)

States	*Total Inhabited Villages (As Per 2001 Census)*	*Villages Electrified (Provisional)*		*Unelectrified Villages*
		Numbers	*%age*	
Arunachal Pradesh	3863	2195	56.8	1629
Assam	25124	22059	87.8	881
Manipur	2315	1997	86.3	318
Meghalaya	5782	3428	59.3	1968
Mizoram	707	570	80.6	137
Nagaland	1278	823	64.4	455
Sikkim	450	425	94.4	25
Tripura	858	491	57.2	301
India	593732	500920	84.4	55785

Source: Ministry of Power, Govt. of India, *quoted in NEFDi Databank downloaded from db.nedfi.com.*

from Sikkim, Assam, Mizoram and Manipur the other five States are far away from the all-India average of 84.4 per cent, the worst defaulters being Arunachal Pradesh, Tripura and Meghalaya. The position is likely to improve when the on-going projects are completed.

Rural Economy

The pattern of agricultural growth has however remained uneven across regions and crops. The NER continues to be a net importer of food grains even for its own consumption. In spite of covering 7.7 per cent of the country's total geographical area, NER produces only 1.5 per cent of the country's total food grain production. Agriculture provides livelihood support to 70 per cent of the population of NER. Table 1.4 gives an idea of state-wise area, production and yield of total food grains in 2009-10, whereas Table 1.5 provides information on State-wise area, production and yield of total cereals in 2009-10.

Table 1.4: State-wise Area, Production and Yield of Total Food grains, 2009-2010

(Area : ' 000 Hectare, Production: '000 Tonne, Yield : Kilogram/Hectare)

States	Area	Production	Yield
Arunachal Pradesh	198.6	308.9	1555
Assam	2695.6	4481.1	1662
Manipur	188.7	338.9	1796
Meghalaya	132.2	239.1	1809
Mizoram	59.6	62.4	1047
Nagaland	282.1	354.2	1256
Sikkim	78.4	117.3	1496
Tripura	254.7	647.9	2544
Total	6549.8	3889.9	1660

Source: Ministry of Agriculture, Govt. of India, Quoted in NEFDi Databank downloaded from db.nedfi.com.

The region produced 6.5 million tonnes of food grains including 6.4 million tonnes of cereals in 2009-10. It is not self-sufficient in food grains and other items. At present, of about 39 lakh hectares under cultivation, nearly 37 lakh or roughly 94 per cent is under food grain production. At about 1660-1790 kg/hectare, land productivity is very low in the region. Despite a vast potential, only 20 per cent of the net sown area is under irrigation. Almost 95 per cent of the region's soil is acidic with *p*H value below 5.6. *Jhum* cultivation, widely practiced in the hills by the tribal

Table 1.5: State-wise Area, Production and Yield of Total Cereals in NER, 2009-2010.

(Area : '000 Hect., Production : '000 Tonne, Yield : Kg./Hect.)

States	Area	Production	Yield
Arunachal Pradesh	189.7	299.2	1577
Assam	2580.3	4416.5	1712
Manipur	174.2	331.7	1904
Meghalaya	128.2	235.6	1839
Mizoram	55.7	55.9	1004
Nagaland	248.6	319.5	1285
Sikkim	65.2	104.4	1601
Tripura	248.2	643.4	2592
Total	3690.1	6406.2	1790

Source: Ministry of Agriculture, Govt. of India. Quoted in NEFDi Databank downloaded from db.nedfi.com

population, has kept productivity low and contributed to deforestation and erosion of soil. The target should be to increase food grain production in the NER to 75 lakh MT in 2010, 87 lakh MT by 2015 and 110 lakh MT in 2020, which would require accelerating the growth rate to 2 per cent in the first phase, 3 per cent in the second and 4 per cent in the third phase. (North Eastern Region Vision 2002: 26).

There should be different strategies for accelerating growth in agriculture in the plains and the hills. In the plains, the goal should be to increase crop intensity by better utilisation of irrigation potential and cultivation of short-duration crops. Controlling the annual floods in the Brahmaputra and Barak valleys and strengthening embankments to control soil erosion should be an important part of strategy for the development of agriculture in Assam and parts of Arunachal Pradesh. Though the Brahmaputra Board has emerged as a regional institution to design, implement and monitor flood management strategies in the valleys of the NER, it has failed to evolve a workable solution. In the plains, increasing the land area (about 1.5 million hectares) under double-cropping to 25 per cent in a phased manner would considerably enhance productivity. Measures such as expanding area under High-Yielding Varieties (HYV), more balanced use of organic manure and chemical fertilisers and pesticides, and steps to balance soil conditions to reduce soil acidity are needed. It is also important to expand the area under cultivation by bringing under cultivation, the cultivable waste land and areas developed under the command area development. This implies increasing the productivity of land in a phased manner (North Eastern Region Vision

2002: 26). It is good that the success of Assam and Tripura in raising production of rice has earned for the two states "Krishi Karman Awards" in 2011, instituted by the Government of India for the first time in that year.

In the hills, the tribal population has, for generations adopted shifting (*jhum*) cultivation. While the strategy should be to wean them away from this practice, this has to be done not through displacement, which would endanger their food security, but through persuasion and demonstration of alternative livelihood systems and building their capacity to engage in productive and sustainable livelihoods. In hilly areas, it is important to expand horticulture, floriculture, plantation crops and organic farming.

Interestingly, the region's agro-climatology is suitable for commercial floriculture, medicinal and aromatic plants, and ornamental horticulture. The North-East has the potential to mimic Holland as a floriculture hub. Already states like Meghalaya, Mizoram and Nagaland are supplying rich shades of anthuriums, liliums, carnations and roses to different parts of the country and abroad. The youth could be trained in standardization and packaging of cut flowers and also in managing the whole production chain.

The region is a mega biodiversity area and a hotspot of generic erosion. The forests have 8,000 of the 15,000 species of flowering plant occurring in India. The species richness is the highest in Arunachal Pradesh, where over 5,000 flowering plants occur, and the lowest is in Tripura with 1,600 species. The region is natural habitat of orchids that are much sought after in Europe, America and West Asia. Almost all the hill states have a favourable climatic condition for commercialization of orchid cultivation and this area needs to be explored. Of the 1,300 species of orchids reported from India, the region has the highest concentration: about 700 species. Meghalaya alone has 124 species of orchids.

Though all the forests of the North-East are repositories of medicinal herbs, Arunachal Pradesh is acknowledged to be the storehouse of an eclectic range of medicinal plants and exotic flora. *Taxus baccata*, also known as the yew tree, the bark of which is used to manufacture Taxol, an anti-cancer medicine, particularly effective in treating ovarian cancer, used to grow profusely along the high reaches of the Meghalaya plateau. Today, the *taxus bccata* is almost extinct. Bio-piracy, coupled with ignorance about the plant's efficacy as a medicine, has made it a threatened species. Several rare species of plants and herbs have been destroyed through destruction of forest cover. Another plant, *Bogonia tessaricapa*, locally known as *rebe*, which was thought to have been extinct was rediscovered in the Arunachal forest in 2004. This plant has long been known as a cure for stomach ailments and its extracts are also used to ward off mountain leeches. There may be several such medicinal plants and herbs which are waiting to be discovered.

The region produces large varieties of pineapples, oranges, strawberries, peaches, pears, plums, cashew nut, and capsicum. The Darrangiri banana market in the Garo Hills is the largest in Asia. The Garo Hills has emerged as possibly the largest producer of pine-apples in Asia and first in cashew nut output in India. The hill district of Tamenglong in Manipur is known for its sweet oranges. Sikkim has the highest production of, and the largest cultivated area of cardamom in India. India is the world's largest ginger producer, accounting for over 50 per cent of the total production, and of that more than half is produced in the north-eastern states, with Meghalaya producing 45,000 tonnes, followed by Arunachal Pradesh (25,000 tonnes), Mizoram (22,000 tonnes) and other States. Ginger is produced as a cash crop mostly in '*jhum*' fields spread over the hills and tribal areas of the entire region. The produce is mostly marketed in the fresh form as a vegetable. Though mainly used in cooking as a flavouring agent and to a smaller extent in medicinal and veterinary preparations, of late it is also being used for the manufacture of several by-products like oil, ginger oleoresins, starch from spent ginger in soft drinks and ginger powder.

Bamboo is another crop native to the region. Bamboo is the lifeline of the region, and 63 out of the136 species found in India occur here. Of the States, Mizoram is heavily dependent on bamboo, as the State harvests 40 per cent of India's 80-million tonnes annual bamboo crop. Bamboo expanses cover nearly 6,500 sq. km in the sub-tropical evergreen forest–about 31 per cent cf Mizoram's area. The "green gold" could make Mizoram a rich state. While the total bamboo yield is about 32,37,689 tonnes per year, consumption is only 28,315 tonnes per year. The surplus can be methodically utilized for generating huge resources (Chatterjee, 2010: 873). Bamboo-based industries for producing laminated walls and ceilings are the need of the hour in a high seismic zone. The youths should be exposed to better technologies for adding value to bamboo. So far the plant has not been cultivated on a commercial scale. Scientists say a bamboo grove of 10 square meters can fetch approximately Rs. 2000 on maturity of approximately 100 bamboos at the rate of Rs. 20 in local prices. This means that the bamboo cultivation can fetch approximately Rs. 20 lakh over a period of five years from a well-organized and well-maintained area of one hectare.

Apart from tea and coffee, natural rubber cultivation has been taken up in a big way in the North-eastern States. In Tripura, where rubber cultivation began in early 1960s, about 4,000 hectares are added to cultivation every year. In Assam, Meghalaya, Mizoram, Manipur, Nagaland and Arunachal Pradesh, rubber cultivation is spreading rapidly even with constraints that were seen as insurmountable nearly a decade ago. In each of these States, average productivity hovers around 1,200 kg per hectare, the national average being around 1,800 kg. A total of 4.5 lakh hectares have been identified as suitable for rubber cultivation in the North-East. The Rubber Board estimates that an investment of Rs. 1.85 lakh is needed for developing a hectare of rubber plantation in Tripura. It takes up to seven years for the rubber plants to be tapped (*The Hindu*, January 18, 2012). Some, however, believe that expansion of rubber cultivation reduces soil fertility and it should be replaced by other crops.

There is tremendous potential for cultivating horticultural crops in the hills, but success depends on the development of rural infrastructure including transportation infrastructure, cold storages, processing facilities and marketing support. Extension services need improvement, with better provision of good quality seeds, inputs and seedlings. At present much of the research in horticulture is conducted by the Horticulture Department of Assam Agricultural University in Jorhat, which needs to be upgraded to a national-level research organisation capable of serving the entire region. The Assam Small Farmers' Agri-business Consortium (ASFAC) station in Guwahati too will have to be upgraded to undertake research and development of horticulture for the benefit of the region as a whole. Expansion of horticulture in tribal areas to replace jhumming is a challenging task and the strategy for this has to be worked out carefully.

The people of the region are predominantly non-vegetarian but the production of meat, fish and eggs is inadequate to meet the demand. Few regions in the world are endowed with so much bio-diversity and evergreen grasslands ideal for dairy, livestock and poultry development and vast wetlands for fisheries. Yet the region imports about 50 per cent of its milk consumption, over 87 per cent of the eggs consumed and almost 55 per cent of its fish consumption from outside (North Eastern Region Vision 2020, p. 28).

The total fish production was 2.77 lakh tonnes in 2008-09 and 2.98 lakh tonnes in 2009-10 of which 2.62 lakh tonnes and 2.77 lakh tonnes, respectively, were inland fish production. The State-wise fish production and inland fish production in NER is given in Tables 1.6 and 1.7.

Table 1.6: State-wise Fish Production in NER:

(In '000 Tonne)

States	*2008-09*	*2009-10*	*2010-11 (Up to 31.12. 2010)**
Arunachal Pradesh	2880	2650	2285
Assam	206150	218822	145618
Manipur	18800	19200	15531
Meghalaya	3959	4210	3184
Mizoram	2891	3042	1899
Nagaland	6175	6360	5250
Sikkim	168	168	150
Tripura	36000	42268	35725

* Figures are Quantity in Tonne.

Source: Ministry of Agriculture, Govt. of India, quoted in NEFDi Databank downloaded from db.nedfi.com.

Table 1.7: Inland Fish Production in NER

(Tonne)

States	*2007-08*	*2008-09*	*2009-10***
Arunachal Pradesh	2830	2880	2650
Assam	190320	206150	218822
Manipur	18600	18800	19200
Meghalaya	4000	3959	4210
Mizoram	3760	2891	3042
Nagaland	5800	6175	6360
Sikkim	175	168	168
Tripura	36245	36000	42268
India	4207346	4637896	4862843

** Figures are provisional.

Source: Ministry of Agriculture and Ministry of Statistics and Programme Implementation, Govt. of India, quoted in NEFDi Databank downloaded from db.nedfi.com.

Nature has already gifted the region with adequate rainfall, a salubrious climate and an undulating topography that is ideal for fish-rearing. Under the World Bank-aided Assam Agricultural Competitiveness Project's Fish Intensification Programme covering *beels* and ponds, fish production has gone up by four to five tines in every *beel* or pond where renovation, desilting and deepening were carried out. And given the high price of every species of fish, the farmer fetched as much as Rs. 60,000 from a one-bigha pond which makes it more profitable than conventional farming. The other good news is the steady growth of fish seed production in Nagaon district where farmers were trained in fish seed production and then assisted to grow spawns and fingerlings.

There is need for incentives to small farmers to convert a part of the agricultural land into fish pond and to adopt the Bangladesh practice of rearing fingerlings first in a small adjacent tank and introduce them in the pond where they become large. But this will succeed only when ponds are protected from leaching of chemical fertilisers or pesticides which points to the need for community management that could facilitate spread of the proven Indonesian model of a single pond based duckery, poultry and fish farming where fish thrives on poultry droppings and horticultural plants cover all sides of a pond enriching the soil. If adopted, on a significant scale, a "blue revolution" could be a reality in Assam and elsewhere in the North-East where wetlands of about 250,000 hectares exist unutilised and capable of massive 'spin offs" in the regional economy. Together with "blue" and "white" revolutions, the North-East could emerge as an agricultural power, get out of "Central Dependency Syndrome" and move on to a sustainable growth path (Rangan Dutta, Statesman, June 27, 2011).

In recent times, the governments of Assam and Meghalaya have embarked on a radical policy shift from developing urban centres to reaching out to rural hamlets with livelihood projects. They will now concentrate on multipurpose livelihoods for the rural poor. Leading economists of the world have found that single livelihoods will not be able to pull those living below the poverty line to catch up with the rest of the population. To come out of the black hole of poverty, people would need at least three livelihoods. This is what the Meghalaya's River Basin and Livelihoods Development Programme aims to do. River basin are good for fish rearing, for rice and vegetable farming, for bee-keeping (apiary) and also for cane and bamboo works, weaving and a host of other related activities (Mukhim, *Statesman*, February 27, 2012).

North-East India lives in its villages. Crop cultivation is still the only occupation, but over the years, agricultural funding has decreased instead of increasing. If adequate attention had been paid to investments in agriculture, floriculture and horticulture, to veterinary services and fisheries, to sericulture and weaving, the states would not have been so economically backward. A thrust to agriculture and allied activities requires significant government initiatives in terms of providing rural infrastructure and extension services. An extensive rural road network is necessary to increase the mobility of people as well as the movement of goods, while the electrification of villages is necessary for increasing crop intensity and spreading rural industrialization. Extension services are critical both for enhancing production and improving marketing and, therefore, need significant upgradation. Establishment of a network of cold storage facilities and information centres and organization of marketing and financial support through self-help groups will have to be initiated on a large scale.

Urban Development

The growth of urban settlements in the North-East is not always an outcome of a social process. Rather it is the result of conscious administrative efforts. The urban pockets have been superimposed upon the traditional tribal set-up partly in carrying out politico-economic dictum and partly in providing for urban facilities to the administrative personnel recruited from outside the territory.

The NER witnessed different urbanization levels before and after the independence of the country. While in the pre-independence period the region was almost rural with less than 5 per cent of its population living in urban settlements, the scenario was very different in the post-independence phase. Right from the onset of the second half of the twentieth century the region started witnessing surprising increase in its level of urbanization. The reasons are diverse. Firstly, there was a massive reorganization of the administrative and political boundaries in the region which resulted in the creation of many new States like Nagaland, Meghalaya, Mizoram and Arunachal Pradesh. Secondly, the region attracted impressive development projects from the State and Central Governments. Thirdly, the contribution of Christian missionaries in the region in terms of the upgradation in the quality of life of the tribal people is no less noteworthy. It invested in the education and infrastructure sectors and thus played an important role in the enhancement of the level of urbanization in the region (Khawas, 2006: 256-57). Besides, several other important factors like the partition of the country, allocation of the specific funds by the Central Government for the development of the urban areas, etc. might have influenced the levels of urbanization in the region.

The States like Mizoram and Arunachal Pradesh which were rural until 1950, started getting urbanized in the post-independence period with tremendous pace altogether. This is particularly true in case of Mizoram where urban population rose from about 25 per cent in 1981, to 46 per cent in 1991 and almost 50 per cent by 2001. Arunachal Pradesh also

Table 1.8: Trends in the Levels of Urbanisation

States	1901	1911	1921	1931	1941	1951	1961	1971	1981	1991	2001
Arunachal Pradesh	0	0	0	0	0	0	0	3.70	6.56	12.80	20.41
Assam	2.34	2.41	2.74	2.92	3.11	4.29	7.21	8.82	9.88	11.10	12.72
Manipur	25.39	21.56	20.83	19.26	19.47	0.50	8.68	13.19	26.42	27.52	23.88
Meghalaya	2.83	3.46	4.07	5.52	6.87	9.66	15.27	14.55	18.07	18.60	19.63
Mizoram	0.00	0.00	0.00	0.00	0.00	3.54	5.36	11.36	24.67	46.10	49.50
Nagaland	3.05	1.63	1.76	1.54	1.85	1.94	5.19	9.95	15.52	17.21	17.74
Sikkim	0.00	0.00	0.00	0.00	0.00	1.99	4.22	9.37	16.15	9.10	11.10
Tripura	3.70	2.98	2.54	2.50	2.45	6.67	9.02	10.43	10.99	15.30	17.02
Northeast	4.20	4.01	3.99	3.65	4.22	3.57	6.87	10.17	16.03	19.72	21.50
India	10.84	10.29	11.18	11.99	13.86	17.29	17.97	19.91	23.34	25.72	27.78

Source: p. 259 of Urbanisation in the *Eastern Himalayas: Emergence and Issues* (ed) Karubaki Datta, 2006, New Delhi, Serials Publications.

witnessed appreciable level of urbanization in the last 30 years which reached almost 21 per cent by 2001.

The State of Manipur which had accommodated over 25 per cent of its population in urban areas by the turn of the 19th century itself, saw continuous decline in the share of urban population, so much so that by 1951 it came down to less than 1 per cent. The share of urban population, however, again started gaining in pace in the post-independence period and reached about 28 per cent by 1991, but again declined to about 24 per cent by 2001. In the rest of the States the levels of urbanization are below 20 per cent even in 2001. Table 1.8 will clear the picture.

Consequently, towns of different sizes have come up in the NER. There were 196 towns in 1991 which rose to 245 in 2001, an addition of 49 towns in a decade, as shown in Table 1.9.

Table 1.9: Number of Towns in 1991 and 2001 in North East India

States	*1991*			*2001*		
	Statutory	*Census*		*Statutory*	*Census*	
	Towns	*Towns*	*Total*	*Towns*	*Towns*	*Total*
Arunachal Pradesh	0	10	10	0	17	17
Assam	75	19	94	80	45	125
Manipur	28	3	31	28	9	37
Meghalaya	7	5	12	10	6	16
Mizoram	22	0	22	1	21	22
Nagaland	8	1	9	8	1	9
Sikkim'	8	0	8	8	1	9
Tripura	12	6	18	13	10	23
Total	160	44	204	148	110	258

Source: p. 275 of *Urbanization in the Eastern Himalayas: Emergence and Issues* (ed) Karubaki Datta.

The largest increase was in Arunachal Pradesh—from 10 to 17. Assam and Tripura also registered sizeable increase. Other States, however, did not witness much addition of new towns in the last decade. Moreover, States like Mizoram and Nagaland did not see any addition of new towns at all.

While most of these towns are emerging as multi-ethnic settlements, there are some which are inhabited by a particular ethnic community. For instance, in Arunachal Pradesh, Zero is inhabited by the Apatanis, Tewang by the Monpas, Teju by the Mishmis, Along by the Galongs, Deomali by the Wanchoos and so on (Sengupta 2006: 314).

Most state capitals and urban centres of the North-East are unplanned. They have grown disproportionately, both in terns of human and vehicular population. Their ability to look after the sewerage and garbage is suspect. Guwahati, with garbage overflowing into the main roads, is a classic example. Shillong, too, is not far behind. The once clear and clean Umkhrah river has turned into a natural sewer absorbing the solid waste of a burgeoning population. It is the same with Imphal, Itanagar, Gangtok and Aizawl. Even urban basic services appear to have failed citizens. Following the rise in land prices owners are filling up their ponds for sale. Constructions are coming up on such land in and around Agartala in a big way defying safety rules. In the early part of August 2009 the Centre signed two agreements with the Asian Development Bank, one for Rs. 1,000 crore for the improvement of urban facilities and amenities in Aizawl, Agartala, Gangtok, Kohima and Shillong and the other for Rs. 500 crore for widening the East-West corridor now under construction. All that the Centre needs to do is to adopt a pragmatic result-oriented approach with proper accountability, and concentrate on completing ongoing projects (*Statesman*, August 12, 2009).

Guwahati, known as the gateway to the region, is developing at a mad pace. One is appalled to find plush residential quarters in the heart of Guwahati city that are shooting up to 12 storeys. This in a region known to be in an active earthquake zone (Zone V)! Land prices in Guwahati and Shillong are skyrocketing! A walk along the roadside near Shillong's pastoral Umiam Lake shows the massive depredation of forests and abrupt instances of urbanization and commercial use of land. The feeder rivers and water-bodies that are supposed to flow into Umiam Lake are now affected by these structures in the lake's catchment areas. Soon after the monsoon is over, the lake starts drying up to the extent that islands on it look like weather-beaten bones.

The authorities in Guwahati are said to have suddenly woken up to the perils of a high seismic zone and decided to go in for a technical audit of about 1,500 multistoried buildings which have come up over the past 10 years. Similarly, the Tripura government has also initiated a move to identify buildings which have sprung up in and around Agartala by ignoring safety regulations (Chakrabarty, *Statesman*, December 12, 2011).

Chief Ministers of North-eastern states have realized rather late in the day that ruralization as opposed to urbanization is the answer to most problems. The more the rush for urbanization, the greater are the problems of overpopulated cities, with their diminishing capacities, to cater to the civic requirements of people.

Minerals

This region is endowed with oil, natural gas and huge mineral resources such as coal, limestone, iron ore, mica, gypsum, gold, sillimanite, fireclay, kaoline, pyrites, different kinds of road-building stones, and uranium. The uranium deposits at Domisariat in the West Khasi district of Meghalaya are of a high grade capable of generating 1500 MW. Efforts by the Uranium Corporation of India Ltd. to mine the ore has met with stiff opposition from the civil society of Meghalaya, led primarily by the Khasi Students' Union. The movement has gained momentum after three rivers in the Jaintia Hills have turned toxic due to mining activities (Mukhim, *Statesman*, March 19, 2012).

Coal deposits are assessed at 371 million tonnes in Assam, 584.01 million tonnes in Meghalaya, 91 million tonnes in Arunachal Pradesh and 17.2 million tonnes in Nagaland. Deposits of nickel-cobalt minerals in the Tuensang and Kohima areas have been discovered.

Oil and Gas

The NER has been pioneer in India in exploration and production of petroleum. Asia's first successful mechanically drilled oil was in Makum (Assam) way back in 1867. This was followed by the first commercial exploration of crude oil at Digboi (Assam) in 1889 making the beginning of oil industry in India. In the year 1959, the Oil India Limited (OIL) and the Oil and Natural Gas Commission (ONGC) were set up in India for exploration and production of hydrocarbons. Crude oil is available at Naharkatiya, Moran, Hugrijan, Rudra Sagar lake in Assam and in Tripura. Oil struck in the Wokha area of Nagaland is officially stated to be of better quality. Oil Refineries have been established at Digboi, Noonmati, Bongaigaon and Numaligarh. Total reserves of oil in the NER are estimated at 158 million tonnes (Chatterjee, 2010:875).

The Government of India has signed a Memorandum of Understanding in July 2011 with Jubilant Oil and Gas Private limited, a firm registered in the Netherlands and listed on the London Stock Exchange but which operates out of Noida near Delhi, for exploration in Tamenglong, Churachandpur and Jiribam districts of Manipur (Laba, *Statesman*, April 2, 2012).

Industry

Apart from tea plantation, oil exploration, some coal mining and extraction of timber, there was little value-addition activities in the NER. Development of the region in a systematic manner took place only after Independence under the Five Year Plans, mainly in the 1960s. During the post-independence plan period, a number of major industries based on the rich mineral and forest resources like the Fertilizer factory at Namrup, cement factory at Bokajan, Paper Mills at Jagi Road and Badarpur have been set up under the Central public sector. In the State public sector also a number of industries have come up (Chatterjee 2010:875). A Green Field Industrial Corridor will be set up in Arunachal Pradesh by the Union Ministry of Commerce, Trade and Industry for which an amount of Rs. 75 crore will be provided by the Central Government. With the setting of this Corridor industrial growth could be visible in the State soon (*The Hindu*, December 5, 2011).

A State-wise principal characteristics of annual survey of industries in NER in 2007-08 is given in Table 1.10

Handicrafts

Handicrafts of the area are a novelty. Wood carving and textiles of Nagaland, basketry and cane work of Tripura and pottery and textiles of Manipur have a huge market not only outside the region but outside India also. Nagaland's handloom and handicrafts are famed for their superior quality. The beautiful hand woven tribal shawls, Naga *mekhalas,* and handbags are exquisitely and intricately designed and have won worldwide appreciation. Naga weavers narrate stories of crimes, passion and adulterer in the linen and give a fabric a personal touch. Since designs from the Naga tradition are not protected by the Intellectual Property Rights (IPR), these are freely copied and the Nagas are losing out on much of what is rightfully theirs.

The women of the North-East are good weavers. They produce beautiful traditional garments for their livelihood. However, the import of foreign products is reducing the demand for the traditional tribal products which provide employment to women.

Trade and Commerce

When the **Look East Policy (LEP)** was conceptualized in the corridors

Table 1.10: State-wise Principal Characteristics of Annual Survey of Industries in NER (2007-2008)

(Value Figures in Rs. Lakh and Others in Number)

States	Factories	Fixed Capital	Productive Capital	Invested Capital	Workers	Total Persons Engaged	Wages to Workers	Total Emolu-ments	Total Input	Gross Output	Depre-ciation	Net Value Added	Rent Paid	Interest Paid
Assam	1859	891081	1237240	1301965	113132	134284	42729	75245	2705324	3104360	71563	327473	6463	36889
Meghalaya	90	61033	116154	83251	4574	5587	2950	4839	110950	171468	6549	53969	1088	4060
Tripura	340	24494	45797	46419	20696	22896	3579	5035	60280	76615	1987	14348	296	1213
Nagaland	104	2792	5201	6953	2494	2974	501	743	9646	13606	244	3716	41	222
Manipur	69	1141	1972	2006	2442	2722	569	681	4623	5825	107	1096	31	81

Source: Compiled from Various Reports of Annual Survey of Industries. Quoted in NEFDi Databank downloaded from db.nedfi.com.

of power in New Delhi, the North-East was nowhere on the radar. It was a foreign policy shift after this country realised that ties with Southeast Asia were as significant as those with the Western world. Also, the growth of China's economic and political clout around the region must have given New Delhi the impetus to start looking eastwards, but mainly through the sea routes. It is in this context that Visakhapatnam became an important sea port and made major gains by trading with and through Southeast Asia. India was not even remotely thinking of any trade through land routes in the North-East.

The improved intensification of economic linkages with the Association of South East Asian Nations (ASEAN) motivated India to enter into the second phase of its LEP, which preeminently emphasizes the development of the North-East because of its proximity to South-East Asia. The North-East India being a landlocked region, its trade and commerce with the rest of India makes it non-viable. It is easier, faster and more lucrative for Meghalaya and Tripura to send their products via Bangladesh. Similarly, it makes sense for Nagaland, Manipur and Mizoram to trade with Myanmar. The LEP envisages the North-East region not as a periphery of India but as a centre of a thriving and integrated economic space linking two dynamic regions. The ethnic origin of the people is also more similar to the people of the South Asian region than that of the Indian mainland. The North-eastern region would be the India's gateway to this vast ASEAN region and a free trade relation is expected to be established between India and the ASEAN countries.

The LEP can bring focus on the North-East, allowing for not only visibility and increasing border trade but also opening prospects for a social intermingling that will result in opportunities in education, health and tourism. The LEP may effectively address the most chronic problems of the youth of the North Eastern Region, i.e. the problem of unemployment. They will get job directly as well as indirectly.

At present two trade centres—one in Manipur at Moreh-Tammu sector, since April 1995 and another in Mizoran at Chaimphai-Rih sector since January 2004 are operating between the two countries. An Integrated Check-post at Moreh on the pattern of the Wagah Check-post is coming up.

The tradable items permissible through Moreh are 22 commodities and there is a proposal to increase it to 44 commodities. Major export items include cement, engineering goods, transport equipment, motorcycles, iron and steel, medicine, chemicals and allied products and cotton yarn. The items imported from Myanmar through barter mechanism include betel nuts, turmeric, red kidney beans (*rajma*), *kuth* roots, gram, resin, dry ginger, etc. The volume of trade at the Moreh-Tamu Border Point in 2001-02 was worth Rs. 95.48 million and in 2009-10 it was Rs. 298.19 million, which indicates an average increase of 39 per cent. The LEP and the related innovative measures to promote and enhance trade link with Southeast Asia provide Manipur with a comparative advantage. The Free Trade Agreement with ASEAN has also opened up newer vistas for trade with these countries.

While the NE could import from Myanmar through the land route items like rice, pulses, beans and teak, the scope for export of finished goods from the NE would open up. The industrial raw materials could arrive in NE from Kolkata via Sittwe port. NE should not be a corridor for transit of goods. There must be processing and value addition in the region. To take advantage of the possibilities, the road network must develop in the NE. Production facilities would have to be set up and warehouses built to supply manufactured items to Myanmar markets smoothly. Besides, facilities at border trading points must be developed. Efforts are under way to develop infrastructure at the border trade point at Phi-Zowkathar in Mizoram sector by upgradation of the Rhi-Tiddim and Rhi-Falam Road segments in Myanmar. There is a proposal for a MoU on the Rhi-Tiddin Road between India and Myanmar, connecting Manipur directly to Tiddim for border trade. Besides, the India-Myanmar-Bangladesh trilateral highway is also on the anvil. The Border Roads Organization is already building the Tamu-Kalayamyo Road that would help in border trade (*The Times of India*, May 4, 2012, 13).

A major portion of the trade between the two countries is unofficial. Businessmen or traders from Imphal, Kohima, Silchar, Aizawl, Shillong, Guwahati and Kolkata work through the local agents at the different trade centres like Moreh, Champhai and Lungmalong on Myanmar border. A large section of the population, including people in public life and administration, educated unemployed youth, common men, women and children are involved in unofficial trade as a means of their earning. The introduction of new trade routes like the proposed railway link between Delhi and Hanoi (Vietnam) will create more job opportunities for both the educated and uneducated youth of NER, uplift the socio-economic conditions of the region, mitigate the insurgency problem in general and check illegal cross border trade of the region in particular (Th. Binarani Devi: 2008, 320).

Although the policy has been in place for a decade and a half, the NER has gained very little. Indeed, there is considerable potential for the policy to benefit the region but that would call for a qualitative change in the relationship with the neighbouring countries, particularly the larger countries of Bangladesh, China and Myanmar to improve connectivity, provide for better management of water resources of the region including flood control, foster trade and improve cultural exchanges.

Service Sector

Tourism

With its moderate climate most of the year, the NER is ideal for tourism. This region offers visitors a rare fiesta of unique natural beauty, brightly painted antique monasteries, challenging rivers, chains of blue, drowsy hills, tribal crafts showcasing the antiquity of protected cultural traditions and indigenous sports that have survived the passage of time. Each State has its own hidden treasures and their mesmerizing appeal underscores the unchained melody that heralds their ancient linkages.

The natural beauty of the region is awesome. If properly addressed, it is a factor which can make the region an international tourist destination. Where one can find enthralling mountain slopes and cool alpine climate on the one hand, and giant water bodies, rivers, torrential rainfall and primary tropical forests on the other! The region can offer tourists diverse and unparalleled experience such as one gets in Switzerland, Brazil or Bali in Indonesia.

This is a sector with a very high potential for generating income and employment. The focus, however, should be on high-value tourism which will require close collaboration with the private sector hospitality industry, building high-quality infrastructure and well-targeted promotion. Several tourist circuits could be developed in the region, depending on the attractions and experiences they present. Annual music and dance carnivals, held in different parts of the North East, with national and international participation, like the Hornbill Festival conducted annually at Kohima in December and Sangai Tourism Festival in Imphal, could attract visitors. Similarly, tourist visits and circuits could be built around the colourful Bihu festival in Assam and Dusshera festival in Manipur. The rich natural beauty, serenity and exotic flora and fauna of the area are invaluable resources for the development of eco-tourism. Unequalled opportunities for mountaineering, trekking, skiing, river-rafting, adventure tourism, studying the rich flora and fauna and the diverse wildlife make the region unique. Boat cruises on the Brahmaputra would be exciting and memorable. However, this should be done in a sustainable manner, keeping in mind the fragile environment.

It is often overlooked that North East is a *Craft Heaven,* and craftsmanship is jealously guarded as a part of the heritage by almost all the tribes in the region. *Craft Tours* can be organized for the visitors. *Tex Tourism* has been a success in many South East Asian countries including Thailand, Laos and Vietnam.

The number of tourists both, foreign and domestic, visiting the North-East in 2009 and 2010 is given in Table 1.11.

Table 1.11: Domestic and Foreign Tourists Visit North East, 2009 and 2010

Tourist Inflow	*2009*	*2010*
No. of Domestic Tourists	5772068	6166269
No. of Foreign Tourists	47658	50950

Source: Ministry of Tourism, Govt. of India, quoted in NEFDi Databank downloaded from db.nedfi.com.

It will appear from Table 1.11 that 57.72 lakh domestic tourists visited North-East in 2009 and 61.66 lakh in 2010, registering an increase of roughly 7 per cent. In the case of foreign tourists the increase was also to the tune of roughly 7 per cent.

So long the foreigners were required to obtain Restricted Area and Protected Area Permits to visit certain areas of the North-East. So strict are the rules that even those from the region who have foreign wives find it difficult to get permits for their spouses and children. With a view to attracting foreigners, the Centre has withdrawn the restriction imposed on the foreigners under the Foreigners (Protected Areas) Order, 1958 of obtaining Protected Area permit to travel to Manipur, Mizoram and Nagaland. This concession was extended to all foreigners excluding Pakistani and Chinese with effect from January 1, 2011. The relief, however, won't be applicable to foreigners who would like to go to Arunachal Pradesh. So Arunachal Pradesh is the only state left in the North-East where foreigners are required to take prior permission before any visit. Citizens of some specified countries, including Pakistan and China, continue to require prior approval of the Ministry of Home Affairs before their visit to these three states (*The Times of India*, January 1, 2011).

Unfortunately, tourism projects are limping in most of the States for dearth of funds and lack of proper planning. If the Centre is really serious to make tourism a trailblazer, it must formulate a uniform tourism policy for the North-East. Only an integrated plan with the cooperation of all the States can explore the region's immense potential. What actually discourages people from visiting the region, particularly Nagaland and Manipur, is not the sense of insecurity but the lack of infrastructure, mostly communications and basic amenities of a desired standard. Individual States with resource constraints can do little unless tourism is treated as an integrated plan encompassing all the North-East States. All the eight States have to adopt a common tourism policy and develop a modern outlook of tourism culture to either make waves or sink together.

Information Technology Industry

Other important services that present an opportunity for development are in the financial sector including banking, and insurance, the information technology industry. The IT industry, however, requires significant capacity building, a larger emphasis within the education system towards mathematics and science, and creating the environment to induce information technology companies to operate in the region. Some information technology companies have found significant potential for sourcing employees in the region, and it is important to create favourable conditions for their operation. Creation of education and training facilities for the youth of the region in Information Technology (IT) and Information Technology Enabling Services (ITES) could provide a great impetus in generating a pool of personnel increasing employment opportunities for the youth.

Banking

Financial infrastructure is essential for economic development. The spread of banks was thin in the NER. Even as late as 1969, just before the nationalization of banks, there were only about 74 bank offices in Assam with deposits of Rs. 33 core. The position has, however, changed perceptibly. In 2010 there were 2277 bank offices in the NER which increased to 2479 in 2011 and the deposits in the banks were a whopping Rs. 97,783 crores in 2011, the state-wise break-up are given in Tables 1.12 and 1.13, respectively.

Education

Education plays a very important role in promotion of economic, social,

Table 1.12: Sate-wise number of offices of Commercial Banks—2010 and 2011

State	*As on March 31st*	
	2010	*2011*
Arunachal Pradesh	81	88
Assam	1494	1558
Manipur	81	84
Meghalaya	214	221
Mizoram	99	101
Nagaland	91	96
Sikkim	77	83
Tripura	240	248
Grand Total (All India)	88203	93080

Note: 1. Data are as per information reported by banks.
2. Data on number of offices include administrative offices.

Source: Master Office File (Latest updated version) on banks, DSIM, RBI. Quoted in NEFDi Databank downloaded from db.nedfi.com.

political and institutional development. Education promotes development of all the sectors including agriculture, industry and social. Sustainable development cannot take place without investments being made in people. It is now widely accepted that the improvements in the quality if people as productive agents, must be a central objective of development policies. Access to educational institutions promoting skill development is a prerequisite for providing trained man power. As per 1991 census literacy rate of NER was 58.09 per cent (All India 52.2%), in 2001 it was 68.5 per cent (all India 64.8%), and in 2011 it was 74.35 per cent (all India 74.94%). Table 1.14 gives an idea about the growth of literacy in this region.

Some of the north-eastern states are ahead of the national average in respect to literacy. Mizoram's effective literacy rate is as high as 91.58 per cent, Tripura with 87.75 per cent is second, Sikkim with a 82.20 per cent of literacy rate occupies third position. Nagaland, Manipur and Meghalaya has a literacy rate 80.11 per cent, 79.85 per cent and 75.48 per cent respectively. However, the performance of Assam (73.18%) and Arunachal Pradesh (66.95%) are below the national average of 74.04 per cent. The most spectacular increase in literacy rate in this decade was registered by Tripura with 14.56 per cent, closely followed by Sikkim (13.39%), Nagaland (13.52%), Meghalaya (12.92%) and Arunachal Pradesh (12.61%).

Table 1.13: State-wise Distribution of Deposits and Credit of Scheduled Commercial Banks in NER, 2011

(*As on March 31*)

State	Deposits				Credit				Credit Deposit Ratio
	Amount (in crores)	Per cent share in total deposits	Per capita deposits (in Rs.)	Deposits per office (in Rs. lakh)	Amount (in crores)	Per cent share in total credit	Per capita credit (in Rs.)	Credit per office (in Rs. lakh)	
Arunachal Pradesh	5422	0.1	43691	6305	1220	0.0	9831	1419	22.50
Assam	59101	1.1	19334	3930	21053	0.5	6887	1400	35.62
Manipur	3537	0.1	14443	4261	1159	0.0	4733	1396	32.77
Meghalaya	9797	0.2	37379	4515	2351	0.1	8970	1083	24.00
Mizoram	2629	0.0	26185	2656	1131	0.0	11265	1142	43.02
Nagaland	5265	0.1	23410	5661	1346	0.0	5985	1447	25.57
Tripura	8731	0.2	24145	3653	2739	0.1	7575	1146	31.37
Sikkim	3301	0.1	53938	4026	1245	0.0	20343	1518	37.72
All India	5426508	100.0	46321	6090	4076867	100.0	34800	4575	76.54

Note: Population per office, per capita deposits and per capita credit figures are worked out on the basis of population figures as on March 1, 2011 supplied by the Office of the Registrar General, Government of India.

Source: *Quarterly Statistics on Deposits and Credit of Scheduled Commercial Banks, March 2010 & 2011, RBI, quoted in NEFDi Databank, downloaded from db.nedfi.com.*

Table 1.14: Literacy rate of North-eastern States and percentage change in literacy: 2001 and 2011

State	Literacy rate (%) 2001	Literacy rate (%) 2011	Decadal difference (%) (2001-2011)	All-India ranking in 2001	All-India ranking in 2011
	(1)	(2)	(3)	(4)	(5)
Arunachal Pradesh	54.34	66.95	12.61	33	34
Assam	63.25	73.18	9.93	25	26
Manipur	69.93	79.85	9.92	22	16
Meghalaya	62.56	75.48	12.92	27	24
Mizoram	88.80	91.58	2.78	2	3
Nagaland	66.59	80.11	13.52	20	15
Sikkim	68.81	82.20	13.39	17	13
Tripura	73.19	87.75	14.56	13	4
All India	64.83	74.04	9.21		

Source: Statement 24 Ranking of States and Union Territories by literacy rate: 2001 and 2011. *www.imaginmor.com/census-of-india-2011.html*

The higher educational institutions like colleges and universities have also come up in nearby urban centres. Considering that the present modern higher learning set-up in this region has an antecedence of a little more than 100 years, the growth in the number of institutions of higher learning here has, indeed been spectacular. With each of the States now having at least one Central university, the latest tally of universities serving this region now stands at eighteen, which includes two Agricultural universities at Jorhat and Imphal. The Department of Biotechnology has set up an Institute of Bio-resources and Sustainable Development at Imphal. The Indian Council of Agricultural Research (ICAR) National Research Centre exists in Nagaland, Arunahcal Pradesh and Assam. There is the North Eastern Space Research Organisation and a regional Centre of the Indira Gandhi National Open University also. Besides, with an Indian Institute of Technology at Guwahati, an Indian Institute of Management and an Indian Institute of Medical Science at Shillong, the Regional Medical College at Imphal, one National Institute of Technology (deemed university) in each of the eight States, the region now hosts a number of institutions of excellence. The number of universities, colleges and polytechnics in this region as on September 30, 2009 is given in Table 1.15.

Table 1.15: Number of Universities, Colleges & Polytechnics

(As on 30th September, 2009)

State	Universities	Arts, Fine Arts, Social Work, Science and Commerce	Engineering/ Technology/ Architecture	Medical	Education/ Teacher Training	Total Colleges	Polytechnics
Arunachal Pradesh	2	17	3	1	1	23	3*
Assam	6	337*	9	7*	40**	546	10
Manipur	1	59	3	1	5	73	3**
Meghalaya	2	88	2	3	4	118	3
Mizoram	1	23	0	2	2	29	2
Nagaland	1	45	0	0	3	74	0
Sikkim	3	5	2	3	2	18	2
Tripura	2	16	2	4	1	29	1
All India	40	14321	2894	2074	3357	25938	1914

Note: ** repeated from 2006-07, * repeated from 2007-08, ^ repeated from 2008-09

Source: Statistics of Higher & Technical Education 2009-10 quoted in NEFDi Databank, downloaded from db.nedfi.com

The higher educational institutions have encouraged the students to go for higher studies. The opportunities in government service for qualified persons have attracted the villagers to modern education. Spread of education has changed the attitude of the villagers in many respects. Now many of them are aware of the various rural development pogrammes and various economic opportunities available outside the village periphery. At the same time, it also created apathy towards agriculture on which their village economy still has a greater dependence.

Healthcare

Focus on other aspects of human development such as basic health needs is equally important for capacity development. The States of the NER have a poorly developed health care delivery system both in terms of healthcare personnel and healthcare institutions and infrastructure especially in rural and tribal areas. The shortage of medical specialists and lack of tertiary facilities in several states needs to be addressed, along with issue such as the high incidence of AIDS, cancer, malaria, and other diseases, and the wide gaps in rural-urban provisioning of basic services. The health and nutrition status of the region especially for children and women requires to be raised.

Table 1.16 shows the population served per doctor, per hospital bed, per hospital and per bed in all allopathic embellishments in the different States of the North East and compares the last three sets of figures with the corresponding all-India averages. The Table shows that the population served per doctor is quite high in all the States of the North East. It also shows that compared to the all-India average, the population served per hospital bed is higher in four out of the eight States of the North East, namely Tripura, Nagaland, Meghalaya and Assam. According to the Figures given in Table 1.16, in all the eight States of the North East, the population served per hospital is higher than the all-India average and the population served per bed in all allopathic establishments is higher than the all-India average in Tripura and Assam (Dasgupta, 2008:77-78).

Table 1.16: Population Served Per Doctor, Per Hospital Bed and Per Hospital in the North East

State	*Population Served per doctor*	*Period to which data relate*	*Population served per hospital bed*	*Population served per hospital*	*Population as on*	*Population served per bed in all allopathic estabs. On 1.1.02*
Arunachal Pradesh	3755	31.12.1999	880	83600	1.1.2002	475
Assam	11980	1.1. 1999	1782	84183	1.1.1991	1410
Manipur	2820	31.12.1991	1378	125737	1.1.2001	931
Meghalaya	5581	31.12.1990	1958	347714	31.3.2000	738
Mizoram	10360	1.1. 1999	863	81000	31.3.2001	465
Nagaland	6292	31.12.1991	1747	99059	31.3.2000	848
Sikkim			834	292000	1.1.2002	449
Tripura	4693	1.1.1999	1800	118185	1.1.2001	1420
All India			1503	66758	1.1.2002	1124

Source: *p. 78 of Globalization and North East India 2008* (Eds) Bamal J. Deb & Others.

North-East India can offer medical treatment to patients from across the border at its hospitals. Training for health personnel from Myanmar and other neighbouring countries could be offered at institutions in the region, such as the North Eastern Indira Gandhi Regional Institute of Health and Medical Sciences and the Indian Institute of Public Health in Shillong and the Regional Institute of Medical Sciences in Imphal.

Problem of Poverty and Its Elimination

Economic growth and social justice are two inseparable objectives of the economic efforts. Therefore, apart from growth acceleration poverty elimination is another important criterion to be studied to judge the positive impact of the new economic policy on an economy. Higher growth rate of the economy does not mean economic development in the real sense of the term. Higher economic growth is not meaningful, if a large section of the people suffers from acute poverty which manifests in poor quality of life, deprivation from basic amenities of life, malnutrition, illiteracy and low human resource development. Thus economic reforms aim not only at a higher rate of economic growth but also at tackling the problem of poverty and unemployment.

An analysis of the percentage of population below poverty line of the North-eastern States during the period 1973-74 to 2004-05 as given in Table 1.17, reveals that all the States except Manipur have achieved the distinction of alleviating the economic condition of their population to a great extent with Sikkim leading the NER States with only 8.40 per cent of its population below the poverty line in 2004-05, followed by Mizoram (17.30%), Arunachal Pradesh (17.60%), Nagaland (18.50%), Assam (19.70%), Tripura (20.10%) and Meghalaya (30.70%) in that order. Meghalaya with 30.70 per cent population below the poverty line is rather on the higher side of the poverty line.

Table 1.17: Per cent of population below Poverty Line

State	*1973-74*	*1983-84*	*1993-94*	*2004-05 (based on MRP Consumption)*
Arunachal Pradesh	51.93	40.88	39.35	17.60
Assam	51.21	40.47	40.86	19.70
Manipur	49.96	37.02	33.78	38.30
Meghalaya	50.20	38.81	37.92	30.70
Mizoram	50.32	36.00	25.66	17.30
Nagaland	50.81	39.25	37.92	18.50
Sikkim	50.86	39.71	41.43	8.40
Tripura	51.00	40.03	39.01	20.10
All India	54.88	44.48	35.97	32.80

Source: Table A 13.2 of India Development Report 2011 (ed) D.M.Nachane, 2011, Oxford University Press, pp. 287-88.

Growth Trajectories

The economy of North-East India has got its definite identity due to its peculiar physical, economic and socio-cultural characteristics. Per Capita Net State Domestic Product (PCNSDP) gives a rough idea about the economic condition of NER with respect to all-India level. Table 1.18 gives the State-wise break-up of Per Capita Net State Domestic Product during the period 1980-81 to 1996-97. It will appear there from that all the States of NER except Arunachal Pradesh and Mizoram are below the all-India level for the years 1985-86 to 1994-95. This Table shows the economic backwardness of the region in general and Assam in particular.

Table 1.18: Per Capita Net State Domestic Product (at 1980-81 prices)

(in Rupees)

State	*1980-81*	*1985-86*	*1990-91*	*1994-95*	*1995-96*	*1996-97*
Arunachal Pradesh	1571	2119	2710	3265	3304	3059
Assam	1284	1510	1544	1585	1606	1628
Manipur	1419	1598	1739	1986	1993	—
Meghalaya	1361	1412	1733	1673	1808	1837
Mizoram	1289	2658	4474	7743	—	—
Nagaland	1448	1653	1916	2270	—	—
Tripura	1307	1240	1646	1898	2113	2197
India	1625	1857	2267	2533	2664	2814

Source: p.200 of *Globalization and North East India* (ed).

In India, the growth rate of income per capita almost tripled from 1.5 per cent during 1951-81 to 4.2 per cent during 1981-2009. Within the latter period, growth accelerated from 2.8 per cent in the 1980s to 4.2 per cent in the 1990s and then surged to 6.1 per cent in 2001-2009. Table 1.19 shows the Net Domestic Product Per Capita Growth Rates (%) in the following North-East States for the period 2001-2009.

Table 1.19: Net State Domestic Product Per Capita Growth Rates in States (%)

State	*2001-09*
Assam	3.53
Arunachal Pradesh	5.34
Meghalaya	3.01
Sikkim	6.19
Tripura	5.85
All-India	6.1

Source: p.49 of *Economic & Political Weekly*, Vol. XLVII No. 3, January 21, 2012.

Sikkim's NSDP was more or less at par with the all-India average while Tripura and Arunachal Pradesh were not much lagging behind.

More or less the same pattern was revealed when the growth pattern of State Domestic Product (SDP) by major sectors from 1981-2007 of seven States of NER, excepting Mizoram which was excluded from the study due to lack of database for the related variables, was analyzed. The SDP data have been classified into three parts: agricultural SDP, industrial SDP and SDP originating from the services sector. The agricultural sector consists of agriculture and allied activities, fishery and forestry. The industrial sector includes mining and quarrying, manufacturing, construction, electricity, gas and water supply. The services sector comprises the rest of the sub-sectors. The SDP data are incorporated in Table 1.20.

Table 1.20: Growth Pattern of SDP by Major Sectors from 1981-2007 (at constant 1999-2000 prices, in % per annum)

States	*Agriculture*	*Industry*	*Services*
Arunachal Pradesh	4.73	11.59	7.52
Assam	1.72	5.17	5.56
Manipur	3.02	7.32	4.15
Meghalaya	3.41	7.72	5.81
Nagaland	8.61	13.60	5.27
Sikkim	5.31	8.57	10.40
Tripura	3.04	11.08	8.24
North-east region (NER)	2.31	6.12	5.82
All-India	3.22	6.43	8.31

Source: *Economic and Political Weekly*, Volume xlvii No.6 dated 11-2-2012, p.73.

As one would expect, there is a considerable variation in the performance of individual states in respect of sectoral growth. It is seen from Table 1.20 that during 1981-2007 four of the North-East States, viz., Arunachal Pradesh, Meghalaya, Nagaland and Sikkim have grown at a rate higher than all-India standards in respect of agricultural SDP. Within the NER, Nagaland has been diagnosed as the top-growing State followed by Sikkim, Arunachal Pradesh, Meghalaya, Tripura, Manipur and Assam. In respect of the industrial sector, all the North East States except Assam have grown at a rate higher than the all-India standards. Within the NER, Nagaland has been identified as the top-growing State in terms of income-generation from the industrial sector, followed by Arunachal Pradesh and Tripura, whereas Assam secured the bottom place in the list. The growth pattern of services sector SDP reveals that Sikkim and Tripura have grown at a rate higher than the all-India standards during the study period. Within the NER, Sikkim has been identified as the top-growing State in terns of income-generation from services, followed by Tripura and Arunachal Pradesh, whereas Manipur secured the bottom place in the list. It also shows that though Assam contributes around 70 per cent of total SDP of NER during the period 1981-2007, its performance in respect of sectoral growth is among the poorest in the region (*Economic and Political Weekly* Vol. xlvii no.6, p.73).

Social and economic progress achieved by the North-eastern States can be assessed by the Human Development Index (HDI) prepared by the Planning Commission. Human Development Index is a composite of variables capturing attainments in three dimensions of human development, viz. economic, educational and health, which is worked out by a combination of measures: per capita monthly expenditure adjusted for inequality, a combination of literacy rate and intensity of formal education, and a combination of life expectancy at age 1 and infant mortality rate. The Human Development Index of the North-eastern States, given in Table 1.21, indicates that the ranks of some States such as Mizoram, and Manipur are quite high throughout this period while that of Nagaland and Sikkim were high for two consecutive decades (1981 and 1991)., and that of Meghalaya for only one year, i.e. in 1981. Other States are below the national average. Compared with other Indian States, levels of socio-economic development of North-Eastern States do not lag much behind.

Table 1.21: Human Development Index by State, 1981, 1991 and 2001

States	*Ranked with respect to all-India 32 States/UTs in*					
	1981		*1991*		*2001*	
	Value	*rank*	*Value*	*rank*	*Value*	*rank*
Arunachal Pradesh	(0.242)	31	(0.328)	29	(0.328)	
Assam	(0.272)	26	(0.348)	26	(0.386)	14
Manipur	(0.461)	4	(0.536)	9	(0.536)	
Meghalaya	(0.317)	21	(0.365)	24	(0.365)	
Mizoram	(0.411)	8	(0.548)	7	(0.548)	
Nagaland	(0.328)	20	(0.486)	11	(0.394)	
Sikkim	(0.342)	18	(0.425)	18	(0.425)	
Tripura	(0.287)	24	(0.389)	22	(0.389)	
India	(0.302)		(0.381)		(0.472)	

Source: Table A 13.1 of India Development Report 2011 (ed) D.M. Nachane, for 1981 and 1991 and Table 17.4 of Globalization and North East India (ed) for 2011.

Environmental Degradation

Sustainable development, that is, 'meeting the present needs without compromising those of the future' (WCD, 1987), involves important inter-generational equity considerations, including those related to the environment. Environment is of importance not only because of its effects on the psychic and non-economic welfare, but also because of its impact on production over the long-term (World Bank, 2000).

Strategies of development such as big river dams by displacing a huge tract of tribal habitat, denudation of forest cover to build roads and other structures are bound to have serious impact on the ecology of the area. Industrialization has brought in its train pollution of the environment. Black carbon or soot emitted by diesel engines is threatening the North-eastern skies and its people. The International Agency for Research on Cancer (IARC), part of WHO, has announced that diesel engine exhaust causes lung cancer in humans (*The Times of India*, June 14, 2012, p.15). The Barapani Lake (local called it Umiam Lake) at Shillong has become polluted due to throwing of all solid garbage of the city (Mukhim, *Statesman*, August 8, 2011). Loktak in Moirang, 50 km south of Imphal, is the largest freshwater lake in the eastern region and is also known as the "Floating Lake" because of the presence of *phumdis*, a heterogeneous mass of vegetation, soil and organic matter in various stages of decomposition. The Centrally-sponsored prestigious 105 MW Loktak hydro-electric power project, commissioned in the late 1980s, draws water from the lake. The water level of the Lake has fallen dangerously making everybody jittery about their very existence (Lama, *Statesman*, April 20, 2009).

There are four major rivers in Meghalaya—the Kupli (Kopili), Umngot, Lukha and the Myntang. The Kupli and Lukha are already heavily polluted. Only the Umngot and Myntang are, perhaps, still pristine. The North Eastern Electric Power Corporation which generates hydro power from the Kupli river, has encountered several problems on account of the low *p*H content of the water. The seepage of acidic water from the coalmines adjoining the Lukha river was responsible for the pollution of the river (Mukhim, *Statesman*, 28 November, 2011).

A lot of tree cover has been lost due to wanton destruction of forests by the timber mafia for quick bucks by illegal felling of trees. The government has even sold parts of Keibul Lamjao National Park in Loktak Lake considered the last sanctuary of the nearly-extinct brow antlered deer, locally called *sangal*. Reports say the government has already sold parts of the park to 14 private individuals, complete with *pattas* (Lama, *Statesman*, November 28, 2011).

There are reports of encroachment on the Intanki National Park in Nagaland by illegal settlers. About one-fourth of the total area of 20,200 hectares have already been encroached and encroachers are buying land in the National park for Rs. 1000 an acre. Similarly the Rangaphar Reserve Forest which earlier covered over 8,800 hectares has shrunk to 176 hectares after fifty years of encroachment (Bera, *Sunday Statesman*, 9 January, 2011).

There is now nationwide concern that the drinking water scenario in India is evolving into a major crisis and tough measures need to be taken. Groundwater, the major source of rural supply, is fast depleting in many areas because of an expanding village irrigation network. In many areas, groundwater levels have shrunk by four to five feet. With the groundwater level decreasing drastically in most of the States in the North-eastern region, a total of 7,067 habitations across the region have been identified as "badly arsenic-affected" and another 29.030 as "fluoride-affected". The situation has deteriorated following the unusual prolonged drought. Even Cherapunjee in Meghalaya, once the wettest place on earth, is now drying up (Chakrabarty, *Statesman*, March 15, 2010).

Civil society groups pointed out that the on-going massive power projects were not based on informed a priori consent of the people. As such, projects would completely alter the life of a river, and hence, disparage climatic stability and affect rainfall, soil quality, underground water and the overall fragile ecology of the region. As the livelihood of tribes, communities and others living in the North East solely depends on cultivation, animal rearing and forest and mineral resources, any attempt to industrialization driven by forces of the capital and the state is bound to frustrate and anger a huge section of indigenous and other people rooted in the region (Biswas, *Statesman*, August 9, 2010).

Water Management

The waters of the Brahmaputra are shared by China, India and Bangladesh. The Tsangpo, also called the Yarlung Tsangpo, the highest river in the world, originates at Tamlung Tso Lake in Western Tibet, southeast of Mount Kailash and Lake Mansarovar, and later forms the South Tibet Valley and the Yarlung Tsangpo Grand Canyon before entering India at Tuting in Arunachal Pradesh. On entering India, the river is called the Siang and it flows for many a mile to meet the Lohit river, where it transforms into the Brahmaputra. Speculation about China building a dam on the Tsangpo at the great Bend, had started since the 1990s. China initially denied the allegation but admitted in April 2010 that it was, indeed, building the Zangmu Dam on the Brahmaputra. But it allayed all fears that the project would impact the downstream flow to India. However, with news that the same river which used to be several kilometres wide at Pasighat in east Siang district of Arunachal Pradesh has narrowed into several channels, leaving behind a bed that is dry and sandy, there are serious concerns about what will happen further down in lower riparian states. Given China's phenomenal thirst for power (hydro, thermal, nuclear, solar) to fuel its ever-growing manufacturing industries, the prospects of it damming every upstream river and/or diverting the flow of those rivers is real (Mukhim, *Statesman*, March 12, 2012).

Meanwhile, the Asia-Pacific Forum of Environmental Journalists has expressed concern over a number of dams on the Brahmaputra inside the Tibetan region of China. The umbrella organization of environmental journalists based in the Asia-Pacific region argues that once the dams on the 2,900-km trans-boundary river are commissioned, there will be a massive ecological effect in the North East and also in Bangladesh. The saline water of the Bay of Bengal will enter south Bangladesh and destroy the aquatic life and agricultural field (Thakuria, *Statesman*, March 11, 2012, p.8).

The Way Forward

The market oriented economic reform programme leads to the process of globalization. Innovation like money and private property which had no place in the traditional tribal economy, are playing a remarkable role in the process of change. New avenues for earning money, job opportunities in public services, government contracts, trading, sale of commercial products etc. already created a new horizon replacing traditional notion of self-sufficiency of a tribal village.

The growing educational standard, economic opportunities, interaction with different ethnic groups, emerging communication system as well as declining land-man ratio etc. are cumulatively playing an effective role for emerging occupational diversification in the North East. The people are now more in favour of doing business, getting contracts of small construction works or white-collar jobs. As a matter of fact, there has been a shift in the sectoral contribution from the primary sector (Agriculture, Fishing, Forestry and Logging, Mining and Quarrying) to the tertiary sector (Construction, Electricity, Gas, Water, Transport, Communication, Trade, Finance and Real Estate, Community and Personal Services).

In Assam, Meghalaya, Mizoram and elsewhere, the service sector the main growth engine, is now largely under the control of local entrepreneurs, be it hospitality, tourism and transport, healthcare, education or construction. Even in manufacturing and financial services where there was little "local" presence before, local entrepreneurs have set up a good number of these. Grant of dealership of vehicles, two-wheelers, petrol pumps and all kinds of "white goods" by national manufacturing companies primarily to "sons of the soil" as a matter of policy or some form of compulsion has prompted the growth of entrepreneurship and associated activities.

While there are legislations to protect land from being sold to non-tribal people on the logical argument that this would make it an unstoppable project, the same legislation is not applied to the tribes who have the right to own and purchase land not only in the hills but in the plains as well.

Community ownership of land and resources which was the hallmark of a tribal society has given way to individual ownership. Absence of a land-ceiling law has spawned a new rich land-owning class in the tribal society, leading to high incidence of landlessness, rural poverty and gross income inequality—features unknown, till recently, in tribal rural society. The emerging tribal rich are engaged in over-exploitation of mines and forests placed under their control in Sixth Schedule areas to reap short term gains regardless of the impact on the environment, ecology and future generations (Chatterjee, 2010: 864-870).

One may look at this stage the long-standing but somewhat erroneous perception that the region has been stagnating largely due to the lack of adequate central concern and investment. The per capita transfers under the aegis of the Finance Commission, Plan transfers and aggregate transfers during plan periods from 1969 to 1985 as shown in Table 1.22, will give an idea about the position of the North-eastern States vis-à-vis the other States. All the North-eastern States (Arunachal Pradesh and Mizoram attained statehood in 1987) are listed in the Special Category States and the disproportionate per-capita transfer of resources is too glaring. While the All India average of per capita transfers during this entire period was Rupees 1,765, it was as high as Rupees 17,998 in Nagaland, followed by Sikkim (Rupees 11,313), Manipur (Rupees 8,528), Meghalaya (Rupees 8,502) , Tripura (Rupees 5,227) and Assam (Rupees 2,650).

Table 1.22: Per Capita transfers under the aegis of Finance Commission, Plan transfers, other transfers and aggregate transfers during Plan periods

[In Rupees]

States	Fourth Plan (1969-74)	Fifth Plan (1974-78)	Annual Plans (1978-80)	Sixth Plan (1980-85)	Total
Assam	472	483	408	1287	2650
Manipur	815	1724	1351	4638	8528
Meghalaya	818	1350	1034	5300	8502
Nagaland	3080	3546	3120	8252	17998
Sikkim	—	1912	2592	6809	11313
Tripura	481	1039	814	2893	5227
Average of All States	248	318	288	911	1765

Source: Annexure X.12 at pages 328-330 of the Report of the Commission on Centre-State Relations, Part I.

The North-eastern States, Himachal Pradesh and Jammu and Kashmir have continued to gain significantly from the awards of the successive Finance Commissions since then.

Arunachal Pradesh has the distinction of receiving 85 per cent of its administrative and development costs from the Centre. The Centre's share for Nagaland and Manipur stood at 80 per cent, Mizoram 72 per cent, Meghalaya and Tripura 70 per cent, Assam 51 per cent and Sikkim 40 per cent (Deb, 2008:20).

The allocation of funds by the Central Government for North East India is high. In fact, Central funding leaves little incentive to raise local taxes and resources—always politically unpleasant—and creates a central dependency syndrome. State revenues are almost non-existent; non-plan expenditure including that spent on security is very high. The total dependence on central funds and direction has promoted passivism and encouraged corruption. It has created a government monopoly in employment which is destroying the work ethic of a modern economy.

The Annual Plan outlay for the year 2012-2013 was Rupees 3342 crore for Arunachal Pradesh, Rupees 10,500 crore for Assam, Rupees 3,500 crore for Manipur, Rupees 3939 crore for Meghalaya, Rupees 2,300 crore for Mizoram, Rupees 2,300 crore for Nagaland, Rupees 1877 crore for Sikkim and Rupees 2250 crore for Tripura. It means an outlay of Rupees 2.409 in Arunachal Pradesh, Rupees 0.334 in Assam, Rupees 1.285 in Manipur, Rupees 1.363 in Meghalaya, Rupees 2.108 in Mizoram, Rupees 1.162 in Nagaland, Rupees 3,104 in Sikkim and Rupees 0.513 in Tripura per thousand person. If we remember the fact that the plan outlay during the same period per thousand person for the neighbouring States of West Bengal, Bihar and Orissa was Rupees 0.2836, 0.222 and 0.411, respectively, then it will help remove the long-standing but somewhat erroneous perception that the North East has been stagnating largely due to the lack of adequate central concern and investment.

As a matter of fact development analysts could raise a question: is the region getting value for money from the approximately Rupees 30,000 crore being spent annually in the region, as stated by no less an authority than Union Minister of State for Commerce Jairam Ramesh? A substantial part of this amount is for the creation of productive assets and investments in roads, industries, technical and scientific education, research and training, telecom, health care, surface communications, etc. Certainly the region is not getting its due 'returns' from these investments due to poor implementation and low quality services. M.S. Swaminathan also does not mince words when he says, "outlay is, however, not getting converted into socially meaningful outcome" (Swaminathan, *The Hindu*, 2009). The Prime Minster has repeatedly expressed his concern over lack of governance and development in the region. He even publicly alleged in December 2008 that corruption in Miizoram under the MNF Government had reached epidemic proportions (*The Hindu*, November 26, 2008). There are charges of corruption against many politicians but North East India does not enjoy the reputation of probing such charges.

A survey conducted by the Association of Democratic Reforms, New Delhi and a Kohima-based youth organization gives an idea about how many rich politicians are there in States considered backward or undeveloped. Nagaland reportedly has 59 crorepatis. The Nagaland People's Front (which rules the State since 2003) tops the list with 26, followed by the Congress 13, the BJP's six, the RJD's two, the NCP and the UNDP one each. There are nine Independents in the category. Former Nagaland Chief Minster K.L. Chisi reportedlly has the highest assets of Rupees 46.77 crore. Nuklutoshi of the NPF has Rupees 41.82 crore, Congress Legislature Party Chief S.I. Jamir has Rupees 35.33 crore and Neiphiu Rio (Chief Minister since 2003) has Rupees 15.13 crore. There is no reason to believe the figures have been manipulated, these being the mandatory disclosures by candidates contesting the elections. They, however, need not worry getting into the taxmen's net because tribals are exempt.

According to the Meghalaya Election Watch, an NGO, the State has as many of 27 Crorepatis—mostly belonging to the Congress. Former Deputy Chief Minister, Deborah C. Marak, reportedly has assets worth Rupees 122 crore—the highest (Chatterjee, 2010: 888).

In the age of globalization no country, far less a region, can live in isolation within a protective cocoon. The world is opening up and so also India. An investment climate, conducive to industrialists, entrepreneurs and others, has to be created so that the LEP, formulated for the economic growth of this region, becomes successful. In the NER, there is still restriction between the States in mobility of human being, goods and services, through the restrictions of Inner Line Permit/Restricted Area Permit etc. and other government restrictions on possession of land entrepreneurship and business permit. People from the plains are not allowed to settle and cannot own properties. In Meghalaya, most cement companies are owned by non-tribal companies operating on the *benami* model.

Establishing peace, security and responsive governance are essential prerequisites for development. An integral part of a vision of development is of peace and harmony, and free from violent confrontations. Armed conflict has taken a heavy toll on economic progress, goodwill and happiness in the region. Governance is weak and there are widespread leakages – of revenues that should have accrued to the public exchequer, of expenditures on various development schemes due to rent-seeking of various kinds, and of large amounts of funds through rigging of contracts, according to the National Institute of Public Finance and Policy (NIPFP) report. It is a fact that armed conflict, going back more than five decades, "has dampened private investment in potentially productive sectors". The NIPFP adds, "nor have the initiatives by the Central and State Governments to accelerate development through various plans had the desired results. The system is full of leakages, perverse incentives towards economically productive initiatives and rent-seeking behaviour." It describes the widespread practices of parallel tax collections, random extortion, kidnapping and similar acts which may be characterized as 'roving banditry.' Added to poor governance, they create a situation of extreme tension and pressure, especially on the weak and vulnerable (*North Eastern Region: Vision 2020*, p.41).

Significantly since 1996 several bold initiatives have been taken by the Central Government by augmenting Central investments in different spheres of the economy with primary focus on the region's infrastructure in order to bring about perceptible changes in economic governance of the region. In fact, state intervention in the economy of the region has become more strident to prepare the ground for absorption of market oriented economic reforms. In the past one decade, central packages, new industrial policy, creation of non-lapsable pool of Central resources, creation of a Department for Development of North Eastern Region (DoNER) in September, 2001 on the recommendations of the Shukla Commission and its subsequent upgradation to a full-fledged ministry in May 2004, and revamping of the North Eastern Council have created the required springboard for development leap forward. The North Eastern Region Vision 2020 document brought about jointly by the Ministry of Development for North Eastern Region and the North Eastern Council provides the blue print for the development of the NER. Since fund is not a constraint, as assured by the Prime Minster himself on a number of occasions, what is required is the machinery, both political and administrative, to translate that vision into a reality.

REFERENCES

Alam, Khorshed (2008),"New Economic Policy and Assam's Economic Performance", In *Globalization and North East India (eds.)* Bimal J. Deb, Keya Sengupta and B. Datta Ray, New Delhi, Concept Publishing Company Lvt. Ltd.

Bera, Sayantan (2011), "Encroachers' paradise", *The Sunday Statesman*, 9 January.

Bhatacharjee, R.P. (2008), "Impact of New Economic Policy in North Eastern Region" In *Globalization and North East India* (eds.) Bimal J. Deb, Keya Sengupta and B. Datta Ray, New Delhi, Concept Publishing Company Pvt. Ltd.

Biswas, Prasenjit, (2010), "Cry, my beloved region", *The Statesman*, August 9, p. 8.

Chakrabarty, Satyabrata, (2010), "Coming soon, major catastrophe", *The Statesman,* March 15, p. 8.

_______, (2011), "Safety with quakes in mind", *The Statesman*, December 12, p. 8.

Chatterjee, Sarajit Kumar (2010), *North-East India: Dispersion and Discontent*, New Delhi, Abhijeet Publications.

Das Gupta, Malabika (2008),"Market-oriented Reforms in Health Care Delivery System and the North East", In *Globalization and North East India* (eds) Bimal J. Deb, Keya Sengupta and B. Datta Ray, New Delhi, Concept Publishing Company Pvt. Ltd.

Datta Ray, B. (2008), "North East India in the Context of New Economic Policy", In *Globalization and North East India* (eds.) Bimal J. Deb, Keya Sengupta and B. Datta Ray, New Delhi, Concept Publishing Company Pvt. Ltd.

Dutta, P.C., and Pradhan, B.C. (2008), "New Economic Policy and Development in NER of India", In *Globalization and North East India* (eds.) Bimal J. Deb, Keya Sengupta and B. Datta Ray, New Delhi, Concept Publishing Company Pvt. Ltd.

Dutta, Rangan (2011), "Need for a 'blue revolution", *The Statesman*, June 27, p. 8.

Dutta, Rangan (2011), "Now need for a white revolution", *The Statesman*, August 8, p. 8.

Deb, Bimal, J., (2008), "North East India and its Council for Development", In *Globalization and North East India* (eds.) Bimal J. Deb, Keya Sengupta and B. Datta Ray, New Delhi, Concept Publishing House.

Debnath, Avijit and Roy, Niranjan, (2012), "Structural Change and Inter-sectoral Linkages: the Case of North-East India", *Economic and Political Weekly*, Vol. xlvii no. 6, February 11, p. 73.

Devi, Th. Binarani, (2008), "India's Look East Policy and Youth of Manipur", In *Globalization and North East India* (eds.) Bimal J. Deb, Keya Sengupta and B. Datta Ray, New Delhi, Concept Publishing Company Pvt. Ltd.

Khawas, Vimal, (2006), "Trend and Levels of Urbanisation in the North-eastern Hill States of India and Related Environmental Issues", In *Urbanisaion in the Eastern Himalayas: Emergence and Issues, (ed.)* Karubaki Datta, New Delhi, Serials Publications.

Kumar, Utsav and Subramanian, Arvind, (2012), "Growth in India's States in the First Decade of the 21st Century: Four Facts", *Economic and Political Weekly,* Vol. XLVII No. 3, January 21, p. 49.

Laba, Yambam, (2012), "Nungba's day in dubious deals", *The Statesman*, April 2, p. 8.

Lama, J.B., (2009), "Saving Loktak is truly saving our life", *The Statesman,* April 20, p. 8.

________, (2011), "Decks being cleared for Chetia's extradition, but…", *The Statesman*, November 28, p. 8.

________, (2012), "Between demands, deadlines and deja vu", *The Statesman,* January 9, p. 8.

________, (2012), "So much for a rail route left to flounder", *The Statesman,* May 28, 2012, p. 8.

Mukhim, Patricia, (2011), "Overwhelmed by garbage", *The Statesman,* August 8, p. 8.

________, (2011), "Mortgaged to mining lobby", *The Statesman*, November 28, p. 8.

________, (2012), "Ruralisation the new mantra", *The Statesman*, February 27, p. 8.

________, (2012), "The China quotient in impending change", *The Statesman,* March 12, p. 8.

________, (2012), "The foreign hand bogeyman", *The Statesman*, March 19, p. 8.

________, (2012), "What's needed is the push from print to practice", *The Statesman*, April 30, p. 8.

Nachane, D.M., (ed), (2011), *India Development Report 2011*, New Delhi, Oxford University Press.

North Eastern Region Vision 2020, (2007), New Delhi, National Institute for Public Finance and Policy.

Report of the Commission on Centre-State Relations, Part I, (Sarkaria Commission), 1988.

Sen Gupta, Surojit, (2006), "A Sociological Study of Urbanisation in Arunachal Pradesh", In *Urbanisation in the Eastern Himalayas: Emergence and Issues, (ed)* Karubaki Datta, New Delhi, Serials Publications.

Singh, A. Rajmani, (2008), "Centrally Sponsored Schemes for Upliftment of Rural Economy of North East India: An Analysis", In *Society, Politics and Development in North East India (*eds) Asok Kumar Ray and Satyabrata Chakraborty, New Delhi, Concept Publishing Company Pvt. Ltd.

Swaminathan, M.S., (2009), "How to develop India's northeast", *The Hindu*, January 19, p. 8.

Thakuria, Nava, (2012), "Waiting for another uprising", *The Statesman*, March 12, p. 8.

WCED (World Commission on Environment and Development), (1987). *Our Common Future* (The Brundtland Commission Report), Oxford University Press, Oxford, UK.

World Bank, (2000), *Entering the 21st Century: World Development Report 1999/2000*, OUP New York.

The Hindu, July 3, (2008), p. 13

_______, December 6, 2011, p. 2.

_______, January 18, 2012.

_______, June 2, 2012, p. 9.

Editorial entitled "Pragmatic approach" in *The Statesman*, August 12, 2009, p. 6 .

The Times of India, January 1, 2011, p. 11.

_______, March 24, 2012, p. 8.

_______, May 4, 2012, p. 13.

_______, June 14, 2012, p. 15

2
A Review of Uneven Pattern of Growth in North-East Region

Mithilesh Kumar Sinha

Prologue

The North-East states of India blessed with Nature's bounties and India's gateway to East Asia, – comprise eight states, namely Arunachal Pradesh, Assam, Nagaland, Manipur, Meghalaya, Mizoram, Tripura and Sikkim. These states are geographically, ethnically and culturally different from the rest of the country.

From times immemorial, India's North East has the meeting point of myriad communities, faiths and cultures. A place renowned for its magical beauty and bewildering diversity, North East India is the home for more than 166 separate tribes speaking in many exotic tongues. Some groups have migrated over the centuries from places as far as South East Asia; they retain their cultural traditions and values but are beginning to adapt to contemporary lifestyles. The lushness of its landscape, the range of communities and geographical and ecological diversity make the North East quite different from other parts of the subcontinent.

Northeastern states are special category states and enjoy 9:1 ratio for external aid. The aid taken from the external agencies is bifurcated in two components of grants and loan. About 90 per cent are grant and about 10 per cent are loan. Total expenditure of eight NE states is almost ₹ 30,000 crores a year which means ₹ 10,000 per person per year is spent annually. ₹ 20,000 crores come as a direct transfer from Central Government to NE states.

However, despite having it all, they lag behind in economic development for myriad reasons. The economies, because of natural constraints have not grown in tandem with the plains, and there stills remains as a vast disparity in terms of both economic development and opportunities. The region as a whole has always lagged behind the rest of India in development. No state has ever had a per capita domestic product above the national average. These ranged from 99 per cent of the national average (Arunachal Pradesh) to 62 per cent (Tripura) in 1990-91. The reforms of the last 20 years have not materially altered this. In 2006-07, the range was 85 per cent to 68 per cent. Assam, Manipur and Nagaland had become relatively worse off over this period. The 2008-09 Economic Survey observed that even when some northeastern states performed well in the early years of the century, that was not enough to pull them out of the low-growth trajectory (Sambrani, 2012).

In brief, the region's economy is generally characterized by low per capita income, low capital formation, inadequate infrastructure facilities, geographical isolation and communication bottleneck, inadequate exploitation of natural resources like mineral resources, hydro power potential, forests etc., low progress in industrial field, lack of private and foreign direct investment and high unemployment rate among the relative high literate people.

Objective of the paper is to analyze the perspective of socio-economic growth and examine the level of inter-state regional disparities in the North-eastern region and identify causes of inter-state disparity and hindering factors to development.

I

Paradoxical Scenario: The story of India's North East, in many ways, is the story of a paradox. On the one hand, it is almost the picture post card perfect land, blue mountains, green valleys and the red rivers, on the other is the high incidence of uneven economic growth. On the one hand, the North East is like the crown on the nation's head, on the other extreme, it is a region yet to taste the fruits of India's rapid economic transformation. It is a cornucopia of diverse ethnic, social and cultural influences, while on the other, it is a region whose true potential is to be recognized, leave alone rejuvenated. On the one hand, tourism in the Seven Sister states is a major attraction. Manipur has a lot to offer too, with attractions like the beautiful Loktak Lake. Mizoram is a dazzling mix of this cross-cultural vibrancy with 87 per cent literacy, the second highest in India. Tripura richly endowed with nature's bounties and is known as the 'Queen of Hills'. It has an ancient culture, tradition and this makes it ideal for special interest tourism. Meghalaya is a blissful paradise in the hills of Northeast.

It is here that Nature mingles with life in a journey towards perpetual happiness. Nagaland, the eastern-most state of India, bordering Myanmar, is small but beautiful, rich in art, culture and crafts and is a virtual treasure-trove of natural resources with a people known equally for their stamina and skills. But, here, tourism sector suffers for the lack of proper infrastructure support. Natural resource in each state is unique but is greatly untapped primarily because of lack of industries and also infrastructure that facilitates industries. North East shares a large international boundary of nearly 4,500 kms with many nations but trade through this border is greatly underutilized (Ganguly, 2010).

The regional economy of the north-east is largely dependent on agriculture, and most other economic activity is small on traditional skills of weaving and handicraft. It's a vicious circle of insurgency, underdevelopment and the resultant poverty that has proved to be the undoing of the region. In fact, the economy of most part of the region has virtually remained stagnant because of lack of business-like situation. People from the region are banking on government jobs rather than spotting economic opportunities. Assam's economy decelerated in the 1990s. Agriculture has grown only at 2.1 per cent per year over the 1980s and 1990s and has further slipped to 1.6 per cent in the 1990s. Manufacturing growth rate in the 1990s was higher at 3.4 per cent compared to 2.4 per cent in the 1980s, while services sector has decreased from 4.9 per cent to 4.5 per cent. Troubled by history and geo-politics, India's North East has remained backward.

II

North-Eastern region presents a picture of wide inter-state disparities in terms of economic and social indicators. Disparity in NER relate to inequality of factor endowments, development of agriculture, industry and other socio-economic growth, employment and reduction of disparities in income and wealth. India has since walked the path of economic liberalization and as is ordained by the laws of economics, in the initial years, the investments have flowed into regions with better infrastructure, ensuring uneven growth and development. While some parts of the economy have witnessed spectacular growth and development, others have lagged behind. Going by the same laws, as disparities become more pronounced, the growth at the initial centres of prosperity will slowly taper off and the capital will seek out low cost destinations which will develop slowly bridging the gap between regions.

By this logic, almost three decades into the process of liberalization, the North East is awaiting its tryst with economic destiny. A virtual treasure-trove of natural resources with a people known equally for their stamina and skills, the region is waiting the spark that will light a million fires of entrepreneurship.

The pace of development in the hilly areas and plains differ considerably. The valleys are economically active areas of the region, the Brahmaputra valley being the most active. Tribal population forms only one-fourth of the population of the North East, despite the fact that in four States, i.e. Mizoram, Meghalaya, Nagaland and Arunachal Pradesh, the tribal people are in majority and in Mizoram, they constitute as high as 95 per cent of the population. Though the region is diverse and heterogeneous, it is also homogeneous in the sense that the social stratification found in other parts of the country is not present in the North East.

There are differences among the eight States in the North-Eastern region with respect to their resource endowments, level of industrialization as well as infrastructural facilities. The industrial sector has mainly grown around tea, petroleum (crude), natural gas etc. in Assam and mining, saw mills and steel fabrication units in other parts of the region.

Growth Story

The North-Eastern states are at the bottom, together accounting for little above one per cent of the national GDP. Though the macroeconomic indicators of North East India show an encouraging trend as all the states except Meghalaya has shown an improvement over the previous years' performance but a comparison of growth within the North East India highlights disparities across the states. The top performing state in the period of 1994-95 to 2001-02 was Tripura with 8.24 per cent average growth in gross domestic product (GSDP) above the national average during the same period. In the period of 2004-05 to 2011-12 the top performing state is Sikkim with 12.62 per cent average growth above the national average growth. While Assam and Manipur grew at less than 5 per cent average in the period of 1994-95 to 2001-02 (average growth 2.21 and 4.26 per cent respectively) and during the period of 2004-05 to 2011-12 the less performing states are Assam, Nagaland and Manipur with average growth of 5.76, 6.32 and 6.33 per cent respectively (Table 2.1).

Table 2.1: Real Growth Rates of North-Eastern States—GSDP per cent at constant prices

	Arunachal Pradesh	*Assam*	*Manipur*	*Meghalaya*	*Mizoram*	*Nagaland*	*Sikkim*	*Tripura*	*All-India*
1994-95	–0.90	2.83	–2.37	3.64	N.A.	7.64	1.49	–0.39	6.40
1995-96	14.24	2.86	4.07	10.54	N.A.	0.14	9.29	8.42	7.30
1996-97	–4.95	2.93	8.95	3.70	N.A.	13.83	6.49	10.63	8.00
1997-98	3.12	0.99	8.77	6.13	N.A.	7.82	7.14	10.27	4.30
1998-99	3.13	–0.22	2.16	9.87	N.A.	–4.01	7.06	9.91	6.70
1999-00	4.01	3.18	12.00	7.79	N.A.	0.80	3.48	7.11	6.40
2000-01	7.07	2.53	–6.35	5.45	4.97	16.60	7.59	5.88	4.35
2001-02	15.70	2.60	6.81	6.89	6.52	11.45	7.88	14.07	5.81
2002-03	–4.31	7.07	–0.46	3.79	10.39	9.45	7.31	6.41	3.84
2003-04	10.94	6.02	10.84	6.78	3.19	5.02	7.89	5.88	8.52
2004-05	16.46	3.74	9.70	7.11	4.15	6.65	7.72	8.14	7.47
2005-06	2.75	3.40	6.35	7.9	6.97	10.22	9.83	5.82	9.48
2006-07	5.25	4.65	2.00	7.74	4.78	7.80	5.97	8.28	9.57
2007-08	12.06	4.82	5.96	4.51	10.98	7.31	7.61	7.70	9.32
2008-09	8.73	5.72	6.56	12.94	13.34	6.34	16.39	9.44	6.72
2009-10	14.80	7.98	7.63	9.03	10.39	4.36	31.87	8.62	8.39
2010-11	7.87	7.34	6.16	9.39	9.18	3.98	8.94	8.74	8.39
2011-12	3.65	8.42	6.24	9.54	N.A.	3.93	N.A.	8.87	6.88
Average 1994-95 to 2001 2002	5.18	2.21	4.26	6.75	5.75	6.78	6.30	8.24	6.96
Average 2004-05 to 2011-2012	8.95	5.76	6.33	8.52	8.54	6.32	12.62	8.20	8.28

Source: Directorate of Economics and Statistics of respective State Governments and for All-India-CSO; Data from 2004-05 Series based on base year 2004-05.

The Northeastern states have shown comparatively higher increase in the average annual growth rate of PCNSDP in the period of 2006-07 to 2011-12 over the previous period of 2000-01 to 2005-06 except Nagaland and Sikkim. During the whole period the state of Tripura has registered highest growth rate among these 8 states. The states of Manipur and Assam had the lowest growth rate (2.22% and 2.42% respectively) in the former period but Assam improved in the latter period and Manipur marginally. The state of Nagaland registered 6.18 per cent in the former period but it witnessed deceleration in the latter period (from 6.18% to 3.72%) (Table 2.2).

Table 2.2: Per Capita Net State Domestic Product of Northeast States at Constant (2004-05) Prices

	Arunachal Pradesh	*Assam*	*Manipur*	*Meghalaya*	*Mizoram*	*Nagaland*	*Sikkim*	*Tripura*	*All India*
2000-01	5.6	1.34	-8.32	3.86	1.17	13.94	2.79	5.77	1.83
2001-02	10.04	0.66	3.98	4.08	3.67	5.04	4.23	13.49	3.66
2002-03	-5.72	4.33	-2.55	2.35	6.87	3.52	6.97	4.75	2.01
2003-04	9.53	4.61	8.69	4.89	0.68	4.88	6.41	4.52	7.02
2004-05	11.53	1.98	7.06	5.62	1.88	1.05	6.45	6.85	5.63
2005-06	0.56	1.60	4.50	6.46	4.72	8.64	8.68	5.30	7.75
2006-07	2.97	3.10	0.25	6.24	1.87	6.05	4.43	7.28	7.89
2007-08	9.56	2.90	3.47	1.92	8.21	6.40	4.72	5.31	8.07
2008-09	5.91	4.61	5.29	11.52	12.18	4.62	11.58	9.27	4.69
2009-10	10.34	6.72	5.62	7.34	7.90	2.60	24.83	8.25	6.58
2010-11	6.06	6.01	4.20	8.11	6.61	2.25	7.85	8.41	6.35
2011-12	1.91	7.24	4.42	8.38	N.A.	1.38	N.A.	8.59	5.59
Average 2000-01 to 2005-06	5.25	2.42	2.22	4.54	3.17	6.18	5.92	6.78	4.65
Average 2006-07 to 2011-12	6.13	5.10	3.87	7.25	6.13	3.72	5.56	7.85	6.53

Source: http://planning commission.gov.in.

The Growth-Income Conundrum

The two states of the Northeast India –Arunachal Pradesh and Sikkim – have the higher per capita income than that of nation. Manipur and Assam are the other states with per capita incomes of less than ₹ 30,000 per annum. Mizoram, Meghalaya and Tripura are relatively better off than Manipur and Assam with per capita incomes of ₹ 45,982, ₹ 42,601 and ₹ 35,799 respectively. Looking at the annual growth in real per capita income since 2004-05, the states of Arunachal Pradesh (7.60%) and Mizoram (7.40%) have shown the best performance in the North East India followed by Tripura, Sikkim and Meghalaya. It is disappointing to see Assam (3.80%) at the bottom of the growth performance chart of India (Table 2.3).

Table 2.3: State-wise Per Capita Incomes and Annual Growth in Real Per Capita Income

States	*Per Capita Income at Current Prices 2009-10 (Rs.)*	*Growth in Real Per Capita Income per Annum 2004-05 to 2009-10 (%)*
Arunachal Pradesh	51644	7.60
Assam	27197	3.80
Manipur	28531	—
Meghalaya	42601	4.20
Mizoram	45982	7.40
Nagaland	—	—
Sikkim	48937	5.80
Tripura	35799	6.50
India	46492	6.90

Source: CSO Estimates as on 08-03-2011.

The Wealth Gap

The wide variation in the proportion of households in the highest wealth quintile across states of the Northeast region exemplifies the magnitude of inequality across the Northeast India. The proportion ranges from eight per in Meghalaya to 30.10 per cent in Mizoram. Sikkim and Arunachal Pradesh are the top two states in the Northeast with more than 20 per cent of households in the highest wealth quintile group. But it is very low in comparison with other states of India. For example, Puducherry, Daman & Diu, Punjab, Lakshadweep, Goa, Delhi and Chandigarh—more than 50 per cent of households are in the highest wealth quintile group. On the other hand, among the North East states, Manipur appears at the top of the poorest states with 22.70 per cent of households in the lowest wealth quintile. Arunachal Pradesh is not far behind with 18.60 per cent of households in the poorest group. Mizoram and Sikkim have less than two per cent of households in the poorest quintile. The gap between the lowest and highest wealth quintile is the narrowest in Meghalaya, Assam, Tripura and Arunachal Pradesh. The low proportion of households in the two extreme quintile groups in these states is an indication of lower inequality since a larger proportion of households are concentrated in the middle quintile group. In fact, more than 30 per cent of households in Meghalaya and Tripura lie in the middle quintile, Sikkim stands out with more than 40 per cent of households in the second highest wealth quintile (Table 2.4).

Table 2.4: State-wise Look at the Percentage of Households in the Lowest and Highest Wealth Quintiles

States	*Lowest Wealth Quintile*	*Highest Wealth Quintile*
Arunachal Pradesh	18.60	20.40
Assam	13.80	13.00
Manipur	22.70	14.00
Meghalaya	9.50	8.00
Mizoram	1.80	24.30
Nagaland	N.A.	N.A.
Sikkim	1.10	30.10
Tripura	10.00	10.70

Source: District Level Household Survey (DLHS), 2007-08.

Manufactured Growth

When it comes to the sectoral share of the gross state domestic product (GSDP), manufacturing accounts for 10 per cent or less of state income in all the north-eastern states. According to the latest period for which data from the Central Statistical Organization (CSO) are available for North East states, 2000-01 to 2007-08, The growth in manufacturing at 1999-2000 prices ranges from 26.60 per cent to 3.50 per cent a year, with the national average standing at 7.76 per cent. Meghalaya ranks at the top mainly due to the large scale cement factories set up in recent years, while Arunachal Pradesh holds the lowest rank among the Northeast states. There are only two states with double-digit growth in the manufacturing sector during this period—Meghalaya and Assam. And remaining states where manufacturing growth has been in range of 9 per cent to 3 per cent (Table 2.5).

Table 2.5: State of Output

(In%)

States	Growth of Manufacturing GSDP (at'99-00 prices) from '00-01 to '07-08	Sectoral Share Manufacturing in GSDP '07-08
Arunachal Pradesh	3.50	2.40
Assam	10.70	10.00
Manipur	5.00	6.30
Meghalaya	26.60	4.70
Mizoram	9.40	1.90
Nagaland	N.A.	N.A.
Sikkim	6.40	3.40
Tripura	4.50	2.50
All India	7.76	15.22

Source: CSO estimates, as on 12.04.2010.

The Number of Factories

The Annual Survey of Industries (ASI) conducted by the Central Statistical Organization (CSO) covers all factories registered under Sections 2m (i) and 2m (ii) of the Factories Act, 1948, that is, those factories employing 10 or more workers using power and those employing 20 or more workers without using power. The data reveals that there is barely any presence of factories in Manipur, Nagaland and Meghalaya. Among North East states, Assam has highest number of factories (2211) and Net added value (Rs. 136.3 lakh) followed by Tripura (363) and net added value (Rs. 42.7 lakh) (Table 2.6).

Table 2.6: Number of Factories and Net Value Added across states of Northeast India

States	Factories in number	Net Value Added (Rs. Lakh per factory)
Arunachal Pradesh	N.A.	N.A.
Assam	2211	136.3
Manipur	72	17.3
Meghalaya	95	551.1
Mizoram	N.A.	N.A.
Nagaland	91	31.0
Sikkim	N.A.	N.A.
Tripura	363	42.7
All India	155,321	339.8

Source: Annual Survey of Industries, 2008-09.

Sectoral Share of Employment

The share of workforce in agriculture, forestry and fishery is more than 50 per cent in the states of NER except Tripura (36.0%) such as Arunachal Pradesh (71.3%), Assam (64.8%), Manipur (57.2%), Meghalaya (67.0%), Mizoram (64.7), Nagaland (70.0%) and Sikkim (54.3%). Workforce engaged in secondary sector is very uneven. In four states less than 10 per cent of the workforce is engaged in secondary sector while in two states less than 20 per cent workforce is engaged in this sector and in only Tripura more than 25 per cent of workforce is engaged in this sector. When it comes to services, all the states of NER have less than 30 per cent of their workforce in the services sector (Table 2.7).

Table 2.7: Sectoral Share of Employment in Percentage

	Primary	*Secondary*	*Tertiary*
Arunachal Pradesh	71.3	5.4	23.2
Assam	64.8	7.3	27.9
Manipur	57.2	16.8	25.9
Meghalaya	67.0	10.9	22.2
Mizoram	64.7	7.9	27.4
Nagaland	70.0	4.8	25.2
Sikkim	54.3	13.5	32.2
Tripura	36.1	29.3	34.6

Note: Primary sector: agriculture, forestry and fishery; Secondary sector: mining and quarrying, manufacturing, construction, electricity, gas and water supply; Tertiary sector: trade, hotel and restaurant, transport, storage, communication, finance, insurance, real estate and other business activities, community, social and personal services.

Source: NSSO-64 round, 2007-08.

Agricultural Scenario

Agriculture continues to be the main source of livelihood security to around 600 million Indians, who have virtually no other source of employment, making growth in this sector critical for the majority of Indians. It is the only sector that directly affects our entire society with its positive or negative growth. Agriculture may continue to be the engine of economic growth. It is the backbone of the national livelihood security system. It is the only sector which can bring inclusiveness in the country because it is the avenue of employment generation and income generation of more than half of the population, and at present it accounts for about 52 per cent of the employment in the country. It is the mainstay of 52 per cent of India's population and the performance of agricultural sector influences the growth of the economy. It is the key to ending hunger. It is vital for India's food security, particularly for the 23 per cent living below poverty line.

The agriculture sector's growth in North East states is almost stagnant in during two periods of 1996-97 to 2003-04 and 2004-05 to 2009-10. Variations in the growth of agriculture are wide as only Nagaland had broken through with high growth in this sector in the period of 1996-97 to 2003-04 but it could not sustain the agricultural growth rate in the period of 2004-05 to 2009-10. In this period Nagaland has registered declined average growth rate of 4.92 per cent. During the period of 1996-97, except Nagaland no state has touched the average growth of 5 per cent. Arunachal Pradesh registered less than 1 per cent whereas Assam and Mizoram recorded negative growth rate. In the period of 2004-05 to 2009-10 Arunachal Pradesh, Assam and Mizoram have improved the growth rate but Manipur, Meghalaya, Sikkim and Tripura have not performed well. Their growth rate of agriculture sector has shown a declining trend (Table 2.8).

Food Challenge

Taking the period 2004-05 to 2008-09, the latest five years for which the data are available with the department of agriculture, four states of the Northeast region with a yield less than 1,500 kg/hectare are Assam, Sikkim, Arunachal Pradesh and Mizoram. If we compare the average food-grain yield across two five-year periods, 1999-2000 to 2003-04 and 2004-05 and 2008-09, we find that Mizoram is the only state to show an even sharper drop, with average food-grain yield falling by more than 700 kg/hectare and has recently launched a programme to end "jhum" cultivation, shifting to permanent farming to stem this decline. Sikkim and Assam too, are the states to show marginal decline, with average food-grain yield falling by 42 and 36 kg/hectare. The states with the improvement in yields over these periods are Tripura and Nagaland by more than 200 kg/hectare (Table 2.9).

Money Management for 8 Sisters

When it comes to ground zero banking penetration, the North East remains light years behind the western and southern states, or even the northern

Table 2.8: Agricultural Growth Rate in Northeastern States

	Arunachal Pradesh	*Assam*	*Manipur*	*Meghalaya*	*Mizoram*	*Nagaland*	*Sikkim*	*Tripura*	*All-India*
1996-97	0.59	-0.37	5.99	6.72	N.A.	12.54	9.95	7.57	9.92
1997-98	-16.09	3.61	11.40	0.79	N.A.	15.18	4.53	1.29	-2.55
1998-99	0.63	-4.27	2.39	3.67	N.A.	5.78	-25.99	7.86	6.32
1999-00	9.85	-0.37	-0.96	14.29	N.A.	12.92	17.30	4.07	0.50
2000-01	13.05	-1.34	4.21	5.92	-7.28	30.60	6.53	-9.47	-0.25
2001-02	-5.22	-0.64	3.66	3.16	0.74	12.92	7.03	21.59	6.25
2002-03	-0.68	1.22	-3.42	6.38	4.04	12.67	6.16	-0.97	-7.24
2003-04	3.69	1.51	14.96	1.81	-1.34	5.51	7.76	5.21	9.96
2004-05	-2.63	-1.35	9.46	6.48	4.35	9.03	5.19	3.42	0.05
2005-06	2.22	2.76	-7.37	4.67	2.60	3.53	3.88	8.25	5.25
2006-07	13.04	-0.99	-2.47	2.25	1.86	2.20	2.25	2.89	3.68
2007-08	7.34	0.67	3.17	3.64	2.95	N.A.	3.23	0.41	4.73
2008-09	2.47	6.43	3.74	8.28	2.48	N.A.	3.64	N.A.	1.58
2009-10	-	2.40	N.A.	N.A.	N.A.	N.A.	N.A.	N.A.	0.22
Average 1996-97 to 2003-04	0.73	-0.08	4.77	5.34	-0.96	13.51	4.16	4.64	2.86
Average 2004-05 to 2009-10	4.49	1.51	1.31	5.06	2.85	4.92	3.64	3.74	3.06

Source: http://planning commission.gov.in.

Table 2.9: Food Facts [Yield (kg/hectare)]

States	*1999-00 to 2003-04*	*2004-05 to 2008-09*
Arunachal Pradesh	1186	1221
Assam	1443	1407
Manipur	2313	2281
Meghalaya	1643	1697
Mizoram	1891	1129
Nagaland	1378	1610
Sikkim	1338	1296
Tripura	2180	2414
All India	1665	1863

Source: Averages Estimated from Agricultural Statistics 2010, Department of Agriculture.

cluster for that matter where banks handle far bigger volumes of business. But what is indeed heartening is that banks are steadily expanding their footprint in this neck of the woods for exploring, hitherto, untapped opportunities.

The country's top banks added 167 branches to shore up their tally to 2,114 till March 2009. At present the average population served per office of scheduled commercial banks in the North East is 21,470. These are far more than the national average of 14,490, suggesting that fewer banks in the region cater to large swathes of the population, in turn, undermining the quality of services. But, on the positive side, a grossly-under-banked region is slated to pave the way for bigger opportunities for the banking fraternity. The region still has miles to go to make banking accessible to every household. If anything, eight-North East sister states are among the poorest in terms of banking penetration. The Northeastern states of Tripura, Meghalaya and Arunachal Pradesh have a very low credit inflow. Mizoram is among the eight states with a moderate CDR of 57.70 per cent and Tripura is at the bottom with lower CDR of 31.60. The North Eastern states collectively control 1.6 per cent of the country's deposits and 0.8 per cent of credit. But, in the last couple of years, 2008 and 2009 business is anything to go by, banks in this region have every reason to chill out. In the North Eastern states, banks deposit mobilization has increased to ₹ 63,247 crore (₹ 50,012 crore) and credit off take grew to ₹ 22,642 crore (₹ 19,529 crore) (Table 2.10).

Table 2.10: Northeastern Banking Matrix

States	Credit			Deposits			CDR
	2009	2008	Change (%)	2009	2008	Change (%)	2010 In %
Arunachal Pradesh	914	817	11.8	3682	2807	31.17	34.40
Assam	15115	13057	15.76	39427	31666	24.51	40.50
Manipur	916	864	6.02	2368	1830	29.40	44.80
Meghalaya	1702	1464	16.26	6157	4811	27.98	32.70
Mizoram	1025	838	22.32	1746	1499	16.48	57.70
Nagaland	1065	867	22.84	3473	2611	33.01	40.20
Sikkim	1066	985	8.22	2517	2073	21.42	49.50
Tripura	1905	1624	17.30	6394	4792	33.43	31.60

Source: Reserve Bank of India.

The Other Growth Story

Rural Road Connectivity

Connectivity is the most basic infrastructure need for development. Studies have shown that government expenditure on roads has the largest impact on reducing rural poverty in India; it has a significant impact on productivity growth and a rupee invested in rural roads has the potential to generate more than ₹ 5 in returns from agricultural production. More than 50 per cent of the habitations were unconnected in 6 states of Northeaster region. The problem is severe in Nagaland. In this state only 5.4 per cent of rural habitations are connected by pucca roads (Table 2.11).

Table 2.11: Share of Habitations to be connected by pucca roads in rural areas of Northeastern States

States	Arunachal Pradesh	Assam	Manipur	Megha-laya	Mizoram	Nagaland	Sikkim	Tripura
Share of habitation	58.4	59.4	44.6	48.4	34.1	5.4	28.7	26.5

Source: NSSO, 64 round, 2007-08.

Literacy

Data from Census 2011 show that the North East States have done well with higher literacy rates. All the states of North East India except Arunachal Pradesh and Assam have literacy rates above than that of nation

(74.04). Assam has laggard in literacy rate from the nation by just a margin of 0.84 per cent. But Arunachal Pradesh is not showing encouraging picture in literacy. It is lagging behind all the states of Northeast India and by 7.04 per cent behind national's literacy rates. Though in respect of female literacy too, the north-east states' performance is above 70 per cent except two states like Arunachal Pradesh and Assam, the gap in literacy of Male and Female is still above 10 per cent in four states – Arunachal Pradesh (14.1%), Manipur (13.3%), Assam (11.8%) and Sikkim (10.9%) as per 2011 Census of India (Table 2.11).

Table 2.11: Literacy Rate

(In%)

States	*Total Literacy*		*Male Literacy*		*Female Literacy*		*Gap in M F Literacy*	
	2011	*2001*	*2011*	*2001*	*2011*	*2001*	*2011*	*2001*
Arunachal Pradesh	67.0	54.74	73.7	64.07	59.6	44.24	14.1	19.83
Assam	73.2	64.28	78.8	71.93	67.0	56.03	11.8	15.9
Manipur	79.8	68.87	86.5	77.87	73.2	59.70	13.3	18.17
Meghalaya	75.5	63.31	77.2	66.14	73.8	60.41	3.4	5.73
Mizoram	91.6	88.49	93.7	90.69	89.4	86.13	4.3	4.56
Nagaland	80.1	67.11	83.3	71.77	76.7	61.92	7.9	9.85
Sikkim	82.2	69.68	87.3	76.73	76.4	61.46	10.9	15.27
Tripura	87.8	73.66	92.2	81.47	83.1	65.41	9.1	16.06
India	74.04	65.18	82.14	75.85	65.46	54.16	16.68	21.69

Source: Census of India, 2001& 2011.

Nourishment

The prevalence of malnutrition in India is among the highest in the world. The North Eastern states are also facing the problem of malnutrition. In this region all the states showing increasing trend of malnutrition from 1992-93 to 2005-06. In Assam the percentage of children under malnutrition is the highest, more than Nation. The situation is equally worrying in Meghalaya where more than 40 per cent of the children under malnutrition (Table 2.12).

Children of Doom

With three years left until the 2015 deadline for achieving the eight globally-agreed Millennium Development Goals (MDGs), India is at a crucial point with some successes and some failures. On the infant mortality indicator, India remains far behind the requisite target. But

Table 2.12: State-wise proportion of children below three years of age (In%) under nourishment

States	*Arunachal Pradesh*	*Assam*	*Manipur*	*Meghalaya*	*Mizoram*	*Nagaland*	*Sikkim*	*Tripura*	*India*
NFHS-1 (1992-93)	32.1	44.1	19.8	36.9	17.2	18.7	na	42.1	47.9
NFHS-2 (1998-99)	21.5	52.2	20.1	28.6	19.8	18.8	15.5	12.1	42.7
NFHS-3 (2005-06)	35.8	55.0	19.5	42.9	14.3	23.6	17.3	35.2	40.4

Source: National Family Health Survey (NFHS).

among the North Eastern states, Manipur, Nagaland and Tripura have achieved the MDG target of 27 per 1,000 live births. Assam and Meghalaya are laggards with !MR exceeding 50 per 1,000 live births. In all the North Eastern states IMR is higher in rural areas than urban areas. In rural areas of all the states MDG target has not been achieved except Manipur and Nagaland (Table 2.13).

Table 2.13: Infant Mortality Rate (per 1,000 live births) in North-eastern Region

States	*Arunachal Pradesh*	*Assam*	*Manipur*	*Meghalaya*	*Mizoram*	*Nagaland*	*Sikkim*	*Tripura*	*India*
Rural	34	60	15	58	47	24	31	29	51
Urban	12	36	9	37	21	20	19	19	31
Total	31	58	14	55	37	23	320	27	47

Source: Sample Registration System.

Girls, Interrupted

The falling child sex ratio is a grim reminder of India's continuing aversion to the girl child. Nagaland registered fall in the rural child sex ratio by more than 35 points. In North Eastern states, state-wise analysis shows a wide disparity in trends. Mizoram has led to a rise in the overall child sex ratio. Nagaland presents a mixed picture with only urban areas showing an improvement. On the other hand, in Arunachal Pradesh, only rural areas have seen a rise in the child sex ratios. According to the Census 2011, all the states have sex-ratio (females per 1000 males) between 889 and 987 (Arunachal 920, Assam 954, Manipur 987, Meghalaya 986, Mizoram 975, Nagaland 931, Sikkim 889, and Tripura 961).

III

From above discussion we find that the North East India is now witnessing a spurt in development of infrastructure, urban development, food, airlines, communication and IT sectors. As a result, the North East is experiencing vibrant social mobility and change. But for desired and equitable development, removal of infrastructure bottlenecks, healthcare, provision of basic minimum services, creating conducive environment for private investment should be the important priority.

A precondition for peace and prosperity is people's participation in decision-making. Maximizing self-governance and participatory planning is critical to inclusive development. Empowerment of people for participatory governance requires devolution of powers and building the planning system right from the village level. This calls for strengthening decentralized institutions—both Panchayati Raj in areas covered under Parts IX and IX-A of the Constitution and traditional village and district development committees in Schedule VI areas. The planning must be from the grassroots level and decentralized institutions should be designed to work in harmony with the traditional community institutions. Maximizing self-governance and participatory planning will help to develop peace and harmony in societies ravaged by insurgency. Indeed, the reports on insurgency in the region are often exaggerated as this is confined to only certain pockets. Nevertheless, the perception has to change for the private investment to flow in.

The region is rich in natural resources such as land, water, minerals and forests. The large river systems have been a source of misery due to floods and land erosion and these have to be converted into a source of wealth and prosperity. It is important to use the vast river systems for agricultural development and hydroelectric potential, and mineral wealth to generate additional employment and incomes.

Equally important is opening up the natural routes of transportation, trade and commerce. It is important to realize that the development of the North East is inextricably intertwined with the fortunes of the neighbouring countries. The 'Look East Policy', which has been the existence for over two decades, has hardly benefited the region; in fact the policy should start from the North Eastern region. These calls for opening up for trade from the North East to East and South East Asia and beyond (Rao, 2008).

A precondition for the development of trade and industry in the region is a quantum jump in the development of agriculture, agro-processing and manufacturing activities. Much of the investments will have to be made by only when the enabling environment is ensured through infrastructure investment, which is most important. Competitive infrastructure will have to be created mainly by the Central and State governments. Large intra-regional investment in connectivity through roads, railways and waterways and in trade routes with neighbouring countries is an essential development of the region.

Development of human resource available in Northeastern region needs to be taken up on the highest priority (Singh, 2005).

An enabling environment for economic activity also requires responsive governance, capacity development of people and institutions and, above all, changes in the mindset from one of security to development orientation in administration. Realizing the vision of peace and prosperity bè able to the people will meet this formidable challenge.

We hope that better counselling, education, healthcare and employment opportunities can surely enhance the pace of development and the quality of life of the North East region and their participation in development activities. The government strategy, pro-development mindset of the NE people and a responsive administration will convert dreams into reality.

REFERENCES

Ganguly, Suvobrata (2010), "Picture Postcard North East on Brink of Tryst with Economic Destiny", *The Business Standard*, May, Sponsored Section.

Rao, M Govinda (2008), "A Development Vision for India's Northeast", *The Business Standard*, August 5.

Sambrani, Shreekant (2012), "Northeast India: A Bridge Not to Burn", *The Business Standard*, August 29.

Singh, Manmohan (2005), "North East 2020", *Yojana*, Vol. 49, December, New Delhi.http://planning commission.gov.in.

3

Challenges of Development and Livelihood Linkages of the People of Border Areas of Arunachal Pradesh: An Empirical Study[1]

Amitava Mitra and *Kaju Nath*

Introduction

Arunachal Pradesh has gone remarkable economic changes within a relative short span of time. The comparatively isolated economics of the various tribal communities of the area which were later recognized as North East Frontier (NEFA) and subsequently Arunachal Pradesh, was gradually integrated after independence and more specifically after Indo-China War of 1962. The State's economy has experienced a remarkable growth over past decades, and it has diversified from an agriculture and forestry subsistence economy into a monetized economy. However, there is a great deal of regional variations in the degree of integration with the market economy. There are wide ranging inter district disparities in terms of availability of infrastructural facilities which are crucial for improving the economic condition of people. For example, most of the districts of the northern and eastern international border areas, with high mountains are less well serviced than the districts in the foothills of Arunachal Pradesh. Hence, in this chapter, an attempt is made to examine the challenges of development, the socio-economic condition as well as

[1] The Paper is based on the 13th Finance Commission sponsored study on Problems of Border Areas in North East India: Implication for Thirteenth Finance Commission (Arunachal Pradesh Chapter). The first author worked as the Principal Investigator and the second author worked as the Research Associate of the Project.

livelihood linkages of the people of international border areas of Arunachal Pradesh. The problems and challenges of development along the border regions have a unique place and significance in the process of national planning due to the specific needs of the people living in the stressful environment conditions. However, the magnitude of the problems differs from region to region depending upon the physiographical condition, socio-cultural set-up etc. In this paper an attempt is made to study the problems of the border areas of Arunachal Pradesh. The present paper deals with all the border blocks of Arunachal Pradesh in general, and two border blocks (bordering with China) in particular. There are six sections in the present paper. The first section concentrates on the data base and methodology. The second sections deals with the background of Arunachal Pradesh as a border State. The third section deals with socio-demographic and economic features of the border blocks. The fourth section concentrates on socio-demographic peculiarities as well as resource base and infrastructural facilities of the surveyed blocks. The section fifth discusses the socio-demographic and economic condition of the surveyed border villages. Finally, the section six deal with the recommendations and conclusions.

SECTION I: DATA BASE AND METHODOLOGY

The present study is basically empirical in nature. It is based on both secondary data as well as primary data. The secondary date regarding demographic and economic characteristics of the district and block level were collected from the last census records, i.e. 2001 census and Human Development Report of Arunachal Pradesh, 2005. However in 2001, the number of border blocks were less in number. Depending on the availability of data, an attempt is made to update the present number of blocks on the basis of the circle data of 2001. The data regarding infrastructural indicators of border districts and blocks were collected from the District Statistical Handbooks. The data regarding physical features, land used/land cover etc., were collected from Arunachal Pradesh Remote Sensing and Application Centre, State Development Report of Arunachal Pradesh and data available from studies conducted by other scholars. Regarding the primary data, a village survey was conducted through a multi-stage sampling technique. The different stages under a technique were as follows:

Stage I : Selection of Border District
Stage II : Selection of Border Blocks
Stage III : Selection of Villages

At Stage I, two border districts namely, viz. Tawang and Anjaw were selected by purposive sampling on the basis of length of boundary and the strategic importance of the respective district. At Stage II, one block in each district, namely Lumla (Tawang) and Chaglagham (Anjaw) were selected by purposive sampling on the basis of their relatives backwardness. Finally, the villages were selected randomly. In addition to it, the focal group discussions were held with the representatives of the communities from various categories.

SECTION II: BACKGROUND OF ARUNACHAL PRADESH AS A BORDER STATE

Arunachal Pradesh is located in the extreme north-eastern corner of India. It is bordered by Bhutan (160 km) on the west, China on the north and north-eastern (1080 km) and Myanmar to the east and south-east (440 km). In fact, Arunachal Pradesh is one among a few states of India which has international border with three countries. The state has a territory of 83,743 square kilometre which is around 2.55 per cent of India's land area and around one-third area of North-East India. As the largest State in North-East India, Arunachal's area is slightly more than that of Assam but its population is 0.11 per cent of India's population and only 2.85 per cent of the population of North-East India. All the States of North East India, except Mizoram, have a population larger than that of Arunachal Pradesh.

Arunachal Pradesh is not only the largest in terms of area but it has the largest international border among the states of North East India. For example, it consists of only 2.55 per cent of India's landmass but it shares 11.65 per cent of India's total international boundary. Out of India's total border with China (3488 km), Myanmar (1643 km) and Bhutan (699 km) Arunachal Pradesh shares 30.96 per cent, 26.78 per cent and 22.89 per cent respectively. At present, Arunachal Pradesh has sixteen districts and out of these sixteen districts, twelve districts have international border. In other words, around 75 per cent of the total districts of the state have international border.

From Map 3.1 it is found that two districts, namely Tawang and West Kameng have international border with both Bhutan and China. As many as seven districts of the State have international border with China alone. Anjaw is the only district which is bordering with both China and Myanmar on the other hand, at the south-eastern tip of the State, two districts i.e. Changlang and Tirap have border with Myanmar. As a whole, the border

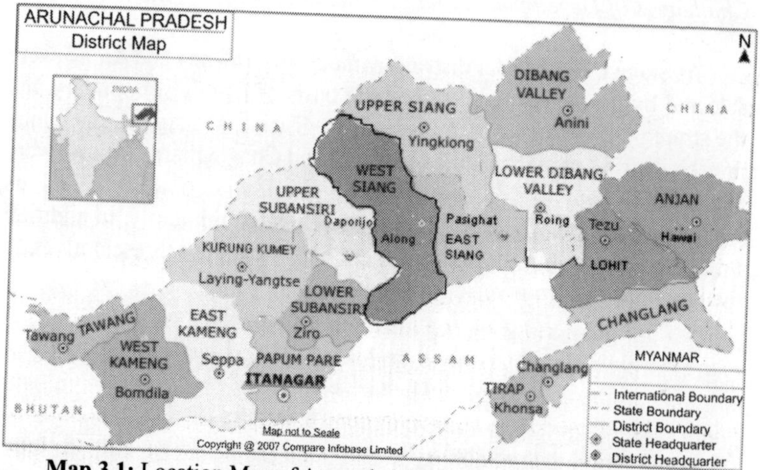

Map 3.1: Location Map of Arunachal Pradesh and its Border Districts

districts consist of 83.17 per cent of the total area of the State, and 64.43 per cent of the total population live in those border districts.

SECTION III: SOCIO-DEMOGRAPHIC AND ECONOMIC FEATURES OF THE BORDER BLOCKS

In this section, an attempt is made to examine the socio-demographic and economic features of the border blocks by taking some indicators depending on the availability of data at the block level. The details are given in Appendix A-1. Arunachal Pradesh has the lowest density of population in the country. However , if we look at the density of people of the border blocks, it was found that twenty two border blocks (out of thirty two) had less than the State average (13 persons per sq.km. in 2001). Around twenty-three border blocks had less than the respective district averages. In fact, it was found that in two of the border blocks of Dibang Valley viz. Anini-Mipi and Etalin-Maliney there was only one person per square km. as many as nine border blocks had density of population of only two persons per square km.

As far as literacy rate is concerned, two five blocks (out of thirty two)had less than the State average (54.3%) and twenty two blocks had less than the respective district averages. In some border blocks like Pongchau-Wakka (Tirap), Chaglagham (Anjaw) the level of literacy was only 15.3 per cent and 15.8 per cent respectively. As far as the composition of Scheduled Tribe population is concerned, as many as twenty-four and twenty one border blocks had higher than the State average and the respective district average respectively. For example, Parsi-Parlo block of Kurung Kumey district had almost cent per cent Scheduled Tribe population. In fact, it is found that all the border blocks of East Kameng, Kurung Kumey, Upper Subansiri, Upper Siang and Tirap district had a concentration of more than 90 per cent Scheduled Tribe population.

The work participation rate of Arunachal Pradesh as a whole is high because of a higher level of female work participation rate, and they are mainly engaged in the primary sector. However, it is found from Appendix A.1 that twenty nine (out of thirty two) border blocks had higher female work participation rate than that of the State average of 44.55 per cent. There are four border blocks where the work participation rate was high as more than 60 per cent. This is because in most of the border blocks, people were mainly employed in the agricultural sector due to a lack of avenues in other sectors like secondary and services sector. As many as twenty two border blocks had a higher percentage of main workers engaged in the agricultural sector than that of the State average of 59.16 per cent.

The availability of household goods in the houses of the border blocks portrays the economic status of the people. Radio is expected to be an important asset for the far-flung border blocks. It was found that the households of twenty one border blocks had less radio sets than the state average. In some border blocks of East Kameng and Kurung Kumey less than ten per cent households possess a radio. As far as the possession of television and telephone are concerned, the picture was even worse. The household of twenty six and twenty nine border blocks possessed television and telephone less than the State average (25.7 and 9.19 per cent respectively). The households of twelve border blocks did not have a single telephone connection.

Thus, the analysis reveals that most of the border blocks of Arunachal are much worse off as compared to the State average and even the respective district averages.

SECTION IV: SURVEYED BLOCKS AT A GLANCE

For a detailed study, two blocks with the Chinese border were selected by purposive sampling. These are Lumla block (in Tawang district) lying to western Chinese border of the State and Chaglagham (Anjaw district) which is to the extreme eastern Chinese border of the State. Both the blocks are very backward in terms of socio-demographic and economic indicators (Appendix A.1). These two blocks were selected for the present study due to their backwardness and unique location (surrounded by China on two sides).

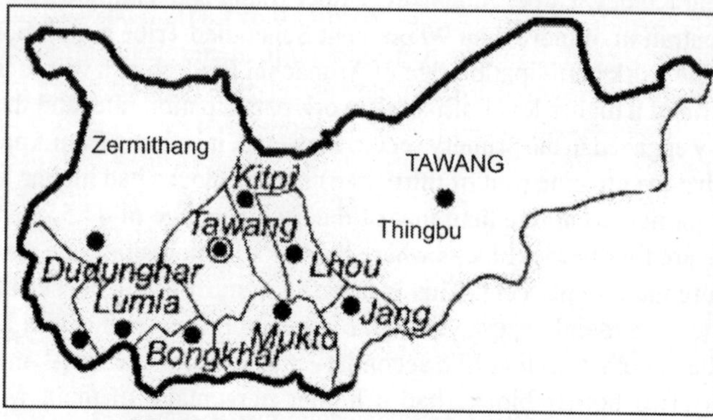

Map 3.2: Location Map of Tawang District

Lumla block alone covered 33.46 per cent of the total area of the district and consisted of 26.89 per cent population of the district. On the other hand, Chaglagham block covered around 30.64 per cent of the total area of the district and consisted of only 12.79 per cent population of the district. In Chaglagham, the density of population was as low as two persons per sq.km and much lower than State average. In fact, the literacy rate of Chaglagham was only 16.8 per cent in 2001 which was much less than the State average and respective district average. Both the blocks had higher composition of Scheduled Tribe population and much higher percentage of main workers engaged in the agricultural sector.

As far as the resources base is concerned, flora and fauna are the important resources base of the surveyed blocks. It was found that in Lumla block 67.61 per cent of area were covered under evergreen forests and 17.78 per cent of area were covered under degraded and deciduous forests. On the other hand, in Chaglagham block, around 63.17 per cent of the total area were covered under evergreen forests and 8.67 per cent were covered under degraded and deciduous forests. Both the blocks had a high percentage of barren land due to snow cover and rocky mountains. In Chaglagham block, a good percentage of area was reported to be under shifting cultivation (Map 3.3).

Both the blocks under study had predominantly agro-based economy. Around 88.19 per cent and 72.17 per cent of main workers were engaged in the agricultural sector for their livelihood in Chaglagham and Lumla blocks respectively. In Lumla block, a good percentage of workers were

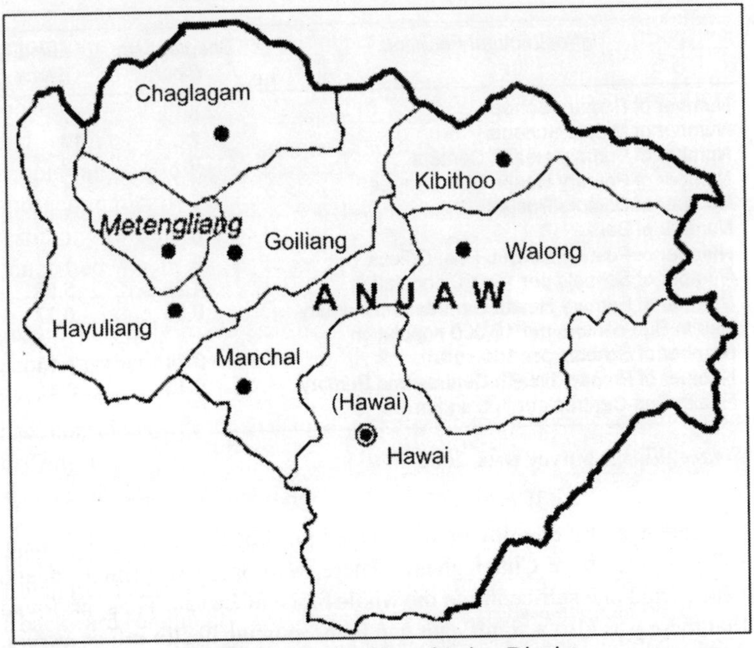

Map 3.3: Location Map of Anjaw District

engaged as labourers in construction activities because of lack of agricultural land. In both the blocks, they produced maize, millet etc. In Chaglagham block, it was found that in most of the village the villagers produced opium illicitly in spite of Government's efforts to reduce its production. The sale of opium was a good source of income for them.

Infrastructural Facilities of the Surveyed Blocks

A study of the existing levels of infrastructure in a block level is a pre-requisite for the formulation of polity for future development. Hence, we try to provide in Table 3.1, the existing infrastructure at the block levels.

When we consider educational infrastructure, the primary schools is regarded as the base for educational development. However, there were only eight primary schools and two middle schools in the surveyed Chaglagham block. Thus, a gap was observed in the existing educational infrastructure in the surveyed blocks. The condition of health infrastructure was pathetic. There was no primary health centre but two-sub-centres in Chaglagham block which covered an area of 1346.2 Sq. km. The hospital

Table 3.1: Infrastructural Facilities of the Surveyed Blocks

Infrastructural Facilities	*Chaglagham Block*	*Lumla Block*
Number of Primary Schools	8	17
Number of Middle Schools	2	13
Number of Primary Health Centers	0	2
Number of Primary Health Sub-Centres	2	1
Number of Doctors Posted	1	1
Number of Banks	0	1
Number of Post Office/Sub Post Offices	2	1
Number of Schools per 10,000 population	4.24	5.58
Number of Primary Health Centres and Primary Health Sub-centers per 10,000 population	0.85	0.37
Number of Schools per 100 sq.km.	0.74	4.13
Number of Primary Health Centres and Primary Health Sub-Centres per 100 sq.km	0.15	0.41

Source: Village Survey Data, 2008.

was managed by one doctor who stayed most of the time in Hayuliang (57 km away from Chaglagham). There were only two primary health centres and one sub-centre in the whole block of Lumla. Thus, we found that there was also a significant gap in the existing health infrastructure. Although the situation was slightly better in Lumla block, in comparison with Chaglagham, yet the situation was way below the desired level of infrastructural development.

SECTION V: PROFILE OF THE SURVEYED VILLAGES

Physical and Demographic Features

In this section, an attempt is made to provide a brief profile of the villages surveyed. The villages surveyed in Chaglagham block are (1) Tabaikun. (2) Tarampa, (3) Tegamna, (4) Taflagham, (5) Apumna and (6) Abuagham. On the other hand, the surveyed villages in Lumla block are: (1) Muchlat, (2) Gorsam, (3) Lumpo, (4) Kharman, and (5) Zeminthang. The details are given in Table 3.2.

Table 3.2 shows that there are variations in the attitude among the surveyed villages. The attitudes of the surveyed villages of Lumla block are within the range of 3000 to 7000 feet above the sea level. However, the villages in the Chaglagham block are in a lower attitude and are within the range of 2000 to 3000 feet above the sea level. The number of

Table 3.2: Characteristics of the Surveyed Villages

Name of Village		Altitude (in feet)	Appropriate Distance from Border (in km)	Number of House-holds	Main occupation	Secondary Occupation
Chaglagham Block	Tabaikun	2465	29	7	Farming	Contract
	Tarampa	2780	32	6	Farming	Contract
	Tegamna	2500	33	14	Farming	Contract
	Taflagam	2680	35	28	Farming	Contract
	Apumna	2600	40	9	Farming	Contract
	Abuagham	2567	34	6	Farming	Contract
Lumla Block	Muchlat	7000	25	25	Farming	Labour
	Gorsam	3000	90	90	Farming	Labour
	Lumpo	6000	45	45	Farming	Labour
	Kharman	4000	38	38	Farming	Labour
	Zemithang	3000	90	90	Farming	Labour

Source: Village Survey Data, 2008.

households in the surveyed villages of Chaglagham block was very few, varying from 6 to 28 but the population of the villages were not so small. For example in Tarampa village, the number of households was only 6 but the population was approximately 236. This is because they lived in a joint family and the size of the family surveyed was on an average 40 persons per family. During the survey, we met a family having 63 members. In fact, Chaglagham block was mainly inhabited by the *Taraons* or *Digaru Mishmi*. Their houses were long and rose on pillars. A corridor ran along the length of the house on the side and the other side was portioned off into a number of rooms, with hearths of their own. Each room was about 12-15 feet long and about 10-20 feet wide. The members of the whole family inhabited each house, and separate rooms were allotted to married couples.

On the other hand, Lumla block was inhabited by the *Monpas* and they were Buddhist by religion. Most of the surveyed villages are located in the steep mountain slopes at an average distance of around 10-15 km from the Chinese Border. The number of households in the surveyed villages varied from 25 to 90. The area was very thinly and sparsely populated. There was limited cultivated land in the surveyed villages due to hilly terrain. The rocky soil and climatic condition was not conducive for cultivation. The villages grow mainly millet, maize and chilly. The main source of livelihood was no doubt agriculture and animal rearing but it was not sufficient for the whole year. Hence, many villagers were found to be working as labourers in Pradhan Mantri Gram Sadak Yojana (PMGSY) and GREF's road construction work. They were also engaged as labourers to carry the loads of defence forces up to the Chinese border.

Economic Features

The main occupation of the surveyed villages of Chaglagham block was agriculture. They mainly practiced shifting cultivation with no fixed recycle period. The crops grown were maize, millet and paddy. The area under maize and millet was much higher than that of paddy. In addition to it, cardamom (big variety) was cultivated in some of the villages. However, few of them sell cardamom in the market. The most important feature of the surveyed villages of Chaglagham block was that all the villages surveyed showed almost ubiquitous cultivation of opium. The area of cultivations ranged from 0.5 acre to 4 acre with yield ranging from 50 gm to 2.5 kg. The sowing of poppy plants started around late September and continued up to December. The crop was harvested between the months of February and April. Opium was smeared on a cloth and dried and thereafter usually stored in a bamboo. The opium was sold at the range between Rs. 400.00 to Rs.1000.00 per tola.

Livelihood Linkages

The question of livelihood linkages is essentially an issue of quality of life, diversification of occupation. In the surveyed villages, the occupational structure outside the household was not usually well-articulated and formalized. Their living was tightly bound up with the household *vis-à-vis* the community and the economy. The local economy was something that could not be isolated from the society, rather, the economy was embedded in the social relations of the family and their community. They undertook a wide range of productive activities in the farm. They grew crops, reared animals, engaged in home-based activities liked making baskets, mat, repairing and construction activities. However, on the off farm they participated in the formal economy through selling or buying of different products in the local markets and sometimes beyond the border. Thus, we found that the villagers in the border area had limited livelihood strategies. It was observed that the majority of villagers were dependent on their livelihood conditions, i.e. agriculture, forestry and animal husbandry. Apart from this combination, the major occupation found in villages of Lumla block was that of wage labour.

Infrastructure and Basic Services

If we undertake an analysis of infrastructural facilities like connectivity, health, education etc. available to these villages, it was found that there was high variation among the surveyed villages. There is only one surveyed village in Chaglagham block and three villages in Lumla block which were within a distance of 1 km from jeepable road. Many villages were not even connected by *Kuchcha* road.

In the surveyed villages of the both the blocks, the medical facilities were hopelessly inadequate. There was only one surveyed village Le.Zemithang which has a primary health centre. In other surveyed villages, the users had to walk more than 5 km for availing themselves of the medical services from primary health centres. It was observed that the primary health centres were managed by the nurses. The doctor was posted, but he was not found in the health centre. Thus, the villages scattered in border areas of Arunachal Pradesh witnessed many untimely deaths due to non-availability of medical services and also because of their strong belief in traditional medical practices. The field investigators of our team heard sad narratives of deaths, many of which could have been avoided through the provision of medical services. Children dying of diarrhoea, young people dying of fever and Tuberculosis, women dying of simple complicacies of pregnancy etc. were common in surveyed villages, which required one days' foot march to reach the nearest health centre. At the same time, their faith was still on traditional system where priests, locally known as *gokham* in Chaglagham block and *Lama*, in Lumla block, were the persons who use to take care of ill people.

There was also lack of educational infrastructure in the surveyed villages. For example, six villages surveyed in Chaglagham block had a primary school located at Taflagham village. Similarly, in Lumla block Zemithang village had only one primary school and Gorsam had one middle school among the surveyed villages. Both the schools lacked basic facilities. Thus, the education of the surveyed villages was restricted up to primary education and middle school only. There was a lack of basic amenities like electricity. All the surveyed villages in Chaglagham block did not have electricity. On the other hand, all the surveyed villages in Lumla block had electricity but the electricity supply was very erratic. Water was available in all the surveyed villages and drinking water was basically delivered from spring. However, water which was supplied through tap, was not available during winter. Sanitation in the surveyed villages was either traditional or in open space. Pigs acted as scavengers, clearing things ranging from rind of an orange to other waste.

SECTION VI: CONCLUSIONS AND RECOMMENDATIONS

On the basis of the findings and observations, the following recommendations have been made to prepare an action plan for further development of the border blocks in general, and surveyed blocks in particular.

It was found that there was a wide infrastructural gap between a majority of the border districts and border blocks with respect to the State average and respective district averages. The gap was wider in case of road density, connectivity and medical and educational facilities. Hence, it is imperative that these facilities should be extended and consolidated so that these border blocks may at least come nearer to the level of the relatively developed blocks. It is true that the cost of construction of road in hilly terrain is very high and difficult, and the cost of construction is around 3 to 4 times higher because of hills cutting and high transport cost of road equipments (as stated by the engineers of border blocks). However, the road has to be constructed at any cost since an increase in road connectivity will lead to improved health and better educational facilities as well as to higher income earnings and better economic development. Further, it will remove the isolation of the people living in the border areas. This will necessitate more allocation of funds in the border blocks on a priority basis for the construction of all-weather roads.

The border blocks also require special attention with regard to the health services sector, since it is observed that in surveyed blocks the medical facilities are hopelessly inadequate. It is no doubt, that there is a felt need in many of the villages to set up more primary health centres (PHCs) since the people have to walk long distances to avail of the modern medical facilities. Our research team also observed that many existing PHCs in the border areas of the State were not-functional due to absenteeism of doctors and nurses. The Government should take immediate steps to fill the vacant posts of medical personnel in all the PHCs especially in border blocks. At the same time the problem of over staffing in the more accessible areas and under-staffing of PHCs in the inaccessible border areas needs to be addressed on a priority basis.

Our research team found that in one of the border blocks there was large scale opium cultivation which was being sold in the open market.

There is no denying the fact that opium is being cultivated because of its economic returns. Therefore, introduction of cash crop could be a viable alternative. Our research team observed that cardamom (big variety) was cultivated in a very large scale in those areas. However, the main problem faced by the producers is that the production drops significantly in 5-6 years period when the plant have to be shifted to another area. The Government agencies should tackle the problem in a planned way since the production of cardamom can act as a very good alternative to opium cultivation. At the same time the other cash crops like orange, plum can also be encouraged to produce particularly during the winter season, which is the opium production season. However, before cultivation of cash crops marketing network should be strengthened.

The flourishing border trade of the past is languishing in the recent years. For example in Chaglagham block, the villagers used to exchange their goods across the border. The main articles exchanged were common salt from Indian side and from the Chinese side it was brass utensils, Tibetan silver coin and food articles. However it is now restricted. The people in the border areas strongly feel that the centre should reintroduce the border trade. In fact, the Central Government may seriously think not only to promote border trade but to use the border outlets for full-fledged international trade in the background of the "Look East Policy".

It is observed that there is a huge potential for hydropower generation in the border blocks. However, substantial investment is required to harness this latent potential. It is also found that there is large potential for developing nature-based and to some extent Buddhism based tourism in the border blocks, provided road, and other basic infrastructural amenities are built up. It is observed that border blocks of Arunachal with its beautiful villages, verdant forests, spectacular rivers and fascinating people has immense potential for eco-tourism. However, tourism requires that infrastructure should be adequately developed. The Department of Tourism needs to draw up a base plan to develop areas selectively and promote certain destinations by providing accommodation and other facilities. The destinations will have to be developed in consonance with the local people. It may be possible to provide a unique experience to tourists by building low cost infrastructure in the villages adjoining block-circle headquarters by using local materials and local inputs. This will create employment opportunities for the local people and will arrest to large scale exodus of people from border areas to administrative centres in search of better jobs and livelihood opportunities.

Appendix A.1
Socio-Demographic and Economic Features of the Border Blocks of Arunachal Pradesh, 2001

Name of Bordered District/ Bordered Block	Density of Population	Literacy Rate	Percentage of ST Population	Work Participation Rate	Percentage of Main Workers Engaged in Agriculture Sector
Tawang District	18	47.3	74.99	55.77	41.89
Tawang	80	62.7	61.52	56.89	21.16
Mukto-Thimpu	15	39.3	81.57	56.30	48.03
Lumla	14	26.6	91.14	53.52	72.17
West Kameng District	10	60.8	49.53	46.06	48.03
Dirang	19	56.6	63.47	45.69	37.10
Kalakthang	13	72.8	48.86	45.79	39.86
Nafra	2	49.2	79.89	42.33	77.65
East Kameng District	14	40.6	86.71	45.38	73.69
Bameng	4	22.3	98.50	54.63	87.88
Chyangtajo	15	26.6	98.60	48.20	85.55
Kurung Kumey District	5	25.7	97.88	53.48	85.82
Sarli	2	17.5	94.47	61.16	89.36
Damin	2	26.0	97.45	58.28	85.83
Koloriang	2	27.5	96.25	48.90	80.22
Parsi-Parlo	2	19.9	99.98	62.08	97.81
Upper Subansiri District	8	50.3	89.53	40.50	68.89
Nacho	2	29.0	97.68	48.32	82.68
Siyum	4	23.8	98.52	52.12	91.50
West Siang District	13	59.5	81.73	41.46	62.25
Mechuka	5	45.5	91.37	46.00	61.64
Monigong	2	21.9	99.27	31.01	85.40
Kaying-Payum	3	33.9	94.41	45.36	78.70
Upper Siang District	5	49.8	78.21	51.27	64.19
Tuting	1	46.2	77.01	57.92	61.73
Singa-Gelling	2	36.7	97.44	63.12	88.47
Dibang Valley District	4	53.0	66.38	51.66	31.69
Anini-Mipi	1	59.5	62.26	47.38	31.92
Etalin-Maliney	1	46.6	56.06	65.46	28.28
Aneli-Arzoo (B)	2	33.5	93.79	46.10	56.67
Lower Dibang Valley District	NA	59.8	43.62	43.62	61.21
Hunli-Kronli	1	48.0	81.18	52.57	64.65
Anjaw District	4	38.4	77.27	51.62	65.99
Hayuliang	6	37.9	76.03	50.01	49.47
Manchal	1	28.2	98.25	49.20	92.79
Chaglagham	2	15.8	96.43	53.58	88.19
Walong	4	41.6	71.94	53.83	61.66
Changlang District	27	51.3	36.16	47.87	72.16
Khimiyang	3	35.8	94.72	56.70	88.58
Nampong-Manmao	13	68.1	51.37	43.87	44.18
Khagam-Miao	20	78.0	32.40	46.23	76.05
Tirap District	43	41.7	83.67	48.91	74.69
Lazu	18	42.5	96.23	54.05	91 .86
Pongcau-Wakka	46	15.3	97.85	53.69	93. 62
Arunachal Pradesh	13	54.3	64.22	44.55	59. 16

Source: Census of India, Final Population Totals 2001, Arunachal Pradesh.

REFERENCES

Das, G., (1995), *Tribes of Arunachal Pradesh in Transition,* Vikas Publication, New Delhi.

Elwin, V., (1998), *A Philosophy for NEFA,* Directorate of Research, Government of Arunachal Pradesh, Itanagar.

Government of Arunachal Pradesh, (2005), *Human Development Report of Arunachal Pradesh*, Itanagar.

Government of Arunachal Pradesh, (Different Issues), *Statistical Abstracts of Arunachal Pradesh*, Itanagar.

Government of India, (2009), *Arunachal Pradesh Development Report*, Planning Commission, New Delhi.

Government of India, (2002), *A Study Report on BADP*, Planning Commission, New Delhi.

Government of Arunachal Pradesh, (2008), *Border Area Development Programme in Arunachal Pradesh*, Department of Planning.

Government of India, (Different Issues), *Census of India Arunachal Pradesh*, New Delhi.

Mitra, A., (2003), *Environment and Nature-Based Tourism*, Kanishka Publishers, New Delhi.

Mitra, A., (2006), Transition of Arunachal's Economy: Opportunities and Challenges for a Less Developed State, *Indian Development Review*, Vol 4 (2).

Singh, S., (1997), *A Resource Atlas of Arunachal Pradesh*, Government of Arunachal Pradesh, Itanagar.

UNDP, (Undated), *Survey of Opium Cultivation in Lohit District*, Arunachal Pradesh.

4

The Livelihood Pattern of the Noctes, Arunachal Pradesh: Continuity and Change

R.P. Athparia

The People

In common parlance, the word Nocte means 'People living in an organized community (Noc-village, and te = the people, i.e., "one who lives in a village" or village people' (Dutta, 1978:9). The Noctes call themselves as the Nagas. They are also known as the Nagas by the people of the adjacent plains area of Assam. The Nocte is a homogenous group. However, dialectically, each village is different from the other. They trace their descent from a remote ancestor, named Khunbao—a chief. Khunbao had two sons—Khunlung and Khunlai. They were succeeded by Tangthok and Tankam. The claims of the Nocte chiefs to royal descent are based on this genealogy. The Ahom chronicles (Barua 1969, Bhuyan; 1929, 1933, 1949 and Devi, 1968) bear evidence to the fact that the Nocte settlements were in existence in the district of Tirap as early as the beginning of the 13th Century. In the Ahom period, and the early British period, the Noctes were referred to as the Bordurias, Pandurias, Namsangias and the Jaipurias etc.

The Land

Once the Tirap district was a part of the old Sadiya Frontier Tract. In 1942, it was made a separate district carving it out of Sadiya Frontier Tract and giving the name after the name of the river Tirap which flows throughout the district.

The district is an arch like South-eastern and South-western prolongations of Arunachal Pradesh adjoining Myanmar and it is the only district of the Pradesh which lies entirely to the south of the Brahmaputra river. It is bounded on the north by the Dibrugarh district, on the south by Myanmar, on the east by the Changlang district and the west by the Sibsagar district of Assam and Mon district of Nagaland. Smallest in area of all the districts of Arunachal Pradesh, Tirap occupies a tract of 2362 sq. km of land.

Social Life

The Nocte society is patrilineal, patriarchal and patrilocal. It is organized under the chief. The chief is called **Lowang.** The existence of chieftainship is an important feature of their community life. The chieftainship system of the Noctes has created two distinct classes. Dutta (1978:98) states that the chieftainship system has greatly affected the social life of the Noctes, leading to the creation of two distinct classes. The existence of the two classes is, however, not so marked among the Wanchos, a neighbouring community. Among the Nocte, the chief and his descendants form a separate class called the **Lowangjat,** while the commoners are called the **Sanajat.** The **Lowanjat** being the ruling class, treats the **Sanajat** as their sub-servant class. In the Lazu area, the commoner's class is called **Panajat.** Each of these two classes consists of many clans and lineage groups called **Ku** or **Mu** with distinct names and numbers in each class. All the clans are exogamous but the tribe is endogamous. The exogamous character of the clans regulates the marriage system of the tribe. But the marriage between members of different clans within a **Chum,** physical division of the village, is under some exceptional circumstance, prohibited. Marriage is not possible between members of all *Chums* as it is believed that certain clans constituting different **Chums**, have had a common ancestry. All clans within a particular **Chum** have a common name.

Land Laws

Agriculture is the basic means of livelihood of the Noctes. The **jhuming** or the slash and burn method is the prime mode of cultivation of the people. The *jhum* plots are locally known as *Haram*. Usually, a piece of land is cleared and trees are cut down and after these, the land is left for some time to dry or rot, and lastly the bushes and the branches of the trees, are burnt. The soil is then stirred with a stick and sowing is done by broad costing. It is to be noted here that the nature of terrain does not permit a radical change from *Jhuming* to permanent cultivation. Lack of sui be Table agricultural land prevents many villages from adopting the permanent cultivation. Today, however, in many villages sufficient land is available for settled cultivation. It has been adopted in addition to terrace cultivation. These methods have been sponsored by the Agriculture Department of Arunachal Pradesh. The people have some interest in settled cultivation. While improving the settled cultivation, the age-old method of *jhuming* has also been simultaneously improved on scientific lines.

There is no land settlement system as found in other settled areas. No cadastral survey has been conducted so far in the Nocte area. The ownership of land can be broadly divided into three categories, namely:

1. Land owned by individual;
2. Land owned by the clan;
3. Common village land.

The Government's attitude to land in Arunachal Pradesh is formulated in three ***Jhum Land Regulations promulgated*** in 1947-48. These regulations give the Nocte people absolute rights over their *Jhum* land which is defined as "all lands which any member or members of a village or a community have a customary right to cultivate by means of shifting cultivation or to utilize by clearing jungle or grazing live stock, provided that such village or community is in permanent location" (Dutta, P.C. 1978:71).

In the areas where the *jhuming* method of cultivation is followed, all lands in principle, belong to the clan or viliage. It is wrong to think that communal ownership of land does not counterance individual rights of possession of any sort. The yield of paddy in the *jhum* field is comparatively low.

The gradient of the mountainous terrain of the Nocte area is suitable for horticulture. There are three h· ·iculture nurseries and 20 people's horticulture gardens in the area. Grafts of mango, lichi, Sapota, orange, sweet lime, grape, guava, pomegranate and banana are planted in the horticulture nurseries. Plantation of pineapple, banana, sweet lime, guava and pomegranate are also done in Khela and Khowsa villages. Pear-grafts, arecanut, seedlings, mango grafts, paddy seeds and sugarcane are raised on a experimental basis in Borduria village.

Though *jhuming* is the traditional mode of cultivation of the Noctes of the studied villages, namely, Lapnan, Laz:ı and Soha, a changeover to other modes have taken place with the passage of time. By all means, attempt of permanent cultivation is made side by side with improved jhum cultivation. Moreover, the *Jhum Land Regulation of 1947* has given the villagers customary rights over the *jhum* land. They have been showing willingness to adopt the new methods and techniques of sedentary cultivation.

In the villages, the local farmers take active interest in the present agricultural development. Then co-operation for implementation of the agricultural schemes is noteworthy. The agricultural shows, exhibitions and demonstrations on the modern system of cultivation have stimulated in them a curiosity and enthusiasm. The development of communications and the establishment of administrative centres in the three villages studied for the purpose, have opened new horizons for social and economic progress of the people.

To inculcate a sense of healthy competition among the cultivators, exhibitions are organized on some auspicious occasions, such as on the Independence Day and Republic Day, and such, and these are attended by the local people in large numbers.

Soil and Crop

The nature of the soil of the Nocte area ranges between sandy loam, loam and clayey-loam. In the Lazu area, the soil is generally shallow and well drained, brown and reddish in colour and comparatively coarse in structure. In the Lapnan village, it is loamy and better developed, having slightly deeper structure. In Soha area, the soil ranges from loamy to clayey loam.The higher regions are suitable for citrus and deciduous plants and other fruits, varieties of cereals and seasonal vegetables. The lower regions are suitable for root crops.

Though the soil condition is suitable for many crops and fruits yet the Noctes grow hill-paddy, millet, arum, chillies, tapioca, maize and some pulses and vegetables. Millet is an important crop and all the rituals and festivals are centred round the cultivation of the millet. There are also some festivals related with the paddy cultivation. The common crops of Lapnan village are: different *ahu* (*champa*), paddy (summer variety) Khons, Mouza, Nyak millet-himoi, arum (*tou*), guard (*chagum*), potato (*akhoni*) etc. In Soha, the Noctes cultivate early variety paddy – Sajong, potato (*kho*), tapioca (*bengkho*), sweet potato (*kho kham*).

Major and Subsidiary crops

Rice is the staple food of all the Noctes. It is grown at all elevations. There are different types of paddy. The early variety ripens in September and the late variety in November, whose grains are bigger in size.

Next to paddy is the millet, another important crop. Main types of millet are finger millet, fox tail millet and job's tear.

Maize is another important crop produced by the Lazu Noctes. Different varieties are grown at different seasons from March to July.

Sweet potato, arum, tapioca etc. are also grown according to the necessity to fulfil the shortage of food or to meet the scarcity of paddy harvest. Potato is a recent crop introduced by the government and its cultivation is steadily growing popular.

The different species of millet, paddy, arum and potato of the three villages are as follows: ***Millet (Himai)*:** Kangsa, Langnan, Kanhan, Kangtu, Hitangtip, Sumiyen. *Paddy (Sajong)* – Khanse, Samyu, Khansit. *Warang paddy* (*Sa ma*) –saliyang, Wangfa, Sasiyang, Khoila, Sakha, Bong rim. *Sima Arum* (*Ta*) – Tuhom, Tusa, Masik, Nyakpha, Yakthat, ItKhuk, Damnya, Rongsomtu. *Potato* (*Tha*) – *Thasong*, Thajya, Singfo tha, Thami, Mukoi tha, Wasaring tha, Po tha, Tha rim, Phung Su, Tha Sa.

Agricultural Implements

The agricultural implements used by the people are **Dao (Lapnan – Dong)**, a small hoe, **Janhum**, iron or bone scrapper (**Kanghe**) for weeding, spade (**Chà**) and knife (**Dongmit**) and a wooden stick. With these implements they cultivate all the crops in *jhum* fields. It takes a long time either to clear or cultivate a small patch of land for *jhum* cultivation. Now-a-days, the government of Arunachal Pradesh is supplying the local cultivators some simple agricultural implements at subsidized rates. However, till 1954-55 the government had supplied the agricultural implements such as axes, spades, pick axes, hand hoe etc. at free of cost. Now, the government besides supplying agricultural tools on subsidized rates, helps the poor cultivators by giving subsidy towards land reclamation, minor irrigation, purchase of seeds, purchase of bullocks for ploughing, and also for improving piggery, poultry and dairy farms. Moreover, the government is providing guidance and training for crops, veterinary and like-stock upgradation.

Seeds and Manures

Traditionally, the people were interested in horticulture rather than *jhum* cultivation and are not in the habit of using of manure in agricultural fields. However, the *jhum* fields are kept fallow for a couple of years for natural regeneration. The *jhum* cycle varies from 10 to 12 years depending upon the number of fields a village possesses. Each *jhum* field has its own name according to location and condition of soil. For example, Lazu village has eleven *jhum* fields, namely Rittong, Hemha, Kehang, Tamchat, Longkare, Rapcha, Nyetho, Thamthung, Rasha, Rennang, and Thencha. Similarly, the *jhum* fields of Soha village are: Pondap, Liiruk, Kangkoi, Langrang, Barak, Phasi, Kholamkong, Sapfakong, Wadakpang, Zatsa and Namli. Traditionally a field is cultivated and planted for two consecutive years after which it is left fallow for a period of 10 to 12 years. In the first year, millet, arum, tapioca and all other vegetables are grown.

Festivals in Agriculture

Along with other agricultural ceremonies, millet and paddy harvest festivals are also observed. At Kapu village, millet and paddy grains are kept in the granary after performing ***Pun Ram*** ceremony. In this ceremony, the Lowang and his wife are entertained with a good meal at the granary itself. The youth dance in the house of the chief. The owner of the granary kills a pig on the occasion.

Similarly, a ceremony called ***Towsat*** at Lazu is performed to bring arum and potato from the field. Special feature of the ceremony is to feed the old men and women with the newly harvested arum and potato.

At Soha, the first rice of millet and paddy is kept on the roof of the house. It is called ***Dichong Bongku.*** Rice is also offered to the fire before consuming by the members of the family. This ceremonial offering is called ***Chongtu Bongku***. The harvested millet and paddy is also kept in the main post of the house. It is called ***Thongdong.***

At Lazu, putting up of fencing in the field is celebrated by performing a ceremony called ***Penhen.*** Before consuming the newly harvested maize, a ceremony called ***Ko Chuk*** is performed. It lasts for three days. On the second day, the maternal uncles are invited for a meal. They are fed with a special item called *Ren* prepared by boiling powdered rice and millet. Selection of new *jhum* sites is done in this ceremony. The dance performed in the ceremony is called ***Je Cha Sam Buon***.

Agricultural Calendar

The Noctes have their own names for the different months of the years. These names are derived from the agricultural activities performed in a particular month. The agricultural calendar is not uniform for the entire tribe. At Soha, a year is called ***Rang ngat***. The months are lunar months and calculated on the basis of the moon's position. A month is called ***Da***

Name of the Village	Local name of the Month	Corres-ponding English Month	Major Agricultural Work	Festival and other activities
(1)	(2)	(3)	(4)	(5)
SOHA	Da si	Jan/Feb	Setting fire to new millet field, clearing the field and sowing of millet	
	Fun Sa	Feb/ March	Planting of paddy seedling, arum and potato	
	Fung dong	March/ April	Planting of arum and potato continues, construction of field huts, clearing of last year's jhum field for Ahu paddy	
	Datu	April/May	Sowing of Ahu paddy	
	Dasang	May/June	Weeding in millet field	Males go to the Assam plains for trade
	Namsa	June/July	Construction of granary	
	Nam dong	July/Aug	Harvesting of millet Starts	
	Dari	Aug/Sept	Weeding of Ahu paddy	Construc-tion of houses
	Dasa	Sept/Oct	Harvesting of Ahu paddy	
	Dattoi	Oct/Nov	Harvesting of Ahu paddy& jungle cutting in the *jhum* field	
	Nam cha	Nov/Dec	Jungle cutting in the new *jhum* field	
	Dafoi	Dec/Jan	Cleaning of the *Jhum* field	
LAZU	Darang	Janaury	Clearing of the *jhum* field	Hakhen
	Rudong	February	Setting fire in the millet field and sowing of millet	Hiwin
	Namdong	March	Road and bridge construction	Phoobi
	Namsa	April	Clearing of last year's *ihum* field for cash crop	Worang
	Dasone	May	Arum, Potato & other cash crop cultivation	Toki
	Dasa	June	Ahu paddy harvesting	Chaki
	Darant	July	Harvesting of millet	Majob
	Dashi	August	Harvesting of millet ends	Ronghen
	Donam	September	Prayer for new cultivation	Kochup
	Daritra	October	Clearing of jungle for cultivation	Donshot
	Dawot	November	Clearing of jungle	Haphab
	Tomre	December	Clearing of cultivating land and store of crops in granary	Wottian

fai by the Soha people. There are four seasons in a year among the Lazu Noctes, these are **Batin** (autumn), **Jokha** (Spring), **Yanba** (Winter) and **Yangjo** (Summer).

The agricultural calendars of Soha and Lazu villages are given above showing the agricultural work done and festivals performed.

Thus, we have observed that the Noctes perform agricultural festivals along with the different agricultural operations. Agricultural festivals have great socio-cultural role in the society. It is seen that the whole year the people remain busy in one or the other activities of the agricultural work.

Agrarian System

For cultivating millet, a *jhum* field is selected through divination from among their fields which had already left fallow for a period of ten years or so. The divination is done by the priest with sample of soil from the fields sometimes without it. Omens are observed by bursting a kind of bamboo or on an egg. The ceremony is commonly known as ***Pitsa*** in Borduria and Thinsa area. In Soha, it is known as ***Wiknok.***

Generally, the ceremony performed in connection with selection of a new *jhum* field, lasts for one day, which is observed as restricted day or ***genna*** (***apiyen***). In Soha village, before selecting the *jhum* field, the priest, *Wiknop* sees the auspicious place by ***taboi tadak*** leaf. The villagers select the *jhum* site according to the convenient. The **Zenna** is locally known as ***Weisampmet.***

After selection of the *jhum* site, the next operation is cutting and clearing of the jungle. This is done by performing ceremonies as the life of the Noctes has a great significance on the jhuming. The ceremony performed on the occasion is called ***hakufap*** (Lazu), ***Bikocok*** (Soha), ***Jatsang ku*** (Laiwang) and so on. The first day of the ceremony is called ***famlam***. On this day, the articles required for the ceremony are collected. The second day is called ***Jatcha***. On this day, old men and women go to the new *jhum* sites and the youngsters to the old field, i.e. the previous years' field. The third day is observed as ***genna***. On this day, nobody goes out of the village. The cutting of *jhum* plot and clearing of the old field starts from the following day.

The third stage of agricultural activity is sowing of millet seeds which have a great significance in the Nocte's life. It is called **Chibin** in Soha, **Hibin** in Lazu, **Chaliwan** in Borduria, **Sarok** in Kolagoan and **Pongtu** in Kothung. The ceremony is performed generally in one day but in Soha it is celebrated for three to four days. On the day of sowing millet, the villagers sacrifice pig and cock in their houses. After sacrifice, the seeds are smeered with the blood of the sacrificed animals. Then it is carried to the *jhum* field, by the women. Before sowing, they make the boundary wall of the field with the help of bamboo or wood. It is called **Kare**. The smeering of seeds with blood is known as **Siron**.

Next day is known as **Weisangmet**. Third day is called **Sadam**. On this day, they clear the land. Fourth day is called **Weisongmet** means **genna** or abstain from doing any work. From the fifth day, they work in the *jhum* field.

Dutta (1978:80) states that the ceremony connected with the sowing of millet seeds in Bordunia and Kolagoan lasts for three to four days. At Bordunia, the second day after sowing the millet is called *Chaban*. On this day and the third day (*Khaksa*) a fair is held in the front of the chief's house. In Lazu, the sowing is done in the month of Janaury (**Darang**) and February (**Rudong**). In these months, ***Hakhen*** and ***Hiwin*** festivals are performed. The **Pongtu** festival of Kolam village last for seven days, it is celebrated to perform the last rites for the dead and ensure welfare of the village.

Paddy sowing is also associated with ceremonies. In Soha, the cultivation done in the month of February and March is locally known as **Fun Sa**. They cultivate a local variety of paddy known as **Sajong**. The ritual observed by the Lazu people in connection with the sowing of paddy is known as **Sake**. Arum and potato are ceremonially planted by the Lazu people. It is called ***bohum***.

Harvest of paddy and millet is an important agricultural operation of the Noctes. Harvest is a joyful and happy occasion and is associated with some festivals. The harvest festival is known as **Kakiyak** in Borduria area, **Ronghuon** (Thinsa, Tupi, Kolagoan, Dadem and nearby villages) and **Chambi** (Kothung village). The harvest of paddy is known as **Chathik** at Lapnan village. At Soha, harvest of millet and paddy is known as **Chomthik.**

The harvest of millet is significant among the Noctes as all socio-religious and socio-cultural activities are intrisingly attached with this agricultural operation. As a matter of fact, this is the biggest festival of the Noctes. It is called **Rong Low** at Borduria, **Rong Rong Paku** at Noksa, **Phoobi** at Lazu and **Hoju** at Kapu. At Soha, harvest of millet is done after performing the **Lambon** ritual.

Like the millet harvest, paddy harvest is also followed by performance of some festivals such as **Chalow** (Borduria, Thinsa, Kolagoan villages), **Loku** (Doidam village) etc. These festivals are celebrated for three to four days with much pump and grandeur. At Borduria, the *Chalow* festival is celebrated as the biggest agricultural festival. All the days of the festivals are passed off in dancing, eating and drinking.

Changing Trends

As reported by the Agricultural Department, the net area sown under agriculture in 1992-93 was 14248 hectares. Out of which 6951 hect. area were current follow land and 19,350 hect. old fallow land. Cultivable waste land was 11,900 hect. The area brought under fertilizer during 1992-93 was 175 hectares. The total barren and uncultivatable land was 1250 hectares. The area brought under plant protection in 1992-93 was 2650 hectares and improved seed in 1992-93 was 1325 hectares. The total horticulture area by the Noctes was 18 hectares and horticulture nurseries 5 hectares. The above figures show that they have now realized the value of improved method of cultivation and the need of horticulture farms. Many people have come forward to reclaim more of the cultivable waste land and thus brought under cultivation. Harnessing of animal power for cultivation is yet to be in force. The ecological set-up and the nature of terrain stand in the way of utilizing the animals for cultivation. A large horticulture gardens at Borduria village is an example of the interest of the people in the cultivation of citrus trees, bananas, pineapples and other fruits. After the establishment of the administrative circles in Khonsa, Lazu and Soha, some changes have taken place in these villages. The villagers of these villages largely depend on the fair price shops for the rice as the yields from the *jhum* fields are not sufficient to feed their growing population. The Government is trying to increase food production in this remote area where people are not self-sufficient in their production, through several schemes such as land development, irrigation, supply of tools and implements, supply of high quality seeds and plants, etc. have been taken up by the Agricultural Department. However, the production of cash crops particularly, the potato has taken a special place in recent years and tea cultivation has been taken place as vital cash crop of the Noctes.

Conclusion

In an attempt to discuss the agricultural laws and practices of the Noctes, various aspects of the society has been observed. It is seen that they practice the old aged jhuming along with other improved variety of agriculture. The economy of the Noctes is rural in nature and the concept of export and import does not exist in their life. In fact, the co-operative societies have played an important role in the transitional period of barter economy to monetary economy. At the far end of the discussion the following observations have been identified:

1. The people have their own conception regarding the quality of land, soil and crops. They are reluctant to adopt new varieties of crops, manures and pesticides.
2. A number of rituals and festivals are associated with the agricultural practices which unveil mystic ancestral relationship.
3. There is no much change of the land reform rules over the last four decades. No cadastral survey has been made in the area.
4. There is no rivalry between the landlords and the agricultural labourers. There are no tenancy rules in the area. The landlords and the tenancy have built up a kind of co-operation among themselves since time immemorially.
5. Income is also derived from the sale of vegetables to the government officials. The villagers near the administrative headquarters earn substantial money by selling fire-woods.

Over and above, all the developmental activities have brought about a change in the outlook of the people. Along with the development of the area, some changes have also taken place in socio-cultural life of the people.

REFERENCES

Barua, B.K., (1969), A Cultural History of Assam (Early Period) Vol X. Gauhati, Department of History and Antiquarian Study.

Bhuyan, S.K., (1929), *Early British Relations with Assam*, Shillong, Govt. Secretariat Press.

Devi, Lakshmi, (1969), *Ahom-Tribal Relations*, Gauhati, Assam Book Depot.

Dutta, Parul, (1978), *The Noctes*, Shillong, Directorate of Research, Arunachal Pradesh.

5

Forest as a Source of Livelihood for the Tribes in Kurung Kumey District, Arunachal Pradesh

Tame Ramya

Introduction

In the present day Arunachal Pradesh, there is a general conformity about the importance of the tribal people on social and cultural practices. As tribal communities constitute the state's cultural diversity, the knowledge and study on those regions require vast amount of data about those people's way of life. The tribal people forming little more than 7 lakh, i.e. 64.22 per cent of the state's total population (2001 Census), embody and nurture the state's cultural and biological diversities. They live in and around naturally origin virgin forests and are concerned with preserving land, protecting language and promoting culture. Some tribal people strive to preserve traditional way of life, while other seeks greater participation in the current state structure.

A total of 26 different major tribes and 110 sub-tribes and minor tribes speaking as many as 42 different dialects with varied size and populaion are living in Arunachal Pradesh (Arunachal Pradesh State Gazetteer, 2010). While coming to Kurung Kumey district, as per the provisional population Census of 2011, the population of this district is pegged at 89,717 with 44,226 males and 45,491 females as compare to 42,518 with 21,117 males and 21,401 females in 2001 Census. The district registered a record decadal growth rate among the districts of Arunachal Pradesh with 111.01 per cent during the decade 2001-2011. The population of this district is predominantly tribal (more than 97%) and the *Nyishis, Bangrus* and the *Puroiks* are the major tribal groups inhabiting the region. The *Nyishis* are demographically the dominant tribe inhabiting in all directions/circles of the district. The *Bangrus*, a relatively small tribe is confined to the western and north-western part of the Sarli circle and in some pockets of Damin circle. They are closely related to the *Nyishis* whom they resemble in dress, festivals, manners and customs, and with whom they often intermarry. The *Puroiks* are confined to the high hills in the district's northern, north-western and western part spanning the areas of Sarli, Nyapin and Phassang circles. The *Puroik* settlements are interspersed with the *Nyishi* and the *Bangru* villages. Their economy is based on food-gathering and big-game hunting. Few of them are now taking to sedentary form of agriculture and the change in their life style is now perceptible, though at minimal level.

The tribal communities in Kurung Kumey district are still left as the most disadvantageous groups by the government and policy makers. These tribal people sometimes fell themselves alienated from the mainstream in terms of actual practice and development behaviour. As a consequence, an antagonistic relationship has been inexistence between the people and government. The government claims that the tribal people are key destroyers of the forest and its resources. On the other hand, the tribal people believe that different developmental projects and incursion of non-indigenous people to their area are adversely affecting their lifestyle and livelihood. Hence, the importance of studying people's livelihood pattern cannot be ignored, as the rural setting refers more dependence on forest than urban areas and diversified practice needs diversified study. This study was carried out in order to have an idea about the tribal lifestyle, to have an understanding of the socio-economic status of tribal people and also to find out the dependence of forest as a source of livelihood among the tribal communities of Kurung Kumey district in Arunachal Pradesh.

Methodology

This paper dicussses about three tribes, viz. the *Nyishi, Bangru* and the *Puroik* in Kurung Kumey district of Arunachal Pradesh. Data were collected from three different sites and from two significant perspectives of livelihood pattern and forest dependence. Through those data, their socio-economic status was analysed and scrutiny is made to find out who are comparatively more dependent on forest resources for their living. It is assumed that, all the three tribal communities are equally dependent on forest for their livelihood. Further, it is also presumed that they have equal impact on forest. The area for the study of tribal communities was as under:

(i) For *Nyishi* tribe—Hiya village, Nyapin Sub-Division, Kurung Kumey District.
(ii) For *Bangru* tribe—Wabia village, Sarli circle, Kurung Kumey District.
(iii) For *Puroik* tribe—Polosang village, Sarli circle, Kurung Kumey District.

People-Forest Interactions

There is no doubt that all people (rural or urban dwellers) have some dependence on forests, at least for contsruction materials and for products such as timbers and papers. However, many people rely heavily on forests for their livelihoods (see Table 4.1). In this regard, rural households heavily relied on natural resources. Studies indicate that as much as 20-25 per cent of rural people's income is derived from environmental resources in developing countries where India is also a part (WRI, 2005; Vedeld *et al.*, 2007). Poor people typically engage more in low-return forest activities, but often fail to accunulate capital from such activities. Meanwhile, the concept of 'forest-dependency' is complicated one. Although it is possible to refer loosely to any people who relied on forest and its products for their livelihood as being to some extent 'forest-dependent', this loose usage blurred fundamental distinctions between different types of relationships. By presenting a fundamental critique of the use of the term 'forest-dependency', Byron and Arnold (1997) argued that it is more useful to present a typology of different types of users. They crafted a vital distinction between people who rely on forest use and have to substitute, and those who use forest products or hold-on in economic activities linking forests, but do so as matter of preference.

The tribal people may be consider as the offspring of forests who depend on the forest for their subsistence and other economic activities. It is reported that about 60 million indigenous people are almost totally dependent on forests (Colchester, 2006). Dubois (1996) reported that the Amazonian Indians have been depending on forests, for centuries, for livelihood through shifting cultivation, hunting, fishing and accumulation of forest products. According to Dembner (1996), the Pygmies of Central African rain forest have traditionally lived by specialising in hunting and gathering wild forest resources, which they consume themselves or trade to neighbouring farmers. Traditionally, tribal communities are well-informed about natural resources on which they are closely dependent. They are considered to be a threat to forest conservation. But, there are instances from different parts of the world that the tribai forest dwellers apply traditional knowledge and new tools and techniques in forest management. Over the past few decades, the magnitude of tribals' Indigenous Knowledge (IK) in managing natural resources and environment has gained increasing recognition.

Table 4.1: Forests Contribution ways to Human Livelihood

Forest Contribution	*Livelihood Pattern*
Household Use (Subsistence)	Timber, fuelwood, wild foods (plants and animals), medicinal plants, grazing for animals, forest-based agriculture, nutrient subsidies for agriculture.
Food Security	Depend on forest foods when crops fail to meet seasonal needs or to provide dietary supplements.
Income Generation	From sale of any products listed above or sale of agricultural or livestock production dependent on forests.
Income from forest-based labour	By working in different forest-based works.

Fisher *et al.,* (1997) has acknowledged three broad categories of interactions between people and forest which may be mention as follows:

(i) People who reside inside forests, often living as hunter-gatherers or shifting cultivators, and who are heavily relied on forests for their livelihood on a subsistence basis. People in this group are often indigenous people or people from ethnic tribal communities. They are, thus, usually outside the mainstream polity and economy.

(ii) People who reside near forests, frequently involve in agriculture outside the forest, and regularly use forest products partly for their own subsistence functions and partly for income generation. For those involved in agriculture, nutrient supplements from forests are often crucial to productivity. Such supplements can be in the form of mulch from leaves gathered in the forest. Another source of nutrient supplement is forest grazing by livestock which alters nutrients from forest biomass into manure.

(iii) People engaged in mercantile activities as trapping, accumulating minerals or forest industries such as logging. Such people may part of a mixed subsistence and cash economy. Distinctness of these people from first two categories may be found from the fact that they depend on income from forest-dependent labour rather than from direct subsistence use of forest products. However, it is worthy to note that this type of people-forest relationship or interaction can exist even in an extremely monetised circumstance.

(iv) The forest products obtained by the tribal communities from the study areas have been grouped as per use and a description of each use type is as below:

Fodder

The major fodder species as enlisted by the *Nyishi* tribe are *takuk-sangney* (*Gynocardia odorata*) and *kulung* (wild banana or *Musa* sp), the former for being palatable, easy to digest and for its milk enhancing properties and the latter for its easy availability and palatability. Traditionally, these people leave their animals and livestock for grazing and feeding in the open areas, *Jhum* fallows and the community forests. Stall feeding is a phenomenon of very recent past and is now seen in practice in some private farms. *Gynocardia* leaves are available only during the monsoon months, whereas wild banana is available through out the year. In addition bamboo foliage also acts as a supplementary fodder. Fodder collection is only for meeting the requirement of their domestic cattle and has been taken up in the recent past.

Fuelwood

The most preferred species for fuelwood is *yahak-sangney (Macranga denticulata*). A local species *yarphu-sangney (Callicarpa arborea*) is also highly preferred for use as firewood. These are very light woods, easily combustible, leave less smoke while burning and dry easily. In addition to these, many inferior wood species are also made use of for fuel wood purposes. The availability of the same is throughout the year and in addition to meeting their subsistence requirement; head loads from the *Jhum* land are also sold in the nearby market. The general rule of collecting only dry and fallen stems and branches is practised. Wood of other species is also made use of for burning, depending on the demand and relative availability.

Construction Material

Timber

Yalluk-sangney (Hollock or *Terminalia myriocarpa*) and *sangnyum-sangney* (*bola* or *Morus laevigata*) are the two timber yielding species most preferred for use in construction and repairs of dwelling houses. In the typical long house of the *Nyishis*, bamboo and roofing leaves of wild banana are also made use of. As a general understanding among the community members, timber for domestic use can be taken from the community forest or the *Jhum* land, irrespective of the ownership of the *Jhum* land. *Mekhahi (Phoebe cooperiana), taram (Alnus sp)* and *jutli (Altingia excelsa)* are the other timber yielding species which are also made use of.

Poles

The houses are rose normally on stilts and the requirement of poles for the same is met from the forests. *Yahak-sangney (Macranga denticulata)* and *yarphu-sangney (Callicarpa arborea)* are the more commonly used species for the same. For construction of their long houses, bamboo also comes in very handy as stilts, struts, purlins and rafters in the same along with the woody species.

Ropes

Ropes made of locally available bamboo, canes and local species *tapetarig* are commonly used for construction works, livestock and other miscellaneous works.

Medicinal Plants

A host of wild flora is used for the traditional medicine of the people of this area. The plants are made use of in curing diseases and disorders ranging from simple cuts and wounds to jaundice. The traditional system is passed by the word of mouth and still a major number of diseases are being cured in this way. These plants are available in the forest area throughout the year and their extraction is need specific. *Dhuna* resin (*Canarium resiniferum*) is also used in households for expelling mosquitoes and is sold in the local markets.

Food

Flora

The wild plants are a major component in the daily dietary consumption of the tribes of the study area. Though the list may be an exhaustive one and for want of detailed survey on the same, a few of them enumerated by the people are *papua-toh, jonko, rara, babuk, buck-barawa*, bamboo shoots etc. Many among these are eaten either raw or in boiled form for their medicinal value. Their availability is generally through out the year, with the intermittent seasonal variations. In addition, variety of tubers, *mekahi (Phoebe cooperiana)* fruits, mature seeds and fruits of *Amoora walichiana* are also made use of for supplementing their diet.

Fauna

Fishing and small game supplement the diet of the villagers. In addition honey is extracted, based on the availability. The honey from the small bees (*Apis florea*) is termed *ngunya* and that from the bigger ones *ngocho (Apis indica*). Besides being used as an effective medicinal supplement, it is also sold in the local market. Honey is available in the months from August to December. *Balam-tapum* (a caterpillar), *ruik* (pupae and frogs) also supplement the diet. A locally available insect known as *tari-pumchii* is a cherished delicacy and people may be seen looking for the same in the river banks and near boulders.

Concerns of Tribal Communities in Relation to Forests

Forests are among the world's most diverse and most endangered ecosystems on the earth. In this context, it is imperative to underline some basic concerns which have yet to be truly taken up for doable forest conservation. Concerns of the tribal communities in relation to forests may be cited as under:

(i) The first concern is that forests are not empty. Forests have been inhabited by the tribal communities for hundreds of thousands of years, well before the creation of most of the modern nation states. Each of those people has a very precise knowledge of the boundaries of the territory they used, owned and managed.

(ii) The second concern is that the tribal people hold the rights to those territories by virtue of being a first settlement. However, these rights are not recognised by most national and state governments, which declare that forests belong to the state. This legal injustice paves the way to destruction of forest through government concessions for large scale exploitation.

(iii) The third concern is that the tribal people hold the knowledge about the forest. Evidence of this is that for centuries they managed to live with the forest while fulfilling all material and spiritual requirements through adept management. The causes of the most present destructive practices is usually in external pressures on forests from government policies rather than in tribal people themselves.

(iv) The fourth and the most vital concern regarding the future of forests is that the tribal people are the ones more directly involved in their conservation because forests not only ensure their livelihoods but are an integral part of their ways of life, where respect for nature is at the nucleus of their culture. They are the "right-holders", not merely a "stake-holders" and as such they are the most keen to protect their resources in the long-run.

The tribal people, thus, constitute a ray of hope for the future of the forests. They have the grip of the rights and knowledge and their physical and cultural survival relies on ensuring their conservation. In many instances, the tribal people are adapting their knowledge to a varying situation, working out and executing options for sustainable and impartial livelihoods, far away from "sustainable development" discourse which governments have barred of the sense it originally conceded.

Findings and Discussion

Land Ownership

Land ownership and land-use pattern are important parametres for livelihood studies. Land ownership for forestry sector shows how the tribal communities are dependent on forest and also its gives a clue to find out the effective utilisation of forest land. In Table 5.2 below, it is shown that total land per capita of the *Nyishi* tribe was (105.72 decimals). The *Bangru* tribe possess a per capita land of 62.48 decimals. In case of the *Puroik* per capita land holding is about 42.35 decimals which was the minimum.

Table 5.2: Per Capita Land Holdings among the Tribes of the Study Area

Tribe	*Land Per Capita*	*Land in Decimal*
Nyishi	105,72	105.72
Bangru	62,48	62.48
Puroik	42,35	42.35

Land-Use in Different Categories

The per capita land by land-use type owned by the three tribes of Kurung Kumey district is shown in Table 5.3. Among the *Nyishis*, per capita land holdings under forestry, agriculture and homestead were 83.24 decimals,

46.05 decimals and 15.38 decimals respectively. Though the amount of forest land per capita is highest among the *Nyishi,* yet the income from forestry was not that maximum. It indicates the unproductive use of forest land. Among the *Bangrus*, per capita land holdings under forestry were 47.00 decimals, 37.95 decimals under agriculture and small amount of 8.25 decimals owned under homestead. Yet, the share of forestry in their income was highest amongst the three tribes, which means they are productive user of forest land. In case of the *Puroiks*, per capita lands possession under forestry was 36.78 decimals, 18.05 decimals under agriculture and 2.35 decimals under homestead.

Table 5.3: Analysis of Per Capita Land Ownership by Land-Use Types among the Tribes of the Study Areas

Land-Use Type	*Per Capita Holdings by Tribes (in Decimal)*		
	Nyishi	*Bangru*	*Puroik*
Forestry	83.24	47.00	36.78
Agriculture	46.05	37.95	18.05
Homestead	15.38	8.25	2.35

Income Analysis

To find out the livelihood pattern, income and sources of income from each of the three tribes data have been interpreted. Income per capita and per family are compared and contribution of each sources of income is provided. The following Table 5.4 shows the per capita income of three tribes of Kurung Kumey district. The highest per capita income was among the *Nyishis* which was Rs. 18,545.25 per annum and minimum was found among the *Puroiks* which was Rs. 6,575. It was also observed that among the *Nyishis*, more family members were involved in income generating activities.

Table 5.4: Per Capita Income of the Tribes of the Study Area

Tribe	*Per Capita Income (in Rupees)*
Nyishi	18,545.25
Bangru	12,685
Puroik	6,575

An analysis of the family income by the respondent households' (Table 5.5) shows that highest family income in the study area was found in the *Nyishi* families, i.e. Rs.17,000 per annum and minimum in the

Puroik families, i.e. Rs. 8,000 per annum. Household with high involvement in different income generating activities generated more income. The *Nyishi* family members were found to be much more involved in different activities among the three tribes in the district.

Table 5.5: Per Family Income of the Tribes of the Study Area

Tribe	*Per Capita Income (in Rupees)*
Nyishi	17,000
Bangru	14,700
Puroik	8,000

Sources of Income of the Tribal Communities

In the following Fig. 5.1, the percentage of the sources of income of the *Nyishi* tribe is given. Results show that maximum income was derived from agriculture (58%) and minimum from service (2%). On the other hand, 25 per cent income was generated from business and 15 per cent was from forestry activities. 50 per cent people were earning member in the 10 families among the *Nyishi* tribe.

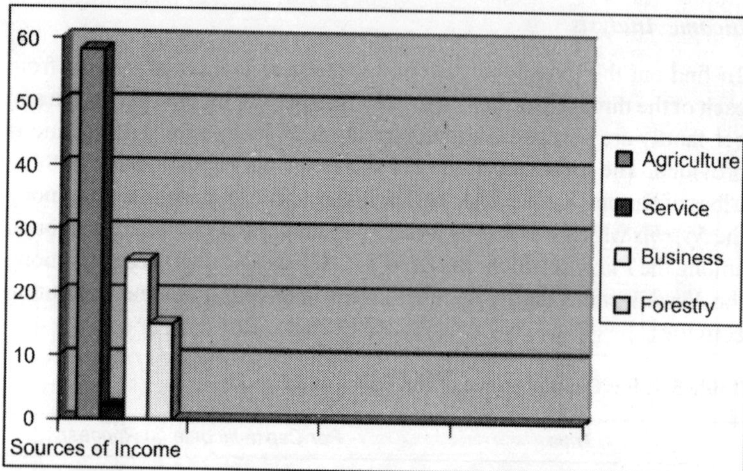

Fig. 5.1: Sources of Income Distribution of Nyishi Tribe

In the case of the *Bangru* tribe, it was found that income was generated from agriculture and service which were 53 per cent and 15 per cent respectively. From forestry activities 21 per cent monetary income was received and a 22 per cent was received from business (details in Fig. 5.2). 21 out of 47 family members in 10 families were working members.

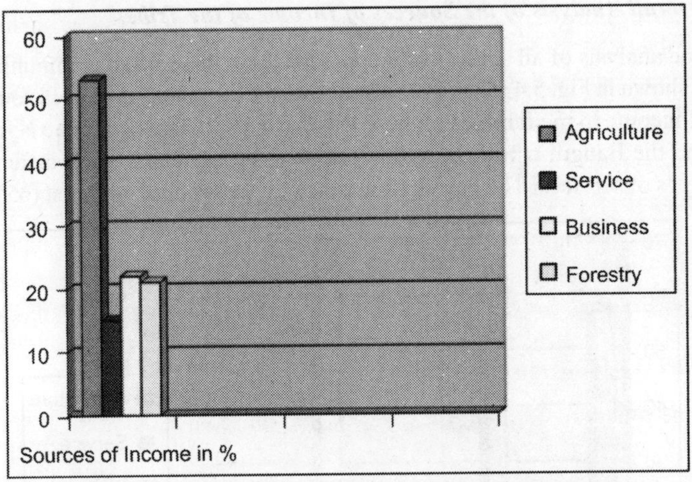

Fig. 5.2: Sources of Income Distribution of Bangru Tribe

The maximum percentage of income of the *Puroik* tribe (Fig. 5.3) is generated from forestry (65%) and and minimal percentage of income from service (2%). About 23 per cent and 10 per cent of the income is generated from agriculture and business respectively. About 27 per cent people of the *Puroiks* contributed monetary support to their families.

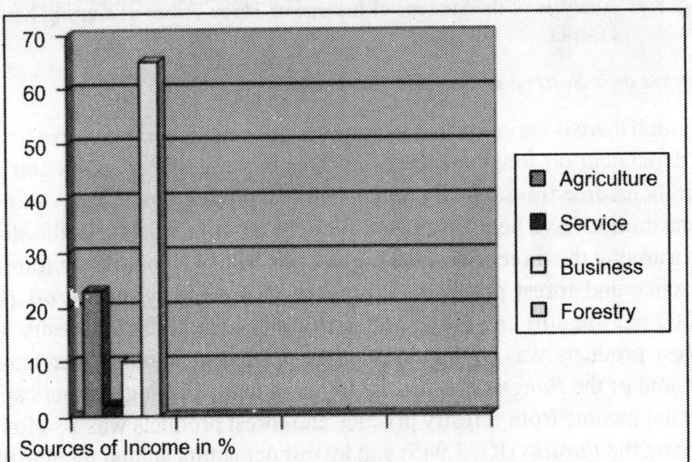

Fig. 5.3: Sources of Income Distribution of Puroik Tribe

Overall Analysis of the Sources of Income of the Tribes

The analysis of all sources of income for these three tribal communities is shown in Fig. 5.4. The figure also shows the contribution of each source of income to the families of these tribal groups. It shows that the Nyishi and the Bangru tribes are more dependent on agriculture and different types of services. The Puroik tribe is heavily dependent on forest (65%).

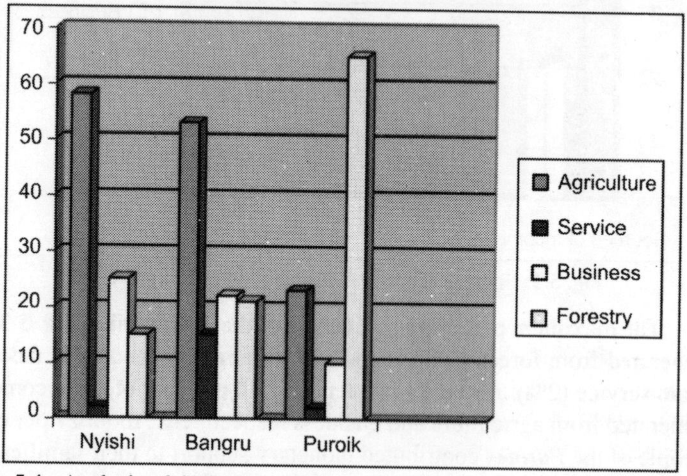

Fig. 5.4: Analysis of the Sources of Income of Three Tribes of Kurung Kumey District

Forest as a Source of Income for Tribes

Though there is variation in the resources utilisation, but each tribal group is dependent on forest resources in the study areas. Per capita and per family income from forestry practice, forest products and share of forest contribution have been calculated for each tribe as follows. In the study area among the three tribes, the highest per family income from forestry practice and forest products (Fig. 5.5) was gained by the *Puroik* (Rs. 7,000 per annum) and the lowest per family income from forestry and forest products was by the *Nyishi* (Rs. 2,700 per annum). Per family income of the *Bangru* was Rs. 4,250 per annum. The highest per capita annual income from forestry practice and forest products was also found among the *Puroiks* (Rs. 3,945) and lowest per capita annual income was observed among the *Bangrus* (Rs. 1,730). It was also observed that per capita annual income from forestry practice and forest products among the *Nyishis* was Rs. 2,365.

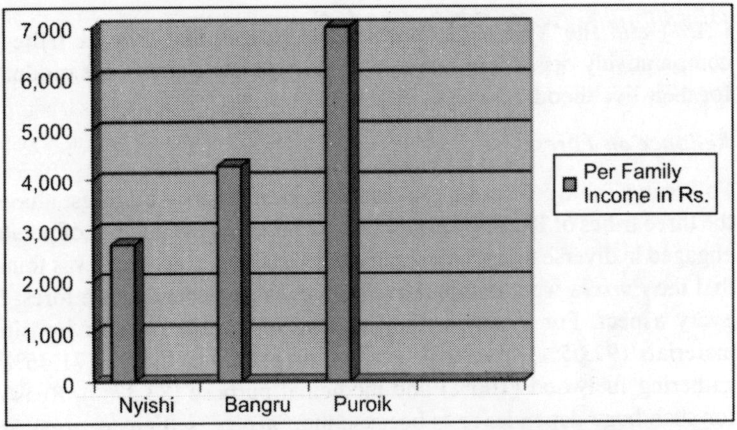

Fig. 5.5: Annual Family Income of the Tribes of Kurung Kumey District from Forestry Practice and Products

From Fig. 5.6, it was observed that total per capita income both forestry and all sectors was high among the *Nyishi* tribe and it also contributes more in total per capita income. The *Puroik* tribe has the highest per capita income in forestry sector as compared to the *Nyishis* and the *Bangrus*.

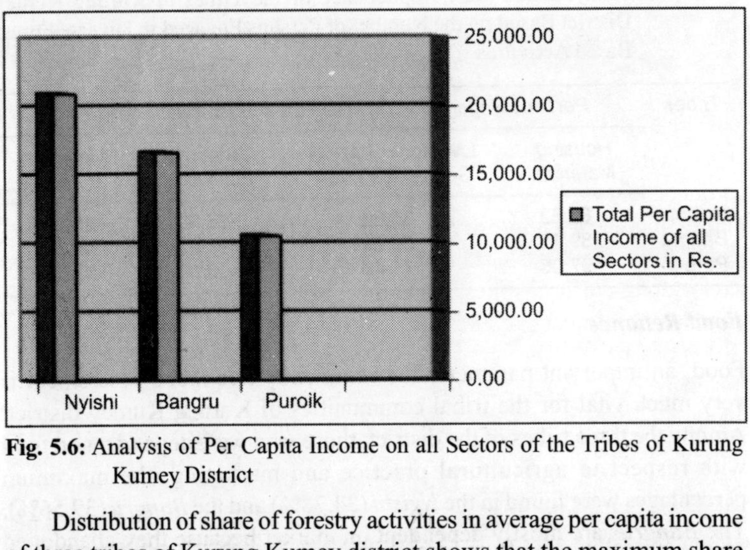

Fig. 5.6: Analysis of Per Capita Income on all Sectors of the Tribes of Kurung Kumey District

Distribution of share of forestry activities in average per capita income of three tribes of Kurung Kumey district shows that the maximum share (65%) of forestry was among the *Puroik* tribe followed by the *Bangru*

(21%) and the *Nyishi* (15%). This indicates that *Puroik* tribe is comparatively depending more on forestry practice and forest products for their livelihood.

Reliance on Forest

Following Table 5.6 shows the distribution of reliance on forest among the three tribes of Kurung Kumey district based on the number of person engaged in diverse forest based activities. From the outcome it was found that the *Puroiks* were comparatively much more dependent on forest in every aspect. For instance, they depend on forest for their housing materials (97.05%), livestock grazing or gathering fodder (71.46%), gathering fuelwood (100%) and medicinal purpose (83.37%). Reason for such huge dependence is because the *Puroiks'* settlement areas are found in such a remote and inaccessible location that the modern-day facilities like building materials, medicines, etc. are unable to reach their settlement area. Whereas, both the *Nyishi* and the *Bangru* settlement areas are found in accessible locations where some building materials like cements, CGI sheets and modern medicines could very easily be brought from nearby towns.

Table 5.6: Analysis of Forest Dependence of the Tribes of Kurung Kumey District Based on the Number of Persons Engaged in Diverse Forest Based Activities

Tribes	*Persons Engaged in Diverse Forest Based Activities (in %)*			
	Housing Materials	*Livestock Grazing/ Gathering Fodder*	*Gathering Fuelwood*	*Medicinal Purpose*
Nyishi	82.63	35.85	96.33	23.17
Bangru	89.11	53.26	98.02	46.72
Puroik	97.05	71.46	100.00	83.37

Food Reliance

Food, an important parameter for community livelihood assessment is very much vital for the tribal communities of Kurung Kumey district. Among the three tribes of the district, those who were dependent on food with respect to agricultural practice and marketing, the maximum percentages were found in the *Nyishi* (34.78%) and the *Bangru* (39.56%). The *Bangrus* are mostly dependent on market because they abandoned their agricultural cultivations since 2009 due to rat menace triggered by the bamboo flowering.

Table 5.7: Analysis of Food Reliance of the Tribes in the Study Area

Tribes	*Patterns of Food Reliance (in %)*		
	Market	*Family Agriculture*	*Both*
Nyishi	18.06	34.78	47.16
Bangru	39.56	21.43	39.01
Puroik	11.26	25.25	63.49

Miscellaneous Findings

Six houses out of thirty (20%) was *pucca* or semi-*pucca*, while other 24 (80%) houses were built of bamboos, wooden planks and wavy CGI sheets. Most of the households especially belong to the *Puroik* community, use traditional hearth for cooking where fuelwood and residues are used; while some *Nyishis* and *Bangrus* are found to be using LPG cylinder for fast cooking along with the traditional hearth. Almost every household of all the three tribes found to collect fuelwood from nearby forests for their domestic use. It is astonishing to note that almost all the households do not have toilets having sanitary latrine barring a few households those having sanitary latrine by their own. It is also found that all the respondents belong to three tribes were a permanent resident of their villages, meaning they haven't migrated from any other places.

Conclusion

This modest but substantial study offers a broad idea of the life, standard of living and land-use pattern of the tribal societies of Kurung Kumey district in Arunachal Pradesh. A precise account about their dependence on forest is also depicted. With this study, it is observed that the role of Government officials for the development of the tribal people are sometimes contradictory. Besides, Government is regrettably dormant for motivating any development strategy in the study areas. The tribal communities are not actively involved with any kind of practice with Government departments and their officials, although a few Panchayat leaders are involved. No any participatory appraisal scheme is running over there in the study areas. There are some Non-Governmental Organisations (NGOs) and few women Self-Help Groups (SHGs), who are functioning intermittently with a short term vision for the welfare of the people. An amalgamated development plan is supposed to play a crucial role for the development of these tribal people. Government's development agencies like District Rural Development Agency (DRDA),

Rural Work Department (RWD), Public Work Department (PWD), Public Health Engineering Department (PHED), and department of Water Resource Development (WRD) needs to actively involved the people in their participatory projects and co-management activities. Literally speaking, the tribal people have got the top precedence to be incorporated as participatory stakeholders of the forest, but they still lack of real access to the participatory forest management. The tribal communities in Arunachal Pradesh as a whole and of Kurung Kumey district in particular can no longer be walked over, as has been always the case. The findings of this humble research study may facilitate to illuminate assured development policy for the well-being of the tribal people. The study is comparative in nature, the outcomes establish through this study can be held as identical to the large scale study.

REFERENCES

Arunachal Pradesh Human Development Report-2005 (2006), Department of Planning, Government of Arunachal Pradesh, Itanagar.

Byron, N. and M. Arnold (1997), *What Futures for the People of the Tropical Forests?* CIFOR Working Paper No. 19. Centre fir International Forestry research, Bogor.

Colchester, M. (2006), *Justice in the Forest: Rural Livelihoods and Forest Law Enforcement.* Forest Perspectives 3, CIFOR, Indonesia.

Dembner, S.A. (1996), *Forest Peoples in the Central African Rain Forest: Focus on the Pygmies.* Unasylva 186 (47), pp. 3-7.

Dubois, J.C.L. (1996), *Uses of Wood and Non-Wood Forest Products by Amazon Forest Dwellers.* Unasylva 186 (47), pp. 8-15.

Fisher, R.J., V. Michael and K. Nitiya (1997), *People and Forests in Asia and the Pacific: Situation and Prospects.* Asia-Pacific Forestry Sector Outlook Study, Working Paper No. 27, Forestry Policy and Planning Division, Rome.

Vedeld, P., A. Angelsen, J. Bojo, E. Sjaastad and G.K. Kobugabe (2007), *Forest Environmental Incomes and the Rural Poor*, Vol.9. Elsevier, pp. 869-879.

World Resources Institute (2005), *The Wealth of the Poor: Managing Ecosystems to Fight Poverty.* WRI Publications.

6

Land, Peasant and Money Lenders : A Study of Assam Proper in Late 19th Century

Lipi Ghosh

"No subject has been more strongly and frequently pressed on our attention than the evil result which spring from the degree to which the landowners are sunk in debt, the asserted rapid increase of their indebtedness and the difficulty they find in extricating themselves from such burden".[1] This impressive sentence of the Famine Commission report expresses the importance of rural indebtedness as a theme of discourse.

About the general picture of rural indebtedness in pre-British India, we have found no reason to believe that the agricultural population of India at any known period of their history has been generally free from debt, although individuals or classes may have fallen into deeper embarrassments under the British rule.[2] It increased rapidly during the last quarter of 19th Century and become one of the acutest problems in the country-side. There was a considerable burden of indebtedness in the rural areas of Assam also. It is said that "the cultivators in Assam born in debt, increases his debt and dies in debt."[3]

The study of the moneylenders in Assam proper, which emerged with a 'new force' as a result of the socio-economic changes of the colonial era, particularly their composition and social roots, their simultaneous activities and the specifications of the rural credit scene, fall within the scope of their paper. A notable feature of the composition was the predominance of alien money-lenders unlike in many regions of India, whose primary motive behind credit transactions was furtherance of their trading interests. Another striking feature was that they were not much interested in acquisition of peasants' holdings.

The cause generating poverty among the rural people, particularly among the peasants, can be summarised. Monetisation of the Assameese economy, introduction of new land system and gradual commercialisation of agriculture in the context of money-short, subsistence oriented Ahom economy with a weak agricultural setting added a set of changes to peasant, production and land and left the very way open for the growth of the power of the money-lenders. Growth of population and stagnation in rural productivity also created poverty among people. "Social ceremonies like marriage, sradha etc. accounted for one-tenth to one-fifth of the total loans and productive purpose like purchase of cattle, seeds, implements etc. and improvement of land only fifteen to thirty per cent. Famines and crop failures were the general causes of loan."[4]

In this context, growing commercialisation of agricultural production, in which the money-lenders had some direct involvements, need a special reference. In fact in Assam, there had occurred a kind of forced commercialisation. The trade in Assam was almost entirely in the hands of the 'Kayas' (the Marwari traders mahajan as they were locally known). Jenkins wrote in a letter to A.J.M. Mills "the trade being solely in the hands of the Marwari traders, the profits mostly go to enrich Rajpootana and do not accumulate in this province."[5] These people before the harvest put forward advances to the poor cultivators on condition that the "maharaj" or money-lenders and rates were fixed before-hand, which in most cases was much lower than the existing market rates. Srijut Lakheswar Barthakur remarked once "the Marwaris had established a new-work of trade connection by which even the petty shops in the remotest part of the country are connected with Calcutta firm."[6] The river borne trade of Kamrup and other districts' trade were also in the hands of these Marwaris.

The alien money-lenders' control was reinforced by the fact that the poor peasants in the context of an utterly inadequate transport system could not sell their produce to outside markets. Mostly he disposed it to the Marwaris middle men in lesser prices at his own village. Even if he sometimes took his produce to other markets like Calcutta, they mostly misread the market demand and there were often wrong speculations and consequent fluctuations in prices for which he suffered heavy losses. In fact, 'had there been an organisation of cultivators they could control the market and get better prices. But until the people advanced in education and learnt to combine and market their commodities better, the existing system could not be improved'.[7]

While such chains of circumstances created poverty among the cultivators, the channel through which cash reached them was a agency of money-lenders – both alien and local. In Assam money-lending had its beginning since a long time and the role of the alien money-lenders was scarcely a development during British rule. From 13th to 17th century, there was an influx of outsiders in Assam and "encouragements were given to such outsiders to settle in Assam as would contribute culturally and materially ... of the latter the "Kaya" or the merchants of Marwar had trading establishments at Joghighopa, Goalpara and Gauhati."[8]

Among the moneylenders, besides these Marwari people the Assam Provincial Banking Enquiry Committee speaks of local people like the Telis and the Johlas, the Kabulis and Government stamp-vendors, clerks and pleaders. In all districts there was also some big landholders, who having saved money lent it out to their fellow villagers.

About the forms of credit, there were three major forms : loans in cash, paddy, and agricultural implements including seeds. The forms of appropriation varied too.

Sometimes the Kayas advanced money as a loan one or two months before harvest. There was a common bargain that one 'dun' (of $3\frac{1}{2}$ seers normally) was to be given after harvest, over and above the number of 'duns' of the current market rate. But Kaya's 'dun' was not the regular $3\frac{1}{2}$ seer but contained more like 4 seers at least.[9] Sometimes money was advanced for which interest rate was $37\frac{1}{2}$ to 75 per cent per annum for small loans. In larger transactions, where a mortgage has given upon movable property its rate was 12 per cent to 20 per cent.[10] Mortgage on houses and lands was uncommon. As regards paddy loans, there was a peculiar system – a man borrowing before the harvest had to pay double at a harvest. Taking payment in Baisakh he had to pay three times the quantity borrowed in Agrahayana and six times in next Baisak.[11] The Marwaris used to keep "*khata*" and the signature or thumb impression of the debtor was taken on a stamp in the *Khata*.[12] Manipulation of such accounts often occurred. Rai Bahadur Nilambar Dutta, tea planter, Dibrugarh was of opinion, "I do not say that respectable Marwaris do it but it is common talk, the Marwaris of the village are in habit of interpolating their khatas."[13]

The form of appropriation common among local village money lenders was insistence on labour service from the indebted peasants. Loans were extended either in cash or in goods in exchange of labour service. In this way, the better of peasants could exploit the poorer ones. The poor people who had no land for cultivation, took the land of well-to-do's either as tenants or as share-croppers. The cultivators who had no cattle often borrowed it on "*morakya*" terms (a *morakya* labour ploughed owner's land with owner's cattle two days and one day his own field). Peasants could also become a part time agricultural labourer and he often sold his family members under "bondha" system. Those people, who had some land but no capital, sometimes gave out part of his lands on rent (*khandua* system) or share cropping (*adhiya*; 50% share) and the rest he cultivated with borrowed cattle on *morakya* term.[14]

About the proportion of this money lending class and the population in debt to the over-all population figure of Assam, Census of Assam from time to time furnishes us with some valuable data.

According to the Census of Assam 1881, the number of money-lenders in the whole province of Assam was 2,414 and the petty shopkeepers engaged in this business were 48,452 making a total of 50,866. There were both male and female money-lenders. Of these people as per 1881 Census, the total number of male money-lenders in Assam proper (including both mercantile men and other general dealers) was 11,884 and that of the female was 3,614, making a total of 15,498.[15] So we find approximately one-third of the total money-lenders in Assam were belonged to our five districts. The census of 1891 returned the total number of money-lenders in the Brahmaputra Valley as 1,193 while in the whole Assam it was 9,801. This figure, however, did not include the number of the petty shopkeepers whose total number was 6,992. Here it is mention-worthy that the Census behind the growth in the number of money-lenders in 1891 is that this year the Census report included the number of the dependants also.[16] While again as per the Census report of 1901 which excluded the number of dependants their number was only, 1,031 in whole Assam, 279 of whom were women and 164 were combined with the agriculture.[17]

About the proportion of population in debt, we find no definite data but revenue officials always went on saying that 'a considerable portion of people are in debt.' One settlement officer wrote : "The independent cultivators in the good villages are generally well off but without much money, but in the bad villages, they are distinctly poor."[18] The Dufferin Enquiry Committee report on the condition of the lower classes provides valuable information. Even though, the report chiefly aimed to prove that the common assertion of most important reports of the province that "the greater portion of population suffer from a daily insufficiency of food" was false,[19] there are numerous example which speak of mass pauperization and indebtedness. In this huge and extensive report, though H.Z. Darrah put forward some example of well-to-do peasants, there are numerous example collected by Rai Guhabhiram Sarma Barua, Rai Sarat

Chandra Banerjee, which contradict Darrah's assertion. Rai Gunabhiram Samar Barua, extra Assistant Commissioner spoke of Jin Ram Kakoti, a cultivator who borrowed Rs. 40 in the year and expected to repay in next year only 'if' the crops were successful.[20] Another typical example was Hati Boru Ahom who for 20 to 25 years was under strained circumstances. He sold his cattle, lands, jewelleries and sent his son to work as a servant for Rs. 6/- a month.[21] Rai Sarat Chandra Banerjee, extra Assistant Commissioner, told even of a well to do *gaonborua* who had a debt.[22] Bolai Kewat, one poor man in Chalchali mauza was in so precarious condition that though he could not pay the year's revenue, yet borrowed at a rate of 75 per cent and sometimes lived in starvation.[23] So the report reveals that majority of cultivators were in a precarious condition.

One significant feature, in this rural credit transaction business was that much land did not fall into the hands of the money-lenders. As noted above, the money-lenders of Assam did not grab peasant holding to any considerable extent. The money-lenders being more alien people had lesser interest in acquisition of land and mortgages on houses and lands were uncommon. W.W. Hunter said that advances to cultivators were made generally on the personal security of the borrower.[24] To quote W.L. Scott, Director of Land Records : "In the Assam Valley ... he (Marwaris mahajan) favours as security or lien on the crop rather than a mortgage on the land."[25] However, when the borrower was unable to pay from the crops he took the land but he had no intention of holding it and sold it to someone who paid a fair price. In this way, sometimes some non-resident non-agriculturists, who had ready money, acquired the lands.

The power of transfer possessed by the cultivators of Assam had also a different history. At the time of annexation the right to transfer agricultural land was neither generally recognised nor practised. Under British rule, new changes were brought in 1859, Jenkins declared the *ryots* were "now considered to have full proprietary rights in their lands of all description." In 1870, the Commissioner of Assam issued settlement rules which recognized a transferable right of *ryots* (subject to registration) who agreed to take out ten years' lease. So, here a distinction is visible between decennial and short term holders.[26] This distinction was continued in the Assam Land and Revenue Regulation of 1886 with only exception that annual settlement holders by ten year's continuous occupation would acquire the same right as decennial settlement holders.[27] In 1879 such rights were extended to '*nisf-khiraj*' (semi-revenue free) estates.[28] Such constrains from earliest time took much time for the people of Assam to be habituated with the newly introduced laws, sanctioning land-transfers.

Again, in the Assam valley tenants had no transferable rights. A draft bill was prepared in 1833 for this purpose but it was not processed further.[29] It can also be said that unlike other provinces of India, in Assam "value of land in few cases reached a stage at which it forms a basis of credit."[30] So with such prevalent laws and lesser interests of money-lenders in land appropriation, in Assam the transfer of land was not a factor of much importance.

Another crucial happening which does not escape our attention was that there was no investment of merchant usury capital in land. Such was the happening, because for Hindus and Brahmins, who formed major part of the local money-lenders, ambition to live a better life and spendthrift nature checked any such flow of capital to land. Likewise, for alien money-lenders improvement of land was their no concern at all. Rather for both groups of money lenders temptation for high rate of interest centred their attention more and more to money-lending business.

Truly speaking as transactions were not between two men of business, often the debtor was compelled to lose everything. But as these money-lenders were indispensable agencies for financing the agricultural sector, they continued in the rural society without having any immediate chance to elimination.

REFERENCES

1. Report of the Famine Commission 1880, Part II, Chapter III, Section IV, p. 120.
2. Selection from papers on Indebtedness and Land transfer, p. 22.
3. Report of the Assam Provincial Banking Enquiry Committee 1929-30, Vol. 2: Evidence p. 491 (Henceforth reference as A.P.B.E.C).
4. P.C Goswami, *The Economic Development of Assam*, Bombay, 1963, p. 60.
5. F. Jenkin's letter to A.J. Moffat Mills, para 21, as found in Mill's Report 1854, Appendix B.
6. Report of the Royal Commission on Agriculture in India, Vol. V : Evidence taken in Assam 1927. Replies to questionnaire by Lakheswar Barthakur (Henceforth referred as R.R.C.).
7. *Ibid.*, Replies by Rai Bahadur K.L. Barua.
8. H.K. Barpujari, *Assam in the Days of the Company*, Gauhati, 1963, p. 262.
9. A.P.B.E.C., 1929-30, vol. 1 : Report, p. 62.
10. W.W. Hunter, *A Statistical Account of Assam*, 1879, sections on capital and interest as found in different volumes.
11. A.P.B.E.C., 1929-30, vol. 1 : Report, p. 60.

12. *Ibid.*, Vol. 2, Evidence, p. 323 (Rai Sahab Dandadhar Barua of Khuntai).
13. *Ibid.*, Vol. II, Evidenee, p. 240.
14. Amalendu Guha, "Assamese Aggrarian Society in late Nineteenth Century", *Indian Economic and Social History Review*, XXVII, 1980, relevant pages.
15. Census of India 1881; Assam Report, p. 307.
16. Census of India 1891; Assam Report, p. 307.
17. Census of India 1901; Assam Report, pp. 161, 164.
18. B.C. Allen, *Assam District Gazetteers*, p. 171.
19. Duffer in Enquiry Committee Report; Note on the Condition of the People of Assam, No. 10, 1888, p. 4.
20. *Ibid.*, Example, 11, p. 55.
21. *Ibid.*, 1888, Example, 19, p. 60.
22. Ibid., Example, 23, p. 64.
23. *Ibid.*, Example, p. 68.
24. Hunter, *op.cit.*, p. 385.
25. R.R.C., 1927, Vol. 5, Evidence.
26. Note on Land Transfer and Agricultural Indebtedness in India 1895, para 54, p. 23 (Henceforth referred as 'Note').
27. Assam Land and Revenue Regulation, Regulation 1, see, 1 and 9.
28. Note 1895, para 57, p. 24.
29. *Ibid.*, para 417, 419, pp. 234-35.
30. R.R.C., 1927, Vol. V; Evidence (Replies by Mr. W.L. Scott, Director of Land Records).

7

Women Workers in Tea Plantation in Upper Assam : A Profile

R.K. Kar and *Sr. Molly Kaniampadickal*

Introduction

Employment of women in non-traditional gainful activities is considered as the critical entry point to the development of a society.

The total female working population in India accounts for approximately 150 million; and around 2 million women are added to the labour force every year. With the growing industrialization rate, the share of women in the organized sector, as a matter of fact, has been steadily increasing (*cf.* Tripathy, 1999: 132).

Access to different types of paid work is, however, by and large, not equal for women and men. With regard to the division of labour between the members of the two sexes *vis-à-vis* the status of women, Quinn (1977:187) observes, "Whatever be the evolutionary history behind men's greater size, strength and energy, writers have considered that these characteristics suit men for heavy labour and thus help explain the near-universal exclusion of women from such tasks as tree felling, ploughing and operation of heavy agricultural machinery as well as hunting and warefare. And the resulting division of labour between the sexes has been argued by some to initiate far-reaching effects on the status of women.

However, whatever outdoor work women may do, they also have the major responsibility for most of the household work, including the care of children and the other members of the family. Women contribute significantly, not only to the economic life everywhere, but also to the proper maintenance of family life through bearing, rearing and upbringing of children as well as by carrying out other household activities. In other words, women everywhere have to carry out both productive and reproductive roles simultaneously.

Several scholars (e.g. Lowie, 1929; Parsons, 1954; Sullerot, 1971; Thompson and Finalyson, 1953) have dealt with the issue of women's gainful ***employment*** and the related matters. Different authors have made their observations in different spheres. Thus, for example, Thompson and Finalyson (*op. cit.*) have seriously questioned the compatibility of women's employment with a proper psychological development of children. They have also argued that the domestic responsibility of women workers adversely affects the quantity, quality and duration of their work. Sullerot (*op. cit*), on the other hand, restricts his observations to some other aspects. He argues that women have become increasingly aware that the surest way of raising their social status and their position in the families is to become earners. According to him, by working, women gain a new sense of power.

Keeping these facts and observations in mind, in the present paper, an attempt has been made to understand the nature and content of the gainful employment of the womenfolk in tea plantation in Upper Assam; and also to have an idea as to their pre-occupation scenario in the familial setting as well as their overall position in the work place.

In order to have a concrete understanding of the issue at hand, some relevant empirical data have also been incorporated in the discourse. These data, incidentally, were generated from 3 selected tea plantations, located in Upper Assam, while carrying out an anthropological project during the period 2008-2010 (*cf.* Kar, 2010).

Tea Workers in Assam

Tea is considered to be the backbone of Assam's economy; and is an important export item for earning a substantial amount of foreign currency for the country. At present there are around 760 full-fledged and 2,500 small-scale (producing green leaf only) tea plantations in Assam. The total number of workers (permanent and casual) engaged in these plantations are around 11 lakhs (Kar, 2010:71).

India's place in the world tea market is unquestionably very high. She occupies the largest area under tea and also produces the largest amount in the world (around 988 million kg. during 2011-12).

The leading states in respect of tea industry in India are Assam (produces around 56%) and West Bengal (approximately 25%).

The origin of tea plantation in India can be traced back to 1774, when Warren Hastings was the Governor General. Experimental commercial production in Assam, however, did not start before 1837. The first experimental tea estate in Assam was established in 1837 at Chabua (**Cha** – tea and **Bua** – to plant) in Dibrugarh District in Upper Assam.

In the early nineteenth century, during the formative days of Assam plantations, the labour scarcity was a constant hindrance to the expansion of tea plantations in Assam (Kar and Barua, 1997: 145-60). At the initial stage, however, the local people like the Kacharis, the Mataks, the Kukis, the Nagas, the Singphos and the Apatanis could be employed with the active assistance of the chiefs of the respective ethnic groups (*cf.* Chakravarty, 1973: 29; Gait, 1926: 254; Harlalka, 1975: 94-7; Roy Burman, 1968: 2; and Sharma, 1987: 8-9). But the arrangements did not prove to be very successful. Prior to 1860 the local labourers, in most of the plantations indulged in a number of protests and revolts (Kar, 1995: 53-5). In course of time, the number of tea plantations steadily increased; and the demand kept growing for larger number of labourers. But the need could not be fulfilled from the local labourers as they had gradually been showing reluctance to work in tea plantation.

By around 1855, the problem became very acute; and the planters started procuring labour from other states of India. The labourers were recruited from various cultural, linguistic and ethnic heritages, mainly from Bengal, Bihar (including Jharkhand), Orissa (Odisha), Madhya Pradesh (including Chhatisgarh), Andhra Pradesh and Tamil Nadu. Desperate poverty and land alienation on the countryside in those areas and the false promises of "Less work and high wages", probably made this huge labour group available for transportation to Assam (Kar, 2001).

A good number of these migrant labourers initially suffered from mal-adjustment; some of them met pre-mature death, others went back home after the expiry of the contracted period; and still others fled away before the expiry of that period. A major section of the migrants, however, survived that stage and had gradually made up their mind to make a permanent settlement in the new habitat in a new economy; and far away from their original homes (Kar, 1986: 143-58).

Sharma (1990: 235) observes that the process of settlement of these labourers in rural areas began as early as in 1868. This section of the labourers is known as *ex-tea labour* despite the fact that most of them have already passed 3-4 generations since they had left the tea gardens. They constitute a sizeable section of the rural population in the tea growing districts of Assam.

There are more than 100 tribe and caste groups that compose the tea labour population of Assam. The details of the different groups along with their native homes have been discussed by Crawford (1924: 344-51). There are at least 32 ethnic groups who were brought from Chotanagpur (Kar, 1999: 21-46).

It is not possible to provide an exact figure as to the numerical strength of the tea and ex-tea labour population, at present residing in Assam. It has, however, been estimated that approximately 20 per cent of the total population of the state is constituted by this section (Kar, 2001).

Women Workers and Tea Plantation

Tea is a labour-intensive industry. It is one of the few industries that mainly depends on women labourers to work in the tea beds. Surveys show that the entire North East India has as many as 60 per cent women workers; in the case of Assam alone 45 per cent women are employed in the tea plantations. The probable factors that contribute towards having such a large number of women workers in the plantations are: (i) the plantation work is only a special kind of agricultural work and is, therefore, familiar to Indian women, the vast majority of whom live in rural areas; (ii) facilities have been given to the male workers to settle in, or in the vicinity of the plantations; and to have their wives and other members of the families with them; (iii) Under the old system, labour contract was based on the principle of utilization of the able-bodied persons of the family of a labourer and fixing the wage rates accordingly; and (iv) many women had to seek employment in order to balance the family budget. Although the contract system has long been abolished, the wage system and the need for supplementary earnings still remain.

Before taking up a discussion on the various aspects of women's economic pursuits and the related issues, it will probably be prudent to have an overall idea as to the nature of the different types of activities in a tea plantation.

In a tea plantation, there are basically 2 types of activities, namely the activities connected with (a) growing and collection of tea leaves, and (b) processing of tea leaves.

Growing and Collection: Most of the activities connected with the growing of tea leaves are generally undertaken by male labourers. The activities include: *Preparing the tea beds; Growing seedlings and Maintaining the nursery; Transplanting the seedlings and Tipping; Pruning and Forking; Weeding and Digging; Manuring*; and *Spraying fof Posticides* and *Pest Control*. Women, engaged in this exercise, generally carry out the tasks of growing seedlings, maintaining the nursery, transplanting the seedlings and tipping etc.

Collecting or *Plucking* of tea leaves is generally better suited to women workers. It is an important operation, because the quality of the manufactured tea depends upon the care and attention with which the plucking is done. The proper plucking consists of *two leaves and a bud.* Anything less than this is considered as *fine plucking*; and inclusion of more leaves as *coarse plucking*. Proper plucking may be considered as a skilful art that demands for tremendous patience on the part of the plucker. May be for this reason, the task is believed to be more suited to women. In India, plucking is done by hand; and women are largely employed in the operation. Plucking wages are generally dependent on the weight of the leaves, plucked; and as such coarse plucking increases the quantity of the crop resulting into increased wage amount to the plucker. Therefore, very often there is a temptation to resort to coarse plucking. In Assam, in most of the areas, the bushes are usually plucked once every 7 or 8 days during the season. The plucking season here usually extends from February/March to October/November.

Processing of Tea Leaves: The operation, undertaken in a factory for the purpose of processing the tea leaves may be described as follows:

After plucking, the leaf is placed on withering lofts where it remains for 18 to 24 hours until it becomes ready for the second process. It is then sent to the rollers where a twist is imparted on the leaf. From the rollers the tea is sent to the fermenting room where it is spread thinly, either on floor or on racks. It remains there for 3 to 4.5 hours when certain chemical changes take place in the leaf. From the fermenting room, the tea goes to the firing machines, where it is dried. The purpose of this operation is to drive off all moisture; and during this process, the tea takes on its traditional black appearance. After firing, the tea is sorted out into various grades, required by trade and is then packed in the chests and dispatched for sale.

The labourers working in the factory are mostly men. Sometimes, women workers are engaged for carrying the tea leaves from one place to another, and also in helping the men workers in packing the leaf in the chests.

Besides these regular phases of work directly connected with the **growing, plucking** and **processing** of tea leaves, there are a good number of other essential services in the plantation. Each labour **line** (a cluster of households forming a unit of settlement) has a **chowkidar**, who works as the **headman**; and each establishment (**office, factory**, **hospital** and **bungalow** of the **executive staff** etc.) has a **chowkidar** who works as a caretaker. There are **Sardars** (Gang leaders) who supervise the labour force at work; there are employees in various cadres in **school, hospital** and **office**; there are **drivers, carpenters, electricians** and people for preparing and repairing fences in the plantation; and some ones are engaged in distributing drinking water and raw tea liquor (*Paniwalla*) to the labour force, actively engaged in the outdoor work, connected with growing and plucking of tea leaf. Further, there are sweepers, peons, bearers and gardeners (*Mali*) etc. in different units of a plantation.

Nature of Employment and Associated Facts: On the basis of the terms of appointment, the workforce is divided into 2 categories, namely Permanent and Temporary (*Faltu*) workers.

The **Plantation Labour Act (PLA), 1951**, along with **Plantation Labour Rules (PLR), 1956** has defined many conditions of labour employment in clear terms, for example:

(i) **Clause 30** of the **Act** provides that every worker shall be allowed **leave with wages** at the following rate:
   (a) One day for every 22 working days for adult.
   (b) One day for every 15 working days for the minor
   (c) In case of sickness, *sickness allowances*, and
   (d) In case of women workers, *maternity allowances* are provided by this clause. Again a woman is not allowed to perform arduous jobs during her pregnancy. In the event of a *miscarriage*, certified by a Doctor, a woman is entitled to *2 to 3 weeks' leave.*

(ii) **Under Clause 8**, in every plantation, effective arrangements shall be made by the employer to provide and maintain sufficient **supply of drinking water** for all workers.

(iii) **Clause 9(1)**: There shall be provided separately for males and females in every plantation a sufficient number of **latrines** and **urinals** of prescribed types.

(iv) **Clause 10(1)**: In every plantation there shall be provided and maintained **free medical facilities** for the workers and their families.

(v) **Clause 15**: The employer is to provide and maintain for every worker and his family, residing in the plantation necessary **housing accommodation.**

(vi) **Section 12**: The emplcyer should provide **Crèches** for the children (below 6 years of age) of the working mothers.

(vii) **Section 14**: Facilities for *education* be provided to children below 12 years of age.

(viii) Section 13: Employer should make provision in his/her plantation of recreational facilities for the workers and their children.

The **Act** also provides that an employer shall provide the workers with **umbrella, blanket, rain coat, slippers** and other allied amenities for the protection of the workers from rain and cold.

The Illustration

As noted earlier, some relevant primary data had been generated during 2008-2010 from 3 selected plantations, namely Dorothy*, Manasi*, (both located in Dibrugarh district) and Dalimi* (Tinsukia district) in Upper Assam.

Data were generated from a randomly selected sample of 500 families having a total population of 2873 (Women-1380, Men-1493) individuals. Standard anthropological method and techniques have been used while generating the mass of data.

Sex-wise distribution of the population by **employment status** during the time of investigation has been presented in Table 7.1. It will be seen from Table 7.1 that approximately 46 per cent (Women – 23.4, Men – 22.6) of the people are employed wherein women's share is relatively slightly more favourable.

Distribution of the employed ones according to sex and the different specific occupational pursuits is presented in Table 7.2. A cursory glance of Table 7.2 makes it apparent that although there are as many as 16 different types of assignments to the workers, majority of them (approximately 87%) are engaged in outdoor work, basically plucking, cutting and cleaning. It will be seen from Table 7.2 that 56 per cent of the outdoor workers are women. Incidentally, 95 per cent of the working women are engaged in plucking and some lighter outdoor work. It will also be seen from the Table 7.2 that there are some works (namely Line

Table 7.1: Sex-wise Distribution of the Population by Employment Status

Sl. No.	*Population Category*	*Population Figure*		
		Women (%)	*Men (%)*	*Total (%)*
1	*2*	*3*	*4*	*5*
1.	Working	672 (23.39)	648 (22.56)	1320 (45.95)
2.	Non-Working	708 (24.64)	845 (29.41)	1553 (54.05)
3.	Grand Total	1380 (48.03)	1493 (51.97)	2873 (100.00)

* For some obvious academic ethical reasons pseudonyms have been preferred.

Table 7.2: Sex-wise Distribution of the Population by Occupation

Sl. No.	*Occupational Pursuit*	*No. of Individuals*		
		Women (%)	*Men (%)*	*Total (%)*
1	*2*	*3*	*4*	*5*
1.	Teacher	1 (0.08)	1 (0.08)	2 (0.15)
2.	Sardar / Sardarin	1 (0.08)	27 (2.05)	28 (2.12)
3.	Line Chowkidar	—	12 (0.91)	12 (0.91)
4.	Plantation Chowkidar	—	6 (0.45)	6 (0.45)
5.	Night Chowkidar	—	6 (0.45)	6 (0.45)
6.	Electrician	—	8 (0.61)	8 (0.61)
7.	Carpenter	—	7 (0.53)	7 (0.53)
8.	Driver	—	14 (1.06)	14 (1.06)
9.	Hospital Work (Unskilled)	9 (0.68)	11 (0.83)	20 (1.52)
10.	Factory (Unskilled)	8 (0.61)	31 (2.35)	39 (2.96)
11.	Outdoor Work (including plucking)	640 (48.48)	502 (38.03)	1142 (86.51)
12.	Others*	12 (0.91)	24 (1.82)	36 (2.73)
13.	Grand Total	671 (50.83)	649 (49.17)	1320 (100.00)

* Paniwala (Distributor of raw tea and drinking water) (9), Mali (Gardener) (6), Sweeper (9), Herdsmen (6) & Peon (6).

Chowkidar, Plantation Chowkidar, Night Chowkidar, Electrician, Carpenter, Driver and Herdsman etc.) that fall exclusively in the man's domain. One woman has been found to be employed as a teacher in a plantation-managed primary school. She has completed her Higher Secondary level courses. It is really a rare opportunity for a woman member of a tea labour family to be a member of the teaching staff.

While dwelling some more on their occupational pursuits, it may be noted that there is only 1 woman who works as a *Sardarin* (female Sardar). The rest of the *Sardar* posts are occupied by the male incumbents.

The Line Chowkidar and the *Sardars* belong to the supervisory staff; they are better paid and also enjoy a better status. Most of these posts are occupied by the male members. For a general unskilled tea worker, the scope for promotion is almost non-existent. The very few posts of *Sardars* and Chowkidars are their ultimate aspiration, and as such, there is keen competition for these posts. With regard to a woman worker, it may be emphasized that the opportunity for a promotion is extremely rare; and stagnation in the occupational status is the characteristic feature.

Bhadra (1997) in the context of the plantation workers in North Bengal also makes a similar observation when she states that in the plantation industry upward occupational mobility is extremely difficult; and in the case of women it hardly exists.

With regard to the different pursuits in a tea plantation, it may relevantly be noted that the people, by and large, show a relatively less preference for the outdoor activities; and the least preferred one is the job of plucking. Any work within or associated with the factory, office, hospital or school is preferred by most of the people. Association with the factory or some technical or allied activities, they believe, provides them with a better status. As noted earlier, women are by and large, engaged in plucking operation, and as such, their felt status in the community is obviously relatively inferior.

With regard to their own realization as to the overall prospect in the present occupation, most of the women labourers feel that by working in the plantation, they have actually become the victims of socio-economic stagnation. For most of them, in the present setting, it is not possible to improve their social as well as economic condition in the near or distant future.

In order to have an overall idea about their income scenario, distribution of the studied families according to their total annual income* has been presented in Table 7.3. Income range has conveniently been divided into 10 slabs. The minimum has been put at Rs. 10,000.00 and below, and the highest at Rs. 50,000.00 and above. It will be seen from Table 7.3 that the modal income of the families lies between Rs. 10,000.00 and 15,000.00 for which the per centile frequency is 31.4. This is followed

Table 7.3: Distribution of the Families according to Annual Income

Sl. No.	*Income Range (Rs.)*	*No. of Families*	*Per centage (%)*
1	2	3	4
1.	Below 10,000.00	3	4
2.	10,000.00-15,000.00	12	2.4
3.	15,000.00-20,000.00	77	15.4
4.	20,000.00-25,000.00	132	26.4
5.	25,000.00-30,000.00	34	6.8
6.	30,000.00-35,000.00	32	6.4
7.	35,000.00-40,000.00	27	5.4
8.	40,000.00-45,000 00	14	2.8
9.	45,000.00-50,000.00	08	1.6
10.	50,000.00 and above	07	1.4
	Grand Total	500	100.00

* Fringe benefits have been converted in to the equivalent cash; and the amount has been added to the total wage to compute the total annual income.

by the slab that ranges from Rs. 20,000.00 to Rs. 25,000.00. There are a total of 132 families (26.4%) in this category.

There are at least 15 families (3.0%) whose annual income is Rs. 45,000.00 and above. The average annual income of a family stands at Rs. 21.49 thousand.

With regard to a relatively large number of women's seeking employment in the tea plantation, it seems, economic compulsion is the main driving force. Most of them spend whatever they earn in meeting the basic needs of the family.

As noted earlier, as per the provision of the PLA, 1951 the workers, by and large, in addition to their wages, have been provided with the following benefits:

- (i) **Rent-free Accommodation:** The floor space covered by each standard type of house is 425 sq.ft., while the total area of the compound is 3000 sq.ft. For the twin quarters, the specifications are: Floor space – 894 sq.ft., and the compound – 5000 sq.ft.
- (ii) **Contributory Provident Fund:** At the rate of 8 per cent of the wage. No provident fund accrues during the probation period (6 months).
- (iii) **Provision of paddy land:** Subject to availability, some amount of cultivable paddy land is provided to a worker to exercise usufractuary right only till retirement.
- (iv) **Free medical attention:** In each of the plantations there is a hospital with its own medical and subsidiary attending staff.
- (v) **Leave with wages:** The workers avail of this benefit as per the provision, incorporated in the **Act**.
- (vi) **Sickness Allowances:** Deserving workers are provided with this benefit.
- (vii) **Maternity benefits:** Women workers do avail of these benefits as and when needed.
- (viii) **Provision of fire wood:** 228 cft per year per family, 114 cft per year per bachelor/spinster.
- (ix) **Subsidised ration and free tea leaf:** 500gm of rice/atta per head per day @ Rs. 50.00 per quintal, and 500gm of tea leaf per month per family.
- (x) **Free cinema shows:** One show in a month plus 4 shows during **Durga/Kali puja**.
- (xi) **Bonus:** Minimum amount of 8.33 per cent of the annual wage.

(xii) **Gratuity:** The workers after retirement get this benefit as per the prevailing rate.

(xiii) **Drinking water provision:** It seems the provision prevails there, only for an eye-wash.

(xiv) **Recreation club:** This too seems to have been provided for name-sake only.

(xv) **Miscellaneous:** One **apron**, one pair of **slipper**, one **umbrella**, one **mosquito net** and one **blanket** in 2 years, and **sunglass, gumboot, jersey** and **hand gloves** for the **sprayers of pesticides and insecticides.**

The fact, however, remains that only the permanent workers are entitled to the social security and most of the other fringe benefits referred to above. Temporary workers are engaged in the plantation to work for a specific period. A temporary appointment is limited to a maximum period of 150 working days. The period from May to November is generally regarded as the busy season in a tea plantation. During this peak plucking season, there are quite a large number of temporary labourers who are employed for the plucking of the tea leaves.

The minimum, wage rates during the time of investigation (November 2009) were as follows: Women – Rs. 58.40; Men – Rs. 58.40 (prior to 1985, the rate was Rs. 1.52 more than that of women); and Children – Rs. 29.00

At present (May 2012), the rates are: Women – Rs. 84.00; Men – Rs. 84.00; and Children – Rs. 42.00.

Working Women vis-à-vis the Economic Plight

As noted earlier economic compulsion seems to be the main driving force for this large number of women seeking employment in the tea plantation. Most of them spend whatever they earn in meeting the expenditure of the basic needs of the family. In other words, their income is, by and large, contributed to the family fund to be utilized for recurring domestic expenditure. As a matter of fact, though an earning member, a woman worker, by and large, very often, does not enjoy the desired liberty in spending her earnings.

It is, however, a fact that a good number of them (more than around 60%) are allowed to keep their income with themselves. But, they need to consult their husbands while spending any amount. In these families, normally the entire amount is spent to meet the recurring family expenditure, needed to maintain it. Most of the women members have to manage the family budget with a sense of responsibility. In many families, the husbands hand over a part of their earnings to their wives for meeting family expenditure. They generally decide together how to spend the entire amount.

In the relatively well-to-do families (very few in number) the women earners can keep their income with themselves; and are allowed to spend the amount as they desire. Their husbands generally do not question them as to the selection of items to be purchased while spending an amount. In other words, these women can exercise their liberty in spending their own earnings.

There are a few widows who, however, have to manage the family budget by themselves alone. Incidentally, there are a good number of families where the husbands spend their entire income on consumption of alcohol; and do not contribute anything to the family expenditure. In these families too the basic needs are managed by the wives from their own income only.

> **Case 1.** *S.O., is a permanent worker in Dorothy Tea Estate (T.E.). She is 34 years old and belongs to the Oraon tribe. She is married and has 3 children – 2 sons and 1 daughter. Her husband M.O. aged 39 years is also a permanent worker in the same plantation. M, incidentally is an alcohol-addict. He drinks regularly; and usually exhausts his earning within around a week of its receipt. As such, he borrows money from others for the rest of the period (around a week again). On receipt of the next wage, he spends an amount for the repayment of the loan; and the rest in buying his regular quota of drinks. Borrowing and repayment of the loan amount is a regular process in his case. Occasionally, after an overdose of drink, he beats his wife. Sometimes, he also quarrels with his neighbours. The entire expenditure for the maintenance of the family is borne by S.O. Due to financial hardship, she could not send her children to school.*

> **Case 2.** *F.S. is 45 years old and belongs to the Savara tribe. She is a permanent worker in Manasi T.E. She is married and has 4 children, of whom 3 are daughters. Her husband D.S. too is a permanent worker in the plantation. He is an alcohol-addict and takes both haria (fermented from rice) and laupani (country liquor prepared from molasses) and spends his entire income on liquor only. Therefore, F.S. has to bear the entire expenses needed for maintaining the family. D.S. not only spends his own*

> *earnings on alcohol, but sometimes also takes some amount of money from F. S's income for the purpose.*
>
> *Their eldest daughter being nubile one, once it so happened that D.S. took some money from an aged person promising that their daughter would be married to him in return. Although the verbal contract was done secretly, very soon it became an open secret. In any case, the contract finally did not materialize due to the intervention of F.S, their daughter and other well-wishers of the family.*

Notwithstanding these habitual borrowing episodes here and there, the fact however, remains that a woman's gainful employment raises the percapita income of a family, and as such, very often also enhances the consumption habits of its members.

Production and Reproduction vis-à-vis the Women Workers

A normal adult woman in a society is traditionally expected to be a wife, mother and a home-maker in the family. But in case of a working woman, alongside the reproductive and domestic responsibilities, she has to play a role in the productive activities too; and as such, she generally confronts some problems that were hitherto unknown. Most of the working women, as a matter of fact, are burdened with a double work-load to dispense with – one in the place of employment and the other on the domestic front.

Evidence from several national surveys about how women feel about the double load of job and home-making have led to the following conclusion by Wright, "*Evidence presented ... makes it reasonably plain that both work and house-keeping roles have costs and benefits attached to them. Working women enjoy an outside income and some increase in independence as a result of it, they get out of the house and so on and so forth. But they also pay for these benefits in reduced free time for themselves, a more hectic pace, and a more complicated life. The life of a housewife, in contrast, is somewhat easier ... and almost certainly, less hectic than that of their employed counterparts*" (cited in Hurlock, 1981).

However, Hate (1969) maintains that the main problem of Indian working women is that of **role-conflict** which stems from their dual responsibilities.

Role-conflict, as a matter of fact, occurs when a person occupies 2 or more positions simultaneously; and expectations are not fulfilled properly. This is very evident in the life of a working woman. In her case, a new additional role is added to her existing role as a housewife and mother. Thus, she is subjected to plurality of role expectations which are mutually incompatible. In addition, they may also feel disturbed if they are too busy or too tired when they return from work to take an active part in their children's interest. As a result of these feelings on the part of the working women, their home lives are generally far from satisfactory; and this is apprehended to have an obvious ramification in the overall life of the members of the entire family. In this backdrop, it will be very relevant to have a comprehensive idea as to the nature and content of the constraints (if any), the working women under discussion confront in their day-to-day family life as well as at the work place.

In order to have an overall idea of the nature of routine activities of the different members of a family *vis-à-vis* the division of labour by sex in particular, let us first discuss in brief the general daily life of the members of the community as a whole.

The daily activities of the people usually vary from season to season; and from person to person (depending on the nature of job requirement), but that is only with regard to the exhaustive details. Essentially, the flow of life is by and large, the same throughout the year.

The labour lines stir themselves to life before the sun rises. The first to get out of the room are the adult women; and then men. To start with, they attend to nature's call, clean their teeth and wash face. After these are over, the women members clean the kitchen (particularly the place where the hearth is located; usually by the side of the outer wall) and utensils; and start preparing breakfast after either taking bath or changing the night clothes.

The adult male members of the families possessing cattle, bring them out of the shed, give them fresh fodder and water, and milk them. The cattle are then driven out for grazing in the field; and are looked after by a herdsman (he is also a member of the labour community and is a whole time worker in the plantation for rendering this service). Those who do not have cattle, help in some domestic work or look after the kitchen garden or do some light repairing work in the fencing or so. Almost every house possesses a kitchen garden within the residential compound.

The breakfast, as a matter of fact, amounts to a brunch and contains either *rooti* (made of atta) and tea (without milk) or rice with some vegetable fry and chilli. Conservative housewives (not many in number) generally take their food after the adult men have eaten. The children may take the company of either of the parents on their option.

After taking the breakfast both women and men go out to their respective jobs in the plantation so as to reach there by 7 a.m. (8 a.m., according to the local plantation time which has since the colonial days been continuing to be 1 hour ahead of the I.S.T.). When a working woman has a baby and there is none in the house to look after the same, she sometimes employs a caretaker (*chanakhela*) for the necessary period on payment. The *chanakhela* may take the baby to the working spot; and remain nearby the mother throughout the day. The mother at regular intervals feeds the baby by breast. In some cases, when it is otherwise negotiable, the *chanakhela* with the baby remains at home; and the working mother, during the break time manages to come back for a while to feed the baby. In the process, however, the days become relatively more hectic and taxing for her.

> **Case. 3.** *R.M. aged 35 years is a permanent worker in Dalimi T.E. She belongs to the Munda tribe. She is illiterate, married and has 3 children, aged 5 years, 3 years and less than 1 year respectively. Her husband also is a permanent worker in the same plantation. Her day generally begins early in the morning at around 4.30 a.m., she does her household chores of preparing food and cleaning the house etc.; and leaves the house for work before 7 a.m. (I.S.T.). She carries packed tiffin with her. When the working bed is close to her quarters, during the break time she goes home to feed her young children; and then again rushes back to work. In the process, very often she cannot manage to have her own tiffin.*
>
> *After returning from work at around 3.30 p.m., once again she continues with her household chores. She normally does not seem to have any time to take care of herself nor can do full justice to her children too. At around 8 p.m. after preparing the dinner, she feeds her children and waits for her husband to return home. Then she takes her food and retires to bed by around 9 p.m. This cycle of activities is repeated every day, with however, some breathing gap on Sundays and holidays.*

Sometimes, the children, left at home are taken care of by the elderly unemployed/retired inmates of the families from the immediate neighbourhood.

> **Case 4.** *S.M. aged 44 years is a permanent worker in Dorothy T.E. She is illiterate and belongs to the Santal tribe. She is married and has 4 children. Their ages are 9, 7, 4 and 2 years*

> *respectively. Her husband too is a permanent worker in Dorothy. Their 2 elderly sons are school-going students. In the morning, she generally gets up from bed before any body else at around 4 a.m. She cleans the house and prepares food for the members of the family. She serves food to her children and husband; and also packs tiffin for her husband, the school-going sons and for her ownself. She leaves for her work at around 7 a.m. Before leaving for the work place, she leaves the 2 younger children in the custody of one of the neighbouring families.*
>
> *After returning from tea bed she takes a bath and also cleans her children before entering the kitchen for the routine activities including the preparation of dinner.*
>
> *After serving the night meals to all the members of the family, she takes her own one at around 7.30 p.m. Then again, some more time is needed for setting everything in order to have a convenient start of the daily cycle of activities, the following morning. She retires to bed at around 9 p.m.*

Ordinarily, the people are to work for 8 hours a day. Thus, they become free at around 3 p.m. But, however, it varies from season to season. During off (non-plucking) season, they can come back by around 1 p.m., or so. But, during plucking season, usually they work overtime. Some women, who need to return home earlier from the work for looking after the children or for some other domestic preoccupations, are permitted to take some helper (usually one's own son/daughter) with them to complete the allotted work earlier.

All the workers, during the working hours in the plantation are provided with raw tea (liquor with salt) by the management for 2 to 3 times a day.

Usually, all the people come back home by around 3.30 p.m. The women members generally do not waste much time in relaxation. They start their daily household chores like cleaning the pots and pans, sweeping the floor and polishing the floor and courtyard with wet rags and soil (courtyard polishing, however, is not done daily). After taking bath they enter the kitchen; and prepare tea and *rooti* for all. Mothers having adult daughters however, need not do it themselves. The daughters do it either entirely by themselves or they help the mothers in preparing the tiffin and tea.

After finishing their afternoon tea, men generally spend the evening by gossiping with the neighbours or going out for a walk inside the labour *lines* or to the nearby villages. Occasional shopping in the nearby shops is also done in the evening only. This is conveniently done by either women or men. Regular marketing and shopping are, however, done on every alternate Friday, the day of their wage payment. It has also been observed that some members of the menfolk stay at home for sometime to feed the cattle and / or to do a little bit of household work like repairing a wall, watering the kitchen garden or the likes. Women members spend time either with their children or in the kitchen, planning for the dinner preparation.

Just when the sun is about to set (dusk), women light lamp in the house and silently pay their homage to God. In many houses a small space is partitioned aside to preserve paddy, safe from rats and mice, in huge baskets; and an altar on the eastern wall in the name of the God (**Bhagawan/Bishnu**). Those who can afford, burn incense on that altar every morning and evening and then pay their silent homage. Otherwise, this is actively used only during some family rituals. In some families some flowers are offered in the name of the God on the altar every morning.

After paying the routine homage to God a woman settles down in the kitchen to cook the dinner. In most of the families this is the only time when a full-fledged cooking (processing of rice, curry and *dal* etc.) is done. Fish and meat are their occasional delicacies. On the day of the wage payment they purchase fish from the plantation market that sits on that day only. Goat is occasionally slaughtered in the *line*; and meat can be had on share basis. Sometimes, in the rainy season many of them indulge in individual fishing using nets and fishing rods in the nearby ditches and drains.

With sunset, the children are back home (from the company of their peers and playmates). Students generally sit with their books. In most of the houses; and very often (but not necessarily daily) men at that time drink *haria* either at home or elsewhere in the neighbourhood in the company of some one's else. In many houses bitterness in the conjugal relationship; and also sometimes in the relationship with the other members of the family starts as one loses control over oneself after being intoxicated. Sometimes this unpleasant affair reaches the extent of physical torture. In some families (though very few in number) however, women also drink *haria* to the extent of losing control over themselves. In those cases, the spirit of hot exchanges between the couple becomes co-dominant. Otherwise, it is always the husband who generally dominates. Occasionally, during the holidays and on festive occasions, many of them get intoxicated during day time also.

In most of the families, the dinner is finished by around 8.30 p.m. Usually, women eat after all other members have taken their meals. In case, the husband is late to return, the wife feeds the children and let them sleep; and she waits for her husband. After the dinner, sometimes the husband and wife chat and relax for a while. Occasionally, the children also join and/or enjoy the gossip. After that they finally retire to bed.

During the holidays, the people usually do not have any definite routine work. Some people conveniently visit the nearest urban centre for making some purchases or enjoying some movie in any cinema hall. Someones go to the nearby plantations/villages to see their friends/relatives. Women do some major cleaning of the house and wash clothes; and occasionally some young women and girls go to the nearby urban centre to enjoy movie in the matinee show with or without some male guardian/escort.

During agricultural season both men and women work in the field in various capacities. Women help actively in sowing and harvesting, but not in the preparation of the land nor in carrying paddy from the field to home.

It is thus apparent that the women workers generally lead a very busy daily life with practically no time to have leisure and relaxation. As a matter of fact, they genuinely need some helping hands to provide relief from the burden of domestic chores. It seems, the husbands, by and large, do not assist their wives to the required extent on the domestic front.

As such, very often, women are overburdened with day-to-day routine activities. This is relatively more acute in the nuclear families. Incidentally, this particular reality of over taxation on their body and mind is very often reflected in their overall deficiencies in the health scenario. However, the disappointing state of affairs in this regard seems to be in conformity with the observation, made by Kapoor (1971) in an allied type of study long back. It goes as, "... *the working wife, especially if she has children, will have to make in many instances, a little greater effort to keep things going and she actually needs more help than is commonly given to her*" (cited in Jha, Mehta and Menon, 1998: 132).

Over and above, the women workers, very often, also have to experience some constraints outside the family domain too, that is, in the workplace. Work condition, as a matter of fact, includes both physical environment as well as the relationship with the supervisors and the fellow workers. These constraints too sometimes negatively contribute towards the maintenance of peace and tranquility in the domestic sphere.

We know that the **PLA, 1951** and the **PLR, 1956** have laid down a good number of provisions in terms of working conditions, but, incidentally the fact remains that the prevailing physical conditions at the work place are, by and large, not very satisfactory. Thus, for example, proper facilities for drinking water, attending to nature's call and sheltering the kids (*crèche*) etc., are lacking in the workplace. Lack of toilet and crèche facilities in many cases, create acute problems for the women workers. At times they are unable to respond to nature's call due to lack of toilets nearby. This problem, coupled with lack of potable drinking water very often leads to some perennial health problem for a good number of workers.

Besides, the nature of the management – worker relationship is also of crucial importance for a worker at work place. The *Sardars*, as we know, are the supervisors at work; they are the *de facto* representatives of the management for a group of labourers at work. Thus, the quality and content of the relationship that prevails between a worker and the work-supervisor does have a lasting impression on the worker's motivation and morale. At times, it has been found that the *Sardars* deal with the women workers in a very unkind way. A concrete case is being shared as an illustration.

> **Case 5.** *S.M. aged 42 years belongs to the Munda tribe. She is a permanent labourer in Dorothy T.E. She is married and her husband too is a permanent worker in the same garden. In the work place, she is very often reprimanded by the Sardar on this or that hypothetical flimsy pretext. Sometimes she has to endure his misbehaviour in the presence of other co-workers even if she talks with another woman worker. One day when the Sardar had been chastising her for talking with a woman co-worker, very politely she wanted to speak a few words to defend herself. The Sardar got furious and refused to listen to her.*
>
> *The matter did not end there. He went ahead and lodged a complaint with the manager about her "misbehaviour". The manager called S.M. to the office and chastised her with a warning that any more complaint against her might cost her job. He too did not allow her any opportunity to defend herself.*

Incidentally, this is not the usual behavior with a male worker even if one of them indulges in gossiping during the working hours.

This differential treatment towards the women workers by the management may be reflective of either subjective gender bias on the part of the members of the supervisory staff or the fact that the women workers enjoy a relatively inferior status in the work place. Further studies are in fact needed to arrive at a decisive conclusion in this regard.

Concluding Observations

It may be highlighted that in the tea plantation women workers are normally more in number; and most of them are engaged in the outdoor activities, especially in the plucking operation. A good number of them are temporary workers; and as such are not entitled to have the privilege of enjoying all the social security benefits as well as other fringe benefits. The physical facilities, available in the work place do not seem to be very satisfactory. In other words, the provisos made in the **P.L.A., 1951** are not available to the workers to the required extent. Some of these facilities (e.g. crèche and toilet) are genuinely needed for the women workers. In many instances, it has also been found that the women workers are differently treated by the management that contributes negatively towards their work environment. In wage rate, however, since 1985 they have been treated at par with their male counterparts. Further, though engaged in gainful employment, barring a very few, they do not seem to enjoy any economic independence in their family life. It has been observed that most of them do not enjoy any relief in their traditional domestic preoccupations because of their outdoor employment.

In fine, it may be emphasized that of late, some young women workers with the background of some formal education have been found to take active part in the Trade Union activities. In the union meetings, they very often become vocal and plead for the protection of their interest as well as self-respect.

REFERENCES

Bhadra, Mita, (1997), "Changing family, authority, role and status of the tea plantation women workers in Darjeeling District", in *Plantation Labourers of North East India.* Edited by R.K. Bhadra and Mita Bhadra. Dibrugarh: N.L. Publishers, pp. 229-46.

Chakravarty, L.N. (1973), *Glimpses of early history of Arunachal.* Shillong: Research Department, Arunachal Pradesh.

Crawford, T.O. (1924), *Handbook of castes and tribes employed on the tea estates in North-East India.* Kolkata: Indian Tea Association.

Gait, E. 1926 (Reprint, 1933), *A history of Assam.* Kolkata: Thacker, Spink and Co.

Harlalka, S.S. (1975), *Tea garden labour in Assam.* Dhubri: People's Publishing House.

Jha, Mehta and Menon (1998), *Status of Indian Women: Crisis and Conflict in Gender Issues.* New Delhi: Kaniska Publishers Distributors.

Kar, R.K. (2010), *Socio-cultural dimension of health and health-seeking behaviour among the tribal workers of tea plantations in Assam: A case study in continuity and change.* An unpublished project report. Dibrugarh: Dibrugarh University.

Kar, R.K. (2001), Anthropological appraisal of a migrant population in Assam, North-East India. *Man and Life*, 27: 139-62.

________, (1999), "A panoramic view of the tea and ex-tea tribes of Assam", in *Identity of Adivasis in Assam.* Edited by Thomas Pulloppillil. Delhi: Indian Publishers Distributors, pp. 21-46.

________, (1995), Assamer Cha-shramik ebong Oraon Upajati. *Nandan* (A Bengali medium journal, published from Kolkata) 31 (6): 53-5.

________, (1986), Absenteeism among tea labour: A case study in cultural ecology. *Man and Life*, 12 (3-4): 143-58.

Kar, R.K. and Tultul Barua. (1997), "Morbidity and health behavior: A case study among the migrant Munda tea labourers", in *Health studies in anthropology.* Edited by Farida Ahmed Das and R.K. Kar. Dibrugarh: Dibrugarh University, pp. 145-60.

Lowie, R.H. (1929), *Primitive society.* London: George Routledge and Sons Ltd.

Parsons, T. (1954), *Essay in Sociological Theory.* New York: Free Press.

Quinn, Naomi. (1977), Anthropological studies on Women's status. *Annual Review of Anthropology.* Durham: Department of Anthropology, Duke University, pp. 181-225.

Roy Burman, B.K. (1968), *Socio-economic process in tea plantations with special reference to tribal labours.* Delhi; Census of India, 1961, Vol. I, part-VII A.

Sharma, J.L. (1987), *Tradition and Change among the migrant Oraons in Assam: A case study.* Unpublished Ph.D. dissertation submitted to Dibrugarh University, Assam.

Sharma, J.L. (1990), "Ex-tea labour settlement in Upper Assam: A case study", in *Tea Garden Labourers of North-East India.* Edited by S. Karotempral and B. Dutta Roy. Shillong: Vendrame Institute.

Sullerot, E. (1971), *Women, Society and Change.* London: World University Press.

Thompson and A. Finalyson. (1953), "Married Women who work in early motherhood." *British Journal of Sociology*, 114: 150-68.

Tripathy, Jayashree, (1999), "Women and their work environment", in *Women in India: A Search for Identity.* Edited by Sharada Rath and Navaneeta Rath. New Delhi: Anmol Publications Pvt. Ltd., pp. 129-47.

8

Resource Utilization among the Tribal Communities of North East India: With Special Reference to the Rabha of Assam

K. Jose SVD

Introduction

Resource is generally defined as something available in supply and that can be used for life support of all living beings at any point of time. This is a total means available most especially for socio-economic, religio-cultural and political development. Resources are also essential for increasing production or profit; including raw material such as mineral wealth, labour force, etc. In sum, resource is a source of supply which is available at the disposal of an individual, a community or a nation for the needs, progress and welfare of the individual members or people collectively.

Resources are things that help to produce goods and services. There are never enough resources to produce all of the goods and services that people want. Four major economic resources are: Land, Labour, Capital and Entrepreneurial ability. When we speak about land it includes natural resources such as timber, oil, coal, iron ore, soil, water, as well as the ground in which these resources are found. It is used for the extraction of minerals and farming, provides the site for factories, office buildings, shopping centres, homes, etc. Labour, Capital and Entrepreneurial ability are essential for bringing the resources to its ultimate form of utilization or consumption. Utilization is the primary method by which asset and its performance is measured and business success determined.

The tribal communities of India generally live in rural setting amidst forests and hilly areas. The precious heritage of the great Indian tradition is an amalgam and harmonious blending of a wide variety of cultures. Often they live a simple life, undertaking agricultural activities and similar allied occupations. So much so they are not in a position to economically compete with other advanced communities of neighbouring towns. They are on various levels of socio-economic and cultural development – from hunting, gathering to pastoral and unskilled workers in industrial sector. Varied ethnicities, diverse languages and different religions among the tribal communities have been harmonized in the traditions of Indian civilization.

About 742 million people, or 72.2 per cent of India's population, live in rural areas. Of these, 89 million belong to the Scheduled Tribes. The Scheduled Tribes are concentrated in the so-called tribal belt of central India, with a second highest concentration in the North East India. According to 2001 Census there are more than 84,326,240 tribal people divided into 445 tribes who form about 8.20 per cent of the total population of India. The main occupations of the tribes are: forestry and food gathering; shifting cultivation, settled agriculture, agricultural labour, animal husbandry and household industry. They generally dwell in forested and hilly areas and highly depend on forests for their cultural, spiritual, and economic needs in varying degrees (www. indiacurrentaffairs.org/ tribal-population-in-country).

When we see the tribes of North East India we understand that they are exposed to modernization and westernization for a prolonged period of time compared to some communities in central India and elsewhere. With regard to the various resources they are plenty in most of the tribal areas of this region. However, some are not able to make the best use of it due to various reasons. The infrastructural bottlenecks like road communication, problem of storing including marketing facilities etc. are among them. North East India, despite its multifaceted potential, is one of the most underrated and least explored regions of the country. The region has an interesting socio-cultural, ethnic, and linguistic diversity, with more than 200 dominant tribes and many sub-tribes that reflect the complex social structure. In terms of its natural resources, the region is identified as one of the world's biodiversity hotspots, with species-rich tropical rainforests supporting diverse flora and fauna, and is the centre of origin of several species, including citrus, cereals, and orchids.

This immense potential, however, is yet translated into economic prosperity. The poverty rate in the region is significantly higher than the national average; the human development indices show poor records, and lack of development plagues the region. The number of industries in the region is significantly low. This is mainly due to the absence or weakness of basic infrastructural facilities, the major constraint to the promotion of entrepreneurial ventures in the region. This is compounded by the protracted civil unrest in many of the north eastern states. The inadequate transport services and connectivity, including the poorly maintained highways and unreliable air connectivity, are some of the factors that debilitate development in the region. To add to this, a sense of psychological alienation from mainland India, whose poor understanding of the region exacerbates the current conditions, only creates a deeper disconnection between the two.

Some of the problems that affect especially the young people, including drug abuse and ongoing insurgency, can be attributed to the lack of employment opportunities and development in the region. There is a perceived need to increase and diversify the sources of income at the community level to help arrest migration and reduce dependence on the government. Some argue that this change can be brought about by the revival and strengthening of traditional institutions for better management of resources and for building peace and development in the region. Governments are taking recourse to these traditional forms of governance and community decision making, once treated as a constraint to development, and reorienting their policies to assign more powers to the local governing councils to rebuild society. Traditional societies and villages are being acknowledged as important functional units. Self-help and self-reliance and community sentiment are strong characteristics of the communities in the North East India that have helped them through many difficult periods.

The present study is basically focused on the number of resources available in tribal areas with special reference to the Rabha of Goalpara, Assam who are undergoing a number of changes amidst socio-economic and cultural realm and making efforts to be relevant in the present day context.

Natural Resource of the Tribal Communities

Soil, water, vegetation, and bio-diversity are abundant in North East India. On the other hand, with no long-term plans for their utility, exploitation of these items is rampant. Therefore, soil erosion, fertility loss, recurrence of floods, extinction of rarest of the flora and fauna, wastage of quality water, low productivity of crops etc. affect the region very adversely.

Even the formation of new development departments unfortunately, does not seem to have improved current conditions. The process of displacement of the tribal people has accelerated exponentially. The moot question then is what is the way out? Do the indigenous people have no room in Democratic Republic of India? What are the obligations of the Indian States? All such questions demand scientific answers and contemporary solutions.

The tribal communities in North East India for a long time were developed in their own genius. When we compare them with other parts of India we can say that they remained isolated and outside the gamut of development. However, that is not entirely true for they flourished under the self-governing institutions. Economic development of a particular geographical area should never be considered only in terms of its quantity of economic resources, but strengthening of its socio-cultural institutions should be taken into serious consideration. So, social and economic sectors are to march ahead hand in hand. In our deliberation though we shall take agriculture and the allied activities as a prime mover of economic development of the people under our study, we shall also look into other available resources including cash crop, namely rubber.

Natural Resources and Livelihood Security

Environmental problems in the North East India have been influenced by the increasing population, the survival needs of the poor, and the economic greed that often typifies commercial interests. They are also aggravated by prevalent economic disparities and unemployment, which are deeply embedded in unsustainable patterns of production, consumption, and exchange; ill-informed policies and programmas; and inappropriate development strategies. Unsustainable extraction of timber for local industries and export markets has disrupted forest ecosystems in states such as Meghalaya, Assam and Arunachal Pradesh, resulting in tremendous loss of biodiversity. In fact a number of natural resource which was available in plenty, has almost vanished out of sight due to the unplanned land utilization patterns in North East India.

Other than forestry, fragile hilly slopes have been extensively used for unsustainable agriculture, mining, and cash crops. These unplanned interventions have had a disturbing impact on the environment. The imperatives of specific local socio-economic and ecological conditions, which alone can determine the relevance and effectiveness of interventions in the hilly states, are seldom incorporated into development policies and programmes for these areas. Besides, most existing policies and programmes relating to these areas do not address the needs and priorities of traditional resource users at the grassroots level. Furthermore, there are inadequate data about the availability, location, and distribution of forest and mineral resources and the level, pattern, and rate of resource consumption and environmental degradation. Lack of applied research and extension services have also resulted in unsuitable land use. Finally, loss of traditional methods in resource management and lack of appropriate institutional arrangements have had adverse effects on people's control over the resources on which they depend for their sustenance (Karki, 2001).

Natural resources are substances that exist naturally in the Earth. They are valuable in manufacturing products, supplying human necessities or comforts, and providing ecosystem services that maintain the health of the biosphere. They include air, land, water, natural gas, coal, oil, petroleum, minerals, wood, topsoil, fauna, flora, forests and wildlife. Renewable natural resources are those that reproduce or renew and include animal life, plants, trees, water, and wind. Non-renewable resources are irreplaceable once extracted from water or soil and include gold, silver, fossil fuels, diamonds, copper, ore and natural gas. Most of the natural resources including minerals, are located in tribal areas. The tribal people are being alienated from their land and forest due to the ongoing deforestation, hydro-electric power generation, industrial growth and mining activities. The natural resources are being exploited in a way, which leads to a process of gradual displacement and denying the basic right of livelihood. Massive investment in construction of dams, power plants, industrialization and mining create wealth to the nation and employment opportunities to various people but all these are hardly of any benefit to the tribal people; rather it leads to their social and cultural deprivation, land alienation, destruction of environment and displacements, which is often without any rehabilitation.

Human development, environmental upgradation, improving the quality of life and recognizing the aspirations of the younger generation are all major concerns in North East India. Certainly economic development is a tangible parameter for a vibrant community and region. The number of rebellious movements will point at the failure to meet their economic needs. The region is rich with resources of coal, oil, tea, water etc. and therefore, it should bring in hope. However, abundance of natural resources in itself will not bring economic sustenance. There is a need to materialize the vision for this vast region with immense potentialities. One often hears complaints that the funds received by the North Eastern region of our country is far less than what is required for our multi-faceted engagements related to development and prosperity; yet one cannot forget the fact that the central funds and amenities remain often underutilized, and larger chunk of it is siphoned off with no remorse of conscience. Thus natural resources though are available in plenty, their utilization for livelihood security have not become a reality in a full measure.

Land, the Most Priced Resource of the Tribal people

Land is central to tribal life around the world. Land and forests are the life support system around which the tribal economy and knowledge systems evolve. The knowledge systems were meant to nurture and manage the resource at its most sustainable level without disturbing the ecological balance. They employ technologies that look primitive and simple, but are ecologically adaptive because their implements were ecologically feasible. The indigenous communities have a deep sentimental attachment and socio-cultural orientation towards the land on which they live. This attachment gives both to an individual and to the community a sense of belonging to a place. It is an important social and cultural phenomenon because it is deeply rooted in their homestead, landed property, relatives, clan and community, in general. One of the beautiful manifestations of this attachment is their aesthetic sensibility that they express through folk songs and dances, beautifully designed hand-woven ethnic attires, wood carvings, beautiful and durable bamboo products, etc.

That brings us to the basic issue of land ownership and laws. Before the introduction of land related laws by the colonial administration, the indigenous people have negligible problem around land. Traditionally they had a three-tier land ownership and control system: 1. Community land, 2. Clan land, and 3. Individual land. Every community had well-defined boundaries and traditional administration systems based on the customary law. The situation has changed considerably today with inevitable alteration in land use and relations. The first external cause of land alienation is higher demand for it for development projects. Alienation processes often come along with the inducement of so-called modernization, development processes, and State laws, which often favour individualism. The second demand comes from the immigrants who encroach on their land. These issues have become important in the context of the development projects, especially major dams, being planned in the region, most of them on tribal land. A consequence of these processes is shortage of land, and ethnic conflicts around it.

For example, in Tripura, land alienation from tribal to non-tribal people is a major issue. This chronic problem has turned the indigenous communities of the state into a minority. Continued refugee influx and illegal migration contributed to population explosion, and resulted in land alienation of the indigenous people. This has led to conflicts for three decades. By the late 1960s refugees from Bangladesh had encroached on 60 per cent of indigenous tribal land. In 1970s Gumti dam was announced, though the tribal people protested they were forced out of their land. It submerged 46.34 sq.km., most of it very plain land that was cultivated by the tribal people. By official count it displaced 2,558 families or 13,500 persons, but about 35,000 people were dependent on these families who were not even counted. The dam has become non-viable now. Some of the affected people demanded the decommissioning and returning the land to the people but the state is not ready for it. The origin of the Tripura tribal insurgency can be traced to this event (Shimray, 2006:10-11).

Some of the indigenous techniques for land and water management developed traditionally in this region are *Zabo* system of terrace farming and *Panikheti* (wet cultivation) in Nagaland, bench terracing cultivation in Sikkim, bamboo drip irrigation system of Jowai in Meghalaya, and sustainable land and water management system of the Apatani in Arunachal Pradesh. There is a need to suitably modify these techniques for individual agro-climatic conditions and to spread the good features of these systems in other parts of the North East India too (Mishra, 2002:98). Most indigenous peoples have a special relationship to the land and territories they inhabit. It is there their ancestors have lived and where their history, knowledge, livelihood practices and believes are evolved and developed. To most indigenous peoples the territory has a sacred or spiritual meaning, which reaches far beyond the productive and economic aspect of the land. For example; in Meghalaya the availability to land is not at all a problem. Even the lime stone and coal fields bring great hope for the indigenous people. However, the question is does the resources truly belong to the people themselves, or are they plundered by the middlemen and others?

Land is instrumental in the formation and shaping of the material and non-material culture of the communities depending on it. Every society, whether industrialized and agriculture-based is closely attached to land, though there is difference in the nature of its relationship to it. Thus management of land is crucial to a society at every stage of its development. The highest benefits can accrue to a society or people only through its effective management. The way land is managed, however, varies not only from one society to another and from place to place, but also from age to age even within the same society. From hunting-gathering through slash and burn to settled and mechanized farming is a long social history of human transition. The plains and valleys usually practice settled cultivation, though its nature varies according to the climate, and from arid, semi-arid to wet zones. While in the hills, though the slash and burn method continues along with terrace cultivation, there has been substantial inevitable change in the land use pattern over the years.

Land occupied a crucial position in the pre-modern, traditional Rabha social life. It continues to be important in their socio-political and cultural life. It is their main sustenance in the absence alternative employment avenues. However, its management and ownership have changed substantially with the passage of time. Traditionally land was a communal asset but with modernization one witnesses the growth of private ownership. This transition from communal to private ownership has brought in a number of negative impacts such as alienation to non-tribal people and concentration of land in the hands of the tribal elite. Scores of legislative measures have not succeeded in addressing this complex issue.

It is essential to know and understand the deeply spiritual and special relationship between indigenous peoples and their land as basic to their existence as such and to all their beliefs, customs, traditions and culture. For the tribal, land is not merely a possession and a means of production. Their land is not a commodity which can be acquired, but a material element to be enjoyed freely and a cultural element around which the whole of their live evolve. This is reaffirmed in Article 25 of the UN Declaration on the Rights of Indigenous Peoples, which stipulates that indigenous peoples have the right to maintain and strengthen their distinctive spiritual relationship with their traditionally-owned or otherwise occupied and used lands, territories, waters and coastal seas and other resources and to uphold their responsibilities to future generations in this regard. The territory is the basis for most indigenous peoples' economies and livelihood strategies, traditional institutions, spiritual well-being and distinct cultural identity. Consequently, loss of ancestral lands threatens their very survival as distinct communities and peoples.

The Tribal Communities in Assam

Assam received its name according to some, from the Sanskrit word *asama,* which means uneven and undulating. To some others, the word

Assam comes from *cham*, which is a Sanskrit cognate for the verb 'to eat'. This interpretation of the name came from the fabled reputation of the land inhabited by people who ate whatever they found. Thus, when the first group of Brahmins came to Assam and found that they were not cannibals, they gave the area and people the name *A-cham*, 'not cannibal people and land'. A third interpretation is that the name came from '*Ahom*'. The historians believe that *Ahom* means 'unequal' or 'unparalleled' (For detailed description of the term Assam (see K. Barua, 1923; and S. Barua, 1928).

Assam is one of the eight states of North East India including Sikkim. It is bounded by Bhutan and Arunachal Pradesh on the north, Meghalaya and Tripura on the south, Manipur, Nagaland and Arunachal Pradesh on the east and Meghalaya and West Bengal and Bangladesh on the west. It covers a territory of 78,523 sq. km, roughly a fourth of it comprising rugged hills and the rest verdant alluvial plains out of which 78,088 sq. km is occupied by rural and 485 sq. km is occupied by urban areas. According to 1991 census, the total population of the state is 22,414,322 out of which 11.09 per cent are urban and 88.89 per cent are rural inhabitants. The state of Assam is divided into 23 districts. Of the total districts, two districts are hills districts. These are Karbi Anglong and North Cachar Hills districts. With a long history of peopling, Assam presents a diverse population composition and accommodates 3,308,570 tribal people accounting for 12.41 per cent of the state's total population as per 2001 Census.

Assam is a land of different tribes, which plays a very important role in the culture and tradition of the State. Almost all of them have rich culture and they develop in their own unique ways. Most of them also have contributed to the composite culture of Assam as well. As there are a very few scientific and comprehensive study on the tribal communities of Assam it is not easy to make an over all observation on the resource utilization of the people of Assam, however, individual tribal communities which are studied longitudinally by the scholars also throw some light on their indigenous resources, marketing strategies, livelihood pattern and other similar themes. When the distribution of tribal population is concerned, it is observed that people are mainly concentrated in the hill and foothill regions, peripheral and low-lying areas of the state, and hence the overall distribution is quite uneven. Again, of the total tribal population in the state, 82.40 per cent live in the plains and the remaining 17.60 per cent in the hills. Assam is the home of as many as 23 tribal groups. Of these 23 tribal groups eight groups have more than 1 per cent of population each, out of the total tribal population of Assam. They are the Boro (40.09%), Mising (17.80%), Karbi (10.68%), Rabha (8.14%), Sonowal-Kachari (7.01%), Tiwa (5.02%), Dimasa (3.35%) and the Deori (1.20%). The eight group together account for 93.29 per cent of the total tribal population in the state. It may be mentioned here that except the Karbi of Karbi Anglong and the Dimasas of N.C. Hills, the rest are plain tribes occupying distinct areas of the state.

The Rabha Tribe is one of the Scheduled Tribes found in Assam. This unique tribe is scattered along the Golaghat, Kamrup and Goalpara districts of the state. Some of the Rabha people also lives in Jalpaiguri and Cooch Behar districts of West Bengal. Almost the whole part of Eastern and Western Dooars are considered as the land of Rabha community. However, in Assam Goalpara district is the heartland of the Rabhas where they live in most numerous villages. Agriculture is the main occupation of Rabha community. Earlier they used to practice shifting cultivation but later on they took the job of settled cultivation. Besides agriculture they are also engaged in forest based activities and handloom weaving. It is the traditional occupation of Rabha women. Now-a-days these people have taken the occupation of teachers and government officials but their development is quite low in respect of other communities. Although, the government has taken many steps for their development but all of them have not born considerable results. Most of the Rabha in this district are merely living a life of subsistence engaged in agricultural operations and some of them are also employed in daily labour.

The tribal communities though small in size, occupy an important position in the society, economy and polity of Assam. Having diverse ethnic origins, yet representing a distinctive socio-cultural system, their own cultural ethos, a unique-way of adaptation to different ecological niches and a distinctive social structure of their own, they seem to respond to processes of social change quite differently to other communities. While on the one hand, their tradition-bound practices continue to exist, on the other hand, they adapt to new wider forces. With this background in mind an attempt is made in this article to understand how new socio-cultural changes are accepted, rejected or adapted by the Rabha, living here. The study is based on both secondary and primary data. While secondary data have been obtained from relevant Census of India publications for the period 1991-2001, necessary primary data have been collected through a field survey. Here below we shall briefly make some observations on the state of Assam and its resources.

Assam and its Resources

A broad view of Assam with regard to various natural resources will throw light on the availability of immense amount of Natural resources in Assam which include mineral resources, power resources and forest resources. Coal, Crude Oil, Natural Gas, Lime Stone, probable reserves of other minerals, all of these give an ample scope for industrialization through fuller utilization of these vast mineral resources. When we see the total area covered by forests in Assam it is 30,807 sq.kms (1991-92), which is 39.2 per cent of the total geographical area of the State. But reserved forest area covers 22 per cent of the total geographical area of the state. National forest policy prescribed national minimum of 33.3 per cent under the productive forest and Assam's per centage of forest area is lower in this respect.

Among all the natural resources of Assam, water resources are considered as one of the most important resources of the state. Water is essential for the survival human, animal and plant life on earth. Besides, water in adequate quantity is very much important for the development of agriculture, fishery, animal husbandry and also for industrial development. As agriculture is the main occupation of the people of Assam, regular and assured supply of water in adequate quantity is very much important for the development of agricultural sector. Power is an essential prerequisite for industrial development. Assam is generously blessed by nature with its huge power potential based on water, natural gas, coal and oil. Assam alone has 28 per cent of the total hydro power potential of the country, which remains under-utilized. In spite of having huge power potential, Assam is lagging behind most of the other states of India in respect of installed capacity as well as per capita consumption of electricity. Livestock and fishery resources are also areas wherein the state can play a vital role in development of the people for a long time to come as it is underutilized till today. In sum mineral resources, forest resources, agricultural resources and water resource are areas the state can make great break through if put into optimum use.

Goalpara District

Goalpara district of Assam is situated on the south bank of the river Brahmaputra. Geographical location of the district is between latitude 25°50′N - 26°10′and longitude 90°07′– 91°05′E at 100 —500 m above the mean sea level (msl). It covers an area of 1,831 sq. km and is bounded by West and East Garo Hill districts of Meghalaya on the South; Kamrup District on the East, Dhubri District on the West and the river Brahmaputra all along the North. The word Goalpara was derived from *Gwaltippika* meaning *Guwali gaon* in Assamese and village of the milkmen in English. In 1826 British accessed Assam and Goalpara was annexed to Assam in 1874.

Total population of the district is 8,22,035 (2001 Census) and male and female ratio is 1,000 : 956. The literacy rate is 47.46 per cent. The Scheduled Tribe (ST) population in the district is 16.10 per cent of the total population and the Scheduled Castes (SC) population is 4.80 per cent. Total working population of the district is 2,74,150 (33.34%). Economy of the district is primarily an agrarian. However, only 18.34 per cent of the population is directly engaged in agriculture as cultivator (12.22%) and agricultural labourers (6.12%). The farmers are basically smallholders. Agro-forestry is the unique practice in the district. Every household grows timber plants as source of cash. Areca nut and banana are the major cash crops in the district. Since last 15 years areca nut has been suffering from ganoderma putting the farm families in economic difficulties. It has compelled the farm households to convert their areca nut orchard to rubber orchard. The major agricultural produces are rice, jute, green gram, black gram and wheat. Major horticultural produces are banana, jack fruit, areca nut and *rabi* vegetables. Most of the rural households keep livestock like cattle, goat and pig and fowl like duck and chicken, at their home stead.

The Study Villages

Our study is based on two villages, namely Matia and Majerburi. Both of these villages are in Matia Tehsil in Goalpara District in Assam. These villages are situated 19 km distance from its Goalpara district headquarters and 136 km distance from its State capital Dispur. In our study area of 2 villages, there are 101 families in total and there are 539 numbers. of total population. 16 families of Majerburi are followers of traditional *Rabha* (Rangdani) religion and 45 families are Christian, whereas in Matia 40 families are traditional worshippers and 20 families are Christian (*ref.* Household Schedule, 2011).

History of Migration

Playfair has tried to trace the original habitat of the Rabhas and the manner of their migration. His monograph 'The Garos' gives an interesting account regarding the migration and settlement of the Bodo group, particularly the Boro-Kachari, the Garo, the Koch and the Rabha. According to him the migrations took place from Tibetan region to Brahmaputra valley and from thence to the Garo Hills of Meghalaya in the remote past (Das, 1960: 2). In a particular way he also holds the view that the Rabhas after migrating from Tibetan region occupied the Garo Hills area and then distributed in Assam plains. He opines that the original home and habitat of the Rabhas was the region bordering the northern slopes of the Garo Hills (Playfair, 1975:18).

Playfair has also observed some linguistic and cultural similarities between the Garos and the Rabhas He has pointed out the remarkable similarities between the dialects of the Rangdani and the two sections of the Garo, i.e. Atong and Ruga. He writes: 'The real facts can never be satisfactorily settled, but in the Rabhas, Koches, Atongs, and Rugas we have the representatives of the original inhabitants of the tract of country which we call the Garo Hills. For this reason, while I class all other Garo divisions with Kacharis, and believe that they represent the primitive Bodo, the Atongs and Rugas are of different stock and have a common origin with the Rabhas and Koches' (Playfair, 1975: 22). Endle (1911) was the first English writer to include the Rabhas in his book entitled 'The Kacharis: Bodo', as a tribe closely allied to the Boro-Kacharis, who were commonly called as Datiyal Kacharis in Darrang district. As regards the origin of the Rabhas he writes, "their origin is but imperfectly known, but they are said to be descended from a Hindu father who lost caste by marrying a Kachari woman" (Endle, 1990: 83). Grierson (1903) holds almost the same view. According to his observation, "Rabha appears to be a Hindu name for the tribe, and many men so called are pure Kacharis" (Playfair, 1975: 19).

All the different views and observations expressed by the scholars may well be summarized in the following words of Gait (1892:232), who identifies the Rabha as a distinct tribe. He writes: "There seems to be a good deal of uncertainty as to who these people really are. In lower Assam it is asserted that they are an offshoot of the Garos, while in Kamrup and Darrang, it is thought that they are Kachari on the road to Hinduism. That they belong to the great Bodo family is certain; but it is not equally clear that the Rabhas are more closely allied to any one tribe of that group than to another. They have their own language (which is fast dying out), and it is not necessary for a Kachari or Garo to become a Rabha on his way to Hinduism. On the whole, therefore, although some Kachari and Garos may have become Rabhas, it seems probable that the Rabhas are in reality a distinct tribe (Grierson, 1995: 357). As mentioned there are no records to tell us regarding the migration and settlement of the Rabhas. Das (1960:48-49) points out that the ancestors of the Rabha tribe migrated from the sub-Himalayan region; north of Tezpur towards the Brahmaputra valley *via* Doangiri to arrive at Bakbua hill near Barpeta. There they rested and later entered Goalpara district. But how far this tradition is genuine and trust worthy no one knows. Hence no detailed account could be traced on the subject of migration of the Rabhas.

There are certain legends prevalent among the Rabhas, an examination of which gives some idea about their route of migration. According to a popular legendary story of the Koch-Rabhas (a Rabha sub-group) the Rabhas migrated from Mongolia through various regions of China *via* North-West Tibet. While others opine that they entered the present Garo Hills crossing the mighty Brahmaputra River. Both the ethnic groups lived side by side for a long period. But after several years due to the fight for supremacy for land the Rabhas were driven out to the plain areas of Assam where they are settled presently. Thus, the traditional stories prevalent among the Rabha and the Garo point to Tibet or the eastern sub-Himalayan region as their ancestral home. Through years of migration and contact with other tribal and non-tribal people the Rabhas have undergone a perceptible transformation. A few sections of the Rabha, who are said to be Hinduized to a great extent, have already lost their traditional customs and dialects. Except for physical features, these groups have lost almost all the traces of a Rabha. But in spite of such social transformation a few groups have preserved their distinctive identity through language, religious practices, cultural expressions, family setting etc.

Economic Engagements of Rabhas

The economy of Rabha is primarily based on agriculture. Throughout the year they sweat it out on the farm lands to make their both ends meet. In order to understand their economic operations we need to observe them closely with regard to their engagement in various activities related to agriculture, tending of various animals, weekly marketing patterns, cottage industry, fishing, food habits and other allied activities from dawn to dusk. Some of the most common variety of rice cultivated by them are *ahu, sali, asra, masri, aijong, bilsa* etc. They not only cultivate rice but also engage themselves in farming of jute, mustard seeds, cotton, sugarcane, maize, pulses, sweet potato and so on. It is observed that very few of them are engaging themselves in trades and other occupations. A few educated Rabhas are engaged in government services, mainly in teaching professions (Field Study, 2012).

Besides agriculture, animal husbandry is also a source of income for the Rabhas. They rear cows, pigs, chickens, goats etc. for household use and for selling. The Rabha men are expert in bamboo crafts, and they also make houses, baskets, fishing traps and other household equipments using bamboo. Fishing is another important economic activity of the Rabha especially during the rainy season. They catch varieties of fishes with the help of fishing traps for household consumption, though some of them also sell a small quantity in the local market. Traditionally rice beer (*Choko*) is a popular and very important item of their food. They offer it also whenever a guest comes to visit their home. They also believe after a hard day's labour rice beer refreshes them. Though there are incidents as a result of excessive drinking their socio-economic condition deteriorated beyond any limit.

Role of Rabha Customary Laws

The general philosophical basis of the concept 'Custom' is that it refers to a set of established patterns of interactive behaviour among humans, which can be objectively verified in a particular social setting, because these behaviours are adopted in everyday routines (Orebech, 2005). 'Law' refers to principles, rules, rights and obligations that govern social interactions and processes.

In North East India, particularly in areas covered by Sixth Schedule of the Constitution, the tribal communities were allowed considerable freedom to operate and develop their traditional institutions through Autonomous District Councils and Regional Councils. The powers of the District Councils include the powers of enacting legislation on customary laws. But while most of the District Councils did not exercise their powers in this direction fully, some faced troubles after they had enacted legislation. These acts of omission and commission indicate that the traditions are not rigid frames of action; there are many cross-currents of interests which are to be mutually accommodated (Burman, 1998:349).

There is a widely held view that the failure to codify customary laws of the tribal people has been a serious impediment to integrated development of the tribal areas. A working group set up by the Reserve Bank of India in July 1976, to study the problems of bank credit in the North East India has mentioned absence of land ownership/land laws, as one of the factors why institutional finance did not flow adequately to the region. In the case of the Rabha in Goalpara district they are guided by customary laws especially with regard to their land and forest produce utilization, their over all development plan, festivals, life cycle ceremonies and other day-to-day life of the people as well (Cfr. Interviews conducted in *Matia-Majerburi* villages, 2011).

Customary laws are integral part of the *Rabha* tribal community, and they consider it as a part of their culture and tradition. They cherish these laws as intrinsic to its identity. But one of the changes that modernization has brought among these tribes is with regards to their legal system. It has resulted in a new identity search among these tribal people because of the feeling that modern trends devalue their culture. The search is expressed, more than anywhere else, in the demand for recognition of their customary laws. Since customary laws are central to the tribal people as it provides the backbone for their culture, they perceive modernization as an effort to impose an alien culture upon them (Kumar, 2005:1).

Among the Rangdani Rabha (one of the most numerous sub-groups of the Rabha) the traditional village council regulates their society. The duties and responsibilities of the village council are confined to the settlement of disputes between the members of the village and to look after the general welfare of the village. Though the council looks after the welfare of women in general, participation of women in the council is still ignored, and men are the sole decision makers of the society. However, the tribal council is gradually modifying the customary laws of the society towards the patrilineal principle and whole society follows the directions of the tribal council even today. The *Tiwa* tribal community traditionally has their own customary laws governing all aspects of their lives, which are administered by organizations and institutions of two categories: secular and non-secular or religious. They have a secular village organization which is headed by the *gaonburha* and assisted by an official called *barika*. The *gaonburha* decides cases (civil and criminal) in a *mel* (traditional assembly of the village arbitrators) and inflicts punishment upon the offenders (Medhi *et al.*, 2006:1-16).

The introduction of the Sixth Schedule in the Constitution was no doubt an important step towards granting autonomy to the tribal people to develop their own genius, but from the very beginning, in Sixth Schedule areas, the District Councils became a bone of contention between State Government and the Councils' authorities. Many limitations have come to light in the process of implementation of the Sixth Schedule which failed to satisfy growing political consciousness of the tribal people.

Consequently, it has affected developmental process in the tribal areas. Customary laws are more suited to needs of the local communities even in the face of rapid changes. This is because customary laws, contrary to popular belief, do not constitute a static legal system but is flexible and adjustable to the changing needs of the times. Therefore, the need to make a serious coordination between the tribal customary laws and laws that govern the State in general is very important when we draw up strategies for the tribal development. Here below we shall see how rubber cultivation has become a major breakthrough among the Rabha of Goalpara district, Assam.

Benefits of Rubber Plantation

In India, rubber was first introduced in Kerala, Tamil Nadu and Karnataka as early as 1902 by the British colonial powers. Since these regions had reached their saturation point in rubber cultivation with very limited scope for further expansion, the Government of India (under Rubber Board) launched rubber development programmes in the North East India (NEI) starting the late 1980s. The rationale for rubber expansion in the NEI was to serve as the effective supplementary income for the tribal communities in the region while meeting the ever-growing domestic demand for natural rubber. Currently, the seven North Eastern states together make up the second largest area planted to rubber in the country at 71,840 ha (11.3%), and produce about four per cent of the total output. Of the total rubber area in the NEI, Tripura accounts for 57 per cent, followed by Assam (25%), Meghalaya (9.5%) and four other states (8%). Thus Tripura, Assam and Meghalaya collectively account for 92 per cent of total rubber area and 96 per cent of rubber production in NEI.

The study uses cross-sectional data collected from 25 rubber smallholders from India's North Eastern state of Assam. The entire sample growers belong to the Rabha (Rangdani) tribal community of Goalpara district who have comparatively small stretches of land both for cultivation of paddy and other cash crops with special reference to rubber. The land use pattern in the study village show that rubber occupies as high as 50 per cent of the total land area in Matia-Majerburi villages, as against 66 per cent in overall Assam. Rice has the second largest area as a single crop, ranging from 15–25 per cent of the low line land. A negligible area of land is used for the cultivation of vegetables, for example brinjal, beans, bitter gourd, pump kin, green gram, etc. which is generally for the home consumption.

However, the labour intensity pattern for the rubber cultivation and caring at regular intervals reveal that majority of farmers use about 10 per cent of the family labour for rubber, 15–20 per cent for agriculture and about 10 per cent for other farming and allied operations. Female work force is higher in agricultural operations and they are also found to be engaged in assisting male members for supplementary works especially related to collecting rubber latex in the lean period of agricultural works. We observed that Rubber Board has come to help the Rabhas especially in the initial years of rubber cultivation, i.e. in the years between 2002-2004. A number of the Rabhas took the benefit of the subsidy schemes and have at present done plantation on 20 to 50 per cent of their total available land, *i.e.* on an average about 5 to 10 acres of land is under rubber plantation among each of the Rabha family under our study.

In the final analysis it is observed that on an average each of the small rubber planters is able to obtain an average 5 kilo dried rubber per day. This is a regular income for the small scale rubber growers. As the tapping is done only on the alternative days the average number of tapping days per month is 15 and the total rubber obtained is more or less 75 kilos which will bring an income of Rs. 8,000 per month. This is a substantial income compared to the small income available from selling of seasonal vegetables, intermittent cash from other labour in the neighbours' field, selling of timber and other irregular and meagre monetary engagements.

Discussion

At present, because of increasing population in tribal areas and contact with people dwelling in plains, who practice unsustainable life style, there are very many threats for the life style of the tribes. The commercial attitude which results in overexploitation of resources on which the sustenance of the tribes was dependent is a major concern, because this is eroding the very resource of the tribes and the unwanted wealth in remote forest areas is bringing in unhealthy attitudes in the tribal areas. In order to prevent this, the traditional items which are to be conserved through protection as they form basic raw material for further crop improvement using the traditional methods. Incentives should also be given to the tribal communities cultivating the traditional food grains and other resources for their sustenance, which are low yielding when compared to high yielding varieties. This is to encourage the tribal people to cultivate the genetically rich, drought resistant and pest tolerant varieties thereby compensating their low yield. Value addition to the traditional rice varieties like *bogma, turia*, and millets can be achieved by means of undertaking bakeries and tying up with commercial business. This is also very much applicable in the case of fruits such as banana, jackfruit, orange, pineapple, mango and lichi among others.

Policy decisions, which might affect the ecological balance of biodiversity, should be taken through prior consultation of the tribal people inhabiting the areas, who may help us with practical suggestions. Otherwise, ultimately the ethnic people are the worst affected in any environmental crisis, as they exist at the bottom line of social strata. Loss of biodiversity results in the loss of cultural diversity, which is the cradle of knowledge on the values of plants. Ignoring the conservation of cultural diversity and the associated traditional ecological knowledge is detrimental for the cause of conservation of biodiversity on which the entire world depends for its survival.

North East India has witnessed lack of development, the tribal land alienation has taken a massive toll on their resources and the magnitude of their unemployment is manifold. The subsistent economy on which they had complete control is now more and more controlled by people who devalue their culture and contribute to impoverishment. What should be our efforts to bring in inclusive policies? Can we proactively respond to the heart beats of the less privileged and marginalized segments of our society? Will we continue to respond to the emerging contemporary challenges of North East India? Can we include others especially the less privileged ones to be a beacon of hope and contribute towards peace and development in North East India? These and other queries ring out loud and clear.

Resource management should become a strategy for any forward looking community. Human resources including people, land, water, forest, minerals and energy resources, are some of the most important ingredients in the life of the people, particularly the tribal communities of a given region (Jain, 1946:7). Many indigenous people except a few are said to be under the grip of a process of impoverishment and extinction most specially because their lands, forest, rivers, mines and all sources of livelihood have almost been taken away in the name of development. As a result, their economic, social and cultural status instead of improving has deteriorated significantly. Resource-rich indigenous people of India are faced with starvation, unemployment, disease, illiteracy and lack of shelter. Market forces are engaged in plundering the rich natural resources of these people. As they dwell amidst hills and forests, over the centuries they have gained precious and vast experience which is reflected in their water harvesting techniques, indigenously developed irrigation channels, construction of cane bridges in hills, and utilization of forest species like floral parts for medicinal purposes. Such invaluable knowledge of theirs needs to be properly documented, and preserved.

Conclusion

While planning is done for a specific community one has to take into account the indigenous ethos of the people considering the diversity and complexity within the local communities. This is to say that while programme for resource development and its utilization is done it should take into consideration the socio-cultural mores of the people under consideration; otherwise the best of the intentions may bring in very little or even adverse impact for a prolonged period of time. It is important to note that communities are far from homogenous and any programme or scheme initiated in the North East India should be tailored to meet the specific needs of the diverse peoples taking adequate care with regard to their present state of over all development perspectives in the region. Resource utilization among the people depends on the availability of the resource yet new resources can often be introduced and adapted within the ecological and cultural parameters of the land and people. This will call for endurance and innovative methods by the economic planners and the indigenous people.

The Rabha like other communities, are severely impacted by poverty and its manifestations, such as low levels of literacy and health care, hunger and malnutrition. They suffer social and political marginalization and remain vulnerable to exploitation. In order to redress this situation and to remove obstacles to their development, a number of programmes may have to be introduced. Certainly the introduction of cash crops for example rubber will prove to be a great step forward. However, it will be important for the tribal people like the Rabha to see that cash crops do not take away the agricultural fields to a phenomenal extent even though this will certainly create an enabling environment for promoting the interests of the Rabha tribe and for harnessing their untapped potential for overall social and economic development. Towards this end, action-oriented programmes and projects are required which specifically address the constraints and opportunities for sustainable livelihood and empowerment of the tribal communities in general and the Rabhas in particular.

REFERENCES

Barua, Keshav Kanta, (1923), *Asamar Athutajatir Uttpattir Bibaran*, Assam, Dhanaraj Gogoi Publication.

Barua, Saniram, (1928), *Assam Buranji*, Mulak man-Citra, Guwahati, T.K. Bandhyapadhyay.

Burman, K.R. (1998), "Changes in the Institution of Family Tribes of North-East and Problem of Codification of Customary Laws". In S. Karotemprel, (Ed.) *The Tribes of North East India,* Shillong, Don Bosco Centre for Indigenous Cultures, pp.349-357.

Das, B.M. (1960), *Ethnic Affinities of the Rabha*, Gauhati University.

Gait, E.A. (1892), *Census of Assam*, 1891, Vol-1, Report

Jose, K., *The Rabhas: Perspectives on their Economy* (unpublished manuscript on the Society and Culture of Rangdani Rabhas of Goalpara, Assam).

Kumar, G.P. (2005). *Legal Implications of Development Induced Displacement in Assam,* Guwahati, North Eastern Social Research Centre, p.1.

Karki. Madhav (2001), Institutional Socio-economic Factors and Enabling Policies for Non-Timber Forest Products-Based Development in North East India. *IFAD Report* No.1145-IN.

Playfair. A (1975). *The Garos* (Reprinted) Gauhati, United Publishers.

Medhi, Birinchi K. and I. Barpujari, (2006). Changing Dynamics of Customary Laws and Traditional Institutions in a Tiwa Village of Assam, *Bull. of Dept. of Anthropology,* Gauhati University, Vol. X.

Mishra, A.K. (2002). 'Integrated Management of Natural Resources of North East India for Sustainable Development in 21st Century'. In B.J. Deb (Ed.) *Development Priorities in North East India.* New Delhi, Concept Publishing Company.

Orebech, Peter, Fred Bosselman, Jes Bjarup, David Callies, Martin Chanock, Hanne Petersen (2005), *The Role of Customary Law in Sustainable Development.* Cambridge University Press.

Rabha, Gabriel (2009), Ethnicity and Cultural Identity of the Rabhas in Assam, Tezpur, Unpublished Manuscript by the author.

Shimray, U.A. (2006), *Tribal Land Alienation in North East India: Laws and Land Relations*, Guwahati, NESRC.

OTHER BIBLIOGRAPHICAL CONSULTATIONS

Deb, B.J. (2002). *Development Priorities in North East India*, Shillong, North East India Council for Social Science Research.

George, K.T., V. Haridasan, and B. Sreekumar (1988), "Role of Government and Structural Changes in Rubber Plantation Industry in India", *Economic and Political Weekly* 23 (48): 158–166.

Grierson, G.A. (1995), Linguistic Survey of India, Vol. III. No. 2.

Kothari, Ashish *et al.*, (eds.) (1998), ***Communities and Conservation: Natural Resource Management in South and Central Asia***, New Delhi, Sage Publications.

Samanta, R.K. (2002), ***India's North East: The Process of Change and Development***, New Delhi, B.R. Publishing Corporation.

9

The Moria Muslims of the Brahmaputra Valley: A Study on Population and Occupational Diversification

P.K. Guha

The characteristics of any population are usually shaped by the geographic, demographic and socio-economic factors. The geographic factors include climate, soil factors, natural resources and transport facilities and all these factors play crucial role in the growth of human population. The demographic factors are dependent more on the socio-economic and cultural factors. The studies in the North East India especially in the Brahmaputra valley, have shown that the geographical factor helped in sustaining various currents of human migration along with its resources (Taher, 1979).

The Brahmaputra Valley extends from the easternmost tip of Upper Brahmaputra Valley near the syntoxial bend of the Eastern Himalayas to the west of Dhubri on the border of Bangladesh and well demarcated by the Eastern Himalayas, Pat Koi and the Naga Hills and the Garo-Khasi-Jaintia and the Mikir Hills. The average level of the valley ranges from 130 m. in the east to 30 m. in the west. The Brahmaputra Valley is wide in Upper Assam and in Lower Assam but it is narrow at Gauhati because at Gauhati the river flows close to the granite hillocks of Shillong plateau. In the north, innumerable tributaries run down from Arunachal Pradesh and the Bhutan Himalayas.

Three major social groups are found among the Muslim groups in the Brahmaputra Valley. They are the Assamese Muslims, the immigrant peasant Muslims from East Bengal and a small group of Urdu speaking Muslims living in the towns and service centres engaged in trade and commerce. The Assamese Muslims are further divided into the Syads, the Sheikhs and the Morias.

The present study discusses on the population and occupational diversification of the Moria Muslims of the Brahmaputra Valley of Assam who earlier engaged in brazier works but now a majority of them are engaged in other occupations like business and services. A discussion has been made on economic variables as working force and occupational characteristics which are determined by the nature and a number of socio-cultural factors.

The Moria Muslims

It is assumed that the word 'Moria' has originated from the beating *(mara)* of hot brass metal for making utensils. Another view is that, the word 'Moria' originated from the term Marshiya or Murjiiay. Murjiiay was the name of a sect of the Muslim, which came to be first known in the Umayyad age (A.H. 40) in 661 A.D. (Saikia,1978). The group came as invaders and later started their carrier as braziers. They are categorized as Other Backward classes.

It may be mentioned that, though they had started their livelihood as braziers but after. the Independence their original profession has been given up due to the implementation of stainless steel, plastic etc. At present only 17.59 per cent workers of them are engaged in brass industry and the rest of the workers are engaged in other occupational activities.

The Moria Muslim villages are both uni-ethnic and multi-ethnic. The villages are surrounded by the Assamese Hindu caste groups like the Brahmin, Kalita, Keot and others and the tribes like the Koch, Mishing and others. The surrounding communities keep harmony with the Moria Muslims which is reflected in their behaviour with their fellow villagers.

The presence of different castes and tribes in the neighbourhood of the Moria Muslims in and around the village, shows a relationship of reciprocity and co-operation among the communities. It has also been observed that other communities usually invite the Moria Muslim at the time of socio-religious rituals and festivals, and this develops a cordial and friendly relation among them. These social and economic relationships have developed between the Moria Muslims and other communities through a process of interaction.

The Moria Muslim follow Islam by religion. They perform all the Islamic religious functions like Id-Ul-Fitre, Id-Uj-Zuha, Muhharam, Bakrid etc. But at the same time they also go to the pandal of Durga-puja to see the idol. In some villages (Pithakhowa, Kakojan, Becheria etc.) the executive members of the Durga-puja committee are also selected from this community. They give subscription for the Durga—puja. In

Kalipuja also they fire crackers. For this reason the Tablique party- an Islamic missionary people preaches Islam to the Morias. The Tabliques do not take food in the Moria houses. It may be mentioned that among the Morias not many observe the *Namaz*. So now Moulovis and other groups of the Muslims are trying to raise the attendance in Moria *Jamat* (mosque) at the time of *Namaz*.

Social History

The history of the Moria Muslims is dated back to the second Mohammedan invasion in 1532 A.D where the Ahoms defeated the Mohammedans. The present Moria Muslims of the Brahmaputra Valley are the descendants of the captives during the battle. This was the second invasion when a Muslim commander of Bengal named Turbak invaded the Ahom territory with guns and cannon and other fire weapons and large battery of artillery. Even then the Ahoms defeated the Muslim invaders in a series of engagements. The final defeat of the Muslims took place in a battle near the river Bharali (Gait, 1926; Barua, 1966; Acharyya 1966; Bandopadhyaya, 1982).

Nine hundred Muslim invaders were taken in prisoners by the Ahom King during this war and were settled in different parts of the Brahmaputra Valley. According to a traditional legend the Ahom Kings first ordered them to cut grass for the king's elephants, but they were found unfit for this work. They were then employed as cultivators, but it appeared they were absolutely ignorant about cultivation. It is saying that one of the Ahom Kings commented, '*naha marai chaha dhan pale*' (Nine hundred Morias had grown only six hundred paddy grains). Next they were ordered to construct houses but they also failed to do this work. After a year, the disgusted Ahom King then released the prisoners so that they could earn their livelihood in whatever way possible for themselves without being a burden on the royal exchequer. Some of the mercenaries had knowledge of welding of brass metal as they had used guns which they repaired themselves. Hence after the release, some of the Muslim mercenaries began the brass metal work as an occupation and settled down in the Brahmaputra Valley.

It may be mentioned that, since the Moria Muslims came as invaders in Assam, they did not bring any females with them. The Ahom King decided to offer them low caste Hindu women.

From the beginning of the settlement of the Moria Muslims in this valley they were assimilated with the Assamese Hindu society. Very little information can be gathered about the Moria Muslims during the British period. W.W. Hunter in his book, '*A Statistical Account of Assam*' mentioned that the braziers formed a distinct and separate community and used to depend entirely upon their trade for their livelihood. The brass workers were paid at the rate of six pence per pound of metal worked up. The Marwari traders used to supply metal to the manufacturer and used to sell the finished utensils to the traders (Hunter, 1879).

Their occupation was not related to the notion of pollution as the brass utensils produced by them were used in the 'Namghars'. In social relationship also, the Syads and Sheikhs try to keep away from the Morias. Due to the social distance maintained by these groups, the Moria Muslims have become an endogamous group (Saifun Nessa, 1984).

Distribution

The Moria populations are distributed in nine districts of the valley—north-west and southern part of Dibrugarh district, southern part of Sibsagar district, central and eastern parts of Jorhat district, Golaghat town of Golaghat dstrict, Dhing and Koliabor areas of Nowgong district, Hajo Malara Islampatti and Uzanbazar of the city of Guwahati of Kamrup district, Mongoldai town of Darrang district, Pithakhowa and Bakula areas of Sonitpur district, Dhakuakhana, Lilabari and North-Lakhimpur town of Lakhimpur district. It has been observed that the Morias prefer to settle near the urban areas to avail of the market facilities for purchasing the raw materials and also for selling out the finished products.

In the village level again, there is a variation in the concentration of the Moria Muslim population. From the field survey, it has been observed that they are distributed only in fifty two villages in the Brahmaputra Valley. The highest concentration is found in Chawlkhowa (10.55 per cent of the total Moria population) village in Dibrugarh District of Upper Brahmaputra Valley (Table 9.1). This village is situated at twelve kilometres east of Dibrugarh town and well connected by regular bus and railways services. A large proportion of this village population is engaged in trade and commerce and services. Of the total number of working population of this village, 29.08 per cent people are engaged in trade and commercial activities and 23.64 per cent working people are engaged in service in railway, court, electricity board, school teacher and private farm in Dibrugarh town.

An analysis of the rural-urban composition of the Moria Muslim is present in Table 9.2. From the calculation it is revealed that 32.06 per cent of the Moria populations of the Brahmaputra Valley live in the urban area as against 4.28 per cent of the Brahmaputra Valley (according to

Table 9.1: Village-wise Total Moria population with Percentage (Total Population 23686)

Name of the district	*Name of the village*	*Total Population*	*Percentage of population*
Kamrup	Hajo Islampatti	783	3.31
	Malara Islampati	482	2.04
	Uzanbazar	635	2.68
Darrang	Vevarghat	632	2.67
Sonitpur	Pithakhowa	1600	6.76
	Gavorugaon	50	0.21
	Niraiati	150	0.63
	Becheria	1210	5.11
	Bakula	815	3.44
Lakhimpur	Shilabari Balijan	490	2.07
	Balijan Tengabari	81	0.34
	Dhekial	384	1.62
	Nawkari	374	1.58
	Lilabari	382	1.61
	Dhokuakhana	399	1.69
Dibrugarh	Laluka	582	2.46
	Chowlkhowa	2500	10.55
	Sadia	446	1.88
	Bakul	320	1.35
	Margherita	110	0.46
Sibsagar	Demoumukh	581	2.45
	Mothadang	341	1.44
	Bagal	382	1.61
	Bambari	20	0.08
Sibsagar	Dopdar	16	0.07
	Panidihing	297	1.25
	Khatopahar	20	0.08
	Amguri	360	1.52
	Gauri Sagar	392	1.66
	Nazira	398	1.68
	Geleki	375	1.58
Jorhat	Veleuguri	80	0.34
	Mudoijan	126	0.53
	Jhanji	94	0.40
	Koliapani	200	0.84
	Badulipukhuri	256	1.08
	Neematighat	221	0.93
Jorhat	Tamulishika	350	1.48
	Fatigasiga	244	1.03
	Naobaisya	286	1.21
	Kakojan	753	3.18
	Gakhirkhowa	209	0.88
	Boloma	56	0.24

(*Contd.*)

Name of the district	Name of the village	Total Population	Percentage of population
Golaghats	Kacharihat	500	2.11
	Kamarbandha	180	0.76
	Moinapar	80	0.34
	Islampatti	800	3.38
Nowgong	Langi	287	1.21
	Jayantipur	925	3.91
	Huntergaon	916	3.87
	Baligaon	801	3.38
	Bilotia	715	3.02

Source: Based on Field Survey, 1988.
(Morias are included in the Census after 1911 as Assamese Muslims).

Table 9.2: Percentage of Rural-Urban Composition of the Moria Population of the Brahmaputra Valley, the Muslims of the Brahmaputra Valley and India.

Areas		Moria	Muslims
Brahmaputra Valley 1988	T	23686	
	R	16093 (67.94 P.C.)	
	U	7593(32.06 P.C)	
Brahmaputra Valley 1971	T		2903153
	R		2778771(95.72 P.C)
	U		124382(4.28 P.C.)
India	T		75512439
1981	R		49834389(65.99 P.C)
	U		25678050(34.01 P.C)

Source: (i) Based on Field Survey, 1988.
(ii) Census of India, 1971, Series-3.
Assam Part II-c (i), Social and Cultural Tables. A.K. Saikia. pp. 4-5.
(iii) Census of India, 1981.
Population gives an idea of the problem.

1971 Census) and India's 34.01 per cent of the total Muslim population (according to 1981 Census). From the analysis it is observed that the Moria population is more urbanised than the other Muslim population of the Brahmaputra Valley.

Density of the Moria Population

The census record of the Moria population between 1872 to 1911 has been very irregular. In the Census of 1872 they were counted excluding those who did not enumerate themselves in the group, so this census does not give the accurate number of people. In the census of 1881 they were not returned as a separate class, which was perhaps due to some measure of the progress they have made towards the orthodox Mohammedans (Census 1881: 101). Moreover, the separate figures for males and females were not shown in the census.

By 1891, the density of the Moria population of this Valley was 0.03 per km^2. According to this census, the districtwise density calculated at Kamrup district was 0.01 per km^2, Nowgong district 0.10 per km^2, Sibsagar district 0.07 per km^2, Lakhimpur district 0.006 per km^2 and Darrang district 0.03 per km^2.

In 1901 census the Moria population recorded a fall from the previous census. As a result the density of the population has also been decreased. The population had considerably fallen off, as they were affected by the disease Kala-azar (Census 1901). According to this census the density of the Moria population was 0.02 per km^2. The districtwise population figures showed a decrease in population density. The density of the Moria population became 0.01 per km^2 in Kamrup district, 0.002 per km^2 in Nowgong district, 0.07 per km^2 in Sibsagar district, 0.02 per km^2 in Lakhimpur district and 0.03 per km^2 in Darrang district (Table 9.3).

Table 9.3: Density of Moria Muslim Population (1891-1911)

Districts		*1891*	*1901*	*1911*
Goalpara	P	—	—	—
	D	—	—	—
Kamrup	P	118	135	1
	D	0.01	0.01	0.001
Nowgong	P	585	13	15
	D	0.10	0.002	0.002
Sibsagar	P	621	611	1040
	D	0.07	0.07	0.12
Lakhimpur	P	88	315	71
	D	0.006	0.02	0.005
Darrang	P	265	161	455
	D	0.03	0.03	0.05
Brahmaputra	P	1677	1235	1582
Valley	D	0.03	0.02	0.03

P = Population D = Density

Source: (i) Census of Assam 1901.
B.C. Allen. Vol. I, Delhi- 1902, pp. 29-30.
(ii) Census of India 1911 Vol.III, Part-I Report J.M.C. Swiney, Shillong 1912.

According to 1911 census the density of the Moria population had slightly increased. It became 0.03 per km^2 in the Brahmaputra Valley. The highest density of population is found in Sibsagar district and it was 0.12 per km^2 (Table 9.3), followed by Darrang district (0.05 per km^2). This increase of population in these two districts was due to migration from Kamrup and Lakhimpur districts, where Kala-azar badly affected the people. After the 1911 Census, the Moria population was merged with the Assamese Muslim population. It has already been mentioned earlier that the separate figures of the Moria Muslim population are not available since 1921.

The detailed field survey on the Moria population in 1988 showed an increase of 0.42 density per km^2 density in the Brahmaputra Valley. The highest density is found in Sibsagar district and it is 1.23 per km^2 followed by Jorhat district (1.01 per km^2) (Table 9.4). In the previous census the highest density found in Sibsagar district. This is due to the fact that they first settled in this district in large number in the historical time from where they migrated to other districts.

Table 9.4: Density of Moria Muslim Population 1988

Districts	Area (in Sq. Km.)	Population	Density
Kamrup	4634.1	1900	0.41
Darrang	3511.1	632	0.18
Sonitpur	5239.7	3825	0.73
Lakhimpur	2318.7	2110	0.91
Dibrugarh	7067.9	3598	0.56
Sibsagar	2587.0	3182	1.23
Jorhat	2846.5	2875	1.01
Golaghat	3545.5	1560	0.44
Nowgong	5693.7	3644	0.64
Brahmaputra Valley	56395.2	23686	0.42

Note: Calculation done on the basis of the area of new districts.

Source: Based on field survey, 1988.

Growth

The growth of the Moria population in any particular place is not regular. According to the 1891 Census, the total Moria population was 1677. But during the time 1891 – 1901 the variation of population had decreased to 26.36 per cent (Table 9.5). This is due to the severe type of Kala-azar and fever (Census 1901: 19). From the districtwise census it has been observed that in Nowgong district the population had sharply fallen with a decrease of 97.78 per cent. This is due to Kala-azar and fever. Record shows that the total death toll rise to 93,824 in Nowgong district due to fever and Kala-azar (Census 1901). The highest growth is found in the Lakhimpur district. The growth rate increases to 257.95 per cent and it is due to migration from other district as this district was free from disease. During the next decade (1901-1911) the population growth increased to 28.09 per cent. Districtwise population shows the highest growth rate in Darrang district (182.61%). This is due to migration from other districts.

Table 9.5: Growth of Moria Population

Name of the districts	*1891 total population*	*1901 total population*	*Decade Variation*	*Percentage of growth*	*1901 total population*	*1911 total population*	*Decade Variation*	*P.C. of growth*
Goalpara	—	—	—	—	—	—	—	—
Kamrup	118	135	+17	+14.41	135	1	–134	–99.26
Nowgong	585	13	–572	–97.78	13	15	+2	+15.38
Sibsagar	621	611	–10	–1.61	611	1040	+429	+70.21
Lakhimpur	88	315	+227	+257.95	315	71	–244	–77.46
Darrang	265	161	-104	–39.25	161	455	+294	+182.61
1891-1911 over all growth	1677	1235	-442	–26.36	1235	1582	+347	+28.09

Source: (i) Census of Assam 1901, B.C. Allen, pp. 29-30.
(ii) Census of India 1911, Vol. III Part-I Report.

During the period (1911-1988) the Moria population showed high rate of growth of 1397.22 per cent. The highest growth rate has been recorded in Kamrup district (189900.00%) (Table 9.6). The highest growth

Table 9.6: Growth of Moria Population, 1911-1988

Name of the Districts	*1911 Total Population*	*1988 Total Population*		*Variation*	*Percentage of Growth*
Kamrup	1	1900		+1899	+189900.00
*Darrang	455	632	=4457	+4002	+879.56
Sonitpur		3825			
*Sibsagar	1040	3182	=7617	+6577	+632.40
Jorhat		2875			
Golaghat	–	1560		–	–
*Lakhimpur	71	2110	=6068	+5997	+8446.48
Dibrugarh		3958			
Nowgong	15	3644		+3629	+24193.33
1911-1988 Overall growth	1582	23686		+22104	+1397.22

* Sonitpur district was created as a separate district from Old Darrang district. Jorhat, Golaghat districts were created from Old Sibsagar district and Dibrugarh also created a new district from Old Lakhimpur district.

Source: (i) Census of India 1911, Vol. III.
(ii) Based on Field Survey, 1988.

rate is found in this district due to the location of Guwahati, the capital of Assam as it gave opportunities to avail facilities for trade and commercial activities, petty jobs etc.

On the basis of the sampled data the classification of age-sex composition has been done and the different groups have been shown in Table 9.8. From the sample survey the entire population has been classified into thirteen age groups for males and females. The age groups are 0-4, 5-9, 10-14, 15-19, 20-24, 25-29, 30-34, 35-39, 40-44, 45-49, 50-54, 55-59, 60+. The population distribution in each age group shows that the females in the age group of 15-29 years outnumber the males. But in other age groups the position is reverse. The causes of high percentage of females show the high birth rate of female child at least in the surveyed villages.

Table 9.7: Age-Sex Structure (Sample Population) 1988

Age group	*Population*	*P.c.*	*Male P.c.*	*Female P.c.*
0-4	648	13.70	7.29	6.41
5-9	686	14.50	7.57	6.93
10-14	603	12.75	7.15	5.60
15-19	437	9.24	4.42	4.82
20-24	493	10.42	4.92	5.50
25-29	442	9.35	4.40	4.95
30-34	322	6.81	4.08	2.73
35-39	279	5.90	3.36	2.54
40-44	187	3.95	2.11	1.84
45-49	185	3.91	2.24	1.67
50-54	130	2.75	1.48	1.27
55-59	106	2.24	1.37	0.87
60+	212	4.48	2.32	2.16
Total	4730	100.00	52.71	47.29

There is a gradual decrease of population beyond the age of 35 years, which shows low mortality among the adult population due to the availability of medical and other amenities. The general longevity of the people is still low and only 4.48 per cent of them can hope to survive upto 60 years of age.

Dependency ratio

The dependency ratio which has been shown in Table 9.8, is found to be 76.89 per cent, of which 79.37 per cent is found in rural areas and 71.05 per cent in urban areas. From the calculation it is revealed that the urban dependency ratio is lower than rural dependency ratio. In the rural areas due to non-availability of sufficient agricultural land, the children of 0-14 years age group do not get jobs in the agricultural field and also in rural areas there is no scope of getting petty jobs for children. In the urban areas, the children of lower age group get jobs in small factories, P.W.D., big shops etc.

Table 9.8: Dependency Ratio of the Moria Muslims (Sample Survey) 1988

Name of the village	*Percentage of population*			*Dependency ratio*
	Upto 14 years	*(15-64) years*	*65+ years*	
Hajo	38.19	60.53	1.28	65.19
Malara (Islampur)	40.87	56.85	2.28	75.91
Vevarghat	29.43	63.61	6.96	57.21
Jayantipur	43.78	54.16	2.06	84.63
Langi	44.25	55.40	0.35	80.50
Naobaisya	39.51	57.34	3.15	74.39
Kakojan	48.07	49.94	1.99	100.27
Laluka	42.61	55.67	1.72	79.63

Source: Total Dependency ratio = 76.89 per cent; Rural Dependency ratio = 79.37 per cent; Urban Dependency ratio = 71.05 per cent. Source : Based on fieldwork, 1988.

Of the above eight sampled villages, the highest dependency ratio is found in Kakojan village, and it is found to be 100.27 per cent. This is due to the fact that 48.07 per cent of the total population are found in the 0-14 years age group and 1.99 per cent people are found in the age group of 65+ years. Both these groups are assumed to be non-workers. But 49.94 per cent people are found in the age-group of 15-64 years, which is mainly the worker group. So, in this village 49.94 per cent people have to feed 50.06 per cent non-workers.

Marital Status

The marital status has been calculated from the eight-sampled village study. Table 9.9 shows that 39.41 per cent are married, of which 37.81 per cent are males and 41.49 per cent are females. The Morias do not prefer early marriage due to their economic backwardness and also due to the influence of Assamese Hindu culture. This may be supported by the fact that the percentage of married males and females under nineteen years are 0.83 and 11.58 respectively. But above twenty years the percentage of married males and females are found to be 99.17 and 88.42 respectively, which show their disinclination to an early marriage.

The percentage of widows is found to be 3.47 which is very low due to prevalence of widow marriage among them. About 0.27 per cent of divorce cases are found in this society of which 0.04 per cent of males and 0.54 per cent of females which are negligible and rarely seen in the community. This is also due to the poor economic condition and the influence of Assamese Hindu culture. The divorce cases are rare due to the inability of returning the 'Denmehar' by the husband, which is fixed at the time of marriage. Moreover, in the Assamese Hindu society a divorce case rarely happens, so this might have also influenced their society.

Table 9.9: Marital Status of Moria Muslims, Villagewise, 1988 (Sample Survey)

Name of the village	*Married*		*Unmarried*		*Widow*	*Divorce*	
	M	*F*	*M*	*F*		*M*	*F*
Hajo	168	166	242	23	–	–	03
	(40.98)	(44.50)	(59.02)	(6.17)			(0.80)
Kakojan	144	139	260	194	15	01	–
	(35.56)	(39.94)	(64.19)	(55.75)	(4.31)	(0.25)	
Jayantipur	208	204	274	201	33	–	05
	(43.15)	(46.05)	(56.85)	(45.37)	(7.45)		(1.13)
Naobaisya	51	48	110	65	11	–	01
	(31.68)	(38.40)	(68.32)	(52.00)	(8.8)		(0.8)
Vevarghat (Islampur)	113	112	225	154	27	–	01
	(33.43)	(38.10)	(66.57)	(52.38)	(9.18)		(0.34)
Langi	62	61	86	72	06	–	–
	(41.89)	(43.88)	(58.11)	(51.80)	(4.32)		
Malara	92	94	143	120	31	–	02
	(39.15)	(38.06)	(60.85)	(48.58)	(12.55)		(0.81)
Laluka	105	97	210	152	18	–	–
	(33.33)	(36.33)	(66.67)	(56.93)	(6.74)		
Total	(37.81)	(41.19)	(62.15)	(50.94)	(7.33)	(0.04)	(0.54)
Grand Total	39.41		56.85		3.47	0.27	

Note: The figures within parentheses indicate percentage.

Source: Data collected from the field survey, 1988.

Villagewise analysis provides more insight into the problem. The percentage of married couples is found to be the highest in Jayantipur village of Nowgong district (total 22.10 per cent of which 43.15 per cent males and 46.05 per cent females) and the lowest is found in Naobaisya village of Jorhat district (total 5.31 of which 31.68 per cent males and 38.40 per cent females).

The practice of late marriage is also in existence. At present rich boys and girls do not prefer to get married early due to their changed outlook. The parents are also against early marriage which may be due to the influence of the Assamese Hindu society. Polygyny is allowed by the Mohammedan law, but it is not seen in this society. It may be the influence of the Assamese Hindu society.

Child-Women Ratio

The data on child women ratio have been collected from the eight sampled villages, and have been shown in Table 9.10. The child women ratio has been found to be 612.48 per thousand, of which rural child women ratio is 612.82 per thousand and urban child women ratio is 611.65 per thousand. The rural and urban child women ratio is almost equal.

The highest child women ratio (797.39 per thousand) is found in Kakojan village. This is due to the higher number of children (18.83%) in 0-4 years age group, than the number of mothers. It shows the high birth rate in this village. The lowest child women ratio (307.19 per thousand) is found in Vevarghat village. This is due to the lesser number of children (7.25 per thousand) in the 0-4 years of age group.

Table 9.10: Villagewise Child Women ratio of Moria Muslims 1988

Name of the village	*Children aged (0-4 years)*	*Women aged (15-44 years)*	*Child women ratio Per 1000*
Hajo	127 (19.60)	200 (18.90)	635
Malara Islampatti	81 (12.5)	112 (10.59)	723.21
Vevarghat Islampatti	47 (7.25)	153 (14.46)	307.19
Jaintipur	130 (20.06)	208 (19.66)	625
Langi	50 (7.72)	67 (6.33)	746.27
Naobaisya	29 (4.48)	56 (5.29)	517.86
Kakojan	122 (18.83)	153 (14.46)	797.39
Laluka	62 (9.57)	109 (10.30)	568.81
Total	648	1058	612.48

Note: The figure in the parentheses indicates the percentage.

Source: Based Sample Survey, 1988.

Fertility Rate

The fertility rate of the Moria population collected from sampled villages is found to be 119.09 per thousand of which 109.48 per thousand in rural areas and 142.39 per thousand in urban areas (Table 9.11). From the data, it seems that the fertility wastage is less in the urban areas than in the rural areas due to the better medical facilities in the urban areas. In the rural areas malnutrition, low standard of living, lack of hygienic sense etc. are responsible for high fertility wastage.

The villagewise general fertility rate provides more insight into the problem. The highest general fertility rate is found in Langi (208.96 per thousand) village of Nawgong district and the lowest is found in Vevarghat (Islampur) village (39.22 per thousand) in Darrang district. The higher rate is found in Langi village due to non-practice of birth control methods offered by the Family Planning Department. The location of this village which is about thirty two kilometres away from Nawgong town makes it impossible for the villagers to avail the medical facilities to control the general fertility rate. On the other, Islampur village is situated one kilometre away from Mangaldoi town of Darrang district, from where the people can get the medical facilities very easily (Table 9.11).

Table 9.11: Fertility Rate of the Moria Muslims (Villagewise) 1988

Name of the village	*No. of birth in a year*	*Women aged (15-44) years*	*General fertility rate per 1000*
Hajo	31	200	155.00
Malara	11	112	98.21
Vevarghat	06	153	39.22
Jayantipur	26	208	125.00
Langi	14	67	208.96
Naobaisya	03	56	53.57
Kakojan	22	153	143.79
Laluka	13	109	119.27
Total	126	1058	119.09

Source: Data collected from the fieldwork, 1988.

Birth Rate and Death Rate

The birth rate per thousand of the Moria Muslim population of the Brahmaputra Valley (26.64) is found to be significantly lower than that of the general population for the state (31). It is due to the acceptance of the birth control methods and also due to their close contact with the urban people. The rural birth rate per thousand is (24.37) is lower than the urban birth rate (32.23) per thousand. It is due to high fertility wastage in the rural area due to the non-availability of proper medical facility at the proper time, malnutrition and lack of hygienic sense (Table 9.12).

The villagewise analysis reveals that the birth rate is highest in Langi village (48.78) due to the availability of proper medical facilities in and around the village and the good transport facility which connects Nowgong town and Tejpur where the proper medical facilities are available.

Further, the death rate per thousand of the Moria Muslim population (11.62) is slightly lower than that of the state (12.5) for general population because of the availability of medical facilities due to more urbanisation. Among the villages, the highest death rate is found at Vevar Ghat (12.65), followed by Malara Islampatti (12.45). It is due to the bad communication system with urban areas, non-availability of proper medical facilities and poor economic condition (Table 9.12).

Table 9.12: Birth and Death Rate of the Moria Muslim Population, 1988 (Sample Survey)

Name of the villages	*Total population*	*Total No. of birth*	*Birth rate per 1000 of population*	*Total No. of deaths*	*Death rate per 1000 of population*
Hajo Islampatti	783	31	39.59	09	11.49
Malara Islampatti	482	11	22.82	06	12.45
Vevar Ghat	632	06	9.49	08	12.65
Laluka	582	13	22.34	06	10.31
Langi	287	14	48.78	03	10.45
Naobaisya	286	03	10.49	03	10.49
Jayantipur	925	26	28.11	11	11.89
Kakojan	753	22	29.22	09	11.95
Total	4730	126	26.64	55	11.62

Note: Rural birth rate is 24.37 and urban birth rate is 32.23. Rural death rate is 11.89 and urban death rate is 10.98.

Source: Based on field survey, 1988.

Types of Family

The field data on type and size of the family collected from the sampled villages, show that the Moria families have members varying from 1 to 20 persons with an average of 6 persons per family. From Table 9.13 it is revealed that 68.67 per cent families are of nuclear type, 13.05 per cent families are of vertically extended type, 8.88 per cent and 9.4 per cent families have been categorised under horizontally extended and broken types of families respectively. The nuclear type of families consists of parents and children. The joint families have been divided into two-vertical extended families constituted of parents, sons, daughter-in-laws and grandchildren and the horizontal extended families formed by brothers, their wives and children who live in the same house using the same kitchen. The broken families are headed either by a widow or by a widower along with their minor children (Table 9.13).

The Jayantipur village in Nowgong district is the most populated village among the sample villages with 146 families. It is to be found that 63.01 per cent families are of nuclear types. The size of the nuclear families varies between 2 to 8 persons. The joint families are less in number, and it is calculated to be only 28.76 per cent (15.75% vertically extended, 13.01 per cent horizontally extended). The average size of the family is 6 persons. The largest size is of 20 persons.

At Hajo Islampatti village of Kamrup district there are 141 households having an average family size of 5 persons. In this village 70.21 per cent families are of nuclear types. The size varies from 2 to 8 persons per family. Only 20.57 per cent joint families are found including both vertically and horizontally extended families. The largest family size is of 18 persons and most of the families fall within the range between 4 to 6 members per family.

Table 9.13: Types of Family (in percentage)

Name of the village	*Nuclear family*	*Vertical extended family*	*Horizontal extended family*	*Broken*	*Total No. of family*
Hajo Islampatti	70.21	17.02	3.55	9.22	141
Malara Islampatti	78.49	7.53	3.23	10.75	93
Vevar Ghat	50.00	15.48	28.57	5.95	84
Laluka	72.82	4.35	4.35	18.48	92
Langi	84.75	3.39	5.08	6.78	59
Naobaisya	77.78	5.56	1.85	14.81	54
Jayantipur	63.01	15.75	13.01	8.22	146
Kakojan	60.83	24.74	11.34	3.09	97
Total	68.57	13.05	8.88	9.4	766

Source: Field Survey, 1988

In Malara Islampatti there are 93 families have an average of 5 persons in each household. The largest family size of is 11 and the lowest size is of 2 members. In this village 78.49 per cent families are nuclear families and the percentage of joint families is only 10.76 including both vertical and horizontal types.

In Vevarghat there are only 84 families having an average of 7 members per family. Largest family size is of 20 persons. In this village the nuclear type of family are 50.00 per cent and the percentage of the joint families, 44.05 per cent.

Laluka village of Dibrugarh district have a total number of 92 families and average number of members per family is 6 persons. The largest family size is of 17 persons. Most of the families are found within the range between 4-6 members. Here 72.82 per cent families are of the nuclear types.

In Langi village there are altogether 59 households having 4 persons per household. The largest family size is of 17 members and the smallest family size is of one member. In this village that 84.75 per cent families are of the nuclear type.

Naobaisya has only 54 families having an average of 5 persons per family. The largest family is of 10 persons, and the smallest is of one member. The dominance of the nuclear type of family is also seen here (77.78%).

Kakojan village has 97 numbers of families with an average of 7 persons per family. The largest family size is of 26 persons and the smallest is of 3 persons. This village has 60.83 per cent families as nuclear type (Table 9.13).

Among the Moria that the joint family system is gradually breaking down into nuclear type. It is because the sons have started staying separately from their parents after getting married and the married brothers also have separated due to shortage of living space, family dispute over properties and other matters.

Literacy

Of all the aspects of population attributes, literacy is the best indication of the people's socio-economic development. The trends of literacy are indicative of the pace at which a particular society is getting transformed (Chandana, 1986).

Literacy among the Moria Muslims has been calculated on the basis of the sampled village survey (Table 9.14). On the basis of the data from eight sampled villages, it is found that the literacy of the Moria Muslims is quite high (64.48%). The high literacy percentage is due to the fact that they are not cultivators and send their children for education. The male literacy rate is 72.29 per cent and female literacy is 55.77 per cent (Table 9.18). It is mainly due to the fact that the guardians are consciousness about education. But the strength of rural literacy (72.20%) is higher than that of the urban literacy (27.80%). It is because of easy availability of jobs in urban area where guardians send their children for earning money, though in the urban areas educational facilities are more. In rural areas the higher literacy rate is due to the non-availability of jobs and all the villages have at least one primary school where the guardians can send their children for education. The percentage of literacy up to primary level is 53.44 per cent. The rate of literacy upto VI to VIII level is 25.54 per cent. Percentage of literacy upto IX to X level is 12.75 per cent. The literacy rate beyond Matric level is significantly low.

From the above discussion it is observed that the higher education is significantly very low among the Moria Muslims as the facilities for higher education is not available in nearby area. Due to economic backwardness most of them go for earning a livelihood at an early age.

Table 9.14: Spatial Distribution of Rural and Urban Literacy, 1988 (Sample Survey)

	T	*M*	*F*
Total	3050 (64.48)	1803 (72.29)	1247 (55.77)
Rural	2202 (72.20)	1313 (72.82)	889 (53.45)
Urban	848 (27.80)	490 (27.18)	358 (28.71)

Note: The figure in the parentheses indicate the percentage.
Source: Based on field survey, 1988.

Marital Relationship with other Communities

The Morias marry among themselves for which Irshad Ali (1974) calls them as kin-community. Ali writes that socio-economic background and network of kinship here helped to create a sense of solidarity among the Morias, so there is a possibility of both hypogamy and hypergamy.

From Table 9.15 it is observed that 88.18 per cent marriages have been slolemnized within the community. 10.86 per cent marriages are performed with the Garia Muslims, 0.21 per cent marriages are performed with the Assamese Hindus, 0.11 per cent with the Bengali Muslims, 0.21 per cent with the Christians, 0.32 per cent with the Bengali Hindus and 0.11 per cent with the tribes. At present the tendency to establish marital relationships with other communities is very slowly increasing. This is due to the occupational diversification and close linkage with communities (Table 9.15).

Marriage Distance

It has been observed that the maximum number of marriages are solemnised within the village. This is due to the poor economic condition and due to communication difficulties. Within the region they have good contact but contact is less with the distant villages. It has also been observed that the marriages are not performed with the villages of Upper Assam and with the villages of Lower Assam because of their inability to spend money on transport. It has also been found that before 1974, they did not have any idea about their concentration and the total number of villages of their own community. For the first time the Moria Muslims had a community conference of their own in Jayantipur village of Nowgong district on 27th January, 1974. From this conference onwards, communication among the Moria Muslims living in districts started. Before that the marriages were confined within the districts. But at present though marriages between the families living in far away villages have increased but the percentage is quite low as it is a recent phenomenon, but the attitude of the people towards distant-marriages is gradually changing (Table 9.16) day by day.

Table 9.15: Marital Relationship with Other communities (in percentage) 1988

Name of the village	*Moria Muslims*	*Garia Muslims*	*Assamese Hindus*	*Bengali Muslims*	*Christian*	*Bengali Hindus*	*Tribe*
Hajo	84.94	15.06	-	-	-	-	-
Vevarghat	78.07	18.42	-	-	-	2.63	0.88
Malara	80.51	16.95	-	0.85	1.69	-	-
Langi	93.44	6.56	-	-	-	-	-
Jayantipur	99.01	0.99	-	-	-	-	-
Naobaisya	87.5	12.5	-	-	-	-	-
Kakojan	91.44	7.14	1.42	-	-	-	-
Laluka	84.69	15.31	-	-	-	-	-
Total	88.18	10.86	0.21	0.11	0.21	0.32	0.11

Source: Based on Sample Survey, 1988.

Occupational Structure

The occupational composition of a group of population is always influenced by economic, demographic and social factors. The size of the labour force, its distribution into various occupations, sexwise participation in different economic activities and the difference in participation rates by age literacy and residence are fair indices of physical resource base, the system of social organisation and the nature of economy prevailing in a region (Chanana, 1980).

It is found that the percentage of the Moria Muslim workers (26.09) is less in comparison with that of the state (28.35) for the total general population (Table 9.18). But at present it is observed from Table 9.17 that out of the total workers 48.06 per cent of population are engaged in trade and commerce, followed by brass industry (17.59%), service (15.96%), transport and communication (10.05%), daily wage labour (5.75%), and agriculture (2.59%) for their livelihood.

Table 9.16: Marriage Distance in Kilometres and in Percentage (including total number of marriage)

Name of the village	*Inside the village*	*Distance in Km*						*Total number of marriage*
		1 to 10	*11 to 20*	*21 to 30*	*31 to 40*	*41 to 50*	*50 +*	
Hajo	105 (63.25)	03 (1.81)	22 (13.26)	24 (14.46)	09 (5.42)	01 (0.60)	02 (1.20)	166
Malara	71 (60.17)	10 (8.48)	06 (5.08)	20 (16.95)	04 (3.39)	03 (2.54)	04 (3.39)	118
Vevarghat	62 (54.39)	08 (7.02)	09 (7.89)	06 (5.26)	22 (19.30)	01 (0.88)	06 (5.26)	114
Langi	29 (47.54)	22 (36.06)	03 (4.92)	03 (4.92)	02 (3.28)	0 0	02 (3.28)	61
Jayantipur	166 (81.77)	05 (2.46)	03 (1.48)	06 (2.96)	16 (7.88)	03 (1.48)	04 (1.97)	203
Kakojan	61 (43.57)	12 (8.57)	20 (14.29)	18 (12.86)	06 (4.29)	08 (5.71)	15 (10.71)	140
Naobaisya	18 (37.5)	02 (4.17)	09 (18.75)	05 (10.42)	01 (2.08)	06 (12.5)	07 (14.58)	48
Laluka	64 (65.31)	05 (5.10)	03 (3.06)	06 (6.12)	0 0	02 (2.04)	18 (18.37)	98
Total	576 (60.76)	67 (7.07)	75 (7.91)	88 (9.28)	60 (6.33)	24 (2.53)	58 (6.12)	948

Source: Based on Sample Survey, 1988.

Trade and Commerce

The village-wise analysis gives an insight into their occupational structure. From the Table 9.17 it is observed that their engagement in trade and commerce is highest in Jayantipur village (77.53%) and then Langi village (73.97%) of Nowgong district. These two villages are well communicated with Nowgong town and Tezpur town of Sonitpur district. Nowgong town is one of the important business centres of the Brahmaputra Valley. These two villages are situated thirty kilometres away from Nowgong town and fourteen kilometres away from Tezpur town—another business centre of the valley. People of these two villages engage in the business of bamboo, wood, contract, big and small stationary and grocery shops. They also supply wood, and bamboo to Nowgong and Tezpur towns.

The Moria muslims of Naobaisya and Kakojan villages of Jorhat district also involved in trade and commerce (61.54 per cent and 50.5 perp cent respectively). Naobaisya is situated twelve kilometres away from Jorhat town.

Table 9.17: Percentage of the Occupational Structure of the Moria Muslims

Name of the village	*Trade And comm.-erce*	*Brass Industry*	*Service*	*Transport & Communication: Pvt. Bus driver*	*Pvt. Bus Cond-uctor*	*A.S.T.C. driver*	*A.S.T.C Condu-ctor*	*Thala wala*	*Taxi driver*	*Truck driver*	*Ricks-haw puller*	*Total*	*Daily labour*	*Agricu-lture*	*Total workers*
Hajo Islampatti	21 (8.64)	158 (65.02)	31 (12.76)	18 (7.41)	07 (2.88)	01 (0.41)	00 (0.00)	01 (0.41)	00 (0.00)	00 (0.00)	00 (0.00)	27 (11.11)	06 (2.47)	00 (0.00)	243 (31.03)
Malara Islampatti	44 (33.84)	17 (13.08)	19 (14.61)	19 (14.61)	04 (3.08)	02 (1.54)	00 (0.00)	05 (3.85)	00 (0.00)	01 (0.77)	00 (0.00)	31 (23.85)	17 (13.08)	02 (1. 54)	130 (26.97)
Islampur (Vevarghat)	102 (58.96)	07 (4.05)	40 (23.12)	01 (0.58)	00 (0.00)	01 (0.58)	01 (0.58)	00 (0.00)	02 (1.15)	04 (2.31)	01 (0.58)	10 (5.78)	08 (4.62)	06 (3.47)	173 (27.37)
Kakojan	101 (50.5)	27 (13.5)	27 (13.5)	15 (7.5)	00 (0.00)	05 (2.5)	00 (0.00)	00 (0.00)	00 (0.00)	00 (0.00)	03 (1.5)	23 (11.5)	09 (4.5)	13 (6.5)	200 (26.56)
Jayantipur	176 (77.53)	06 (2.65)	32 (14.10)	03 (1.32)	00 (0.00)	00 (0.00)	00 (0.00)	00 (0.00)	00 (0.00)	02 (0.88)	00 (0.00)	05 (2.2)	03 (1.32)	05 (2.2)	227 (25.54)
Naobaisya	48 (61.54)	01 (1.28)	08 (10.26)	02 (2.57)	00 (0.00)	01 (1.28)	00 (0.00)	00 (0.00)	05 (6.41)	06 (7.69)	01 (1.28)	15 (19.23)	05 (6.41)	01 (1.28)	78 (27.27)
Langi	54 (73.97)	00 (0.00)	09 (12.33)	00 (0.00)	00 (0.00)	00 (0.00)	00 (0.00)	00 (0.00)	00 (0.00)	00 (0.00)	00 (0.00)	00 (0.00)	05 (6.85)	05 (6.85)	73 (25.44)
Laluka	47 (42.73)	01 (0.91)	31 (28.18)	04 (3.64)	00 (0.00)	00 (0.00)	00 (0.00)	00 (0.00)	05 (4.54)	04 (3.64)	00 (0.00)	13 (11.82)	18 (16.36)	00 (0.00)	110 (18.90)
Total	593 (48.06)	217 (17.59)	197 (15.96)	62 (5.02)	11 (0.89)	10 (0.81)	01 (0.08)	06 (0.49)	12 (0.97)	17 (1.38)	05 (0.41)	124 (10.05)	71 (5.75)	32 (2.59)	1234 (26.09)

Note: The figures in the parentheses indicate the percentage.
Source: Based on sample survey, 1988.

The people who are engaged in business, regularly visit the Jorhat town through bus service. Majority of them are the owners of stationery and grocery shops, some among them purchase stationery items from Calcutta also.

The people of Kakojan village situated about 18 km from Jorhat town are mainly engaged in cow and buffalo business. They purchase cows and buffalo from the Nishi and the Nath communities of Majuli (largest Riverine Island) island which is 25 kms away from this village and sell them directly to the villagers in Nagaland—30 kms away from the village. They make good profit out of it.

Islampur Vevarghat is a village of Darrang district where 58.96 per cent people are engaged in trade. This village is three km away from Mangoldoi—a district headquarters of the Darrang district. They are mainly shop keepers, either grocery or stationery. They purchase stationery articles from Gauhati and from Calcutta also.

Laluka, a village of Dibrugarh district and situated 3 km away from Dibrugarh town and well communicated by road transport. Only 42.73 per cent of the people are engaged in trade and commerce in Dibrugarh. They are engaged as contractors, shop keepers etc. and do the Government as well as private works. A few of them are owners of private buses and trucks which run between Gauhati and Dibrugarh as night service. A few of them have automobile parts shops.

At Malara Islampatty village in Kamrup district, situated 30 km away from Gauhati, only 33.84 per cent of people are engaged in trade. They run petty business and are mainly engaged in mobile business selling stationery articles in different villages where the Kalita, Nath, and the Garia Muslims live. A very few of them have their own shop of stationery or grocery. Only a few remain engaged in trade (8.64%). This is because almost all the families are engaged in brass industry. But only 8.64 per cent people are engaged in brass utensil shop within the village or in Hajo town. A few of them are the owners of stationery and grocery shops in Hajo town.

Brass and Allied industries

Trade and commerce is followed by brass industry and allied business. Only 17.59 per cent of the Moria people are engaged in brass industry, blacksmithy, goldsmithy etc. At present the demand of hand made brass utensils has fallen down due to the popularity of machine-made brass utensils, high rate of raw materials and the tendency of the common people to purchase utensils of stainless steel and plastic.

From Table 9.17, it is observed that 65.2 per cent of people of Hajo

Islampatty of Kamrup district are engaged in brass and allied industries followed by Kakojan (13.5%) of Jorhat district, Malara Islampatty (13.08%) of Kamrup district, Vevarghat (4.05%) of Mongoldoi district, Jayantipur (2.65%) of Nowgong district, Naobaisya (1.28%) of Jorhat dstrict, Laluka (0.91%) of Dibrugarh district, and none in Langi village of Nowgong district.

Services

Brass and allied industries are followed by service. Of the total workforce 15.96 per cent are engaged in service. People of villages adjacent to the urban areas are engaged in service in local factories, Government and private farms etc. Since community people do not prefer higher education, very few of them are found to be engaged in service in the higher category. From Table 9.17 it is also observed that in Laluka 28.18 per cent of people are engaged in service. This village is in close proximity of the Dibrugarh town, followed by Islampur (Vevarghat) (23.12%) and also in close proximity of the Mangoldoi town, followed by Malara Islampatti (14.61%), Jayantipur (14.10%), Kakojan (13.5%), Hajo Islampatti (12.76%), Langi (12.33%) and Naobaisya (10.26%).

Transport and Communication

Of the total workforce 10.05 per cent people are engaged in transport and communication.

From Table 9.17 it is observed that in transport and communication 23.85 per cent people are engaged at Malara Islampatty of Kamrup district, 19.23 per cent people are engaged at Naobaisya village of Jorhat district, 11.85 per cent people are engaged in Laluka village, 11.5 per cent people are engaged in Kakojan village of Jorhat district, 5.78 per cent people are at Vevarghat, 2.2 per cent people are engaged in Jayantipur village and none in Langi village of Nowgong district.

Daily Labour and Agriculture

Of the total number of workers 5.75 per cent are earning their livelihood on daily wage basis. The people are engaged as labourers in agricultural field at the time of sowing and harvest season of the land of the Garia Muslims and Assamese Hindu caste group, in the construction of houses either in the village or in the towns, in brass industry and in road construction etc.

From the total number of daily wage earners, about 16.36 per cent of labourers are from Laluka. Being in close proximity to the Dibrugarh town the villagers get absorbed in the town area in various jobs. About 13.08 per cent of people are engaged in Malara Islampatty.

Of the total number of workers only 2.59 per cent people are engaged in agriculture. This community is mainly landless but some of them have agricultural lands which they use either for self-consumption or for commercial purposes. But average land holding per family is not encouraging. But some of them do cultivation on *Adhi* system (Share cropping) in the agricultural field of the Garia Muslims and Assamese Hindu caste groups. In all the villages less than 10.00 per cent Moria practice agriculture. They have less than 2.0 bighas of land, except those who live at Kakojan village of Jorhat district. There they have 3.16 bighas of land per family.

On the basis of the sample survey, when the percentage of the occupational structure of the rural areas is compared with the urban areas (Table 9.18), it shows that the percentage of workers is significantly high (71.39) in rural areas but the same is quite low (28.61) in urban areas. It is mainly due to the high literacy rate (72.20%) of the people of the rural areas. From this table it is also observed that, 59.59 per cent of rural people are engaged in trade and commerce as compared to the people of urban area (28.61%). This is mainly because the big businessmen go to the village and purchase the articles like bamboo, cane, wood etc. from them. In some rural areas, the people are engaged in selling of cows and buffaloes which they purchase from other villages and sell it to the urban centres. Moreover, the villagers who are owners of big and small shops, in urban centres, live in rural areas. Thus the trade and commerce is

Table 9.18: Rural-urban composition of the percentage of the occupational structure of the Moria Muslims (Sample Survey, 1988)

	Trade and commerce	*Brass Industry*	*Service*	*Transport and communi-cation*	*Daily labour*	*Agriculture*	*Total workers*
Total	593 (48.06)	217 (17.59)	197 (15.96)	124 (10.05)	71 (5.75)	32 (2.59)	1234 (26.09)
Rural	525 (59.59)	58 (6.58)	135 (15.32)	84 (9.53)	47 (5.33)	32 (3.63)	881 (71.39)
Urban	68 (19.26)	159 (45.04)	62 (17.56)	40 (11.33)	24 (6.80)	00 (0.00)	353 (28.61)

Source: Based on Sample Survey, 1988.

significantly high in rural areas. On the other hand, 45.04 per cent of urban workers are engaged in brass industry which is significantly high when it is compared with the rural workers (6.58%). It is mainly due to the fact that the raw materials for brass industry are easily available in the urban area. Therefore, the percentage of workers in brass industry is significantly high in urban areas.

Occupational Distinctiveness

The eight sampled villages show that the workers have been divided into six types viz, Trade and Commerce (T), Brass Industry (B), Service (S), Transport and Communication (TC), Daily labour (DL) and Agriculture (A).

Following to Betal (1972), the mean and standard deviations (6) for the selected occupations have been calculated to determine the occupational distinctiveness ($\overline{x}$).

Table 9.19: Degree of Distinctiveness

Occupations	$\overline{x}$	6	$\overline{x+6}$	$\overline{x-6}$	$\overline{x+6}$	$\overline{x-6}$	$\overline{x+36}$	$\overline{x-36}$
T	74.13	46.68	120.81	27.45	167.49	–19.23	214.17	–65.91
B	27.13	50.23	77.36	–23.1	127.59	–73.33	177.82	–123.56
S	24.63	10.78	35.41	13.85	46.19	3.07	56.97	–7.71
TC	15.5	10.09	25.59	5.41	35.68	–4.68	45.77	–14.77
DL	8.88	5.28	14.16	3.6	19.44	–1.68	24.72	–6.96
A	4.00	4.06	8.06	–0.06	12.12	–4.12	16.18	–8.18

From Table (9.19) it is revealed that, trade and commerce is predominant in Jayantipur village of Nowgong district followed by Langi village, Naobaisya village of Jorhat district and Islampur (Vevarghat) of Darrang district. Brass industry is highly specialised in Hajo followed by Kakojan and Malara. Service is predominant at Laluka, followed by Islampur. Workers in transport and communication are found at Malara Islampatty, followed by Naobaisya village, Laluka, Hajo Islampatty of Kamrup, Kakojan village of Jorhat district. Daily labour is found in Laluka, followed by Malara Islampatty, Langi village and Naobaisya. Agricultural workers are present in three villages. These are Langi village, Kakojan village and Islampur (Vevarghat).

It may be mentioned from the above discussion that the diverse occupation is seen among the Moria Muslims in almost all the districts. At present they are not engaged in any fixed occupation. Their occupations depend on the location, ecological settings and the socio-environmental influence. The test of homogeneity shows chi² value = 698.46 which is highly significant at 0.1 per cent of probability, thereby suggesting that the villages differ from each other in respect of occupational pattern.

Income and Expenditure Pattern

It has been already mentioned that 26.09 per cent of the Moria Muslim workers have to feed 73.91 per cent of non-earning dependants. It has also been mentioned that though their primary occupation was brass industry since the time of the Ahom kings but at present occupational diversification is seen among the Moria Muslims.

The sample survey (Table 9.20) also shows that the monthly average income per Moria Muslim household is Rs. 851.47 in the study area. The monthly per capita income is found to be Rs.137.33 for the Moria Muslim population as against Rs. 546.00 for general population of the state. The villagewise analysis on the basis of the sample survey shows that per capita income is the highest (Rs.186.59) at Jayantipur village and the lowest at Vevarghat (Rs.105.46).

Table 9.20: Monthly Per Capita Income of Moria Muslim Population

Name of the village	*Number of household*	*Total no. of persons*	*Average family members per household*	*Average monthly income per household (in rupee)*	*Monthly Per Capita income (in rupee)*
Hajo Islampatti	141	783	5.5	742.49	134.99
Islampur Vevarghat	84	632	7.5	790.97	105.46
Laluka	96	582	6.06	861.32	142.13
Langi	59	287	4.86	800.71	164.76
Naobaisya	54	286	5.3	623.46	117.63
Jayantipur	146	925	6.34	1183.00	186.59
Kakojan	96	753	7.84	846.91	108.02
Malara Islampatti	93	482	5.18	709.98	137.06
Total	769	4730	6.2	851.47	137.33

Source: Based on Sample Survey, 1988.

On the other hand when the monthly per capita income of the urban areas and the rural areas are compared, it is seen that, per capita monthly income of the rural area is Rs.138.79 and that of the urban area is Rs.137.26 which is almost equal (Table 9.21). This is mainly due to the availability of transport, metalled road, facility and literacy. The people of the rural areas can very easily reach the urban areas where petty jobs and business facilities are available.

However, the income pattern of the Moria Muslims varies from one village to another. On the basis of the sample survey their economic status can be classified into four distinct groups. These are as follows:

1. High income group with Rs. 1200 per month per household or a little more.
2. Medium income group up to Rs. 600 to Rs. 1200 per month per household.
3. Low income group up to Rs.600 per month per household.
4. Unknown income group. Per household income is very low and hence negligible.

Table 9.21: Rural-Urban composition of Monthly Per Capita Income of Moria Muslim population, 1988 (in rupees) (Sample Survey)

	Number of household	*Total no. of persons*	*Average family members per household*	*Average monthly income per household (in rupee)*	*Monthly per capita Income*
Total	769	4730	6.2	851.47	137.33
Rural	532	3365	6.33	878.57	138.79
Urban	237	1365	5.76	790.62	137.26

Source: Based on sample survey, 1988.

To determine the income per household of the Moria Muslims 766 households have been taken into consideration (Table 9.22). The percentage of households (59.14) having an income of less than Rs. 600.00 and the percentage of households (13.98) having a low income which is not considerable as only 5.38 per cent of households are in the higher income group (Rs.1200+) at Malara Islampatti. The reason behind this is mainly due to the bad transport communication, low literacy (50.41%) rate among the intensive studied villages. On the other hand, higher percentage (30.82) in the higher income group is found at Jayantipur village. It has been discussed previously that this village is having a good communication system and well connected with business centres and with a high literacy (74.70%) rate. For this reason the percentage of the higher income group is found to be more, compared with other villages.

When the income pattern of the rural areas and urban areas is compared, it is observed that in the rural areas the percentage of households (44.28) having an income (Table 9.23) of less than Rs.600 is higher than the percentage of households (36.91) having an income less

Table 9.22: Percentage of Moria Muslim Households in Different Income Groups (In Rupees), 1988 (Sample Survey)

Name of the village	*Unknown*	*Low upto 600*	*Medium 600-1200*	*High 1200+*	*Total No. of households*
Hajo Islampatti	06 (4.26)	46 (32.62)	74 (52.48)	15 (10.64)	141
Malara Islampatti	13 (13.98)	55 (59.14)	20 (21.50)	05 (5.38)	93
Islampur Vevarghat	03 (3.57)	42 (50.00)	24 (28.57)	15 (17.86)	84
Jayantipur	04 (2.74)	74 (50.68)	23 (15.76)	45 (30.82)	146
Langi	02 (3.39)	21 (35.60)	25 (42.37)	11 (18.64)	59
Naobaisya	05 (9.26)	25 (46.29)	20 (37.04)	04 (7.41)	54
Kakojan	0 (0.00)	19 (19.59)	53 (54.64)	25 (25.77)	97
Laluka	0 (0.00)	40 (43.48)	26 (28.26)	26 (28.26)	92
Total	33 (4.31)	322 (42.04)	265 (34.59)	146 (19.06)	766

Source: Based on sample survey, 1988.

Figures in the parentheses indicate the percentage

than Rs.600 in urban area. In the higher income group (Rs.1200+) also the percentage of households (19.69) in rural areas is higher than the percentage of households (17.59) in the urban areas. This is mainly due to the high rural literacy (72.20) rate and good communication with the urban areas.

Table 9.23: Rural Urban composition of the percentage of Moria Muslim Households in Different Income Group (in Rupees), 1988 (Sample Survey)

	Unknown	*Low upto 600*	*Medium upto 600-1200*	*High 1200+*	*Total no. of households*
Total	33 (4.31)	322 (42.04)	265 (34.59)	146 (19.06)	766
Rural	27 (5.07)	236 (44.28)	165 (30.96)	105 (19.69)	533 (69.58)
Urban	06 (2.58)	86 (36.91)	100 (42.92)	41 (17.59)	233 (30.42)

Note: Figures in the parentheses indicate the percentage.

Source: Based on Sample Survey, 1988.

The test of homogeneity shows Chi^2 value =71.28 which is highly significant at 0.1 per cent probability, thereby suggesting that the villages differ from each other in respect of per family income.

From the survey it is revealed that an average monthly expenditure per Moria Muslim household is Rs.781.11 (Table 9.24) as against an income of Rs.851.47. Further per capita monthly expenditure of the Moria Muslim is Rs.126.95, while the per capita monthly income is Rs.137.33. Though it shows a small surplus budget but only 19.06 per cent of the Moria Muslim people belong to the high income group, 34.59 per cent belong to middle income group but the rest (46.35%) are below the minimum income level. Thus, the average per capita income and expenditure does not indicate the general level of the standard of living. So, the average budget of these families is always a deficit one.

It is also found from the survey that the common items for consumption of an average family consist of rice and rice products, flour and flour products, vegetables, egg, fish, meat (mutton, chicken, beef), salt, mustard oil, spices, molasses, sugar, tea, milk and milk products, tobacco, betel nut, etc. Clothing such as *lungi*, *dhoti*, trousers, shirt, *saree*, *mekhala, chaddar,* and half pant are common items for general use. Kerosene, firewood are commonly used as fuel. Rich families use cooking gas as cooking fuel.

However, the survey shows (Table 9.25) that most of the expenditure is incurred on foodstuff (67.95%) as against 0.89 per cent in luxury goods. For that reason they cannot afford to spend enough on recreation (1.22%), education (5.40%), medicine (3.75%), fairs and festivals (2.28%), transport (5.02%), house construction (4.69%). From this point of view the Moria Muslims are economically backward in all respects.

A villagewise analysis shows that the highest amount of monthly expenditure is incurred by a Moria Muslim family in Jayantipur village (Rs. 918.08), while lowest in Naobaisya village (Rs. 630.00). It is only because that a deficit budget is a common affair in a Moria Muslims household.

Conclusion

The present work on the Moria Muslims of the Brahmaputra Valley provides an interesting study, primarily from the population geographic point of view. Beginning from the geographical setting and economic and social conditions of the area the study includes the interpretation and analysis of the distribution, density, growth and size of the Morias, their

Table 9.24: Average per household and per capita monthly expenditure of the Moria Muslim Population for Different Consumption Items, 1988 (in Rupees) (Sample Survey)

Village/ Items	Hajo Islampatti		Malara		Islampur (Vevarghat)		Jayantipur		Langi		Naobaisya		Kakojan		Laluka		Total	
	H.H	Capita	H.H	Capita	H.H	Capita	H.H	Capita	H.H	Capita	H.H	Capita	H.H	Capita	H.H	Capita	H.H	Capita
Food staff	475.00 (63.96)	86.36	483.91 (67.11)	93.42	564.83 (71.08)	75.31	590.33 (64.30)	93.11	570.90 (71.69)	117.47	460.91 (73.16)	86.96	575.60 (69.68)	73.42	557.10 (64.19)	91.93	534.82 (67.95)	86.26
Cloth	78.33 (10.55)	14.24	75.80 (10.51)	14.63	70.00 (8.81)	9.33	80.45 (8.76)	12.69	70.00 (8.79)	14.40	50.75 (8.06)	9.58	85.91 (10.39)	10.96	99.48 (11.46)	16.42	76.34 (9.70)	12.31
Luxury	10.50 (1.41)	1.91	5.00 (0.69)	0.97	4.90 (0.62)	0.65	11.20 (1.22)	1.77	3.60 (0.45)	9.74	3.10 (0.49)	0.58	4.60 (0.55)	0.59	12.92 (1.49)	2.13	6.98 (0.89)	1.13
Education	40.60 (5.47)	7.38	32.43 (4.50)	6.26	31.80 (4.00)	4.24	50.30 (5.48)	7.93	35.45 (4.45)	7.29	20.65 (3.28)	3.90	35.10 (4.25)	4.48	37.28 (4.30)	6.15	35.45 (4.50)	5.72
Medicine	35.40 (4.77)	6.44	28.82 (4.00)	5.56	25.75 (3.24)	3.43	30.85 (3.36)	4.87	24.90 (3.13)	5.12	20.40 (3.24)	3.85	29.30 (3.55)	3.74	40.91 (4.71)	6.75	29.54 (3.75)	4.76
Fairs & festivals	21.20 (2.86)	3.85	15.90 (2.21)	3.07	16.30 (2.05)	2.17	21.20 (2.31)	3.34	16.40 (2.06)	3.37	10.80 (1.71)	2.04	15.25 (1.85)	1.94	26.70 (3.08)	4.41	17.97 (2.28)	2.90
Recreation	15.25 (2.05)	2.77	8.40 (1.16)	1.62	6.45 (0.81)	0.86	12.30 (1.34)	1.94	5.80 (0.73)	1.19	5.65 (0.90)	1.07	5.80 (0.70)	0.74	17.22 (1.98)	2.84	9.61 (1.22)	1.55
Transport	35.82 (4.82)	6.51	34.83 (4.83)	6.72	41.00 (5.16)	5.47	50.80 (5.53)	8.01	40.20 (5.05)	8.27	30.45 (4.83)	5.74	41.75 (5.05)	5.32	41.26 (4.75)	6.81	39.51 (5.02)	6.37
House Construction	30.50 (4.11)	5.55	35.96 (4.99)	6.94	33.65 (4.23)	4.49	70.65 (7.70)	11.14	29.10 (3.65)	5.99	27.30 (4.33)	5.15	32.85 (3.98)	4.19	35.09 (4.04)	5.79	36.89 (4.69)	5.95
Total expenditure	742.60	135.01	721.05	139.19	794.68	105.95	918.08	144.80	796.35	163.84	630.00	118.87	826.16	105.38	867.96	143.23	787.11	126.95

Source : Based on sample survey, 1988.

The figures in the parentheses indicate the percentage of expenditure of different items of consumption to total expenditure

Table 9.25: Rural Urban average per household and per capita monthly expenditure of the Moria Muslim Population for different consumption

Items	*Food stuff*		*Cloth*		*Luxury*		*Education*		*Medicine*		*Fairs & festivals*		*Recreation*		*Transport*		*House construction*		*Total*	
	H.H	*Capita*	*H.H*	*Capita*	*H.H*	*Capita*	*H.H*	*Capita*	*H.H*	*Capita*	*H.H.*	*Capita*	*H.H*	*Capita*	*H.H*	*Capita*	*H.H.*	*Capita*	*H.H.*	*Capita*
Total	534.82 (67.95)	86.26	76.34 (9.70)	12.31	6.98 (0.89)	1.13	35.45 (4.50)	5.72	29.54 (3.75)	4.76	17.97 (2.28)	2.90	9.61 (1.22)	1.55	39.51 (5.02)	6.37	36.89 (4.69)	5.95	787.11	126.95
Rural	445.15 (64.97)	85.48	72.15 (10.53)	11.39	05.4 (0.79)	0.85	34.29 (5.00)	5.41	26.67 (3.89)	4.21	15.98 (2.33)	2.52	07.4 (1.08)	1.17	39.84 (5.82)	6.29	38.25 (5.58)	6.04	685.13	108.24
Urban	516.05 (64.08)	89.59	88.91 (11.04)	15.44	11.71 (1.45)	2.03	38.94 (4.84)	6.76	38.16 (4.74)	6.62	23.95 (2.97)	4.16	16.24 (2.02)	2.82	38.54 (4.79)	6.69	32.79 (4.07)	5.69	805.29	139.81

Source: Based on sample survey, 1988.

The figures in the parentheses indicate the percentage of rural-urban composition of different items of consumption to total expenditure.

demographic, socio-economic and socio-cultural characteristics. An attempt is made to show the distinctive character of this group of population from the rest of the area.

The Morias are distributed only in nine districts out of eighteen districts in the valley. It is observed that they generally prefer to settle in or around the urban areas for their profession.

It is urgently required to make systematic plans and policies to improve the economic condition and the spread of higher education among the Morias. More developmental schemes need to be implemented for their betterment. Emphasis should be given on the development of their economic condition and education.

Their traditional brass industry should be improved by giving loan and subsidy from the State Government at least to those families who are still interested to keep their traditional identity in this industry. At present only a very few families of Ḥajo Islampatti get this loan irregularly from *Gaonlia* (rural) Bank. The loan is required to be given regularly through the *Goanlia* (rural) Bank. The youths need to be given proper training to compete with the machine-made brass utensils. The training centres should be opened at the selected areas or villages, to cater their need. Co-operative societies should be opened among the workers through which they can sell their finished products for their economic enrichment. The price of the finished articles will be fixed according to their quality and craftsmanship and the wages should be determined according to the degree or skill of the artisan and the quantity of the products. If it is done then the following effect may be made:

(i) Traditional brass industry will survive and revitalize and will be expanded in the villages. Its commercial value also will be increased.
(ii) The illiterate and semiliterate youths may be engaged in their traditional industry in their own villages.
(iii) Their standard of living will be improved.
(iv) Personal interest will grow to develop their own skill.

Besides this industry, the weaving cane industry etc. should be introduced by giving them proper training and financial assistance.

Primary education is available in almost all the villages. So middle or secondary schools should be established in or near the villages, so that the guardians can send their children for high school education. Emphasis should be given to establish colleges in selected areas in their locality where the youths can avail of opportunity in getting higher education.

The study shows their socio-economic development, which could be made under the supervision of the State Government. The main focus should be given on their traditional brass industry, other cottage industries and the higher education. All these will surely help the Moria Muslims to achieve a prestigious status in the society at large.

REFERENCES

Acharyya, N.N., (1966), *The History of Medieval Assam*, (1st edition), pp. 95-96, and 53. Dutta Barua & Company, Gauhati, Assam.

Ali Irshad, A.N.M., (1974), 'Social Relations among the Assamese Muslims in Rural and Urban Situations', Ph.D. Thesis, unpublished, p. 99, 224. Gauhati University, Gauhati.

________, (1974), 'Occupational mobility through generations among the Assamese Muslims', in B.M. Das (ed.).

Contemporary Anthropological Research in North-East India. pp. 93-100. Dibrugarh University, Dibrugarh.

Bandopadhyaya, Rakhaldas (1982), *Banglar Itihas* (Vol. II). (Bengali) pp. 211-212. Manmohan Prakashani, Calcutta.

Barua, K.L., (1966), *Early History of Kamrup*, pp. 193-194 (2nd edition), Dutta Barua, Lawyer's Book Stall, Gauhati.

Betal, H.R., (1972), 'Quantitative Mapping of Midnapur', Unpublished Ph.D. Thesis, Calcutta University, cited in H.K. Mandal's *Human Adaptation In Malwa Region: A Study of Habitat, Economy and Society*, Ph.D. Thesis, (unpublished) Calcutta University, Calcutta.

Census of India (1881), Office of the Superintendent of Govt. Printing India. Calcutta. p. 101.

_______, (1891), Assam. E.A. Gait, Vol. II, Shillong.

_______, (1901), Assam, Vol.I. B.C. Allen, pp. 19, New Delhi.

_______, (1911), Assam, Vol.III, Part-I, Report. J.Mc. Swiney, Shillong.

_______, (1921), Assam. Vol.III, Part.I, Report. G.T. Lloyd. Shillong.

_______, (1971), Series-3. Assam Part-II-C (i). Social and Cultural Tables, A.K. Saikia, pp. 4-5.

Chandana, R.C., (1986), *A Geography of Population: Concepts, Determinants and Patterns*, Kalyani Publishers, New Delhi.

Chanana, C., (1980), *Rural Settlements in South Africa, ME* MERB Bookshelf, New Delhi.

Datta, J.M. (1962), Demographic Notes on Harappa a Skeletons. In *Human Skeleton Remains from Harappa,* Calcutta Anthropological Survey of India.

Gait, Edward., (1926), *A History of Assam.* (2nd Edition), pp. 92-95. LBS Publication, Gauhati.

Hunter, W.W., (1879), *A Statistical Account of Assam*, Vol.I, pp. 261, Trubner and Co., London.

Nessa, Saifun, (1984), 'Emergence of the Assamese Muslim Society: A Social Analysis', M.Phil. Unpublished Dissertation pp. 109, 118. North Eastern Hill University, Shillong.

Saikia, M., (1978), *Assam-Muslim Relation and its Cultural Significance*, p. 142. Luit Printers, Golaghat.

Taher, M., (1979), 'Scheduled Caste Population in Assam: A Spatial Analysis', *North-Eastern Geographer,* Vol. II, No. 1 & 2.

10

Mizo Economy : Problem and Prospect

Mita Sarkar (Das)

I

The Mizo people (Mizo : Mizo hnam) are an ethnic group native to North-East India, western Burma (Myanmar) and eastern Bangladesh who speak any of various Kukish languages.

The present Indian state of Mizoram (literally "Mizland") was called the Lushai Hills and was a district of Assam, before it became a Union Territory and afterwards a full-fledged state. The Lushai people were the first Mizo people to have an external exposure and hence the ethnicity was initially known as the Lushai people. The demand for a distinct political territory for the people of the Lushai Hills resulted in the creation of a separate Union Territory and afterwards the State of Mizoram. In this struggle, one of the powerful factors was the movement to call themselves Mizo, rather than by distinct tribal names such as the Paite, Lushei, Ralte, Gangte, Mara, Pawi, Hmar etc. Their languages (of which the largest is Lushai Duhilian District dialect) belong to the Tibeto-Burman, their brethren are the Chins in the adjacent Chin State of Burma, as well as the Kukis.

Sandwiched between Burma in the east and south and Bangladesh in the west with a total of 630 sq. miles, Mizoram is inhabited by the Mizo people and the minority Chakma (Mizo:Takam) and the Reang (Bru Mizo Tuikuk) communities. Historically speaking, the Mizo people are a part of the great waves of the Mongoloid races spilling over into the eastern and North Eastern India from Tibet and Yunnan province in the 18th century. Their sojourn in western Burma, into which they eventually drifted around the 7th century, lasted about ten centuries, the Mizo people came under the influence of the British missionaries in the 19th century. The spread of education by Christian Missionaries led to the high percentage of 91.58 per cent literacy.

Religion

A great majority of the ethnic Mizo people are Christians. The major Christian denominators are Presbyterian (Majority), Baptist, The Salvation Army, Lairam Jesus Christ Baptist Church (LIKBK), Seventh-day Adventist, Evangelical Church of Maraland (ECM), Congregational Church of India (Maraland) in the southern district of Saiha, Roman Catholic and Pentecostal. The Mizo indigenous religion Hnam Sakhu has gained momentum since the 1950s, and has a large following. It is based on the animistic monotheistic religion practiced by the ancient Mizo people.

Historical Perspective

During the later part of the British rule, the people in the Lushai Hills as well as in the Manipur hills felt that the British administration was trying to adopt the policy of control through the Chiefs of the community. There were several rebellions against the British rule and as a result, an anti-Chief movement gained ground and in 1946, a political party named *Mizo Common People's Union* (MCPU) was formed. In the event of India being independent, the *Mizo Union*, formerly known as *Mizo Common People's Union* declared that Mizoram should be with Assam rather than adjoined with Burma, which the pro-Chief party advocated.

But, in reality, with the independence of India, the secessionist group in MCPU favoured joining Burma. The separation of India from Burma in the year 1937, the partition of India in 1947 and the administrative extension over the Indian part of the area negatively impacted the free mobility of the inhabitants, despite the existing rules that allowed free cross-over across India-Burma and India-East Pakistan (now India-Bangladesh) international border. These territorial demarcations were never accepted by the people and resulted in March 1966 as the Mizo National Front uprising.

Sociolinguistic Mosaic

The multi-ethnic and pluralistic state of Mizoram exhibits a co-existence of different communities, such as the Mizo (majority) who includes the

Lusei, Gangte, Pawi, and the Lakher, or Mara, the Riang (Mizo: Tuikuk), and the Chakma (Mizo: Takam).

Lai

With the promulgation of the Constitution of India as a Soverign Democratic Republic in 1950, the Lai people of Southern part of Mizoram (a segment of the much larger population of Lai/Chin) – have been given constitutional safeguard by granting them an Autonomous District Council under the Sixth Schedule of the Constitution of India. Lawngtlai was created as the Headquarters of Lai Autonomous District Council.Their language has been strictly maintained in the community and even their education. Maintenance of language as a symbol of identity has been included up to Middle school standard. The Lai Autonomous District Council managed their education from Primary to Middle stage in which the state government (Mizoram) has no control and interference. Due to the spread of Christianity, education also spread and moulded their social life. The Lai people speak both Lai and Mizo languages.

Mara

The Mara, earlier known as the Lakher, is the predominant community of the southern district of Saiha. The demand for a separate Lakher hills district in 1945 led to the formation of an organized political party called Mara Freedom Party. An autonomous district council, Mara Autonomous District Council under the Sixth Schedule of the Indian Constitution was given to them. Their struggle for identity, having passed through several politico-historical events, now plays an important part in the political horizon. Their maintenance of language as a symbol of identity has been supported by their education. Due to the spread of Christianity, education has also spread and moulded their social life. The Mara people have a native-like understanding of Mizo language.

Political, Linguistic and Economic Scenario

Consequent to Indian independence, the democratic change in administrative set-up of Mizoram led to an anti-Chief movement. The agitation brought forward the general mass feeling against the autocratic Chiefs and support for the *Mizo Union*. In 1955, the demand regarding the formation of a separate hills state was put forward in a tribal leaders meeting in Aizawl, due to the feeling that involvement of the Assam Government during the mautam famine was unsatisfactory. The introduction of Assamese as the official language of Assam in 1960 led to the protest against the Official Language Act of 1961. This was followed by the *Mizo National Front* uprising in March 1966 resulting in the attack of the military installations in Aizawl, Lunglei and other towns which followed by the declaration of independence of Mizoram by the Mizo National Front , formerly known as Mizo National Famine Front. Mizoram was declared Union Territory on January 21, 1972. The whole atmosphere was still surcharged with the feelings of anti-Non-Mizo attitude. Pu Laldenga, the President of Mizo National Front, signed peace accord in 1986 with the Government of India, stating Mizoram was the integral part of India. Pu Laldenga came to the ministry in the interim government which was formed in coalition with Congress in 1987 and the Statehood of Mizoram was proclaimed on February 20, 1987.

The economy of Mizoram is largely dependant on agriculture. The agrarian economy accounts for the livelihood of more than 70 per cent of the state's populace. The craggy hilly terrains are not conducive to cultivation of crops. However, a regular distribution rainfall for the whole length of the year and the fertile temperate soil has resulted in the springing up of the dense forest enveloped in the lush foliage. In spite of the ragged terrains, the favourable climatic condition and the rich soil have led to extensive *Jhum* cultivation in the state. Horticultural crops are also grown for economic purposes. Agriculture forms the primary sector in the economy of Mizoram. Thus all subsidiary industries also happened to be agro-based. Several food processing units are mushrooming all over the state, and the government is optimistic that the increase in the production in spices, fruits and vegetables as well as cultivation of cash crops in the coming years will led to a burgeoning food processing industry in the state.

Mizoram houses a small repository of minerals. Thus mining also contributes to a small part of the economy. In fact, majority of the mines in Mizoram dig up the hard tertiary rocks that are used as building materials. A large number of small scale industries that sell exquisite bamboo works as well as handloom made apparels also contribute to the state's economy. Another core sector of the economy, i.e. tourism contributes largely to the state's revenue. The state is also beginning to exploit the untapped hydro electric power potential and is also endeavouring to explore the medicinal values of the various herbs that grow in plenitude in the state forest.

Present Demand for Inclusion in 8th Schedule

With 91.58 per cent literacy, the second highest in Indian states, Mizoram is now leading towards the spread of education in a substantial manner, the recognition of Mizo Tawng in the 8th Schedule of the Constitution of Indian , is an undercurrent demand that is evident in various aspects of social and political life. Though the term Mizo is often used to name a nation it is rather an umbrella term to denote the various tribes. A number of dialects are still spoken under the umbrella of Mizo. But contrary to the above statement the research team of the Art and Culture Department of Government of Mizoram had mentioned that the term Mizo has a dipper meaning than the former historians' belief. In the systematic classification they published, it shows Mizo is the name of the nation which may have an ancient origin somewhere in Central Asia and comprising eleven tribes : the Aso, Chho, Halam, Gangte, Lai (Pawi), Lusei, Mara, Mui-Khumi, Paite (Zomi), Ratle and the Thado (Kuki). Each of them has numerous clans, (e.g. Sailo, Chhakchhuak, Kawlni, Khupchawng, Thiak, Chawngthu, etc.) and these clans contains at least five sub-clans.

II

Mizoram Districts: Formation and Administrations

Mizoram a Union Territory of the Indian Union, situated on the north-eastern corner of India was carved out of the then State of Assam on January 21, 1972 under the provision of the North-Eastern Areas (Re-organisation) Act, 1971. It is bounded on the North by Cachar District of Assam and Manipur, on the East and South by Chin and Arakan Hills of Burma (Myanmar) and on the West by Chittagong Hill Tracts of Bangladesh and the State of Tripura. Briefly, its boundary with Assam, Tripura and Manipur extends 12,366 and 95 kms respectively. The tropic of cancer runs through the State. It covers an area of 8143 sq. miles, i.e. 21,087 sq.km. and has mostly a hilly steep terrain. The average height of the hills and ranges is about 900 metres. The boundary with Burma (Myanmar) extends 404 km. And with Bangladesh 318 kms. Thus, it occupies an area of great strategic importance, having a total boundary length of 772 km. with Bangaldesh and Myanmar. The State, in fact, runs lengthwise length being twice the breath. The State comprises eight districts—Aizawl, Lunglei, Champhai, Mamit, Kolasib, Serchhip, Saiha and Lawngtlai.

Table 10.1: Names and Areas of the Districts and Sub-divisions

Sl. No.	Name of District	Name of Hqs.	Area in Sq.kms	Sl. No.	Name of Sub-division	Area in Sq.Kms.
1	2	3	4	5	6	7
1.	Aizawl	Aizawl	3576.31	1.	Aizawl (Sadar)	1543.60
				2.	Sakawrdai	1037.48
				3.	Saitual	995.23
2.	Lunglei	Lunglei	4538.00	4	Lunglei	3178.57
				5.	Tlabung	880.01
				6.	Hnahthial	479.42
3.	Champhai	Champhai	3185.83	7.	Champhai	985.73
				8	Khawzawl	932.92
				9.	Ngopa	1267.18
4.	Mamit	Mamit	3025.75	10.	Mamit	785.94
				11.	Kawrthah	948.56
				12.	W. Phaileng	1290.25
5.	Kolasib	Kolasib	1382.51	13.	Kolasib	200.12
				14.	Vairengte	206.18
				15.	Kawnpui	796.21
6.	Serchhip	Serchhip	1421.60	16.	Serchhip	801.21
				17.	N. Vanlaiphai	457.17
				18.	Thenzawl	163.22
7.	Saiha	Saiha	1399.90	19.	Saiha	457.17
				20.	Tuipang	942.73
8.	Lawngtlai	Lawngtlai	2557.10	21.	Lawngtlai	1304.84
				22.	Tuichhak	565.91
				23.	Chawngte	686.35
		Total	21087.00			21087.00

Source: Statistical Handbook, Mizoram-2000, Directorate of Economics and Statistics, Mizoram.

For administrative convenience, 23 sub-divisions have been carved out of eight districts such as 3 in Aizawl, 3 in Lunglei, 3 in Champhai, 3 in Mamit, 3 in Kolasib, 3 in Cerchhip, 2 in Saiha and 3 in Lawngtlai which can be seen at Table 10.1 showing the names and areas of the districts and sub-divisions.

Besides, 22 Rural Development Blocks with a view to bringing about a socio-economic transformation in the lives of the rural poor Mizos, have been in the operation. Table 10.2 indicates the names of districts, Rural Development Blocks and their areas in square kilometres.

These Blocks function under the control of the Department of Rural Development. But, the officers, who man these Blocks, are of Mizoram Civil Service cadre. The Rural development Department does not have its own cadre officers to man these Blocks. An imperative need is that

Table 10.2: Names of Districts, Rural Development Blocks and their Areas

Sl. No	*Name of Block*	*District*	*Area in Sq.Km.*
1.	Aibawk	Aizawl	616.88
2.	Darlawn	Do	1037.48
3.	Phullen	Do	515.15
4.	Thingsulthiliah	Do	874.13
5.	Tlangnuam	Do	532.67
	Sub-total		3576.31
6.	Ngopa	Champhai	891.77
7.	Khawbung	Do	705.98
8.	Khawzawl	Do	1588.08
	Sub-total		3185.83
9.	Reiek	Mamit	937.42
10.	W. Phaileng	Do	999.57
11.	Zawlnuam	Do	1088.76
	Sub-total		3025.75
12.	E. Lungdar	Serchhip	623.00
13.	Serchhip	Do	798.60
	Sub-total		1421.60
14.	Thingdawl	Kolasib	1382.51
	Sub-total		1382.52
15.	Bunghmun	Lunglei	1389.26
16.	Hnahthial	Do	985.39
17.	Lungsen	Do	1046.29
18.	Lungleli	Do	1117.66
	Sub-total		1382.52
19.	Chawngte	Lawngtli	686.35
20.	Lawngtlai	Do	1304.84
	Sub-total		1991.19
21.	Sangau	Saiha	565.91
22.	Tuipang	Do	1399.90
	1965.81	1965.81	1965.81
	1965.81	1965.81	1965.81

Department should have its own cadre of officers to implement the development schemes efficiently and effectively.

III

Mizo Economy: The Problem

Mizoram, according to the Census of 2011, has a population of 10,97,206 with 5,55,339 males and 5,41,867 females. They are predominantly tribesmen and Christians. The density of population is 52 sq.km. However, the population growth rate has shown upward trends during the period of ten years of 2001-2011 (23.58%). 5,25,435 Mizos live in the rural areas while the urban population is of 5,71,771. Sex ratio is of 976 females per 1000 males.

The urban population has been increasing owing mainly to the heavy influx of villagers from the interior places neighbouring Myanmar during the disturbances and political, administrative and economic reasons and also a heavy influx foreign nationals (Burma and Bangladesh) especially after the status of Union Territoryhood and Statehood. But, this urbanization which refers to an increase in population living in urban areas and is governed by social, cultural and economic factors, has brought about social and other problems like slums diseases, sanitation, water supply, traffic, health services, poverty and unemployment. The Mizos like urban life without their democratic or political participation. Democratic or political participation means power to decide issues and sources of action, control of the apparatus created to give effect to such choice or decisions. The Government of Mizoram has created and notified 23 towns including the city of Aizawl but has not so far provided for the pattern / structure of urban governance / administration. Instead, the village councils meant for the rural governance have been allowed by the political structure of the State to continue functioning in 23 notified towns which are contrary to the fundamentals/principles of urban local governance.

In literacy, the State as per 2011 census, claims about 91.3 per cent. The percentage of literacy in rural and urban areas is 84.1 and 97.6 respectively. Female literacy is 89.3. Thus, the literacy rate has gone up from 88.8 per cent to 91.3 per cent in the past ten years.

Agriculture is the chief occupation of Mizo people. The Mizo way of cultivating land is/was very primitive and wasteful. It is also destructive of the forest wealth. The practice of what is called *jhum*, a slash and burn method of cultivation, is / was popularly known as shifting cultivation. In the shifting cultivation, there are no permanent sites for cultivation and there is no permanent ownership of land. Individual households do not have absolute ownership right over the land cultivated by them, their rights are of the nature of usufruct. As soon as, they stop cultivating the land, their right ceases. Briefly, the land belongs to the community (government). But the major breakthrough in the development of Mizoram has been in the field of agriculture. The traditional pattern of jhuming is gradually giving way to modern methods of production, permanent and terrace cultivation. Thus, there has been progressive change in attitude of the Mizo people towards the patterns of agriculture after the elevation of the Mizo Hills to the status of Union Territory of Mizoram and subsequent to statehood (Mizoram). Briefly, agriculture in Mizoram has already become commercial and money crops oriented.

As has been experienced, the tribal socio-economic arrangements owing to internal weakness have been allowed to readily surrender to the alien economic patterns or capitalist economy. And gradually the egalitarian social bases / values of the Mizo society have given way to a stratified structure / system where land has emerged as the most precious possession, and the hitherto unknown process of land alienation on one hand and land concentration on the other appears as natural phenomenon in the Mizo society. This happens because the country has consciously pursued the capitalist path of modernization. So, the system of land arrangement in the country including Mizoram is an unavoidable phase towards privatization of land. This, no doubt, has encouraged the policy-makers in the state to opt for individualization of land at a faster rate. A number of land legislations and other protective land regulations framed/ enacted by the State Government, as is experienced, debar the non-tribesmen from owning landed property in the State, no doubt, but these have also generated a process of progressive concentration of landed property in the hands of the emerging local middle class or a small group of well-off people and have tended to aggravate the situation of rural poverty by pushing an increasingly larger sections of the small and marginal farmers to the status of landed peasants, landless agricultural labouers and share-croppers. Thus, the privatization of land and changing property relations has led to the growth of unknown phenomenon like land alienation by well-off-natives, uneven distribution of land among individual households, absentee landlordism, intermediary rights, realization of rent from land, money lending, encroachment of community land, exploitative groups based on antagonistic relations of production, land mortgage, and perpetuation of the existing disparities of wealth. The merging well-off-natives/middle class in the State are neither opposed to the landed gentry, nor to the Indian capitalist class. Therefore, it is suggested that the Government of Mizoram on priority basis, should initiate a legislation to bring out both an agrarian reforms and land reform measures to ensure the economic and social welfare of the tiller of the land that is peasant, the tenant and the landless labourers. This also holds the key to a broad based social change in the State.

The economy of the territory was not exposed to the modernization process because of its being inaccessible, isolated, neglected, backward, underdeveloped and restrictive legislations and regulations, i.e. imposition of Inner Line Regulation, 1873 enacted/framed not only during the British rule but also during the post-independence period for many years. These wounded the sentiments of a section of Mizos very badly, who triggered of an armed revolt in 1966 against the Government of India and persisted in protracted political strife for the independence of the territory till the Memorandum of Settlement between the Government of India and the Mizo National Front was signed in June, 1966. Briefly, political pressures from the leaders of the erstwhile Mizo Hills District Council for larger autonomy and the political uprising led to further changes in the administration of the land by elevating the district to the Union Territory of Mizoram as per the provisions of the North-Eastern Areas (Recognisation) Act, 1971. But, in order to get the Union Territory administration fully involved in the modernization process, socio-cultural and politico-economic transformation of the Mizo and also acting as a counter-insurgency forces, a provision of the Legislative Assembly and a Council Ministers was made in the Government of Union Territories (Amendment) Act, 1971. Accordingly, Mizoram became Union Territory on January 21, 1972 with 33 elected and nominated members and a council of ministers. To the Act, the Mizo Hills District Council would stand dissolved and ceased to exist from the date on which the Legislative Assembly of the Union Territory of Mizoram would be constructed. The Pawis, the Lakhers and the Chakmas demanded more autonomy for their areas in the new political status. So the Pawi-Lakher Regional Council was trifurcated into three Regional Councils which were later elevated to the status of the District Councils, viz. Lai District Council, Mara District Council and Chakma District Council with their headquarters at Lawngtlai (now District), Saiha (district) and Chawngte (Sub-Division). Later the Union Territory of Mizoram attained the status of the 23rd State of the Indian Union on February 20, 1987. It is, thus, clear from the provisions of the Sixth Schedule that the civil administration of the Autonomous District in the State is placed with the two authorities, viz. Deputy Commissioner representing the State Government and the Chief executive Member of the Executive Committee heading the District Council. There is, thus, dual form of administration functioning independently of each other.

It has been experienced that after Mizoram became Union Territory and State, the Central Government has been generous with its pursue and pumped more funds in this fledging territory for infrastructural development, rapid economic growth, social development/social justice and generation of productive employment than perhaps in any other comparable population. This enlarging money economy due to expansion of development activities has helped growth of classes/neo-middle rich class and the poor, which are on the increase day by day in the present society. The local elites have been the policy-makers and also the executors of the planning priorities and policies to have a just Mizo society based on the principle of 'destructive justice'. Besides, there are also several restrictive enactments like Inner Line Regulation to prevent the entry of the plains' businessmen/traders and rich contractors to this regulated State to protect the poor tribesmen from exploitation. There is, no doubt truth in it. But, it is experienced that these restrictive enactments and the Inner Line Regulation cannot stop/prevent the exploitation of the many poor Mizos by the emerging class of neo-middle rich, so long as a distribution of poverty, income, education, power/authority and prestige within the Mizo society continue. Because those groups of people, who acquire more property, and education come to wield more powers than others and thereby help the beginning of exploitation of the poor by those class/groups controlling the material means of production and the mode of production not only in terms of exchange but also in terms of allocation of the means of livelihood. So economic power is dialectically related to political power. This phenomenon is now very much visible in the Mizo society. The gulf between the rich and the poor is widening day by day due to modernization based on capitalist lines. In terms of political economy, what is taking place, is anti-development/modernization through development. Briefly, a few persons in the Mizo society are beneficiaries and have become very rich in recent years whereas majority of the Mizo people are still on the old standard of living. It is, thus, obvious that the tribal economy has been exposed to the onslaught of the capitalist economy during the last few decades despite the Inner Line Regulation and other restrictive enactments and constitutional provisions. The budget of the State is not that much growth oriented. Revenue, which is collected from different sources, is too meagre. The State has, no doubt, still a dependant economy and no worth naming development of industrial infrastructures even after three decades of its administration. Briefly, Mizoram is non-industrial State.

IV

Mizo Economy: The Future Prospect

No faster development can take place in the State, if this is to remain a close community and shut its door on people from outside the territory.

The State has been a closed community for hundreds of years, and that is precisely the cause of its low economic development arising out of history. This condition has to be rethought and it has to be in terms of larger cooperative endeavour. To achieve this end the Inner Line Regulation may have to be modified. A narrow economic approach or bureaucratic approach must give place to a new enlightened and progressive policies for bringing about the basic socio-economic changes which will certainly contribute to secularization, modernistaion, political and emotional integration at a rapid rate. Since, January 21, 1972 the administration of the Mizoram Union Territory began to function. The Chief Commissioner was appointed by the President of India to carry out the territory administration till the constitution of the territory legislature and subsequent formation of government. The Chief commissioner/Lt. Governor/Governor was/is assisted by a Council of Ministers and a set of officers such as Chief Secretary, Development Commissioner, Secretaries and others.

The Government of Union Territories (Amendment) Act, 1971 provided for the cretion of a legislature in Mizoram. So the first and the other eight elections to the Mizoram Legislative Assembly were held in 1972, 1978, 1979, 1984, 1987, 1989, 1993 and 1998. After the results of the election polls, the governments by both national and regional political parties securing majority seats or more party candidates elected, have been formed to transact the entire business of the government and its various departments.

To the Act, the Mizos enjoy a special safeguard under Article 371 (B) of the Constitution of India to protect their religious practices, customary and economic interests, which no other States in the plains areas enjoy. They have been given complete internal home rule to manage their own affairs by their own genius financed by the Government of India. As is true, only because of the parliamentary apparatus, the Mizo people have begun to see more and more of that today. The Mizos governs the Mizos. The Ministers, MLAs and most of the officials are the Mizo. The non-Mizos in Mizoram are working in partnership with the Mizo for the constructive socio-economic transformation of the Mizo society. By and large, the destiny of the Mizoram remains in the hands of the Mizo people. So the local people must contribute their intelligent and instructed judgment to the task of bringing about just and non-exploitative socio-economic order in the State. It is, of course, a challenging task in the existing capitalist socio-economic order which the Mizo people must share with determination, conviction and seated fast integrity.

REFERENCES

Abbi, B.L., *North East Region: Problem, Prospect and Development*. Centre for Research and Industrial Development, Chandigarh.

Datta Ray, B. (1983), *The Emergence and Role of Middle Class in North-East India*. Uppal Publishing House. New Delhi.

Chakravarty, P. (1999), *The Inner Line Regulation of the North-East India*. Linkman Publication, West Bengal.

Misra, N.L. (1989), *Responsive Administration with Special Reference to District Administration*.

Nivedan, N. (1980), *The Dagger Brigade*. Lansars Publishers, Delhi.

Vergheese, C.G. (1997), *A History of the Mizos*. Volume I & II. Vikash Publishing House, N. Delhi.

11

Rural Naga Women as Natural Resource Managers: Issues and Challenges

Lucy Zehol

Introduction

In this chapter I have tried to look at the human-environment relations that concentrate mainly on the local context and the internal society dynamics as the drivers of ecological change. I have also tried to apply a political ecology framework in understanding the dynamics of the resource frontier in the context of Nagaland. Borrowing what Nancy Peluso and Michael Watts have to say about political ecology, is the fact that it provide tools for thinking about conflicts and struggles engendered by the forms of access to, and control over resources. Its attentiveness to power relations inherent in defining, controlling, and managing nature suggests an alternative way of viewing the link between environment and political action, (Peluso and Watts 2001:24-25). Political ecology studies often begin by mapping the different actors involved in the particular conflict, ranging from powerful ones like the state, or multilateral institutions or corporations to the weaker ones such as communities, local non-governmental organizations (NGOs). My focus is on gender issues among the Khezhas of Khezhakeno, and from this experience attempts are made to relate to the broader debate on socially equitable future for the Naga in particular and the tribal society at large. In the context of Nagaland, besides the many aspects of natural resources, is today the related conflict concerned of nature as resource issues. As we will see the right to, and control of, resource extraction is closely related with issues of land ownership. As it appears, the 'commodification of nature is an extremely critical socio-ecological process that seems to alter peoples' relationship to, and engagement with, nature as well as their mode of dwelling and perceptions of the environment. Nature is thus turned into extractable resources, commodities for market exchange. In a different manner it can be said that a new 'nature regime' is taking over (Escobar 2008). The capitalist regime is characterized by the twin processes of governmentalization and commodification of nature. With this theoretical framework, I hope this chapter will help in our reflection on how to build an environmentally sustainable and socially equitable future.

This information has been gathered primarily based on anthropological fieldwork tradition at a Naga village known as Khezhakeno. Ancestral home to most of the Naga tribes, Khezhakeno is believed to be the village of origin for almost all Naga tribes. Legend has it that most Naga tribes once settled in this village before dispersing to other parts of Nagaland. Khezhakeno appears to be an important place in the migration route of the Naga tribes. The Khezhas are part of the tribe known as 'Eastern Angamis' during the British colonial period and are today part of the Chakhesang Naga tribe in the post-colonial period. Khezhakeno is situated in Phek district of Nagaland. Personally, I think that insisting on in-depth knowledge of particular setting remain critical (Zehol & Zehol, 2009).

Rural Khezhas Women

Rural Khezhas Naga women are those most directly dependent on natural resources for their immediate livelihood and food security. In other words, these are critical sources of livehood and basic necessities for the villagers. However, in the natural resource management, there are differences between the roles and responsibilities of women and men due to the socially constructed division of labour.

Natural resource management means the management of resources such as water, land, forest, food/vegetable, plants and animals with a particular focus on how management affects the equality of life for both present and future generations. Natural resource management is a vital area where both the rural and urban communities depend directly on surrounding natural resources for its ecological benefits and resources such as access to land, forests, sources of water, pastures and fields etc. and is crucial both for lives and livelihoods in the community. We will focus on land and forest as important natural resources for the people of Nagaland.

Land

Land is one of the most important productive natural resources for the people of Nagaland. One can invest in this natural capital for productive activity to generate wealth. It is a store house for minerals and forest resources of various kinds. In the present age of globalization, this natural capital is movable and can be converted into economic goods, e.g. used as mortgage to secure loan. This natural capital can also be privatized and ownership changed. While men can inherit the most important and productive wealth, land for 'free', it does not apply to the Naga women the same way. There are certainly gender biases when it comes to land ownership with numerous existing inequalities. In this Naga village, the land holding tenure system is customarily defined and owned privately by individuals, a group of clans or sub-clans except the sacred forest which is community owned, known as Abvunhou and Ngade in Khezhakeno. It is an interesting observation that despite the denuded of forest cover in other part of Nagaland traditional forms of protection and management are able to hold against the prospect of profitable resource extraction from these sacred forest at least in the case of my study village (Zehol & Zehol, 2009). Woman's lack of land rights can not only reduce the well being of family but also deprive her socially and culturally. Hence, the effective exclusion of women from possession and control of land is largely the basis of their 'subordination' and dependence on men in rural India. In family relationship, while there are many 'cooperative outcomes' beneficial for all the household members, the different members have 'strictly conflicting interests in the set of cooperative arrangements'. Hence, the bargaining power of men and women within the cooperative conflict will depend much on their resources and power outside the family or household. The rural Naga women are socially powerless and resourceless and are likely to remain in that situation even when the outcome of cooperative conflict is unsatisfactory. It would be unfavorable for women to leave the household. But in case of breakdown of cooperative arrangements, the fallback position of women is worse, which is reflected in their lack of entitlement to resources, consumption and decision making outside the family and within it. Hence, gaining ownership of land would strengthen women's position and their position within marriage. Thus woman's access to land rights can secure sustainable livelihoods with increased productivity, reduce level of feminization of poverty, gain better social relationships and cultural values. These are source of prestige and power and will increase bargaining power of women with a fallback position in case of breakdown of cooperative arrangements.

However, the Naga women's access to land resources and user's rights are mediated by the Naga customary laws, and control rights are often subjected to the Naga customary laws, which are one-sided and biased. Regarding the principles relating to the relationship between the men and women show that rules were more favourable for men as husbands than women as wives, especially where inheritance of properties was concerned. In the customary law of the village as in the other Naga villages, women had no equal rights with men in the political or administrative sphere though their role was seen to be very essential for the proper functioning of the society. The recognition of the Naga customary laws in Article 371 (A) of the Constitution of India further marginalizes women.

Forest

In Nagaland, out of the total geographical area of 16,579 sq. km, 89 per cent area is privately owned and only 9.1 per cent is owned by the State Government. The Department of Forest and Ecology has observed that roughly 33 per cent or 2,843 sq. km of the total 8,629 sq. km of classified forests were degraded in 1996-97. While women have no direct role or much say in the community forest management, effective forest resource management and its wise utilization, will provide both men and women with ecological benefits, life support systems and resources. This will positively benefit women with a comparative advantage when forest resources are abundant and are used for sustainable livelihoods as it will greatly reduce work load and drudgery on women and enhance women's nutritional status due to the biodiversity of resources. Case study done by NEPED showed how women though, working on the land and nurturing its resources had very little participation in aforestation project of the Nagaland Empowerment of People and Economic Development (NEPED) with the full control rights over the trees. In reality, use and control of forest resources is determined not by lack of or constraint of natural resources but by whether the user has the rights to use productive resources, especially land. Natural resource degradation will adversely affect women more with an increasing work load and drudgery as they have to travel longer distances to fetch resources such as NTFPs, MAPs, fodder etc. for household use. One interesting observation is, if the family cannot produce enough food, the women are often labelled as being lazy and not diligent, and have a low status in the society even though they play a crucial role in contributing to family food security. Hence, investment in additional work without availability of additional labour and means of production will only increase women's work load, burden and drudgery.

Gender Division of Labour

The gender division of labour depicts power relation and inequalities in sharing of works. Men partake in activities that need physical strength and stamina but are seasonal. Men also do activities that have economic value such as collecting timber and marketing cash crops. Women are attached to activities mainly for sustaining livelihood that are invisible and unaccounted. There is a gender gap in sharing the workload attached to **resources and value**. Thus, the gender differentiated roles and responsibilities in natural resource management and interventions must address the specific needs and opportunities of rural women and men, particularly the poorest, to reduce inequalities, stimulate growth and reverse environmental loss and degradation.

Women remain important and are key to family food and nutrition as they play major role as farmers and producers. However, their access to resources and opportunities to enable them to move from subsistence agriculture to higher value chains has been constrained and is much lower than men. Women lack market access for their agricultural produce. However, they face a number of barriers such as poor infrastructure, poor road condition and connectivity, lower mobility due to gender division of labour, socially constructed roles assigning women in reproductive sector and care economy, lack of access to training and marketing information due to low literacy rate and denial of access to productive resources due to cultural factors. Apart from efficiency gains, food security and welfare gains are also strongly linked to the provision of greater economic opportunities to women. It is well known that resources and incomes controlled by women are more likely to be used to improve family food consumption and welfare reducing child malnutrition and an increased overall well-being of the family. In addition, enabling poor women access to market opportunities and resources would lead to women's economic empowerment. This will result in overcoming overall subordination of women due to cultural and other factors. However, women lack good access even to local markets. Often, transportation and infrastructure are critical to link producers with these markets. Thus, building capacity to manage marketing businesses with related support is a priority for both producers and policy makers. Women may not necessarily be the source of solutions to environmental problems. Groups of women as well as men may act in environmentally damaging ways and women's apparent closeness to nature may stem from their lack of opportunities outside the household and the social relations in society than their biological makeup. Sustainable development, therefore, depends on removing women's subordination and oppression as well as their poverty, not simply grafting on women as a group or lumping women's varied interests together. Gender approach to the environment policy therefore, should attempt to understand the differences that exist between women and men in households and between subgroups within communities (differences in workloads and use of resources, knowledge and skills, social status, etc.). Besides, an attempt should be made to understand power structures and relations, thus recognizing the rights and responsibilities of women and men that exist in communities. These may be partly hidden and may not be obvious without careful investigation. For example, traditional rights of access to land and the products it yields may often be problematic for women as women may not have control over farm products and earnings. These rights might not be written or codified. The socially constructed gender division of labour with women in reproductive, productive and community organizing works give women less time to invest in their human capital or for capacity building for social networking. The agricultural extension training programmes hardly have women participants. This further marginalizes women. Sustainable development in Nagaland depends primarily on a balanced approach that includes biodiversity conservation, sustainable management of existing land and forests, reduced exploitation of new forest resources, adapting efficient agricultural systems and building proper marketing linkages. Expansion of agricultural area into accessible primary forest should also be checked through adaption of better farming practices. In general, environmental and resource degradation increases women's workload and drudgery. It increases the distances for the women to walk to collect firewood and water. Recognizing women's need for environmental resources, not only for crop production but also for fuel and water, and incorporating these concerns into plans and policies for environmental management, would release more time for women for income generation, child care and personal development.

The Issue and the Challenge

The Naga women as much as their men have a special relationship with nature that gives them a particular stake in and a special ability to undertake eco-management. However, the issue that disturbs me is that of lack of engagement with the issue of gender equity in the Naga society and how this impinges on the welfare, efficiency and sustainability of effort towards eco-management. At best, there is an occasional mention of women's actual or potential role in eco-management projects. Indeed, many are arguing for a strengthening or replication of traditional community institutions for local resource management, paying little attention to the unequal social relations—especially unequal gender relations—these institutions typically embody.

For example, the Government of Nagaland initiated the concept of communitisation of Public Institutions and Services Acts (2002) in order to build partnership between government and the people through delegation of management responsibilities to the community so that the performance of the public utilities improves in areas such as health, water supply, education, forest, bio-diversity, tourism, electricity etc. But the issue is what shape should community institution for eco-management take? It is a well known fact that there are a number of environmental thinkers favouring the reviving or replicating of traditional institutions as they assume that the past tradition constituted a period of ecological stability and social harmony. Evidence provides a very different picture. Undoubtedly, colonialism contributed to environmental decline, yet what is at stake here are the inegalitarian social relations and values that most traditional institutions embody. Many of the community based institutional arrangements that have emerged in recent years through the encouragement of governmental or NGOs are forced to be entrenching, even exacerbating, gender inequalities. Pre-colonial Naga societies were characterized by strong gender hierarchies, not just in terms of norms and perceptions but in terms of deeply embedded aspects relating in particular: (a) gender division of labour, (b) property rights, (c) jural authority and access to public decision-making forums. Moreover, these elements of gender inequality underlie not only most of the noted negative effects of environmental degradation, they point to the little attention being given to women's concerns in the emergent village institution like the village council. As noted, the gender division of labour is the basis for women's having a double work burden. Women's lack of ownership in land increases their dependence. And above all, due to their low representation in decision-making forums, they have little say in the rules governing natural resource management now being framed.

Rendering these hierarchical structures historically invisibly also make invisible their continuation in the post colonial period. Today, these forms of inequalities persist, although in less stark forms. The gender division of labour continues to be unequal with women bearing a double work burden. Although acquired property may be allow to be inherited by women, significant inequalities remain, especially in relation to ancestral landed property. And despite an improvement in women's education, there is still a wide gap in relation to men at all levels, but especially at higher levels of decision-making. Nagaland has not seen even one woman candidate elected for assembly election till date. And particularly due to their low representation in decision making forums, (lack of critical mass of women) they have little say in the rules governing natural resource management now being framed. This is a very central argument, that although is understand by self-respecting development workers and bureaucrats dealing with development, unfortunately not often brought into actual policy (Kirpal, 1995).

Conclusion

A misrepresentation of the past prevents the identification and hence the challenging of the institutional and social constraints that the Naga woman continues to face and allows traditional inequalities to persist in emergent institutions for environmental change and efficient eco-management for the Naga society at large. Women are not passive victims of environmental degradation but to be effective agents for changing their situation requires the ability to transform in their own interest, the formal structures that control natural use and abuse including existing socio-economic and political barriers.

REFERENCES

Escobar, Arturo (2008), *Territories of Difference: Place, Movement, Life, Redes*. Durham, NC: Duke University Press.

Kirpal, P. (1995), *Culture and Development*. New Delhi: Har-Anand Publications.

Peluso, Nancy Lee and Michael Watts (2001), *Violent Environments.* Ithaca & London: Cornell University Press.

Zehol, Lucy and Kevekha Kevin Zehol (2009), *The Legendary Naga Village—A Reader* (Khezhakeno). Dimapur: Heritage Publication House.

12
Livelihood Pattern and Health Care of the AO Nagas in Rural Setting in Mokokchung District, Nagaland

Pranjal Boruah

Introduction

Livelihoods is an aggregate measure of how people or a given population (as small as a household of a single person) make their living within the limit imposed by the environmental, social, economic and political conditions of the society within which they live. This determines the totality of human welfare of a household at the micro level, and a community, a region or a nation at macro level (Ajala, 2008). The term 'Livelihood' implies the capability and capacity to survive (Gregory, 2008).

Life and livelihood are linked to the biological and physical world in a complex way. Humans are bound by their physical and biological environment in terms of provision of food, water, shelter and other environmentally related services. However, links to the environment are more than a rational and positivistic issue. They also encompass values and symbols, ranging from identity and solidarity to property control and power relations. This includes values and systems of norms as significant parts of the management of resources, influencing human health and other viable of life and livelihood. Cultural systems influence the way in which resource utilisation and environmental impact accrue to various groups in the society.

The tribal communities of India have distinctive problems because of their special kind of placement in difficult areas and circumstances in which they live. The first and foremost characteristic of the tribal economy is the close relationship between their economic life and the natural environment or habitat, which is, in general, the forest (Mehta, 1994). Technology, life and livelihood strategy of a tribal group depends on the nature of habitation, environment and resources (Sahadevan, 2009).

The present study is an attempt to analyse the livelihood pattern of the Ao Nagas, in rural setting in Mokokchung district, Nagaland. The empirical data presented in this paper have been generated through field investigation in three homogeneous Ao Naga villages, namely Lirmen, Yajang-A and Yajang-B under Japokong range in Mokokchung district. The total households of the village Lirmen is 130 and that of Yajang-A is 101 and Yajang-B is 28. Standard anthropological techniques have been used in the collection of field data.

Ethnography of Ao Nagas

The Aos, a major Naga tribe, are the principal inhabitants of Mokokchung district of Nagaland state in Indian Union. According to mythology of the Aos, they claim that their ancestors emerged from the stone (Jamir and Lanunnungsung, 2005). The name Ao means went or went away (Aier, 1990). They call themselves *'Ni-so-meh'* and *'Sa-mai-na'* (Sen, 1987). The Ao Naga belongs to Mongoloid stock. They speak Tibeto-Burman language and are divided into *Chungli*, *Mongsen* and *Chungki* sections based on their dialect.

The Ao is an endogamous tribe divided into different clans such as *Longkomer*, *Longchar*, *Jamir*, *Lamtor*, *Imchen*, *Walling*, *Pongen*, *Ozukum*, *Tsudir* etc. Clan exogamy remains the most important marriage rule among the Aos. In Ao society, they prescribe the rule of marriage both for widows, widowers as also for divorces.

Nuclear type of families is predominantly found in the Ao community as after the marriage, the newly married couple lives separately in a new house constructed by the husband. Inheritance is in the male line and in case of absence of sons, only the close agnatic male members inherit the property, particularly the landed property. A daughter cannot inherit the landed property.

Village council (*putu menden*) is the highest authority in a Ao village and all the members of this village council exercise their supreme power collectively in their village administration. The Aos are Christian by religion at present but traditionally they were animist. They have faith in supernatural powers and also believe in ghosts and spirit.

The Ao people have their own dress and ornaments which are distinct from other Naga tribes. They had several festivals in year and most of the festivals were centred round to their agricultural activities and celebrated with feasting. But after Christianity, the Ao Naga have abandoned most of their traditional festivals, however, they still continue to perform the traditional *moatsu* festival with certain change and modification.

The Daily Activities of the People

The people are mostly *jhum* cultivators and so they are engaged in their *jhum* field for the entire year. Both men and women go out to their respective *jhum* field by completing their breakfast before 7.30 A.M.

The children those who go to schools get ready at 7.30 after taking meal. Majority of the children do not go to school and play outside. Some boys and girls generally look after their infant and toddler brothers and sisters during day time in the absence of their parents. The adult daughters do the household work and also help mothers in preparing food. The unemployed young boys help their fathers in domestic works and in the *jhum* field. Some of them go out in search of job on daily wage basis. Sometimes they spend their time by hunting in the forest.

Elderly people who are too old to work in the agricultural field, work on some basketry (for domestic use only), and fencing or in the kitchen garden, or simply sit down and wait for the day to pass. Generally, the menfolk if sometimes do not go to the *jhum* field, get busy with work on basketry, repairing of their house and some other occasional tasks like bamboo work etc. The womenfolk also sometimes do not go to their *jhum* field and engage themselves in domestic works and other relevant activities.

Usually, the people work in the *jhum* field up to 4.30 P.M. and thereafter they come back to their respective home. While coming back from the field they carry betel leaf, various roots and shoots, broomstick, firewood etc. with their baskets. Usually they sell the betel leaves on the way.

After reaching home both men and women take bath. The womenfolk get busy in the preparation of night meal. Mothers having adult daughters need not do by themselves. The daughters do it either entirely by themselves or help their mothers in household works.

The men folk generally spend the evening by gossiping with the neighbours. Some of them go to fetch water in bamboo pipes. Usually both men and women and the children (if needed) also fetch water in bamboo pipes as required. Occasional shopping in the nearby shops is also done in evening by the menfolk. Some members of the men folk in the evening stay at home to feed the cattle and to do a little bit household work. After having the night meal, which is usually finished by around 8 pm, they go to sleep.

On Sunday, the people do not have any definite routine work. They do not go to the *jhum* field and do any work on that day. Just after completing the usual morning works all the family members get ready to go to the Church to pray. The Church time is from 10 AM and by this time all the people complete their bath and morning meal. At 11 AM the Church is over and all the people come out gossiping with each other. The village council members sit in their respective place and hold their meetings on that day as they do not get free time to discuss about village matter except on Sunday. The womenfolk also hold their meeting on that day. Some people visit to their friends/relatives in the nearby villages and some go the nearest town to purchase their necessary items.

Economic Life

The people have predominantly agricultural economy. They are traditionally shifting cultivators. Land is the most important natural resource from which the Ao derived their subsistence. Generally, at the time of establishing a new village, the founding leaders used to reserve certain portion of land for residential sites as well as *jhum* lands in the village. Shifting cultivable land is kept secured by the village community and the residential sites are aligned in rows and also at different places. Each clan possesses the land both for residential and for the purpose of cultivation. Again, in the vicinity of the village, there are protected pockets of lands for forest, bamboo groves and pastures owned by different clans. All the distant lands which individuals or clan cannot claim, belong to the village. Each village has certain areas of common land such as sites for worship, cemetery, water tanks, ground etc. All the land disputes arising in the village are referred to the village council (*putu menden*) who gives the verdicts in presence of both the parties according to their customary law.

In the villages under study the *jhum* cycle is ideally of ten years duration. Under the prevailing system, a field is put under cultivation for two years continuously and then abandoned for ten years in favour of another new tract.

Though agriculture is the primary occupation of the people, however, with the inroad of education as well as because of increase in the population, some of the people have gradually been taking up service and business as the primary occupations. However, agricultural pursuits are also maintained alongside by some of them.

Trade in forest products: Besides the annual agricultural produce in the form of paddy and some other vegetables, the economy of the people is also enriched by certain products collected from the neighbouring forests. The chief among these are fire wood, thatch and *tokopat* for roofing, broom stick and some amount of timber used in house construction. Some people sell forest products in the market. The women collect dried twigs, branches and barks of trees to be used as firewood. The sale of firewood collected from the forest has become an important source of earning for many villagers. As they follow the *jhum* cycle of 10 years duration, greater re-growth of forest is possible and therefore, extraction of firewood from their respective *jhum* fields is not difficult. Firewood selling is a male occupation.

To meet certain requirements of the village, timber is extracted from the village reserve forest which is under the control of the village authority. The money obtained from the sale is used for the construction of community building such as Church and school and for village development. Any timber extracted from *jhum* fields may be individually sold to earn some cash by individual villager. Other forest products such as thatch and *tokopat* (leaf of a kind of palm tree) are used by the villagers for their own house roofing and in need, they sale these to each other among them. However, a few families earn some cash from the sale of broom stick in the nearby market. Whenever they are in need of cash they sell some *jhum* products such as sweet potato, pumpkin and cucumber etc. They sale their products in the nearby markets and thus, these market places play an important role in the economic life of the people.

The cane and bamboo works practised throughout the tract by every household. As Nagaland is rich in bamboo and cane, this abundance has made them common objective to be used for the construction of dwellings, furniture, utensils and other necessaries of daily life.

Animal husbandry: The people are fond of rearing animals like pig, fowls, cow etc. to supplement their household income and also to meet the domestic requirements of meat. Water buffalo are kept by few villagers for use as draught animals. Buffalo meat is also consumed by them.

Poultry keeping is universal though number of fowls in a household is not high. There is hardly any buying and selling of poultry within the village. Poultry is reared mainly for occasional domestic consumption and to enrich meals on festive occasions. The Aos greatly relish pork and so, pigs are kept in most of the households. Pork is taken on the occasions of Christmas, New Year's Day, wedding celebration, house-warming, etc. Pigs are kept properly barricaded so that these cannot damage the kitchen garden of any villager.

Kitchen gardening and horticulture: There are little kitchen gardening activities among the Aos. Vegetables mostly come from the *jhum* fields. Generally in their residential area they also cultivate orange, pear and pineapple. Some of them also possess these in far area from the residence. Besides, they also cultivate betel-nut and betel leaf in these areas. These are the only commercial horticultures among them.

Hunting and fishing: The people sustain their economy by hunting and fishing also. The forests of Aos are a fine hunting ground for certain animals such as monkey, bears, deer, jackal, wild boars, elephant etc. As hunting is very important for the livelihood of the Aos, they start practising it from childhood. The youngsters accompany the hunting parties whenever they get an opportunity. They hunt wild birds and animals both individually and in groups. When an animal is killed, the man who makes the fatal attack gets the major share. The rest of the meat is shared equally by all the other members of the hunting team. Generally, they use their own indigenous methods for hunting. However as a weapon, gun, spear, etc. are used.

The Aos are also expert in fishing and they adopt various methods in the operation. All the people of the three villages under study, go for fishing in their near by river side. Annually, they go for community fishing in the month of October. The date and time of commencement is fixed in the annual meeting by the village council. All the *arju* (traditional age group system) members, village council members and other oldest person who have retired from the village administration work, together go for fishing. They start early in the morning and stay there in the night. Community fishing is a masculine task and according to their custom, no female person can participate and observe in this community fishing. Fishing expeditions are carried out in groups of persons by making small dykes in the streams with bamboo and mud and leafy branches. The water thus accumulated is poisoned with the mixture of particular kind of seeds of a tree or by bleaching powder. The catching of fish is done in the morning 3.00 O'clock. Then all the people together have a feast there and come back to their residence. After reaching their residential area, they gather in the ground of the village with their fishes. Then the *arju* members divide the fishes by age-wise among the people who went for fishing. The highest portion goes to the oldest person among the people. Though the people annually go for community fishing but in general, they go any time for fishing for household consumption.

Consumption Pattern: The crops produced in a season by the Aos are not consumed instantly. The whole production of paddy in a year is primarily meant to last the whole year. Therefore, everybody feels the necessity of storing it in a secured place, away from fire and various agents of mass destruction. In some of the traditional dwelling houses paddy is stored inside containers made of bamboo which are placed at a corner of the house. Now-a-days, the granaries for storing paddy are built little away from the main dwelling house. Apart from paddy other seasonal crops like gourd, pumpkin etc. are also stored inside the granary.

Even the meat of animals killed in a hunting expedition or from market is not immediately consumed; a portion is smoked over the family hearth and preserved on a platform above the hearth for future consumption. By continuous exposure to the heat of fire the meat cannot be infected by pests or household flies. Similarly, fish and other food items are also preserved in the same manner. Apart from paddy, pulses and vegetables, juice of fruits are normally preserved for use throughout the year. In preservation of this item no chemical is used.

Every village has devices to face any dire eventualities like famine and fire. For such occasions the village Church and Church based women's society maintain reserve of paddy. Such reserves are built by way of tithe to be contributed by every household at the rate of one tenth of its agricultural produce. Similarly, the village women's society also builds up a store of paddy through collection from its members.

Normally, the people take three meals a day, i.e. early morning, mid-day and evening. A meal consists of cooked rice and a curry, either vegetable or meat or fish and sauce of dry fish and chilli. Use of mustard oil is rare and they prefer generally the boiled items. The vegetables and to some extent, the meat are stewed and a small quantity of salt and spices are added to improve the taste. For the working persons in the field, a meal is very necessary in the mid day. For this purpose, when they go to the field they carry these food items in a packet. Though the consumption of rice beer was common in the past, only a few persons at present have the habit of drinking. Majority of the people do not consume rice beer since after embracing Christianity. The alternative beverage is tea. Fruit juice is also taken by them. The traditional food items of the Aos are fermented fish and fermented pulse. They are also fond of meats like chicken, beef, pork, and meat of dog. Cooking is performed by women mostly, however it may also be done by the male individuals according to their convenience.

Nature of Spending: The daily expenses in a household are generally met from the cash earned through the sale of forest and *jhum* products. In a few households nearly all day-to-day expenditure is met with salary of the working members. During November and December, many villagers sell some paddy from their stores to sustain the expenses of Christmas which include buying of new clothes for both young and old.

The daily household expenditure cover purchase of various items such as cigarette, *bidi*, soap, salt, mustard oil, pulses, potato, sugar, kerosene oil, tea leaves, beef and pork etc. They buy these items from the village shop or nearby market. Other contingent expenses of a household include purchase of shirts, trousers, shoes, wrist watches, books and stationery for school and college going children, and also a few cosmetic items and medicine.

Some of the expenditures are also incurred by travelling by bus and hired taxi. They go by bus and taxi to Mokokchung, Dimapur, Jorhat and so on, and they also visit these places for health check-up, shopping, for attending to official matters or for mere recreational purposes. A little expenditure is also done by house tax and by electric bill.

Most of the parents spend some amount of money on children's education. The educational facilities in the villages under study are up to primary and middle level. Therefore, education for the children as long as they stay in the village is not very expensive. However, if one studies outside the village, expenditure on education becomes comparatively high. A few householders have sent their children to Mokokchung, Tuli, Dimapur and Hyderabad for undertaking higher studies. Thus, they have to remit a fair sum of money for every boy and girl studying outside.

Marriage and death also includes some amount of expenditure. The minimum expenditure in negotiated marriage involves the cost of the meat of pig/cow and tea to be offered to the invitees and villagers. Funeral rites do not involve much expenditure. The deceased person's family has to arrange for the burial and a simple post funeral prayer meeting.

The nature and extent of expenditure varies from one household to another depending on the level of income. The majority of the people live at the bare subsistence level economy. Only a handful of the people enjoy a life better than those of the others because of the regular cash income earned in the form of salary.

Environmental Health

The health of the Ao people is strongly influenced by their environment and their lifestyle and that these factors produce marked inequalities of health.

The houses of Aos are constructed from bamboo and *toko* leaves are used for roofing. All the houses are of temporary construction, and there are two rooms on an average for every household. One room is being used as living room and the other one is kitchen. The houses do not seem to be very clean. The floor in most of the houses is dirty. The people sit and sleep on the floor without putting anything on it. After meal they wash their mouths and hands where they sit and the interspaces allow the water go down. In case home delivery, it has been observed that discharges come out from the delivery mother also go down between the interspaces of the floor.

In most of the houses, there are no proper windows and other means of light and ventilation. Because of scarcity of light and air, at any time of the day the inner side of a house always remains dark and stuffy. The situation worsens because of the smoke that is generated from the hearths that remain lit for almost 24 hours at least in winter season. The smoke that billows all the time from the hearth affects the living room also. This constant exposure to smoke affects lungs and eyes. During winter, they feel very cold due to bamboo construction of the houses, which may be considered as an important factor contributing towards the frequent incidence of cough, cold, pneumonia etc.

Personal Hygiene and Sanitation: The people are not very conscious about personal hygiene and cleanliness. Both men and women take bath only one time after returning home from the *jhum* field. During the winter many of them do not take bath regularly. Use of toilet soap has been found to be reasonably infrequent.

The children as well as the elderly members are very often found to be in dirty clothes. Most of them wash their cloth on Sunday as they get time. A majority of them brush their teeth with charcoal. Trimming of nails is not done at regular intervals. Sometimes these become very long and dirt accumulates under the same, and they generally do not wash hands before taking meals.

Proper toilet facilities are very important health factors as most of the diseases are borne from open field or *kachcha* type of toilets. During the study it has been observed that all the households have *kachcha* type of toilets. The people go to these latrines with bare foot and they do not use a separate cloth for it. They are also not conscious about the use of toilet soap after defecation.

Since the people under study are widely distributed in the hills in rural setting, they totally depend on the river and spring water for drinking as well as for other purposes. This water is carried through the pipe or canal system towards the village area, where they usually have a big tank to store. All the people carry water in bamboo pipes from these tanks.

Due to scarcity of water and as the tanks are far away from their individual houses, they also store water in iron drums and in the bamboo pipes for 3-4 days and these are not properly washed. In rainy season, they also store the rain water and it is seen only in the tin roofed houses. The preserved water, however, mostly remains uncovered. So, these households are at the high risk due to water pollution because when the water is left open, a large number of micro-organisms from their surroundings get mixed with water causing water borne diseases. Some households also possess overhead cemented tanks where they store the rain water. The only problem with the overhead tanks is that they do not clean the tank regularly so microbes get developed in these tanks. The households are not aware of this type of pollution and this resulted in some diseases. As the people are not getting satisfactory quality of water and as they keep water in open containers inside the house, all these factors together contribute to diarrhoea, cholera, typhoid, jaundice, malaria and gastro-enteritis to these poor households.

Food Habit: Health has a direct relation with the intake of food and drinks that help one in carrying out the physiological processes for living. The ecology, on the other-hand, is responsible for availability or deficiency of different food items in different environmental settings. The staple food of the people is rice. The people generally take three major meals a day, i.e. early in the morning, in the mid of the day and in the evening without much restriction of the food items. They do not have any idea of the need of a balanced diet. People are fond of the flesh food, and they believe that these foods contain all the required nutrients for the body. These items are not in regular menu and these are taken less frequently than vegetables.

Ignorance of the need of additional nutrients during pregnancy, post-natal period and after protracted illness etc., seem to be common feature among the people. Due to the nutritional deficiency and because of the poverty, a number of diseases may originate among them. Anaemia, general weakness and eye problem etc., are some of the frequently incident nutrition related diseases among the people. Except a few educated women, others are not concerned about the balanced diet of their children. The supplementary feeding is not different from the diet of the other family members, and they also do not maintain any proper time schedule for feeding their babies.

Health Resources and Utilization

As a health resource in Lirmen village, there is only one dispensary with a pharmacist, one nurse and one midwife. But infrastructure of the dispensary is very poor and where facilities of treatment for minor diseases are available. The people of this village first consult with the pharmacist or nurse for their diseases and depending on the nature and severity of the disease they give medicines. If they are not cured even after using medicine, the people then go to Morioni, Dimapur, Mokokchung for better treatment.

In Yajang-A village, there is one health sub-centre with one nurse and one midwife. The infrastructure of the sub-centre is also very poor and it is not in regular service. Most of the time, the nurse is not available in the sub-centre and used to get transfer within a short duration. So, the people of this village have to depend on modern health resources available in the nearest town for allopathic treatment. But there is a reputed herbal medicine man and a magico-religious man in Yajang-A village. People of this village mostly depend on these two experts, depending on their nature of the diseases. In case of harm of evil spirit and snake bite they approach the magico-religious man.

For all other disease, they first approach the herbal medicine man, as they believe that he can diagnose the actual disease and cure it. It has been reported that the medicine man could cure some diseases which are not cured by the modern medicines. Their economic condition is a factor, for which they approach the traditional medicine man. It is their assumption that if they go to modern practitioners they have to spend a large amount and sometimes even the patient is not cured. The traditional medicine man never demand any amount from them and most of the time, he gives free check-up. The medicine man diagnoses the case first and depending on the nature of the disease, he gives his prepared medicine. In case, the disease is not curable by him, he advises the particular case to take help from modern resources. Sometimes, in some minor cases, he prescribes the medicines to take from the pharmacy nearest to them. Thus, the medicine man serves both traditional herbal practices as well as modern allopathic practices.

In the village Yajang-B, there is no health sub-centre or dispensary. So, the people of this village go to the nearest town Haluwating and Amguri for Allopathic treatment. As the transportation facility is not good, the people of Yajang-A and Yajang-B villages have to come on foot or have to hire taxi from Haluwating to reach these modern resources at the cost of rupees 600-700. The people of Yajang-B village originally came from Yajang-A village and from same clan. Therefore, they by and large depend on the medicine man of Yajang-A. The people first approach to the herbal medicine man in time of their diseases. If the disease is not curable by him then according to his suggestion they take the help of other modern (allopathic) health resources where available. For snake biting, and wrath of malevolent spirit they take the help of magico-religious man of Yajang-A.

Maternal and Child Health Care

From conception to delivery of the child the Aos by and large do not have any idea of medical check-up. They do not seem to be very much concerned about the necessity of some special care of the mothers' health. It is due to the non availability of adequate health resources and health education among the people.

The Ao women carry more of the work burden of the household and therefore have less time to seek out health care services making them disadvantaged relative to men in their access and utilization of health care services. They do not get much leisure in the midst of their multifarious pre-occupation. From early morning till night women generally remain busy with their work at home as well as in *jhum* field in addition to the child bearing and child rearing exercises. The pregnant women are also to continue these daily works till the time of delivery. Some elderly women commented that there are some cases where women delivered a baby immediately after returning from the *jhum* field. They believe that if they do hard work, the delivery will be normal. As nuclear family predominates among the Ao Nagas, the pregnant women are bound to perform their daily activities for their consumption.

However, a few educated women are found to take health check-up during pregnancy period from the physician of nearest town. Besides, the health centres are far away from their villages and it is difficult for them to cover a long distance, as the transportation facility is not sound. Most of them cover it by walk.

Most of the deliveries are carried out at home by traditional midwives. Sometimes a trained midwife or nurse is called if available. A woman is likely to be taken to a clinic or hospital when she has serious complications.

As there is no proper health centre and no health professional, the people are not aware about the importance of vaccination. They do not know that to save their children from malignant diseases (Tetanus, T.B., Diphtheria, Whooping Cough, Polio, and Measles) vaccination is must. Most of the children suffer from various diseases such as fever, diarrhoa, cough, measles, jaundice, malaria, typhoid etc. In some cases death episodes are also recorded from these diseases. Though all kinds of necessary vaccinations are free supplied by the Government but people are deprived from it as, available health centres have got no scientific equipment to store the vaccines safely. Besides, the health centres where the vaccines are available are far away from their villages and their communication problems do not allow them to receive these. However, O.P.V. (Oral Polio Vaccine) under compulsory programme is given to all of their issues which are supplied by the government time to time at a free cost.

A few of them have got the knowledge of vaccination, but due to their poor economic conditions they cannot get it from the nearest private health resources where these are available. Due to lack of proper health resources they cannot give proper health check-up to their children. As a result, the children die without getting proper health check-up timely. In this context, Babu and Rao (2006) opined, "The problem of child health care of the scheduled tribe is a complex one and is not comparable with the general caste population or even scheduled castes segment. Promotion of modern health care among the tribal societies depends on their capacity to receive it, their stage of socio-cultural revolution, ecological settings and mode of economy and so on."

Summary and Conclusion

The present chapter attempts a brief appraisal of the livelihood pattern of the Ao Nagas, a major tribe of Nagaland in North East India. The Ao people are traditionally shifting cultivators and have predominantly agricultural economy.

Cultivation as a main occupation brings all adult members in a household to remain engaged in agricultural activities in one way or another. Very young children and aged persons are, however, exempted from tasks in the field. The men and women have specific areas of specialization in economic activities including agriculture. The women are primarily the house keepers in the Ao society. However, like other tribes of Nagaland, among the Ao, the women play a very important role in shifting cultivation. Their principal tasks in the field include preparation of the soil, sowing, weeding and harvesting. Felling of trees, clearing of jungle and firing are masculine tasks.

Besides the annual agricultural produce in the form of paddy and some other vegetables, the economy of the people is also enriched by certain products collected from the neighbouring forests. The chief among these are firewood, thatch and *tokopat* for roofing, broom stick and some amount of timber used in house construction. The people sustain their economy by hunting and fishing also.

The majority of the people live at the bare subsistence level economy. Only a handful of the people enjoy a life better than those of the others because of the regular cash income earned in the form of salary.

The health of the Ao people is strongly influenced by their environment and their lifestyle. They still have to subscribe their traditional medicare system as the modern medicare system is not accessible to them. Health facilities do not reach them because the norms prescribed by the State Government for establishing Primary Health Centres and Health Sub-Centres are inappropriate in their localities.

Though government health departments have introduced many needful schemes for the well-being of the society but these are yet to reach in such rural areas. There is need of proper investigation and inspection to implement the government health schemes in these rural areas.

The people, by and large, have not been able to receive more that seventh or eighth standard of education due to economic constraints. So, health education programme for the people in general and for the women in particular, is highly needed to promote health awareness among them. Further, road communication is one of the major problems of these rural people, it should be improved with the help of new technology.

REFERENCES

Aier, I.T.A. (1990), *The Religion of The Ao Nagas,* Jorhat: Assam Printing Works (Pvt.) Ltd.

Ajala, O.A. (2008), Livelihoods Pattern of Negede Weyto Community in Lake Tana Shore, Bahir Dar Ethiopia. *Ethiopian Journal of Environmental Studies and Management*. Vol. 1 (1): 19-30.

Babu, M.S. & P.D. Rao (2006), Child Care among Racha Koyaks: A Tribal Group from Andhra Pradesh. *Man and Life*. Vol. 32 (3-4): 67-74.

Gregory, S. (2008), *Development, Livelihood and Empowerment,* Kerala: IRISH.

Mehta, P.C. (1994), *Voluntary Organisations and Tribal Development.* Udaipur: Shiva Publishers Distributors.

Jamir, N.T. and A. Lanunungsang (2005), *Naga Society and Culture*. Jorhat: Borkatoki and Co. Pvt. Ltd.

Sahadevan, V. (2009), Interaction Pattern and Livelihood Strategies of an Artisan Tribe. *Stud Tribes Tribals*, 7 (1): 27-30.

SEN, S. (1987), *Tribes of Nagaland,* New Delhi: Mittal Publications.

13

Agricultural growth in Nagaland: Some Issues

Manoj Kumar Singh

Introduction

Agricultural crisis in India in recent years is the combination of economic, ecological, technological and institutional factors (Behra & Mishra, 2007). It is pointed out that the recent agricultural deceleration is due to combination of policy fatigue, institutional fatigue and ecological fatigue. The analysis of growth at the all India level in recent years confirms that government expenditure in agriculture including public investment, subsidy for fertilizer and electricity consumption in agriculture are the main factors affecting agricultural production in India.

Agricultural prices have a positive significant impact on its production. Exogenous variables like rainfall and population are also important. However, the recent agrarian crisis has been resulted by various factors. The present crisis is attributed due to technological, ecological, socio-economic and other policy related factors (Reddy and Galab, 2006).

Lack of an interesting farming approach (Desai, 2002), weak agricultural and extension network, restriction on agricultural trade and processing, inadequate public expenditure on rural infrastructure (Sharma and Gulati, 2005). However, the experts called for 43rd National Development Council in May 2007, opined that technological fatigue is one of the important reasons for the agrarian crisis started from mid of 1950s. The same reasons have been supported by the Prime Minister as "One feature that stands out is the lack of any breakthrough in agricultural production technology in recent years. There is technology fatigue, which need to be addressed", (GOI, 2007). Moreover, the poor performance of agriculture experienced in recent years is not because of technological fatigue but mainly because of policy fatigue (Narayana Moorthy, A., 2007).

Since the eco system of hill area regions is very different from the 'Plains', it is essential to focus on the agriculture of the hill districts of Nagaland in a different manner. Nagaland is a primarily an agricultural state although its share in the country's total areas and production is very small. The contribution of agriculture in state domestic product is about 30 per cent and population dependent on agriculture for their livelihood is about 75-78 per cent. The development of the hills is primarily linked with the development of agriculture and its allied activities. Since the hills are constraint in the development of large scale industry. Due to infrastructure constraints, the development of the service sector remains the prime focus. People in hills have been primarily engaged in subsistence agriculture. The contribution of Nagaland to country's total food grain and sugarcane production is negligence.

I

Growth of Agriculture in Nagaland

Share of Agriculture in State Domestic Product in Nagaland

Nagaland traditionally dependent on agriculture for a higher growth in state domestic product, have witnessed almost stagnant in agricultural share in SDP from 1993-94 to 2005-06. The share in SDP has shown a

Table 13.1: Share of agriculture in State Domestic Product in Nagaland

Year	*Share of agriculture in GSDP (in %)*
1993-1994	24.4
1994-1995	25.3
1995-1996	22.9
1996-1997	23.1
1997-1998	24.6
1998-1999	27.1
1999-2000	30.5
2001-2002	31.60
2002-2003	32.86
2003-2004	32.67
2004-2005	33.17
2005-2006	33.41

Source: Statistical Handbook, Government of Nagaland.

stagnant trend that is between 1993-94 to 2005-06 as evident from Table 13.1. It is also observed that in 1990s the share of contribution of agriculture and allied sector to GSDP was less than 30 per cent in Nagaland. The percentage share of contribution of agriculture and allied sector to GSDP is more than 30 per cent. This is the only state in India where the share of agricultural contribution to GSDP has been increasing after reforms period.

Growth Rate in Agriculture

It is observed that in 1990s and early 2005 the growth rate of Agriculture sector in Nagaland is above the national agricultural growth rate but from 2005-06 and onwards the agricultural growth rate decelerated to 2.20 in 2006-07, that is below National agricultural growth rate.

If we analyse average annual growth rate of agriculture sector for two periods of 1996-97 to 2003-04 and 2004-2005 to 2009-10, we find that in the period of 1996-97 to 2003-04 the percentage of average annual growth rate of agriculture sector was 13.5 per cent but in the later period (2004-05 to 2009-10) it decelerated to 4.92 per cent that is a huge gap of the agricultural growth rate between two periods.

Table 13.2: Agricultural Growth Rate in Nagaland

Year	*Growth rate in Agriculture (in %)*
1996-1997	12.54
1997-1998	15.18
1998-1999	5.78
1999-2000	12.92
2000-2001	30.60
2001-2002	12.92
2002-2003	12.67
2003-2004	5.54
2004-2005	9.03
2005-2006	3.53
2006-2007	2.20
2007-2008	N.A
2008-2009	N.A
2009-2010	N.A
Average 1996-97 to 2003-04	13.51
Average 2004-05 to 2009-10	4.92

Source: Planning Commission, Government of India.

Land use pattern in Nagaland: With the growth of commercial agriculture and horticulture in Nagaland, the need for irrigation facilities is being increasingly felt. Nagaland though ranked second in terms of

Net Irrigated Area of Net Sown Area among the North East States but the percentage of Net Irrigated Area in Nagaland is as low as 24.1 per cent of net area sown.

Table 13.3: Pattern of Land Use in Nagaland (2007-08)

Net Irrigated area or % of Net area sown	*Net area sown (Unit Million Hectares)*
24.1	316

Area under total cereals has declined in 2007-08 (–2.51%) while productions of total cereals in the same period have taken quantum jump over previous year (40.10%). Area under pulses has dipped down (–21.2%) over the previous period. Area under total oilseeds have shown upward trend. In the year 2007-08 it registered an increase (8.21%) over the previous period and production of oilseeds in 2007-08 has witnessed positive growth (6.29%) over previous period.

Area and production of commercial crops have also shown positive growth of 14.76 per cent and 7.43 per cent respectively. On the whole the productions of principal crops are not showing much encouraging growth. It is also a matter of concern.

Table 13.4: Area and Production of Principal Crops

Crop	*Area Production*	*(Area in hectares; Production in MT) (2003-04 to 2007-08)*				
		2003-04	*2004-05*	*2005-06*	*2006-07*	*2007-08*
Total Cereals	A	233140	228280 (-2.09)	234200 (2.60)	256880 (9.68)	250440 (-2.51)
	P	385260	382910 (-0.61)	381940 (-0.25)	391110 (2.40)	446260 (14.10)
Pulses	A	30000	28680 (-4.4)	29710 (3.59)	37500 (26.22)	30060 (-19.84)
	P	28900	23080 (-20.13)	35767 (54.96)	45000 (25.81)	35460 (-21.2)
Total Oilseeds	A	61270	64500 (5.27)	68637 (6.41)	70210 (2.29)	75980 (8.21)
	P	69960	82810 (18.36)	63550 (-23.25)	63030 (-0.81)	67000 (6.29)
Total commercial crops	A	14660	21530 (46.86)	22590 (4.92)	15510 (-31.34)	17800 (14.76)
	P	190450	252800 (32.73)	327540 (29.56)	303680 (-7.28)	326270 (7.43)

Source: Statistical Hand Book of Nagaland 2008.

II

Inter-District Disparities in Nagaland

District-wise data related to agricultural area, production and productivity available so that there is district-wise variation in area, production and productivity of three major crops—cereals, pulses, and oilseeds. It is observed that the area under agricultural activities is high in Kohima and Tuensang in respect of cereals, whereas in Zunheboto and some other districts agricultural activities is less. Productivity of agricultural output per hectare is highest in Dimapur district whereas lowest productivity has been registered in Zunheboto district. There is high gap of agricultural productivity per hectare among districts of the State. The district of Dimapur has witnessed 223 tonnes per hectare whereas Zunheboto only 162 tonnes per hectare.

Again in respect of productivity of pulses per hectare, Dimapur district is the top performer that is 155 tonnes per hectare, whereas, Mokokchung is the bottom performer where productivity per hectare is only 112 tonnes. If we analyse the variation of productivity per hectare in respect of oilseeds, we find that again Dimapur is the top performer where productivity per hectare is 111 tonnes. The District of Kohima is bottom performer in this respect.

Dimapur is top performer in all the type of crops because of use of fertilizer, good seeds, good manure, and plain agricultural land area. But other districts are hilly and applying modern tools of agriculture is not possible; that is why traditional tools are in practice. Consequently, productivity per hectare is lower than the district of Dimapur.

There is much variation in gross potential created and net irrigated area under crops district-wise. In Kohima, Mokokchung, Phek and Zunheboto districts, total potential created in 2006-07 was 13339.45, 10941.85, 14125.40 and 10187.70 hectares respectively but in comparison the area of net irrigated in all the four districts is very less, that are 52.69 per cent, 51.12 per cent, 66.84 per cent, and 60.10 per cent respectively. The percentage of net irrigated area to total potential created shows that not more than 55 per cent of total potential created was made. If we observe total potential created for irrigation we find that there is much district-wise variation.

The above discussion on the basis of district-wise data base, we can draw inference that irrigation facilities are affecting the agricultural production and productivity in districts particularly and in Nagaland in

Table 13.5: District-wise Area, production and productivity of cereals, pulses and oilseeds in Nagaland (2007-08)

(Area in hectare/Production in MT)

District	Cereals			Pulses			Oil seeds		
	Area	Production	Productivity per hectare	Area	Production	Productivity per hectare	Area	Production	Productivity per hectare
Kohima	39140	67460	72.35	4000	4590	114.75	9000	6980	77.55
Phek	30990	54620	176.25	3560	4050	113.76	8570	6970	81.33
Zunheboto	22860	37020	161.94	2780	3100	111.51	12280	11570	94.21
Wokha	29210	49000	167.75	3640	4640	127.47	7890	6250	79.21
Mokokchung	29380	49980	170.11	4020	4510	112.18	8290	6680	80.57
Tuensang	39760	70910	178.34	6700	7630	113.88	11260	9990	88.72
Mon	26600	44800	168.42	3400	3990	115.31	8860	7620	86
Dimapur	32500	72470	222.98	1900	2950	155.26	9830	10940	111.29
Nagaland	250440	446260		30060	35460		75980	67000	

Source: Statistical Hand Book of Nagaland 2008.

Table 13.6: Total potential created (Gross) and Net Irrigated Area under crops as per M.I. census report (Area in hectares)

Sl. No.	*Name of District*	*1987-88*		*1993-94*		*2000-01*		*2006-07*	
		Total potential created (Gross)	*Total net irrigated area under crops*	*Total potential created (Gross)*	*Total net irrigated area under crops*	*Total potential created (Gross)*	*Total net irrigated area under crops*	*Total potential created (Gross)*	*Total net irrigated area under crops*
1.	Dimapur	–	–	–	–	34104.85	8176.35	28362.20	14444.63
2.	Kohima	19483.70	18018.60	19483.70	14777.96	17693.84	10033.66	13393.45	7056.81
3.	Mokokchung	4513.00	4513.00	5029.75	4513.00	9593.65	4019.77	10941.85	5601.69
4.	Mon	2149.10	2149.10	2149.10	1441.96	2980.33	2030.62	3197.63	2332.30
5.	Phek	1380.70	13380.70	13380.70	9390.11	12069.12	8881.44	14125.40	9441.95
6.	Tuensang	5321.00	5313.70	5321.00	3997.87	10920.08	6407.80	7940.20	6476.49
7.	Wokha	2705.30	2705.30	2775.90	2173.36	3440.74	2054.45	4023.80	2269.15
8.	Zunheboto	4612.90	4612.90	2049.40	1450.65	9722.40	6254.80	10187.70	6120.50
9.	Kiphrie	–	–	–	–	–	–	2374.25	1500.50
10.	Longleng	–	–	–	–	–	–	2314.00	1337.00
11.	Peren	–	–	–	–	–	–	6357.58	4382.17
	Total	52165.70	50693.30	50189.55	37744.91	100525.01	47858.89	103217.85	60963.19

Source: Irrigation and Flood Control Department Nagaland.

general. The State of Nagaland has sharp variation in productivity per hectare of farm output.

III

Constraints, Suggestions and Conclusion

Slow agricultural growth is a concern for policy makers as some two-thirds of Nagaland's population depend on rural employment for a living. Current agricultural practices are neither economically nor environmentally sustainable and Nagaland's yields for many agricultural commodities are low. Poorly maintained irrigation systems and almost Universal lack of good extension services are among the factors responsible. Farming access to markets is hampered by poor roads, rudimentary market infrastructure and excessive regulation.

In Nagaland farmers are facing many difficulties that are:

- In the hills small agricultural holdings are also affecting the economy of the State and the farmers are unable to introduce modern technology in their holdings due to which production is badly affected.
- Due to deforestation in the state habitat of the wild animals are distributed therefore food chain is being disturbed and thus fraying away from the forest into the residential area in search of food animals, these become man eater.
- Globally urbanisation is an increasing trend. Nagaland is fastly moving to the Urbanization. Agricultural lands are badly affected due to expansion of urbanisation resulting in reduction of agricultural land and thereby affecting reduction of crop production.
- Due to the lack of proper roads and transportation, hilly farmers are unable to transport products to the markets and ultimately most of their raw products get damaged and thereby affecting the economy of farmers.
- Several pests, diseases and weeds flourish due to rich humid climatic conditions of the State. Some pests like white grub are threat to hill farmers especially in rain-fed farming areas.

Suggestions

- To boost the agricultural productivity irrigation facilities should be provided in hilly area to reduce dependency on the nature.

Government should check that fund provided by them, is properly used for construction of canal for irrigation because due to corruption most of the work done is of very low quality.

- Rural and agro-based industries should be developed so that the pressure of population on agriculture may be minimized. Due to this migration of the farmers will be minimized.
- Urbanization is providing opportunities of jobs but reducing the agricultural lands due to which farmers are compelled to sell their farming lands for the multistorey buildings construction. Instead wasteland should be given for expansion of urbanisation and protect agricultural land.
- Proper roads construction from villages to markets and better transportation facilities should be given priority so that farmers can sell the crops.
- Research and development facilities should be developed and expanded keeping in mind to the topographical, geographical and climatically conditions of the state. Adequate arrangements should be launched to educate the farmers.
- Since size of the holdings for farming in hilly area are very small, so collective farming should be emphasized by the government to increase production. By this collective farming modern technology can be easily used by the farmers.
- There are no proper credit facilities in hilly areas so as to boost the agricultural farming; proper credit facilities should also be given which can provide easy and cheap credit to farmer in those areas. Rural Bank should be set-up.
- There are some agricultural crops which need very less care and labour like Jaiyal, Jhangora, Burans etc. So such types of crops should be cultivated in Nagaland to gain more profits.

Conclusion

From analysis made in this chapter it can be concluded that the share of agricultural contribution to State GDP is still high. It is a matter of concern that the agricultural growth rate in early 2000 decelerated. We also find that there is district-wise variation in area, production and productivity in agriculture sector. It is the fact that many constraints to agricultural development in the State are prevailing those should have been overcome for the acceleration of pace of agricultural growth from subsistence level to commercial level.

REFERENCE

Behera, B. and P. Mishra (2007), *Acceleration in Agricultural growth in India: Suggestive Policy Framework*, Vol. 42, No. 42, October 20.

Desai, B.M. (2002), "Terms of Trade ,Trade and Technological Change, Strategies for Agricultural Growth", *Economic and Political Weekly*, Vol. 37, No. 8.

Government of India (2007), "Inaugural Address of Dr. Manmohan Singh, the Prime Minister of India, 53rd meeting of the National Development Council, Government of India, New Delhi, May, 29.

Narayanamoorthy, A. (2007), "Fertilizer Consumption after Decontrol; Myth and Realities", *Artha Vijnana*, Vol. 37, No. 4.

Reddy, V.R and S. Galab (2006), "Agrarian Crisis: Looking Beyond Debt Trap", *Economic and Political Weekly*, Vol. 41, No. 19, May 13.

Sharma, P. and A. Gulati (2005), "Can the Budget Boost Agricultural Performances", *Economic and Political Weekly*. Vol. 40. No. 21.

Statistical Hand Book, Government of Nagaland, (2008).

14

The Naga Land Use System : Economy, Harmony and Relationship

Mita Sarkar (Das)

Like any other traditional society, the economy of the Naga society is predominantly agrarian in nature. The livelihood of the Naga depends largely on the local natural resources. The given ecology, land and forest constitute the basic foundation of their culture and social system. In other words, the Nagas draw their livelihood sustenance from the traditional agricultural system. In the society, the use of land is the nucleus of all socio-economic activities and work participation. The dominant land use system and traditional economic activities are *Jhum* or *Jhuming* ("slash and burn" or "Sweden" agriculture or referred to as shifting cultivation; In North Eastern region of India it is popularly known as *Jhum*), sedentary terraced wet-rice cultivation and forestry. *Jhum* system, according to Payn as quoted in Hodson (1911:15) is, "The primitive mode of agriculture all over the world and widely practiced, even yet, wherein virgin forest land is abundant, for in such circumstances it is the most economical method, because it produces the largest net return". The National Sample Survey (NSS 44th Round, 1990) defines shifting cultivation as, "an agricultural system in which impermanent clearings are crcpped for shorter periods in years than they are fallow."

The Nagas use simple technology for agricultural purpose, which fits well with their ecological surroundings. Moreover, their economy can be said to be of a subsistence type and always aimed at producing crops for their family consumption. "The family is a unit of food production, consumption, distribution and of property ownership" (Singh *et al.*, 1994: XIV). Therefore, the Naga economy can be broadly categorized as "production-consumption economies".

The early writers on the Nagas like Hodson (1911), Hutton (1921), Fürer-Haimendorf of (1936) record the Naga occupation or domestic life as: *Jhum* system of cultivation, terraced field [settled cultivation], manufacturing [spinning and weaving, pottery, wood work, metal work, basketry], food gathering [mushrooms, roots, fruits, herbs, honey collection, etc.], hunting, fishing, and livestock.

Traditionally, in sedentary terraced cultivation, a mono-cropping of rice [*Oryza sativa*] is practiced. Such cultivation system is mostly located on narrow river valleys. In shifting cultivation, multiple cropping systems are practiced. Even among the various Naga groups, the agricultural practices vary from one community to another. For instance, the Naga groups like the Tangkul, Mao, Chakhesang, Zeliangrong, and the Maring practice both *jhuming* and wet traced cultivation.

Traditional Land Use System : Uniqueness of Nagas

The Naga village is well-defined unit having their own village territory, land and forest. The units of this structural village system are comprised households of different clans. Villages are complementary component having interdependent relationships: socially, economically and culturally. Also, the village system and its functions are a source of their tradition and culture.

Indeed, the village represents a social, political and cultural unit and each village is an independent unit. The village functions as a compact and well-knit society where the traditional customs and disciplines were observed. A Naga village state has (i) population, (ii) territory, and (iii) sovereignty as its components. The Naga village was in the past an independent unit and accordingly enjoyed the right of sovereignty. Every village state pursued an independent foreign policy and implemented its own customary laws on all walks of life towards its citizens. Each village state had its own defence system. Administration is indigenous and independent. Its economy was local and self-sufficient. In the village, customary laws were strictly enforced. Every Naga obeyed these laws for he himself was the maker of the laws. Laws of the *Morung* (dormitory) or of the society – all these were accepted in the making of these laws. Each village state enjoyed the absolute rights to make war and peace. It pursued one independent policy of its own.

The village is often irregular in settlement patterns and situated mainly on hills tops or the shoulder of a spur, where it is warm, well defended, and there is adequate supply of water. The reason for choosing hill tops for their settlement was a strategic one and it was a necessity of time as they had to keep constant vigil over the invading enemies. It has been stated that "Naga communities are organized very strongly around the principle of the village as a unit, ruled over by an autocratic chief." The villages are sovereign state in nature and always a social, political and religious unit. The village community is a compact well-knit society where the customs and traditions are regulated accordingly. During the times of head hunting or inter-village feuds, hostility and fear of enemy invasion was a common phenomenon. "This may, to certain extent, account for the divergence of dialects from one village to the next one" (Horman, 2000:66). In the case of the Tangkhul Nagas, every village have their own respective village language and in most of the cases it is not intelligible to one another. However, there is one common language called Tangkhul tui (Tangkhul language). This language is intelligible to the whole Tangkhul Naga community.

The first settlers of each village had carved out enough land which enabled them to become self-sufficient. Horman (2000) pointed out that the popular practice in the Naga world for villages is to send people out of their inhabitants to form a new colony, or to exploit the territories of the villages, so as to reduce the population in the village. After sometimes such newly formed colonies became independent, retaining only sentimental links with the mother village. Thus, they eventually became consciously defensive, and it explains their strategic choice of hill tops as sites for their village. Persons belonging to the families of the same stock in the male line form themselves into a clan. Members of the clan work together and form a village under the authority of the eldest of the clan who takes the title of the headman or village chief. The village itself is their identity in terms of society, culture, tradition and economic status.

Before the advent of the British colonialism , villages were isolated from one another and inter-village trading and interaction were limited, except few friendly villages. During those times, trade relations between the neighbouring villages were minimal with the exception of some of the friendly villages. The different villages including villages of the same community were living in a constant state of feud. Hodson (1911:130) states that "the origin of many of the village feuds is lost to memory, but the heritage of hate persisted in full vigor".

The Nagas seldom shift or move their villages sites. However, in recent times, there are some cases where new villages have been established. As said, villages have their own demarcated boundaries, viz. streams, rivers, ridges or stone. Though there are inevitable inter-village boundary disputes, which is a common phenomenon even now. Hitherto, the spatial ties of marriage, politics, and trade among the various villages creates an extensive network of relations.

Administrative Institution

The village system plays a significant role in the Naga society. Among the Konyak Nagas, the powerful village chief called *Ang* units the village as the embodiment of its fertility and cohesion (Furer-Haimendrof, 1969). Among the Lotha Nagas, Tangkhul Nagas and the Rengma Nagas, the unity of the village is expressed with the hereditary clan or village chief. The Ao Nagas have village council organization. Among the Tangkhul Nagas, villages are ruled by the hereditary chief called *Awunga*. But *Awunga* does not acquire his position by chance but usually deserves it. He is usually the unanimous choice of the head of all the clans residing the village. The village chief administer in consultation with The Village Council.

Village Chief: As noted, the office of the village chief is hereditary passing down to the eldest son. The chief is prominent at all social religious gatherings of the village [in olden days, the village chief played triple roles: secular, religious and ceremonial]. After the advent of Christianity and its subsequent prosylitisation, the role of religious activities are taken over by the local Christian priest. But as the head of the village administration, his duty is to summon and preside over both the village public meeting and council. In any function either executive or judiciary, the village council is bounded by the various unwritten customary laws which have to be followed accordingly.

By tradition, the village chief is the nominal owner of village territory, land and forests. But in practice, the land and forest belongs to the whole village community. Each *bona fide* household of the village has the right to possess properties like homestead, kitchen garden, paddy field, garden, fishpond and woodland.

Village Council: In the village council as per custom, all the clans in village have one or two representatives. Every village has about 5 to 8 clans. The councillors are either elected or appointed by the respective clan members. To be councillor one has to attain certain qualifications. Any married person (marriage being considered as a sign of maturity) is eligible to hold the office of the councilor. He continues in office as long as he commands the confidence of his clan. He may hold office for a long time, but the office is not hereditary.

The functions of the village council are broadly executive, administrative and judicial. The councillors are the real body in whom the highest power of the village state is vested. They are at the helms of affairs of the village in war and in peace; they can amend the unwritten laws, which are the rigidly followed. [Although, in application of actual laws in day-to-day administration, there are variations from one Naga group to another.]

The most important of the village is the community and natural resources (land and forest). The Naga concept of territory is located on objects and places they possessed and controlled which are inherited and immutable. Within the given village territory and land, there are different patterns of land use and landownership. The land use system revolves around the basic question of how land is used by the society and its members. Each household has the right to possess paddy fields, gardens and woodlands.

Land Use System

The land use system of the Naga encompasses the tenure of land as well as ownership of land in the village. The land use system includes all the different types of land utilization in the given village territory. Besides, in land use system, there are two way relations, that is, between the land tenure system including ownership and cultivation of land. One has to keep in mind that there are slight differences in the pattern of land use among those villages traditionally practicising shifting cultivation and sedentary terraced cultivation.

We can broadly categorise land use system in the Naga village into three divisions: (i) village settlement area, (ii) community land and clan's land, and (iii) forests.

Village Settlement Area

Generally, the Naga village settlement is either compact, shapeless-nucleated or of lineated form. The houses are aligned along one or more paths, that is, align with the main road or footpaths.

Broadly, the land use in settlement area can be divided into the following types: (a) homestead, (b) home garden or kitchen garden, (c) public open ground, (d) roads and footpaths, (e) village spring ponds, and (f) burial ground. In settlement area each household has got its own homestead, kitchen garden and compound. The size of the village settlement area varies from village to village.

Homestead and kitchen garden are individually owned by the household whereas, other land, like roads, footpaths and public ground, belongs to the village community. In the village, every household has its own homestead land and home garden. The third land use is open public ground. In open public ground, activities like village public meetings, festivals, as well as space for the children. The community maintains the village's common roads but footpaths are taken care of by the individual households. Public places like school, church, and community hall are built in public land. Usually the burial ground is located at the outskirts of the village.

Community and Clan's Land

The community land consists of undivided land, which belongs to the village community. Any bonafide household is free to use such land for any agricultural purposes and domestic consumption. It may be pointed out that this might be owned by an individual household or by the lineage members in the name of the head of the lineage temporarily. As long as the household operates the land for agricultural pursuit either by shifting of cultivation or other purposes the household has full right to build fence or ditch around the area to protect from the wild animals and cattle. Once the household stops the agricultural operations, the plots automatically revert back to the community land. This particularly happens in the case of small-scale shifting cultivation, and crop farming. In case of sedentary terraced cultivation, such plot eventually became private property.

In community land every *bona fide* household has the right to use and occupy without paying any land revenue to the village authority. Any individual household cannot claim more land than what one can actively make use of. Household members cannot bar any person/member from occupying or using any vacant plot of land by claiming that it is within their occupation or has otherwise acquired it unless there is incontrovertible evidence of his actual use of the plot. "Whatever may be the position in the statute, shifting cultivation is frequently associated with the tradition of communal ownership of land. Very frequently, individual households do not have absolute ownership right over the land cultivated by them. They can hold the land so long as they make effective use of the same. As soon as they stop their operations, their right ceases" (Ngajokpa, 2000).

There are certain customary provisions in using the community land. When one household or person operates agricultural and other related economic activities, the occupant has the right to fence the plot or ditch surrounding the land, although the village chief and his councillor lay down certain provisions about the size of the area or plot which one can operate. If a person vacates or does not make use of the land under his actual occupation, the land/plot reverts to the community. In this case, there is no proprietary, heritable or transferable right on the community land, the use and occupation is purely of temporary nature especially seasonal agricultural cultivation.

However, there are traditional rights of a person to acquire ownership if the individual household has made permanent improvement on it by way of construction of permanent building or cultivation of permanent crops and plants like fruit trees or converting into sedentary terraced paddy field or fish pond. The Naga society evolved sedentary terraced cultivation mainly in the form of wetland cultivation of paddy in the river valleys.

The land of the clan like community land, is free to access and extract the resources but is limited to clan members only. This type of land system exists only in certain Naga villages. Many Naga villages do not have any land system of the clan. This type of land use is less significant in the Naga society.

Forests and Ownership of Land

Forests and its products are indispensable economic asset of the Nagas. The forest situated around the village settlement areas are under active use by the villagers. Almost all the houses in the villages are made of forest produce – the thatch roof or roofing leaves, the post and the walling made of timber and bamboos, the tying canes and creepers. Firewood used for domestic fuel, is directly obtained from the forests. However, the extraction of forest products is limited to the household consumption. In some villages, some portion of the village forest land and woodland or farm is owned by individual household.

The term 'ownership' encompasses such questions as to who has the rights to use a particular plot of land, who exercises control and who has legal claim to certain portions of village land and forests. Broadly the rights over land are of two types: those that belong to individual households and those that belong to the community. In fact, these two types of ownership are intrinsically linked with the two system of cultivation. Generally, in the case of shifting cultivation land is collectively owned, but in terraced cultivation, the land is owned by the individual households. Each Naga village headman (village chief) has his own definite village territory. Theoretically, the headman of the village owns the land in his name. But in practice, land is held by the village community as a whole. The village headman, as a nominal owner of the village land can never portion out any part of the village land to anybody. For the Nagas land tenure system embodies certain customary laws and under such rules and procedures the individual household has the rights in the use of basic resources of land and water in the community's land and forests.

There are four different kinds of land in the Naga society. Most of the households owned land and worked on the family land. A second kind of land is operational holding that is, leased land from the families. In addition a household works on the land owned by the clan or the village. A fourth type of land is one where a household manages land owned by the village. The land owned by the households is managed at different levels. For instance, sedentary terraced agricultural fields are generally owned by individual households and considered as private property with ownership entitlement.

Land ownership is an important economic component of the Naga society. In olden days, the wealth of the household was measured in terms of landed and domestic properties, that is, how much the individual household owned the land and domestic animals [cattle and Mithun]. Broadly, we can categorise individual household owned land as 'ancestral land' and 'acquired land'. *Ancestral land*, as the name suggests, is that land which is passed down to the male line from generation to generation. *Acquired land* on the other hand, is the land obtained by purchasing or barters by an individual. In the process land can be re-classified as ancestral land when it is passed down to the children of the one who has acquired it.

Forest (Woodland/Farm) Ownership : In some cases, forest area is divided into number of plots and is owned by the individual household. Such an area is considered as household's reserved forest. In this household reserve forest no one is allowed to encroach and no one is allowed to set fire or collect any forest products. The owner is free to manage and use the forest.

The Naga society having patriarchal social system, does not permit the immovable property especially agricultural land and house to pass down to women. Such properties have to be handed over only to the males. Also, like homestead and sedentary terraced fields, household's owned forest/woodland are important immovable property. The household can sell or mortgage this type of forest at any time. It is because of the selling and buying system there is inevitable disparity in the land holding.

Inheritance and Transfer of Land

The land use system and its customary practices are transmitted from generation to generation. In the Naga society, only males can permanently inherit the landed properties. The same general rule of inheritance persists in other Naga groups (Hutton, 1921; Ngajokpa, 2000). If a man leaves no son, the inherited properties will go to his brother or to the nearest male cousin.

As mentioned, the four main important household properties are homestead, terraced paddy field, *Jhum* areas and the forest owned by the household. The importance of the landownership in the society is apparent, as for the Nagas, their lives directly depend on it. Individually acquired land and property are transferred from generation to generation. Such old practices have been sustaining since they first settled in the village site. At the same time, individual ownership is a kind of practice that would mean possession of land with rights to use it or dispose it in any manner according to the customary practices.

Land transfer or sale of land is possible within the prescribed limits and requires certain social and customary sanctions. No land is to be sold, mortgaged, leased, bartered and gifted or otherwise transferred by the Nagas to any non-Nagas. Although individual owned land is sold according to individual's consent, there is the inevitable customary sanction that one has to follow the traditions. The selling should be done within the village; one cannot even sell it to residents of other villages except the people in the village itself.

Land selling and transfer follows four stages. In the first stage of selling or mortgage or bartering of land is to be conducted among the nearest family members. In case the immediate family members cannot purchase the land, a seller scouts among the members of the clan who wishes to obtain the land. In case no such purchaser is available, the village community is approached for the willingness to buy the land. A person can sell the land within the three layers of the community just described. However, a person can resort to selling to outsiders only after the three stages have been exhausted. Selling of land to outsiders is not a simple task. An important stipulation of selling of land to outsiders is that the buyers of the land have to become *bona fide* and members of the village and must permanently settle down in the village.

According to the custom the son must inherit the landed properties of the family at the time of their marriages. The property is divided and allotted among the sons, while the eldest son gets slightly more than the equal share. Indeed, patrilineal family system is dominated by virilocal marriage and patrilocal residence after marriage. The sons have the exclusive right of property inheritance and the obligation to support parents in their old age.

Earlier we have mentioned that the Nagas follow patriarchal system where women do not inherint family ancestral land, either agricultural or homestead. But the women are taken care of by the father, brothers or husband. The Naga women never complain about the lack of land security, for an unmarried daughter(s) is often taken care by the brother(s) when their parents are dead. At the time of marriage the parents often give certain gifts to their daughter like paddy, buffalo and cow. It is the husband's duty to take care of his wife and children.

Changes in Land Use System

The land as well as ownership of land and its relation to the community have undergone changes in course of time. The changes have occurred for many reasons. Traditionally, the Naga community manages their village land and forest in the following order: (i) Village authority headed by village chief manages the village territory and land. Any inter-village land dispute and intra-village land dispute are taken care of by the village authority. (ii) All the *bona fide* households of the village have the right to use community land for agriculral purposes, expand or make it permanent for cultivation. (iii) The one who clears the virgin forest for cultivation purpose will be recognized as the 'holder' of the field at least till it is left fallow. This fallow land will revert back as community land.

In recent times, the land use system and tenure system face inevitable threat especially to the community land and forest. Broadly, the changes are attributed due to the socio-economic transition and population pressure. Mergence of 'elite households' and appearnce of money economy in the village are slowly replacing the traditional barter system. Transfer of money takes place now when the ownership of land changes. Another ınevitable change is the influence of exogenous forces and internal transformation in the household economic system.

The emergence of elite household can be traced back to the colonial period. The introduction of currency value by the British had led to the alteration of the local standard of wealth, power and influence to some extent. The British introduced Western system of education which was assisted by the Christian missionaries to bring the Nagas in touch with the modern civilization and used the educated class as link between the rulers and ruled. With the rise of the elite households including the preacher, pastor, educated class—who worked for the British administrators, the position of the traditional power (traditional institution) holders seemed to have weakened to some extent. This conversion of Christianity in fact resulted in the erosion of traditional belief system as well as the institutions. At the same time, this led to the gradual transformation in value systems, catalyzed by the increasing influence of market forces.

It is further emphasized that 'power' and 'status' attached to the land were directly affected. And land was considered the most important factor gaining status and influence in the society. But now it is challenged by the introduction of currency and education. The two factors, education and newly formed wealth based on currency put pressure for modifying the traditional land ownership system. The money economy had multiple roles as an agent of change. With this regard, owned land is available as a commodity in which sale and purchase is possible. Eventually the best portion of the land was under the ownership of rich households.

The other intervention that has led to the change in the land use is inappropriate developmental schemes mainly from the state mechanism. No doubt development schemes have been promoted in the region but this has been taken up without considering the ecological parameters. The villagers have readily accepted income generation schemes introduced by various agencies [Government as well as NGOs] especially those related to horticulture, cash crop promotion or commercial based afforestation. Moreover, the promotion of income-generation schemes affecting a change in land use patterns, has also resulted to competition of land. For instance, more and more commercial plantations and tertiary shifting cultivation activities operate in the community land.

The village territory and land becomes the bond which tied the members of the village community. Traditionally, in the Naga society, land use system and tenure are not codified in written basis but it is based on oral tradition. This could have made an easy target for the individual household to extend land and claim as private ownership. If a particular plot of land is operated by one individual household on the community land and make permanent improvement on it, and continues to occupy it, that land in course of time, is recognized as his/her private property. This goes to show the increasing tendency of individual ownership of land.

This eventually shrinks the community land in the long run. Another possible factor for shrinking village community land is certain development activities or projects in the form of reclamation of the plot of land by the government. Such initiatives pave the way and encourage the state machinery to control land. Even though there is a clear cut demarcation between privately owned land and community land. In reality the village community land are often usurped and turned into individual land. Such processes become the inevitable situation.

Territorial Concept and Ecological Relationship

The interrelationship between territorial, ecology and economic system operates within the given village land. The uses of natural resources are often regulated by the social and cultural practices. In order to understand the Nagas' traditional and ecological relationship we use Cohen's (1976) concept of 'multidimensional approaches' in understanding ecology and its orientation of the society. According to Cohen, the theory yields four major ecological orientations. The four ecological orientations are : (a) the Instrumental or Means Orientation, (b) the Territorial Orientation, (c) the Sentimental Orientation, and (d) the Symbolic Orientation. Here, we shall consider only means, territory and sentimental.

The Paradigm of Naga Ecological Analysis

Orientation of Ecology	*Means*	*Traditional*	*Sentimental*
Purpose Mode of Adaption	Natural Resource Livelihood and Economic Sustenance of the community	Control Traditional Institution	Attachment Sense of belongingness and prestige
Regulative Mechanism	Traditional and local knowledge system	Collective decision making	Social System based on traditions and customs
Types of Environmental Organisation	Land and Properties of Values	Territorial Rights and Boundaries	Village Systems

Source: Cohen's concept is modified in the Naga context.

(a) Means of Instrumental Orientation

Means or instrumental orientation relates to the environmental and space as a resource or the locus of resources. The points in space or features of the environment may serve as resources because of their own qualities, their location or both. Natural resource refers to an individual or community.

In the Naga society, surrounding natural resources are the primary means of sustaining their livelihood system. Village territory, land and forest are their sole life support system. The Nagas depend on the local ecological knowledge system in the regulation as well as utilization of the natural resources with the inherent source of Nagas' local sustainable level without disturbing the ecosystem. The technologies that the Nagas employed, are still primitive, simple and ecologically adaptive. In other words, the Nagas employed environmentally feasible implements.

The Nagas also organized the ecological parameter as 'property value' in their given village system. The property values in the sense of an individual household's landed properties and forest. However, the community maintains the common properties. The belief that the natural landscape is sacred and that the God has given to the people' as a tribe, is known to themselves.

(b) Territorial Orientation

The territorial orientation relates to the environment in terms of control over the territory and territorial resources, be it in the form of physical dominance or traditional institutional-based regulation. Historically, the struggle for control over territory is a major and persistent feature of human society. Form (1954:321) states that "the ecological processes in terms of territorial control and its accompanying regulative mechanisms for 'dominance'."

The same concept exists in the Naga society. In every village, respective village territory, land and forest, and the areas are demarcated either by streams, rivers, ridges or stones. The land and territory provides an important element of psychological security, its sense of belonging and roots. The Naga society is one with its territory, whose rhythm is obeyed and it maintains innumerable ecological links. The dominant control of territory is the most important aspects because all the social, cultural and economic activities operate within the given village land. By tradition, the village land and forest are controlled by the village community. Such territorial system in fact upholds the communitarian social system.

(c) Sentimental Orientation

The sentimental orientation refers to the space in terms of psychological attachment to the area. The sense of attachment conveys both to an individual as well as the community; attachment may be the result of a sense of belonging to the place, or it may be derived from a place's prestige. Cohen (1976) observed that, "Within the sentimental orientation two related, fundamentally dissimilar, modes are distinguished. The primordial represents attachment to a place or territory rooted in birth or traditions. Hence, it is less institutionalized than the prestige, which represents the social sentiment. The prestige orientation generates attachment to the place where one is living as 'home'." Cohen further emphasises that the prestige mode relates to the environment in terms of social evaluation according to its various features, from houses and neighbourhoods to whole region, derived, in principle, from the worthiness of those associated with them.

The sentimental orientation is one important social and cultural phenomenon in the Naga social system. The Nagas once settled, seldom move from the place they live. The essential components in the village system are individual household, clan and community. Moreover, sentimental aspect is deeply rooted to their homestead, landed properties, relatives, clan and village community in general. One beautiful manifestation in this sentimental attachment is "aesthetic-sensibility". The Nagas' aesthetical tastes are displayed through their folk song and dance, beautifully designed hand-woven ethnic attires and carvings in wood.

Every individual belongs to their respective village. They are also identified with that village. This sense belongingness provides the social status as well as security. The concept of "my village, my home and my clan" is strongly accentuated in the society. The village in which they are born, builds up strong solidary institutions. This social solidarity regulates the relationship between people in the form of kinship, clan organization, friendship and neighbourhood. The fact is such orientation sustains the custom and traditional system of the Nagas.

Remarks

We have noted the ecological concept and territoriality in the sense, how Nagas understand the ecology and resources. The village land and forest provides an important element in their livelihood system also, security and sense of belongingness. Historical roots are strongly founded with the land they live. In fact, land is more than just a habitat or a political boundary; it is the basis of their economic and culture systems. Thus, the Nagas are one of those ecological entities moulding a landscape such that there is harmony in the relationship.

Indeed, village territory, land and forest are the basic foundation of the livelihood. And the most important uniqueness of the Nagas is land use system, which is inherent and immutable . The land is communally owned with, collective responsibility and cannot be alienated in any circumstances. Any individual Naga has to follow the tradition in transferring the landed properties. The essential orientation in the Naga traditions is that the concept of 'my village', 'my home' and 'my clan' is never ceased in fact strongly accentuated in the tradition. The land in which they are born, and is build up a strong institution. For the Nagas, land is very much sacrosanct and immutable in any circumstance, and its uniqueness lies in the traditional land use system. Such tradition sustains the Naga cultural root and politics.

REFERENCES

Achary, S.K. (1990), "Ethnic Process in North-Eastern India", in D. Pakem (ed.), *Nationality, Ethnicity and Cultural Identity in North East India*. Omsons Publications, pp. 69-108, New Delhi.

Ansari, A. Ibqal, (1999), "Minorities and the Constitution Making in India," in D.L. Seth and Gurpreet Mahajan (eds.), *Minority Identities and the Nation-State*, Oxford University Press, New Delhi.

Chaube, S.K., (1973), *Hill Politics in North East India*, New Delhi: Orient Longman Limited.

Cohen, S.G. (1978) Review of Anthropology Columbia, Columbia Univ. Press.

Devi, Bimol, (2000), "Administrative Changes in the Hill Areas of Manipur", in Horman (ed.), *The Rising Manipur*, Manas Publications, New Delhi.

Elwin, Varrier, (1969), *The Nagas in the Nineteenth Century*, Bombay.

Form, W.H., (1954), *"The Place of Societal Structure in the Determination of Land Use: Some implication.* Oxford Publication.

Furer-Haimendrof, C. Von, (1969), *The Konyak Nagas: An Indian Frontier Tribe*, New York: Rineheart and Publishing House, New York.

Gait, Edward, (1990) [1905], *A History of Assam, Guwahati* : Lawyer's Book Stall.

Hodson, T.C. (1911), *The Naga Tribes of Manipur*, Macmillan, USA.

Horman, J. (2000), *The Rising Manipur*. Manas Publication, New Delhi.

Hutton, J. (1968), *The Sema Nagas*. Oxford University Press. New Delhi.

Mills, J.P., (1926), *The AO Nagas*, Macmillan, London.

Milton, J. Esman, (1994), *Ethnic Politics*, Ithaca: Comell University. U.S.A.

Ngajokpa, F., (2000), "Land Use System of the Marams" in M. Horam (ed), *The Rising Manipur*, Manas Publications, New Delhi.

Phanjoubam, Tarapot, (1997), *Drug Abuse and Illicit Traficking in North East India*: Vikas Publishing House, New Delhi.

15

Traditional Wisdom as a Strategy of Management of Land Resources and Maintaining Basic Source of Livelihood: A Study Among the Lepchas of North Sikkim Himalaya

Sudhansu Gangopadhyay

Introduction

The age-long attachment with the nature has developed some basic qualities in their indigenous knowledge which has active and eco-friendly role for the management of land in order to generate agriculture resources in the harsh mountainous environment of North Sikkim Himalaya where the Lepchas are living since long past. The Lepchas are believed to be indigenous people who are found concentrated in North district of Sikkim. Again, the core area of habitation of the Lepchas in the district is Dzongu area lying to the west of the Tista river or lying along the bank of the *Tolungchu*, a tributary of the *Tista* river though their concentration is also found as mixed habitation along with other ethnic groups of Nepali, Bhutia in the east of the *Tista* river. But their concentration does not go beyond Chungthang of the district, though their distribution is also seen in other districts with maximum concentration in the east followed by west and south district. According to 2001 census, the Lepchas constitute about 7.50% per cent population (40,568) of total Sikkim population (54,0851) based on their mother tongue. Similarly in respect of district-wise concentration during 1991 census year, north district tops in having Lepcha population (9,899) followed by east (7,863), west (7,501) and south

(4,591). It is also seen that the concentration of the Lepcha population is found in two areas in North district which are: (1) Dzongu area (core habitation) and (2) outside Dzongu area (mixed habitation zone). Again Dzongu area is further divided into two based on its location. These are Tolungchu and Ring Khola. Again *Dzongu* is named as upper Dzongu which is seen to the north of Ring Khola and has reputation for its ruggedness and inaccessible terrain. On the other hand, lower Dzongu is lying to the south of this Khola which has lower elevation in comparison to upper Dzongu. So, in totality the Lepcha concentration is found in three areas such as lower Dzongu, upper Dzongu and non-Dzongu area.

The Lepcha being the inhabitants of rough terrain of middle Sikkim Tista valley, were believed to be dependent on collection of forest products in many ways and to have had familiarity with cultivation of dry varieties of paddy and millet type crops in the high hills of Toloungu valley with the help of slash and burn method of cultivation. But in the beginning of the last century, the Lepcha are seen to have followed the practice in changing mode of land use by way of introducing cardamom on the slope cultivation or wet paddy cultivation in dry terrace probably due to the contact with the Nepali immigrants or exposure with new agricultural methods in recent times. In this context it would not be unjustified to observe the variation in management of land resources and to see impression of antique features in characteristics of land use pattern if the Lepcha settlements are selected from locations of different ecological set up marked by altitudinal variation, degree of accessibility and habitation of the ethnic groups. It would throw light on traditional wisdom in land management and on how to adapt and maintain the survival strategy in this respect.

Objectives

The main objectives of this write up is to see variation in management of land resources among the Lepchas which are guided by altitudinal variation, degree of remoteness and ethnic setup. However, the management of land resource is reflected in traditional wisdom which is seen in identification of land category; way of cultivation; crops grown, variety of season; techniques of sowing, harvesting, implements used, preparation of land, use of high yielding variety and chemical fertilizer, water management and level of production. It is seemed that characteristic features in management of land resource and in maintaining survival strategy would throw light on underlying principles behind the variation in the backdrop of eco-cultural set up of the Lepcha habitation.

Table 15.1: Eco-cultural Situations of the Villages

Sl No.	*Village*		*Zones where located*	*Altitudinal Characteristics*		*Remoteness/ Distance from district headquarter*	*How to approach from district headquarter*	*Terrain Character*
	Name	*Ethnic concentration*		*Average Altitudinal Zones (At the level of Tista Valley) (in metre)*	*Altitudinal Range at Village Level (in metre)*			
1.	Kajor	Lepcha, Nepalee and Bhotia (Mixed habitation of ethnic groups)	Middle Tista Valley (Outside Zongu area), Eastern part of Teesta.	1200-1800	800-1700	4 km	Vehicle frequent service available	Gentle slope with terraces at places.
2.	Lingdong	Exclusively Lepcha	Middle Tista Valley (Upper Zongu, but near to Lower Zongu) Western part of Tista river	1200-1800	800-1700	12 km	Vehicle available but service not frequent	Rough terrain with narrow terraces.
3.	Shipgyer	Exclusively Lepcha	Middle Tista Valley (Upper Zongu with high hills) Western part of Tista	1200-1800	1300-2000	25 km	Major part inaccessible while vehicle ply upto the border of Toong.	Very rough terrain with very narrow terrace.

In order to note down the variation in respect of land resources among the Lepchas, three Lepcha villages – Lingdong, Shipgyer and Kajor have been selected from different eco-cultural situations marked by altitudinal characteristics, remoteness and ethnic composition. The eco-cultural situations of the three villages are given below:

Eco-cultural Situation of the Villages

It is observed from the eco-cultural situation of the villages that Shipgyer has rugged terrain and maximum inaccessibility while Lingdong is not having rugged terrain to that extent. But it is connected by jeepable road from Mangan district Headquarters but service is not frequent. Again Kajor is well connected in Mangan at a distance of 4 km. In respect of ethnic compostion, Shipgyer and Lingdong is lying in Dzongu area where the Lepcha are considered as dominant community and restriction is imposed for other communities to live permanently. But Kajor is lying in non-restricted zone where the Lepcha, Nepali and the Bhutia are the inhabitants.

Traditional Idea about Nature and Land

Indigenous idea on nature and land may be considered as the latent strength to utilize the natural resources effectively. The Lepcha being the inhabitants of the middle Tista Valley, basically have good idea on slope, hill top and hill spur, i.e. sloping land coming out from hill top and descending with valley bottom. They are also familiar with local weather condition, flora and fauna of the area.

The Lepchas identify sloppy land as *rop matro*, while they mark plain land as *potang*. They also know ins and outs of slope. That is why, they mark convex and concave slope as *Chu-kiyung* and *Koop-kiyung* respectively. Even they mark hill spur as *sugor*. *Kiyung* is the name for the stream. Large stone is known as *Long* while land slide is called by *Rit*. Being inhabitant in the hilly areas, the Lepcha have fair idea on altitudinal variation qualitatively. The upper, middle and lower altitudinal part is familier to them as *sayasu*, *liangbak* and *dang* respectively.

The high hill slope of Dzongu area (Lepcha habitat) has developed poor soil type. But the Lepchas have fair idea on soil type at their own level. They divide soil into three types according to colour and condition of soil. They are black (*fat anok bu*) soil, white soil (*fayor*) and red soil (*fat aharibu*). Normally paddy and maize grow well in black soil while ginger in the red soil. The presence and size of stone may be said as best indicator of good / bad soil. Accordingly, the Lepcha have own marking identity. As for example *fat jug* is marked by less and small size stone, while a *fat-dungrup* means much stone and poor depth of soil.

The Lepchas know the change of weather condition mainly by the advent of flower and floral variety of nature and by nature of wind. Basically they have two seasons known as *Sujong lavo* and *Soum lavo*. *Sujong lavo* is known as winter season which they feel by cold wind mainly. During this time, no flower except *Pedongrip* is seen. During this time, they feel touch of wind known as *suchuk kiyar kong* which comes from higher zone of north Sikkim. It stretches between November and February. The another season, *soum lavo* is felt by the presence of hot wind known as *suchuk lang* coming from south Sikkim. During this time, flower of different varieties known as *kursong*, *pedong* and *kuchen* appear. Rainfall occurs during this time. It lasts between March and October.

Management of Land Resources

The effective land management depends on identification of farm land category which ultimately governs selection of crops, type of farming and types of techniques. Again the basis of identification of farm land has been developed by the Lepchas through indigenous knowledge on nature, land, soil and local weather. Therefore, it is necessary to discuss farm land category based on local perception and subsequently farm land category is to be taken into account following the study of three villages in order to see crop varieties, farming methods and techniques and commercialization in agriculture if any in keeping parity with land.

Farming Land Category based on Local Perception

As perceived by the Lepchas, the wet land comprises *Khetjami* known as *areniyot*. This land grows paddy (*jo*) in the terrace field known as *kathem* though dry paddy is found to grow on high slope under slash and burn method. Normally *areniyot* (paddy land) is found in the low height (*dang*) where slopes become low. The wet land is divided into two types based on the qualities of alluvial coverage with its colour, stony coverage and retention quality of water as per idea of survey and settlement department. But the Lepchas think this type of land as permanent and cultivated land known as *Rangji niyot kunchet*. They do not have finer idea on classification of paddy land but they have different varieties of paddy and different methods of cultivation basically guided by local slope, terrain and weather condition.

Similarly, the dry land available in the Lepcha habitat, comprises *sodyum pregsheet* (temporary cultivated land), *niyot som* (dry cultivated land) and *sing* (kitchen garden land). The degree of slope soil condition and nature of dryness divides the land into three types. The existence of *sodyum pregsheet* is rare but its imprints are still left out in small patches in higher slope of the hills. This kind of land has greater slope, poor depth of soil and presence of much stone. This kind of soil is locally known as *fat-dung-up*. The one year cultivation called *namkat* while fallow land for 2/3 years is known as *sodyum nam nyat som lyat bu*. Thus this land is divided into two as mentioned on the basis of holding.

Secondly, *nyat som* (dry cultivated land) is normally found in the mid-altitudinal level or foot hill zone. It is an eroded type though the presence of stones and pebbles and also thickness of soil vary from place to place. Normally, it is rain-fed. The degree of terracing divides the land into three types, i.e. *kathem*, *fat jug* and *fat ajen*. The word *kathem* means presence of terracing while fat jug is leveled as good land in terms of thickness of soil, less stone and black type. On the other hand, *fat ajen* means vary bad land in terms of soil and having more stones. However, this type of soil becomes favourable for the growth of maize, ginger as well as millet type of crops. Out of it, *fat jug* bears good management quality in terms of resource utilization.

The fourth category of land is known as *sing* which is carefully utilized and nurtured due to close proximity of settlement units. Water is distributed to this place by bamboo post or water channel. In this area, fruit trees like guava, papaya are grown along with vegetables such as *raisag*. This kind of land lies in the medium height of the hill range. The height varies between 2000 to 4000 feet. Ginger also grows in this type of land.

Apart from dry land there is another category of land which is named after cardamom cultivation. It is locally known as *lanchi sum* in Lepcha and *alanchi kheti* in Nepali (cardamom land). The land is basically sloppy area. Cardamom growth on slope without any use of plough or spade. This land though basically grows cardamom, allows different kind of trees known as *kartoosh*, *urtish*, *chilawnai*, the last two provide shade to the cardamom plants. It is found lying in the hill slope stretching out from middle hill slope to nearly river bed of Tista.

Farm Land category

We shall now to see area under farm land category in different habitats of the Lepchas, i.e. Dzongu and non-Dzongu area on the basis of ecological condition, i.e. terrain, height and soil condition after having its land category based on people's perception.

Table 15.2: Farm Land Category

Area in hector

Sl. No.	*Village*			*Location*	*In percentage to total geographical area*					
					Farm Land				*Non Farm Land*	
	Name	*Average altitude in metre*	*Total Geog. Area**		*Cardamom Land*	*Wet Land*	*Dry Land including Banjo land*	*Farm Land Total*	*Cultivable Waste Land*	*Land not fit for Cultivation*
1.	Kajor#	1200	261	Middle Tista Valley (non-Dzongu area)	23	3	16	42	2	56
2.	Lingdong	1300	473	Middle Tista Valley (Upper Dzongu area)	20	7	30	57	Nil	43
3.	Shipgyer	1600	1636	Middle Tista Valley (Upper Dzongu area)	7	Nil	23	30	1	69

\# Outside Dzongu

* Wasteland

Source: (Based on Census of India, 1991).

Table 15.2 shows that Shipgyer has maximum land under not fit for cultivation (69% total geographical area) among two other villages under study probably almost same is the condition due to its rough terrain. Similarly land under dry, wet and cardamom cultivation is also less in this village due to inhospitable terrain. Wet land and cardamom cultivation is mostly concentrated in the area where slope is gentle. It is believed that west facing and gentle slope village like Kajor have higher concentration of cardamom as the west facing land gets less sun.

Farming Methods and Techniques

It is observed that terrain condition and slope may be governing factors in broadcasting or putting seeds in the hole. Similarly, water availability along with gentle slope controls the degree of transplantation method.

In case of Kajor village, transplantation of method of paddy in wet terrace, broadcasting in dry terrace in mid-altitude and putting seed in the holes in case of the sloppy land are usual phenomena. Transplantation is also followed in case of *kodo* which is done in dry terrace. But it is planted in field of maize one month before harvesting of maize. *Fapor* is broadcast and cultivated in the second/third year in dry terrace. Otherwise soil fertility would be lost, if it is cultivated in the first year. Wheat is also sown by broadcast. It is to be noted that the village Kajor produces one crop in one calendar year by and large though a little amount of land is devoted for mixed cropping like maize and buckwheat. This type of land grows paddy, maize, millet, wheat, buckwheat, potato and other root crops in general. Maize is dominant cereal cultivated in more than 80 per cent of total cultivated areas followed by paddy (nearly 15 per cent of total land). The land under cultivated fallow is insignificant (2% area of total geographical area).

Spades are used for digging the soil. They also use stick, *kanta* for the same purpose particularly in the stony and sloppy area. The hole would be made by a stick known as *tangel.* Plough is used in places where terrace is well developed and covered with less stone. Spade is more popular than the plough in the village which is indicated by plough spade ratio.

Cattledungs are generally used as manure. Apart from this, leaves fallen from the trees during off season are burnt. The ashes are spread through out the land. This type of manuring is done in the land away from the settlement or in the slope where organic manures are difficult to carry.

People get water from *Jhora* (small stream) and divert the same to the cultivated fields through bamboo funnels.

The Lepchas of Kajor grow high yielding variety of wheat and paddy though use of high yielding variety wheat is much rare. They also use chemical fertilizer. Maize is now shown by broadcast instead of sowing in holes.

Kajor due to having gentle slope and less sun shine, cool climate by and large west facing coverage and having different trees like *chilawani*, *kartoosh*, grow cardamom of *golsoi* variety in general in an area covering 23 per cent of total geographical area. It blossoms during May-June and it is harvested during October-November. It requires weeding for three times. Weeding, harvesting and drying operation are done in three stages in course of getting cardamom finally. The Lepchas are the owners where Nepalies work as labourers. Female participation is badly required in giving readymade shape of the cardamom. It is sold through merchants residing at Mangan.

In case of Shipgyer village, resistance is offered by rugged terrain, high altitude and absence of irrigation facilities for the growth of cultivation. Therefore, only dry farming is practiced. Nearly one-sixth of dry cultivated land is put under cultivation for a year so as to enable other farm areas to gain their recuperation capacity.

The age old slash and burn method, i.e. shifting cultivation is in vogue in this village. The land is kept fallow for four years for the regeneration of forest at the cost of two years farming. Therefore, total 25 per cent area of total cultivated land including 10 per cent of it as homestead land, allow cultivation only for a year.

Degree of slope governs broadcasting on slope or putting seed in the hole. Due to its sloppy land, maize is put in the hole at an interval of half metre in temporary fields. But *kodo* and *fapor* are broadcast and these are grown in homestead land by transplantation method. Wheat and barly are raised from homestead fields. Dry paddy varieties like *tokmojo*, *chobyojo* are grown in the rugged terrain and dry land.

Slash and burn method is practiced in different stages, i.e. (i) selection of land, (ii) cutting and clearing of forest, (iii) drying and burning of decayed materials, (iv) showing of seeds, (v) weeding, and (vi) harvesting. The top of hill, steep slope or rocky surface are not usually considered for shifting cultivation. Trees are cut in the months of January and February. Large trees are cut from a certain height, while the smaller one are cut from the ground. Subsequently, the trunks of trees are laid along contour lines in order to prevent soil erosion. The trees and bushes get dried for about one month and firing takes place by fifteenth of March. The burnt materials are turned into organic manure. The spade is normally in use for digging soil. Sticks and *kantas* are also used to dig soil particularly in stony areas and in the slopes. Plough is rarely used and plough spade ratio is 1 : 13.

Ashes of burnt trees and bushes are normally used as manure in temporary fields but cattle dungs is used if available, in permanent homestead land.

Crops of temporary field are rainfed, but crops of homestead/ permanent fields get water from small streams.

A few of them use chemical fertilizer. The use of high yielding variety is not common due to inaccessibility in rough terrain. *Sonalika* a high yielding wheat variety is used by few of them. The high yielding variety is not very popular due to its high cost.

Cardamom is only cash crop. *Ramsoi* variety grows well in the village because it is suited to high altitude. *Golsoi* variety is also grown to a limited extent. Steep slope, rugged terrain, moist and cold climate are not congenial for the production of cardamom in this region.

In case of Lingdong village, the higher hill slope (*Sodyum pregsheet*) having poor depth of soil and presence of much stone has developed cultivation under slash and burn method (*Namkeet*). This type of cultivation though it is rare, seems to be best possible of management if its slope, soil quality and presence of stone are considered. Again they are careful in the way of cutting trees at height of half feet from the ground in case of small plants or lopping branches. They sometimes cut larger plants or unuseful trees at the height of 2-3 feet from the ground. They allow regeneration period for 2-3 years for the growth of the forest and restoration of soil fertility. For one year they allow to convert the forest residues into fertilizer, prevent of soil erosion by way of broadcast or putting seeds into hole and rasing of certain 2/3 crops.

Similarly, terracing (*Kathem*) has been adopted in medium hill slope primarily for rasing of crops suitable for different quality of soil, presence of stone and availability of water.

The way of gardening by careful nursing and watering, helps them to raise some fruits, vegetable and ginger. This has become possible due to its close proximity to settlement unit.

Another simple way to utilize to hill slope specially down side is through raising of cardamom which has become possible by way of planting trees in order to provide shade to the cardamom plants for its growth.

Thus slash and burn method (*sodyum tot/sodyum sok*), terracing (*kathem*), gardening (*sing*) and cardamom plantation (*jebrong*) have been in use to utilize different types of land in the village of Lingdong.

Crops Grown, Crops Variety and Crop Season

It is observed that the method of cultivation varies according to broad land types. But it is also fact that the management of land is also greatly influenced by its soil quality, presence of stones and gravel, quality of terracing, availability of water, slope at finer level etc. On the basis of different qualities of land as perceived by the Lepchas, the land utilization and management are reflected at different tiers of land in terms of crops grown, crops variety and growing seasons.

The temporary cultivated land (*sodium pregseet*) starts its holding only for one year after allowing land for 2/3 years of regeneration period. The land grows paddy, minor millet locally known as *fapor* and beans of larger size locally known as *taktip*. The only paddy variety known as *tokmorjo* which thrives with little water and become resistants to hill slope at higher part is preferred by them in this type of land. Due to little requirement of water, this paddy variety is leveled as dry paddy variety. This kind of paddy is grown during June-December with the help of monsoon rain. After the harvest of it in December, the land grows millet type of crop *fapar* and large size bean type of plant, i.e. *toktip* in the marginal side of the field. Considering the harsh type of land dry quality of seed of crop is preferred by them.

The wet land, i.e. *niyot* is meant for the growth of different types of paddy cultivation mainly since it requires terrace land, depth of soil and presence of stone and gravel in least amount and availability of water. Different types of paddy, such as *atey, darmarey, thapachini, jakop, champasiri, etc.* are grown in this land. All these types require more water and grow by transplantation method. Out of these varieties, water accumulation is better required for *champasiri*. The production rate seems to be better in relation to other varieties. The grain appears to be lengthy in size. The transplantation process for all the varieties is completed by 15th June and harvesting is done by the middle of December.

The *niyot som* (dry land) is meant for the growth of maize (*kuncham*), wheat (*kokiu*) and millet type of crops, i.e. *fapar* (*karhu*), *kodo* (*mong*). It also grows ginger (*singhi/adoa*) to some extent. It is observed that all types of crops as mentioned, grow in *niyot som* though maize, wheat normally prefer to grow in *fatjug* (good land), and millet type of crops, i.e. *fapar* (*korhu*), *kodo* (*mong*) are found to grow in *fat ajen* (bad dry land). Similarly, ginger prefers to grow in better type of dry land where less stone, good soil and terracing exist. There are different varieties of maize, wheat, ginger and millet types of crop. Out of them, millet types of crops do not have any attachment for growth in higher and lower altitudinal tier. Again large size crop like ginger known at *singhi timbu* is seen sometimes to grow in better types of dry land. In respect of maize, *kuncham dari* (medium size) is preferably attached with higher altitudinal tier, while *kuncham mu* (large size) has attachment with lower altitudinal tier. On the other hand, wheat belonging to *kocher*, and *kokshi* varieties specially grow in higher altitudinal tier while *kokiu* variety would grow in lower altitudinal tier. The crop season is influenced by the altitudinal tier and therefore, varieties grow at higher altitudinal set up, take much more time to attain maturity. Maize normally is shown during 2nd week of January–February end while it is harvested during June 2nd week–July end. The sowing time of *fapar* (millet type) is October while its harvesting time is April–May. Another millet type crop *kodo* is sown in February and it is reaped in the month of December. The growing season of wheat starts in October and ends in April. Thus the season becomes lengthy if it is grown in higher altitudinal tier. The growing season of *kokiu*, variety of wheat grown in wet land of paddy field is found to start after the harvest of paddy, i.e. in the month of December. The growing season of ginger starts from March and ends at next March though ginger grown in the side of dry field along with maize is found to be shown before maize and to be reaped after maize.

The another category of dry land lying to the adjoining area of homestead unit is now-a-days in maximum use by ginger cultivation, though fruit trees and vegetables are found to grow. However, ginger variety known as *singhi chimbu* (small size) is found to grow in this type of land because it requires careful nurturing.

The cardamom land, i.e. *lanchi sung* is meant for the growth of cardamom exclusively. If the cardamom land is situated in the east facing slope, the same has to get much heat which is not good for better production of cardamom. However, considering heat and rough terrain, *saune* variety and *tamrop timbu* (large size) varities of cardamom is preferred by them, though other type of *ramsey* variety of this crop is also found to grow.

Techniques of Sowing and Harvesting Implements used and Preparation of Land

The change of any natural resource like land in the form of its usability does not depend only on crop selection or choice of crop variety but also on showing techniques and implements used. The preparation of land in special form before any stage of agricultural operation has some short of indication towards management skill.

In case of temporary cultivated land *sodyum pregsheet* sowing is made following the method of putting seed into the hole. The holes are made on the hill slope at the interval of 6 inches. The hill slope has been laid by the community in making hole instead of broadcasting as normally followed in gentle slope of lower hills. The implement used for cutting the trees, plants grown during regeneration period in temporary cultivated land is *banchari*. A wooden stick (*tangel*) is used to make holes in order to put seed in it. This kind of cultivation known as *nam kat* found in high hill slopes with forest species to grow, has some merits of land management in such situation. For example, allowing useful trees, converting forest residues as manure (*kung-niyom-asar-busha-lut*) by way of getting dried under sun and little fire, prevention of soil erosion by way of cutting trees at certain height or by way of placement of cut down trees along the line of contour may be said as useful attempt to combat with the harsh terrain. Again getting two/three crops in one season may be considered as an added advantage.

The sowing method for the crops—maize, wheat and minor millets – *kodo*, *fapar* in dry cultivated land '*nyot som*' lying at mid and low altitudinal tier is followed by broadcasting method which is in tune with gentle slope. Again, this land is made fertile with the application of cowdung (*bek-yit*/*gai-ka-mal*). The sowing method between temporary dry cultivated (*sodyum pregsheet*) and dry cultivated land (*niyot som*) is so different in relation with height and slope that the sowing method is known as *jothang* in temporary cultivated land and *jomal* in dry cultivated land. In cultivation, spades are used for digging the soil. They also use stick, *kanta* for the same purpose particularly in stony and sloppy area. Sickle is also used during harvest. The use of plough is also used in dry cultivated land where terrace is well developed with less stone.

In wet land, transplantation method is followed due to well developed terrace field and availability of water. This method is known as *joat lee* in Lepcha which is popularly known as *bijon fat* in Nepali. It is ended by 15th June. Normally plough is the usual agricultural inplement in this field.

In homestead land (*sing*) persona! care is attached in planting vegetables, ginger and they are also very attentive in removing weeds and in raising the crops/vegetables etc. Cow dung is also used. Plough or spade is used in digging soil. *Kanta* is used to remove stones.

In cardamom land, weeding, clearing is much more important than any other operation like preparation of land, sowing etc. Weeding is required three times, i.e. before flowering, after flowering and before harvesting. In cardamom land, fresh plantation is needed only at the interval of five six year normally. But new plantation is required even after one year if the plants get damaged due to much sunshine.

Seed Requirement

It is seen that seed amount is less required in temporary dry cultivated land where it is put in the hole, but the seed is required almost double in dry cultivated/wet land where broadcasting/transplantation is followed. But the production rate is little less in temporary dry cultivated land. Production appears to be little high in wet cultivated land. This may be due to that application of cattle dung, good soil and availability of water in wet land, and these may be the factors in maintaining production rate at a reasonable level.

Water Management

For the purpose of proper distribution of water through out paddy field, they take the help of earthen dam, i.e. *aripo* (Lepcha term) or *ali* (Nepali term). With the help of *aripo* water is also passing down smoothly without any damage to land. They also take the help of bamboo (*tofong*) in order to channelize water to proper site where it is required actually. In making *tofong*, a kind of bamboo locally known as *podyung* is used by them. This kind of bamboo is widely available in this locality. This kind of irrigation is seen in the village and use of bamboo is seen much to distribute water in the village of rough terrain specially in Shipgyer village.

High Yielding Variety and Chemical Fertilizer

Normally, the Lepcha prefer to grow to local varieties though they also use high yielding variety VL-61, *kalra* varieties of paddy now-a-days. It is used preferably at lower height due to requirement of more water and higher temperature.

Normally, they use cow dung though chemical fertilizer is seen to be used in very few cases in recent times. The use is seen much in the villages which are very close to communication network or in the villge of with good terrace land. As a result of it, Kajor uses chemical fertilizer to a great extent.Similarly, Lingdong uses the same to a great extent due to its gentle slope. Shipgyer uses less due to its high hill and rough slope.

Production Level: The three villages, i.e Shipgyer, Lingdong and Kajor lying in different eco-cultural zones, i.e Dzongu and non-Dzongu area of North Sikkim respectively, have different level of production which reflects traditional wisdom and is tuned with harsh environment. It is observed that in rough terrain and high hill slopes of Shipgyer village, seed is put in the hole of temporary farming land (*Jhum* cultivation) and therefore, seed is also required in less amount. Production rate is also less. However, production is little bit fare in wet cultivated land where transplantation method is followed with higher seed requirement. But in case of dry cultivated land broadcasting is done with less requirement of seed in relation to wet land and production is little less in relation to wet land. Application of cattle dung, good soil or availability of water might be the factor in maintaining the production at a reasonable level in harsh mountainous situation. But, in case of cardamom, high production is tuned with west facing slope favouring less sunshine for the longer time of the day and gentle slope with soil coverage and coverage of tall trees since cardamom requires less sunshine with the scope of draining rain water. Kajor is better example for this case.

The choice of seed variety is also the factor to cope with environmental drawback. As for example, *saune* a variety of cardamom, is widely grown by virtue of its adopting with little warm and moist climate as seen in Lingdong village of Dzongu area. *Tokmorjo*, a variety of local paddy is well suited to harsh and high hill with little water as observed in Shipgyer village.

In the context of environmental background, out of three villages Shipgyer village has maximum land under hill slope cultivation followed by Lingdong village, while Kajor has no hill slope cultivation due to its gentle slope. Therefore Shipgyer and Kajor villages have to put seed in the hole in high hill due to their rough terrain which ultimately lead to lower production in two land types. However, in gentle slope with good soil coverage of Kajor and Lingdong production is better in wet land and also in dry land in some situation. In addition in dry terrace field of three villages where plough does not work due to stone in the soil, production is also less.

Traditional Wisdom as Survival Strategy

The traditional wisdom as seen in identification of land category; way of cultivation; crops grown, variety of season; techniques of sowing, harvesting, implements used; preparation of land, use of high yielding variety and chemical fertilizer, water management and level of production has thrown light on survival strategy in the context of different environmental background of the three villages. The situation of survival strategy is given in the Table below.

Table 15.3: Situation of survival strategy

Sl. No.	*Agricultural Features*	*Village Names, Average Altitude and Zone*		
		1. Kajor (1200 m), Non-Dzongu	*2. Lingdong (1300m), Upper Dzongu*	*3. Shipgyer (1600m) Upper Dzongu*
1.	Land Type	Dry terrace, wet terrace and cardamom land	Jhum land, Dry land of three types depending on soil, presence of stones and quality of terrace; wet land and cardamom land	Jhum land, Dry land, Homestead land, Cardamom Land.
2.	Way of Cultivation	Terrace Cultivation (wet and dry terrace), Plough Cultivation with use of spade in little and Cardamom on hillslope	Terrace Cultivation (wet and dry terrace), Jhum Cultivation on high hill, Plough Cultivation with use of spade in little and Cardamom on hill slope	Terrace Cultivation (dry terrace) and homestead cultivation. Land lies in medium height, Spade Cultivation, Jhum Cultivation on high hill and Cardamom on hill slope
3.	Crops Grown	Paddy, maize, millet, wheat, buckwheat, potato and other root crops, cardamom	Paddy, maize, millet, wheat, buckwheat, potato and other root crops, cardamom, vegetables such as raisag and ginger grown in homestead land	Fruit trees like guava, papaya grown along with vegetables such as raisag and ginger grown in homestead land, Dry paddy, Minor millet buckwheat and maize in Jhum land. Cardamom on hill slope.
4.	Season	Cardamom-flowering (May-June), Harvesting (October-November), wheat and potato grown in winter, other cereals grown in summer	Paddy sown by middle of June and harvesting by middle of December Wheat in winter though maturity length is wider. Maize in summer. Ginger takes to grow between March–March. Cardamom—May-June to October-November.	Paddy, maize and minor millet grown in summer, wheat in winter. Buckwheat grown in between summer and winter (September-November).

Table 15.3: (*Contd.*)

Sl. No	*Agricultural Features*	*Village Names, Average Altitude and Zone*		
		1. Kajor (1200m)	*2. Lingdong (1300m)*	*3. Shipgyer (1600m) U.Zon*
5.	Techniques of Sowing and Harvesting	Transplantation method in wet terrace for paddy. Maize broadcast in dry terrace though seed put in the hole in stony land. Wheat broadcast in dry terrace. Minor millet transplanted in terrace.	Transplantation method in well developed terrace. Putting seed in the hole in high hill while broadcasting in dry terrce. Vegetables and ginger in homestead land.	Maize put in hole in high hill slope, Minor millet and fapar broadcast in the high hillslope. Maize broadcast in permanent field, minor millet transplanted in the same field. Wheat and barley raised from the field. Tokmojo and Chobyojo dry paddy grown.
6.	Implements used	Major use of spade with plough in well developed terrace; Kanta and stick used in hill slope.	Plough and spade both used in terrace and high hill, Kanta and stick used in hill slope.	Mainly spade used with use of kanta and stick. Plough used in homestead land.
7.	Land Preparation	Digging the soil by Spade. Leaves fallen from trees during off season burnt and used as manure.	Cutting trees avoiding uaeful trees and converting those into manure by drying, litting fire twigs and leaves in Jhum land. Preparing soil by plough and spade in terrace.	Cutting trees avoiding uaeful trees and converting manure by drying, litting fire twigs and leaves in Jhum land. Preparing soil mainly by spade.
8	Use of high yielding variety and chemical fertilizer	Use of high yielding variety is seen in case of wheat but limited in case of paddy. However, use of chemical fertilizer is becoming high gradually.	V.L-61, Kalra as high yielding paddy variety. However, use of chemical fertilizer is becoming high.	Use of high yielding variety is limited duo to inaccessibility, though high yielding variety seeds are used in case of wheat to a limited extent. Use of chemical fertilizer is aiso very limited.
9.	Level of production	Well in case of cardamom. Good in case of paddy and maize.	Good in wet terrace and wet terrace field. Medium in case of cardamom.	Fair to poor, Good in case of Cardamom
10.	Water management	Earthen bundh along contour to prevent water movement unnecessarily and soil erosion. Bamboo funnel and earthen channel used for water distribution.	Earthen bundh along contour to prevent water movement unnecessarily and soil erosion. Bamboo funnel and earthen channel used for water distribution.	Earthen bundh along contour to prevent water movement unnecessarily and soil erosion. Bamboo funnel mainly used for water distribution

Conclusion

It is seen that land management pattern among the Lepchas is basically. guided by degree of rough terrain and altitudinal variation, though remoteness and combination in ethnic set-up bears impression on use of high yielding seeds or chemical fertilizer and also degree of paddy cultivation being in high intensity in dry or wet land which is aptly and mainly done by the Nepalee labourers. These Nepalese labourers mainly live in Kajor (lying outside Dzongu area), while they live mainly during cultivation season at Lingdong and Shipgyer, upper Dzongu village temporarily. Again, Shipgyer has also thin concentration of the Nepaleese population.

It is also seen that there are different practices in the pattern of land management in various types of land lying in different altitudes, ethnic combination and remoteness of the villages. Distribution of water through bamboo funnel or earthen channel depending on slope and terrain is observed in the villages. Contour bundh is usual phenomenon in the villages to check soil erosion or to distribute water in a regulated way. The features of agricultural practices as discussed in different heads of the paper are put in a table against the villages and their backdrop of average altitude and situation in respective zone in order to explain the land management among the Lepchas of North Sikkim in different set- ups.

The traditional wisdom, i.e. indigenous idea and thoughts or people's perception about natural environment, way of cultivation, farming methods and techniques, idea on organizational network to prepare farming land, indigenous way on controlling water in order to have uniform distribution of it which may be considered as the latent strength to utilize the natural resources in their own way. The way of their land management also conforms to the principles of preserving and conserving the natural resources also.

Therefore, it may be said that the heritage of management of natural resources continues to operate through the latent force of traditional wisdom. But this wisdom has become weakened gradually with the introduction of modern management through science and technology, opening up new avenues for livelihood, contact with outside world through development of communication net work and increasing education. However, it is suggested that there are some basic positive qualities in the traditional wisdom in tribal societies which are to be utilized for the management of natural resources as and when necessary even in the era of modern management due to its eco-friendly role and easy understanding at the cognitive level of tribal people.

REFERENCES

Cohen, S.G. 1978 Review of Anthropology Columbia Univ. Press, Columbia.

Gangopadhyay, S. (1988), 'Nature of Human Adaptation in the Tista valley of Sikkim: A Geographical Analysis', Ph.D. thesis, Calcutta University.

Gorer, G. (1938), *Himalyan Village : An Account of the Lepchas of Sikkim*, Introduction by J.H. Hutton, London.

Government of India (1991), Census of India, Series-22, General Population Tables and Primary Census Abstract, Part IIA and IIB.

Government of India 2001 Census Annexure 6A

PART TWO

SOCIAL LANDSCAPE

16
The Tribal Situation of North East India

Manis Kumar Raha

Pandit Jawaharlal Nehru, the first Prime Minister of the independent India, had a heart full of sympathy towards the tribal people of India. We can feel his pulse when we read what he said once about the tribal people of India in general and the tribal people of North East India in particular. He wrote:

> We should have a receptive attitude to the tribal people. There is a great deal we can learn from them. Particularly in the frontier areas, and having learnt we must try to help and co-operate. They are extremely disciplined people, often a great deal more democratic than most other in India …

Like a large number of Indian population Pandit Nehru also liked this north-eastern part of India very much. 'He had a soft corner in his heart for this region. He travelled throughout the length and breadth of India in order to discover India but north-east India fascinated him greatly' (Raha, 2008:119).

> He was very much charmed with north-eastern region of our country, its varied culture, its natural beauty and was deeply concerned with its neglect and backwardness (Panigrahi, 1993:171).

It is not Pandit Nehru only but anybody and everybody will be charmed the beauty of the north-eastern part of India and also be sympathetic with the simple, sober and beautiful life-style of the people living there.

> "Ecologically this region is somewhat unique in comparison to other parts of India. High mountain, snow bound region, deep

> forest, undulated terrain, network of rivers and rivulets, plateau and plain land with high rainfall and moist weather have made. this region unique in all respects (Raha: *ibid.* 11).

People living in this region belong to different ethnic groups with different bio-genetical make up. 'They bear different livelihood patterns, different social organizations, different methods of social control, and different world-view. They profess different religions, speak different languages and love to live in different types of settlements' (*ibid.*). Their varied types of colourful dresses and ornaments, their own dances and music, their joyful festivities, all attract the attention of the people outside. 'Though diversity is the basic feature among the people of North-East India, yet an undercurrent of unity and similarity is found if one goes deep into their culture' *(ibid.)*.

In North-East India the tribal people live in different ecological conditions. Hills, forests, plains, in all these geographical situations the tribal people of this region live by closely interacting with the nature.

> "Nestled within the complex of the sub-Himalayan ranges, the Indo-Burmese hills of Nagaland, Manipur and Mizoram and the erosion surfaces of the Meghalaya plateau, the tribes of north-east India have a world of their own (Ahmed, 1983 *cf* Nayak, 2008:168)

According to Choudhury. 'The northern and eastern mountain ranges and the southern plateau' have provided the tribal people a very suitable habitat. In the Brahmaputra valley also there are suitable sites for the tribal people. A good number of the tribal people have also found suitable place for living on the northern bank of the river and also in the river islands (Nayak, 2008:170).

> The tribal habitat in the entire region thus displays a remarkable diversity in their physical setting and ecological parameters forcing them to make adjustments and also to make the most effective use of the varying natural resources in accordance with their technological equipment and social resources. The economic and social as well as cultural responses of the tribes thus confirm to the varying qualities of their respective habitats. (*ibid.*: 172)

Population

According to 2011 Census the total population (Provisional) of all the eight States of North-eastern India which include Arunachal Pradesh, Assam, Manipur, Meghalaya, Mizoram, Nagaland, Sikkim and Tripura, is 45,587,982 forming 3.77 per cent of the total population of India. Out of this population 51.13 per cent are males and 48.87 per cent females. Again as we look into the distribution of population (Table 16.1) in different States according to 2011 Census (Provisional) the overwhelming majority (68.37%) live in Assam. Next to Assam comes Tripura where 8.05 per cent of the total population of North-eastern States live. The other states namely Meghalaya (6.50%) and Manipur (5.97%) and have population more than 5.00 per cent each. Nagaland (4.34%), Arunachal Pradesh (3.03%) and Mizoram (2.39%) have less than 5.00 per cent. Sikkim covers only 1.33 per cent of the population of N.E. India. When we look at the population strength of these North-eastern States in the total population of India (1,210,193,422) according to 2011 Census (Provisional), we find that except Assam (2.58%) each of the remaining states has below 1.00 per cent of the total population of India. Mizoram has the lowest strength (0.09%). So according to 2011 Census among these eight states, highest population (31,169,272) is in Assam and the lowest (6,07,688) is in Sikkim.

Table 16.1: Sex-wise Distribution of Population in North-eastern States, 2011 Census (Provisional)

States/UT	*Total population*			*% of the total Population of the State/UT in the total population of NE*	*% of the total population of the State/UT in the total population of India*
	Persons	*Males*	*Females*		
Arunachal Pradesh	1,382,611	720,232	662,379	3.03	0.11
Assam	31,169,272	15,954,927	15,214,345	68.37	2.58
Manipur	2,721,756	1,369,764	1,351,992	5.97	0.23
Meghalaya	2,964,007	1,492,668	1,471,339	6.50	0.25
Mizoram	1,091,014	552,339	538,675	2.39	0.09
Nagaland	1,980,602	1,025,707	954,895	4.34	0.16
Sikkim	607,688	321,661	286,027	1.33	0.05
Tripura	3,671,032	1,871,867	1,779,165	8.05	0.30
Total	45,587,982	23,309,165	22,278,817	99.98	3.77
India	1,210,193,422	623,724,248	586,469,174		

Source: Census of India, 2011, Provisional Population Totals (Figures at a glance).

Scheduled Tribes

According to 2001 Census the total Scheduled Tribe population of North-east India is 10,465,898 forming 12.41 per cent of the total Scheduled Tribe population (84,326,240) of India. This total Scheduled Tribe population of NE India covers 26.93% of the total population of NE India. When we look at the distribution of the Scheduled Tribe population in the total population of the respective states, we see that in Mizoram 94.46% of the total population of this State belong to the Scheduled Tribes. That means almost all the people of Mizoram are Scheduled Tribes. Next comes Nagaland where 89.15 per cent of the total population are covered by the Scheduled Tribes population. Then comes Meghalaya (85.99%) followed by Arunachal Pradesh (64.22%). The Scheduled Tribe population of Assam form only 12.40 per cent of the total population of Assam.

Then again if we examine the distribution of Scheduled Tribe population of different states of this region in the total Scheduled Tribe population of N.E. India, we see that the Scheduled Tribe population of Assam have secured highest number (31.61%) in the total Scheduled Tribe population of N.E. India. Meghalaya has the second position in this regard covering 19.04 per cent followed by Nagaland (18.02%). The Scheduled Tribe population of Arunachal Pradesh has the lowest strength (6.74%) in the total Scheduled Tribe population of N.E. India (Table 16.2).

Table 16.2: Distribution of Scheduled Tribe Population in Different States of N.E. India, Census 2001

States/UT	*Total population*	*Total S.T. population*	*% of S.T. Population in the Total Population of the State/India*	*% of the S.T. Population to the total S.T. population of N.E. India*
Arunachal Pradesh	1,097,968	705,158	64.22	6.74
Assam	26,655,528	3,308,570	12.40	31.61
Manipur	2,166,788	741,141	34.19	7.08
Meghalaya	2,318,822	1,992,862	85.99	19.04
Mizoram	888,573	839,310	94.46	8.02
Nagaland	1,990,036	1,774,026	89.15	16.95
Sikkim	540,851	111,405	20.60	1.06
Tripura	3,199,203	993,426	31.17	9.49
Total	38,857,769	10,465,898	26.93	12.41
India	1,028,610,328	84,326,240	8.20	

Source: Ministry of Tribal Affairs, Govt. of India, Annual Report: 2008-09.

As already said there are a total of 10,465,898 Scheduled Tribes inhabiting North East India. These people are distributed in varied number in all the eight states of this region. Out of these 10,465,898 Scheduled Tribe population a little over half (50.63%) are males and a little less than half (49.37%) females, the sex-ratio being 975 females per 1000 males. Except Arunachal Pradesh, in all other states of this region, the number of males is slightly higher than that of the females. In Arunachal Pradesh the reverse is the case. The number of females is slightly higher (50.08%) than that of the males (49.92%).

When we look at the sex-ratio of these Scheduled Tribes of different states (Table 16.3), we see that only in Arunachal Pradesh there is higher ratio for the females (1003 females per 1000 males) and in Meghalaya they are equal (1000 females per 1000 males). But in other states, females are lower than per 1000 males. Nagaland has the lowest sex-ratio (943 females per 1000 males) followed by Sikkim (957 females per 1000 males).

Table 16.3: Sex-wise Distribution of the Scheduled Tribe Population in different States of North East India, 2001

State/UT	*Scheduled Tribe Population*					
	Person	*Male*		*Female*		*Sex-ratio*
		No.	*%*	*No.*	*%*	
Arunachal Pradesh	705,158	352,017	49.92	353,141	50.08	1003
Assam	3,308,570	1,678,117	50.72	1,630,453	49.28	972
Manipur	741,141	374,319	50.51	366,822	49.49	980
Meghalaya	1,992,862	996,567	50.01	996,295	49.99	1000
Mizoram	839,310	422,963	50.39	416,347	49.61	984
Nagaland	1,774,026	913,203	51.48	860,823	48.52	943
Sikkim	111,405	56,940	51.11	54,465	48.89	957
Tripura	993,426	504,320	50.77	489,106	49.23	970
Total	10,465,898	5,298,446	50.63	5,167,452	49.37	975

Source: Census of India, 2001.

In the North Eeastern region of India a large number of the Scheduled Tribes live. They are living there from time immemorial. While some of these tribes are autochthones of this region, some came to this region from outside in some remote past. According to Chatterjee there are 134 Scheduled Tribes inhabiting North East India excluding Sikkim (2010: 40-41). Now, if we add four Scheduled Tribes of Sikkim the total number of the Scheduled Tribes becomes 138. While some of these tribes are formed of several tribes, some others have a number of sub-tribes. According to the *Annual Report of 2009-10* of the Ministry of Tribal

Affairs, Government of India, there are 310 such tribes and sub-tribes spread over in different states of North East India (2009: 47-58). According to this report Arunachal Pradesh has 16 Scheduled Tribes, Assam has 15 Scheduled Tribes in the Autonomous Districts of Karbi Anglong and North Cachar Hills and 14 Scheduled Tribes in the State of Assam including the Bodo Land Territorial Areas District but excluding Autonomous Districts of Karbi Anglong and North Cachar Hills. In Manipur there are 33 Scheduled Tribes, Meghalaya 17, Mizoram 15, Nagaland 5, Sikkim 4, and in Tripura 19 (2009:47-58). Again in Arunachal Pradesh there are 18 such tribes/sub-tribes included in some tribes. In the autonomous Districts of Karbi Anglong and North Cachar Hills there are 58 such tribes and sub-tribes and in the state of Assam including Bodo Land Territorial Areas District they are 16 in number in Manipur 33, Meghalaya 61, Mizoram 58, Nagaland 5, Sikkim 8 and in Tripura 49 (Chatterjee, 2010:40-41) such tribes and sub-tribes within some certain Scheduled Tribes.

Now let us see which are those tribes and sub-tribes who are grouped with tribes. From the said *Annual Report* of Ministry of Tribal Affairs, we get that in Arunachal Pradesh, the Mishmi Tribe includes tribe like the Idu and the Taroan. In the autonomous districts of Karbi Anglong and North Cachar Hills of Assam the Dimasa includes the Kachari, the Khasi are grouped with the Jaintia, Synteng, Pnar, War, Bhoi and the Lyngngam. Again the Synteng here have also been shown as the separate tribe. In this area the category 'Any Kuki Tribes' also includes 37 other tribes. In Meghalaya the Dimasa includes the Kachari, the Khasi includes the Jaintia, Synteng, Pnar, War, Bhoi and the Lyngngam. Here again the Synteng have also been shown as a separate tribe. 'Any Kuki Tribes' in Meghalaya include 37 other tribes. In Mizoram the Khasi and the Jaintia in a similar way, consist of the Khasi, Synteng, Pnar, War, Bhoi and the Lyngngam. Here also the Synteng have also been shown as a separate tribe. Similarly, here like other areas 'Any Kuki Tribes' include the same 37 other tribes. In Sikkim the Bhotia includes tribes/sub-tribes like the Chumbipa, Dopthapa, Dukpa, Kagetey, Sherpa, Tibetan, Tromopa and the Yobmo. In Tripura, a number of tribes like the Halam, Bengshel, Dub, Kaipeng, Kalai, Karbong, Lengui, Mussum, Rupini, Sukchap, and the Thangchep have been grouped together. In Tripura again the Kuki include 17 sub-tribes, the Munda include the Kaur and the Noatia include the Murashing. Again as we come to Assam one of the categories is 'Any Mizo (Lushai) tribes' but it has not been mentioned in the Report who are actually these Mizo (Lushai) tribes. Similarly, here 'Any Naga tribes' have not been spelt out as to who those Naga tribes are. The same is the case with 'Any Mizo (Lushai) tribes' and 'Any Kuki tribes' of Manipur. In Meghalaya while the name of tribes included in the group 'Any Kuki tribes' has been given, no tribes have been mentioned under 'Any Mizo (Lushai) tribes'. The same thing has happened in Mizoram. In Tripura the name of the sub-tribes of the Kuki tribe have, of course, been mentioned. On the other hand, in Arunachal Pradesh in cases of the Naga no tribes or sub-tribes have been mentioned by name (Chatterjee, 2012: 390-411).

When we look at the Census of 2001 (Chatterjee, 2012: 390-411) we mark that the number of Scheduled Tribes as returned by the Census of 2001, is quite different from what we get from the reports of the Ministry of Tribal Affairs, Government of India. We have already shown those figures as mentioned in the report of the Ministry of Tribal Affairs. Now according to 2001 Census there were a total of 98 Scheduled Tribes in Arunachal Pradesh plus some 'Generic Tribes'. But there is no mention about the number and name of those 'Generic Tribes'. Assam had 14 Scheduled Tribes in the autonomous district of Assam comprised Karbi Anglong and North Cachar Hill districts and 9 in the State of Assam excluding the autonomous districts. Here also live some 'Generic Tribes'. In Manipur the number of Scheduled Tribes as mentioned by Census 2001, was 29 excluding some 'Generic Tribes'. Meghalaya had 18 Scheduled Tribes (plus 'Generic Tribes'), Mizoram 14 (plus 'Generic Tribes'), Nagaland 5 (plus 'Generic Tribes'), Sikkim 4 (plus 'Generic Tribes') and Tripura 19 (plus 'Generic Tribes').

Now when we look at the tribes/sub-tribes included or added to some of the tribes in some states, we get from the said *Annual Report* and also from Chatterjee (2012) that in Arunachal Pradesh with the Mishmi, the Idu and the Taroan were added in 2002, with the Singpho, the Hrusso, Tagin, Khamba and the Adi were added in 2002. In Assam, in the autonomous districts of Karbi Anglong and North Cachar Hills districts we get the Khasi including the Jaintia, Synteng, Pnar, War, Bhoi and the Lyngngam. But the 'Any Kuki Tribes' include 37 tribes and/or sub-tribes. The Census 2001 has specifically named these 37 tribes/sub-tribes. In case of the Mikir, the Karbi were the substitute for Mikir in 2002. Again with the Synteng, the Lalung were added in 2002. But here no specific tribe was named for 'Any Mizo (Lushai) tribes' and 'Any Naga tribes'. In the state of Assam excluding the autonomous districts with the Rabha, the Dimasa Hajong, Singpho, Khamti and the Garo were added in 2002. In Manipur the Vaiphui were substituted by the Veiphei in 2002; with the Zou, the Poumai Naga, Tarao, Kharam and 'Any Kuki Tribes' were added in 2002. But in Manipur the names of 'Any Mizo tribes', '(Lushai) tribes' as also 'Any Kuki Tribes' were not spelt out. Meghalaya has also tribes/ sub-tribes included in some tribes. Here the Kachari were included with the Dimasa, the Jaintia, Synteng, Pnar and the War were included in the Khasi group. The Lyngngam were included with the Bhoi, 37 Scheduled Tribes/sub-tribes were included in 'Any Kuki Tribes' (names of such tribes has specifically been mentioned) (Chatterjee, 2012: *ibid.*).

In Mizoram we see that the Dimasa included the Kachari, the Khasi and Jaintia included the Khasi Synteng or Pnar, War, Bhoi or Lyngngam. 'Any Kuki Tribes' included 37 tribes (names of tribes were specifically mentioned). Finally, with the Synteng the Paite were added in 2002. But in this state in case of the 'Any Mizo (Lushai) Tribes' and 'Any Naga tribes' no tribe was specifically named. Here also the Khasi include the Khasi Syntengs or Pnar, War, Bhoi or Lyngngam. But 37 tribes/Sub-tribes included in 'Any Kuki Tribes' have been named in Nagaland out of five tribes, the Naga include 19 tribes.

Sikkim had two tribes earlier but in 2002 two more tribes, the Limboo and the Tamang were included. But in this State the Bhotia include the Chumbipa, Dopthapa, Dukpa, Kagate, Sherpa, Tibetan, Tromopa and the Yolmo.

As already said Tripura has 19 Scheduled Tribes. Now out of these tribes, the Halam includes the Bengshel, Dub, Kaipeng, Kaloi, Karbong, Lengui, Mussum, Rupini, Sukuchep, and the Thangchep. All these were added with the Halam in 2002. Here the Naotia also include the Murashing. But the Kuki include sub-tribes like the Batte, Belalhut, Chhalya, Fun, Hajango, Jangtei, Kharent, Khephong, Kuntei, Laifant, Lentei, Mizel, Namte, Paitu, Paite, Rangchan, Rangkhole and the Thangluya.

Besides the above grouping of the tribes in a particular tribe which definitely causes some problem in specifically identifying a tribe from the other, there are some other problems also which one will face while identifying some tribes of different parts of India as also of North East India (Raha 1999). In North East India (Singh, 1994) many of the tribes have more than one name or included in some broad generic term. We can cite many such examples from the tribes of North East India (Singh, 1994). For example the Lhota Naga call themselves as the Kyon. The Aka are also called by another name, the Hrusso. According to Mackenzie (1884) both the Aka and the Hrusso are synonymous. The Anals of Manipur are also known as the Pakan. The Apatani are variously referred to as the Anka, Auk, Apa Tanang, Auka Meri, Tenal and also as the Tanu.

The Gangte of Manipur are also known as the Rangte. In western Assam, the Kachari are represented by the Mech. But they are again represented as the Bodo in central Assam. In the North Cachar Hills they call themselves as the Hojai and also as the Dimasa. They are also known as the Sonowal and the Thengal in the eastern part of the Brahmaputra Valley. But in the plain of Cachar they are known as the Barman. In Nagaland the Kacharis are also known as the Koirat and the Dimafisa. In Sikkim the Kagate are also known as the Yolmo. Sunders (1898) confused the Rabhas with the Garo as both practiced matriliny.

The Garo sometimes prefer to be identified as the Mande or Achik meaning hill men or hill dwellers. Very good example is the Purum of Manipur. In 1936 Prof. T. C. Das (1945) found 305 Purums in Manipur. In 1951 they were reduced only to 43 and in 1961 to 82. The 1971 Census failed to return any Purum. In 1975 Das Gupta (1985) also failed to trace out any Purum. The Purums according to Das Gupta, have been renamed as the Chote. But 2001 Census has returned 2762 Chote and 571 Purum. The *Annual Report* 2009-2010 of Ministry of Tribal Affairs, Government of India has also mentioned the Chote and the Purum as two separate Scheduled Tribes. According to Das Gupta 'all the Purum villages have this prefix because Purum is the type of land in which they inhabit though the villagers call themselves as the Chote. To the Meitai or any village group, the Chote and the Purum Tampak may be known as only Purum, and this might have resulted in confusion for others' (1985:35). In connection with the change of identity of the Purums, Danda thinks.

> Thus the self-perpetuating Purum system when exposed to various solidarity movements, the Purums should not normally have any difficulty in assuming new identities without discarding the old (1991:117).

Hiyang (Khiyang) and others think that the Chote or Chothe is the original name of the tribe which is now, oscillating between two words 'Chothe' and 'Purum' (1985: 6-25). But according to Arun Kumar the views of the Purums informants were that the Purums were the geographically localized Chothe and the name of the tribe as such was Chothe. All Purums identified themselves as the Chothe (1998: 69-70). Again according to Shakespeare (1912), Hodson (1911) and Das (1945) the Purums or Chothe are the Old Kuki Tribe. McCullock (1859) has considered them as the Kuki Tribe. But Arun Kumar has observed that the Purum/Chothe 'villages are polarized to the acceptance of Naga ethnicity' (*ibid.*:71). Raha thinks that 'this process in itself is an exciting proposition, the proper understanding of which would be able to add a new dimension to group dynamics in the context of Northeast India' (2005:257).

Let us now come to the Lushais. Srikrishan found them to disassociate themselves from the blanket term 'Kuki' and adopted a new name 'Mizo'. Later on some other tribes like the Poi, Relte, Lakhen and to some extent the Darlong also accepted the term 'Mizo' (1995:274). According to some scholars the term 'Naga' came to existence only in 1954. According to Hokishe Sema (1986) 'for long this appellation of 'Naga' was resented to by these people (of Tuensang)' 'till political expedience cause it to be accepted as describing the separate identity of these people as distinct from other ethnic tribal people and also from the people in the country at large'. Now the Naga group includes a large number of tribes like the Ao, Angami, Kacha, Lhota, Kabui, Zounuo-Keyhonous, Zemi, Sema, Rengma, Chang, Konyak etc. Similarly, the Adi is not a single group but includes a group of tribes like the Gallong, Minyong, Padam, Pasi, Bori, Pailibo, Ramo and others. Again the Eastern Monpas have adopted a new name, Sartang for their tribe. The Abor are now calling themselves as the Adi, the Dafla as the Nishi and also the Bangni, the Mpui as the Kabui and so on. In Nagaland and Meghalaya the Karbi have been returned as the Mikir. They are also known as the Karbi in Arunachal Pradesh though they were earlier known as the Mikir. They also prefer to be known as the Arleng. The Khamba of Arunachal Pradesh also describe them as the Kham Zayu. The Khamiyang of Arunachal Pradesh are also known as the Khamjang. The Koch Rabha are sometimes confused as the Koch (Raha, 1989: 32-39; Singh, 1994:1014-1019).

The Lepcha of Sikkim are also known by the term Rong, Rongkup or Mutanchi Rongkup. The Lish of Arunachal Pradesh are also known as the Yobin. The Miji of Arunachal Pradesh prefer to be called by the term Sajalong. There are another term, Taraon by which the Digaru Mishmi can be identified. The Miju Mishmi are also known as the Kaman. The Hualngo Mizo have a second name called the Chhakchhuak. The Pang Mizo prefer to be called as the Pangkhua and the Pawi Mizo as the Lai, or Chin. Though the Riang are known as the Riang in Tripura but in Mizoram they are also known as the Tuikuk. Besides the above there are many other tribes who are also called in different other names. It is even seen that while a tribe is known by a particular name in a state, they are called by different name in some other state. This sometimes may create confusion and lead to some identity problem (Singh, 1995; Raha, 1999: 104-122).

Tribal Division

Many of the tribes of North East India are divided into a number of divisions or sub-tribes. For example, the Wancho society is divided into two district divisions, namely Wangham or the Chief's groups and Wangpan or the group of the commoners (Raha, 2006:36). According to Dutta this Wancho society is characterized by the existence of 'Class distinction', a system uncommon among the tribal (1987:3). 'There are four classes each one of which is laid on the foundation of class and sub-class unity and received varied degree of social cognizance' (Dutta, 1990:123). The superior most of these four classes is the Wangham. Then comes the Wangsas followed by the Wangsus. The lowest of these classes is the Wangpan. But in some other areas like the Moujan group of villages, the two main divisions of the the Wancho are the Wangjan and the Panjan. In some other areas they are divided into the Wangsa and the Pansa.

The Apatani are divided into two horizontal endogamous classes, Mite and Mura (Furer-Haimendorf, 1962:73) . While Mite or Mithe belong to the patricians, the Mora or Mura to the plebian or slave.

The Tangsa is divided into two divisions such as the Tangwa and the Pangwa. But the Tangsa who live near Myanmar border, have the Lungchang, the Moklum, Jogli, Lungri, Havi, Mosang, etc. as sub-tribes (Singh, 1995:1108-1128).

The Ramo on the other hand, are divided into two economic classes, high and low or slaves (Dhasmana, 1979: 158-159). According to Dhasmana, the high class Ramo claims the ownership of all agricultural lands, forest, hunting grounds, fishing spots and streams etc. But the members of both elevated and emancipated slaves have to take permission from the members of the high class for the use of the same (1979:159).

The Adi are divided into a number of sub-tribes like the Padam, Minyong, Panggi, Simong, Karko, Bori, Bokar, Pailibo, Pasi, Milang and the Ashing. In the past all these sub-tribes were included into a broad generic term, Abor (Raha, 2006:47). The Nocte also have two distinct classes—one chief's class or the Laueangjat and commoners' class or the Sanajat (Dowerah, 2006:100). The Aka have two territorial divisions namely the Hrusso and the Korou but the social, economic and cultural activities of these two divisions remaining the same (Nimachow, 2006:45). The Singpho are divided into four classes and these are the Myung, Lubrung, Shangai and the Mirip (Chowdhury, 2004:131).

The Sema Naga society is divided into two distinct classes- the Chiefs' class and the commoners' class. The commoners (Mughemi) are inevitably tied to the chiefs' villages. The chief of a particular village provides the commoner under him with land as soon as the latter marries 'with the understanding that he will do work in his field...' (Kumar, 2005:99). The Ao Naga as reported by Kumar, are also divided into two groups—the Chogli and the Mongsen.

In Assam, the Mishing are divided into two broad divisions namely the Barogam and the Dahgam. 'These two are further subdivided into Pagro, Chayengia, Ayengia, Dambukial, Samuguria and so on (Mipun, 1993:20).

We now come down to Meghalaya where we find, as Gurdon has mentioned, the Syntengs or Pnar are divided into the Synteng proper, Nongtung and the Kharwang, the War into the War proper and the War Pnar, the Bhoi into the Jinthong, Mynri, Ryngkhong and the Khasi-Bhoi (Gurdon, 2002:62). The Garo are divided into five exogamous divisions called *Chatchi*. These *Chatchis* are the Sangma, Marak, Momin, Shira and the Areng though originally the Garo had two groups, namely Sangma and Marak (Marak, 1997:75). According to Bose 'three other Chatchis, Momin, Shira and Arleng have been formed by class originally belonging to the Sangma *Chatchi* (1985:XIV).

The Karbi or Mikir are divided into four broad social groups, namely the Chinthong, Ronghang, Amri and the Dumrali. The Karbi or Mikir are divided into the Zayu, Kham, Nonghe, Chungpho, Popa etc. The Miji are divided into two broad groups like the Nibuith or the group with high status and the Khialing or group with low status. The Mao Naga have three groups like the Paomata, La Paona and the Imemei. The Rabha have sub-tribes like the Pati, Moitoria, Bitliha, Kocha, Shonga etc. (Raha, 1989:43).

Moities

In North East India, some tribal groups are divided into two moieties. The moieties are the primary division by which the tribe is made up of two exogamous groups. But moity system is found only among a few tribes. The Minyong are divided into two moieties like the Kumin and the Kuri. The Monsang also have two moieties and these are the Simpu and the Rinhe (Singh, 1994). The Angami Naga are also divided into two exogamous sub-groups or moieties called the Kepezoma and the Kepepfuma (Hutton, 1969:111). Similarly, the Khiamngam Naga have two moieties called the Lam and the Shiu.

'The Khiamngan Naga being divided into two exogamous moieties, indeed have the most ideal form of moity system' (Das, 1993:130).

According to Hutton moity system is present among different sections of the Angami (1969:111). The Zounuo-Keyhonou are divided into two large sections, namely the Thevo and the Tepa (Das: *ibid.*).The Chakhru Naga are divided into two moieties called the Chuzo and the Thevo. Both are exogamous in nature. The Moyon of Manipur have the Simphuti and the Jingven moieties. The Tangsa Jugli also have two moieties which are Khanglim and Khanham (Singh, 1994). There are some tribal groups of North East India who also have moity system.

Clan

In India as also in North East India most of the tribal groups are divided into a number of clans or sibs. The clan is a compromise kin group and unilineal and exogamous in nature. It controls marriage and residential unity and group solidarity. In many cases the clans are totemic. In case of the totemic clans, the members do not eat, kill, injure, hunt, hurt or any way harm the totemic objects which may be animal, plant, inanimate objects or heavenly bodies. The clans are always exogamous; no one should marry in his or her own clan. There are some clans which are territorial also. The clans are either patrilineal or matrilineal. In a few cases they may be bilateral. However, we shall now look into the clans of the tribal groups of North East India.

The Idu Mishimis are divided into a number of clans such as Pulu, Mendo, Mega, Lingi and Minchichi (Dutta Choudhury, 1995:256). They believe that these clans have descended from a common ancestor, Anya, and have equal status (Barua, 1960:44). The Ramo also have several clans and these are Komi, Koling, Koje, Kodung, Kochung, Chijee, Yourdung, Samun and Samiur (Dutta Chowdhury, 1995:120; Dhasmana, 1979:94-95). The two subdivisions of the Apatani, i.e. *Mite* and *Mura* are subdivided into a number of clans, called *Halu*, Kimle, Noda, Taru, Taro, Taku, Kago, Haj, Dani, Puna, etc. are the clans of the *Mite* subdivision. The *Mura* subdivision has clans like Dasu, Dora, Miri, Dani, Pura, etc. certain *Mura* clans are attached to certain *Mite* clans. For example, Dasu and Dora clans are attached to Kimle, Miri and Hidu clans of *Mura* sub-division are attached to Noda clan of *Mite*. Fermu is attached to Taku, Puma to Haj and so on (Fürer-Haimendorf, 1962:66).

The clan among the Tangsa-Lungri is known as *Ipham.* The clans among this tribe are Kimkhak, Sidia, Liche, Jochi, Riadia etc. Many of these clans are divided again into sub-clans (Dutta, 1959:52). All these clans have equal status (Husain, 1995:341).

The Dirang Morpa are divided into a number of clans or *khang*. Faichurpal, Gunpapa, Baquipam and Shorthefa are the *khang* of the Dirang Morpa.

The Lalung are divided into 12 clans known as *nane* or *kul*. These clans are Macharang, Madur, Maloi, Dafor, Sukai, Amfli, Kasa, Cholong, Amchong, Kakhor, Darfong and Loron (Thakur, 1994:145-146) Syam Choudhuri and Das have found that 'The number of Lalung clans are not uniform in any of the present day villages. Commonly three or four of them are clustered together' (1973:57). These clustered are known as the *maharis*. Many of these clans are divided into sub-clans. The Baite, one of the Kuki tribes, have five sub-clans called Darnei, Nampui, Ngamlai, Ngirsim and Thiete (Pakhem, 1984:278-279). The Thadou Kuki on the other hand, consist of twenty nine clans. In the Zounuo-Keyhonou society the clan (*Thenu*) is 'an organization of well defined smaller groups…A *thenu* or clan grows by continuous multiplication of its parts…' (Das, 1993:118-119). There are four clans among these people, and these are Pavoma, Kirhazuma, Zerima and Rochuma (*ibid.*). The Chang Naga have some clans, namely Chongpo, Ung, Lumao, Kangcho and Kudamji (Kumar 2005:101). The Maring have four clans and these are Dongsa, Charanga, Kansouwa and Makunga. These clans are considered as the major clans of the society. Apart from these major clans there are some other clans which have limited distribution (Das, 1985:56). The Mishing traces origin of their clans from the name of their forefathers or from the names of the deities. Some of their clans are Kuli, Khutum, Koman, Kogyung, Doley , Pegu, Pangging, Mipun, Lagachu etc. (Mispun 1993:21). Because of the presence of double bilineal system descent, the Semsa have both *patri* and *matri clans* (Danda & Ghatak, 1985:50-60).

Marriage

Marriage, which 'is a socially approved relationship of one or more persons with one or more persons involving cohabitation, socio-economic co-operation and reciprocal rights and obligations between partners entering into union', (Raha 2007:23) is a universal institution. It is present in all human societies, and so it is also present among the tribal groups all over North East India.

Marital Status

Normally among human beings four different marital statuses such as unmarried, married, widowed and divorced/separated, are found. Among the tribal people of North East India the same four types are present but in variable number. While the number of unmarried Scheduled Tribe persons was more than half of the total population everywhere (Arunachal 56.3%, Assam 57.5%, Manipur 61%, Meghalaya 58.4%, Mizoram 58.3%, Nagaland 65.3%, Sikkim 58.5% and Tripura 54.3%), the strength of the married persons varied from 32.00 per cent to 42.00 per cent (Arunachal 36.7%, Assam 39.1%, Manipur 36.1%, Meghalaya 34.9% Mizoram 36.2%, Nagaland 32.4%, Sikkim 37.4% and Tripura 42.9%) according to 2001 Census. Everywhere the number of widowed persons was below 4.0 per cent. The number of divorced or separated persons was below 1.0 per cent except in Mizoram where the same was 2.4 per cent.

Marriage: Child and Adult

Among the Scheduled Tribes of North East India the incidence of child marriage is negligible. In Arunachal Pradesh it was 14.5 per cent and in Tripura 6.4 per cent. In other states no trace of child marriage is found. Everywhere in North East India adult marriage is the rule (Singh, 1996).

Endogamy and Exogamy

The tribal groups in North East India are in general endogamous. According to Singh (1996) while all the tribal groups of Mizoram, Manipur, Arunachal Pradesh, Assam, Sikkim and Tripura were endogamous, 83.3 per cent tribes of Nagaland and 93.3 per cent of Meghalaya were endogamous. Again almost all the tribal groups in all thé states practice moity and clan exogamy.

Monogamy, Polygyny and Polyandry

Among the Scheduled Tribes of North East India, Monogamy is the societal profile. All of them practice monogamy. After monogamy comes polygyny in numerical strength. According to Singh (1996) in Mizoram 12.5 per cent cases non-sororal and 6.3 cases sororal polygyny were present. In Manipur 9.5 per cent non-sororal and 4.8 per cent sororal, in Nagaland 27.8 per cent non-sororal and no-sororal polygyny, in Meghalaya 29.6 per cent non-sororal and 7.4 per cent sororal and in Assam 38.7 per cent cases of non-sororal and 17.3 per cent cases of sororal polygyny were found to be present. In Arunachal Pradesh the incidence of polygyny was quite high (58.1% non-sororal and 43.9% sororal). In Sikkim 14.3 per cent marriages were non-sororal, but the sororal polygyny was non-existent. In Tripura there was no polygynous form of marriage as reported by Singh (1996). On the other hand, polyandry is found only in Arunachal Pradesh. Singh (1996) found only 9.7 per cent cases of polyandry among some tribal groups of Arunachal Pradesh. Those who practiced polyandry are the Galong, Ramo, Khamba, Meruba and the Monpa.

Cross-Cousin Marriage

Cross-cousin marriage (MBD type) according to Singh (1996) was present in a large number of tribes. Highest number of CCM (MBD) was found in Manipur (76.2%) followed by Arunachal Pradesh (74.2%). Lowest number of tribes having CCM (MBD) is found in Tripura (21.1%). In other states of North East India the strength of CCM (MBD) was Mizoram 25.3%, Nagaland 44.4%, Meghalaya 53.3%, Sikkim 42.9 per cent and Assam 35.5 per cent. But Cross-Cousin Marriage (FSD type) is not that strong. Highest number of CCM (FSD) is present in Nagaland (38.9%) followed by Meghalaya (26.7%), Tripura 21.01 per cent and Assam 19.4 per cent. In Manipur CCM (FSD) has the lowest strength. Of course, there are tribes among whom both types of CCM are present (Singh, 1996).

Sororate and Levirate

Both sororate and levirate are found among most of the tribes of all the states of North East India. But there is restriction in marrying deceased elder brother's widow. In all states of North East India sororate varied from 52.6 per cent to 25.7 per cent. Levirate was lowest (14.3%) in Sikkim and highest in Arunachal Pradesh (72.6%) according to Singh (1996).

Divorce and Remarriage

Both divorce and remarriage of the divorcees and widows are allowed in almost all the tribes of North East India. But the number of divorcees and widows is significant now.

Family

Among all the tribes of all the states of North East India nuclear type of family has the highest strength. The extended type of families have occupied the next higher position. The families among almost all the tribes are patrilineal in nature with patrilocal residence and patriprotestal authority. But only a few tribes, namely the Khasi, Garo, Rabha, Lalung, Syntengs, Panikoch and a few others, live in the matriarchaol society with matrilineal families and matrilocal or duolocal residences.

Making a Living

The tribal people of North East India have different sources of earning livelihood. But mostly they depend on agriculture. Among them both settled and shifting or *Jhum* types of cultivation are present. Normally shifting cultivation is done in the hilly and plateau region by some tribes. Shifting cultivation was practised among the Adi group of tribes who include the Gallong, Minigong, Padam, Bokar Pangi, and others. The Aka, Dogla, Nishi, Tangsa, Wancho and others of Arunachal Pradesh, the Chakma, Garo, Khasi, Jayantia and others of Assam, and Meghalaya, Mizo of Mizoram, the Naga of Nagaland, the Angami, Kabui, Maring and others of Manipur, the Halam, Jamatia, Mag, Noatia and others of Tripura also practiced shifting cultivation. Many of them are still practicing this type of cultivation (Danda, 1998:65). According to 2001 only 42.0 per cent of the total Scheduled Tribe population of Arunachal Pradesh are workers. In Assam 43.2 per cent, in Manipur 44.1 per cent, in Meghalaya 42.81 per cent, in Mizoram 51.7 per cent, in Nagaland 42.31 per cent, in Sikkim 48.6 per cent and in Tripura 29.69 per cent are workers. It means more half of the total S.T. population of Arunachal Pradesh, Assam, Manipur, Meghalaya and Nagaland are non-workers or dependants. In Tripura a little over 70 per cent are non-workers or dependants. Only in Mizoram a little less than half of the total Scheduled Tribe population are non-workers. It means that everywhere in North East India a very large number of Scheduled Tribe populations depend on the income of their earners.

Now let us see the distribution of the main workers and marginal workers in the total Scheduled Tribe workers. In Arunachal Pradesh the total main workers is 84.42 per cent of the total workers. In Assam they are 74.6 per cent, in Manipur 73.8 per cent, in Mizoram 76.5 per cent, in Meghalaya 76.5 per cent, Nagaland 82.2 per cent, and Sikkim77.6 per cent and in Tripura 69.6 per cent are main workers in the total workers. This means that the remaining Scheduled Tribe workers are marginal workers.

Everywhere in Northeast India agriculture is the main source of livelihood, as already said. In Arunachal Pradesh 75.1 per cent, Assam 70.6 per cent, Manipur 69.7 per cent, Meghalaya 56.2 per cent, Mizoram 60.0 per cent, Nagaland 72.7 per cent, Sikkim 54.2 per cent and in Tripura 45.9 per cent of the main workers are cultivators. Everywhere except Tripura, 'other type of occupation' hold the next higher number of the main workers. In Tripura agricultural labourers have the next higher strength (29.7%) according to 2001 Census.

System of Social Control

All the tribal groups of North East India have their own system of social control. They are 'well known for their decentralized and democratic government. They have had well-developed self-governing independent institutions from time immemorial' (Chatterjee, 2010:201). The lowest unit of such institutions is village council. Different tribes here have different names for such village council. Among the Sherdukpen it is called *Dzong* or *Jung*, among the Akas *Mellay* or *Raiz*, among the Apatani *Buliang*, among the Mishmis *Abbala*, among the Kabui Naga, *Pei-Kai*, among the Lalung *Buni*, among the Khasi *Rangbah Shnong* etc. The village councils of all the tribes 'derive their authority from ancient times, and they are the expression of the will and power of the whole people' (*ibid.*:2002). The village council is constituted of the accepted secular and sacred leaders of the village but the head of all families of the village can attend the meeting. The functions of the village councils of most of the tribes are three-fold—judicial, administrative and development.

In Arunachal Pradesh 'democracy is the fundamental characteristics of almost all tribes ….' (Dutta, 2004:17). Each of these tribes has its own traditional system of social control and administrative system. These systems are in most of the cases institutionalized. The village council of these tribes, the socio-political body, are formed of elders. Among the Monpa the council of elders is known as *Mangma*. The *Isorgens* or chiefs are elected and they look after the maintenance of law and order of the society (*ibid.)*. Among the Sherdukpen the village council is known as *Jung* which consists of a headman, a few members, a courier and a watchman. *Mele* or *Raiz* is the village council for the Aka. It is constituted of the *Gaoburah* (headman), his two assistants *borah* and *gibba* and some members (*ibid.*:17-18). The village council of the Apatani (*Buliang*) is composed of the clan representatives. Among the Garo each village council is made of the headman of the village (*Laskar*), and some elders. Half of the elders are nominated by the executive committee of district council and the other half by election of the adult members of the village ….' (Marak, 1997:58).

Among the Kuki of Manipur 'village is the highest political unit, and chief of the villages and his council of Ministers function within a territorial jurisdiction (Gangte, 1982:55, Gangte, 1993:124). Every Kuki villages has a chief which is hereditary in nature.

Hodson during early part of the twentieth century marked that in Manipur 'the centre of the State was the Raja'. He did not take direct part in the administration except presiding over the meeting of the *Darbars*, but 'all was made to serve his interests' (2003:59). But the 'whole structure of traditional kingship was very systematic and contained many detailed elements (Saha, 1994:128). But later on 'chieftainship ultimately gave way to a type of village council ....' (Das, 1985:87).

The Adis have a very well known indigenous institution of local self-government, called *kebang* (Dutta, 2004:18). According to Roy (1966) this *kebang* 'in a true sense, a government by the people and for the people'. 'This council exercises highest legal and judicial power' (Dutta *ibid.*). The *Phari*, among the Kaman Mishmis, is the council of elders. The members of this body are the representatives of various clans. Similarly, the *Ngothun* of the Noctes and the *Wangsu-Wangsa* of the Wanchos are the village council of elders. Among these tribal groups administration of justice and management of village affairs is quite democratic ....' *(ibid.*:19).

The Lalung have the council of elders which is the highest secular body, and this body looks after the functions of the village (Syam Choudhuri & Das, 1973: 37-38).

Among the Bhotia of Lachen and Lachung areas of Sikkim *dzumsa* is the traditional administrative system of the villages. 'The *dzumsa* or general council is directed by a group of people who are elected or designated by villages to run the village administration. In some other parts of Sikkim the Panchayat system was introduced in 1975 (Subba, 2008:277).

The Riang of Tripura traditionally had 'four-tier political organization of which three have disintegrated' (Bera, 2010:52). The traditional administrative unit is mainly village based. Though the chieftainship was abolished in 1955 after the enactment of Acquisition of Chiefs' Rights Act, 1954, still there is chief in every Riang village (*ibid.*: 53).

Religion

Among the tribal people of North East India different religious belief and practices are found to be present. The animism and Buddhism are probably the early religions prevalent among them. Later on they embraced Hinduism and Christianity.

According to 2001 Census (Bhatt & Bhargava, 2005:37-63) the three main religions are practiced in different States of North East India. These are Hinduism, Christianity and Buddhism. There are some other religions present in these states but the number of the followers of these religions is not many.

Table 16.1: Population wise Distribution of Different Religion, 2001

States/UT	Hinduism	Christians	Buddhism	Islam	Other Religions
	%	%	%	%	%
Arunachal Pradesh	34.54	18.70	12.99	2.02	31.75
Assam	64.87	3.70	0.19	30.91	0.33
Manipur	41.92	39.70	0.17	8.06	10.15
Meghalaya	13.27	70.01	0.24	4.49	11.99
Mizoram	3.54	86.67	7.92	1.46	0.41
Nagaland	7.67	89.14	0.31	2.37	0.51
Sikkim	60.89	6.69	28.07	1.45	2.90
Tripura	85.59	3.23	3.09	7.94	0.15

The number of followers of Hinduism is higher than other religions in Arunachal Pradesh (34.54%), Assam (64.87%), Manipur (41.92%), Sikkim (60.89%) and Tripura (85.59%). So we see that the overwhelming majority of Tripura are Hindus, and in Assam and Sikkim the Hindus number much over 50 per cent of the total population. But in Manipur though Hinduism covers little less than half of the total population, still the number of the Hindus in this state is much over the followers of any other religion.

Christianity covers overwhelming majority of Meghalaya (70.01%), Mizoram (86.67%) and Nagaland (89.14%).

When we count the next higher number of followers of any religion, we find that in Arunachal Pradesh Christianity (18.70%), followed by Buddhism (12.99%), in Assam Islam (30.91%), in Manipur Christianity (39.70%) followed by Islam (8.06%), in Meghalaya Hinduism (13.27%), in Mizoram Buddhism (7.92%), in Nagaland Hinduism (7.67%), in Sikkim Buddhism (28.07%) followed by Christianity (6.69%) and in Tripura Islam (7.94%), have the next higher number.

As already said Buddhism, Hinduism and Christianity are the three main religion of North East India. The Nah of Arunachal Pradesh are Buddhists. They also believe in a number of deities and spirits. Both Lama and *Nyibu* (local priest) play important role in rituals and festivals (Bora, 2006:92). In case of the Tangsa, their religious life and pantheon of deities have close similarity with Hindu gods and goddesses. Their methods of worship are also similar to those of the Hindus (Rao, 2006:140). Besides many other tribes of Arunachal Pradesh like the Khampti, Singpo, Tikkak Tangsa and some others practice Theravada Buddhism whereas the Monpa, Sherdukpen, Nah, Memba, Khamba, Meyor and the Zhakring are the followers of Mahayana Buddhism or Vajrayana or Lamaistic Buddhism (Tripathy, 2006:163). The Adis and also tribes of the Tani group 'have deeprooted faith on the supreme governing power of the universe whom they call *Donyi-Polo'* (God) (Rukbo, 1998:57). *Donyi-Polo* 'is essentially an intellectual and ideological persuit based on nature. Truth is the essence of it' (Ering, 2004:37). Boring has also stated that the Tani group of people who believe and worship *Donyi-Polo* 'is the weightiest origin of all things, beings, spirits, time and forces' (2004:39). The *Donyi-Polo* usually refers to Sun (*Donyi*) and Moon (*Polo*) (Chakraborty 2004:53). The Bokars have strong faith in soul which is the essence of their religion. They also worship physical and natural objects. They keep strong faith on *Donyi-Polo* that means Sun and Moon (Banerjee 2004:144). The Nyishi follow animism and believe that so long they continue to appease the spirits (*Weyis*) through offerings and sacrifices, they are secured (Rikam, 2004:180).

The Kukis of Manipur believe in supernaturalism. They have the concept of *Chung Pathien* or the source of 'All Creations' which refers to the 'highest benevolent God who lives in heaven or sky' (Gangte 1993:161). They also have a number of spirits like the Gamhoise, Joumi, Kulsamnu, Chomnu, Gaomei etc.

The Nocte religion is based on certain beliefs and rituals. They believe in the presence of different supernatural beings whom they call as *Jauban*, *Jongban* and *Tesong*. 'He dwells on the earth and is the cause of all happenings in their life' (Dutta, 1978:223).

The traditional religion of the Zounuo-Keyhonuo is *Krunanu*. The most significant aspect of this religion 'is the observance of *menu* and *kenu*. While *menu* is actually a forbidden, non-working day, *Kenu* is a taboo of any kind to be observed by an individual or a family' (Das 1993:132). But in general the Nagas have accepted Christianity to a great extent. 'Due to obvious reason, the conversion was more rapid in post-independence period and majority of the Nagas became Christians only then' (Kumar, 2005:140).

The Lalung are believers of animism. Their religion 'is an integral part of the overall pattern of social conduct in all spheres, secular, sacerdotal and spiritual' (Syam Choudhuri & Das, 1973:133).

The religion of the Mishing is at present, 'a synthetic product of animism and Hinduism' (Mipun 1993:25). They call their religion as *Kewalia* or *Kalhanghali* or *Nishamlia*. They are also worshippers of different spirits (*ibid.*).

The Sherpa of Sikkim practice Buddhism. They belong to the *Nyingmapa* sect (Raha 2001:81). Subba also finds the Lepcha and the Bhotia as Buddhist by religion. Some of the Lepcha are also Christians. Some others are nature worshippers also (2008:259, 274).

The Riangs are mostly Hindus though some of them have been baptized to Christianity . 'The religion of Riang, both in principle and practice, contains elements of animism, animatism, dream, divination, fertility cult, magic, polytheism, taboo, totemism and witchcraft' (Bera, 2010:54).

So we see that the people of Northeast India who also include Scheduled Tribe people, practice different religions. No doubt majority of the people have embraced major religions like Hinduism, Buddhism, Christianity and Islam, still there are some people in this region who are believers of certain other religions like Sikhism, Jainism, etc. The tribal people of this North East region have mainly embraced Hinduism, Buddhism and Christianity.

The tribal people here embracing all these religions, have different deities, and spirits and also celebrate a number of festivals and rituals in different months and seasons of the year. The believers of different religions have different sites for performing the rituals and worships like the temples, monasteries, church etc. where they undertake worships, prayers etc. and also make offerings and sacrifices whenever required. They also have religious practitioners or priests and also magical performers like Shamans. The tribal people participate in many festivals and rituals whole heartedly and pass these enjoyable and joyful days keeping aside the miseries hazards and problems of their life temporarily.

During the colonial rule the British Government did not like to disturb the isolated condition of the tribal areas. Because of their policy of keeping the tribal people in isolation, '....the tribal people of this country received very little of the modern facilities and western thought the British brought to this country and granted to the Indian people' (Raha, 1989:XXIII). Elwin also noticed this.

> The British Government (was) inclined on the whole, to leave the tribesmen alone partly because the task of administration especially in the wild border areas, was difficult and unrewarding, partly from a desire to quarantine the tribes from possible political infection and partly because a number of officers sincerely held the view that the people were better and happier as they were.... (Elwin, 1960).

This was true for the northeastern part of India also. Many areas of this region were out of bounds for the general Indian mass. As a result a large number of the tribal people were deprived of whatever little development the colonial administration did in other parts of India.

However, in the post independence period the national Government focused its attention towards Northeast India, and sanctioned and implemented a number of development projects for the overall improvement of the region. The constitutional benefits also reached the area. As a result of all these development programmes, constitutional facilities, construction of a network of roads, modern education, modern communication, impact of Hinduism and Christianity, urbanization and finally globalization brought and are still bringing marked changes in the life of the people in general and tribal people of North East India in particular.

At the end I must confess that to write a brief account on the life and activities of so many colourful tribal groups inhabiting all the eight states of Northeast India is a very difficult task. These large number of the tribal groups live in different ecological settings, have different economic activities, different social and political organizations, different life cycle rituals, different religious faiths and so on. All these variables make this part of India a very complex cultural mosaic.

REFERENCES

Ahmad, A., (1993), 'Education of the Scheduled Tribes: Some aspects of Inequality'. Workshop on Indicators of Equity in Education, October 24-28, NIEPA (Mimeo), New Delhi.

Arun Kumar, M.C., (1998), Debate among the Purums, *Man & Life*, Vol. 24, No.1+2.

Banerjee, B., (2004), Religious Beliefs and Practices among the Bokars of Arunachal Pradesh. In *Understanding Tribal Religion* (Eds)., Tamo Mibang & Sarit Choudhury. New Delhi, Mittal Publications

Barua, T.K.M., (1960), *The Idu Mishmis.* Shillong, Adviser to the Government of Assam.

Bera, G.K., (2010), *The Riang of Tripura.* Guwahati, Sanskriti.

Bora, B.K., (2006), Cultural Heritage of the Nah. *In Cultural Heritage of Arunachal Pradesh.* (Eds) N. Nagaraju & Byomkesh Tripathy. New Delhi, Indus Publishing Co.

Boring, G., (2006), Oral Tradition: An Important Source of Adi History. In *Cultural Heritage of Arunachal Pradesh* (Ed.) N. Nagaraju & Byomkesh Tripathy. New Delhi, Indus Publishing Co.

Boring, K., (2004), Philosophy of Donyi Polo. In *Understanding Tribal Religion* (Eds.) T. Mibang & S. Chaudhury. New Delhi, Mittal Publication.

Bose, J.K., (1985), *Culture Change among the Garos* Calcutta, Institute of Social Research and Applied Anthropology.

Chakraborty, B., (2004), 'Religion and Culture of Abo Tani in both the Hemispheres. In *Understanding Tribal Religion (Eds.)* Tamo Mibang & S. Chaudhuri, New Delhi, Mittal Publications.

Chatterjee, S., (2010), *North-East India: Dispersion and Discontent (in two vols)*. Delhi, Abhijeet Publications

Chatterjee, S., (2012), *SCs, STs and OBCs in the Indian Polity*. New Delhi, Abhijeet Publications.

Choudhury, S., (2004), An Ethnographic Note on the Singphos of Lohit. In *Tribes of Arunachal Pradesh*. (Eds.) B. Dhar & P.C. Coomar. New Delhi, Abhijeet Publications.

Danda, A., (1994), Shifting Cultivation in North-East India. In *Journal of Indian Anth. Society* Vol. 29, No. 1+2.

Danda, D. & S. Ghatak, (1985), *The Semsa and Their Habitat*. Calcutta, Anthropological Survey of India.

Dhasmana, M.M., (1979), *The Ramos of Arunachal Pradesh*, New Delhi, Concept Publishing Co. Pvt. Ltd.

Das, N.K., (1993), *Kinship, Politics and Law in Naga Society*. Calcutta, Anthropological Survey of India.

Das, R., (1985), *Manipur Tribal Scene*. New Delhi, Inter-India Publications.

Das, T.C., (1945), *The Purums: An Old Kuki Tribe of Manipur*, Calcutta, University of Calcutta.

Das Gupta, B.K., (1985), Present day Purum (Chote) Society with special reference to Marriage Alliance. In *Purum (Chote) Revisited* (Eds.). B.K. Das Gupta & Others, Calcutta, Anthropological Survey of India.

Dowerah, V., (2006), Cultural Heritage of the Noete. In *Cultural Heritage of Arunachal Pradesh* (Eds.) N. Nagaraju & Byomkesh Tripathy, New Delhi, Indus Publishing Co.

Dutta, P., (1959), *The Tangsas of Namchic and Tirap Villeys*. Shillong, North East Frontier Agency.

Dutta, P., (1978), *The Noctes*. Directorate of Research, Government of Arunachal Pradesh.

Dutta, P., (2004), A Note on the People of Arunachal: Their Culture and Matters of Anthropological Interest. In *Tribes of Arunachal Pradesh* (Eds.) Bibhash Dhar & Palash Ch. Coomar, New Delhi, Abhijeet Publications.

Dutta Choudhury, S., (1995), Mishmi: Idu. In *People of India: Arunachal Pradesh*, Vol. XIV (Ed) K.S. Singh. Calcutta, Seagull Books.

Dutta Choudhury, S., (1995), Adi: Ramo. In *People of India, Arunachal Pradesh*, Vol. XIV (Ed.) K.S. Singh, Calcutta, Seagull Books.

Elwin, V., (1960), *A Philosophy for NEFA*. Adviser to the Government of Assam, Shillong.

Erring, O., (2004), Philosophy of Donyi Polo. In *Understanding Tribal Religion* (Eds.) Tamo Mibang & Sarit K. Chaudhuri. New Delhi, Mittal Publications.

Furer-Haimendorf, C.von., (1962), *The Apatani and their Neighbours*. London, Routledge & Kegan Paul.

Gangte, T.S., (1993), *Nehru and Northeast India*. New Delhi, S. Chand & Co.

Gangte, T.S., (1993), *The Kukis of Manipur*. New Delhi, Gyan Publishing House.

Gurdon, P.R., (2002) (1906), *The Khasis*. Delhi, Low Price Publications.

Hiyang (Khiyang), T., (1985), The Original History of the Chothe (Chote) Tribe. In *Purum (Chote) Revisited* (Eds.) B.K. Dasgupta and others. Calcutta, Anthropological Survey of India.

Hodson, T.C., (2003), The Meitheis Delhi, Low Price Publications.

_______, (1908), *The Meitheis*. Delhi, Low Price Publication.

Hodson, T.C., (1911), *The Naga Tribes of Manipur*. London.

Hussain, M., (1995), Tangsa: Lugri. In *People of India, Arunachal Pradesh*, Vol. XIV, (Ed) K.S. Singh, Calcutta, Seagull Books.

Hutton, J.H., (1969) (or 1927), *The Angami Nagas*. London, MacMillan & Co.

Kumar, B.B., (2005), *Naga Identity*. New Delhi, Concept Publishing Co. Pvt. Ltd.

Mackenzie, A., (2005), *The North East Frontier of India*, New Delhi, Mittal Publications.

Marak, K.R., (1997), *Tradition and Modernity in Matrilineal Tribal Society*. New Delhi, Inter-India Publications.

McCullock, (1859), *Account of the Valley Manipur*. London

Mipun, J., 1993, *The Mishings (Miris) of Assam*. New Delhi Gian Publishing House.

Nayak, D.K., 2008, Geographical Background to Tribal Situation in North-East India. In *North-East India: The Human Interface* (Ed.) M.K. Raha & Aloke Kumar Ghosh. New Delhi. Gyan Publishing House.

Nimachow, G., (2006), A Note on Marriage Practices in the Aka Community. In *Marriage and Culture* (Eds.) Tamo Mibang & M.C. Behera. New Delhi, Mittal Publications.

Pakhem, B., (1984), The Biates. In *Tribes of Northeast India* (Eds.) S. Karotemprel, Calcutta, Firma K.L.M Pvt. Ltd.

Panigrahi, C., (1993), Jawaharlal Nehru and the North East. In *Nehru and Northeast India* (Ed.) T.S. Gangte. New Delhi, S.Chand & Co. Ltd.

Raha, M.K., 1989a, *Tribal India: Problem Development Prospect*, Vol. I, New Delhi, Gian Publishing House.

Raha, M.K., (1989b), *Matriliny to Patriliny: A Study of the Rabha Society*. New Delhi, Gian Publishing House.

Raha, M.K., (1999), The Tribes of India: Patterns and Problems of Identity. In *Contemporary Society: Tribal Studies*. New Delhi, Concept Publishing.

Raha, M.K., (2005), The Purum: Cultural Drift and Problem of Identity. In *North East India in Perspective* (Eds.) R.K. Das & D. Basu, New Delhi, Akansha Publishing House.

Raha, M.K. & S. Bhui (2005), The Tribal Societies of Arunachal Pradesh: A Structure Analysis. Men & Life, Vol. 31, No. 3 & 4.

Raha, M.K., (2006), Aspects of Social Organization of Some Tribal Societies of

Arunachal Pradesh. In *Cultural Heritage of Arunachal Pradesh* (Eds) N. Nagarajun & Byomkesh Tripathy. New Delhi, Indus Publishing Co.

Raha, M. K., (2008), 'Introduction'. In *North-East India: The Human Interface* (Eds) M.K. Raha & Aloke Kumar Ghosh. New Delhi, Gyan Publishing House.

Raha, M.K., (2008), North-East India and Nehru. In *North-East India: The Human Interfaces* (Eds.) M.K. Raha & Aloke Kumar Ghosh. New Delhi, Gyan Publishing House.

Rao, N.S., (2006), Tangsa Religion and Philosophy: A Note on Lord Rang-Frah. In *Cultural Heritage of Arunachal Pradesh* (Eds.) N. Nagarajun & B. Tripathy, New Delhi, Indus Publishing Co.

Rikam, N., (2004), The Faith and Philosophy of the Nyishis. In *Understanding Tribal Religion* (Eds.)Tamo Mibang & S. Chaudhury. New Delhi, Mittal Publications.

Roy, Sachin, (1966), *Aspects of Padam Minyong Culture*. Shillong, North East Frontier Agency.

Rubko, Talom, (1998), Donyi-Polo Faith and Practice of the Adi. In *Indigenous Faith and Practices of the Tribes of Arunachal Pradesh*. Itanagar, Himalayan Publishers.

Saha, R.K., (1994), *Valley Society of Manipur*, Calcutta, Punthi-Pustak.

Sema, Hokishe, (1986), *Emergence of Nagaland*, New Delhi.

Shakespeare, (1912), Lushai-Kuki Clans. London.

Singh, K.S., (1994), *The Scheduled Tribe: People of India,* Delhi, Oxford Univ. Press.

Singh, K.S., (1996), *Identity, Ecology, Social Organizatin, Economy, Linkages and Development Process: A Quantitative Profile*, Delhi, Oxford Univ. Press.

Shree Krishan, (1995), Language Identity and Linguistic Situation along the North-eastern Border. In *The People of the Himalayas* (Ed.) M.K. Raha, Calcutta, Anthropological Survey of India.

Subba, J.R., (2008), *History, Culture and Customs of Sikkim*, New Delhi, Gyan Publishing House.

Sunders, D.H.E., (1895), Survey and Settlement Report of the Western Duars in the District of Jalpaiguri, 1889-1895, Calcutta

Syam Choudhury, N.K & M.M. Das, (1973), *The Lalung Society: A Theme For Analytical Ethnography*. Calcutta, Anthropological Survey of India.

Thakur, A.K., (2006), Marriage and Social Control: A brief study of the Marginals. In *Marriage and Culture: Reflection from Tribal Societies of Arunachal Pradesh*, New Delhi, Mittal Publications.

Tripathy, B., (2006), Theravada Buddhism in Arunachal Pradesh. In *Cultural Heritage of Arunachal Pradesh*. New Delhi, Indus Publishing Co.

17
Globalization and Tribal Identities in North East India

Gadadhara Mohapatra

Introduction

The quest for identity is a basic sub-concern of globalization process, where the creation of viable identities was a fundamental issue. India is a scene of interplay of both modernization and struggles against globalization. On the one hand, it acknowledges the positive sides of India's integration to global economy, on the other, it also cautions the increasing levels of inequality, poverty and social conflicts and the threat that globalization puts to local and regional identity as a result of overwhelming processes of globalization. India is changing; however, the pace of change varied from time to time, group to group and region to region. The basic social institutions of India's countryside such as village, the joint family system and the caste and tribe relation are under great transformation. The process of liberalization, privatization and globalization (LPG) in the last two decades have witnessed the interlinked phenomena of industrialization and rapid economic growth for the country as a whole, a slowdown of agriculture, and an intensification of social conflicts (Walker, 2008:557). Poverty related conflicts are already in existence in the rural parts of India. Studies on poverty and conflicts in contemporary India, show that there are more conflicts between the poverty affected social groups and others in the rural areas in recent decades, and poverty related conflicts have positive and negative potential in the context of political and economic reforms (Anand Kumar, 2004:191). In the era of LPG, the areas inhabited by indigenous people have been subjected to incessant social unrests and protests (Meher, 2009:457).These forces or processes have created new poverty zones in the country, further marginalizing the tribal people. The pathologies of our time are that these mining and industrial projects are destroying the local eco-system and causing loss of livelihood of the self-sustaining tribal communities. The globalization processes have serious implications on the culture of the tribal people. The alienation of the land and other resources which are both their physical sustenance and the centre of their culture, is an attack on their very identity. Besides, globalization imposes an homogeneous consumerist culture and value system on society. In order to ensure the growth of consumerism, globalization has to depoliticize the minority which gets its benefits, destroy their social conscience and desensitize them to the impoverishment of the majority. It thus combines individualism with a culture where everyone looks after his/her own interests at the cost of others (Kothari, 1991:556; Fernades, 2006: 56). The middle class wants a consumerist lifestyle (Petras, 1994:2071). This class supports it because they "see a definite advantage for themselves in a globalization which effectively improves their living standards even as it leaves the mass of the population without any obvious benefit, and, in some cases, may even worsen their material conditions" (Ghosh, 1997: 3). Globalization is a threat to the local culture in North East India and has often been situated in the context of fundamentalism, a part of religious movement. In this region, religious fundamentalism results in shortage of resources and more unrest, and the latter can strengthen exclusive ethnic identities and conflict (Fernandes, 2006:52). Land alienation among the tribal people is both an economic issue and an attack on their culture and identity. Globalization has heightened the crisis in the North-East, showing the need for civil society to search for an alternative value system (*ibid.*: 6). Fundamentalism too plays the role of hiding growing chronic poverty and food insecurity. The problem of food and nutrition security has become more important in the trade liberalization and globalization regime in the developing country like India. The problem is much more significant in North-Eastern region of India that has been lagging far behind the other states in respect of agricultural production especially of food items, industries and the development of human capital (De, 2010:98). The entire North-Eastern region of India is deficit in food production. Along with the worsening problem of landlessness, a significant section of the people suffers from environment, development and conflict-induced displacement. However, food insecurity of the North-East has been ignored so far due to the excessive engagement with questions of 'identity' and 'insurgency' in the region (Husain, 2004: 4515). In addition to environment-induced displacement, the perpetual ethnic conflicts based on exclusivist ethnicity have also induced massive internal displacement of population in the entire North-East. The political environment of generalized violence has been an existential reality both in Assam and Tripura since the early 1980s (*ibid.*: 4516).

It is within this theoretical and conceptual framework, this paper focuses on the socio-cultural implications of globalization and the changing face of tribal identity in North East India. The paper illustrates the social change among the tribal communities in the era of globalization. It also problematises how globalization as a process, further heightened the social conflict among various ethnic groups in North-East region and the subsequent loss of identity and local culture. Finally, it provides a critical appraisal of the tribal development programmes in the region.

Sociology of Globalization and Identity

The roots of 'Sociology of Globalization' can be traced back to the writings of social theorists or the three formative thinkers: Karl Marx, Emile Durkheim and Max Weber who represent 'classical sociology'. Of all classical theorists, Karl Marx was most explicitly committed to a globalizing theory of modernization. Globalization caused an enormous increase in the power of the capitalist class because it opened up new markets for it. The establishment of a 'world market' for modern industry gave a cosmopolitan character not only to production but also to consumption (Waters, 1995:8). Hence, Marx's analysis of modernity and globalization is of capitalist commodification. Durkehim's genuine legacy to globalization is his theories of structural specialization (differentiation) and culture. To the extent that the institutions of societies become specialized, commitment to such institutions as the state must be weakened because they are more narrow in their compass. In parallel, the national culture must progressively become more weak and abstract in order to encompass intra-societal diversity. All of this implies that industrialization tends to weaken collective commitments and open up the way for dismantling the boundaries between societies.Weber (1978) identified rationalization as the globalizing solvent. He was fundamentally concerned with the success of rationalization, with its spread from the seedbed origins of calvinistic Protestantism to infest all Western cultures and to set up an iron cage for all moderns. According to Weber, rationalization implies that all cultures will become characterized by the depersonalization of social relationships, the refinement of techniques of calculation, the enhancement of the importance of specialized knowledge, and the extension of technically rational control over both natural and social processes (Brubaker, 1984:2; Waters, 1995:8). Contemporary sociological theorists especially Robertson (1992) and Giddens (1990; 2000) identified the phenomenon called globalization through the mediating category of Modernity.

The definitions of globalization most frequently encountered in the literature are those of Robertson, who sees it as 'the compression of the world into a single place' and 'the intensification of consciousness of the world as a whole'... both concrete global interdependence and consciousness of the global whole (Robertson, 1992: 8). He argues that globalization refers to the 'global human condition'.

Cultural approaches to globalization focused on several factors, one of them being religion. Religion played a vital role in the process of globalization, initially through the expansion of the world religions of Islam and Christianity, and later through the secularization process in Protestantism. Recent developments were, however, challenging the secularization thesis. What was instead being observed was resurgence of religion in terms of what were being named as fundamentalist movements. Fundamentalism was seen by Robertson as an attempt to declare a social identity, a search for a new consciousness in the face of the infinite fragmentation that was taking place in a global society. Fundamentalists identified and opposed the agents of secularism and sought to restructure the political, social, cultural and economic relations and institutions, according to traditional religious beliefs and practices. Hence, the fundamental movements were of apolitical and political in nature and could be divided into two categories such as: the emergence of new religious movements and the wave of religious nationalist movements (D'Souza, 2005:328). Modernization, Giddens (1990) maintained, with its basic tendency to differentiation, increased the possibilities of choice, but on the other hand created, problems of identity formation at both the individual and collective levels. MacDonald (1999) also argued that both individuals and groups that were marginalized by globalization struggled to establish coherent identities that were being threatened by contradictory social imperatives (Bendle, 2002:3; D'Souza 2005:335). Identity in pre-modern societies was seen as synonymous with the 'core' or centre of existence. Post-modernist views rejected the notion of 'core' and considered identity to be conceived of as something more superficial, transient, multiple and manipulable, something that emerged as a product of discourse. Giddens (1990) saw the transformations in self-identity as one of the requirements in the dialectic of the local-global conditions. In other words, the greater the detraditionalization of a society, the more was the need to negotiate lifestyle choices from the diversity of option (*ibid.*: 7). The formation of identity also became the key component in the social dynamics of high modernity or globalization as reflected in the works of Heelas, Lash and Morris (1996). Heelas explained that in traditional societies, identity was inscribed and based on an authoritarian taken-for-grantedness, whereas in a detraditionalized society, identity was constructed and persons acquired opportunities to critically reflect upon and even reject what traditional society generally offered. Identity was no longer seen as involving the self's non-reflective, unquestioning 'inscription' within a tradition, rather it was seen as emerging in a discourse. It was seen in a globalized society as a shift from the passive level of acceptance to the active level of reflexivity and critique (Bendle, 2002:7 and D'Souza, 2005:336).

Singh (2002) recognizes that globalization was bound to put pressure on Indian cultures which he generally understands as an acceleration towards homogenizing cultural forms and activities (lifestyles, dress, food etc.) in the country. However, he asserts that the social structure and cultural system in India are intrinsically based on pluralism and diversity. Indian society (both caste and tribe) is segmented in communities which enjoy enormous cultural autonomy. This provides enormous cultural resilience to communities in India to filter the effects of globalization through refractorary and prismatic adaptation (*ibid.* 64). Moreover there is an enhanced sense of self-consciousness and awareness of identity. Those elements of globalization are resented that encroach upon or does not promote the core cultural values of society. So, globalization has both facets – homogenization and (cultural) identity enhancement. In case of the Indian diaspora, he finds the trends of cultural fusion. Further, in India, at the level of popular culture of music, dance, dramatic, cinema etc., the trend is one of fusion of traditional Indian forms or styles with western or global forms or styles. Singh regards this emergent popular (fusion) culture, as posing a threat to the indigenous local, regional or ethnic identity of cultural traditions in so far as it abstracts culture from people's rhythm of life and its natural expressiveness or vitality, and converts its new packaging into a community (*ibid.*, 103). In this process, the traditional identities, deeply embedded in a community life (caste, class, tribe, principles of hierarchy and reciprocity), are metamorphosed into a faceless audience. This, he thinks, is not entirely due to globalization, but rather intrinsic to the very paradigm of modernization which we along with the humanity will fully celebrate.

Oommen (1998) talks of cultural impact of globalization and the "Birth of a New World Society." For him, the consequences of globalization should be viewed through four interrelated processes—homogenisation, pluralisation, traditionalisation and hybridisation. These four processes, operating independently and in interaction with one another, give birth to a new world society. Importantly, this should not be understood as a movement from tradition to modernity, simplicity to complexity, and heterogeneity to homogeneity, but rather as a phenomenon that produces new permutations and combinations giving birth to variety and pluralism. Jan Aart Scholte argues that globalization is characterized by the 'transcendence of boundaries' (Schlote, 2000). Such relations are becoming more significant as communication and production increasingly occur without regard to geographic constraints, transborder organizations of many kinds proliferate, and more people become aware of the world as a single whole. Pushed by the structural forces of capitalism and rationalism, propelled by actor initiatives such as technological innovations or regulatory decisions, the transformation is creating a new world. Anand Kumar (2011) states that the process of globalization is often situated within the discourse of globality and global sociology. Globalization has been explored primarily with reference to the processes and institutions of world economy and international relations. However, the socio-cultural and political aspects of this process have been recognized through the lenses of nation, ethnicity, migration, multiculturalism, global governance, new media and communication systems, and transnational civil society.

Discourse on Identity

The concept of identity is closely associated with the idea of culture. Identities can be formed through the cultures and subcultures to which people belong or in which people participate. Stephen Frosh describes the view that identity draws from culture but is not simply formed by it: Recent sociological and psychological theories have stressed that a person's identity is in fact something multiple and potentially fluid, constructed through experience and linguistically coded. In developing their identities people draw upon culturally available resources in their immediate social networks and in society as a whole. The process of identity construction is, therefore, one upon which the contradictions and dispositions of the surrounding socio-cultural environment have a profound impact (Frosh, 1999). However, different theories of identity see the relationship between culture and identity in different ways. Those influenced by modern theories of culture and identity are more likely to see identity as originating in a fairly straightforward way from involvement in particular cultures and sub-cultures (Harlambos and Holborn 2008: 665-66). The term identity first gained salience through the work of the psychologist Erikson (1968). While Erikson associates identity as a definition of personhood that is, with sameness or continuity of the self across time and space, other authors emphasize uniqueness, that is, those characteristics that differentiate a person from other people or the whole of humankind (Bornman, 2003). Erikson uses the term identity *crisis* to refer to individuals who have lost a sense of sameness or continuity. While he regards an identity crisis as a normal and passing stage in adolescent development, he holds that it should be regarded as pathological in adults. He typifies a healthy state of identity development as an invigorating subjective awareness of sameness and continuity. Although Erikson theorizes on identity from a psychoanalytic point of view, he also emphasizes the role of the environment, and particularly the social environment, in the development of identity. He uses the term psychosocial identity in this regard. Psychosocial identity refers to the awareness of who a person is, both as individual and as a member of a family, various societal groups and a particular society (*Ibid.*).

India is an emerging economic power and is one of the fastest growing countries in the world. It has impressive growth rates, which seem to have their basis in the recent policies of liberalization, privatization and globalization (LPG). However, the impact of globalization on social and cultural values in India needs further elaboration. Studies on globalization and indigenous peoples in Asia reflect that globalization comes to the local communities largely through the market. New goods may be seen on the television or come to be known through other ways. But it is through the market that they become available to be consumed or can be used by people. It is also through the market that producers come to know what they can sell. Often they may not know the use of to which their products are put to. For instance, only recently, after the logging ban imposed by the Indian Supreme Court, indigenous women in the North-Eastern states of Meghalaya, India, began selling the bark of a local tree, but had no idea at all of the uses of that bark. The indigenous peoples of Andhra Pradesh, India had for decades been collecting and selling gum called *karaya* without any idea of its use in making dentures (Nathan, Kelkar and Walter (eds.), 2004: 293-94). On account of the changes brought about by nationalist projects and due to globalization, tribes are studied as subjects of modernization and development, or as their victims. The study of tribes as victims, in conjunction with the issue of ecological degradation, has given way to rethinking development policies (Xaxa, 2003). Correspondingly, tribes have come to occupy greater space in contemporary discourse on alternative development or the general issue of protection on environment and ecology. As more attention is paid to attempts by the tribal groups to engage in movements to alter their social situation as well as greater attention to their self-representation, questions of human rights, transnational communication and re-imagining ethnicity and identity are the emerging issues in contemporary India.

Studies on governance, reforms and development among the Scheduled Tribes in India in the era of globalization, reflect the deplorable condition of the tribal people created by the forces of globalization (Louis, 2007). The tribal people continue to be the most isolated, deprived and marginalized segment of the Indian population. Keeping this fact in mind, the framers of the constitution made specific provisions for their upliftment. But, these have not really benefited the tribal communities at large. With introduction of liberalization, privatization and globalization, the rights of the tribal people have been further violated. Yet they continue to wage relentless war to safeguard their interests and rights. During the last six decades the tribal people have been subjected to innumerable forms of oppression and exploitation. Scholars have often identified the significant changes that have occurred in the intervening period in the population matrix of the tribal areas. In many cases, they have been reduced to a minority (Sharma 1995:24). Moreover, a new generation of migrant population—children of officials, traders, contractors and such like have majored who forcefully claim equal status with the tribal people as 'sons of the soil'. Moreover, among the tribal people themselves, a small group comprising the educated, has emerged with no interest in the local traditions—they are anxious to join the 'other side'. Thus, tribal people's undisputed command over their habitat is not only being questioned *de jure* by the state and other exotic interests but even by an influential section of the local population itself, making their position still more vulnerable (*ibid.*: 24).

Globalization and Tribes of North East India

India is the homeland of a large number of ethnic groups and cultures.

These communities, believed to be the earliest inhabitants of the century, live in the forests, hills, plateaus and naturally isolated regions and are differently terms as *Vanyajati* (forest-caste), *Vanavasi* (forest-inhabitants), *Pahariya* (hillmen), *Adimjati* (primitive caste), *Adivasi* (original settler), *Janjati* (folk communities) and several such other names signifying either their ecological or economic or historical and cultural characteristics. Among these nomenclatures the most popular term is "*Adivasi*" while the constitutional name for them is *Anusuchit Janajati* (Scheduled Tribe). The Scheduled Tribes (STs) are indigenous, have their own distinctive culture, are geographically isolated and are generally living in lower socio-economic conditions. For centuries, the tribal groups have remained outside the realm of national development processes due to their habitation in forests and hilly tracts. After independence, Government of India scheduled tribal groups in the Constitution and provided special provisions for their welfare and development as in the case of SCs. There are about 654 ST communities across the States in India and 75 of the STs are most backward and are termed as the Primitive Tribal Groups. Most of the tribal areas are hilly, inaccessible, undulating plateau lands in the forest areas of the country resulting in the bypassing of general developmental programmes. Due to this, infrastructure and development facilities in tribal areas for education, roads, healthcare, communication, drinking water, sanitation etc. have lagged behind compared to other areas which have resulted in further widening the gaps of development between the tribal people and the general population for a long time. Apart from the demographic features, on the social milieu of the tribal people it is noticed that the tribal population has a strong culture and value with which they have organized their social, cultural, economic and political practices and structures. This is precisely why they continue to remain a distinct people in spite of every attempt by the dominant caste and class to bring them into 'mainstream' (Louis, 2007). The adivasi ethos recognizes and respects the basic and fundamental truth that the harmonious relationship between the human community, animal kingdom and the environment should be maintained at any cost. In this process they also respect and value human labour.

The term 'ethnicity' sometimes confuses one with other terms like tribe, people, cultural group, linguistic group, religious group, community etc. In the context of North East India, the term 'ethnic group' is a recent sociological alternative to the term 'tribe' which is considered to be out of date and a pejorative term. But these terms to the same set of confused facts and units of 'original people' as differentiated from units of 'newer people' occupying the same space. The striking demographic feature of North East India is that the hills are predominantly inhabited by the Scheduled Tribe communities, while in the plains the dominant population belongs to other communities. Moreover, no significant Scheduled Caste population is found in the hills. It is not an easy task to determine the ethnic affinities of the population of North East India. Broadly speaking the Scheduled Tribe population in the hills as also in the plains has Mongoloid features. The Aryan speaking people in the plains have mainly Caucasoid features. However, as from the ancient times various ethnic elements have entered this region and have merged with other ethnic elements, it is impossible to analyze the elements separately (Sharma, T.C. & Majumdar, D.N., 1980).

Studies on ethnic movements in North East India (Singh, 1982) shows that the first step of this movement is to assert the identity around certain social problems and the next step is to concretize the identity by forming an ethnic association. The third step is to claim for a separate administrative arrangement, so that the group concerned can preserve their cultural heritage and language etc. The final step is to demand a separate administrative unit comprising the areas where the ethno-cultural group forms a majority. Just after formation of Mizo district council the Pawi-Lakhers demanded a separate District Council. So also the Jaintias desired to achieve their separate District Council. In Nagaland though there has been a somewhat common Naga identity since the formation of the Naga club, the tribal identities have remain strong. However, another phenomenon to be noted here is the merger of smaller identities to form bigger identities making it convenient to raise political demands.The Zeliangrong movement is a case in point (Kabui, 1982). The Kabuis, Roungmas and the Jemis who are closely akin to each other and spread over in three states, Assam, Manipur and Nagaland, have merged their identities to claim a separate homeland for themselves. The same is the case with the PanKuki movement trying to unite all the fragmentary Kuki groups into one strong ethno-cultural identity (Pakem, B, 1990:27-30).

Definitions of the term 'tribe' may vary from time to time depending upon who are the 'newer people'. The first usage of the term 'tribe' was with reference to the biblical people of Israel to certain divisions of political units of ancient Rome from Latin 'tribus'. It refers to a certain group of people without any emotive connotation. It was with its appearance in Middle English that has brought about vagueness and plurality of meanings in its usage. This coincided with the age of British colonialism. The colonial administrators began to apply the term pejoratively to people in colonial area by calling them as primitive, uncivilized, conservative, and inferior. The 'original people' were then looked down upon by 'newer people' quite different from the traditions and loyalties of the latter. The post colonial administrators as 'newer people' also followed suit and viewed the 'original people' as socially and economically backward. The Constitution of India bears ample testimony to this fact so far as the hill people of North East India are concerned. As in the colonial era, the specific backward community becomes a minority group compared to the main or dominant national group. The only difference between the 'newer people' and the 'new people' is that the former had a cross-national background and the latter have a cross-cultural background. Scholars belonging to the latter group had, consciously or unconsciously, neglected the issues of society while drifting towards the policy of national integration. Even established scholars like Verrier Elwin (1939; 1960) had discarded his 'national park; policy in favour of the middle-of-the-road' policy to suit the changing times, which would have ultimately led to the policy of 'integration' had Elwin lived longer (Pakem, 1990:112). The members of a tribal group or a backward community have accepted the term 'tribe' and 'backwardness' for quite sometimes after independence. After realizing the derogatory nature of such terms, there has been a quest for an alternative term to designate their identy. While the hill people have now started calling themselves 'hill people', 'hill men', 'community', or by particular name of the community like the Khasi, Mizo, Naga, etc., and currently by the term 'indigenous people' to cover the original people of the valleys as well, scholars have more or less accepted the term 'ethnicity' or 'ethnic group' as a viable alternative.

North-Eastern Region (NER) of India comprises of eight states such as Assam, Arunachal Pradesh, Meghalaya, Mizoram, Manipur, Nagaland, Sikkim and Tripura. In terms of ethnic groups, the region is identified as the home of mongoloid people. These groups of people are mostly categorized as the Scheduled Tribes (STs) by the Constitution. While mainland Indian states were reorganized along linguistic lines based on the report of the States Reorganization Commission constituted in 1953, North East India was reorganized on ethnic lines. Thus, it is a general notion that Mizoram state belongs to the Mizos, Nagaland to the Nagas, Manipur to the Meiteis and Meghalaya to the Khasi, Jaintia and the Garos. These ethnic states were created after decades of struggle for political autonomy and the creation of such ethnic states have sharpened the divisions (Haokip, 2012: 84). The political autonomy movements among the tribes began during the colonial period, but the formation of separate states on ethnic line was done only after independence (Rath, 2006:40).The North East India experienced the formation of more tribal states than the central India and has also experienced stronger militant struggles. As North East India shares the international border, such militancy makes the region more politically sensitive. The Government of India has, therefore, tried to appease the agitated tribes by allowing the formation of more ethnic states in this region. In the North East, the movement percolated down to the grassroots level; the leaders at the centre of the movement kept contact with the people of the inaccessible tracts through the village chiefs. The local problems in the North East and central India have shaped their respective autonomy movements in terms of their objectives and strategy. The demand for greater Nagaland or Nagalim, with unification of the Naga-inhabited areas of Manipur, Arunachal Pradesh and Assam is certainly not the same as the demand for greater Jharkhand with the tribal-inhabited districts of Orissa, West Bengal and Madhya Pradesh. While the former witness extreme militancy, the latter sticks to democratic means. North East India has been experiencing radicalism through its militancy; the Naxalite-based radicalism of the central tribal region does not find a fertile ground to grow in the North East. In the North East, the feature of autonomy has evolved from the conflict between the traditionalists and the pro-modern elite. Traditionalists are the chiefs who want to protect their power and local resources by invoking a secessionist demand. The modernists are the educated elite who prefer control over resources as well as a share in the benefits of state-owned development projects. They demand political autonomy, which essentially calls for decentralization of national power and resources to the locals (*ibid.*, 41).

North East India presents a resource abundant economy which continued to remain backward in comparative perspective with other regions. However, the backwardness of the economy could be attributed as much due to geo-political constraints as to retrograde policies pursued by the constituent states, a fact which impeded the process of transformation of traditional economy to having the semblance of a modern one. Tradition and identity issues had lulled the region to a zone of complacency and inaction and the only grace point was the safety net of the region which operated through the community based socio-economic structure prevailing in the tribal areas. An agricultural economy with shifting cultivation predominating, together with total absence of infrastructure and restrictive land market militated against the development process in the region and a result, when the new economic policy (NEP) came into force the requirements of change could hardly be made applicable to the economy in a radical manner. In the region as a whole, there was no long term perspective of development, now withstanding the creation of North Eastern Council. Further, the internal security scenario was not conducive either to development. The concept of the tribal development had also made no dent in the situation. The region despite massive flow of Central resources, remained to lay behind in basic infrastructure, power generation, mineral development, cross border trade and agricultural productivity. The NEP has opened up great opportunities to bring about structural changes in the economy, although the challenges are daunting as well. The State Governments of the region have started showing the requisite political will to surge ahead by reaping the benefits of NEP. Significantly, since 1996 several bold initiatives were taken by the Central Government by augmenting Central investments in different spheres of the economy with primary focus on the region's infrastructure in order to bring about perceptible changes in economic governance of the region. In fact, state intervention in the economy of the region has become more strident to prepare the ground for absorption of market oriented economic reforms. In the past one decade, central packages, new industrial policy, creation of non-lapsable pool of central resources, upgradation of various Ministries and revamping of the North Eastern Council have created the required springboard for developmental initiatives forward. Indeed the success of India's Look East Policy hinges on the overall development of the region as a whole. However, one has to guard against lopsided planning and faulty implementation. It is the high time to initiate proactive measures to address issues like militancy, political extremism and insurgency by evolving a region specific community participation in the process of development. The new economic policy has undoubtedly opened up the possibilities of harnessing immense potentials of the North East region for developmental imperatives which had hitherto remained illusive in the absence of economic infrastructure and strong political will. Evidently the decline in agricultural growth rate and retrograde industrial policies only contributed to a stagnating situation. No doubt, the idea of regional planning was invoked in early seventies with the establishment of the North Eastern Council but it made no head way whatsoever. Of late, a new realization has dawned on the political leadership that the region can emerge as a vibrant economic zone on the strength of exclusive and proactive central initiatives which prominently include non-lapsable pool of resources and industrial and investment promotion policy. In addition, Look East Policy expectations have generated a positive outlook in favour of making the region a prominent hub for international trade and commerce. The eleventh Five Year Plan has also focused on the exploration of huge resources of the North East for economic development of the region. A step in the right direction has been on highlighting public-private partnership in investment in the field of road and air connectivity, power generation and mineral development. The improved security scenario in the region and the all-out effort of the DoNER Ministry is all set to bring the benefits of globalization to the region's doorsteps to get over the skewed development profile.

The tendency among researchers and policymakers in using the term "North East" is itself problematic as the region represents a varied cultural mosaic and has never considered itself to be one compact unit. Udayon Mishra states that New Delhi suffers from a strong misconception and has failed to appreciate the complex nature of the problem (Mishra, 2000). North Eastern region on India has around 7 per cent of the total geographical area of the country but around 4 per cent of the population. Around 60 per cent of the population of NER reside in Assam. In most of the all-India studies, Assam is taken as a proper representative state of NER. The justification is in terms of the size of population, since a very small percentage of the total population of India (0.02%) is residing in the remaining seven States. Thus, the demographic perspective of socio-economic analysis leads to marginalization of the remaining states in the domain of social studies (Sinha *et al.*, 2010: vii). The old sense of loyalties to one's own clan, tribe and race is slowly disappearing and a new sense of common identity of the tribal people, a tribal consciousness or tribal corporate personality is emerging among the Indian tribal, people due to the impact of Christianity and modern education (Thomas, 1993 :75). S.K. Barpujari shares that for centuries the Naga had been living in a world of their own leading a traditional life constantly warring against one another more often than not hunting human heads. After their conversion to the new religion, wanton killing was realized as a sin in the light of the teachings of Christ and hostility was replaced by love. A sense of solidarity among the diverse groups of the Naga or Nagaism emerged (Barpujari, 1984:107,109). The Nagaism has the tendency of going beyond the Naga unity even to include people outside the tribes. As Barpujari himself attests: "In other words, they have realized the necessity of peace, toleration and coexistence with their own men and neighbours in the plains" (*ibid.*, 108). The characteristic "resilence and openendedness" that redefine the "social boundary definition and boundary maintenance" is found among other tribal people also. "A communitarian self understanding transcending the segmental sociolinguistic identities" is noted by Khubchandani (1992) in several compact regions such as Jharkhand, Gondwana, Bhilbhoomi, Arunachal and Bodoland. The Jharkhand movement represents a characteristic articulation of syncretic identity, welding together the aspirations of tribal groups belonging to different ancestries (Austric, Dravidian and Indo-Aryan) while the Bodoland agitation, on the other, presents an alliance of different ethnic groups belonging to the Bodo group of Tibeto-Burman language family (Khubchandani, 1992: 95). Nirmal Minz (1990) also has pointed out an emerging tribal consciousness in relation to its tradition and history and in relation to outsiders.

In the pre-colonial period most of the communities of North East India were not conscious about their ethnic identities and their world was confined to their family, clans, and villages. The first sociological process has been to develop an ethno-tribal identity which was acquired in the phase of colonial administration. Different cultural-linguistic communities want to retain their traditions and relative prestige while desiring to improve their social, economic, and political status. All these issues involve competition, conflict and power struggle (Pakem, 1990:1). Regarding the cultural identity movements in North East India, the ethnic group concerned would assert its identity around certain social problems which will ultimately lead to some demands from the state so that the group can preserve its cultural heritage, language etc. As a matter of fact most of the problems in Nortrh-east India emanate from linguistic considerations. But at the same time while cultural identity may separate similar ethnic groups, there are also instances where it brings different ethnic groups to consolidate themselves against any out-groups.

Scholars investigating around the issues of ethnic formation among the various hill people of North East India, generally outlines three stages of ethnic formation – the dormant, calmed and active ethnicity (Pakem, 1990:116). Dormant ethnicity is always out there. As the sociologists would say it is a given or constant. This is all the more true in the context of North East India. But it is sometimes necessary to find out the level of intensity and ethnic awareness of the people concerned. The ethnic intensity, awareness, and behaviour of any people can be affected by impersonal social forces such as social and geographical mobility. These are also affected by human agencies as well, such as governments and politicians. In the early stages of ethnic formation, economic development and education may create ethnic consciousness among the people who shared some objective ethnic characteristics. For example, the gap in the economic or educational level between any two people may further strengthen the "we" and "they" attitude. When any of these and other factors are present, ethnic awareness starts germinating. Of course, in its embryonic stage the ethnic consciousness does not go beyond dormant ethnicity as among the various tribes of Arunachal Pradesh. Unlike other areas of North East India, political awareness has not fully penetrated the interior places of Arunachal Pradesh. Such dormant ethnicity is equated with ethnic quietism. In other areas of the North-Eastern region where the first stage is over, ethnic formation is well on its way. This stage is generally marked with ethnic resentment. It is at this stage that the governments and the politicians used steps to suppress or calm down the process of such ethnic formation. In many parts of the hill areas of the region, there is either a suppressed or a calmed ethnicity. Ethnic groups in Meghalaya may be cited as example of such calmed ethnicity after initial ethnic resentment (*ibid.*, 117).

From ethnic quietism and ethnic resentment, the other most formidable stage in ethnic formation is ethnic millitancy. It is at this stage that ethnic mobilization takes place. It may take place at the level of political participation through the formalities of regional political parties. Most of the regional parties reflected their respective ethnic aspiration (Pakem, 1990), the latest being that of the hill districts and the plain tribes of Assam. At another level, ethnic mobilization is for the achievement of socio-economic modernization. Unlike elsewhere, in the hill areas of the North-Eastern region the important consideration for each socio-economic modernization is not so much on account of class consciousness as in new group consciousness. The question of regional imbalance has been stressed from time to time. What is actually behind the slogan of regional imbalance is the new group consciousness which thrives on common identity of clan, culture, language, race or religion. Because of this, it has been suggested elsewhere (Pakem, 1990) that economic development through various Five Year Plans had failed to weaken ethnic formation as expected in places other than North East India. Huge financial investments had been pumped to Manipur and Nagaland but insurgency continues unabated. This leads to the concept of ethnonationalism which is the highest level of ethnic militancy. This type of militancy is represented by insurgent groups of Manipur, Mizoram, Nagaland, and Tripura. But ethnonationalism has something to do with the principle of self-determination which aims at autonomy only and not for secession. The moment ethnic groups demand for secession the final stage of ethnic formation has been reached and the formal process of nationality begins. Thus, it is clear from the above discussion on ethnic formation among the local people that the ethnic consciousness as a political force is gaining ground in North East India. It is also true that some ethnic groups are still dormant and others are either suppressed or calmed for sometimes. But active ethnicity is also vigorously pursued. The final stage of ethnic formation is however, the active ethnic mobilization towards nationality formation. Commenting on the history of ethnicity, Jackson (1984:213) says: The history of ethnicity is largely a record of the movements and conflicts and resolutions and renewed conflicts of ethnic and related identities.This is also true of the history of ethnicity in North East India (Pakem, 1990:118). Civil strife, together with conflicts between and within states, is common in the region and remains a significant constraint on development. Differences in culture, tribal links, and political aspirations are one set of explanations for the current unrest in the region. But there is much global evidence that poverty, competition for limited resources, and underdevelopment are major catalysts of conflict. Poverty and other economic factors are seldom the direct causes of conflict but they can aggravate existing tensions, tipping the balance towards conflict rather than a search for negotiated peaceful solutions.

The most important trend that has emerged in recent years is the assertion of tribal identity (Chacko, 2005, *Foreword:* 11). Assertions have been made on the basis of region, ethnicity, language, among other elements. The tribal religion is now being interpreted as being different from other religion. They are returning to their own religions as demonstrates over the last two censuses. Further, tribal people have started writing about themselves. The tribal literature has proliferated; the tribal artists are at work seeking self-expression. Though some tribal languages are losing ground, others are holding out. There is a demand supported by linguists for imparting education at primary level in the tribal languages, which will help them to maintain self-respect and identity. Lastly, there are movements for self-role to enable the tribes to maintain their control over resources and to manage in situation that promote their own development while maintaining their culture and identity. All tribal movements today are an expression of the deeply felt-sense of identity (*ibid.*, 11-12). The socio-economic forces of modernization and development have no doubt brought some benefits to the people of some areas, but the benefits accrued to them have been largely outweighed by the harm. Development induced displacement, involuntary migration and resettlement have caused the marginalization of the tribal people and presented enormous problems to them. The new economic regime has led to the privatization and marketisation of the economy revelling it to be a powerful threat to the survival of tribal communities (Singh, 2008). According to one estimate between 1950 and 1990 state development projects, (irrigation projects, mines, thermal power plants, wildlife sanctuaries, industries), have displaced 213 lakh persons; 85 per cent of them are tribal people (Fernandes & Paranjpe, 1997). The government is aware of both (a) the eroding resources base and socio-cultural heritage of the tribal population through a combination of development interventions, commercial interest, and lack of effective legal protection of the tribal people; and (b) the disruption of life and environment of the tribal populations owing to unimaginative, insensitive package of relief. The emerging tribal consciousness has two aspects: desire for self-identity and desire for transcending loyalties. These are not conflicting ideologies. A desire for common humanity does not mean denying one's particular identity based on tradition. No group in the world has discarded willingly their traditional sense of identity. This does not necessarily obstruct developing a universal sense of community based on universal humanness. The tribal self-identity need not hinder national integration. Such a sense of openendedness was not altogether absent even in earlier periods. For example in the traditional matriarchal society of the Khasis, their high priestess, Khyriem, who represented their common ancestress, was expected to marry a non-Khasi. In the Mizo life, as Thanzauva notes, the idea of Zawlbuk, which in the past was exclusively meant for men and for particular clan or village, is showing signs of a "fellowship of openness" church (Thanzauva, 1989: 105-6). National policies must be formulated taking tribal cultural identity as the base for national integration, and all have to learn that only self-respect of communities will create a sensible national community. A new India could be created, not by destroying dalit or tribal self-respect but by promoting tribal culture and language, the sources of their self-respect and self identity. A.G. Noorani's evaluations that the Naga unrest is due to the "appeasement" policy of Article 371 (A) lacks understanding of and sensitivity to minority cultures. Cultural revival among the tribal communities of India has become a major tool of their awakening. For many tribal communities, cultural revival has therefore become a way of reasserting themselves as a people with a right to an identity of their own and a life with dignity, which includes demanding their right over their livelihood. In order to identify the implications of cultural revival, it is essential to understand the nature of the tribal cultures. Even some tribal leaders focus only on the externals of languages, dances and songs and ignore the kernel or the values and the worldview on which they are based. *The core that the externals express combines their values, social system, identity and sustenance.* Because it is intrinsic to their identity, the tribal people resent any imposition on them. For example, the communities of the North East feel that the "one State one nation" thinking tends "to take the degree of Aryanisation as the measure of Indianisation". Identities in North East are mostly constructed around ethno-nationalisms. In the context of North East in spite of claims of uniqueness of an identity, the identities have undergone tremendous evolution and have been hybridised with or without ethno-politics of exclusivity. Studies on the evolution of these identities highlights the transition and transformations that have shaped the Ao Naga, the Mizo and Arunachalee identities (Barthakur, 2006:8-9; Baral, 2006:4). If the transformations have occurred by the state power imposing alien institutions and practices, and by the intrusion of cultural and religious forces from outside semiotically, such forces have also contributed to the strengthening of an identity culturally. Within the generic representation of the Naga, the Mizo and Arunachalee identities it is important to note the internal heterogeneity within the generic as problematic as the conflict between ethnonationalism and the nation state. Therefore, identities in the North East can best be understood to have been placed between conflicts of self/other binary, in an in-betweenness that is simultaneously historicized and dehistoricized (Baral, 2004:4).

Ethnic conflicts are manifested in varying degrees and intensities. The consequences are often seen in the economic deprivation of some groups of people. In the context of Manipur, conflicts are observed at three different levels. First, intra-ethnic conflict, i.e. which occurred within an ethnic group, such as that between the Kuki and the Hmar in 1960 and that between the Thadou Kuki and the Paite Zomi in 1997 to 1998, within the generic ethnic group commonly known as the Chin-Kuki.The issue of nomenclature was the basis of these conflicts. Second, inter-ethnic conflict, i.e. the conflict between two or more ethnic groups, such as that between the Naga and the Kuki tribes in 1992 and subsequently between the Meitei and the Pangal in the valley in 1993. Finally, the conflict is directed against the state and it is the state *versus* people (Anand Kumar *et al.*, 2011:28). The Jhumias of Tripura (*Tripuris, Jamatias and Reangs*) are among the poorest of the poor in the state. The poverty of the shifting cultivators of the state and the remoteness of the areas in which they live make them vulnerable to extremist attacks. Usually the shifting cultivators are not attacked by non-tribal extremists because their hamlets are in remote hill areas far away from the habitations of the non-tribal people.

The recent ethnic violence that has rocked the twin districts of Chirang and Kokrajhar in western **Assam**, bordering **Bhutan**, reflects that the gloomy faces of the relief camp inmates are darker than the overcast skies, and tell the story of their sufferings. The spate of violence has spared none in these two districts, irrespective of community. This is an apparent sign that the Bodoland Territorial Council (BTC)—a Sixth Schedule administrative arrangement in which the two districts fall—and the state government have not learnt any lessons from the ethnic clash that bled Udalguri district in 2008. Over one lakh people were displaced and many killed in the 2008 ethnic violence in Udalguri, which is also under BTC. The BTC covers four districts—Kokrajhar, Chirang, Baksa and Udalguri (*The Times of India*, 2012: July 25).

Mega development projects like multipurpose river dams and large scale mining generate benefits for the few relatively better off sections of population while marginalizing and excluding the poorer tribal people (Oommen, 1998). The majority of the latter become the victims of development. It is found that in large mining projects the tribal people lose their land not only to the project authorities, but also to the non-tribal outsiders who had converged on these areas and corner both land and the new economic opportunities in commerce and petty industry (Fernandes, 2006; Government of India, 2002: 458). The ambitious power generation plan may satisfy the requirements of the North Eastern Region (NER) states, as they are entitled to free 12 per cent of power generated from central projects. However, from the long-run point of view, four problems need to be addressed. First, the large number of hydel projects envisaged for Arunachal will require compensatory afforestation under the Forest Conservation Act, 1980. The lower Subansiri dam has already encountered some objections from wildlife authorities. Given the large forest cover of the state, compensatory afforestation will have to be done elsewhere, and this issue has to be addressed now and not at the project stage. Second, while the state prefers 'run-off the-river' project for instance the Gumti dam in Tripura which is often demanded that it should now be decommissioned; Assam has been asking for dams which also mitigate its flood problem (World Bank, 2007). Finally, the low population density of hill states, and their far-flung villages mean high transmission losses. Yet, barring Nagaland none of the states has seriously investigated the use of relatively lowcost micro-hydel power for loads of up to 5 kW for domestic users (NER Vision, 2020: 174). In the past, errors and oversights occurred on some hydropower projects. It is useful to review these to ensure these are not repeated in the future. Projects may also lose their utility, such as the project on the Gumti in Tripura (upgraded installed capacity of 15 megawatts, but outputs diminishing over the last 30 years). This project also submerged about 45,000 hectares area and displaced about 9,000 tribal families. There have been suggestions to analyze if it would now make economic and political sense to decommission the dam, and resettle about 30,000 landless tribal families in the state on the rich silt-laden reservoir bed. This could make Tripura self-sufficient in grain, help ethnic reconciliation and ecological restoration, and would send a message across the region that water resource development will not take place at the cost of legitimate human and tribal interests. It is important to build this trust before large-scale projects are implemented. The 105 megawatt Loktak project in Manipur did not pay sufficient consideration to the unique lake ecosystem and livelihood factors; the ongoing Pagladiya project did not recognize the political separation of beneficiaries and affected people. In some such cases, renegotiation and technical corrections are feasible, and should be carried out (World Bank, 2007:63). In the North East India, with commercial crops being encouraged, the community ownership system is breaking down. CPRs are not quite compatible with commercial crops. The state, which encourages these crops, also needs to take these communities towards individual ownership. So it deals only with man, considered the head of the family, even among the matrilineal Garo and Khasi tribes of Meghalaya.

Tribal Development Programmes

After independence, planned development started and broadly three different approaches were advanced such as isolationist, assimilationist and integrationist. The first approach was a legacy of the British regime, and is usually described as 'leave them untouched.' The policy was to isolate the tribal population from the masses. The British took deliberate efforts not to develop communication in the tribal areas. The tribal people were kept away from the rest of the population. Verrier Elwin (1934) supported the establishment of a sort of 'National park' or 'specimens in a human Zoo' of the tribal people and advised that their contact with the outside should be reduced to the minimum. But this approach was not followed for long. The 'assimilationist' approach is the approach which paved the way for the tribal people to mingle with the neighbouring non-tribal people. In India, the process of assimilation took place in different parts of the country, resulting in the gradual acceptance of Hindu culture by the tribal people. The main criticism against this approach was that this tried to change the tribal people by imposing the non-tribal customs and traditions. The advocates of this view supported a direct assimilation without waiting for a slow and long-drawn change over. The approach is also considered to be a failure. The past experience of the policies of isolation and assimilation, forced the planners to take the middle way between the two, which is called the integrationist approach. This approach was mainly the brain child of Jawaharlal Nehru. The policy of integration consists of two types of measures for Tribal development such as protective and promotional measures. Nehru's *Tribal Panchsheel* is prominently advocated in the fundamental principles of the policy of Tribal integration. The elements of the policy of integration provided in the *Tribal Panchsheel* are taken as the best intended approach to tribal development and integration. But in some cases the tribal situation at the operational level reveals a disappointing picture because the policy principles have not been implemented in letter and spirit as suggested. The Constitution of India, adopted soon after independence, defines the rights and privileges of the castes, minorities, tribal groups and the weaker sections of society. These are covered by the fundamental rights as well as the directive principles of the state policy. The policy of positive discrimination favoring the weakest communities amongst the caste groups, the tribes and the backward classes as been implemented covering about 50 per cent of the population. Reservations are provided for these communities in educational institutions, political offices and government services. The tribal policy of the government has consistently aimed at encouraging their autonomous growth with protection to their local culture. To protect their rights in land and forest resources, etc., the law prohibits outsiders from purchasing their property or to settle down on their land by purchasing estate which is their preserve. There is an inner line protection policy pursued by the government which protects tribal people from intrusion by outsiders from other states or the foreigners. Cultural autonomy and the rights of minorities to pursue their religion and cultural practices are constitutionally guaranteed. This includes tribal people who by law enjoy privileges in running their own educational, cultural and social institutions. These measures have, however, been less successful in maintaining the autonomy of the tribal local cultures.

The tribal dimension of chronic poverty is most pronounced in the context of conflicts and movements. The ever-increasing exploitation of the tribal people and elimination of their lands led to revolts and rebellion in many parts of India. 'Leave them alone' (or 'exclusion') as in the hills of North East and 'light' administration (or 'partial exclusion') elsewhere was the response of the Imperial Regime in the face of determined resistance to their advancement and consolidation. The dawn of independence ushered in a new era of high hopes and soaring aspirations with an ebullient nation committed to the ideals of democracy, equity and social justice. The cause of weaker sections, particularly the tribal people, was accepted as a national task with clear premises and constitutional commitments. But the hopes were belied. The tribal people in fact faced regression as the personalized administration gave way to an amorphous faceless system. The influx of immigrants, alienation of their lands and underdevelopment are three major problems of the tribal communities. According to the Bhuria Committee Report, 1995, "Notwithstanding the rhetoric of the past four decades, on account of absence of effective democratic decentralization at even district levels, demands and agitations for separate states in the country have taken root in Jharkhand, Bodoland, Uttarakhand, etc. Iniquitous policies and actions and economic imbalance have led to resentment among the deprived regions. Assertions on the basis of region, ethnicity, languages, etc. have been made. They have come to feel that without the political power of a state, they are not able to claim their rightful due" (Anand Kumar, 2003:170).

Conclusion

The issue of tribal development engaged the attention of the planners, administrators and people's representatives since the planning process started in the country. Despite almost six decades of planning, the Scheduled Tribes continue to lag far behind in terms of infrastructure facilities and in all human development indicators. On the other hand, due to economic activities like industrialization, mining, multipurpose projects, cultivation of commercial crops in CPRs etc. a large section of the tribal population has been driven out from their own natural habitats and are facing social-cultural problems. Implementation of various anti-exploitation legislations such as Land Transfer Regulations, Money Lending (Regulations) Act, etc. is not up to the mark. Furthermore, the process of globalization in India has an adverse impact on the tribal people in India. The most important trend that has emerged in the era of globalization is the assertion of tribal identity on the basis of region, ethnicity, and languages. The major components in a variety of mobilizations both in pre- and post-economic reforms period includes movements for environmental protection (*Narmada Bachao*), states reorganization (Jharkhand, Uttarakhand, and Chhattisgarh), political separation (the separatist movements of the North-Eastern Tribal people), and resistance to globalization (Kashipur, Odisha). Such conflicting situations and mass mobilizations have brought the issue of chronic poverty of tribal India. Further it draws the attention of national media and policy makers prompting the governments to come forward with a variety of anti-poverty measures and development packages. The socio-economic forces of modernization and development have no doubt brought some benefits to the people of respective areas but the benefits accrued to them been largely out weighted. Development induced displacement; involuntary resettlement has also caused the marginalization of the tribal people and present enormous problems for them. The new economic regime has led to privatization and marketization of economy which is a powerful threat to the survival of the tribal communities. The socio-cultural change among the tribal communities has certainly empowered the tribal people; however, their cultural identity is under severe stress. Inter and intra ethnic conflict in Manipur and the recent ethnic violence in Chirang and Kokrajhar in western part of Assam, are the instances of poverty related conflicts which are existent in rural parts of North East India. It is not too late to rise above the politics of exclusion, marginalization and social discrimination. Hence, effort should be made to preserve the fast vanishing tribal culture and traditions in tribal pockets of India.

REFERENCES

Baral, Kailash C. and Kar, Prafulla (eds.) (2004). *Identities: Local and Global*. Delhi: Pencraft International.

Barpujari, S.K. (1984). 'Christianity and its impact on the Nagas', in *The Tribes of North East India*, ed. by Sebastian Karotemprel, Calcutta: Firma KLM.

Bendle, Mervyn F. (2002), 'The Crisis of Identity in High Modernity', *British Journal of Sociology*, 53 (1): 1-18.

Bornman, E, (2003), 'Struggles of identity in the age of Globalization.' Communication*: South African Journal for Communication Theory and Research.*

Brubaker, R. (1984), *The Limits of Rationality*, London: Allen & Unwin.

Chacko (ed.) (2005), *Tribal Communities and Social Change*, New Delhi: Sage Publications.

De, U.K. (2000), 'Food Security and PDS in Tripura: A Policy Intervention'. Paper presented at the National Level Seminar on Food, Nutrition and Food Security – Public Distribution System in North East India organized by NEICSSR from 27th to 28th, November.

D'Souza, Leela. (2005), *The Sociology of religion: a historical review*, Jaipur: Rawat Publications.

Elwin, Verrier (1939), *The Baiga,* John Murray, Albemarie Street, London.

Elwin, Verrier (1960), *A Philosophy for NEFA*, Shillong.

Erikson, E. (1968), *Identity: Youth and Crisis*, New York: Norton.

Fernandes, Walter. 'Challenges to Culture in the context of Globalization'. Available at: http://www.holycrossjustice.org/pdf

Fernandes, Walter. (2006), 'Globalization, Culture and Fundamentalism: Impact on Northeastern India'. in Somayaji, Sakarama *et al.* (ed). 2006. *Sociology of Globalization: Perspectives from India*. Jaipur: Rawat Publications.

Fernades, Walter. (2006), 'Development-induced Displacement and Tribal Women', in Govinda Chandra Rath (ed.) *Tribal Development in India: The Contemporary Debate*, New Delhi: Sage Publications.

Frosh, S. (1999), 'Identity' in A. Bullock and S. Trombley (eds.) The New Frontana Dictonary of Modern Thought, London: Harper Collins.

Giddens, A. (1990), *The Consequences of Modernity*. Cambridge: Polity Press.

Giddens, A. (2000), *Runaway World.* London: Routledge.

Ghosh, Jayati. (1997), 'Gender and Macro-Economic Policy in India Since 1991', *Women's Link*, 3 (n.4, October-December), pp. 3-11.

Haokip, Thongkholal. (2012), 'Is there a Pan-North East Identity and Solidarity', *Economic and Political Weekly,* September 8, pp. 84-85.

Haralambos, M. & Martin Holborn. (2008), *Sociology Themes and Perspectives*, London: Harper Collins Publishers, Seventh edition.

Heelas, P.; Lash, S. and Morris, P. (eds.) (1995), *Detraditionalization*, Blackwell: Oxford.

Hussain, Monirul. (2004), 'Food Security and the North East', *Economic and Political Weekly*, October 9, pp. 4515- 16.

Hussain, Wasbir (2004), 'India's North East: The Problem', paper presented as part of the "Interaction on the North East", *Observer Research Foundation*, New Delhi, November 18.

Jackson, Robert H. 'Ethnicity', in Sartori, Giovanni, (ed.) (1994), *Social Concepts: A Systematic Analysis*. Sage Publications, Beverly Hills, Carlifornia, pp. 205-33.

Khubchandani Lachman, M. (1992), *Tribal Identity*, Shimla: Indian Institute of Advanced Study.

Kothari, Rajni. (1995), 'Globalization and Revival of Tradition: Dual Attack on Model of Democratic Nation-Building', *Economic and Political Weekly,* March 25, pp. 625-33.

Kumar, Anand. (2003), 'Political Sociology of Poverty in India: Between Politics of Poverty and Poverty of Politics', *CPRC-IIPA Working Paper No.* 3, pp. 144-96.

Kumar, Anand. (2011), *Understanding Globalization and Emerging India*. New Delhi: Palm Leaf Publications.

Kumar, Anand *et al*. (2011), 'Situating Conflict and Poverty in Manipur', *CPRC-IIPA Working Paper No*. 37, pp. 1-79.

Kabui, Gangmumei. (1982), The Zeliangrong Movement: An Historical Study of Gangmumei Kabui, in K.S. Singh (Ed) *Tribal Movement in India*, Vol. 1, Manohar Publications, New Delhi.

Louis, Prakash. (2007), 'Governance, Reforms and Development: Scheduled Tribes in India in the Era of Globalization', in Kameshwar Choudhary (ed.). *Globalization, Governance Reforms and Development in India*, New Delhi: Sage Publications.

Minz, Nirmal. (1990), 'Dalit-Tribe: A search for Common Ideology', in Towards a Common Dalit Ideology, ed. by A.P. Nirmal, Madras: Gurukul Lutheran Theological College and Research Institute.

Misra, Udayon (2000), *The Periphery Strikes Back: Challenges to the Nation-State in Assam and Nagaland*. Shimla: Indian Institute of Advance Studies.

Meher, Rajkishor. (2009),'Globalization, Displacement and the Livelihood Issues of Tribals and Agriculture Dependent Poor People: The Case of Mineral-based Industries in India'. *Journal of Developing Societies* 25, 4, pp. 457-80.

MoDNER & NEC. (2008), North Eastern Region Vision 2020, Volume 1, available at: *http://tripura.nic.in/portal/More_Info/document/central/NE%20Vision.pdf*

Nathan, Dev *et al*. (Eds). (2004), *Globalization and Indigenous Peoples in Asia: Changing the Local-Global Interface*. New Delhi: Sage Publications.

Oommen, T.K. (1998), 'Emerging Diversity: Birth of a New World Society'. *The Times of India*. New Delhi: October 30.

Pakem, B. (ed.) (1990) *Nationality, Ethnicity and Cultural Identity in North East India*, New Delhi: Omsons Publications.

Petras, James (1994), 'Cultural Imperialism in the Late 20th Century', *Economic and Political Weekly*, 29 (n. 32, August 6), pp. 2070-73.

Rath, Govinda Chandra (2006), *Tribal Development in India: The Contemporary Debate*. New Delhi, Sage Publications.

Robertson, R. (1992), *Globalization*. London: Sage Publications.

Scholte, Jan Yart. (2000) *Globalization: A Critical Introduction*. New York: Palgrave Macmillan.

Sharma, B.D. (1995) *Globalization: The Tribal Encounter*. New Delhi: Har-Anand Publications.

Sharma, T.C. & Majumdar, D.N. (1980), Eastern Himalayas: A Study on Anthropology and Tribalism, Cosmo Publication, New Delhi.

Sinha, Amitabha & K.S. Chakraborty. (2010), *Reflections on Economy and Society in Tripura*, New Delhi, Akansha Publishing House.

Singh, K.S. (1982), Tribal Movement in India, Manohar Publisher, New Delhi.

Singh, Yogendra. (2002), *Culture Change in India: Identity and Globalization*. Jaipur: Rawat Publications.

Times of India. July 25, (2012), 'Assam riots: Community no bar in ethnic clash', available at *http://articles.timesofindia.indiatimes.com*

Thomas, T. Jacob, (1993) Indian Tribal Culture: A Rediscovery of Gospel Values. In *Indian Journal of Theology*, Vol. 35, No. 2, pp. 64-76.

Thanzauva, K. (1989), 'Theology of Zawlbuk', in Towards a Tribal Theology:The Mizo Perspective edited by K. Thanzauva, Mizoram: Mizo Theological Conference.

Waters, M. (1995) *Globalization*, London: Routledge.

Weber, M. (1978) *Economy and Society*. Berkeley: California University Press.

World Bank. (2007) Development and Growth in North East India: The Natural Resources, Water and Environment Nexus Strategy Report, South Asian Region Sustainable Development Department, Environment & Water Resource Management Unit, Washington D.C.

Walker, K.L.M. (2008), 'Neoliberalism on the ground in rural India: Predatory growth, agrarian crisis, internal colonization, and the intensification of class struggle'. *Journal of Peasant Studies*, 35 (4), pp. 557-620.

Xaxa, Virginius. (1999), 'Transformation of Tribes in India: Terms of Discourse'. *Economic and Political Weekly*, June 12-18, pp. 1519-24.

18
A Discourse on Societal Development

Tamo Mibang

As human being, we are too much close to the earth. We adjust ourselves with its surroundings. We get energy, heat, light, air and water. Our body is a synthesis of cosmic forces. Being intelligent animals, we not only adapt ourselves with surrounding environment, but also create an environment of our own for a coherent and harmonious society. We have created an environment of our own cultural geography. We preserve cultural identity and promote our culture through humility, tolerance and assimilation. We ought to assimilate the best elements from all directions to enrich our culture.

The wave of globalization is sweeping the world today. The globe is shrinking to a global village. A European or an American of whom we were talking about as a story, decades ago, is now sitting with us in university classroom, in research institute to learn and share his ideas to advance knowledge and to create knowledge society. There is no geographical barrier for a knowledge society. The world is open to all. Being a by-product of this society, why should not the so-called educated youths break their narrow domestic wall? Language, religion and culture are not matters over which people should quarrel. One can learn and speak as many languages as possible to earn more friends.

As a matter of fact, the world survives on inter-dependence. If there is a seed of conflict in man, there can also be the seed of dependence and mutual support. Conflict is an integral part of life as we are confronted daily with situation that force us to make choices, to decide options for survival. For peace and progress we shall have to move away from the direction of conflict towards inter-dependence. When we see the pages of history, we find the period of conflict is less than that of interdependence. We should transform every negative aspect into a positive one. Mutual respect is born from our awareness towards inter-dependence. As social animals we have hope, aspiration and expectations under all circumstances. Human society is based on co-operation and mutual expectations. We can cite an instance from nature itself. We, human beings exhale carbon dioxide, and it becomes food for the plants. In return, plants give out oxygen which becomes our source of existence. It is an Universal truth that every product, even a cup of tea or a newspaper, which reaches every door, is the result of co-operative effort of many people beyond the boundaries of caste, creed, sex and religion. In business and industry, the extent of success is directly related to co-operation and co-ordination among various supporting units. In an operation theatre, a patient is saved through the time framed co-ordinated care and efforts of the doctors.

Non-violence is the need for social harmony. It cannot be limited to small number of people in a room but to infuse the idea of harmony into the whole community. We have the responsibility towards ourselves, towards our parents and children. To keep quiet at the critical juncture would be violence unto us, unto our society. The so called civil society is to raise voice against violence, communal tension for restoration of environment of tranquillity in the society; to remain as source of inspiration of the people. Volunteer efforts with community spirit can only counter balance not only violence against women, child traffic and communal problems but also the present day corrupted politicians, bureaucrats and state machineries against domination of the society. Today, around the world, civil society has come a long way as non-profit voluntary organizations to work for the benefit of the people which are a hallmark of free and democratic societies. Civil societies should step in to advocate for weaker section where governments failed to deliver services like health, education etc. This way, it ensures that government is doing its job providing accessible education, health coverage, water supply, housing and above all better roads and transportations to the citizens that they really deserve. Thus, it not only works for civil rights as we understand but also helps to make change happen and make it lasting.

When we see a weaker person, say a beggar, in the street or railway stations/compartments, how we respond to his feeling. May be with a few coins, which may hardly get him a cup of tea. Of course, a noble hearted gentlemen may even give ₹ 10 or more, and some do not give at all. This way, in metro cities, a beggar, sometimes collects some amount in a day. That is how we share our resources. When a relative is suffering, we share food, money and clothes. When famine occurs in an area, we share our food; when there is a fire accident or other natural calamities like earthquake, aids used to pour in even from foreign countries. That is how, as human beings, we help each other and how we remain inter-dependent. Men were born dependent, live inter-dependent and shall die dependent as even the last ritual is performed with mutual support and co-operation. I think this is the way of life. Whatever you earn, return something to your society and give a part of your time to social work. Particularly the so called educated people, who are proud of calling themselves Elite! The term Elite should not connote exploitation of the weaker but service to the society. The educated people must view issues with broader perspectives. The normal test of a society is how it treats the children, the needy, the sick, the women and the old citizens who are in the shadows of life.

Today, in Arunachal two groups of educated people are emerging – one is over zealous who like to see change in the State with revolutionary spirit; why their state should not have big hydro projects, industries or factories; why the state should not be opened to tourists to boost the local economy so that the state comes up at par with other states of India in terms of economic development. The second group is more concerned about the people and the future of the state – why development process should not be accelerated in tune with the aspirations of the people slowly and steadily so that local demography, socio-cultural life of the people remain undisturbed and the Inner Line Regulation should continue to stand to protect them against cultural exploitation. They fear that discontinuance of this system would jeopardize the interest of the people resulting large-scale influx of people from all sides and could create a demographic and cultural imbalance. In the process, this will bring a fresh political turmoil in the region. It clearly indicates that the state policy should concern to protect the interest of the tribal people for all the time so that there is less repercussions of today's political liberality. Though Article 19 of the Constitution of India grants the rights of freedom of assembly, association, movement and residence throughout the country, practice of profession, Clause (5) restricts us the exercise of movement in tribal areas for the protection of interest of the tribal. To them revolutionary changes would create a gap, which they cannot bridge up so easily with the advance of time. In nutshell, in tribal world developmental schemes should be slow and steady so that the innocent people are not taken by surprise. The socio-economic transformation should take place peacefully not in a revolutionary spirit. They also feel that for a long time, the people were in dilemma. Neither could they exploit the resources particularly water nor they allow others to exploit. The strategy should be to exploit the resources – forest, water, mineral to optimum use in tune with aspirations of the people and to generate revenue of their own. The so called today's development must be eco-friendly and sustainable.

However, in North East India, there has been popular opposition against mega dam projects for the reasons that dams would affect the fertile valleys, verdant forest with unique bio-diversity and finally will put tremendous pressure on human lives and livelihood. The starting point of any project whether major or minor is the land and forest of the people, the first stakeholder, whose support is the first requisite.

It is observed that the consideration of NEFA administration, now Arunachal Pradesh, was to train up the tribal people to do their own work. Once they realize that the future is theirs, with motivation, they would do their best to keep their heads high. Pt. Nehru, said that these areas have to progress in their own way. They have their own likes. They do not like something alien to be imposed upon them. No individual can grow in alien surroundings, habits, or customs. How are we going to keep these two things together? It is not an easy problem. We have to find a *via media*. And that can only succeed if the people are in harmony with it and there is no element of compulsion about it. That approach also has ultimately to be applied through their own people (Elwin: p. 206).

He further continues that the first thing, therefore, is to train their own people who can work among them and that will be far more effective than for outsiders to try ... we have to make them progress, but progress does not mean just an attempt to duplicate what we have got in any part of India. It may not be suitable to them. It may not be suitable even to India. But there are many things in India which are suitable to them. They will adopt them gradually. Any element of imposition has to be absent so far as possible and so people have to be trained to train others. It may not be a very rapid progress. Every kind of training takes time. Whatever profession you may adopt, it takes years to train people, engineers, doctors and so on (Elwin 1957 : 207). In the beginning, Nehru's policy was followed by the NEFA administration in letter and spirit. Tribal youth were given education and trained for various professions, viz. administration, medicine, engineering, education and so on. It is amazing that now literacy rate has come up to 66.95 per cent (Census 2011) and today practically all the areas have been taken over by the tribal themselves. But the question is that how the quantity matches with the quality of mind. It is in this context, with farsighted vision, Pt. Nehru said that we should judge results, not by statistics or the amount of money spent, but by the quality of human character that is evolved. How judiciously they manage the funds, how developmental activities are being executed and how benefits percolate down to the targeted groups and to what extent they are accountable to the people are the questions of the masses at grassroot level. The Nehru-Elwin Policy seems to be of less relevance in Arunachal due to fast changing socio-economic developmental activities.

The changing social scenario in Arunachal Pradesh seems to make a sad reading to many who could feel the pulse of the society. The inter-tribal tension that took place among some groups of the tribal people during 2005 at Roing, Along, Paighat and in 2012 at state capital, Itanagar may be an indicator of the future of the state. It has been observed that in the last few years, there has been law and order problems in two districts, viz. Tirap, Changlang and the capital complex, Itanagar. The State government has a crucial role to play to restore the image of Arunachal Pradesh which was well known as an island of peace a few years ago. With optimistic note Taba Ajum observes " the state government can do wonders if they address law and order problems with honest instinct; if law and order is under control, Arunachal can dream of becoming a developed state in true sense." In a multi-lingual and pluri-cultural state like Arunachal, tolerance to each other's culture is very important.

When we see the demography of the state, we rather find Arunachal, a mini-India with a population of 13,82,611 (Census 2011). However, the tribal population is below one million. There are myriad tribal groups. Apart from the tribal groups like the Monpas, Sherdukpens, Mijis, Akas, Nyishis, Sulungs, Apatanis, Tagins, Hill Miris, Galos, Adis, Mishmis, Khamptis, Singphos, Noctes, Wanchos, Tangsas, including many other minor tribes in the state, other brethren from various parts of the country live here amicably for decades with their cultural heritage. Every community has the right to celebrate their festivals like Durga Puja, Bihu, Onam, Dussera, Holi, Viswakarma Puja, Idu'l-Fitr, Christmas and so on. The tribal people of the state have a proud record of mingling themselves with the current of Indian culture and civilization. The spirit of the nation itself is 'Unity in Diversity'. The strength of the nation lies in it.

They have a number of local festivals, such as Unying-Aran, Solung of the Adis, Mopin of the Galos, Reh of the Idu Mishmis, Dree of the Apatanis, Nyokum of the Nyishis, Lossar of the Monpas, Si-Donyi of the Tagins Mol of the Thangsas, Solo Loku of the Noctes and Sangken of the Khamtis which are celebrated in the villages and towns like Tawang,

Bomdila, Seppa, Itanagar, Ziro, Along, Pasighat, Yingkiong, Roing, Tezu, Changlang, Khonsa, round the year. The main objective of celebrating the festivals in the towns these days is to highlight the rich cultural heritage of the people as well as to enable the cross section of people to participate so that we inculcate a spirit of unity and solidarity among ourselves. They participate in festivals as it binds them together and promotes unity and integrity. Festival is not an individual affair. They celebrate the festivals of various tribes so as to evolve and promote composite culture in the state to pave the way for a greater identity, i.e Arunachalee identity. Important towns like Itanagar, Bomdila, Ziro, Aalo, Pasighat, Roing, Tezu, Khonsa and Changlang have now become the centre of cultural convergence and from there culture spread towards all directions. Not only that, the perception of the people is that the festivals would become a tourist attraction in days to come. A number of important villages for instance, Rumgong Kombo and Jomo of West Siang district, Riga of East Siang and Damro of Upper Siang district which are representative of their cultural heritage, would automatically come under its ambit.

In a free society every citizen has the right to respect each other's culture. Article 51-A (e) of the Constitution of India specifies as "to promote harmony and the spirit of common brotherhood amongst all the people of India transcending religion, linguistic and regional or sectional diversities". Further, the Article emphasizes on to value and preserve the rich heritage of our composite culture. It is a cherished goal of the people of India, which should be realized by each and every citizen. We shall have to overcome intolerance, which stems from invisible assumption. The state shall have to create awareness of constitutional rights and responsibilities among the citizens and also sensitise them, particularly the youth, the values embodied in our constitution. However, to realize it, value based education seems to be the option. In many cases, it is found in the present day that educated people themselves hardly respect the cultural ethos; for which one is not able to find answers. Who is going to educate the educated people? Is it that university degree alone makes one educated? Is it that educated one becomes so insensitive towards the social reality ? Everyone of us has to introspect ourselves, and rationalize emerging social issues and fallouts. We must view them with long-term perspectives. Educated people should be above the sectarian tendencies. Education does not only prepare for life but it initiates the life long process of learning and it is life itself.

The maxim goes on that well begun is half done, which is applicable to our educational programme. Innovative approaches in educational curriculum are needed to sensitize our young minds by imparting knowledge of cultural history to ensure the values of co-operation and co-existence. In a pluralistic society there could be forces to divide people on ethnic, religious, linguistic, cultural and economic grounds. In a democratic set up everyone has his right to safeguard one's interest and fight against discrimination and seek redress for grievances.

There are many issues such as poverty, illiteracy, employment problems, regional disparity, exploitation of weak, etc. to be addressed on priority basis. The civil society has to create, expand, safeguard the space of commonality through its institutions like the Kebang of the Adis, Abela of Idu Mishmis, Buliang of Apatanis, and so on. Moral story telling to youths and traditions of cultural exchange among the tribal groups must strive in its pursuit of peaceful co-existence.

What the senior citizens want is a harmonious and peaceful society which ensures progress and prosperity. It is pertinent that fundamental duties should be emphasized at every phase of education. The youth must be prepared to assume their roles as responsible citizens of the country. Inculcation of noble idealism in them is an investment of the nation. They are ultimate hope of the future of the nation.

The social fabric should not be damaged because of personal or fractional political interest. Without unity, co-operation and sense of oneness people cannot achieve anything. It is beyond anybody's doubt that physical or political unity without emotional unity would be of less meaning. To change a society, political development should tune with social and economic progress. We must consider each other as brothers and sisters so far our life and property are concerned and must built mutual trust in every sphere of life so that we lead a life of peace, happiness and prosperity.

REFERENCE

Arunachal Pradesh, (2012), *The Arunachal Times* (Vol. 24, No. 197, Saturday, December 29, 2012).

Elwin, V. (1957); *A Philosophy for NEFA*, Directorate of Research, NEFA, Shillong.

19

Landscape, People and Sustainability in the Northern Frontier of North East India: A Theoretical Understanding

Ranjana Ray

Introduction

North East India is presently known as the land of seven sisters, covering the political divisions of the states of Arunachal Pradesh, Assam, Manipur, Meghalaya, Mizoram, Nagaland and Tripura (Sengupta, 1994: vii-ix). Sikkim has been added in the North East India in recent years. Geographically the North East is marked by the Eastern **Himalayas**, Northeast Hills (**Patkai-Naga Hills** and **Lushai Hills**), the Brahmaputra and the Barak Valley. The North East is situated at a strategic point with international borders of China and Tibet on the north, Myanmar on the north-east and Bangladesh on the west. It is connected to the rest of India through a narrow corridor between Nepal and Bangladesh. Because of its location it has gained political importance, more so in post-independent times.

North-Eastern Part of India attracted major attention of Government of India since 1911 after the last emperor of Ming dynasty attacked this part of India starting the border conflict with China (Choudhury, 1978). Last Indo-Chinese war of 1962 aggravated the border conflict, and the area gained more attention of the central administration. This area, better known as Greater Assam, was largely under control of the Ahom kings with their specific policy with the hill communities. British Administration demarcated the border zones as North East Frontier Area (NEFA). International boundary was demarcated by treaties, which resulted in the

McMohan line (Choudhuri, 1976). From time immemorial the people of North East had a distinctive cultural tradition, enhanced in respective of ecological territories. The land is marked by diversity in culture. The present work has focus on the northern most part of the region, presently distinguished as the state of Arunachal Pradesh. The state is divided into 16 districts with its capital at Itanagar. The districts are, Tawang, West Kameng, East Kameng, Papumpare, Upper Subansiri, Lower Subansiri, East Siang, West Siang, Upper Siang, Dibang valley, and Lower Dibang valley, Lohit, Chnaglang, Tirap, Kurung Kumey and Anjaw.

Landscape

The state of Arunachal Pradesh can be divided into four distinct physiographic zones. These are the Brahmaputra plains, Naga-Patkoi ranges, Mishmi Hills, and the Himalayan ranges. The Brahmaputra plains are at an average height of 100 m from the mean sea level. From the plains the land rises abruptly until it reaches the high peaks of the Eastern Himalayas.

Although the topography of Arunachal Pradesh is rugged, hilly and wild, it is the most beautiful place to be in. The name of the state means that it is the land of rising sun. It covers an area of 83,743sq. km (Report: Ministry of Power, 2009). It shares international borders with China on the north, Myanmar on the east and Bhutan on the west. On its southern and southeastern sides lie Indian states of Assam and Nagaland respectively. 82 per cent of the total area of the state is covered by forest. The state is marked by mighty mountains; snow capped peaks, numerous turbulent rivers and streams and deep gorges. The landscape is further characterized by very rich and diverse fauna and flora. Climate also varies greatly. It is subtropical in the southern part near the plains of the Brahmaputra. North of this zone along the Siwalik hills into the higher altitudes the climate becomes temperate, alpine and in the north large areas experience heavy snow during the winters.

The state is mainly located on the hilly tracts of the Eastern Himalayas. The geology of the Eastern Himalayas is divided into three physiographic domains. They are the sub-Himalayan Sivaliks, the Lesser Himalayas, the Greater Himalayas and the northern most zones, the Trans Himalayan Tibetan plateau zone. The last one has got low relief and is 30-40 km wide. All important passes are located on this zone.

The Greater Himalayas are the zone of very high relief. It has more than 6000 m height from the main sea level. The highest peak of the state is Kangte, which lies in the west Kameng district. The Lesser or Lower Himalayas has got an elevation of 2500 to 4000 m above mean sea level and is 80 to 90 km wide. This portion is thrust along the south-east direction against the Mishmi Hills. Its southern limit is defined by a fault. The sub-Himalayan zone rises from the plains of Brahmaputra along the foot hill fault (web: powermin.nic.in/whats_new/PFR/AP/Bhareli.pdf).

The area has a rich source of mineral wealth in the form of dolomite, graphite, quartzite, limestone, coal, marble, oil and natural gas (Dutta and Ahmad, 1995).

The major rivers of this area are the Siang, Kameng, Subansiri, Kamla, Lohit, Dibang Noa-Dehing and the Tirap and their tributaries. The state receives heavy rainfall, which gives rise to luxuriant forest growth and network of rivers, streams and lakes.

Diversity in altitudinal gradients of land and climatic condition has given rise to wide varieties of plants and animal life. The ecosystem varies from region to region. The great wealth of natural life and human culture have emerged through time. The area is a hot spot of biodiversity (Myers *et al.,* 2000). The state lies at the junction of Palaeoarctic, Indo-Chinese and Indo-Malyan bio-geographical region (Darlington, 1957; ICIMOD, 2012). Arunachal Pradesh still preserves the biodiversity and is unique in the world in this sense.

The true tropical dense forests of the North East start from the lower hills and valleys, known as, "Terai", reaching up to 3000 m. The vegetation of the state largely consists of the tropical and sub-tropical evergreen forests interspersed with grasslands and temperate forests in the high hills. The lowland tropical evergreen and semi-ever green forests are found up to 1500 m. Temperate oak and conifer forests occur at higher altitudes. Most of the wooded areas are not virgin forests. These are of secondary nature owing to the frequent destruction of forests by shifting cultivation practiced from early times by the local people. Primary forests are limited to comparatively less accessible areas.

This zone is best known for the variety of fauna and flora. Tiger, elephant, leopard, gaur, sambar, chital, hog deer, swamp deer, buffalo, rhinoceros and many other smaller mammals are found in this belt. Arunachal Pradesh is perhaps the only State which has four major cats, i.e. tiger (*Panthera tigris*), leopard (*Panthera pardus*), clouded leopard (*Neofelis nebulosa*) and snow leopard (*Panthera uncia*). Lesser cats like the golden cat, leopard cat and the marbled cat are also found here. As many as 25 species of mammals included in Schedule–I of the Wildlife (Protection) Act, 1972 inhabit the area. The landscape includes several well-known protected areas such as Namdapha National Park and Tiger Reserve. Ten wildlife sanctuaries and two national parks have been established in the state. Seven species of primates, i.e. hoolock gibbon, slow loris, Assamese macaque, rhesus macaque, pig-tailed macaque, stump-tailed macaque, and capped langur are also found in the forests of the State. This is the only state where all the 3 great antelopes of India, i.e. serow, goral and takin are found. The highly endangered hispid hare (*caprolagus hispidus*) is also found in low grassy areas of the State.

People

Besides harbouring an extremely rich biodiversity, this landscape is home to diverse ethnic communities with unique socio-cultural traditions. However, there are numerous environmental and socio-economic discrepancies impacting the existence of both the region's biodiversity and its people. Striking a balance between traditional resource use patterns, globalization, sustainable development, and biodiversity conservation in the region is the challenge at hand for the policy makers, as well as the people themselves (ICIMOD, 2012).

Considering the rugged terrain, inaccessible forests and snow covered tracts, Arunchal Pradesh is a thinly populated state, having a total population of 1,382,611 as per Census of India 2011. The number of tribal communities reported through the state according to various sources range from 20 to 29. The Anthropological Survey of India has identified a total of 66 communities in Arunachal Pradesh. Out of these 63 are tribes (Singh, 1995) and 25 are recognized as Scheduled Tribes (Dutta and Ahmad, 1995). According to Sarkar twenty nine major tribal communities and more than eighty sub-tribes had been recognized (Sarkar, 2002: 109). Identification had been done on the basis of differences in language, dialect, socio-economic condition, political organization, religion etc. Some of the major tribes mentioned by various scholars are, the Adi, Nyishi, Apatani, Bugun, Galo, Hrusso, Koro, Meyor, Monpa, Tagin, Mishmi, Sajolang, Sartang, Tai Khamti, Yobin, Singpho, Sherdukpen, Khamba, Tangshang and the Memba.

Although the tribes are different from each other but there is somewhat broad affinity among them. In general they have a mongoloid origin and speak language belonging to Tibeto-Burman family. The languages and dialects are often not mutually intelligible between one group and the other. For communication the medium is some kind of broken Assamese, known as, Nefamese.

Ethnological history for the peopling of the region is not clear. Except a few Neolithic celts nothing tangible is found for the prehistoric period of Arunachal Pradesh (Dutta and Ahmad, 1995: 10). Some scholars like Elwin (1958) had studied the myths of the people and identified connection with the mythological stories of the *Purusha Sukta* of *Rig Veda*.

According to the Arunachal Pradesh Government, the region was mentioned in the Hindu texts *Kalika Purana* and *Mahabharata*, and is attested to be the *Prabhu* Mountains of the *Puranas,* and was the land where sage Parashuram washed away his sins and the sage *Vyasa* meditated. King *Bhishmaka* founded his kingdom in the region and Lord Krishna married his consort Rukmini from this kingdom (*http://en.wikipedia.org/wiki/Arunachal_pradesh#cite_note-6*). The Tawang monastery located in North West part of Tawang, gives some idea about the Buddhist time in the region. Written records were kept in the monasteries.

The Monpa and Sherdukpen keep a kind of record of their past and according to that the Monpas occupied their territory in Arunachal Pradesh sometimes around 500 BCE to 600 CE. In general Tibet and Bhutan had a kind of loose control over the area in the north and the region bordering Myanmer and the plains of Brahmaputra were under the control of Ahom kings of Assam. The region was annexed under British regime in 1858. However, most Arunachali tribes remained in practice, largely autonomous until Indian independence and the formalization of indigenous administration in 1947 (Choudhury, 1978).

However, undoubted written evidence first comes in the chronicles of the Ahoms, the *Buranjis* (Dutta and Ahmad, 1995). It appears that the plains were ruled by Chutiayas and Kalitas in ancient times. The Ahom kings of Assam ruled the area during the medieval times. This is recorded in the Mughal chronicles. The British annexed the area in 1858 (Bareh, 2001). In fact due to the ruggedness of the terrain and difficult geographical accessibility of the region not much information is found about the area and people until the end of nineteenth century and beginning of twentieth century. With the Chinese aggression and the strategic position of the area the concept of North East Frontier (NEFA) emerged during 1911-1914 and the British led extensive survey and exploration of the area (Choudhury, 1978).

It may also be conceded that the earlier accounts of the people of the area are not always clear in terms of anthropological definitions because most of the information of nineteenth century came from the administrators, civil servants, military personnel, travellers and missionaries. But none of them were trained in anthropological methodologies. Mostly general accounts were given (Vidyarthi, 1986). Some important writings of nineteenth century belong to Robinson (1841), Hodson (1848) and Peal (1896). Comparatively extensive study was made by Risley when he was the Census Commissioner for the people of Bengal, Bihar and Assam (Risley, 1891). This had special emphasis on tribes and castes of Bengal Presidency. Gazetteers were important contributions to the written accounts of different districts. Volume XI published in 1928 contained information on some tribes of erstwhile NEFA. There were a number of monographs written on different tribes of North East India during the colonial times but not any for the tribes residing in the Frontier Area. A scheme was taken up under the supervision of Verrier Elwin (1959), the then Adviser to the NEFA administration for Tribal affairs (Vidyarthi, 1986: 11). The first monograph was on the Daflas. Subsequently several monographs on the tribes, such as, the Sherdukpens, Idu Mishmis, Gallong, Aka and others came up in the form of The People of NEFA series (Vidyarthi, 1986). Furer Haimendorf (1947, 1982) made substantial contribution to the study of different sections of Naga tribes. The research work on the people of Arunachal Pradesh was subsequently carried out by a number of renowned scholars. Anthropological Survey of India has a vital role to play in writing treatise on the People of India. Arunachal Pradesh had been studied intensively in this respect (Singh, 1994; Dutta and Ahmad, 1995). In recent times vigorous researches are carried out on the people of Arunachal Pradesh, especially on the primitive tribes with formation of Arunachal Institute for Tribal Studies in the Rajib Gandhi University in 1985.

Anthropological Survey of India had identified 63 tribal languages, out of which 62 belong to Tibeto-Burman family and the rest to Siamese-Chinese sub-family of language. According to them there are 63 tribal groups in Arunachal Pradesh. There are also a number of migrant communities from the neighbouring states and countries. The list of Scheduled Tribes prepared by the Arunachal Pradesh Government consists of 25 Scheduled Tribes. Anthropological Survey of India divided the area into five cultural zones on the basis of cultural affinity within the state. From East to west these cultural zones are as follows (Dutta and Ahmad, 1995):

(a) The Mon cultural zone covers the Tawang and west Kameng districts and is mainly inhabited by the Monpas and Sherdukpens. To this zone belong other groups, viz. the Akas, Mijis and the Khowas.

(b) The Nishi cultural zone includes the Bangnis of the east Kameng district, the Nishis of lower and upper Subasisri districts and two unique communities, the Sulungs and the Apatanis. Other groups in this zone are the Nas, Tagins, Mikirs and the Hill MIris.

(c) The Adi cultural zone is extended from the eastern part of Upper Subansiri district to the western part of Dibang Valley district. The zone includes all the Adi sub-groups and the Khambas, Membas and the Mishing/Miri.

(d) The Mishmi cultural zone includes the districts of Dibang and Lohit valley. Three sub-groups of the Mishmi community predominates in the zone. Other people in this zone are the Khamptis, Khamiyans, Deoris, Chakmas and the Tibetans. A small group known as the Zakhrings/ Meyors also live in the area.

(e) The Nocte-Tangsa cultural zone extends over Tirap and Chanlang districts. The Noctes, Wanchos and the Tangsas are the predominating groups in this zone. The Singhpos, Sonawal Kacharis, and the Lisus also live in the zone.

People and Landscape

Although people of Arunachal Pradesh are in the focus of present day administration, knowledge about all the communities residing in the region is not adequate. Population migration in the area is studied on the basis of material culture, language, religion and socio-economic pattern. Reviewing the ethnic affinity of the people of the state, Kar (1994) suggested that the tribes, such as, the Aka, Nishi, Tagin, Hill Miri, Apa Tani, Adi and the Mishmi residing in central Arunachal Pradesh belong to one broad ethnic group. The Monpa and the Sherdukpen of western Arunachal Pradesh are closer to the Tibetan and the Bhutanese. The Nocte and the Wancho inhabiting eastern Arunachal Pradesh have similarities with the Naga and probably migrated from east and south east part of the country. Kar (1994: 13-14) listed 24 main tribes in the Arunachal Pradesh.

Rath (1994) made some ethnographic analysis of a number of tribes of Arunachal Pradesh. He found that Aka or Hruso lives in long houses; administration is carried out by village council, headed by chieftains. They keep slaves and are shifting cultivators. The Apatani are considered as an important tribe having a unique way of terrace cultivation. They live on a high plateau, about 1500 m from the main sea level. This group is well organized with respect to village set up land ownership. There are upper class and commoners as well as slave in the Apatani society. The Apatanis are considered as good farmers with age old method of irrigating their terraced fields. They are also producing good textiles, iron implements and a kind of vegetable ash, called *Khar*. These they trade with other communities for Mithun, other live stocks, beads, small prayer bells etc. The Monpas are specially mentioned because they live in permanent houses made of stone and wood. The usual family pattern is nuclear. Their primary occupation is plough cultivation coupled with animal husbandry. The Wanchus and the Noctes are *jhum* cultivators but they own the cultivable land individually. The Sherdukpen are mainly traders. They act as middle men between plains of Assam and the hills. They sell ponies to the Monpas of Tawang and carry out cattle trade with Bhutan. The Sulung is a tribe considered to be still in the hunting-gathering stage.

Sarkar (2002) made a study of the ecological adaptation of the tribes of Arunachal Pradesh. His study is centred on the altitudinal difference of the habitat of different tribes of the state. He identified three ecological regions. One is located on the high altitude with steep gradient lying between 1800 m to 3300 m. The second zone is on the valleys at the altitude of 900 m to 1800 m. The third zone is on the foothills along the flat plains of Arunachal Pradesh. He also had classified the zones according to the vegetation pattern. The first zone is under temperate forest cover, the second under ever green sub-tropical forest and the last one is with tropical semi-evergreen forest. He has compared the material culture of the respective tribes living in the three zones and come to the conclusion that tribal economy of the state is very much influenced by the ecology. He has concluded that environment of the habitat of each tribe influences its material culture and livelihood pattern as well as subsequent political organization.

Distribution pattern of the tribal habitation shows that most of the people of the state lives in the lesser Himalayan zone and the plains along the foothills. Although there is not much evidence regarding the history of peopling of the area, it can very well be said that the area was not inhabited until Holocene time period. The geological history suggests that climatic fluctuation of Pleistocene period coupled with the rugged terrain and large scale tectonic movement in the tracts of the Himalayas did not invite population migration in the area during Pleistocene times. The late Pleistocene and early Holocene had suffered from great tectonic movements giving rise to faults and thrusts (Khayingshing Luirei *et al.*, 2012), which perhaps was not congenial for human habitation. From the palaeo-geographical and geological evidences it may be suggested that people perhaps entered the zone in the later Holocene times.

There is a distinct grouping of the indigenous people in the state. These people were considered as tribes by the British and later by Government of India. They are distinct from communities who imigrated in recent times. Population migration in the early times had taken place in several stages over the time. This is evident because of the fact that the tribes though speak in languages with, Tibeto-Burman stock hardly can understand each other's languages (Rath, 1994; Vidyarthi, 1986). Each group had started with their own mode of life style by forming ecological niche in the particular environment they occupied. Perhaps hunting, gathering, animal husbandry and shifting cultivation were the primordial modes of subsistence in the area.

The Sulung tribe is foragers and their staple food is sago. The overall material culture of the tribe shows that they subsist on simple economy of gathering (Pertin, 2005). Scholars consider that they could be a remnant of a group with prehistoric mode of subsistence. However, it is apparent that majority of the tribal groups live on shifting cultivation, which again may be considered as belonging to a stage of earliest form of cultivation of the Neolithic times. However, these are assumptions without any concrete evidence.

Transhumance nature of subsistence pattern leads to large scale population movement within the zone as well as triggers trans-border migration. Specially the political border does not always merge with the geographical barrier. The indigenous people entered the region from the vicinity areas with the knowledge of subsistence in the form of hunting gathering, pastoralism and shifting cultivation. The developed mode of plough cultivation and terrace cultivation coupled with unique system of irrigation were developed after the peoples' interaction with the suitable terrain. Out of the two major methods of subsistence, hunting, gathering and cultivation, cultivation can be categorized into slash and burn and settled types. The last is again of two types, terrace cultivation and heavy plough cultivation. Although it appears from all the studies that the tribes of Arunachal Pradesh are mostly *Jhum* or shifting cultivators. These people also utilize resources in their primary form. This includes gathering, hunting, fishing and fowling. All the tribes are skilful hunters.

The Puroik or Sulung are considered as most primitive of the tribes in the area. They have taken up the name Puroik because Sulung means slave. They live on hilly terrains of Papumpare, Kurung, Kumey, east Kameng and some parts of lower and upper Subansiri districts (Pertin,

2005). They live in dense forests of high hills. They are considered as bonded labours of the Nyishis (Bangnis), Akas and the Mijis. They are highly specialized hunters. They hunt regularly. Fishing and fowling are regular pursuits for livelihood. They also collect some wild roots, leaves, fruits and nuts but they are specialized in the collection of sago from the wildly growing dwarf sago palms. At present they are being rehabilitated with land for shifting cultivation and with stocks for animal husbandry.

All other tribes follow hunting and gathering for supplementing food supply. Researches among the tribes have been done for understanding of the subsistence mechanism, and it was found that they hunt for various reasons, namely, for food, for earning cash, for rituals and for protecting crops. Elephant catching is an important activity of some groups. Usually they use simple hunting weapons, such as, spear, bow and arrow, nets, traps etc. Fire arms are recent introduction. People do not hunt indiscriminately. There are restriction in hunting by observing social taboo, maintaining seasonality of availability, thereby giving time for rejuvenation of natural resources and maintaining balance in the resources of the nature. Collection, fishing and fowling are equally important among the tribes. Collections of plants are done for food, fodder, house building and for furniture material. Medicinal plants also have great value among the different tribes. Botanical Survey of India has identified a large number of plants with medicinal value. People have survived in the area for long by prescribing ante dotes and curatives from natural resources for many diseases. Fishing is carried out in rivers, lakes and other water bodies. Fowling is done in the forests and in the surrounds of the homestead. However, for all these they generally use simple technologies and maintain balance in resource utilization by means of restricted utilization, which is prescribed by customary laws.

Slash and burn method of cultivation, as discussed earlier, is a method of cultivation followed by most of the people. In this aspect too simple technology is used and specific traditional ways and customs are there for judicious land use. Customary laws take care of over utilization and abuse of nature. Land is either held collectively or individually but people have to be accountable to the society for its proper use and must refrain from misuse.

Among the settled agriculturists the Apatanis are well known for the unique method of irrigation and terrace cultivation. The Monpas are next to the Apatanis in expertise of agriculture.

Trade is another important aspect of economy. As mentioned earlier

Sherdukpen solely depend on trade. The Apatanis are expert traders and so are many other tribes of the area.

Whole gamut of material culture and related social condition vary with the pattern of resource utilization. The tribal groups of Arunachal Pradesh have highly ordered and organized systems of functioning in their villages. All matters relating to community as a whole are decided in the village level. The traditional village council is a judicio-administrative body consisting of mature and influential elders. Most of them have chieftainship who preside over the village council. There is existence of class on the basis of status. There are upper aristocrat class and commoners and slaves as well. With the change in the Central admintration system, the slaves are declared free, and they are now considered as commoners. It is not unusual to find women chieftains, who are addressed as 'rani'.

Although the Britith and thereafter the Indian Government had introduced Panchayet system but traditional political institutes still function within the villages, may be in a little different style. Plants, animals, birds, and fish are considered as community properties and people tend and protect them with sustainability. However, modern technology, developed mode of communication with metal roads, has brought change and threat to the environment and sustainability within the traditional survival mechanism. Globalization is one great threat to the cultural milieu of the region. At present ethnicity, socio-economy and sustainability of these are at stake, mainly due to globalization.

For maintaining and planning development in sustainable manner several points are to be kept in consideration by the policy makers. It is found that certain territoriality is maintained by the local group. Each group is responsible for protection of its territory. Land and resources are held as community property. Customary laws are there to preserve and ensure sustainability. State must focus and emphasize on indigenous method of resource utilization and preservation of indigenous knowledge as opposed to commercializing it. The task is not an easy one. Progress must not be nipped. People should be given access to modern knowledge and be educated to be at par with the modern world but proper cognizance should be given to the customary laws and traditional values of the people of the land, so that the people may live in harmony in the given space of their own choice. Development, and its sustainability should be planned and formulated with active participation of people in every sphere of the decision making, and policy formation.

REFERENCES

Bareh, H.M. (2001), *Encyclopaedia of North East India.* Mittal Publications. New Delhi.

Choudhury, D.P. (1978), *The North East Frontier of India 1865-1914.* The Asiatic Society. Calcutta.

Darlington, P.J., (1957), *Zoogeography.* John Wiley & Son. New York.

Dutta, P. and S.I. Ahmad, (ed) (1995), *People of India: Arunachal Pradesh.* Vol. XIV, Anthropological Survey of India and Seagull Books. Calcutta.

Elwin, V. (1958), *Myths of the North East Frontiers of India.* North East Frontier Agency. Govt. of India.Shillong

________, (1959), *India's North East Frontier in the Nineteenth Century.* Oxford University Press. London.

Furer Himendorf, C. von (1947). *Ethnographic notes on tribes of Subansiri Region.* Shillong.

________, (1982), *Highlanders of Arunachal Pradesh.* Vikas Publishing House. New Delhi.

Geography of India (2012) http://geography.about.com/od/indiamaps/a/indianstaes.htm

Hodson, B.H. (1848). On the Aborigines of Eastern Frontier, *Journal of the Asiatic Society of Bengal.* Vol. 18, Part II, pp. 967-75.

ICIMOD (2012), *Towards developing the Brahmaputra-Salween Landscape – Report on the experts regional consultation for transboundary biodiversity management and climate change adaptation.* ICIMOD Working Paper 2012/4. Kathmandu: ICIMOD.

Kar, R.K. (1994) The tribes of North East India: An overview. In *Tribes of North East India.* Sarthak Sengupta (Ed.). Gyan Publishing House. New Delhi. pp. 37-52.

Myes, N. Mittermeier, R. A., Mittermeier, C. A. da Fousca, G. A. B. and Kent J. (2000), Biodiversity hot spot for conservation priorities. *Nature,* 403: 853-858.

Ministry of Power, (2009), *Bhareli Project,* Government of India (powermin.nic.in/whats_new/PFR/AP/Bhareli.pdf)

Pertin, David, (2005), The Puroiks (Sulungs) of Arunachal Pradesh – their settlement and socio-economic upliftment. in Chaudhuri, Sarit Kumar and Sucheta Sen Chaudhuri, (ed) *Primitive Tribes in Contemporary India: Concept, Ethnography and Demography*. Mittal Publications. New Delhi. pp. 367-368

Peal, S.E. (1896), Eastern Nagas of Tirap and the Nomadic. *Journal of the Asiatic Society of Bengal.* Vol. 65, Part III, pp. 9-17.

Rath, S.N. (1994), The Emerging Ethnographic Profiles of the Eastern Himalayas: Notes on some tribes of Arunachal Pradesh. In *Tribes of North East India.* (ed) Sarthak Sengupta, New Delhi, Gyan Publishing House.

Risley, H.H. (1891), Tribes and Castes of Bengal (Ethnographic Glossary) Calcutta.

Robinson, W. (1841) (reprinted in 1975), *A Descriptive account of Assam.* Ostell and Lepáge. London.

Sengupta, Sarthak. (1994), *Tribes of North East India.* New Delhi, Gyan Publishing House.

Sarkar, Jayanta, (2002), Ecological Adaptation among the tribes of Arunachal Pradesh. In *Tribal Studies in North East India.* (ed.) Sarthak Sengupta. Mittal Publication. New Delhi. Pp. 109-115.

Singh , K.S. (1994), *People of India*, Vol.IX, Anthropological Survey of India. Calcutta.

Vidyarthy, L.P. (1986), *Art and Cultures of North East India.* Publication Division, Ministry of Information and Broadcasting, Government of India. New Delhi.

Khayingshing Luirei, Surendra S. Bhakuni, Pradeep Srivastava, and N. Suresh, (2012), Late Pleistocene – Holocene tectonic activities in the frontal part of NE Himalaya between Siang and Dibang river valleys, Arunachal Pradesh, India. *Zeitschrift für Geomorphologie,* Vol. 56,4, 477–493 (published online April 2012) website: http://en.wikipedia.org/wiki/Arunachal_pradesh#cite_note-6).

20

Traditional Coping and Adaptive Strategies Employed during Flood Amongst the Mishings of Dhemaji District, Assam

Dipa Patir and *N.K. Gogoi*

Introduction

Water is a source of life for all living organism. Ironically the same water in the form of floods takes away thousands of lives. Floods have ravaged several thousands of lives in India. It is one of the very well recorded natural phenomena since it recurs every year, yet the concerned agencies could do very little to mitigate the problems. Nevertheless, the extent of damages it had caused attracted focused attention of the planners and academia alike. With increasing human interventions and rapid developmental activities, the adverse effects of floods are being loudly felt today.

However, a number of communities around the world have tried to reorient their life-style to cope with this hazard with the help of indigenous coping and adaptive strategies and in many cases they seem to be successful.

In this context works of a few scholars of International and National repute are worth mentioning –

> Roger Few (2003) in his paper "Flooding, Vulnerability and Coping Strategies; Local responses to a global threats" reviews recent theoretical and applied research on vulnerability and adaptive capacity of household and communities in flood prone areas.

Lars Otto Naess, Guri Bang, Siri Eriksen, Jonas Vevatne (2005) in their research paper "Institutional Adaptation to Climate Change: Flood responses at the municipal level in Norway" had examined the role the institutions play in climate adaptation in Norway using examples from two municipalities in the context of institutional responses to floods.

Dukens, J. (2007) worked on the "Herders People of Chitral District of Pakistan" where flash flood is the frequent event. In her work she studied how the villagers, most of the time, manage to save their lives and how they know to interpret local environmental signals and where the hazardous places are.

GEAG (Gorakhpur Environmental Action), 2007 on "Adaptive Capacity of Communities to Cope with Flood Situation" is a documentation of community based agricultural and non-agricultural practices. In this documents efforts were made to compile such knowledge and practices related to agriculture and related issues which have helped communities in developing their adaptive capacities in response to flood of the area.

A.L. Mary and A.E. Majule (2009) in their paper "Impacts of Climate Change, Variability and Adaptation Strategies on Agriculture in Semi Arid Areas of Tanzania : The case of Manyoni District in Singida Region, Tanzania" carried out their study in two villages of Kamenyanga and Kintinku of Manyoni District, Central Tanzania. The overall objective of this study was to understand local communities' perceptions on climate and variability issues and establish its impacts and adaptation strategies within agricultural sector.

B.A. Gyampoh, S. Amisah, M. Idinoba and J. Nkem (2009) in their paper "Using Traditional Knowledge to Cope with Climate Change in Rural Ghana" focused on rural communities in the Offin river basin and highlighted the value of blending traditional and scientific knowledge in strategies for coping with climate change and variability.

Nguyen Van Sanh, Nguyen Duy Can (2009) worked on "Local Community Institutions to cope with the Flood Situation of the Mekong Region". The study was undertaken during 2008 in bordering flood-prone areas between Cambodia and Vietnam, covering four provinces: Takeo, Svey Rieng (Cambodia) and their adjacent An Giang and Dong Thap (Vietnam).

Sanjoy Hazarika (2006) in his paper "Living Intelligently with Flood" studied the improving quality of flood awareness and strengthening local to undertake measures related to disaster preparedness, risk mitigation, prevention and coping with the threats posed by flooding in the flood affected area of Jorhat and Golaghat districts.

Partha J. Das, Dadul Chutiya and Nirupam Hazarika, (2009) worked on the topic "Adjusting to Floods on Brahmaputra Plains", the study was carried out by 'Aaranyak' an environmental research organization in North-East India based in Guwahati, Assam, for the International Centre for Integrated Mountain Development (ICIMOD), as part of a regional project on 'Assessing Local Adaptation Strategies : Too Much, Too Little Water'. Here they have emphasized on the traditional coping and adaptation to flood by the affected people, both Mishing and non-Mishing of Dhakuakhana and Dhemaji districts.

Floods in Assam

Floods cause great distress whenever these damaged crops and property and endangered lives. The term Flood is generally defined as a relatively high flow or a stage in a river and the inundation of low land which might result therefrom. In a broader sense the term 'Flood' is used to convey all outflows due to jamming or blocking of rivers by landslides, an inadequate drainage to carry away surface water speedily. In other sense we can say that floods are temporary inundation of large regions as a result of an increase in reservoir, or of rivers flooding their banks because of heavy rains, high winds, cyclones, storm surge along coast, tsunami, melting snow, dam bursts or breaches of embankment.

Assam is situated in a high rainfall area with an average annual rainfall of 2,546 millimetres. About 60 to 70 per cent of the monsoon rain is received within a span of 3-4 months (May to August). The high rainfall in a limited time span causes major problems in the form of floods, erosion, and drainage congestion in the plains districts of the Brahmaputra and Barak Valleys. The recurring floods have extensively damaged the rural economy of the state. There has been extensive sand casting of fertile land, especially on the north bank of the Brahmaputra, and river bank erosion throughout the state forcing many rural families to migrate to towns and other non-flood areas.

Flash flood occurs due to shallow depth of the rivers owing to silt deposition on the river bed which has decreased the capacity of water discharges of various tributaries. The floods in the Sunitpur, Lakhimpur and Dhemaji districts are due to low carrying capacity of water by the river because of huge siltation on the river bed and as a result the river tends to flow in many directions.

In Dhemaji district the situation of intensive water logging and erosion is also caused due to excessive human intervention on the upper reaches of the rivers and huge construction of physical structures like bridges, roads etc., on the run-off water system with very little openings to maintain the natural flow/drainage of water which resulted in inundation of huge areas of Jonai Block, Sissiborgaon Block and Dhemaji Block of Dhemaji District. Similarly, the huge extraction and mining of boulders from the upper reaches of the rivers Simen, Demow, Jalakiashuti, Gai, Jiadhal etc. has increased the current of the rivers manifold leading to intensive erosion both on the upper reaches as well as on the bank line on plains.

Affect of Floods

Flood hazards affect all aspects of the land, lives, and livelihoods of communities living in the region to a significant degree. Both floods and flash floods caused people to leave homeless and displaced, destroy crops, and eventually rendering the soil unsuitable for any form of cultivation, damage public property, and damage development infrastructure. Victims who become destitute, suffer from trauma and shock. Thousands of hectares of fertile land in hundreds of villages with crops, settlements, and infrastructure have been lost to the river due to frequent shifting of the river course and erosion of river banks. Sand casting has proved to be one of the worst hazards because it results in degradation of thousands of acres of farm land and wetlands due to deposition of debris, mainly coarse sand particles, by flood waters.

The indigenous communities who have been living in such flood prone area have developed mechanisms over time and these have become ingrained in their lifestyles and traditions. There have been observable modifications and innovations in their house types, economic activity, food storage, food procurement and processing, livestock rearing etc. Their skill in traditional craft and knowledge of flood and weather prediction help them immensely to cope with and adapt to the immediate and long-term impacts of such hazards.

The Micro-field

The Micro-field selected for the present study is ideally one with a long history of floods and associated hazards over at least three decades and inhabited by one of the most suffered indigenous community, i.e. the Mishing community who has learned to live with floods over a long period of time.

Six different villages are selected from the district of Dhemaji under three Development Blocks. Under the Dhemaji Development Block Dihiri and Kekuri villages are selected for the study. These two villages are about 3-4 km away from N.H. 52 or Jiadhal Chariali. In Dihiri village there are all total 213 households and its population is 1867 (2011 census). In Kekuri village there are 210 households and the total population of the village is 1915 persons (2011 Census).

Munmuni Chapori village under Gali Gaon Panchayat is located on the bank of river Brahmaputra and is situated about 10 km away from the N.H. 52 or Lai Mekuri Tiniali. In this village the total number of households is 300 and its total population is 1900.

Arun Chapori village under Misamara Gaon Panchayat is located near the bank of river Brahmaputra and river Dikhari which is situated 5 km away from N.H. 52 or from Telam Tiniali. It also comes under the Murkung Selek Tribal Development Block of Jonai Sub-Division of Dhemaji district. At Arun Chapori the total number of households is 150 and total population is 970 persons.

Bhangidia village and Borchapori village are another two villages selected for the study located under Namoni Tangani Gaon Panchayat of Sissi Borgaon Development Block in Dhemaji district. These two villages are located on the bank of river Brahmaputra and river Tongani respectively. There are in all total 113 numbers of households in Bhangidia village and its total population is 554 (2011Census). At Borchapori village there are all total 158 number of households and the number of population is 1058 (2011Census). The two villages are situated approximately 30-35km away from Silapathar town.

All these six villages have a long history of multiple water-induced hazards, mainly floods, flash floods, bank erosion, and breaching of the embankment.

The present paper attempts to bring to light the indigenous communities' traditional coping and adaptation strategies employed during flood. It is also pertinent here to examine whether the traditional coping capacities and adaptation strategies are still useful in dealing with the changing nature of the multiple water-induced disasters.

Our findings may be discussed as follows :

***1. Disaster preparedness and Indigenous technology*:** As the villagers have been experiencing flood every year, the people have developed their system of anticipation, preparation, coping and recovery. In all these overlapping systems of response, the people have heavily depended on their indigenous knowledge. Consequently, every flood experiences have enriched their knowledge which they readily use in mitigating the flood risk.

A. Stock procurement: Preparation starts as soon as or before the rainy season starts. Families try to store as much food as they can. Women of the house prepare to store food and firewood. The capacity to store food depends entirely on the economic condition of the family. However, those who could not afford by themselves borrow money from the moneylender to buy food items. Enough fodder for livestocks is stored in the higher and dry places. Male members of the family are responsible for collecting fodder for the cattle, and they usually go to the river bank for collecting fodder.

B. Structural Changes: Houses on raised stilts (height up to 5 to 12 feet) is a practice of the Mishing community to mitigate damage caused by flood. They build their houses on raised wooden or bamboo stilts. The affluent families prefer using concrete pillars. The platform is made up of timber or bamboo matting. Roof is either thatched or of CGI sheet and is always sloping. It has been observed that the wear and tear of the houses is less and thus repairing and maintenance intervals are long. The lower part of the house is used to provide shelter to animals that every household rears and in river side villages where people lived in flood plain animals were provided shelter on the raised home with people.

During flood the affected people tend to cling to their own homestead as long as possible. When water level comes to the above danger level they make another platform inside their stilt-house out of bamboo and wood. As the water level rises they increase the height of the platform and if not possible they move to the ceiling of the house. When water level comes above the platform they keep a raft ready inside the house. The fire place is made on the raft where they usually cook. Another raft which is kept outside the house is used to dry paddy in between the rain. The matured paddies which are damaged in the paddy field were collected by using boat. The paddies are deseeded with legs. The paddies which get damaged inside the granary are kept suspended in water putting them in 'thoila' (jute bags) for future use. When required they take out a bag from the water and dry it under the sun using a raft or fry paddies in a large frying pan. But when everything is inundated, people take shelter in the nearby refugee camp or on the roadside in make-shift shelter.

***2. Behavioral change as coping and adaptation strategies*:** Both floods and flash floods leave people homeless and displaced, destroy crops, damage public property, and damage development infrastructure; people have to face many problems in adjusting with the disrupted environmental condition. The indigenous communities living in these areas have developed mechanisms over times that have become ingrained in their lifestyles and traditions. The people have adopted different strategies to cope with the flood situation. The strategies may be in the form of behavioral change related to food habits and sanitation habits. A study undertaken at the studied villages, observes that when flood hits, the food habit of the people changes both in quality and quantity.

A. Change in food habit: The Mishing people usually take meal thrice a day with fish or meat but during flood instead of three meals a day, at best, they could manage two meals. Sometimes, they cooked for one day and the same food is judiciously taken for two to three days. A few others tried to survive on dry food like 'muri', 'chira' etc., or had rice with only green chilly and salt. Some people have to spend whole day partaking only 'apong' (rice-beer). The poorest peoples who do not have anything to eat during flood, eat 'posola' (tender inner stem of banana plant). Some of them also starve in spite of having food materials due to lack of fuel.

Women are severely affected both during and after floods because of the physical and mental hardships they face in looking after the family kitchen and the children. Usually it is the women who arrange for or collect water for drinking and other domestic purposes during floods. In a typical marooned situation which continues for several days to several weeks they experience a lot of difficulty in cooking, attending to children, and taking care of livestock and poultry. Hardships increase all the more when they are taking shelter on raised bamboo platforms inside the house as this is often a makeshift arrangement within a narrow space. Before flood women of every households make 'apong', traditional rice beer, mainly the black apong because at the time of flood there is scarcity of drinking water and they use apong as drinking water and the solid waste that is left out after filtration of the apong, is used for filtering water to make it potable . The same solid waste is also used as fodder for pigs.

B. Change in sanitary habit: Maintaining health and sanitation is the greatest challenge for women during floods. The adult males use raft made of banana tree stems (called '*bhur*' in Assamese) or country boats to go out to the jungle for answering the call of nature; children manage do it in near the house by using raft or sometimes relieve themselves inside the house. Women had to wait till dusk or have to row their rafts to the isolated places or to places covered by trees to bathe or to respond to nature's call. People, who take shelter in the nearby refugee camp or on the roadside after making make-shift shelter, are forced to take bath in open space without caring for privacy or modesty.

C. Change in Religious practice: Crisis rituals in any community are unfailingly performed at the right time, right way and right place. It is more so in the case of any death rituals. Among the Mishings the ultimate death ritual called *Dodgung* is performed with profound owe and reverence, and this requires extensive preparation with huge manpower and material resource. But owing to the recurring floods in the area a bereaved family can not afford to perform the same at the stipulated time of one month after death and same may be kept in abeyance. Therefore, going by a religious sanction the same ritual may be performed after one or more years when the family and his kinsmen become economically strong enough to arrange all the required provisions for the ritual. The same ritual may be performed for a number of deceased kinsmen who have died over this long period of abeyance.

D. Change in economic activity :

(i) Agriculture is the primary means of sustenance of the Mishing community and paddy is their staple crop. Although they do not grow seasonal rice varieties like *'sali'* (summer variety) because of flood waters, yet, they manage to grow *'bao'* (deep water paddy) in normal flood water. *'Bao'* is a local variety adapted to a watery environment and it is not easily affected by floods. Some farmers cultivate mix indigenous varieties of summer rice (*ahu*) and deep-water rice (*bao*) to keep option in case one variety fails and to optimize the use of land. In a 'normal' year, when the floods are not so prolonged and virulent, both rice varieties survive. However, early flooding in April or May might damage the summer rice while the better-adapted *bao* survives and ensures food security. Agriculture has been affected almost every year since 1950. The consecutive floods of 2007 and 2008 left almost the entire area of agricultural land in flood plain region of the river Brahmaputra and its tributaries, irreparably damaged.

So, the Mishing community living in that area has adopted new strategies by growing '*bao*' paddy which is not affected easily by flood. Sand deposits covered the entire landmass up to an average height of four to six feet and made it totally unfit for any type of conventional agriculture. This has made them to try locally-developed techniques for growing vegetables in homestead gardens. As a result, many villagers have started growing vegetables like potatoes, pumpkins, gourds, green chilies, black gram and lemons using pit culture. They also cultivate mustard in large quantity.

(ii) The coping strategy also includes generating alternative source of income which majority of them are seen being engaged into. Any opportunity at hand is conveniently turned into earning source with limited available resources. For instance, the small wooden dinghy that a family possesses is immediately put in service for ferrying people on the inundated roads; or by laying bamboo poles over the breached culvert facilitating commuters to cross over for a petty sum of money.

(iii) Fishing, although is an integral part of this reverine community, it is more intensified during and after flood. It not only supplements food supply but also adds to the family coffers. People catches fish whereever it is possible. They mainly use '*langi jal*' (Gill net) in strong current water and in low level current water they use '*dingora*' (Eel trap). Surplus fishes are sold to the local traders who in turn sell the fishes at higher prices in nearby towns. The villagers dry the smaller fishes on bamboo platforms for a few days and sell the dried fish to the traders of nearby village or towns.

(iv) Some people collect drifting timber from the Brahmaputra River, risking their lives at times, and sell the timber. Others make wooden furniture from driftwood and trees in and around the village and sell them. A few of them are skilled boat makers and they are always in demand in the area. Collecting fuel wood and selling them in the market also brings some money to a number of families.

(v) Daily-wage earning opportunities become limited during and after flood. Most of the people go out of the village seeking manual labour like earth cutting, construction labourers etc., and at the end of the day whatever they earn could feed the family for the night. A few able adults move out to distant towns and cities and become rickshaw pullers. The remittances they send back home help in sustenance of their families during the floods. However, majority could not manage any alternative source of income so they have to borrow from their relatives or from the money lenders. Selling of their valuable assets of the family, ornaments and livestock are also common.

(vi) Traditional rice-wine making (*apong*) is an age-old practice and wine is prepared only for domestic consumption. During flood wine making and selling the same becomes an alternative source of income for most of the families. Almost every households make '*apong*' (traditional rice beer) mainly the black *apong* which substitutes drinking water because at that time there is scarcity of drinking water. Sale of this black wine fetches a good amount of remittance to meet the food requirement of the families. Moreover, the Mishing black apong is equally popular and is in high demand among the non-Mishing population too.

(vii) The Mishing women are skilled weaver and they weave most of their garments at home. Mishing textile and design has a good demand among the neighbouring Assamese communities. This skill of theirs not only empowers the Mishing women in general but also enables them to contribute economically to the family at the time of crisis.

(viii) The Mishing community is known for their husbandry of indigenous species of pigs and poultry although they are also known to rear goats, cows and buffalos. The Mishings of these studied villages maintain a steady supply chain of these indigenous species of pigs and fouls to various towns and cities of Upper Assam. There is a weekly (every Wednesday) chartered boat to ferry these live-stocks from the northern bank to the southern bank of the river Brahmaputra catering to the demands from the towns and cities of Upper Assam. This (almost) monopoly in trade also helps the community to fall back upon during the time of crisis.

***3. Indigenous knowledge of flood prediction*:** The Mishing community of Dhemaji district has a rich treasure of indigenous knowledge based on which they claim to be able to predict flood, and this acts as an early warning system. They have a keen sense of observation upon nature, animals and birds by which they seem to provide an early warning of flood.

(i) Weather and Flood Predictions based on animal behaviour

(a) On the early morning of '*Makar Sankranti*' if the cattle are found to stay standing under their shed and there is a visible sign of restlessness among them, this indicates a forthcoming flood.

(b) If on the very next day of '*Makar Sankranti*', a day which is celebrated as '*Garu Bihu*' when the cattle, usually cows and buffaloes, are taken out to the water front to give them a ceremonial bath, exhibit unusual behaviour it is believed that the flood is inevitable.

(c) On any ordinary day if cow, goat, buffalo, and pig become very restless and make unusual moos and grunts in their shed it indicates a forthcoming disaster more likely a flood or earthquake.

(d) When insects' like-locust, grasshopper etc. come out from their hide and fly randomly and enter house, this situation suggests a sudden change in the weather condition, more occasionally a flood.

(e) When colonies of ants shift their shelter to higher places with their eggs and food stuff; it indicates a definite forthcoming heavy downpour or flood.

(f) If swarms of mosquitoes all of a sudden come out at any time of the day and attack their prey violently this indicates an approaching flash flood.

(g) When foxes howl irritably at higher place it indicates an impending prolonged dry spell and when they howl from a low lying location a flood is anticipated.

(h) It is believed that doves chirp monotonously for a long time before an imminent flood.

(i) A mysterious bird locally known as *Mulung* (Owl/*Strix flammea*) cries before a devastating flood.

(j) A bird having local name *Chatak* (*Pelargopsis capensis*) cries mournfully before flood.

(k) A drastic change in weather is indicated by random fly and suicidal action of full grown termite.

(l) Dog bathes frequently before an impending flood.

(m) A bird locally known as *Kurkur* (Osprey/*Pandion haliaetus*) cries and sways in the sky indicating an imminent devastating flood.

(n) Toads and frogs make continuous sounds before torrential rain and devastating flood.

(ii) Prediction on the basis of Observation on nature:

(a) If the moon inclines towards south it implies a forthcoming devastating flood.

(b) If cloud gathers in the south-west direction it indicates a probable storm; in south-east direction it indicates a rain and flood and in north-west it indicates normal rain.

(c) When cloud floats from northeast towards southwest it indicates a forthcoming flood.

(d) If the moon bears an aura of red tinge it indicates forthcoming torrential rainfall within three days.

(e) Wind blowing in southwest direction is invariably followed by a strong storm and heavy downpour.

(f) When rain starts on Wednesday or Thursday it envisages torrential rain fall in next 22 days. If it rains on Monday it lasts for 8 consecutive days. A rain on Tuesday or Saturday may continue for at least 3 days. And rain on Sunday goes on for a longer duration too.

(g) When rainbow extends from north-east to south-west and if it is clearly visible then a devastating flood is inevitable.

(h) When thunderbolt strikes on the northern sky it indicates heavy rainfall and flood. On south-western sky it augurs a devastating storm, and on the south-eastern sky it indicates a prolonged rain and possible flood and on north-western sky it indicates normal rain.

(i) Untimely and massive flowering on bamboo bush increases the probability of devastating flood.

(j) If mango trees bear more flowers than the flowers of Jackfruits it indicates more rain and flood.

(k) When *Simolu* (Silk-cotton tree/*Bombax ceiba*) blooms flower at an earlier date than normal flowering period, it indicates a forthcoming flood.

(l) When a species of grass plant locally known as *Torapat* (*Alpinia alughas*) shoots out a new bud with a tint of silt, it indicates a devastating flood.

(m) Based on their earlier observations when people come to know that there has been rain in the adjacent hills of Arunachal Pradesh then these people in the plains have just

6 to 10 hours of time to save their lives and properties from a flash flood which is bound to occur.

(iii) Prediction by religious specialist and beliefs.

(a) The Mishing shaman is believed to have the power to forecast the nature of the weather for the forthcoming days through a ritual calculation based on the signs on the heart of the pig sacrificed in *Dubur Puja*.

(b) The Shaman may forecast weather based on dreams.

(c) According to the position of Saturn (based on Assamese almanac) at a given period of time of the year, and if it is said to reign over water then an intermittent occurrence of flood is predicted.

***(iv) Community warning system*:** The community has a well practiced information broadcasting and warning system. The villagers used to alarm people at downstream mostly through personnel communication which is relayed through verbal media or at times by beating drums, bronze cymbals and gongs. The Mishing people are usually very mobile within their own territory, and they are seen moving from one place to another either to graze their cattle or to collect fuel wood or roots and tubers. While doing so they keep strict vigil on the trend of the river flow and the vulnerable areas (specially the dykes). If anything unusual is noticed the information is immediately relayed to the villagers so as to take necessary precautionary measures. In some areas they also use public announcing system to disseminate information.

From the preceding discussions we can say that the community under study has by now learned how to live with the flood by making optimum use of the indigenous technology. They have vivid knowledge of the immediate environment within which they inhabit. They are seasoned by the long time and perpetual experience with the flood which perhaps enabled them to cope and adapt to such crisis situation with strategies and innovations purely indigenous in nature.

REFERENCE

Das, P.J., (2009), Understanding Local Adaptation to Climate Induced Water

Hazard—A case study in the eastern Assam flood plains of the Brahmaputra river basin, India. Researcher's workshop on climate change and migration in Asia and the Pacific, organized by ADB, IOM & ADPC, dt. 14th September, Manila (Philippines).

Dukens, J. (2007), *Herders of Chitral: the Lost Messengers?, Local Knowledge on Disaster Preparedness in Chitral District, Pakistan.* Publ. International Centre for Mountain Development: Kathmandu, Nepal, Indigenous Knowledge for Disaster Risk Reduction in South Asia.

Few Roger (2003), "Flooding, Vulnerability and Coping Strategies; Local responses to a global threats". *Journal of Progress in Development Studies,* Vol. 3, No.1, pp. 43-58.

GEAG (2007), *Adaptive capacities of communities to cope with flood situation: A documentation of community based agricultural and non-agricultural practices.* Gorakhpur: Gorakhpur Environmental Action Group. Post Box # 60, Gorakhpur-273001.

Gyampoh, B.A.S. Amisah, M. Idinoba and J. Nkem (2009), *Using Traditional Knowledge to Cope with Climate Change in Rural Ghana.* Food and Agriculture Organization of the United Nations, Rome, 2009, Published in Unasylva No. 231/232 Vol. 60, 2009/1-2.

Hazarika. S., (2006), Living Intelligently with Floods, Centre of North East Studies, The World Bank, 1818H-Street, NW Washington DC-2033, USA.

Lars Otto Naess; Guri Bang; Siri Eriksen; Jonas Vevatne (2005), Institutional Adaptation to Climate Change: Flood responses at the municipal level in Norway. *Journal of Global Environment Change*, vol. 15, pp. 125-138.

Mary A.L. and A.E. Majule, (2009), "*Impacts of Climate Change, Variability and Adaptation Strategies on Agriculture in Semi Arid Areas of Tanzania: The case of Manyoni District in Singida Region, Tanzania.* Institute of Resource Assessment (IRA), University of Dar-es-Salaam, P.O. Box 35097, Dar-es-salaam, Tanzania.

Nguyen Van Sanh, Nguyen Duy Can (2009), *Local Community Institutions to cope with the Flood Situation of the Mekong Region.* Mekong Delta Development Institute, Vietnam.

21

Education is Abandoned in a Tribal Village: An Empirical Study on the Mishings Villages in Assam

Dilip Kumar Bhuyan

As a process, education is as old as the progression of human race. Right from the time of evolution of human beings, education began in one form or the other. Knowledge and skills related to processes of fulfilling basic human needs, such as gathering food, hunting, covering the body, preparing tools, protecting oneself etc. These were passed on from one generation to the next. During the early period education was totally informal in nature; nevertheless it was bound by certain well defined objectives. These objectives were to fulfil the immediate needs pertaining to bodily wants such as hunger, thirst, protection, etc. and enhance the level of comfort. Thereafter with the growth of civilization, the need of formal education for the development of the individual as well as the society was realized and gradually education got institutionalized.

During the post-independence period in India there has been a growing tendency towards change in all the spheres of society. In India, the villagers are subject. These changes have touching and stressing impact on social, economic, political and cultural lives of the rural people. It cannot be denied that there is only a predominant cause or factor, i.e. education which is related to any change. Therefore, it may be noted that education plays a vital role in bringing about change in society from traditional to modern status. In the contemporary period, because of impact of industrialization and westernization, the society as a whole and consequently the pattern of education has largely been changed. The spread of education in the post-independent India has made room for modernization of her economy, health and hygiene, age old beliefs and practices of the people and political participation etc. It further makes the villagers aware of the development in different aspects of life. One of the latent functions of education is to orient the people towards modernization. Education has tremendous potentiality to motivate the village people for change and modernization. Moreover, education is seen to play a vital role in eradicating the evils of traditional society such as superstitious beliefs and practices, caste purity and pollution and gender discrimination etc. It has not only provided a job opportunity to the people but also educated them in the field of economy, health and hygiene, political awareness etc. In short, education plays decisive role in drifting away the villagers from tradition to modernity. In fact, a person's access to educational institution for most people becomes a great concern in the changing scenario. Several measures adopted by the Government of India as progressive measures, need to be inter-linked with access to education and change or development of the rural people. Education provides the people an opportunity to receive something new to any society by replacing the traditional values of the society. It also brings to the society new ideas, fashion, dress, dietary system, housing pattern, new kind of recreation, political beliefs, saving habits, use of new agriculture methods, etc. The rural people who are educated, are aware of modernity or rationality and thereby change their traditional attitudes. So, change comes into a society with the speared of education.

In the primitive communities, the transmission of cultural heritage was mainly a function performed by the institution of family. It was within the family that the child was introduced to the world of social reality. On the other hand, in the present day society the educational institutions have taken up the responsibilities of socialization and imparting formal education to the children. The schools and colleges are entrusted the task of providing of knowledge for the physical, mental and intellectual development of children and to train them for specialized trades and professions. In the present time, the term education, therefore, refers to formal schooling. The principal onus of the article was to discuss the role of education as cultivation rational ability among the villagers of some villages of Assam. The spread of education among the villagers in the context of India is an important factors because of the fact that India lives in her villages. In fact the social change *vis-à-vis* progress and the development of the villagers in the paramount need of the hour. It is also a fact that a vast section of rural people even today has been practicing traditional beliefs and practices, and thereby makes room for the continuance of old age traditions. There is no denying the fact that unless this section of population is guided by rational thinking any development effort of the government as well as of the other non-governmental agencies would yield no result. But how they can be motivated towards rational thinking. In this regard education can certainly play a decisive role in the motivating the rural people for giving up traditional practices and to welcome change and development through the rational ability. Education, here we refer to as the formal schooling through which an individual receives some new ideas, motivates him to come out from tradition.

The author has conducted an empirical study on the four villages in Lakhimpur district of Assam, likes to give an account of the relationship between education and social change taking place in the studied villages. The four studied villages were—Panigaon which is regarded as developed village in terms of proximity to urban centre, Bochagoan—which is considered as developed village, Burhaburhi—which is treated as backward village and Kanhi Dower—which is regarded as the tribal village as well as backward village. Here, we have discussed about only one village, i.e. Kanhi Dower. Regarding the origin and naming of the village it may be mentioned that Kanhi Dower is associated with a mythical legend. The old people think that there is a 'Dower' (like pond) ahead of the village which was created by the rivers, Subansiri and Khabalu. It is believed that the Dower (pond) provides brass and bell metal to the people who are required for performance of religious functions. Because of this fact, the village is known as Kanhi (means kind of utensil) Dower. It is reported that the village was established in about 1930.

The village Kanhi Dower is situated at a distance of 30 km South—East corner from the North Lakhimpur town. The village falls under Telahi Development Block and North Lakhimpur Revenue Circle which are at a distance of about 20 km. and 30km. respectively from the village. It may be noted that this village is a non-cluster village, according to census report 2001. The village is connected with NH 52 by a PWD road. The entrance portion of the road say about 1.5km is Kacha and households are scattered throughout the PWD road. The total households in the village are 58 and the total population are 199 of which 103 are males and 96 are females. The village is entirely a tribal village and its inhabitants are the Mishings who are listed as Scheduled Tribe. Among the plain tribes numerically after the Bodo, the Mishing are the second largest tribe in Assam and constituted 2.07 per cent of the total population of the state according to Census of India, 1991. The Mishings belong to the Tibeto-Burman family of Indo-Chinese group. Basically, the Mishings community may be regarded as an aboriginal ethnic group of Assam, and they are particularly scattered in 6 districts out of 27 districts in Assam, namely Lakhimpur, Dhemaji, Dibrugarh, Sonitpur, Jorhat, and Sibasagar districts. They are the inhabitants of the riverside areas and their primary occupation is agriculture. The language of the Mishings is Mishing, and they adopted Roman script in respect of language.

Educational institution is one of the prime components of any change in any type of society. In the rural areas a quite number of educational institutions were established before Independence and post independence period. But in the village Kanhi Dower we find that only one Lower Primary School was established in the year 1956. It is learnt that the boys and girls of the village pursue higher study in Om Prakash Dinodia College, Panigaon which is located at a distance of 20 km. It may be noted that in the village Kanhi Dower, there is no High School (Secondary level) as well as Middle School (upper primary) till now and therefore both the boys and girls of the village go to the nearest high school, which is located at Agarmile, at a distance of 4 km from the village Kanhi Dower. Moreover, in the village, there is no organization but there are a few numbers of Self Help Groups (SHGs) operating in the village with a view to develop economic conditions of the people of the village.

Occupation is an important component of social background of individuals which determines to a great extent, one's mode of living, thinking, behaviour etc. The rural people basically depend upon on agriculture. But now-a-days there has been a shift from agricultural occupation to non-agricultural occupation due to availability of various tools and equipments. In this regards Desai remarks "Like all other phenomena the rural society too has been changing since its emergence, its technology, economy and social institutions, its ideology, art and religion, have undergone a ceaseless change. This change has sometimes been imperceptibly slow, sometimes strikingly rapid and at some moments even qualitative in character resulting in to the transformation of one type of rural society into another one type" (1969:87). During the field or investigation 56 respondents (96.56%) were found to depend upon cultivation, otherwise (1.72%) respondents were engaged in government service and another one (1.72%) respondent is engaged in semi-government service.

Education is an important tool by which we can judge whether particular society is advanced or not. The standard of a society can be judged by knowing the educational standard of the people. Education is a prerequisite for transformation of a society from traditional to modern status. It is further required to understand the developmental programmes of the government. Economic well being and better standard of living of the people depend upon acquiring of education. According to Cole and Cox (1968:p-401) "Education changes the horizon, standard and perspectives of people. The horizon acceptable to a person at one time in his life way, as a result of learning may be highly unacceptable at another time. One becomes dissatisfied with the existing state of one's knowledge, with the conditions under which one lives, with his social situation and with ones previous goals and the means one has developed for achieving them. One not only becomes dissatisfied, one seeks new knowledge or new sets of conditions and relationships which are not only more satisfying one but more worthwhile to others and to the social system in which one lives" (Cole & Cox 1968:401). This statement has justified the need of putting emphasis on education for development or change of individual and society. It cannot be denied that education widens the mental horizon of the people. It further paves the way for social and occupational mobility. With regards to the role of education in social development or change Borthakur stated that (1994: P-153) "Education once spread in a society, no doubt, will have propound sociological repercussions on the economy and social structure of the society. It is important for social development and it is also the indicator of social development" (1994:153). Based on our enquiry it was founds that in this village 14 (24.14%) respondents was found illiterate, 62.06 per cent respondents have reading up to class X standard and 6.90 per cent respondents have passed HSLC exam i.e. class X standard and H.S i.e. class XII standard. But there is no respondent having graduate and post graduate degree.

It is now considered essential to point out the role of education is bringing about a change in the attitudes of rural people. The concept of attitude helps us in understanding the direction of behavior and action. A change in behavior is usually preceded by a change in the thought patterns of an individual. Attitudes are a significant aspect of thought patterns and thus considered to be important factor of social change. Therefore, the term education has been given a specific connotation in the present study to mean only formal education, which is imparted through such educational institutions like schools and colleges. The village Kanhi Dower has not noticed any change due to spread of education. It is because of the fact that villages attributed the reason of static nature to their isolation from the district headquarters. It is a fact that this village is located far way from the district headquarter town.

In this study an attempt has been made to probe the role of education in the adoption of scientific method of agriculture by the villagers. The investigation of this issue is concerned with only those who adopted agriculture as their main or secondary occupation and as such information regarding adopted of improved methods in agriculture was collected only from those who practiced agriculture. The field data suggest that large majority of (i.e. 100%) the cultivators are accustomed with single crop cultivation and they have not adopted improved methods in agriculture. It may be stated have that village level worker (Gram Sevak) plays decisive role in disseminating information about improved methods of production among the villagers. The study interestingly finds that the Gram Sevak did not visit any residence of the farmers of the village Kanhi Dower. Moreover, the role of Gram Sevak in diffusing information about improved methods of farming is very insignificant. A large majority of respondents has viewed that there is no relationship between education and adoption of scientific methods in agriculture. During the course of field enquiry we could gather that illiteracy, non availability of input of improved methods of cultivation at village level, if training and motivation to orient the farmers to adopt improved methods of farming etc. were some of the reasons of non-adoption of scientific methods of cultivation by a large majority of respondents. All villagers are of the view that they are unaware about formation of Field Management Committee (FMC) in the villages. The entire situation of the universe of the study is that all the respondants (100%) were unsatisfied with the role of the Agriculture Department. The findings suggest that Agriculture Department of the State Government has much more to do in the matter of diffusion of knowledge about improved methods of cultivation among the villagers as well as motivating and guiding the farmers towards this end.

This study discloses that education has a role in regard to political participation of the villagers. By political participation we mean the involvement of individuals in the political activities such as becoming members of political party, contesting elections, castling vote in elections and showing interest in politics etc. It was found that 96.55 per cent of the village Kanhi Dower were not members of any political party. In a democratic country franchise is one of the important components. The findings of this study suggest that the voters are not politically conscious about casting their votes. Another key concept of this study is that saving habit of the villagers. The act of savings is a subjective one. It is implied that certain external stimuli are responsible for generating it. Education acts as external stimulation which promotes aspiration among the villagers for the formation of savings habit for betterment in future. Borthakur remarks "It is necessary to state here that saving money depends upon many factors. Needless to say that there is an urge on every earning member to save money. But if the entire income of each month is spent on consumption, then nothing would be left for saving. Sometimes, a rich man may have less saving than comparatively less well off person in terms of income. But the urge to save money depends upon one's aspiration. A person having aspiration for betterment for future, tends to save money irrespective of his economic standing" (1994:178).

It was seen that in case of village Kanhi Dower, first, due to lack of adequate education and secondly, because of poverty and thirdly, due to long distance to the bank, saving habit has not been developed among the villagers. The present study reveals that education cannot be able to play important role in arousing the idea of savings among the villagers which in turn not helped them to form saving habit in them. The Self-Help Groups play a vital role in regard to the enlistment of economic structure of the rural people. But the study finds that in the village Kanhi Dower a few numbers of SHGs executed various schemes. With regard to the formation of saving habit among the villagers there are some problems. The study highlights that hand to mouth living condition, unemployment, expanses to children's education and large size of family are some of the problems that have stood against the villagers in the formation of savings habit.

Finally, it can be concluded that the villagers whose educational level is minimum X[th] standard and onward, have welcomed change in different aspects of life irrespective of caste and tribe etc. This is not only reflected in the village Kanhi Dower which is a Scheduled Tribe village, it is also found that this village is backward in almost every aspect of life. The state of backwardness of the villagers of the village Kanhi Dower may also be attributed to non-attainment of higher educational level by majority of the villagers. This suggests that education and social changes are closely related to each other but this is not the case with this village.

REFERENCES

Cole, W.E. and Cox, R.L. (1968), *Social Foundation of Education*, America Book, New York.

Desai, A. R., (Ed.) (1969), *Rural Sociology in India*, Popular Prakashan, Bombay.

Borthakur, B.N. (1994), *Communication and Village Development*. Institute of Social Reasearch and Applied Anthropology, Culcutta.

22

Identity Crisis Within: The Problem of the Kabui

M.C. Arunkumar and Akhuan Gangmei

Identity is neither rigid nor concrete. It is too fluid in nature. Social scientists basically use three paradigms to explain the reality of this phenomenon: the primordial, the instrumentalist and the combination of the both. The first stream of thought believes that the ethnic differences among the people are given, they are inherited by them. These differences engender the form of ethnic conflict between the groups. The second stream of thought or paradigm believes that the ethnic differences are not given; they are created by the elite, who could be politicians, teachers, religious leaders, etc. It manipulates the social cleavage for the attainment of their goal. Sometimes the ethnic differences culminate in the form of ethnic conflicts, riots, autonomy movement or insurgency. Besides, the bases of social cleavages, which are turned into ethnic groups, are not always real. Some of them are even invented or constructed by the elite. The third advocates the combination of the both. The first two approaches divide the issue into bipolarity rather than to address the issue.

The identity crisis within same group of people poses a number of questions. The debates over the nomenclature of people whom the Constitution of India recognizes as the Kabui has become more and more complex. The nomenclature is challenged by a quarter of the same people who like to rename the tribe as the Rongmei. The heat of the controversy has further become complex with the formation of a larger identity of Zeliangrong that embraces three different tribes, the Zemei, the Liangmei and the Rongmei (Kabui). The nomenclature, Zelaingrong, is the combination of three syllables of the names of the tribes: Ze, Liang and

Rong. Among the Kabuis (Rongmeis), it seems that those who prefer the name, Kabui adopt the first paradigm in retaining the name, Kabui; whereas those who advocate for larger identity like Zeliangrong consider the second in asserting the new name of a larger tribe.

Tracing the history of the controversy is necessary in order to understand the debate over the identity and its dynamics. On 15 February, 1925, there was a first ever formal conference of the tribe and discussed the need for unity of their tribe, uniformity of their customary laws and the development of *Hao-Keithel,* (literal meaning, the tribal market) near Majorkhul, within the heart of the Imphal town. It was established in 1911. The members present in the conference continue to hold meetings, conferences etc. Meeting was convened, at least once, every month. Such meeting was known as *Agaangmei* (literally, the public) meetings (Zeliangrong Union, 1929, reprint 2009:3).

In course of time, the nascent association gradually develops to be an apex body of the entire tribe. It settled inter-village disputes, acted as the apex body to deal with cases under customary laws and acted above the *Peikai* (village authorities) of individual villages. It is true that prior to this body, inter-village feuds among themselves were order of the day, without any common authority to settle the disputes. The limit of the customary laws was the village concerned. The formation of the apex body was the response to the new challenges that had been brought by the colonial rule and its administration. Since Manipur lost her independence in 1891, the British imposed new structure of administration in the State that affected not only to the dominant group but also the tribal polities. To stand united for facing the colonial imposition on the tribe, formation of the apex body was a historical necessity. Initially, the association had no formal office and structure. It also did not have any written constitution. The headmen of different villages played extended duties; they sat together to take collective decision. They codified customary laws under the leadership of the association. Later, the code was recognized by the British administration in the State. State administrators took the codified customary laws for the adjudication and settlement of tribal cases. As the Kabui villages were distributed in the hill and plain areas of the State, their villages were far away from each other. As it was very difficult for the association to convene meeting every month, they started sitting in different villages at interval times. The sitting held at Tammenglong came to be known as *Kabui-Chingsang. Kabui Chingsang* functioned as regional units of the same body. Likewise, for Imphal sitting, they called *Agaangmei.*

On 7-8 March, 1934, the regional units both *Agaangmei* and *Kabui Chingsang* organized a joint meeting at Keishamthong Kabuikhul, a Kabui colony in Imphal. The conference announced that the association would be formally known as the *Kabui Samiti.* The *Kabui Samiti* convened another conference at the same place on 21-22 October, 1934 to facilitate the King of Manipur Maharaj Churachand Singh on his achievement of the British title, KCSI as well as to normalize the misunderstandings and ill feelings existing between the hill people and plains people since the execution of Haipou Jadonang, a Kabui leader, by the British government in 1931.

Like the parental association, *Kabui Samiti* had no formal secretary or president earlier. One Mr. Atorsing, one of the main conveners of the first *Agaangmei* conference of 1925, used to sit as the chairman in most of the meetings of the *Samiti.* In order to overcome the inconveniences in functioning, *Kabui Samiti* was divided into two administrative regions on geographical basis. The *Kabui Samiti* in valley region came to be known as the *Imphal Sadar Area Kabui Samiti* with its office at Imphal. This *Samiti* consisted of fifteen members nominated from the headmen and prominent leaders of the Kabui colonies in Imphal. Similarly, another set of fifteen members nominated from the hill areas functioned as the *West Tamenglong Area Kabui Samiti* with its office at Tamenglong Headquarters. Each unit had the full powers to function as the *Kabui Samiti* in their respective areas. The decisions of each unit were binding to their respective Kabui villages. However, on rare occasion, the *Kabui Samiti* had joint meeting to discuss very important issues.

In 1940, there was a joint conference of the *Samiti* at *Sawombung Kabui Khul,* a village 15 km from Imphal, on the agenda of reformation of social customs in the tune of changing times and development of modern education. Soon after the joint meeting, the *Samiti* became defunct for more than three years during the Second World War. The war brought a drastic change in the State; the Imphal valley witnessed a series of bombings in 1942. In 1945, the *Samiti* came back again with a new name, as the *Kabui Association.* This time, the Association had its written constitution for the first time. Very soon, the Association had to change its name again as the *Kabui Naga Association* in September 1945 following an allotment of a plot of land in the name of the Kabui Naga Association by Mr. Steward, the then Political Agent of Manipur. This Association was also divided into Hill area and Plain area having an area committee each. Each area was further subdivided into Northern and

Southern divisions with one division committee each. All the committees were elected bodies under its Constitution.

On 15 February, 1947, a conference of representatives of different Kabui villages at Keishamthong, Imphal was organized. The Conference resolved to form an organization comprising the entire *Kabuis* of Manipur and *Kacha Nagas* of Naga Hills of Assam. To bring different cognate tribes of this region, the Conference coined a new nomenclature as *Zeliangrong* to cover the Kabui and Kacha Naga (namely the *Zemei, Liangmei, Rongmei, Puimei,* etc.). The new organization formed was named as the *Zeliangrong Council*, with its Head Office at Kohima (now in Nagaland) and branch offices at *Imphal, Tamenglong* (both in Manipur), *Haflong* and *Birema* (both in Assam). The *Kabui Naga Association* meeting at Dailong on December 14,1947, also opted for the newly coined nomenclature (Zeliangrong) and accordingly changed its name as the Manipur Zeliangrong Union (MZU) but its Constitution and hierarchy of offices remained as same.

The Union started taking active role in the political activities of the State. They even contested and won two seats (see Kamei, 2004:193-194) in the first ever Assembly Election of Manipur in 1948, under the Manipur State Constitution, 1947. It also tried to explore all the possible means for their political future in post-colonial period. In the wake of the Naga armed struggle for independence started in 1950s, they discussed to organize over ground civil organizations. But, it did not come into light after the Annual General Meeting of *MZU* on February 26, 1960 at Zoute-Pabram. The meeting aimed for wider political identity and hence the name MZU also changed into the Zeliangrong Naga Union (ZNU) by omitting the word Manipur and inserting 'Naga' (Zeliangrong Union 1929, 2009:6; Kamei 2004:211).

On 14 March, 1976, ZNU and Maram General Board (the Maram is another scheduled tribe in Manipur) jointly performed a customary rite of *Chuk Sumei* at Majorkhul for the unification of both the tribes as one people of same origin. They tried to replace the name of their tribes as *Maram + Zeliangrong* or *Haomei* (Zeliangrong Union, 1929, reprint 2009:7).

Again, on 15 October 1976, the special meeting of ZNU at Longmai (Noney), a village on National Highway 37, discussed the proposal for replacement of the nomenclature of *Zeliangrong* by what they claimed to be 'original' name—*Haomei/Hamei.* The proposal was rejected by many. Moreover, they could not find any other alternative name to cover these cognate tribes and hence, they retained the name, Zeliangrong. Again, on

26 February, 1985, ZNU at Chingmeirong unanimously passed a resolution to use Hamei *(Haomei)* as common name for the tribes: the *Zemei, Liangmei, Rongmei/Kabui, Puiron, Kourang, Maram* and the *Thangal* which were considered to be kindred tribes of the same origin. They also passed another resolution to bring out a common language for Zeliangrong based on the existing languages of its 'sub-groups'. The cognate tribes under Zeliangrong have their own languages. The meeting did not adopt any specific resolution towards these changes under discussion. In 1995, the Union Assembly held at Jalukie, a village in Nagaland, approved to change the name ZNU into Zeliangrong Union by omitting the word "Naga" from it, as proposed by a local organization called the Zeliangrong Hojam. To them, the use of "Naga" in association with the name of the tribe and the Union carries no meaning.

Apart from the flip-flop issues in the nomenclature of the organization, some critical problems arise as it does not cover some of the sub-groups of the 'tribe' in Zeliangrong. In 1959, the Puimei/Inpui group (of Manipur) made a formal complaint that the newly coined tribal nomenclature, Zeliangrong covered only the Zemei, Liangmei and the Rongmei. The Puimei/Inpui felt that they were left out. They demanded to include a syllable *Pui* from their tribe's name *Puimei/Inpui* in nomenclature and suggested the name should be the *Zeliangrong+pui.* Interestingly, the executive members of MZU appreciated the Puimei's argument; but they clarified that *Zeliangrong* was the name of the organization and the name of tribe is *Hamei/Haomei.* The committee decided to adopt name of the larger tribe as the *Hamei/Haomei* and the same name should also be the name of the organization in the next Annual General Meeting of the Union. For time being, the Puimei did not say anything against the Zeliangrong movement. In 1998, the Union Assembly at Namdailong, a village in Assam, again reaffirmed the earlier resolutions in the favour of *Hamei/Haomei* nomenclature. But the issue is still unresolved; debates are going on.

The Inpui/Puimei Case

The Inpui tribe has a population of 11,000 persons, mainly concentrated in 15 villages: 9 in Tamengrong and three each in Imphal and Senapati districts. They also live in Nagaland. In the past, several Inpui villages had totally assimilated into other neighbouring tribes. It is noteworthy that the Inpui tribe is constitutionally recognized along with the Kabui. It is ambiguous and controversial; moreover the tribe does not like to be recognized in such a way. Mr. Hibou Khumba, a key informant, said that, according to the legends and origin myth of the Inpui, the cave of Ramting Kabin from where the Inpui originated, was located in Makuilongdi near the present Oaklong village under Mao-Maram subdivision in the Senapati district, Manipur. The original men and women settled there for many generations. After many generations, their population increased and hence they migrated from their original settlement to other places.

Expressing the Inpui tribe is a separate tribe (neither a part of the Kabui or a cognate tribe of Zeliangrong), they formed an association under the banner of Inpui Group on 20 March, 2002. The Group later developed into the Inpui (Kabui) Naga Union, Manipur and Nagaland. They claimed that 'Inpuirwan' is the original name of their tribe. The names like Kowpoi, Kaupui, Koupooee, Kapui, Kabui, Puiron, Pooeeron, Puimei, Inpuimei, etc. are misnomers of the tribe, used by the British and others. Mr. Abungswan, a *lambu*, an administrative post, from Haochong village, migrated to Yurembam village, Imphal, was the first Inpui who got formally registered as the Kabui under the government of Manipur (Khumba, 2012). To the Inpuis, there is a fear of being dominated by the Rongmeis who are demographically superior to them in both social and cultural senses. This fear is the root cause of identity crisis among the Inpuis. The Inpuis thought that the Rongmei is different from the Kabui. They argued that the Sungbu is the original ethnonyme of the Rongmei. So they claim that Kabui is another name of the Inpui; they are different from the Rongmeis. A section of the tribes whom the Government of India recognizes as the Kabui subscribes this view. But, there is still confusion over the ethnic boundary of the Kabui. Sometimes the Kabui is used synonymously as the Rongmei. Sometimes the same name (the Kabui) is used only to mean the Inpui and plain dwellers of the tribe. The Inpuis however claim that the Inpuis are the real Kabui. The Rongmeis (here they mean both hill and plain) may dominate the Inpui as the former is far superior in demographic size, education, leadership; but they cannot deny our claim of being the real Kabui (Khumba, 2012).

The Inpui argue that the name Kabui is an Inpui word which means big house. Professor Gangmumei Kamei (2004), a renowned historian, however, denies this claim. He opines that the Kabui is an old name referred to in several historical literatures, literary texts and chronicles of Manipur. The claim that the Inpui was older than Kabui is simply baseless. The Inpui origin of the Kabui will put the Rongmei out of historical texts; this is a historical crime. He further explains that, in course of time, the societies within the tribes have changed in various ways.

Gradually, the Inpuis/Puimei began to move for a separate linguistic identity and finally, for their separate ethnic identity (Kamei, 2004:12).

Some believe the name Kabui is a Meitei word, used as early as the first century AD. The Meitei are the dominant group in the State. They formed the State in 33 AD according to their Royal Chronicles. The term Kabui or Kapui has been extensively used to mean the 'Rongmei' people in the chronicles of the Meiteis before the coming of British (Kamei, 2004:13). Therefore, Professor Kamei concludes that the claim that the Kabui was originated from the Inpui is a wrong proposition. He notes that the Inpui/Puimei consist of people of Liangmei and Rongmei origin who are ethnically common but speaking different languages (Kamei, 2004:15).

A different view on the Inpui is expressed, in an interview, by Mr. Makuningpu Kabui, General Scretary, *Kabui Samiti,* Manipur and D.L. Kabui, President, *Kabui Dharma Sabha*, Manipur. They said that Inpuis are the people who settled down in Manipur since long time back. They were probably recruited from somewhere in Burma by the then King of Manipur and helped in the military services of the then Kings of Manipur. They married with the Kabui women and lived in Manipur since then. They further said that, though there are similarities in culture, customs and traditions, they are linguistically more akin to Kuki-Chin groups. They are now concentrated in nine villages in Imphal, Senapati and Tamengrong districts of Manipur.

On 1 December, 1963, in the Naga Hills District before the statehood of Nagaland, the Kabui was recognized as a Scheduled Tribe. In Nagaland, the Zemei and the Liangmei were recognized as Scheduled Tribes. the Rongmei was not recognized as some of the Rongmei leaders refused to accept the name Kabui. They argued that it was a name given by the Meitei and British administrators. The controversy was centred on the origin and connotation of the name Kabui. Unlike the stand of Professor Gangmumei Kamei, some of them (Rongmei) even opined that the name Kabui should mean only the Inpui/Puimei. On the other hand, the leaders of the Inpuis say, the Puimei/Inpui claim is based on the fact that the word 'Kabui' is derived from 'Puimei'. Therefore, the Kabui should mean only the Inpui/Puimei. They demand to recognize their tribe as the Puimei or Inpui instead of the entry as the Kabui in Schedule List of Indian tribes.

The Inp ıis still recall the bitter experience on the day of formation of the Zeliangrong. They still think that the formation gave a serious blow to the identity of the smaller Inpui tribe. Their plead was not heard properly. Thereafter the Inpui tribe had to form a separate organization, later it turned to the Inpui Naga Union, Manipur and Nagaland. They separate from the Zelaingrong identity as well as from the Rongmeis or the Kabuis.

Rongmei-Kabui Cleavage

There was no Rongmei-Kabui divide in the early days. They were all Kabuis. During the colonial period, the hit and trial methods in British administration gave a brutal blow not only to the administration but also to the relationship between different sections of the people. The foreign hands made a everlasting confusion over the identity of the tribes.

As a part of their policies, the tribal people living in the hill areas were totally chastised with some economic incentives and western ways of life. The conversion to Christianity in the colonial setting thereby brought a serious division between the hill- and plain-people in general (Hindus in the plain and Christians in the hill areas) and Christian and non-Christian among the Kabuis. In the colonial times, western education through missionary works and charity started. They trained many people in different fields; some of them became evangelists. They worked tirelessly in spreading the Christian doctrines in different parts of the Manipur. The converted individuals had different perspectives and world views from those who were not.

The Kabuis living in the valleys were not ready to adopt Christianity. It might have been due to the limited activities of Christian missionaries in the valley areas under a British administrative policy. And they tried to maintain their own traditional belief system and ways of life.

The Kabuis living in the hill areas were readily Christianized. The first Christian church in the Kabui areas was established in 1914 at Keishamthong Kabui village, Imphal. Maipak alias Namrijinang and his wife were converted to Christianity in the same year. He was the first ever Christian convert among the Kabuis (see Kamei, 2004:284-285). Ironically, Christianity could not attract majority of the Kabuis living in the valley. The tireless efforts of Christian missionaries could convert many Kabuis/Rongmeis who inhabited the hill areas.

As a response to Christianity, there came up Heraka cult mostly in the hill areas under the leadership of Haipou Jadonang and Rani Gaidinliu, Kabui Dharma Sabha and Tingkao Ragwang Chapriak (TRC) in the valley areas.TRC came into being in 1994 and its first ever temple is at Chingmeirong, Imphal. It is named after the supreme God, Tingkao Ragwang (the Heavenly God, the Supreme God). They also believe in the existence of many gods and deities who are assigned by the heavenly

God to look after the different aspects of the world, nature and humans. They formed the State Level Gaan Ngai Celebration Committee, Manipur. Gaan Ngai is one of the major festivals of the Kabui/Rongmei. They celebrate it at the State Level every year. This is associated with their identity, they believe. There are TRC temple in Assam and Nagaland.

There is another level of identity crisis of this tribe. There are three schools of thought over their identity: Kabui is the name of the tribe; Rongmei is the real name and they are different tribes. Each school advocates various theories of origin, migration and cultural affinities. Mr. G. Makuga, retired, Nagaland Civil Services and writer, claimed that Gongphungring is the place of origin of the Rongmei Nagas according to the legends of their forefathers. It is located at Makuilongdi or Makhel near Oaklong under Mao-Maram subdivision. In the ancient past they live inside the earth and in course of time men emerge out of the earth through a hole of the cave called Ramting Kabin which is probably located at Gongphungring. He believed that the three kindred tribes of Zeliangrong, namely the Zemei, Liangmei and the Rongmei like other preceding Naga tribes such as the Ao, Angami, Sema, Lotha, Rengma, Tangkhul, Mao, and others perhaps might migrated from Burma and followed the advanced Naga tribes through Barail southerly route traversing through the impassable hill tracts along the Barak river in order to avoid the conflict with other advanced tribes. These three sub-tribes migrated almost at the same time, the Laingmei, one of three groups, followed the Angami tribe towards the north whereas the second group consisting the Zemei turned towards the north west hills and the third group, the Rongmei followed the first and the second up to the west hills tract of Manipur where the Rongmei Nagas made their home land and settled there permanently. But his narration has certain self-contradictory elements. He traced the place of origin to northern district of Manipur and at the same time, he claimed that the Rongmeis migrated from the south towards the west hills tract of Manipur making their homeland there without any chance to move further. He also claimed that the Kabui is derived from out of the Mpui or Apui.

Many pro-Rongmeis (those who prefer to use Rongmei over Kabui) think that the word 'Kabui' has a derogatory connotation. To them, the word sounds like word that signifies 'male sexual organ'. Another ground for their rejection is that the name is associated with 'a group of people' who were sweepers or of low level occupation in Imphal town area. It reminds them the low level occupation (Kamei, 2008:24-25, an interview with Mr. Makuningpu Kabui, General Secretary, Kabui Samiti on July 16, 2012).

On the other hand, Mr. Manthoi Thaimei (1995) argues that the name, Rongmei indicates geographical position. He says that '*Rong*' is 'south', '*-mei*' is 'man' and hence Rongmei means 'man of the south or southerners'. He cites examples that the tribe having the directional connotation. The name Rengmei (a tribe in Manipur) means 'man of the north or northerner'. From this, he likes to suggest that the name Rongmei was wishfully used as an honorific epithet and later became the name of the tribe. He further says that this group of people is not of recent origin. He also assumed that, in those remote past, this group of people, the Rongmei, was the only people originally living in these solitary hill ranges (presently in Tamenglong District of Manipur), and the other groups living in this part of Manipur came much later. He also said that the land where the Rengmei people were originally living in the ancient past was known as Renglam. This often referred to in the folk songs of the Rongmeis as "Apui Renglam," which means motherland of the northerner. It is a fact that the Rongmeis of the ancient days were migrating from north to the southern side, and as such they were the southern neighbours of the Rengmei people, the people of the north. He also talks about the Rongmeis' migration. A section of educated elites of this tribe demand for using Rongmei as tribe's name. They feel the word Kabui bears some derogatory meanings.

There are also a number of theories regarding the origin of the name Kabui. To them the word has no derogatory meaning. One of the theories argues that it is derived from the word Kambuimei. The word is still used in the rite of *Nashan Kanmei* and whenever the village elders give blessings to the family they use the word—"Tu Kambui Jang Kambuimei Subamlatho" (literal meaning, "Be plentiful in life with abundant and ever inexhaustible wealth"). So the name Kabui is derived from the term Kambuimei (prosperity).

In an interview with Mr. Chandrasingh Haomei, an advisour of the Zeliangrong Union and a free lance researcher, he said that there were 7777 households at Makui Longdi, a mythical place. The people there were known as Haomei/Hamei. From there, a section of group of people were moved to the valley in search of their lost mithun but settled down there. In Liangmei dialect, mithun is called *Kabui*. The word is derived from *Kabui louwamei* or *Kabui Luimei* (literal meaning, the followers of the foot print of the mithun). The word *Kabui* itself is the shorten form of Kabui Louwamei or Kabui Luimei.

In due course of time, they migrated towards the south. The people believe that they originally came out of a cave called Mahou-*Taobei*, situated at Ramting-Kabim, a mythical place. The place is mythically placed somewhere on the north-western direction of the Senapati district of Manipur. They came out of the cave due to scarcity of food, in search of a wider place (Kamei, 2004; Thaimei, 1995). They even reached Ningthi (present Shalangthen, in Churachandpur District, Manipur).

The idea of Kabui derivation from *Kabui louwamei* or *Kabui Luimei* is refuted by Mr. D.L. Kabui, President, Kabui Dharma Sabha in an interview. He says that, in Liangmei language, the mithun is known as *Buichang*; *Kabui* is buffalo. The mithuns live in the high hills, not in the swampy areas. He thus argued that the Kabui cosmogony and place of origin should be traced from the south, not from the north. According to him, Rason or *Kapu-Kana Bam* (*Kapu* means father, *Kana* means son and *Bam* means place) is the place of origin which is located at Laimatonching, a place in the northern part of Churachandpur district. It is the place from where seven brothers of Ragong migrated to different directions.

According to him, it is not necessary to look into the origin of the word/term. One should look at how old the term is used over the ages. He points out use of the word Kabui in various forms Kabui Maimu, Kabui Salang Maiba, Kabui Tomba, Kabui Lamsang and Kabuiru, mentioned in historical texts like *Cheitharol Kumpapa, Poireiton Khunthok* and historical epics of the Moirang. He said the Kabuis believe that Kabui Salang Maiba was the seventh and last incarnation of the Ragang, the mythical hero. The Kabuis and different ethnic groups of Manipur observe 2012 as year of Kabui Salang Maiba remembering his contribution to the growth of Manipur in general and the Kabui tribe in particular. Mr. D.L. Kabui also argued that it was customary that the Kabuis had to dwell the place where the Palace of the King of Manipur would be constructed. The places such as Mahabali, Ramjikhul, Langthabal in Imphal and Thaninkhul in Bishnupur district are the living examples. In these places, the Kings of Manipur constructed their palaces.

Mr. G. Makuga (1995) goes a little beyond the present debate over the Kabui-Rongmei; he said the two names represent different tribes. The Rongmei and the Kabui are not identical. They are different tribes. He said that the confusion was made by the British official reports. The British authorities entered the presumptive name of tribes residing in the hill tract between Cachar and Manipur valley on their first entry into Manipur without proper enquiry from village to village and without minute study of the villages. In spite of the similarities and affinities between the Kabui and the Rongmei, these two tribes are different. The Kabui and the

Rongmei have their independent languages, customs, arts and culture. The Kabui used to call the Rongmeis as the Rongbangsang (literal meaning, very clumsy and ignorant people).

Way out: Common Identity or Different Identities

There are differences of opinions and conflicting views among the leaders of the tribe over the question of the Inpuis in Zeliangrong, over the question of name of the tribe Rongmei or Kabui. Because of these differences the villages are well segregated with one or other identity. One can ask question if these differences and conflicts are mainly generated by their religious and political affiliations. From the fact that the name Kabui is preferred mainly by a section of the tribe inhabiting in the valley areas, while the name Rongmei is preferred by the section of the same tribe living in the hill areas. Majority of the valley section who prefer Kabui as the name of the tribe, are non-Christian. They follow their traditional religion. Majority of the hill section are Christian. The Naga secessionist movement that see Christianity as a common thread of the Naga societies and its open call for "Nagalim for Christ" sharpen the dividing line between the Kabui-preference and the Rongmei-preference. Another important fact is that there are three or four Assembly segments where the hill section of this ethnic group predominate the areas. These segments are reserved seats for the Scheduled Tribes. Therefore, there are three or four MLAs in the State Assembly elected from these segments. As they always prefer the Rongmei over the Kabui, they have all possible means for lobbying State government. Though the valley section of the tribe are numerous, their villages are scattered in different Assembly segments. There is least chance of electing a Kabui-preferred MLA in the Assembly. Due to various factors, the internal division of the tribe over their identity becomes widened along the hill-valley divide.

The independent assertions of the cognate tribes of the Zeliangrong and theoretical crisis among the members of this larger identity recalls each of them their separate identities on the basis of religion, customs, tradition, language and geographical variations. The effort of Zeliangrong Naga Union to gain recognition of the Zeliangrong as the name of the tribe did not meet any success. This adds more confusion in the Kabui-Rongmei debate.

In addition to the internal debate, recently Indian Parliament has *amended the Constitution (Scheduled Tribes) Order,* 1950 *to modify the list of Scheduled Tribes in the States of Manipur and Arunachal Pradesh* under the provisions of Constitution (Scheduled Tribes) Order (Amendment) Act, 2011. Earlier, there are 33 communities appearing in the list of the Schedule Tribes in Manipur. The new Amendment Act inserts new tribes in the list. They are the Inpui, the Rongmei, the Liangmai, the Zeme, the Thangal and the Mate. The new Scheduled tribe status for the Rongmei brings exaltation to pro-Rongmeis and anti-Kabuis. However, many persons feel that the insertion of the Rongmei as independent tribe is arbitrary in nature. This does not solve the crisis between the Kabui and the Rongmei over the nomenclature of their tribe. The Kabui is already in the list of Scheduled Tribes; the new insertion of the Rongmei is not in place of the Kabui. Therefore, the two names become two ethnic entities at least in the Constitution of India. It had been done without proper examination of the debate by the Indian Parliament.

After the Rongmei is also included in the Scheduled List of Indian tribes, the debate over the name of the ethnic group comes up again. The debate seems turns towards ugly scene as there is no visible sign of reconciliation. On 7 July, 2012, an interaction programme was organized at Sangaiprou, a Kabui village, Imphal West to have a free talk on the nomenclature of the tribe. There are still four lines of thought and their arguments:

1. The Kabui should be retained as it has been used for long.
2. The Rongmei should replace the Kabui.
3. A new name should be used such as Hao Makammei.
4. Asserting Zelianrong as a tribe would solve the problem.

REFERENCES

Kamei, Gangmumei, (2004), *A History of the Zeliangrong Nagas: From Makhel to Rani Gaidinliu,* Spectrum Publications, Delhi.

Kamei, Gangmumei *et al.*, (2008), *Souvenir: Majorkhul Day Diamond Jublee*, Souvenir Commitee, Imphal.

Khumba, K. Alung (ed.), (2012), *The Inpui Nagas: Traditional Culture and Christianity*, Kendriya Vidyalaya, Guwahati.

Makuga, G., (1994), *Introduction to the Rongmei Nagas*, Imphal.

Thaimei, Mngthoi, (1995), in Naorem Sanajaoba (ed.), *Manipur: Past and Present Vol. III,* Mittal Publications, New Delhi.

Zelianrong Union (2009), *The Constitution of the Zeliangrong Union*, Imphal pp. 3-9.

23

Understanding Maan Social Formation: A Note on a Lesser Known Tribe of Meghalaya

Sarit K. Chaudhuri

The Maan[1], a little known Scheduled Tribe of Meghalaya is residing in West Garo Hills with around 1000 individuals who are scattered in six villages under Selsela Block[2]. In Assamese, the word 'Maan' means 'Burmese migrant' and the people of this community also believe that they belong to this category (Barua,1994: 133).This district as a whole is bounded on the north and west by the district of Goalpara of Assam, on the east by the West Khasi Hills district of Meghalaya and on the south by the Mymensing district of Bangladesh. In fact, Meghalaya is a predominantly tribal state and the Khasi, the Jaintia and the Garo constitute the dominant tribes who are known for their matrilineal heritage. As per the *People of India Survey* (1994: xi) the state is having altogether 25 communities out of which 15 are Scheduled Tribes and others are non-tribal communities (Pakem, Roy and Basu,1994).

It may be noteworthy to mention here that Selsela Block as a whole is identified as a backward block and all the six villages, where Maans are living, are also considered as backward villages as per official record of the Government of Meghalaya. The names of these villages are Haldibari, Sankarpara, Rajangola, Deldela, Bongal Khata and Shyam Nagar. All these villages can be divided into two clusters viz. A and B. Then first three villages can be placed under Cluster A where remaining three villages can be placed under Cluster B. These Clusters A and B work as two separate corporate functional units though they are linked together by a central authority which in turn helps to maintain the wider ethnic social solidarity.

In terms of road communication within Cluster A, it may be mentioned that Haldibari is a road side village, whereas Sankarpara and Rajangola both are placed about more than a kilometre away from Haldibari bus stand without any pucca road. During rainy season villagers of Haldibari have to come at Haldibari market or bus stand by small boats as it is situated in a low land area surrounded by a small rivulet. All these three villages are multi-ethnic in nature and comprise of the Maan, the Koch and the Garos whereas the villages, viz. Bongal Khata and Shyam Nagar are roadside village. But Deldela is comparatively an interior village as it is situated about 4 kilometres away from the Chibinang bus stop and connected by an earthen road. As per administrative category the village Deldela comes under Ronkhula village which is again multi ethnic like Shyamnagar and Bongal Khata. But in Ronkhula the Maan and the Rabhas live separately and the habitational area of the Maans is locally recognized as Deldela village (Chaudhuri, 2003:217).

The present study is based on the fieldwork done in all these villages for about two and half months starting from January to March in the year 1995. In order to understand the Maan social formation whole work is divided in to certain subheading to share basic ethnographic information along with the historicity of the tribe to relocate their position with reference to time and space.

Historical Background

If we look at the history of Assam then we shall be able to trace that Purnananda Buragohain and Bodan Chandra Borphukan, the two kings of Assam, faught with each other due to some of their internal problems. During that time Badan Chandra tried to get help from the Maan King of Burma in order to win that battle. That made a scope for the Maan soldiers to enter into Assam for the first time in the history of Assam in response to his request. Following that, for another two successive periods they invaded Assam. During their invasion they entered in Goalpara, then Silhet and Chittagong. Though this route later they tried to invade areas under the control of the then Britishers and proceeded towards Cachar where they were confronted with British soldiers in 1824. But unfortunately the Maan soldiers were severely defeated and consequently fled away in different areas. In 1825 Assam where their main concentration was present, came under the Britishers. The then chiefs of the Maan soldiers, Champhukan and Bagali Phukan send one Buddhist monk as a middleman to the British Cornel for a treaty. That treaty finally took place and accordingly the Maans were agreed to leave Assam and back to their homeland in Burma. But the Britishers with the help of some of those Maan soldiers who took shelter under the British, captured Lusai, Naga and Garo Hills. Naturally British administrators were pleased with their efficiency and gladly rehabilitated those Maan soldiers in Masakpara, situated at the border of Goalpara and Garo Hills. From that area in later phase some of the Maan migrated to Bongal Khata and Ronkhula (Deldela) village. In 1895 some of those areas were given to them by the then British administrator without any tax (*Nakrach*). But it is a well known fact that they did not agree to take that area without giving any tax as it went beyond the spirit of great warriors. However, the Britishers requested the Maans to help them in their convenient ways. Today the Maans of Meghalaya is the descendants of those Burmese soldiers (Maan, 1969:3)[3].

The most significant and striking phenomena is that none of their female counterpart came along with them. Naturally those soldiers as well as their progenies who ultimately settled down in the Garo Hills after relinquishing their duty as hired soldiers, took their wives from different neighbouring communities, viz. the Rabha, the Koch, the Garo, the Hajong, the Kachari and various Assamese caste groups in order to maintain their family life which in turn helped for the formation of the Maan ethnic identity.

Language

Due to extensive intermixture with the neighbouring communities they lost their original Burmese language. Now they speak among themselves with a mixed language of Assamese and Bengalese with greater inclination towards the former one. But this also varies among the villagers of Clusters A and B due to influences of neighbouring communities. A few Maans who have wider exposures in relation to the business or services, especially those who are better educated, can even speak English and Hindi. Naturally their language differs whenever they interact with different groups of people. They have completely forgotten their original Maan script (Burmese script) and have taken up Assamese scripts for day-to-day communication. But most of them proudly refer two important kinship terminologies, viz. *Amei* and *Aphou* by which they call their mother and father respectively. Undoubtedly these two terms are Burmese in origin and transcended from their forefathers (*ibid.*)

Barua (1994) mentioned that after the formation of Meghalaya in 1972, the Maan and the other Hinduised communities like the Rabha, the Hajong, the Koch and the Rajbanshis had become minorities in the state which directly or indirectly grew a sense of insecurity and feeling of discrimination against them by the numerically dominant Christian tribe like the Garo, the Khasi and the Jaintia.

Naturally, the Maan along with their neighbouring communities like the Hajong, the Koch and the Rabha had formed a composite group rallying around certain common features[4].

Aspects of Social Structure

On the broader social perspective the Maan do not carry a sense of superiority or inferiority in relation to their neighbouring communities. Though they have certain marriage restriction with these communities but at the same time their society has made a provision to accept those community members in case of affinal relationship by converting their religion to Buddhism. They do not have any inter community restriction regarding marriage with any Buddhist community. But as a whole they expressed reservation about the marriage with Muslim boys or girls though they have close economic interactions with them. This might be of recent origin as the case of ceremonial kinship with the aged Muslim member is evident among the Maan of Deldela village which symbolizes a closer social interaction in the past. Perhaps, such emerging feeling among the Maan against a community is linked with their antipathy about the dominant Muslim population who have taken a major control over the agricultural land and production process in the bordering areas of the Garo hills.

The very socio-economic condition of this small tribe provides counter frame of popular traditional notion about the tribe as an egalitarian formation. Heterogeneous historical processes which had ultimately led to the Maan social formation may help us to have an idea how this society has acculturated various cultural traits from composite cultural groups and ultimately formed very complex social code of conduct which is pivoted around the Buddhist religious tradition.

Village Economy

If we take a look to their economic systems then we will be able to find out that inequality is very much reflected and accordingly their life styles are also varying. In each studied village there are a few families who are evident to be economically well placed in comparison to the rest of their population. Undoubtedly their whole economic structure is pivoted round the agriculture. Basically they are settled agriculturist though some of them started shifting to some other occupational avenues, viz. business, government services, school teacher etc. Educational status of the Maan is not encouraging at all. But those who are educated, are eagerly looking for alternative occupational opportunities as they are very much aware of the various constraints which have affected their agrarian system badly. In fact, except a few families, most of the Maan families do not have any cultivable land which paved the way for the formation of two broad classes, viz. land-holding and landless classes. But these too broad classes do not present the complex agrarian network which the system contains. There are so many intermediary classes with overlapping multiplicity of class characters. All shorts of agrarian categories, viz. tenants, share cropper, absentee landlord, agricultural labourer etc. are very much inbuilt. Sometimes a marginal farmer or a rich farmer simultaneously playing multiple roles, and this is not a typical feature of the Maan economy rather may be considered as symbolizing local agrarian structure.

It is a well known fact in the locality that long back, since the formation of Haldibari village, the Maans were very much land owning community. But how and why such a land holding community gradually being marginalized that needs to be looked at from historicity of the people and the place.

As we know that the Maan is a Buddhist community and such religious affiliation generated a spatial linkage with the other Buddhist communities of North-Eastern India, especially who are located in Upper Assam and Arunachal Pradesh. As a result of that some of them used to visit these places and in turn some Buddhist monks also came to reside in their *Buddha Vihar* in order to preach Buddhism among them. As a result of such close interactionsome how an idea or rumour was floated among the Maan villagers that in some parts of Arunachal and Upper Assam cultivable lands were very easily available in a very low price. And it had so pervasive effect that many Maan families sold their land in Haldibari area and then they proceeded towards Arunachal[5] and Upper Assam. But finally they became very much frustrated seeing that cultivable lands are not easily available, and more over those lands are not very much suitable for cultivation. However, somehow they tried for few months to settle there. Then finding no alternative way a large number of families came back to their homeland but in the process became landless labourers. Some of the Maans tried to strive by settling there and marrying members of various Buddhist communities. A few Maans were also died in course of such migration. Some of the Maans also sold their cultivable land as those lands turned into wasteland due to the excessive presence of sand of small tributaries flowing adjacent to their cultivable lands.

Since long the Maan have a very close interaction with the Bengali Muslims through Rajabala weekly market which is considered as one of the biggest as well as oldest in that area. They used to sell their surplus production to the Muslims of Rajabala. Naturally, in case of any urgency or to meet the expenses of marriage or their significant rituals, economically poor Maan villagers used to take loan from them. Those who were unable to pay back the same with interest, had to transfer their cultivable land to them. During that time transfer to tribal land to non-tribal people was not prohibited. A section of the Maans who were landholders but not hardworking at all, had also sold their land to their neighbouring communities and earned instant money to run their families. Almost similar incidents were reported from Deldela village. However, in Haldibari area, most of the land were transferred to the Muslims of Rajabala and Silkata areas. Through these processes land alienation had taken place and agrarian stratification gradually emerged among the Maan in terms of the possession of cultivable lands.

In general land is individually owned though in Deldela area they are having common grazing ground which is given for the villagers of Ronkhula as a whole where both the Maan and the Rabha people inhabit. Traditionally landed properties are transferred from father to son. But some of the Maan families have started giving their daughters a portion of such valuable agrarian resource.

Such economic stratification certainly has an effect on the techno-operational aspects of the agricultural production. Because the members of the upper economic section can utilize their resources in best possible ways which in turn help to make their economic base more stable. However, none of them tried to introduce improved agricultural inputs to make the overall situation much healthier. Of course, those who have substantial areas of land are also trying to produce another crop (*ravi*) in a year. But due to the lack of artificial irrigational facilities their effort did not provide desirable outcome.

Three types of agricultural labourers are available, such as, (i) Agricultural daily labourers who are locally called as *Kamla* though also include day labourers who are in great demand during agricultural season. (ii) *Masra Chakar* means contract labourers for the whole agricultural season. Generally, this category includes male Maan members who work under their own community members or even under the affluent neighbouring communities. During agricultural season they stay in the house of owners and getting 250 to 300 rupees per month along with food and shelter[6]. Generally female members are not taken for such contract. (iii) *Bacharia Chakar* which means labourer employed for yearly contract. Usually, quite well off land owning Maans are keeping such male or female labourers. They have to work during agricultural season at the same time they also assist in other domestic works for which some munds of paddy they earn yearly as per the nature of contract he or she has with his or her employer.

Economic stratification also reflects in terms of the various social rituals. For example, previously *Boro Bia* was a status symbol and highly prestigious marriage forms. In contemporary period *Chotobia* has also emerged as a status symbol. But this variety of marriage also is hardly practiced as love marriage (*mangala*), the most popular and most usual form of marriage among the upcoming young generation. Though community has a negative sanction as per their written social norms but undoubtedly it is one of the most practiced forms of marriage in that locality across the communities.

Village Polity

It is observed that there is a close interrelation between the economy and power structure. In fact, political powers are in control by those Maans who have the economic potentialities. Like many other tribes of Meghalaya, the Maan have their own traditional political organization for the management of their villages. It can be mentioned here that in case of Cluster A that means Haldibari, Rajangola and Sankarpara, they have a common headman, popularly called *Gaon Bura*, who is generally assisted by other elder male members of the village. In order to assist such headman they have a provision of *Dakra* (a messenger) for the whole village who gets some remuneration from the villagers as a whole. Though the post of village headman is not hereditary at all but some sort of kinship bond are traced from the list of previous village headmen. This again shows some sort of relationship between the power structure and kinship bondage. In case of a selection of a new village headman his knowledge, age, experience, social acceptability and economic ability are also taken into consideration. Females are so far not allowed to interfere in their traditional polity structure. However, new authoritative structure in the form of Village Council and District Council are very much effective. In fact this emerging power structure has reduced the importance of a *Gaonbura* to a great extent though this is still helpful for the maintenance of intercommunity solidarity. It may be noteworthy to mention here that they have codified laws which bind each and every village within the wider Maan social organization and help to maintain the community solidarity. Here comes the question of religious functionaries who also take active part in relation to the codification of code of conduct during the annual general Buddhist conference where the Maans of all six villages meet together and discuss various problems and prospects of their society as a whole.

For existing composite nature of community distribution which includes the Garos and migrant Bengali Hindus and Muslims, a non-statutory village council was formed to look after the common interest as mentioned earlier. Such council consists of a president, a secretary and several other members. Naturally each of the community has a chance to send a representative in the village council. Generally their (Maan) village headman is always incorporated within such structure of village council.

Religious Beliefs and Practices

Religion plays a central role towards the formation of the Maan ethnic identity. Instead of high intermixture this religious thread still holds the key of their social solidarity. As we know that at present they are Buddhist by religion and belong to Hinayana sect of Buddhism. Of course, if we trace the history of their religion then we will be able to find out that it is true that a section of the Maan took shelter under the then Britishers and settled in West Garo Hills. Then they started marrying different communities in order to form a Maan society. During those days they were not Buddhist and used to worship local Gods and Goddesses and had a habit of drinking and dancing with necessary musical instruments. They had their own religion specialist also, viz. *Deosi* (Priest) and *Thangdhara* (assistant of the Priest). In course of time some of the Buddhist monks from Burma came to know about their existence in West Garo Hills. Then at first Urimala and later Unandra and Uchandra, all Buddhist monks, came from Burma and revived Buddhism among the Maan by establishing *Vihar* (Buddhist temple) for each Maan village. At present one *Vihar* is jointly shared by the Maan of Haldibari, Rajangola and Sankarpara. But for remaining three villages, all of them are having such monastery.

So far the religious functionaries are concerned for each temple they have one *Changdeka/Sang Deka* and one *Pathek*. *Changdeka* is responsible for the maintenance of *Vihar* and day-to-day activities, viz.

lighting candles to Lord Buddha. It is his responsibility to make proper arrangement for the *Bhante* or *Sraman* (both are Buddhist monks–but first one is higher in rank) whenever they will come to visit or stay in connection with various Buddhist rituals and also as per the invitation of the villagers. The *Pathek* is considered as the Buddhist village priest higher in status than the *Changdeka*. In the absence of the *Bhante* or *Sraman* or others higher Buddhist monks, he has to perform all necessary rituals as per Buddhist tradition. These posts of the *Changdeka* and the *Pathek* are not hereditary in nature. These posts are considered as very sacred and specially the *Pathek* must have to follow the *Panchashil* or five principles of Buddhism (abstain from drinking wine and luxurious way of life, abstain from killing animals for consumption and ritual purposes, righteous thought and righteous deeds). After the death of such religious functionaries it is the responsibility of the villagers including village headman to find out a person to take the responsibility of such sacred rites and duties in relation to the philosophy of Buddhism. Similarly, the *Bhante* or *Sraman* are not hereditary positions, they attain sainthood or *Vikshooship* by having training in Buddhist philosophy through Pali or Sanskrit language by staying in *Buddha Vihara* for a considerable period. Their duty is to give religious teaching to the people as well as to participate in various rituals as mentioned earlier. Most of the *Bhante*s are staying in the *Buddha Vihar* of Upper Assam, Arunachal and Shillong. Majority of such sacred specialists belong to the Khamti, the Singpho and the Assamese communities. Some of the monks have also emerged from the Maan tribe and most of them stay in the *Buddha Vihar* of Upper Assam. Generally these Maan monks take leading role in various festivals as well as ritual performances. Earlier they had a good contact with the Buddhist monks of Burma but with the drawing of political boundary with Burma that contact is lost completely.

Consolidation of Ethnic Identity

An objective understanding to the contemporary social situation of this lesser known tribe reveals that initiation of Buddhism didn't dissolve much of their socio-economic problems rather it has created some contested domains. But it has inculcated a certain cultural values which helped in maintenance of their ethnic boundary. It is evident that in spite of negative sanction to the tribe exogamy frequency of such marriage is quite significant which are explained in terms of poor economy, week population strength; close inter-community linkages etc. (Chaudhuri,

2002:137). Acceptance to Buddhism is the prime frame of negotiation which has created space with in the Maan social formation. Multiple case studies can be sited to supplement such stand.

Conclusions

The whole discourse reveals how historicity and culture as a process of negotiation helped in the social formation of the Maan tribe of Meghalaya. Their demographic scenario and more specifically, nature of their agrarian economy, educational status etc., help us to understand the predicament of a lesser known tribe in an advance tribal state of North East India. Obviously, like many other smaller communities or tribes, the Maans have hardly got any meaningful attention from the state even after reorganization which is run by their dominant tribal brethren. Inequality is not only the part of the Maan social formation but it also remained at the core of wider socio-political systems promoted by state machinery where their voices are hardly reached or in other words, their extreme weak numerical strength hardly matters in the politics of 'vote bank' which usually channels state sponsored developmental initiatives.

NOTES

1. The name of the tribe is spelled as 'Maan' in some writings including three of my project reports and one publication (Chaudhuri, 2003). However, looking at the pronunciation and the way community write it as their surname I thought it is more appropriate to use 'Maan' which I have used in this paper and in my another publication related to the identity issue of this tribe (Chaudhuri, 2002).
2. We don't get any Census figure reflecting the actual Maan population. Barua (1994:133) referred to this population figure which he collected from District Council authority. However, during my fieldwork I had carried out complete enumeration of six Maan villages though so far I didn't try to bring out the actual population structure. However, it was definitely closer to the figure given above and currently it must have increased much further.
3. This is a ten-page document written by Debendra Lal Maan of Bongalkata village in Assamese who was a member of *Assam Sahitya Sabha*. This booklet incorporated minutes of the meeting held on 6th May of 1969 in the Buddhist monastery located at Deldela village where the manuscript was red out and approved by the villagers under the leadership of Maniram Maan. One copy was given to me during my fieldwork in 1995 among this community.

4. All of them are dependent on agriculture with poor numerical strength and sharing habitat in relation to the Garos who are the dominant tribe largely dependent on the shifting hill cultivation. As mentioned earlier that the Maaṅ are having affinal ties with these Hinduaised communities provided they accept Buddhism.
5. Recently Omak Daring, anthropologist as well as reseracher of Arunachal Institute of Tribal Studies, Rajib Gandhi University who went for doing fieldwork among the Adi Samoa of Lohit district, came to know about the presence of some Maan population in those areas.
6. This labour charge must have been changed within twelve years time span as this study is done in 1995.

REFERENCES

Barua, S. (1994), *Maan, in People of India : Meghalaya* , eds. Pakem, B.; S.Roy and A. Basu, Seagull Books, Calcutta, pp.133-139.

Chaudhuri, S.K. (2003), The Anthropology of lesser Known tribes, *The Anthropology of North East India: A text book*, eds., T.B. Subba and G.C. Ghosh, Orient Longman, New Delhi.

Chaudhuri, S.K. (2003), The Maans of Garo Hills: A Study on Change, *Transition, Change and Transformation: Impacting the Tribes of India*, (eds) J. Sarkar and J. Chakraborty, Anthropological Survey of India. Kolkata, pp. 216-227.

Maan, D. (1969), *Maan of Garo Hills* (in Assamese), People of Maan Community, Dhubri.

Pakem, B.; S. Roy and A.Basu (1994), *People of India : Meghalaya*, Vol. xxxii, Seagull Books, Calcutta.

24

A Sociological Study of Urban Neighbourhood in Shillong City

Surojit Sen Gupta

Urbanization is the process of becoming urban, moving to cities, changing from agriculture to other pursuits common to cities, such as trade, manufacturing, industry and management and corresponding changes of behaviour patterns. It is the process of expansion in the entire system of inter-relationships by which a population maintains itself in its habitat (Hawley, 1981). An increase in the size of towns and cities leading to the growth of urban population, is the most significant dimension of urbanization.

The term urban is used demographically and sociologically. In the demographic sense, it emphasis on the size and density of the population, and nature of work of the majority of the adult males. Sociologically, it focuses on heterogeneity, impersonality, interdependence and the quality of life. Tonnies (1957) differentiated between *gemeinschaft* (rural) and *gesellschaft* (urban) communities in terms of social relationships and values. The former is one in which social bonds are based on close personalities of kinship and friendship and the emphasis is on tradition and informality, while in the latter, impersonal and secondary relationships predominate and the interaction of people is formal, contractual and dependent on the special function or service they perform.

Sociologists do not attach much importance to the size of population in the city because the minimum population standards vary greatly. A city is an administratively defined unit of territory containing "a relatively large, dense and permanent settlement of socially heterogeneous individuals" (Wirth, 1938). Urban refers to a set of specialized, non-agricultural activities that are characteristic of, but not exclusive to city dwellers. A ruling class with a capacity for taxation and capital accumulation and writing and its application to predictive sciences, artistic expression, and trade for vital materials are the kinds of specialized activities necessary to the definition of the emergence of a truly urban place. George Simmel, (1950) has also stressed on dense living conditions, rapidity of changes and impersonal interaction in urban settings. Anderson (1953) holds that urbanization involves not only movement of population to cities but also change in the migrant's attitudes, beliefs, values and behaviour patterns.

Urbanization as a structural process of change is generally related to industrialization but it is not always the results of industrialization. Urbanization results due to the concentration of large-scale and small-scale industrial and commercial, financial and administrative set-up in the cities; technological development in transport and communication, cultural and recreational activities. According to M.S.A. Rao (1970), urbanization is a complex multifaceted process comprising ideological, cultural, historical, demographic, comparative, traditional and sociological elements. To him, urbanization is a two-way process and occurs along different axes—administrative, political, commercial, religious and educational—giving rise to several types of urbanism. These different axes give rise to different types of contact which the city has with the villagers leading to distinct patterns of urbanization.

Urbanization implies a cultural and social psychological process whereby people acquire the material and non-material culture, including behavioural patterns, forms of organization, and ideas that originated in, or are distinctive of the city. Urbanization may be made more precise and meaningful when interpreted as aspects of diffusion and acculturation. Urbanization may manifest either as intra-society or inter-society diffusion, that is, urban culture may spread to various parts of the same society or it may cross cultural or national boundaries and spread to other societies. It involves both borrowing and lending.

Defining the Concept of Neighbourhood

A neighbourhood is usually thought of more in geographical terms as a distinct part of a town or city, which may be distinct by virtue of certain boundaries and marked out from other neighbourhoods by a certain homogeneity of housing within the area. As a corollary of the similarity of housing, there can be expected a certain homogeneity of social class within the given neighbourhood. The geographical, or physical elements and the social ones do not always go together.

The Advanced Learner's Oxford Dictionary (1974-1982) defines neighbourhood as people living in a district; area near the place. According to compact Oxford Dictionary and Thesaurus, 'neighbourhood is a district within a town or city'.

Neighbourhood is generally used as a smaller version of the local community. It has been conceived in two distinct ways: (i) It has been defined as simply a locality and the people living in it, and (ii) it has been seen as a social fact, a type of group and it is common in most cultures to think of spatial collections of units of some importance and the belief that spatial collectivity leads to social interaction and the development of shared values and action pattern is also widespread.

A neighbourhood is a territory, a small area within larger settlement. It contains dwellings occupied by people, and usually has community facilities and buildings for other uses. The residents come into contact with one another and interact. They are neighbours on the basis of propinquity, that is, nearness, regardless of any other social ties. A neighbourhood is both a physical place and a social community. In sum, a neighborhood is a limited territory within a larger urban area where people inhabit dwellings and interact socially.

One of the very influential and popular schools of thought in urban sociology was the Ecological or Chicago school in the first half of the 20th century. Scholars like Park and Burgess, with the ecological orientation differentiated between localities within a city. These "neighbourhoods" or " natural areas" (Park, 1929, 1952) had particular affinities or aversions to one another resulting overall in an urban ecology-a spatial division of the city, that corresponds to the functional division of labour occurring within it. The examples of these areas were the central business district, exclusive residential areas, areas of heavy or light industry, slums, ghettos, immigrant communities (Flanagan, 1999).

According to Tuan Yi-Fi (1974), 'Neighbourhood' and 'Community' denote concepts popular with planners and social workers. They provide a framework for organizing the complex human ecology of a city into manageable sub-areas; they are also social ideals feeding on the belief that the health of society depends on the frequency of neighbourly acts and the sense of communal membership.

Thus unlike traditional neighbourhood which denotes localities with ethnic enclaves or settlements of families with identical values, ideals and lifestyles, there are the places where relationships between neighbours are close, direct and intimate as opposed to the cosmopolitan heterogeneous urban settlements.

The National Commission on neighbourhoods struggled with definition and finally concluded (1979) with the following observation – that, each neighbourhood is what the inhabitants make of it. The only genuinely accurate delineation of neighbourhood is done by the people who live there, work there, retire there, and take pride in themselves as well as their community. Albert Hunter (1974) refers to such areas defined by residents as "Symbolic Communities". He describes them as social objects with two main elements; cognition and sentiment. The cognitive element is displayed when residents give a name to their neighbourhood and define, at least in their own minds, particular boundaries. Sentiments reflect their attachment to the neighbourhood and their evaluation of its quality.

Roger S. Ahlbrandt, Jr. and James V. Cunningham (1979) have taken a functional approach. The urban neighbourhood, as it has unfolded, has come to take on many functions. These include the neighbourhood as a community, as a market, as a service area, as a provider of shelter, as an arena for improving quality of life, as a political force and as an actual or potential level of government. M. Leanne Lachman and Anthony Downs (1978) have emphasized shared participation and view points among which are: (a) use of the same space as a focal point for personal interaction; (b) a common relationship with nearby institution, such as church or school; (c) a real estate entity; (d) a political entity; and (e) an instrument for exclusion. Neighbourhoods are geographic units within which certain social relationships exist although the intensity of these relationships and their importance in the lives of individuals vary tremendously.

Urban Neighbourhood

According to Carpenter (1933), the neighbourhood is to be found in towns and cities especially in residential areas which are not over-densely populated and which possess a population for the most part homogeneous and exhibiting a low rate of mobility. The characteristic processes of urbanism are, however, hostile to the preservation of neighbourhood life in that they promote a high degree of population density, a low rate of permanency, of residence and considerable heterogeneity of population.

Ruth Glass (1948) have given two alternative definitions of neighbourhood. In the first definition she defines neighbourhood as 'a distinct territorial group, distinct by virtue of the specific physical characteristics of the area and the specific social characteristics of its inhabitants'. Glass's second definition on neighborhood is less clearly objective when neighbourhood is described as 'a territorial group, the members of which meet on common ground within their own area for primary social activities and for organized and spontaneous social contacts'.

Both Ross (1938) and Reimer (1952) suggest that the neighbourhood is a place of retreat from the total urban life; it is a place where the individual can relax, with as little strain as possible, with people of his own sort. This means that he expects to find rest in the neighbourhood from the varied social contacts of city life, and their attendant social adjustments, in a social area where he can expect the people around him to think and act as he himself does.

City of Shillong

Shillong the capital of Meghalaya, is situated at an altitude of 1561 metre above the mean sea level. On its west and south lies the Bangladesh plain, to the east the Barak valley and to the north valley of the Brahmaputra (Assam plain). Shillong is situated in the East Khasi Hills District and is linked by National Highway No. 40 with the state capital of Assam at a distance of 103 km. In the past there were a few clusters of scattered hamlets under the jurisdiction of the Syiem of Mylliem. In 1866, Shillong became the Provisional headquarters of the Khasi and Jaintia Hill districts. Again in 1874, Shillong was made the capital of the Assam Province. Between 1905 and 1912 Shillong was turned into summer capital of newly created province of Eastern Bengal and Assam. Since, then Shillong had remained the capital of Assam. However, in 1972 Meghalaya attained its full statehood and Shilling became the capital of the state.

During the past few decades or so the city has undergone a radical transformation from a hill resort to a multifunctional service centre, catering to a host of administrative and other service functions not only for the state but for the entire North East Region. From a small village in 1866 to a Class-I city today, the city has grown to cater the needs of the state as an enclave of modernization in the midst of the rural-tribal hinterland that continues without any significant change. Thus, urbanization is spreading rapidly in Shillong and its population is becoming more cosmopolitan in nature which is not only affecting the social condition but also the economic life style of the people. Due to its varied functions and high rate of urbanization the population of Shillong city has increased at a rapid pace. This has resulted to the development of new settlements under urban areas.

Methodology

The universe of the study is Laban locality in Shillong city and the study is based on the empirical survey of the respondents in the locality. The unit of observation is the family and the respondents were the adult members of the household. Through the use of random sampling method 87 households were selected for the present study. A random sampling was drawn from the universe in such a way that every unit in the universe has equal probability.

Historically Laban is one of the oldest locality of the Shillong city. It has its own importance as one of the oldest residential area in the greater Shillong. In the olden times, Laban was the name referred to by the villager as the city of Shillong. Laban is included in the Municipal Ward No. 24 (Laban West) and 25 (Laban East). Since the area is old, Laban locality is now becoming congested with ills of the city life like the water crices, garbage problems, and housing problems to mention some. The number of basic amenities such as electricity and goods accessibility etc, also vary greatly between one residential area and the other at Laban. The residential area at Laban are considered as a mixed residential area which includes both low class and high class residential areas. The degree of congestion or number of houses at Laban per unit also indicates the category of the residential type, like congested as well as spaciously built areas. Thus, the residential segregation can be easily identified on the basis of general conditions such as exterior look, building materials, age of the house etc.

Laban, being a municipal area, people of diverse ethnic backgrounds prefer to reside at Laban. Moreover, the basic social character and ethnic composition of Laban remains the same that is mixed ethnic locality.

Neighbourhood, for purpose of this study has been defined as a small community usually a colony or ward, characterized by a limited area, common sharing of certain services and amenities and sufficient physical proximity to develop face to face relationship. In this background, the study of urban neighbourhood at Laban which is located in the core area of Shillong city will focus on the socio-economic and cultural conditions of the city in particular and society in general.

Result and Discussion

The several components which make up the personal background of the respondents in the present study comprise of age, marital status, type of family and economic standing on personal and family level. Thus, there is an attempt to focus on the background of the respondents through component associations.

We have classified our respondents according to age groups and assume that their views are bound to be influenced by their age. The respondents have been divided into four age groups. Out of the total 87 respondents the majority of the respondents 43, which accounts for 49.42 per cent, fall in the age group between (51-60). This was followed by 26 respondents, that is 29.88 per cent, fall in the age group (41-50). Respondents who have reported that their age is above 61, have their percentage is 12.64. And only 8.04 per cent that is 7 respondents falls in the age group of (30-40). Therefore, on the basis of the data on the age structure of the respondents it was found that majority of them come from the age group between (51-60). Regarding the sex composition of the respondents, male constitute (63) 72.41 per cent and female (24) 27.58 per cent out of 87 respondents.

The marital status of the sample studied constituted that out of 87 respondents, majority of them were married (83.90%). There were only 5.74 per cent respondents who were unmarried and similarly 8.04 per cent and 2.29 per cent respectively were divorcees and separated.

Regarding the religious background of the respondents it was seen that majority of the respondents are Christians that is 42.52 per cent. These includes Catholics, Presbyterians Baptist and other denominations as well. Followers of various forms of Hinduism constituted 27.58 per cent. This was followed by the Muslims 12.64 per cent. Respondents who follow the traditional religion of the Khasis, i.e. *Seng Khasi* accounts for 8.04 per cent, 3.44 per cent was Buddhist and a small segment of the percentage that is 5.74 constituted the followers of religion like Sikhism and Jainism.

In this study of urban neighbourhood we tried to uncover from our respondents, about their place of birth. To this 82.75 per cent of the respondents were born in the state of Meghalaya and 17.24 per cent reported that they were born in states other than Meghalaya. In response to the information about whether their place of birth was rural or urban, it was found that majority of them were born in urban areas (89.65%) and the rest (10.34%) of them were born in rural areas. We also enquired whether the respondents were permanent settlers of the Laban locality of Shillong and found that as much as 75.86 per cent had been the permanent residents of the locality. Respondents among the non-permanent residents of this locality accounted for 24.13 per cent.

Family is the bridge between an individual and the community. It acts as the communicator of social expectations and norms, mediator of individual and collective interests and regulator of persons in the context of group relations. Keeping this view, the respondents of the present study were asked to provide information about their types of family. And to this response it was found that, majority of the respondents belong to the nuclear family (83.90%) and only (16.9%) belong to the joint family. Data in relation to respondents' present occupation reveals that majority had reported to be in business and Government services (43.67% and 36.78%) respectively. While 13.79 per cent of the respondents occupation were in teaching professions, only 5.74 per cent of respondents fall under any other profession which include doctors, engineers, advocates, pastors etc. This analysis clearly shows that the respondents of this study came from the white collar class where they had an occupational status.

The ethnic background of the respondents plays an important factor in the present study of urban neighbourhood of a cosmopolitan city of North East, i.e. Shillong. A considerable number of them were the Khasis (35.63%). Next to them were the Bengalis (29.88%). The Hindustanis (17.24%) and the Assamese (5.74%) were relatively less in numbers. Among the others (11.49%) the Nepalis, Oriyas, Manipuris, Garualies, Tamils and others were counted.

Every locality has a special importance where people reside. It was interesting to know what were the unique facilities available to the respondents in their neighbourhood, which were not found elsewhere. To this, 44.82 per cent of the respondents reported that they had good neighbourhood. Safety and security by 20.68 per cent and sufficient water facility by 18.39 per cent were reported to be other categories of responses. 13.79 per cent of the respondents informed of a pollution free zone and only 2.29 per cent indicated nearness to the market. Thus, good neighbourhood, safety, security etc. played a major role and people had their choice for selection of their residence. We also enquired from the respondents about their attachment to the neighbourhood, where they reside. All of them responded that the neighbourhood they reside were their choicest place to live in.

Similarly, it was interesting to know from the respondents whether they were aware of their neighbours. And it was found that all the respondents were aware of their neighbours and they informally always visited to the neighbour's house. We were also interested to know from our respondents whether any barriers like occupational status, community affiliation etc. did come in between neighbourhood interaction. In response to this 87.35 per cent of the respondents said that they did not have such problem and only 12.64 per cent reported that to some extent they maintained the distance with their neighbours.

Our further enquiry from the respondents was that whether language became any barrier for communication among the neighbours. To this query 91.95 per cent of the respondents answered that they did not face any such communication problem, whereas only 8.04 per cent did face some problem with language while communicating with their neighbours. At the same time all the respondents reported that in neighbourhood most of the time they use a common *lingua-franca* i.e., broken Hindi and English while interacting with their neighbours.

To understand the relationship of the different ethnic groups in the neighbourhood, we enquired from the respondents to identify their close circle of friends. To this query, most of the respondents mentioned about their intimate friends, most of whom did not belong to their own community. For example, the Bengali respondents reported that their intimate friends were the Khasi, Nepali and the Garwali. We further enquired from our respondents to mention at least 3 names of the families from their neighbourhood with whom they had most intimate relations. The answer received was that the respondents' intimate relation in the neighbourhood was of mixed group. For instance, a Khasi respondent said that his most intimate neighbours were the Bengalis, Manipuris, Nepalis and others. Thus from this study it is evident that there is no social segregation in the neighbourhood.

We were also interested to know from our respondents that in case any problem came to the neighbourhood, how they faced it. The answer received was that all the neighbours came together to solve the problem, as it was a matter of the neighbourhood. Enquiring about celebrating any function in the neighbourhood, the response received was that in case, such celebration was done, all the neighbours came forward with great excitement.

Our interest was also to know, whether there was any kind of women council that existed in the neighbourhood. The response for this was that, formally there was no such council, but informally the women in the neighbourhood had a very close interaction and understanding, and if anything untoward happened the whole neighbourhood came forward and the entire women stood united against that. Then again 72.36 per cent of the respondents stated that women in the neighbourhood did share at time articles/commodities among themselves.

We also sought to explore from this study that whether all the neighbours did come together when any cleaning drive activity took place in their neighbourhood. In the analysis of data, it was found that 100.00 per cent of the respondents were of the view that, they all used to join hands together in the cleaning drive as it was a common matter for their neighboruhood.

With a view to understand the views of the respondents on religions of other social groups in their neighbourhood, we enquired about their opinion. It is evident that 94.25 per cent were respectful to other religions. During religious festivities organized by different communities in the neighbourhood 80-00 per cent of the respondents admitted that they were invited to participate.

Conclusion

From the above, we draw the lesson that the neighbourhood under study in the city of Shillong, indicated the symptoms of mixed social experience found in urban centres elsewhere. Inter-ethnic relationships within the neighbourhood generally appears to be harmonious not only in the economic field, but also in a social context. Various ethnic groups in the neighbourhood are almost equally important and apparently there is nothing to indicate sectorisation or polarization of different ethnic communities in the neighbourhood. Thus, today residents of a neighbourhood might not attach territorial markers to identify as closely as they would attach other kinds of markers, for instance, certain kinds of music, participation in particular kinds of activities etc. Moreover, there is simultaneous emergence of multiple identities or switching from one maker to another. The geographical unit of space is not the solitary determinant of identity, lifestyle and ties. Today, it is hard to find traditional neighbourhoods in terms of architectural form and style and the traditional neighbourhoods in modern cities poses a number of questions. In our study, we have observed that like any other urban centres in the neighbourhood there is intimate ties. But this does not mean that all neighbours share direct and intimate relations, neither does this suggest that intimate relationships can be sustained by territorial boundaries alone. At the same time, there is enough evidence to suggest that neighbourhood in urban areas are not only geographical or administrative units but represents certain specific life styles with melting pot, where people from several cultures come and converge to become one urban mass with distinct culture.

REFERENCES

Ahlbrandt, R.S. Jr. and Cunningham, J.V., (1979), *A New Public Policy for Neighbourhood Preservation*, Prager, New York.

Anderson, Nels, (1959), *The Urban Community: A World Perspective*, Routlege and Kegan Paul, London.

Carpenter, N., (1933), *Encyclopedia of the Social Sciences*, New York.

Flanagan W.G., (1999), *Urban Sociology: Images and Structure*, Allan and Bacon, Boston.

Glass, Ruth, (1948), *The Social Background of a Plan*, London.

Hawley, A.H., (1981), *Urban Society: An Ecological Approach*, The Ronald Press, New York.

Hunter, A., (1974), *"Symbolic Communities" The Persistence of Change in Chicago Communities*, University of Chicago Press, Chicago.

Lachman, and Downs, A., (1978), The Role of Neighbourhoods in Mature Metropolis in C.L. Leven (ed), *The Mature Metropolis*, Lexingtion, M.A. Lexington, Book.

National Commission on Neighbourhood, (1979), *Neighbourhood, People, Building, Neighbourhoods*, (with a two volume appendix), Government Printing Office, Washington.

Park, Robert E., (1952), *The City for Human Ecology*: II, The Free Press, New York.

Rao, M.S.A., (1970), *Urbanization and Social Change: A Study of Rural Community on a Metropolitan Fringe*, Orient Longman, New Delhi.

Reimer, S., (1952), *The Modern City*, New York.

Ross, E.A., (1938), *Principles of Sociology*, New York.

Simmel, G., (1950), *The Metropolic and Mental Life*, Free Press, New York.

Toennies, F., (1987), *Community and Society*, New York : Harpercollins.

Tuan Yi-Fi, (1982), American Cities: Symbolism, Imagery and Perception, in Bourne Larry S., (1982), *Internal Structure of the City Readings on Urban Form, Growth, and Policy*, OUP, New York Oxford.

Wirth, L., (1938), 'Urbanism as a way of Life', *American Journal of Sociology* XLIV.

25
The Ao Nagas

J.J. Roy Burman

The Ao Naga is one of the sixteen major tribes inhabiting Nagaland – one of the states of Northeast India. According to a traditional story, the Aos sprang up from 'Longtrok', which means six stones. In the famous Ao folk-tale, 'Longkongla', a hornbill feather turns into a stone, the stone into a bamboo vessel and later into a baby boy—the first Ao Naga. (internet). The Aos are believed to have migrated from Mongolia through South-east Asia to Nagaland.

The etymology of the word Ao, according to local traditions means, 'those who went away'. As per legends the people who left Chungliyimti village and crossed the river Dikhu and settled elsewhere, were designated as 'Aor' or Ao by the people who stayed back. The people who stayed back are—the Sangtam, Chang, Phom and the Konyak—commonly called 'Mirir'. The Aos belong to the Mongoloid race and speak a language which belongs to Tibeto-Burman language group.

The Aos claim that there was a written script which was inscribed on the skin of an animal and hung on a wall. But one day when the humans were away in the field, a dog pulled it down and ate it up. From that day it is believed that all information about the Aos was limited to memory and was communicated from one generation to another through the word of mouth. The real home of the Ao Naga tribe is the catchments of the five ranges in Mokochung District of Nagaland lying between the river Dikhu on the east and the plains of Assam on the west.

The territory comprising Mokochung district covers an area of 1,615 sq. km. It is bound by Wokha district in the south west, Zunheboto district in the south east, Tuensang district in the east, Mon district in the north-east and Assam in the west. There are 102 Ao villages under Mokokchung district (Longkumer, 2009). The Ao area is demarcated into six administrative zones.

Among all the Naga tribes, the Aos were the most privileged ones and advanced ones since the British reached and colonised them first. Along with the colonisers the Christian missionaries embarked upon the Ao Nagas and spread western education and medicinal practices. The Aos registered all their joy and sorrows of their living through their folk songs, tales and ballads. These reflect their enjoyment of life and are preserved in their oral tradition as the Aos did not have any written literature. Whatever written literature is available in Ao, it mirrors the cultural values inscribed in the oral tradition handed down from one generation to the other based on memory and knowledge of a few learned elders and oral narrators.

The Ao Nagas did not exist it total exclusion as is often assumed. Though head hunting practice was common among them between villages, the Aos did cross the village for small time trading. Iron and shell beads were procured from outside. Salt too was procured from outside. They did go even to the small markets in Assam for purchases. During the Ahom-Kachari contest over supremacy over Assam, the Ahoms approached the Nagas including the Aos to assist them in defending the Kachari. The Ahom kings recruited the Nagas into their regiments who fought against the Kacharis. The Ahom king too took refuge in the hills to hide from the enemy. In gratitude the Ahom king gave not only valuable presents but also granted arable plots of land called *Khels* and fishing rights over waters known as *Bhils* on the understanding that the Nagas would resist from any predatory attacks on the plains. These lands were called Naga-Khat and were managed by Assamese agents known as *the Naga-Kotoki*.

The Aos came under the British rule by about the middle of nineteenth century after coming into contact with the Christian missionaries. Though the British used some amount of might to subdue the Aos, they allowed some amount of autonomy into the day-to-day affairs of the village. But the appointment of the *Dobhashis* (Interpreters) and *Gaonburas* (Headmen) in the villages affected the administration considerably. These posts were mainly meant for facilitating the administration to maintain the law and order and for collection of house taxes. The traditional village government still acts as a tribunal for adjudication of petty cases, and the district administration intervened only in cases which the village authority could not settle at their level of administration.

The Aos enjoy the Constitutional provisions which have been marked for the state of Nagaland as a whole. Under the Constitution of India, provisions for safeguarding social and religious practices, customary justice and landed property of the Nagas are included in Article 371A (1). This Article provides for safeguarding the religious, social, customary laws and procedure, administration of civil and criminal justice involving decisions according to the Naga customary laws with regard to transfer of land and its resources.

Prior to the British rule, the Ao Nagas like other Naga tribes had head-hunting practices. They dearly defended their territories and did not tolerate any outside intrusion into their village. Due to this their villages used to be located on summits of hills, on a high saddle, or more frequently on the ridge of some spur running down from a high ridge. Longkumer (2009) writes that a typical Ao Naga village is characterized by (i) multi-clan population, (ii) a Village Council, (iii) the age-set grades and (iv) the *khels.*

Settlement Pattern

The Ao Naga villages are usually of nuclear type as all the houses are huddled together. The villages are kept very neat and clean. Their women folk work hard to keep tidy the homesteads and the adjoining areas. The hamlets of the village or the *Khels* are built according to clan affiliations. Each *Khel* is usually uni-clan based. The houses are built along the streets. In most of the cases the household size varies between 3-5. But proportion of single or two member households is very high. This trend is to be seen more in the recent years as many of the households have moved out to cities and left behind their old folks to fend for themselves.

Most of the Ao houses in the villages are of *kutcha* type with the walls and the floor being built of bamboo mattings. The roofs are thatched with grass. But now a days many of the houses are of wooden frame and wall with tin roofs. Many concrete houses too are gradually coming up as people are becoming affluent. Usually each house has a small balcony in front and a hall in the centre. In the centre of the hall usually the fire is lighted for cooking and keeping the house warm. On the top of the central fire a wooden frame is hung to dry the firewood and smoking the meat and seeds. On the backside of the hall a platform is placed to wash clothes and dry vegetables and seeds. On the side of the hall a small balcony is built to store water and firewood.

The household granaries, usually a one roomed structure, is

constructed a little away from the settlement to save it from accidental fire. Presently some of the households are also constructing *pucca* graneries next to their homesteads.

In the olden days when head hunting was in practice, the Aos used to have a bachelor's dormitory or *Areju* located next to the village entry gate. Next to the *areju* a long war drum used to be placed. These days the *areju* is rarely to be found. In place of the bachelor's dormitory they have youth clubs.

Previously the Aos were not very careful about their sanitation and used to have toilets on bamboo or wooden platforms for the pigs to clean off the excreta. These days pit toilets with sceptic tanks have become popular.

Most of the villages have now electricity. No wonder many households have refrigerator, TV, dish antenna, cable connections and DVD players. People do listen to news and watch movies at home. People also get to read news papers published in Dimapur and Mokokchung. One newspaper in Ao language is published in Mokokchung.

Each village has at least one church as everybody has been converted to Christianity. Similarly, every clan in the village has at least one graveyard to themselves. At least one sports field and a library is usually to be found in every Ao village. Community halls are also commonly to be found.

Longevity among the Aos is very high as death rate veers around 14. Old men and women aged 80-90 years are a common sight in Ao villages. Almost 30 per cent of the Ao population in any Ao Naga village is above 50 years of age.

Food Habit

The Ao Nagas have strictly non-vegetarian food habit. They relish pork, beef, chicken, fish or any game they hunt in the forest. They hunt deer, monkeys, rabbits, wild boars, rats and different kinds of birds. The Aos also are fond of wild fruits, vegetables, mushroom and bamboo shoots collected from the forests. Rice is their staple diet. They consume maize as well. Previously they used to drink a lot of rice beer, but due to the influence of Christianity they have now given it up. However, many of them are found to drink foreign liquor brewed in India.

The Nagas—both male and female, were very fond of smoking tobacco. Some of the Aos use small bamboo pipes or metal pipes to smoke. Many raised their own tobacco in the fields. The women in the present times, however, do not smoke that much. Even the men have largely given up the habit. Occasionally they sip nicotine water (Smith, 1925). In the very recent times, some of the youth have been reported to become drug addicts.

Dress and Ornaments

In the olden days the Aos used to be very scantily dressed. The men would wear only a loin cloth attached to a string in the waist. The women too used to wear a wrapper hung from the waist without covering their breasts. After Christianization and coming into contact with outsiders, the men mostly wear pant and shirt. Many of them wear shorts when at home or even in the markets. They are mostly smartly dressed when attending the church services. The young men are mostly seen in jeans and T-shirts. Women are found to wear wrappers from the waist and blouse to cover their body.

The old men and women both used to wear a lot of ornaments like bead and brass or silver necklaces. They also used to pierce their earlobes for putting on rings. These days though the women continue to wear necklaces, men have given up wearing them. Until recently tattoo marks were very common among the Aos, particularly the women as they were used as a symbol of marriage (Singh: 1994).

Economy

The main economy among the Ao Nagas is agriculture. Majority of the people practise *jhum* or swidden cultivation. They fell the trees at selected patches of forests in the month of December-January and let them dry for about three months. Towards the end of March or beginning of April they burn the wood and spread the ashes equally on the soil for fertilization. Immediately after that they sow seeds of many types of vegetables and maize. After some time they sow the seeds of paddy. In August the weeding in the fields take place. The paddy is harvested in September and threshing of the crops takes place subsequently. All the activities involve very simple instruments or equipments. Hoe and dibble sticks are commonly used as no ploughing is involved.

In the present days wet rice cultivation in terraced fields have become quite popular. Many people do both jhuming and wet rice cultivation. Many of the Aos who have moved out, practise paddy cultivation on terraces by hiring labour. Exchange of labour system too is quite popular.

Usually neighbours in the *Khels* form groups to enter into exchange system. Many old people who cannot cultivate by themselves, too take advantage of this system.

Share cropping is practiced sometimes as many people have moved out of their villages or do not have adequate manpower at home, particularly in old age. Sharing can be done on the basis of 50:50 ratio or 30:70 ratio of the crops harvested. The latter system is locally called *Thikka* and the owner of the land stipulates his share of 30 per cent of his share prior to the cultivation and whatever amount may be grown – even if there is a crop failure due to inclement weather.

Because of the government incentives and Bank subsidies and loans many Aos are now practising horticulture. Cash crops, vegetables and fruits are usually raised through horticulture. The horticultural fields are usually placed a bit out of the village settlements. Many Nagas engage non-tribal plainsmen and the Nepalese to raise paddy and work in the horticulture fields.

Many Ao Nagas are also employed in many services. Many of them serve as school teachers, fourth grade and third grade employees. Many of them have even become senior government servants. Many of them are working in far off cities like Dimapur, Guwahati and Delhi. Government service is very much coveted and people also adopt any means to get a government job.

Though the Aos have virtually given up regular hunting and gathering practices, many people are reported to go hunting in the forests with guns. They are fond of sporting deer, wild boars and monkeys. Traps are laid to trap small games like porcupine, rabbit and mouse. Different kinds of birds too are shot down. Collective fishing is yet very common. The Aos of Chanki village go down to the Assam border and in association with the Assamese villagers they do collective fishing. The catch is commonly shared among both the groups.

Most of the Ao women have kitchen gardens a little away from the village settlement. Usually cash crops and vegetables are raised in the gardens and often sold in the market. Crops such as tapioca, are raised for making fodder to be fed to the pigs. Animal husbandry too is common in the villages. Many of the households raise pigs. While earlier the pigs were largely kept open, these days are found to be reared in pens. The pigs are fed with fodder grown in the kitchen gardens and also collected from the forests. Fowls too are raised by most of the households. They are mostly raised in the open.

Basket weaving also provides supplementary income to the Aos, particularly to the elderly people and poor households. The people fetch the bamboos from the nearby forests to weave the baskets. They sell these usually within the village. Some time they also sell these in the town markets as well.

The Naga shawls have become quite popular even outside the state of Nagaland and are sold in the markets of Guwahati, Shillong etc. The Ao Naga shawls are particularly very colourful and finely designed. The shawls have become popular in cities like Delhi as well. No wonder, earlier the Ao women used to weave these in leisure, today these are being produced commercially for the market.

In some of the Ao villages firewood is being collected commercially and sold in the towns such as Mokokchung and even to others in the villages. The wood is brought to the roadside and transported in mini trucks to the destination. Sometimes the wood is collected from the forests privately owned, and the owner is paid 50 per cent of the price. Some of the Aos sell broom sticks also for an income. Pottery is another means to supplement the income. But pottery is done in a very few Ao villages.

Of late the Aos have taken to commercial cultivation of vegetables and fruits for selling outside. Oranges are grown in large quantity along with pineapple. Aloevera a medicinal plant too is raised commercially and marketed outside the state, mainly to the pharmaceutical companies.

Social Structure

Kinship and Marriage

The Aos practise the principle of unilineal descent. They are a patrilineal tribe with exogamous clans. All the male members of a clan refer to each other as *pacha* and female members as *pachalari.* The founding clan of the village is called *Tanik.* Clan exogamy is strictly maintained and any violation results in severe punishment. It is mainly through clan membership that an individual's social standing is established in society. In the kinship terminology the terms used to address the various relations are based on clan membership. A man's agnates are all regarded as father, brother and son depending on their age. The mother's brother too plays a crucial role during ceremonies and moments of crisis. They can intervene in matters of marriage, funeral, divorce and inheritance, should there be any dispute.

The clan membership is very important with regard to ownership of land and political association. The founding clan usually has control over majority of the land holdings in the village and the traditional leadership also hinges on the matter of clan antecedence. The founding clan members usually enjoy greater advantage over the rest.

The hierarchical order of the clans is governed by the migration of the clans in the village. The occupation of land for cultivation and settlement as well as reserved forests distinguishes the founding clan from the clan who settled in the village later. The later migrating clans are often found to attach themselves to the founding clan but their origins are never forgotten. The oral tradition has ensured that the love and history of the people are preserved and handed down. The founding clans have certain rights and privileges and even each man is regarded as equal to the other; the concept of *Emkumri* (or the founding clan) has certain prestige attached. The system of governance established by the first settling clan has to be accepted by the later migrants. However, the migrant clan members can take part equally in executing the established norms.

The founding clans usually have more lands—jhum, paddy, horticultural and forests in the vicinity of the settlements and the latecomers have to obtain permission for making use of them. This ensued into a kind of patron-client relationship.

Should any clan member migrate outside he forfeits all claim over the clan lands. Though he can sell his private land, he can do so only to one of his clan members. In this way land never gets fragmented. In the present time some of the forest lands are declared protected and even clan members cannot make use of them without permission of the Village Council or Village Government.

Gerontocracy is quite strongly evident among the Ao Nagas. Special respect has to be shown towards the clan elders. In ceremonies best portion of the meat is given to the oldest member. In funeral ceremonies the clan elder has to deliver an eulogy at first.

Most of the Ao people are divided into two moieties—Chungli and Mongsen. Each of the moieties has its own dialect and customary laws. Among the Mongsen speaking villages, the village government is called *Samen Menchen* (Literally meaning meat-sharing rule) and among the Chungli speaking villages, the village government is called *Putu Menden* (Literally meaning—generation rule). The tenure of these two types of local traditional government is not fixed as each village follows its own system of rules. The local village government based on age-set system is called *Yanga Menchen* (Age-set rule) and the tenure is fixed.

Chungli is the dominant language as around 60 per cent of the AO Naga speak it. Chungli is usually used in the church services and therefore, even the Mongsen speaking Ao can speak and understand Chungli. Mongsen is spoken more usually in the western part of the Ao territory. Changki is another linguistic group among the Aos but it is confined to just three villages. Strictly speaking, the literary work between the Ao and other Naga peoples was initiated only after the advent of the Christian missionaries from America in 1872. The spread of the gospel among the Naga peoples encouraged the writing of the hitherto unwritten languages. The missionaries who served these peoples, developed script systems for most of the Naga languages. It was Edward Winter Clark who settled in the Ao territory in 1876 and turned the Ao language into a written form through Roman script. His efforts fructified better after the translation of the Bible into Ao language.

Marriage

Clan exogamy is strictly adhered to. But marriage between certain specific clans too is prohibited as they are considered to be closely related. Traditionally the Aos had a very elaborate wedding ceremony, but these days a simple western type Christian wedding system is followed. Marriage is finalised with a formal engagement. The wedding takes place in the church. But still now the groom's parents and maternal uncle settles the marriage by making some presentation to the bride's parents. It is the groom's family which bears most of the marriage expenditure. During the wedding clan members of both sides meet each other and get introduced. Here the clan history is told and importance of the alliance between the two groups through marriage is emphasized. Monogamy is the usual practice but sororate is seen sometimes with the demise of the wife at an early age.

Neolocal rule of residence after marriage is preferred among the Aos. Within a short time after marriage the groom usually builds a new house for himself close his parents house. If no land is available, a new site is chosen within the father's village.

Divorce

Divorce is not very common among the Aos. Fidelity and lifelong partnership between the married couples is very much cherished. In rare cases of difference between the couples the clan members of both sides try to resolve them. In case a divorce becomes inevitable , the landed property remains with the husband and other property is shared. After divorce, usually the sons remain with the father and the daughters go with the mother.

Inheritance

Usually among the Aos the eldest son inherits all property. But among some of the clans the youngest son inherits the parent's house and the eldest son gets the agricultural plots. The eldest son then distributes the property among all the brothers. If there are no sons, the ancestral property will go to the next brother and his eldest son will inherit the property and so on. The inherited land by the eldest son cannot be sold off. Among some clans the agricultural implements, household things, paddy and so on are shared equally among the brothers.

If any woman has amassed wealth during her lifetime, the property can be shared equally among her sons after her death. But in some cases the clan makes a claim on her property. The pigs and proceeds of the kitchen garden usually belongs to the woman. The immovable property like beads necklace, ornaments etc. are inherited by the daughters.

Status of Women

The Ao women enjoy a fair amount of liberty along with men. The household decisions are usually taken by women. But women cannot inherit any landed property. Although they take part equally in the community festivals, they are not permitted to seat equally with men in the Village Council meetings and play any role in the decision making process of the village as a whole. But presently within the church women have their own welfare committees.

Longkumer (2009) observes, "The women do all the household works and also agricultural works. They are the main workers in the agricultural sector. Except for ploughing they do all the works in the field. The girl child is given education but sons are preferred. While sons may be taught in private mission schools the daughters are educated in government schools. Even if a girl does well and finds a good job, her social status is enhanced only when she gets married."

Political Organization

The Ao Naga villages, in addition to clans, have an elaborate system of age-grade and age set which play a crucial role in village governance. In this system, one need not be a member of the founding clan to assume power. In this type of village government the grades move up progressively every three years or so and the councillors are drawn up from the age set (*Yanga semen*) system directly, when they reach the traditionally prescribed age set grade that automatically ensures entry into the village government.

In the age-grade system all the boys who have reached the age of sixteen or so enter the *yanga*. For three years they will remain in the same age-grade and it is considered to be the recruitment period. After three years they will progressively move up to the next age-grade and this will continue till the last grade is reached. The members of each grade remain the same throughout. As each grade moves up, their responsibilities and duties towards the village administration increases as well as the hierarchical power.

Though the Aos participate in the running of the State in good numbers and S.C. Jamir was Chief Minister of Nagaland for a long time. Some AOs had joined the Naga militancy. Some Aos had also joined the armed militancy. But now the situation has cooled down and only some distraught youth not doing very well in studies, are in the underground government of the Nagas. The underground still wields influence and power to affect the over ground politics.

Customary Laws

The Aos inhabiting the villages by and large operate according to the customary laws laid down through the oral traditions. Seldom do they approach the courts provided by the State. Normally the disputes are resolved by the Village Councils.

The *Gaon Bura* post that was introduced by the British yet continues in running the village administration. The *Gaon Buras* were appointed by the British as an intermediary between the State and the people. They collected house taxes on behalf of the State and mitigated the local disputes. These days the *Gaon Buras* function as clan representatives. Men with qualities and oratory skills are selected as the *Gaon Buras*. The Gaon Buras are usually retired army personnel, teachers and government employees. They are permanent members of the traditional Village Council or *Semen Menchen*. Each village may have 10-12 *Gaon Buras* depending on the number of clans and *Khels* in the village.

Village Council

A Village Council consists of members chosen by the villagers in accordance with the prevailing customary practices and usages, the same being approved by the State government, provided that hereditary village chiefs, the *Gaon Buras* and the *Angs* are *ex-officio* members of such council and that they have voting rights. Any Indian person more than 25 years old can be elected as a member of the Village Council. The tenure of the Village Council is for five years. It can be extended by one year through gazette notification of the State Government. Wide ranging functions and powers are conferred upon the Village Council for developmental works as well as the administration of justice which are backed with the provisions for adequate resources with which they conduct their work. Thus a traditional institution has been retained for modern statecraft as long as they are applicable and deemed appropriate. The decisions of the Village Council are arrived at through long open debates. There is active participation of the villagers in such meetings.

Village Development Board

Through the initiative of the State Government since 1980s every village in Nagaland has been provided with a Village Development Board (VDB) for taking up developmental activities at the grassroot level. Such Board is to be seen at every Ao Naga village as well. The VDBs operate under the aegis of the Village Council. The developmental funds of the Central Government are channelized by the State Government through the VDB. The Board comprises at least two female members. Also 25 per cent of the funds are earmarked for the development of the women. The developmental funds are sent annually and almost the entire work is executed by the community. The funds are shared equally or kept in the village account. The District Commissioner (DC) is the chairman of all the VDBs. Every VDB has a bank account in which the DC and the VDB secretary are joint signatories. The VDBs have a Matching Grant scheme whereby a Fixed Deposit is maintained by the village community and this fund is used during emergencies.

Longkumer (*op. cit.*) observes, "It is seen that the modern state machinery is incorporated into the administration of the village using the age-old traditional power structure based on customary laws concerning civil and criminal justice as long as they are applicable and deemed appropriate. The modern system has been adapted and interwoven into the traditional village political framework without disturbing or doing away with the customary and traditional ways of village governance. The developmental programmes and allocation of funds, resources and implementation of such activities are done through the Village Councils and VDB."

Education

The Ao Nagas are a highly educated society. This tribe was first among other Naga tribes to have adopted western education. The literacy rate among them is more than 84 per cent according to the 2001 Census.

Care for education is very high among all the Naga tribes and so is it for the Aos. Almost every child is sent to school. The number of graduates too is quite high among them. Many villages boast of post-graduate men and women as well. Apart from the government, the Christian missionaries too help them in attaining education. Almost every *Khel* has a primary school and a library. There is virtually no Ao village without a high school. Many villages and *Khels* in them have Students Union as well. They are affiliated to the *Ao Kaketshir Mungdag* (Ao Students Conference). The Ao Students Union at the village level are also tied up with the students union at the Hill Range level. The Student Unions organize sports and games during the winter holidays. They also conduct cultural meets and competitions among different villages.

Apart from the Students Unions the villages have various youth clubs. The clubs organize variety shows, particularly during Christmas time. They too organize cultural meets and picnics.

Religion

Prior to the advent of British rule and coming of the Christian missionaries, the Aos had a religion of their own which was close to animism. Belief in supernatural beings, forces and spirits was very common among them. They were very superstitious as well. They used to hunt heads of other villagers for augmenting their manliness. They used to sacrifice many animals during the rituals and ceremonies. But after embracing Christianity they gave up all these habits, and now they worship and pray in the churches like the western people do. Due to this, the Aos lost many of their folk songs, music, dances and folklores. However, the Aos still have retained some of their festivals attached to the agricultural cycle.

Tsumgeng Mo, the harvest festival celebrated in August is their main festival. *Ungma* is the ancestral village of the Ao Nagas where it is celebrated most vigorously. Hundreds of Aos from Tuensang and Zunheboto districts assemble to celebrate *Tsungrengmo* or the festival of blessing. It is a thanks giving ceremony, named after the person who initiated it. Before the festivities begin, the village gates, known as *Sungkum* are closed and entry or exit is restricted and regulated for the day. The natives wear traditional colourful attire, sing songs and perform their ritual dances to express their gratitude to god for giving a high yield. The festival also provides opportunities for the younger generations to display their skills and physical strength.

REFERENCES

Longkumer, J. (2009), *Change and Continuity in Tribal Villages: A Sociological Study*, New Delhi: Akansha Publishing House.

Singh, K.S. (1994), *The Scheduled Tribes*, New Delhi: Oxford University Press.

Smith, W.C. (1925), *The Ao Naga Tribe of Assam*, London: Macmillan & Co.

26

The Riang of Tripura: An Ethnographic Profile

Goutam Kumar Bera

The tribal population of India has been living, since centuries together, in different ecological conditions and is found in all parts of the country. The present chapter attempts to make an overview of the Riang society, in a particular geographical area, to generate information in the light of ecology, habitat, demography, language, economy, social system, religion, politics, acculturation, the processes of change and so on in terms of the dimensions of time and space.

II

Tripura, a small hilly state, having an area of 10,486 sq. km[1], is situated in the north-eastern sector of India[2]. The state bears an extreme length of 183.5 km. and extreme breadth of 112.7 kms. During the erstwhile colonial rule the area was known as Hill Tipperah. Bounded by the Cachar district of Assam and the Mizo Hills of Mizoram in the eastern side, by Comilla and a part of Noakhali districts of Bangladesh in the western side, by the districts of Chittagong and a part of Noakhali in the southern side, and by the Sylhet district of Bangladesh in the Northern side the state forms its jurisdiction.

The early history of Tripura, particularly prior to the fifteenth century, is shrouded in mists of legend and tradition. It is believed that the erstwhile State of Tripura derived its name from King Tripur, the fortieth descendant in the dynasty. According to *Rajmala* (chronicles of Tripura kings) scribed by Kailash Chandra Singha (1896:2) the name of the State has come from the words *Tui* (water) and *Pra* (near) meaning land adjoining water. However, other scholars believe that the name Tripura is the Sanskritized form of *Tipra*, a tribe to which the ruling family belonged. W. W. Hunter

(1876:357) opines that the nomenclature was done in honour of the *Tripureswari* temple located at Udaipur built around 1501 A.D. by Dhanya Manikya who ruled the State between 1490 and 1515 A.D.

According to *Rajmala* the rulers of Tripura are the descendants of Dhruhya, the third son of Yayati of the lunar dynasty. Scholars who believe in the historicity of *Rajmala*, opine that Tripura was a very ancient State and its connection can be traced to the *Sabha Parba* and *Bhisma Parba* of the epic *Mahabharata*. Singha (1896:8), however, mentions that a branch of the Shan dynasty of Upper Burma formed an independent kingdom at Kamrup. The descendants of this dynasty were driven away by the tribal people of Kamrup. The eldest son of this defeated king established an independent kingdom in the Naga Hills which later on came to be known as Heremba or Cachar kingdom with its capital at Dimapur and the younger son migrated to the northern side of Cachar where he established the ancient kingdom of Tripura.

Several rulers including Shamser Gazi, who was once a Revenue Clerk under the ruler, ruled Tripura. Krishnamoni, who assumed the title Krishna Manikya after the death of Shamser Gazi, ruled Tripura from A.D. 1760 to 1783. *Maharaja* Bir Bikram Kishore Manikya was the last ruling king of Tripura. He succeeded his father Birendra Kishore in 1923 and ruled till 17th May, 1947. The formal integration of Tripura took place on 19th October 1949 but it gained statehood on the 21st day of January, 1972.

III

Brief Ethnographic Account

The present study attempts to look into the structure of the Riang society to get a normative pattern of a tribal society of Tripura, and it will also be a major concern to decipher the process of transformation that has taken place in their society through the passage of time (Bera, 2003, Bera and Bera, 2008).

The Riang are the second largest tribal group of Tripura with a population of 1,65,103 according to the census records of 2001. As evident from their legend, they migrated from Burma to Tripura through the forest-clad regions of Chittagong hill tract. After settling down in Tripura, the Riang got patronage from the ruling Tripuri kings of Tripura as defence personnel in the army of the State. But primarily the Riang are shifting hill cultivators. They have a dialect of their own, and have still retained their individual identity by changing to their traditional core cultural markers. Today the Riang are not only numerically the second largest tribal group of Tripura, but also they are an important group from the cultural point of view who have carved out a special position in the whole of the human surface of the state in general and in the map of the scheduled tribes of Tripura in particular. At the present day they are sporadically distributed in all the districts of Tripura where the largest contribution has been found in North Tripura district followed by South Tripura district, Dhalai district and West Tripura district. The possible reason behind such uneven population strength is internal migration over a period of historical time substantiated with reasons. The following table substantiates their population strength in all the four districts.

Table 26.1: Distribution of Riang as per 2001 Census

District	*Total Population 165103*	*Percentage*
West Tripura District	2975	1.80
South Tripura District	49698	30.10
Dhalai District	32151	19.47
North Tripura District	80279	48.62

The Riang, on whom the present study has been conducted, are unevenly distributed over the whole state. Even within the state, internal migration took place as is evident from the census records. But this pattern of migration is available from 1971 only after Tripura achieved statehood. The trend of population dynamics in respect of the Riang over the last century is given below.

Table 26.2: Trend of Population Dynamics in respect of Riang (1901-2001)

Census years	*Riang population*	*Total Scheduled Tribe population*	*% of Riang population to all ST population*
1901	15115	91679	16.49
1911	22433	111308	20.15
1921	28959	171610	16.87
1931	35881	192240	18.66
1941	40347	256991	15.70
1951	48471	237953	20.37
1961	56597	360070	15.72
1971	64722	450544	14.37
1981	84004	583960	14.39
1991	111606	853345	13.08
2001	165103	993426	16.62

It is evident from the above records that over the century (1901-2001) their average population strength had been 16.58 per cent of the total tribal population of the state. Entering into Tripura centuries back through Chittagang hill tract, they first settled in the nearby areas like Bagafa, Gandachhara and Amarpur. The answer to their possible route of migration is laid in the Riang movement led by Ratanmani against Maharaja Bir Bikram during 1940-42, for which many left Amarpur, Udaipur and Belonia out of the fear of prosecution by the royal force. Some others, declined to be involved in the movement, migrated northeastward and settled mainly in the North Tripura district. The Riang villages are located on *tilla* (hillock) deep in the forest and the concentration of the Riang is found on the eastern side of the state in all the districts particularly far east of the metal road which bifurcates the state from north to south. Each village is situated far off the communicable roads and one has to trek on foot through the forested patch to reach a Riang village.

The Riang prefer to live in uniethnic settlement. However, in multiethnic settlement they exclusively form a hamlet of their own, which is called *kami*. But the Bengali words *pada, bari* and *para* have come into their vocabulary while making nomenclature of a settlement. A village is generally named after its founder, or headman, or the nearby river, or the topographical feature. The settlements of the Riang are forestclad hill ranges, and they construct their dwelling places on the *tilla* of the hill ranges. All the hillocks have patches of forest, which have widely grown vegetation.

The Riang call themselves *Bru*, which, in their language, means 'man'. The term Riang is, however, the widely used appellation to denote this tribe. Early references of the Riang (Reyanga) are available from the accounts of Lewin (1869), Dalton (1872), and Scott (1900). Lewin (*ibid.*) states that the Tipperah, the Lushai and the Kuki belonged to the *Toungtha* group and the Tipperah comprised the Pooran, the Nowuttea, the Osuie and the Reeang (Riang) who migrated to Chittagong from Hill Tipperah. Scott (*ibid.*) in the *Gazetteer of Upper Burma and the Shan States*, refers to the Riang as the Yang Hsek, Yang Lam and the Yang Wan Kun. According to Stirling, quoted by Scott (*ibid.*), ethnically and culturally these tribes were different but linguistically they were identical. The language spoken by them was radically the same as that of the speakers of the southern Shan States. There was some diversity in the names of the tribes—the Yang Hsek called themselves Riang (or Riang Rioi); the Yang Wan Kun used the form Riang Rong; and the Yang Lam occasionally gave the name Riang. These tribes have been living in the Shan States for a long time and the Yang Lam had amalgamated with the Shans to a much greater extent than the other two tribes. The Yang Wan Kun showed some cultural affinity with that of the Palaung and Kachin. These tribes professed Buddhism.

Sen (1337 *Tripurabda*) in his historical account narrates that the Riang had a prominent place for their integrity and valour in the army of Tripura kings. In the fifteenth century, *Maharaja* Dhanya Manikya defeated the Pathan army with the help of Rai Kacham and Rai Kachag, two Riang army generals. Another legend accounted in the chronicle of Sen (1337 *Tripurabda*) narrates how the Riang submitted their allegiance to the Maharaja Govinda Manikya of Tripura. Some Riangs, while travelling on rafts of bamboo in the *Gomati* river, broke a thread fastened across the river on the occasion of the worship of *Toibuma*, the Goddess of river. This ensured a quarrel between the Riang and the officials of the king and resulted in a revolt. The queen, Gunabati, pardoned the Riang who were ordered for decapitation, after obtaining the oath of allegiance from them, In return, she offered them her own milk in a pot and a slab of stone.

The Riang are unable to explain the etymological significance of the term Riang. However, Gan Chaudhuri (1983) narrates two interpretations. The Riang claim that they are the children of the famous saint Kashyapa; so they are *Kshatriyas* belonging *Maldhara jati*, i.e. conservative Hindus who use the sacred necklace of basil plants. Tradition has it that in the *Kshatriya-nidhan-yagna* by the outrageous Brahmin Parasuram, only a boy and a girl survived. They too died after some time. Mahadeva had preserved their soul into a stone till the death of Parasuram. The stone remained in the hermitage under custody of Kashyapa. In a battle between an elephant and a tortoise, the stone was under the foot of the tortoise. Suddenly the bird *Garuda* swooped down and took away the combatants and the stone. The bird collected them but could not eat anything. So the hungry bird asked the sage Kashyapa for advice. The saint disclosed what was inside the stone and advised the bird to eat the animals and hatch the stone. The bird after eating the elephant and the tortoise made a long journey taking with him the stone and took rest on the peak of the hill called *Sibrang Khong* near the Jampui range in the north-eastern corner of Tripura. There it hatched the stone from which came out a girl and a boy called *Devlakshmi* and *Dev Tarani* respectively who were the ancestors of the Riang. In the language of the Riang *Garuda* is called *Biangma*. The term *Biangma* is said to have been corrupted first into

Biang and then to *Riang*. Hence, the Riang claim themselves to be *Bihanga putra*. The myth appears to be a blending of the Hindu and animistic thoughts. It has, however, been found that *Dev Tarani* and *Devlakshmi* figure prominently in the myth of creation of the Riang. The following genealogy attests the creation myth.

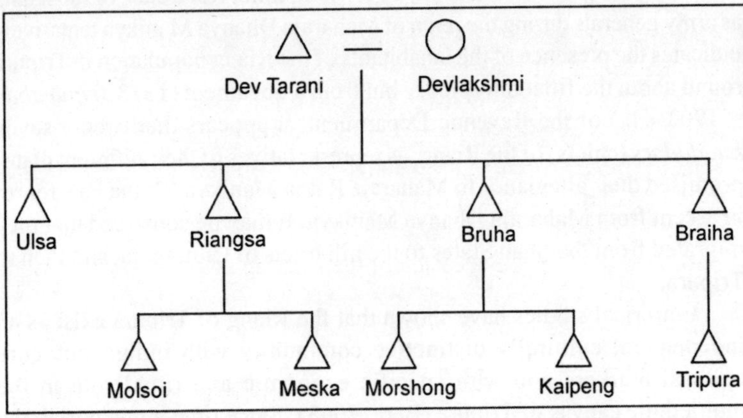

Fig. 26.1: Genealogy of creation Myth

The other myth as stated by Gan Chaudhuri (*ibid.*) runs through the versions of the Uchai tribe. They say that in course of migration from the Burma-Arakan regions towards the Hill Tracts of Chittagong and Tripura, the Riang moved first and the Uchai followed them. The advanced party is called *Riangsa*, and the rear party *Ulsa*, which is now corrupted into Uchai. The myth points out the waves of migration.

Mukherjee (1959) narrates another account, which states that a king of Tripura married a Riang woman named Toimtoima. Being oppressed by Kas Kau, a Riang king, the first four of the six sons of *Molsoi* (at present it is a Riang clan), namely, *Iongsika*, *Paisika*, *Taileongha*, *Toikluha*, *Sandkha* and *Mandakha*, went to see the king of Tripura on bamboo rafts to redress their grievances. They reached a place, called 'Taipra' in between two tributaries, namely, *Sarma* and *Raima*, of the *Gomati* river, where the king was performing *kermi* (it is a communal ritual when eight deities are worshipped for fertility, and also when epidemic of pox and cholera breaks out). The four Riang men appeared there without the permission of the king. This enraged the king who ordered them to be sacrificed before the deity of *Ker*. The intervention of the queen saved their lives.

Singh (1994) attests that the Riang originated from *Bruha*, the eldest son of *Dev Tarani* and *Devlakshmi*, the siblings, born out of two stones created by God. Other scholars have also suggested their possible migration from further east.

It appears that the tribal populations of Tripura have been inhabiting since long the present state from a very long time. Reference of the Riang as army generals during the reign of Maharaja Dhanya Manikya tentatively indicates the presence of the inhabitants of the Riang population in Tripura round about the fifteenth century but from a document (1313 *Tripurabda* = 1903 A.D.) of the Revenue Department, it appears that twenty seven *huddadars* (chiefs) of the Riang, as representatives of their different clans, promised their allegiance to Maharaja Ratna Manikya (Ratna Fa), fourth in ascent from Maharaja Dhanya Manikya. It may be construed that they migrated from the Shan States to the hill tracts of Chittagong and then to Tripura.

Empirical studies have shown that the Riang of Tripura exist as an independent culturally distinctive community with indigenous core cultural markers and with specific economic and ritual role in the multiethnic canvas of Tripura (Bera, 2003). Since time immemorial, the Riang have been in close contact with neighbouring ethnic groups, predominantly the tribal people. During the era of Tripura *Raj*, influx of Hindu castes, as a result of large-scale immigration into their territory, have affected their ethnic environment. Thus aliens have affected their indigenous culture, society and agrarian system. The strengthening of feudatory states of Tripuri kings in the mid fifteenth century intensified this.

Language

Grierson (1928) refers to the Riang (or Yin) as belonging to the Palaung-Wa group of the Austro-Asiatic family of languages, although at present the language spoken by them belongs to the Bara (Bodo) group of the Tibeto-Burman family of languages. Singh (1994) states that they speak in Riang language among themselves, but use Kok Borok and Bengali to communicate with others. However, the empirical observations of the author ascertain that they speak in *Kau Bru*, a dialect of the major Kok Borok language, which comes under the Tibeto-Burman language. The term *Kau* signifies 'language' and *Bru* signifies 'man', hence the language of man.

The *lingua franca* of Tripura is Kok Borok and the Riang

communicate in that language with other tribal groups, but not all. A few Riang, who have come in contact with the caste populations of Tripura, are able to communicate in Bengali. Literate Riangs who have attained higher education are able to communicate in English.

However, the Riang do not have a script of own. But the language Kok Borok has a script now, which is still at the stage of controversy. The State Government of Tripura led by the Left Front introduced Kok Borok in Bengali script as a medium of instruction at the primary school stage. In accordance with it the Left Front ruled Tripura Tribal Areas Autonomous District Council (TTAADC) has passed a regulation to teach tribal students Kok Borok in the Bengali script. But at the present day it seems that there is a political controversy over the selection of the script. The hill regional parties, including the Tripura Upajati Juba Samity (TUJS), TNV and the Tribal National Conference have opted in favour of the Roman script. The Congress (I)-TUJS led Government introduced Roman as the script of Kok Borok in 1989-90. The All Tripura Tiger Force (ATTF) had also been in favour of Roman script. The *Bru* Socio-Cultural Organization, a voluntary social organization of the *Bru* (Riang), which aims at promoting *Bru* (Riang) culture, has introduced Roman script for *Kau Bru*. However, it has similarity with the Kok Borok, and it awaits recognition (Bera, 2003, 2005).

Economic Resources

The economic activities of the Riang mainly comprise subsistence economy like food gathering, and also food producing, rearing of domestic animals, basketry and mat weaving. The food gathering activity consists of the collection of roots, tubers and vegetables, fishing and hunting. However, with the continuous receding of forests, dependence on food gathering has been decreasing. The forests of Tripura offer scope to collect edible products like leaves, vegetables, fruits, roots and tubers. The commonly collected items are *muia* (bamboo shoot), *muikutu* (arum), *khanga* (wild brinjal), *raicak* (soft top of cone), *thalik thampai* (wild banana), *mai khomi* (mushroom), etc. Fishing is done by males in the streams, rivers, marshy lands and lakes for consumption at home. The usual methods of fishing are trapping, catching, killing and poisoning through the juice of *ruo* (a creeper). Hunting of wild games is done individually, communally or by a small group. Only males go for hunting and females are prohibited, as it is a taboo among them. The food producing economy of the Riang centres on *huk* or *jhum*.

The food producing economy of the Riang centres on *huk* or *jhum* carried out on *tilla* (hillock) or hill slopes once in a year as a traditional practice, and *kheto* or settled cultivation on *lunga* (valley between two hillocks) and *kheto* (plain land) during both *Kharif* and *Rabi* seasons. According to a report of the Tripura Rehabilitation Plantation Corporation Limited, shifting hill cultivation, popularly known as *jhum*, is carried on Government *khas* land, proposed Reserved Forests, Protected Forests and Reserved Forests, which are estimated to be about 25,000 hectares. At present there are about 26,000 families involved in *jhum* cultivation in the state of Tripura. Both men and women participate in agrarian operations. In *jhum* major activities like selection of exact site, cutting and clearing of forest patch, firing of woods, clearing the debris, sowing, weeding, etc. are done communally.

The Riang consider *hathai* or *tilla* (hillock covered with forest) as the suitable type of land meant for shifting cultivation. The implement used to clear the forest patch is called *da-khuntha* (big dagger). In *jhum* field they have a multiple choice of food production which includes six varieties of paddy [*Bety* (scented paddy), *Kowprouh*, *Gilong*, *Badia*, *Garo* and *Mikru* (*Kamin*)]; two types of jute [*Paih* and *Bongi*]; *Mesta* [*Paih-mukhoi*]; three types of Beans [*Subai* - long, Subai-blu - medium and *Kosoi* - flat]; seven varieties of vegetables [*Khauh-khlu* (white scented pumpkin), *Chakma* (gourd or cucurbit), *Thamso* (chilli), *Phanthao* (round brinjal), *Phanthao-brouh* (long brinjal), *Khaukhling* and *Haiching* (courgette)]; four types of leafy vegetables [*Mandar*, *Moilao-mandar*, *Khundru-phoi* and *Usnoi*]; five types of tuber [*Tha*, *Theingo*, *Manai*, *Kormo-wouksa* and *Kormo-ksom*]; three types of cereals [*Plao-masinga, Maisoi* and *Plao-maisoi*]; two types of sugarcane [*Masinga* and *Haduma-masinga*]; three types of oil seeds [*Sping, Sping-kphuai* and *Sping-kson*]; cotton [*Khu*]; and other plants like *Lela-kchauh*, *Lela-ksom* and *Ashu*.

Technologically shifting cultivation and settled cultivation lie in two different scales of evolutionary ladder. Hence, the nature and extent of qualitative assessment of people and their practice vary to a multiple degree. The Riang are believed to possess an expertise in *jhum* cultivation since they have the acumen of selecting a good *tilla* (hillock) covered with old forest, shrubs and bamboo plantation. Moreover, the elevation of the *tilla* (hillock) also counts a lot to the potential *jhum* cultivator. Owing to heavy rainfall the cultivable area is constantly rain fed. An individual never owns a *jhum* land and employment of labour is free. It is customary on the part of the Riang to arrange for a team of operators before the start of actual operation. They have the tradition of employment of labour on mutual aid basis who are not hired on the basis of payment. It is also mandatory on the part of the cultivator to stay in the *charnouh* (bamboo pole house) built especially at the *jhum* site for watching the area. Management of operation through group dynamics is the end part of *jhum* operation.

Ideally almost all Riang villages are located on hillocks or elevated areas having patch of forests. Each household is widely spaced and the in between region is covered with wildly grown vegetation. The construction of a house depends on a suitable site and hence the nearest household generally occupies a distant land. The site for *jhum* cultivation is generally located outside the village though a village does not have a stable boundary as the *jhum* fields shift every year leaving behind the already cultivated site as fallow land.

The area of land used for crop is not fixed and also beyond any standard measurement where seeds of different crops are mixed and sown simultaneously. Among the Riang the system of shifting cultivation is known as *hukba*; *huk* (shifting) and *ba* (cultivation). The deep emotional attachment for the traditional system of tillage is amply borne out by the songs of love and work and also by the rituals connected with it. Over and above these strongly felt ties, those who have no land of their own to till or have insufficient land for cultivation resort to *huk* cultivation. They have a strong belief in dream and divination for selecting a site irrespective of the fact that it is used for *jhum* or for construction of a house.

During the months of *Osa* (*Aswin* = September-October) and *Kehchi* (*Kartik* = October- November) a *huk* site is selected, which is called *huk-naimo*. While the type of soil is an important consideration, preference is usually given to the thickly grown forestland and also to a type of land, which has bamboo plantation. Although, ten to twelve years constitute an ideal regeneration cycle of *jhum*, but partly because of the non-availability of ideal *huk* land at a convenient distance from the dwelling place, the normal practice of cultivation is on the land which has been previously tilled six or seven years ago. It seems there lies a dichotomy between the ideal and the actual, which possibly helps in understanding the shift of paradigm that actually happens through the performance of *huk* operation. There is no formal procedure for allotment of land to a particular individual. The Riang, therefore, divide the particular forested areas among themselves by way of mutual adjustment. Disputes in this respect are practically unknown, perhaps, because of their strong community ties and common interest in *hukba* (shifting cultivation). It is to be noted here that a very large area is not tilled every year, but the command area is substantially larger to an extent of ten to twelve times of the actually tilled area. It merits a little explanation. The command area depends upon two factors, viz. (i) the period of consecutive cultivation, and (ii) the period of the *jhum* cycle. In Tripura the period of consecutive cultivation is only one year while the period of *jhum* cycle is about ten to twelve years, leaving aside its certain local variations. A *huk* cultivator after one year of cultivation quits the field and looks for a second one. At the end of next year he goes to the third, thus every year a field is taken up till the eleventh year (ten year cycle) or the thirteenth year (twelve year cycle) when the cultivator returns to the original first plot, now considered ready for re-use or to any other suitable plot in the first locality. Meanwhile all the ten or twelve plots used earlier remain fallow and are not put to use. This follows that if a *huk* cultivator cultivates one standard hectare every year, he then allows another nine standard hectares to remain fallow simultaneously when the *jhum* cycle is taken for ten years. In other words, for every standard hectare of actual cultivation, a total area of ten standard hectares becomes unavailable for any other cultivation in a ten-year cycle.

The site is confirmed by putting the symbol of ownership with the help of an engraved bamboo at the entrance of the main passage after *huk-naimo* (selection of site). This is called *wakhar-kaimo* to avoid trespassing by another cultivator. This is followed by *huk-haomo* (clearing of the forest) by *dao* or *takkal* (dagger). The quantum of land determines the number of labour force required. On an average, it takes one full day with brief intervals for meals, etc. for five to seven persons to cut and fell trees, shrubs and bamboo that stand on one *kani* (17280 sq. ft. or 40 per cent of an acre) of land. The clearing operations are, however, performed on socialistic principles for a number of days usually on mutual aid basis called *yago-kshilaimo*. Thus everyone works on everybody's land. Only the owner provides the meals. Among the Riang an agrarian labourer is called a *yago, which* is applicable for both male and female labourer. The deployment of this workforce takes place in *huk* land, which is totally managed on the basis of mutual aid, and hence no cash payment is done for this operation of *yago-kshilaimo*. Each labourer works in a particular field by rotation and at one day he employs a man who was his one time master in a different land and employed him as labourer. Hence, the concept of labour force in a *huk* land is principally a socialistic way of division of labour.

It is desirable to finish the clearing operations by the end of *Khasoing* (*Magh* = middle of February). The felled trees are allowed to dry up in the sun for about two months. Before firing the dried wood a ritual is performed at the site of cultivation by the *aukchai* (priest) when a pig or a fowl is sacrificed in anticipation of a good crop. The owner also performs another ritual at his dwelling place where he sacrifices a fowl in his courtyard. He also keeps rice grain, cotton and a coin in a *kotra* (container) and places it on the roof of the *verandah* in anticipation of a rich crop. After the fowl is sacrificed the owner throws away the ingredients of the container to a far off place. The ritual performed at the *huk* land is called *hata mailymi* and the domestic ritual is called *yachauhmo*.

During the month of *Choileng* (*Chaitra* = March-April) the dried up leaves, woods and bamboo are set on fire that are reduced to ashes within a few hours. This is called *huk-saomo* and is exclusively done by the men folk only. The soil also gets burnt to about one feet depth. It is, however, noted that large useful trees are neither felled nor put to fire, but are allowed to remain *in situ*. Only the lower branches are cut and utmost care is taken to save these trees from the spreading fire. These standing trees are regarded as the boundary marks between the adjacent individually owned *huk* clearings, only because no fencing is made to demarcate the areas on hill slopes, which look as if commonly owned. Another common but interesting practice is to construct temporary field huts either on raised bamboo poles (*charnouh* or *noksha*) or on treetops with branches chopped off called *noksha-prowo*. Such two-sloped field having the roof of *walai* (bamboo leaves) are erected in the midst of their area of *huk* cultivation to keep a vigil against wild animals like elephants, deer, boars, monkeys and so on. This is called *hachuk-karmi* or *kamo*.

There is a short interval between the phases of *huk-saomo* (burning of forest) and sowing of seeds. During this period before the onset of first monsoon both male and female members clear the ashes and charred parts of the wood and make the soil ready for tilling. This operation is called *huk-khumo*.

In the month of *Sajlang (Baisakh* = April-May) seeds of paddy, sesamum, maize, cotton, vegetables and fruits like pumpkin, melon and cucumber are mixed together in baskets. The seeds are kept in a special type of basket and carried on the back of the cultivator. Whereas the females carry the basket called *kaisni*, the males carry *chinpai*, which differs in shape and size. The males, keeping the body parallel to the hill slope, dig the soil with *da-khuntha*. While the right hand is used for digging, left hand is simultaneously used to pick up seeds from the *chinpai* for sowing. The females follow the trail of the males.

The operation of *huk-tangmo* (weeding) is done thrice by both sexes to ward off bamboo shoots and other weeds. The first weeding starts in

Ashari (Jaistha = May-June) and is called *hagra*. The second and the last weeding called *maiyagu* takes place in *Srao* (*Ashad* = June-July) and *Drumboi (Sravan* = July-August) respectively. Weeding is done in rotation from the first tilled land to the last tilled land. During weeding young boys and girls sing and dance with the rhythm of drum beating. The drumbeater is a male who leads the team with the voice of chorus song. During the weeding season a ritual called *hatataimi* is observed if the growing crops wither. This ritual is performed by the *aukchai* (priest) when a fowl (cock) is sacrificed and is offered to the land along with *khoi* (parched paddy). One thing is taken care of that a particular kind of weed called *artum*, usually accompanying the bamboo trees, are not weeded out as this species is believed to act as a sort of fertilizer when placed by the side of the growing crop.

Before harvesting the paddy the *aukchai* (priest) performs the ritual called *hata maiklumi* by way of sacrificing a pig and/or a fowl in the *huk* field. From the beginning of *Keingrai* (*Bhadra* = August-September) onwards till *Osa* (*Aswin* = September-October) the operation of *mai-rao* or *mai-raimi* (harvesting) is completed where both males and females participate. After the crops ripen, harvesting is done as per the maturity of the crops. The fastest grown paddy is *Bety*, which is harvested during *Srao* (*Ashad* = June-July) and *Drumboi* (*Sravan* = July-August). The last paddy to be harvested is *Kowprouh* during *Keingrai* (*Bhadra* = August-September). Vegetables are taken out as per the requirement of consumption. The late crops are mesta, jute and cotton and are exclusively grown in *huk* field. Oil seeds particularly sesamum takes the maximum time, which is harvested in *Osa* (*Aswin* = September-October). The paddy grown in *huk* is typical to the Riang, which they retain at home for self-consumption.

The *huk* land of the Riang not only reflects an arena of economic pursuit but also it is the place and time where the young people show their excellence in cultural activities particularly in drum beating, love song composition and singing, and dancing. The present author has been able to collect some love songs of the Riang sung during *huk* operation. One such example is cited here to substantiate the feeling of the people who are involved in it.

Men: *Khandu mundoini parbatwa*
Kuni chaknoimalainami.

In the deep forest you were alone and I caught sight of you but I am unable to comprehend how and why God has sent you.

Women: *Khato modi ba mailya*
Shelumo byuilya maibi
Kain khamtakatuimdi
Maiya hunfa talidi.

I search in vain for the one whom I want. Though surrounded by men but none of them is the one I want. How unlucky I am! I don't know what to do!

Together: *Kamchala kuiyi ranfra*
Unuo pathea khuiyi bagneby,
Khanana di, khanana di
Rishadi, rishadi, rishadi.

Lend us your golden ears, listen patiently to all what we say: work hard, work hard, and work hard.

The singing and dancing along with the beating of drums generally takes place when weeding starts in stages. As the crops grow in sizes and get ripened, merry making increases till these attain the stage of harvesting.

The *jhum* land area in Tripura is yet to receive its due importance in the Land Tenure System of Tripura since there is no *Jhum* Land Regulation Act in the state of Tripura as is prevalent in the other neighbouring states of northeast, namely Arunachal Pradesh, Meghalaya and Nagaland.

At the present day all the forest areas of the state have been brought under the Forest Laws and Rules. The important ones among these are *Indian Forest Act, 1927; Tripura Forest Rules; Forest (Conservation) Act, 1980; Tripura Forest (Conservation) Rules* and so on. The implementation of all these Rules and Acts created 3588.183 sq. km. of Reserved Forests, 587.633 sq. km. of Proposed Reserved Forests, and 2116.874 sq. kms. of Unclassed Government Forests in this state with a consideration for the Scheduled Tribes and other forest dwellers for deriving all benefits by working in the forests. The Forest (Conservation) Act and its Rules allowed forest land to be diverted for use for non-forestry purposes with the receipt of same area of *khas* land by Forest Department and Compensation. These have accelerated the process of getting the Government forestland for serving the inhabitants in public interest.

Of late, there is a remarkable development in this arena, which aims to look into a wider network of the tribal habitation keeping in view their traditional rights over forest. Naming it as *The Scheduled Tribes and Other Traditional Forest Dwellers (Recognition of Forest Rights) Act, 2006 (No. 2 of 2007)* the Government of India notified it for operation with effect from 31st December, 2007. Accordingly, *The Scheduled Tribes and Other Traditional Forest Dwellers (Recognition of Forest Rights) Rules, 2007* were promulgated for implementing the provisions of the Act notified on 1st January, 2008.

The major legal rights recognized under the Act were:

- Right to cultivate forestland to the extent under occupation, subject to a ceiling of 4 hectares.
- Right to collect, use and dispose of minor forest produce.
- Right inside forests, which are traditional and customary, e.g. grazing.

The persons who will get the right are:

- Scheduled Tribes who have been living in and depending on forests for their livelihood prior to 13th December, 2005.
- Other traditional forest dwellers who have been living in and depending on forests for their livelihood, for three generations (i.e. 75 years prior to 13th December, 2005).

The duties of the right holders are:

To ensure sustainable use, conservation of bio-diversity and maintenance of ecological balance and thereby strengthening the conservation regime of the forests.

Social Structure

The social structure of the Riang can better be understood through the study on Riang clan structure, kinship system and behaviour, marriage pattern and family type. The Riang accommodate a number of consanguineal kin group units called *panji* (clan), which are based on the rule of patrilineal descent. The *panji-haro* (clan structure) seemingly assumes the form of a bisection of the community having two segments of *Molsoi* and *Meska* clans from each of which the other *haro* or *huda* (sub-clans) have developed (Mukherjee, 1959).

Molsoi	*Meska*
Dalbong	Raikchak
Sagarai	Charkhi
Nowkham	Musa
Apeta	Tuimuiafa
Changpreng	Wairem
Iakstam	Tamyakcha

Mukherjee (*ibid.*) further throws light on the structural development of the Riang clan structure through the following genealogy.

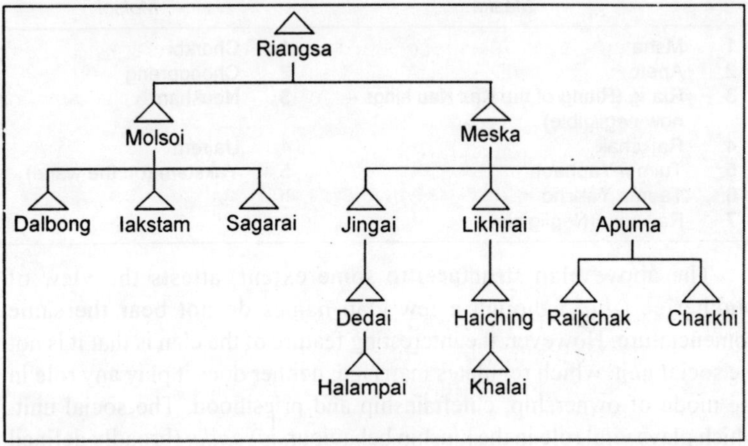

Fig. 26.2: Structural development of the Riang clan structure through Geneology

The basic clan structure 'appears as a segmented genealogical structure remaining confined within a few generations. *Molsoi* and *Meska*, which are the major clans, have exerted enormous stabilizing influence on the Riang clan structure. The structure has developed along patrilineal line, but the affiliation of *Raikchak* and *Charkhi* sub clans to *Meska* has been achieved through matriliny' (*op. cit.*).

Whereas Mukherjee has explained the clan structure of the Riang, having fourteen clans, assuming the form of a bisection of the community, Gan Chaudhuri (1983) argues that the structure as stated by Mukherjee is empirically not observed in any study. Deviating from the earlier study of Mukherjee (1959), Gan Chaudhuri suggests the existence of only twelve clans, namely, *Changpreng, Charkhi, Malsoi, Meska, Musa, Noukham, Oairem, Raikchak, Tam-Yak-Cha, Tooimoiafa* and *Yakstam*.

The present study suggests the existence of fourteen clans, the name, spelling and etymological significance may not resemble the earlier two studies. But after several round of collection of data and cross-checking the same from various sources including highly literate informants and persons with academic background of the discipline of Linguistics, the present author has come to the conclusion that the Riang have fourteen clans where a sense of hierarchy is maintained through legends. The names of the clans under the apparent form of dual organization are:

Riang Clans

	Meska		*Molsoi*
1.	Msha	1.	Chorkhi
2.	Apeto	2.	Chongpreng
3.	Riang (Riang of the Kas Kau kings – now negligible)	3.	Noukham
4.	Raikchak	4.	Uairem
5.	Tuimui Yaphaoh	5.	Yakstam (on the wane)
6.	Tauma Yakcho		
7.	Raiksom (Negligible)		

The above clan structure, to some extent, attests the view of Mukherjee (*ibid.*) though a few clan names do not bear the same nomenclature. However, the interesting feature of the clan is that it is not the social unit, which regulates marriage; neither does it play any role in the mode of ownership, chieftainship and priesthood. The social unit, which plays vital role in the kinship behaviour, is *sandai* (broadly defined lineage) a homogeneous, patriarchal and patrilineal group.

The Riang kinship system embodies two basic concepts—*sandai* and *houchu*, which broadly refer to agnates and affines. It is also contemplated here that all consanguineal kins not necessarily belong to *sandai* and all *houchu* members are not affines too (*houchu* spelt as *hokchu* by earlier scholars). These two fundamental principles are explained in *Kau Bru* as *buithithahani erungtungha bududuhaphaim* (they are of same blood and same tree) and *houchuthaha kailaimi* (those who could not be married). The *sandai* encompasses persons of the father's agnatic lineage group comprising primarily two ascending and two descending generations from the ego. It also includes collaterals like a man's father's father and his brothers and their children, his father and father's brothers and their children, his brothers, his own and brother's children and their grandchildren.

In classifying the relatives as *houchu*, the principle of bilateral reckoning has been employed. The concept of *houchu* includes some of the relatives on the father's side and most of the relatives on the mother's side, who are affinal kin in the general sense. Affiliation to a clan though signifies consanguinity in a general sense because of the belief in common descent, in reality all the clansmen are regarded as *sandai*. Invariably the *sandai* must be of the same clan, whereas the *houchu* may be of the same clan or a different clan.

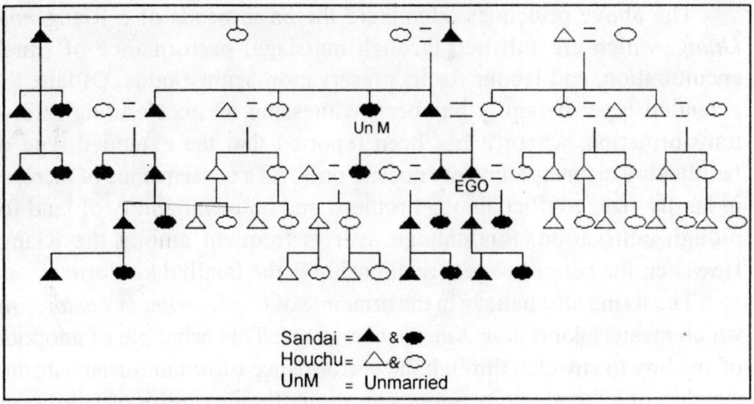

Fig. 26.3: Riang Kinship System.

The head of the family, both in principle and practice, ensures cooperation among the members of the family, job distribution, maintenance of social relations with agnates and cognates, performances of rituals and imbibes family tradition. As a rule of inheritance the family property passes through the males and remains confined among the *sandai*, a man, his sons and brothers, father's brother's sons and their grandsons and so on, but exclusively to the exclusion of the women. In the event of a man having no male child, the *sandai* can bequeath a share to a married daughter living permanently in that family. The rest of the property passes on to the deceased man's brothers and their children, failing, to distant *sandai*. On widowhood, a woman is entitled to a very small share of her deceased husband's property, provided she continues to live in her deceased husband's family under the care of the *sandai* and does not remarry. The *jhum* land can be inherited by an individual as per the customary laws of the Riang in patrilineal line and in this case the general rule of inheritance plays an important role.

In *Kau Bru*, a family is called *nok-khung* which entails four principles.

(a) *Bisabutof naikhe jatigusthi bangnu* = to propagate progeny to have kin.

(b) *Dandharma khenia* = to attain virtue.

(c) *Bisabutaina tangani toinaijate* = to educate children in tribal *gusthini sriangami* (Riang) culture.

(d) *Maiba khumba rangpaicha bangnai* = to live amidst paddy and richness.

The above principles adumbrate the basic needs of a Riang *nok-khung*, which are fulfilled through marriage, performance of ritual, enculturation, and labour for its preservation against odds. Of late, the extended type of family has been witnessing an accelerating rate of transformation, where it has been reported that the extended type of families are disintegrating into nuclear ones. As a consequence of increase in family size, conflict among brothers, and non-availability of land for plough cultivation, this change over is frequent among the Riang. However, the core of *sandai* relationship is the familial kin form.

The Riang also believe in the principle of *bisakroirimi* or *hasaharini*, which means adoption in *Kau Bru* language. This principle of adoption of any boy to any clan through the performance of *sandaiharimi* rite and worship of a female deity *Songruma* shows the flexibility of family and kinship structure. An instance of almost similar type of adoption has been shown by Kandre (1967) in his work among the Yao, a hill tribe inhabiting the southern fringe of the Chinese area.

In the event of the adoption among the Riang the adopted son loses all socio-ceremonial ties with his biological parents, his natal *sandai* and his own kin group owing to his assimilation to the kinship structure of the new family and the new *sandai*. In principle it is preferred that the boy to be adopted should come from the *sandai* group, falling from the clan of the man, failing from any other clan. The boy, after adoption, takes the clan name of the man who adopts him. If the boy is the member of the same clan, no ritual performances are observed, otherwise *sandaiharimi* is observed in the presence of an assembly of the elderly members of all the clans and the village headman, where the biological father of the boy ceremonially hands over his son to the man who adopts him. Thus the boy being absorbed in the new family becomes the legitimate heir of the man who adopts him.

The Riang follow two principles in marriage, *viz*., *halakcham* and *halakchaya* and two concepts in the alignment of relatives. Under the marriage system of *halakcham* one envisages the proper relationship in which marriage can take place between person of the same generation, with the exception of one's own brother and sister. The other system, i.e. *halakchaya* envisages the forbidden relationship in which persons of different generations are involved in marriage. The latter case seems to be impossible in practice, though theoretically it is possible.

Among the Riang the *sandai* of the same generation can form *halakcham* relationship in which children of two male siblings could marry. It is, in other words, paternal parallel cousin marriage. On the other hand, cross cousins and the children of two female siblings stood in the *halakchaya* relationship and hence marriage between them is not possible. Of late, there has been flexibility in marriage rules and hence cousin marriage of all types is taking place. The above principles justify that the Riang, in principle, have family endogamy (here family means extended type of family) and marriage between the children of two male siblings is the traditional practice based on their particular notion of kinship.

While analyzing the above principle of marriage, Mukherjee (1960) attests that 'all types of cousin marriage show that there is no interest feeling with regard to any of them. The frequency of these marriages also establishes that marriage with one's father's brother's daughter is the predominant form of cousin marriage. The low frequency of cross cousin marriage, their absence in the grandfather's generation and the non-alignment of paternal and maternal uncles and aunts with parents-in-law, possibly suggest that cross cousin marriage was introduced later. One may uphold the theory that the non-identity of the above kind, in view of the terminological identity of all the cousins with the siblings, is not an antithesis to the practice of cross cousin marriage. But it may be advocated that this latter identity might have occurred later when the Riang introduced custom of cross cousin marriage owing to the dispersal of familial kin, because of the shortage of land and quarrels among the brothers, or that the Riang might have found no objection to marrying cross cousins who were originally in the *halakchaya* relationship, as they are classed with parallel cousins and siblings. The frequency of parallel cousin marriages is declining by generation, partially because of the breakdown of joint households, moreover, largely owing to the waning intensity of the feeling of *sandai* bonds and, finally, for economic reasons (possession of plough land and trade in cash crops). What is significant is that parallel cousins are socially very important in the family.'

Marriage among the Riang is known as *kailaimi*. Monogamy is the most prevalent type of marriage. But polygyny, sororate and levirate are permissible in the society. Remarriage of divorced and widow are permissible. Marriage between a bachelor and a divorcee woman or between a spinster and a divorced man is called *kaklai kalaime* and that between a divorcee woman and a divorced man is called *kakloi lalaimi*. Widow remarriage is called *randiranda lalaimi*. Marriage of a widower with a spinster is called *sockchokbaisikik*. A man can marry his elder brother's widow but not his younger brother's widow (*waiyrao*). He can marry his wife's younger sister but not his wife's elder sister (*waiyrao*). Marriage by capture (*toikhaitlamo*), intrusion (*haiuhphaimi*) and elopement (*broitoikhailaimi*) has been reported to be practised in the past. Divorce (*kaklaimi*) is also permissible in the society.

Social Control

A Riang king named Kas Kau ruled the Riang, before their migration to Tripura. His autocracy and oppression led some Riang leaders, namely Iongsika, Paisika, Taileongha, and Toikluha to submit to the king of Tripura, Ratna Manikya. The king honoured them and nominated one of the leaders as the chief of the Riang community with the title, *Rai*.

Traditionally the Riang had four-tier political organization of which three have disintegrated. The first one, known as *ata*, ran under the king Kas Kau and his thirteen attendants. The second one, known as *saia*, ran under the *Rai* having twelve officials who functioned as councillors, messengers, storekeepers, rent collectors, drum beaters, flutists, generals and so on. These two units existed till the fourth decade of the present century. The third unit, which had executive and judicial functions, comprised three administrative chiefs, called *Chaudhuri Sardars* for three administrative divisions—Belonia (Madhuripur), Udaipur and Amarpur, the three major areas of the Riang concentration in the past. The fourth unit ran under *Holui Chaudhuri* of each village and the *Sardar* of each hamlet. They were assisted by *Karbari* (messenger) and the council of elders of each hamlet. The post of chief is not hereditary in nature. It is apparent that in the past the Riang had institutions of self-governance. But the state of affairs during the princely period have radically changed specially after India achieved her independence in general and Tripura's accession to Indian Union on the 15th of October, 1949, in particular.

Now the Riang have entered into the vortex of communal, regional, national and international politics. However, the traditional administrative patterns are mainly village based and confined to the community itself. Though officially the village chieftainship abolished in principle in 1955 after the enactment of Acquisition of Chiefs Rights Act, 1954, yet in practice the chief of a village exists among the Riang, who maintain a council of his own. The tribal village council now stands as a relic of the past, which arbitrarily comprises the following persons, viz.:

Holui Chaudhuri or Kami Fang	*Chief of the Riang in the village*
Karpang or Karbari	Manager, Store Keeper
Aukchai	Priest
Kandal	Peon and body Guard
Daoa	Messenger

However, it is contemplated here that the above authority structure is a very rare phenomenon in a Riang village and wherever it is present it remains as an unofficial council. Hence, officially the tribal village council has withered away. Since 1962, the village councils have been replaced by a uniform pattern of statutory *Panchayati Raj* and the administrative responsibility of the village has been shifted from the chief to the *panchayat*, which is a democratic institution formed by adult franchise.

Due to dissolution of the traditional tribal administrative setup resulting from their merging into the general stream of the Government administration, an apprehension of loss of traditional tribal culture arose. To resolve such apprehension and to allow more freedom and autonomy to the tribes practising their traditional ways, the Autonomous district Council (ADC) bill was introduced in 1979, and keeping in view the process of state building as the central purpose, the Tripura Tribal Area Autonomous District Council (TTAADC) was formed in 1985 under the Sixth Schedule of the Constitution of India. Except in maintenance of law and order, the ADC has autonomy in all matters of tribal development and administration.

Religious Beliefs and Practices

The Census of India 1991 enumerates 91.28 per cent of the Riang as Hindu, 8.50 per cent as Christians, 0.14 per cent professing Buddhism, 0.06 per cent professing Islam, and 0.02 per cent subscribing to other religion. Religion of the Riang, both in principle and practice, contains elements of animism, animatism, dream, divination, fertility cult, magic, polytheism, taboo, totemism and witchcraft. The continuance of animistic beliefs and acceptance of religious beliefs of greater Sanskritic canopy constitute the core of their religion. Hinduism has left an impact on their indigenous beliefs and practices.

The Riang believe in *fala* (soul) and in its existence. It is believed that while a person is asleep, his or her soul can leave the body, take the form of a *leincha* (grass hopper) and roam about here and there, come back and re-enter into the body. Belief in dream and divination occupies a major place in their material life. While selecting a site for household or *jhum* cultivation they depend on dream revelation. The other belief is in divination, which is a mystical way of knowing before hand, the future of unforeseen things.

The Riang sorcerers practise both imitative and contagious magic. The magicians prescribe amulets and talisman to ward off evil spirits, cure disease, befriend a person, cause divorce or unite a person. Apart from these, the Riang believe in a number of Gods and Goddesses. The names are given below:

Buraha	*A male god dreaded for his power of destruction*
Haicukma	Wife of Buraha.
Jampira & Kalpira	Sons of Buraha.
Thuinairao	The king of Riang deities; God of death.
Soinairao	Recorder of virtue and vice; equated with Chitragupta who writes the destiny according to Hindu concept.
Sibrai	A male God.
Taocing Chaungma	Wife of Sibrai.
Toibuma	Goddess of water.

However, it may be noted that whatever may be the role of each deity; specific deities are worshipped for a specific purpose in a number of rituals not alone but together with two or three deities. The major specified deities who are regularly worshipped are *Buraha*, *Thuinairao*, *Soinairao*, *Bonirao*, *Toibuma*, *Motaikotorma Songruma* and *Mainokma*.

As a result of close contact with the neighbouring Hindu communities, different Hindu deities, and the cult of Vaishnavism have found place in the religious life of the Riang. Mention may be made of *Mahadeva*, *Lakshmi*, *Krishna*, *Kali*, *Durga* and so on. For about the past seven decades Vaishnavism has created a dent and an enormous influence among the Riang, which has also encouraged them to resort to vegetarianism in principle. The sacred specialist or priest among the Riang is called *aukchai* who is also a Riang by ethnic identity. One can only become an *aukchai* if he is a married man (with one wife only).

Discussion

The given ethnographic details of the Riang state the cognition of two universes of the Riang in terms of the myth of their creation and ethnicity and mechanisms of maintenance of the Riang ethnic boundary. The cognition of their identity as *Bru*, language as *Kau Bru*, and population dynamics over a century have been discussed. Apart from these the factors that constitute a Riang society have been dealt upon through the description of social structure comprising the details of social units and institutions like clan, lineage, family, kinship, marriage and so on; religious beliefs and practices, economic organization; and the mechanism of social control. The description given through the help of earlier works and the present empirical study signifies the structure and pattern of the society and also the current of change (i.e. transformation), which the Riang have been witnessing in the dynamics of time and space.

Social change resulting into transformation of the Riang society lays its foundation in the history of the Riang in Tripura. The Riang came in contact with the ruling community of the State of Tripura round about the fifteenth century. In the last decade of the nineteenth century they came in contact with the Magh, a tribal community. Later on, their contact with other tribal groups, namely the Jamatia, Halam, Noatia and others began, and around 1930s they came in contact with the Bengali Hindus who started pouring into Tripura in large numbers by this time. Around 1935, the Riang came in contact with a member of the Noatia tribe, who accepted Vaisnavism and made attempts at Bagafa region to proselytize the Riang. A detailed discussion about such proselytizing has been delineated elsewhere (*cf.* 2005) where the reformistic movement has been highlighted in a systemic way. Pouring in of the Hindu Vaishnavites followed this and regular contact with the Hindus increased by 1944 due to steady inroad of Hindu refugees from the neighbouring districts of erstwhile East Pakistan (now Bangladesh) and their settlement in the neighbourhood of the Riang hamlets.

It is apparent that the process of transformation took place in stages. The first contact with the ruling community was self-initiated and friendly, which resulted in the voluntary political submission to the king due to internal dissension among the Riang. Moreover, the worshipping of Hindu Gods and Goddesses by the ruling chiefs also influenced their religion. Hindu religious thoughts began to shed light on the Riang culture since this contact. The next contact during 1880s with the Magh resulted in a shift in their traditional practice of *jhum* economy. They learnt the technology of plough cultivation from the Magh. The settlement pattern also started changing due to the transformation of forestlands used for shifting cultivation. The third impact was Vaishnavism, which discouraged the tribal theology based on sacrifice of animal and it also led to acceptance of vegetarianism. The removal of the tribal chiefs against the customary laws marked another footstep for social change. The establishment of the Bengali refugee settlements was another landmark whose effect opened the channels of close and regular contact with alien culture resulting in to and fro flows of culture traits. Another landmark that brought on transformation in the Riang society was the Riang movement of 1940-42.

There are other spheres of changes too, which lie at the ideological as well as substantive levels. At the family level, the extended family structure has been under a considerable process of breaking down resulting into the formation of smaller units called nuclear family as is evident from the empirical study conducted in several villages. The link between the clans and the political organization has broken down owing to the disorganization of the council of the chiefs. This can be further substantiated with the fact that no more the villages are named or identified in the name of clan chiefs. At the present day, there is no leader for each clan. The clan rituals, which could consolidate the members of respective clans, have almost ceased to exist. At the level of kinship behaviour, the intensity of the *sandai* bond has been lessened and ritual for the animation of relationship among the agnates is not performed these days. The institution of marriage has also witnessed changes in the light of the form of marriage, i.e. to say, marriage by capture, intrusion and elopement are obsolete now. Moreover, there is decline in the frequency of parallel cousin marriage, which has started weakening of the *sandai* bond of kinship structure.

The council of the chiefs has disorganized and the chief is no longer a leader. Hence, the disputes over ownership of land, etc. are now settled by the court of law. The bachelor and youth dormitory system, as an institution, ceased to exist and is rated as a matter of the past now. The Riang have shown considerable change in terms of economic mobility. Many have taken to plough cultivation. The exchange of service in agricultural activity has now become a weak organization. The exchange of labour called *yago kshilaimo* is now a practice of bygone days and is only practised in the operation of *jhum* cultivation. However, this has been replaced by employment of agricultural labourer on daily wage basis. They have also started growing new varieties of paddy. The wage earning through labour in land is a new source of income among the Riang.

For over three decades, what has affected more in Tripura is the problem of insurgency in this hill state of north-eastern India that has deep roots in the socio-economic conditions of the state. The connivance of dominant political rule over these decades in the violence does not undermine the importance of the deeper socio-economic causes behind the violence. The society in Tripura, both tribal and non-tribal, reflects inequalities and divisions. Non-tribal immigrants have imposed their social and cultural practices on the tribal social system. One of the basic resources, land, which the tribal people have owned over generations, have now become the property of the immigrant non-tribal people. On the contrary, it is a debatable issue to discuss whether the tribal people have really become a part of the mainstream of the society or not. It, therefore, seems apparent that a section of the tribal people have resorted to violence due to threat of immigrant culture and for fear of land alienation. As a result several insurgent groups emerge out on political and ethnic lines that have a bearing on individual society. The Riang too, as an important tribal community of the state, could not remain outside this system that has been prevailing over decades.

However, there is also a positive note of development. One of the major changes that has effected the Riang of Tripura is that they have been able to get more benefits under the scheme of tribal development, firstly, because they are identified as the Primitive Group of People by the Ministry of Tribal Affairs, Government of India and secondly due to their habitations in such an area of the state which is labelled as the ADC area of the state. This, in a way, provides freedom and autonomy to the tribal population of the state where the focused area is state building as a central concern as is practised in other states in this part of north-eastern India that is governed by the Sixth Schedule of the Constitution of India. In addition to this the recent implementation of *The Scheduled Tribes and Other Traditional Forest Dwellers (Recognition of Forest Rights) Act, 2006 (No. 2 of 2007)* and *The Scheduled Tribes and Other Traditional Forest Dwellers (Recognition of Forest Rights) Rules, 2007* provides their traditional rights over forest.

NOTES

1. The area of Tripura has been shown as 10,486 sq. km., as per the records of the Registrar General of India attested by the Surveyor General of India, though K.S. Singh (*cf. People of India*) and Samarjit Kar (*cf. Tripuray Bedate Ele*) mention it 10,477 sq. kms. Some private publications mention it to be 10,491 sq. km., and the Department of Information, Culture and Tourism, Government of Tripura mentions it 10,491.69 sq. km.
2. The geographical position as per the records of the Registrar General of India attested by the Surveyor General of India, is between 22° 56′ and 24° 32′ north latitude and 91° 21′ and 92°21′ east longitude, though the Department of Information, Culture and Tourism, Government of Tripura mentions it to be between 22° 56′ and 24° 32′ north latitude and 90° 09′ and 92° 20′ east longitude.

REFERENCES

Bera Gautam Kumar, (2003), 'The Riangs of Tripura in the changing scenario'.

In J. Sarkar and J. Chakraborty (eds.) *Transition, Change and Transformation: Impacting the tribes in India*. Kolkata. Anthropological Survey of India, pp. 139-168.

Bera Gautam Kumar, (2005), 'Social Mobility Movement among the Bru (Riang) of Tripura. In S. K. Chaudhuri and Sucheta Sen Chaudhuri (eds.) *Primitive Tribes in Contemporary India,* Vol. 2. New Delhi: Mittal Publications. pp. 349–359.

Bera Gautam Kumar and Nishi Bera, (2008), *Echoes From The Hillocks: A Compendium on the Tribes of Tripura.* Agartala: Tripura Bani Prakashani.

Census of India (2001), Office of the Registrar General, India. New Delhi.

Dalton, E. T., (1872), *Descriptive Ethnology of Bengal*. Calcutta. Indian Studies: Past and Present (Reprinted in 1973).

Gan Chaudhuri, J., (1983), *The Riangs of Tripura*. Tripura. Directorate of Tribal Research.

Grierson, (1928), *Linguistic Survey of India*. Vol. I, Part II. Calcutta. Government Printing.

Hunter, W.W., (1876), *The Statistical Account of Bengal*. New York. Harper and Row.

Kandre, P., (1967), 'Autonomy and Integration of social Systems: the Iu Mien (yao) Mountain Population and their Neighbourhood'. In P. Kunstadter (eds.) *Southeast Asian Tribes, Minorities and Nations.* Princeton.

Lewin, T. H., (1869), *The Hill Tracts of Chittagong and the Dwellers therein.* Calcutta.

Mukherjee, B., (1959), 'The Riang'. *Bulletin of the Department of Anthropology.* VIII (1):1-107.

Mukherjee, B., (1960) 'Cousin Marriage among the Riang'. *Anthropos.* 55. Fasc. 5-6 : 734-738.

Scott, George J., (1900), *Gazetteer of Upper Burma and the Shan State*. Rangoon. I (1).

Sen, Kaliprasanna (Ed). (1337), *Tripurabda. Sree Rajmala*. Vol. I. Agartala.

Singh, K.S., (1994), *The Scheduled Tribes*. (Ed.). Calcutta. Anthropological Survey of India and Oxford University Press.

Singha, Kailash Chandra, (1986), *Rajmala*. Agartala.

PART THREE

BIO-DEMOGRAPHIC LANDSCAPE

27

Demographic Scenario of North East India: A Glance

Debashis Basu

Introduction

The states of North-east India comprising Assam, Meghalaya, Manipur, Nagaland, Arunachal Pradesh, Mizoram, Tripura and Sikkim share a population of 3.68 per cent of total population of India. This northeastern part of India bordering International boundaries with Bangladesh, Bhutan, China, and Myanmar has given shelter to a large number of tribal population mostly affiliating to the Mongoloid stock and living in the hills and plains in most of the states. A large number of caste groups also live there making a paradise for the anthropologists and sociologists. These eight states accommodating both tribal and non-tribal populations, have their respective age-old traditional cultures, beliefs, practices which have imprints on different aspects of livelihood patterns and demographic variables. These may have direct or indirect impacts on their respective population. To begin with Assam has larger share of 68.37 per cent followed by Tripura (8.05%), Meghalaya (6.05%), Manipur (5.97%), Nagaland (4.34%), Arunachal Pradesh (3.03%), Mizoram (2.39%). The same list ends with the smallest state of Sikkim being 1.33 per cent of total population of northeastern India. In any population the impacts of demographic variables like infant mortality rate, child mortality rate, adult mortality rate, economic condition, nutritional aspect, etc. are foremost indicators of population well-being. In the following pages some of the demographic aspects of those states in North-eastern India have been discussed. The child mortality rate among other demographic indicators is reported to be influenced by different biophysical and geographical variables (including rainfall, productivity of agricultural lands, topography/temperature, and market access through road networks), socio-economic and health care indicators out of which the health programme initiatives have a major contribution to reduce the under-five mortality rate (Kumar *et al.*, 2012). Out of other demographic variables there is a strong cross-sectional relationship between (adult) mortality and the rate of fertility. As Lee (2003) and Galor (2004) have mentioned about the consequence of the well-known demographic transition after drawing the relationship which control for various determinants of fertility, particularly income and human capital indicators, and after attempting to control the endogeneity of mortality. Infant mortality, by international standards, is defined as the death of a child less than 1 year of age, i.e. rate of the death of infants aged 0-1 per 1,000 live births. Measurement of this variable is more robust than infant mortality (Ahmad, Lopez, & Inoue, 2000). Therefore, under 5 mortality (referred to throughout as child mortality) is expected to reinforce the results found with infant mortality. Infant mortality, incidentally, varies more than adult mortality. This mortality in the demographic transition, first falls as a result of the adoption of better medical technologies, better hygiene, and better access to medical care (all of which are a function of per capita income) (Bloom and Canning, 2003). Mortality among the children, i.e. child mortality is a widely accepted indicator of well-being. Identifying factors are important as high rates signal lower socio-economic development (Anderson, Romani, Phillips, & van Zyl, 2002, Sen, 1998). To be more precise, there exists a long standing tradition in the literature on the effects of income distribution (relative income hypothesis) and per capita income (the absolute income hypothesis), on mortality and other health outcomes. Country-level analyses have found that mortality is correlated with per capita income (Preston, 1975; Pritchett & Summers, 1996; Rodgers, 1979). Others have focused on the importance of income inequality (Marmot, 2002; Wilkinson, 1996, 1997).

Among the other factors the economy that makes an impact on demographic situation is economic condition which as mentioned by Becker (1960) through quality-quantity theory, that stresses the role of income as a determinant of the fall in fertility. Chowdhury (1988) and Schultz (1978) opine that fertility is an important correlate of child survival. Like child survival, the total fertility rate (TFR) is also influenced by economic and cultural factors (Bongaarts, 1978). The direct determinants are intermediate fertility variables known to influence both the quality and quantity of children demanded (Becker & Lewis, 1973;

Bongaarts, 1978; Hill, 2003). Such direct determinants are not widely available at the aggregate level. Exploring the relationship between mortality and fertility is, therefore, limited (Schultz, 1978).

In this chapter an attempt has been made to assess the status of population and its dimensions with reference to some selective demographic indicators from North-eastern Indian states with reference to the national demographic perspectives.

Population Size and Sex Ratio

North-east India being marked with hilly, terrains, inaccessible roads comprises Assam, Meghalaya, Manipur, Arunachal Pradesh, Mizoram, Tripura, Nagaland and Sikkim shares a population of 45,587,982 being equal to 3.68 per cent of total population of India. The largest state of Assam's population size is 31,169,272 and the Sikkim in terms of population remains smallest state (6,07,688) in 2011.

In Table 27.1 the population of the North-eastern States and India for 2001 and 2011 along with percentage decadal growth, difference in decadal growth, average annual exponential growth rate, Sex Ratio (females per 1000 males) of total population, child population (0-6 years), and Population (7 Years and above) have been described. So far the population of India, 2011 is concerned Assam among other North-eastern States is having larger share of 2.58 per cent which is followed by the Tripura (0.30%), Meghalaya (0.24%), Manipur (0.22%), Nagaland (0.16%), Arunachal Pradesh (0.11%) and Mizoram (0.09%). The smallest state in terms of population being the Sikkim (0.05%). In other words, the whole north-eastern part of India shares a proportion being 3.68 per cent of total population of India. During 1991-2001 period highest percentage decadal growth is observed in the state of Nagaland (64.53) and the lowest percentage decadal growth is found in the state of Tripura 16.03. During 2001-2011 period all the North-eastern States show lower percentage decadal growth as compared to the period of 1991-2001. The most striking percentage decadal growth is observed to be –0.47 per cent in the state of Nagaland. The differences in decadal growth among all the North-eastern States shows that all the states record negative percentage of decadal growth in nature, among which Nagaland exhibit highest negative percentage decadal growth being –65.0 per cent. The values of average annual exponential growth rates among all the North-eastern States also show similar trend of negative growth rate with the state of Nagaland showing highest value of the same being 0.05 for both the periods of 1991-2001 and 2001-2011, respectively.

Table 27.1. Population and sex ratio of North-eastern States and India

Sl. No	State	Total population		Percentage decadal growth		Difference in decadal growth	Average annual exponential growth rate		Sex Ratio (females per 1000 males)					
									Total Pop.		Child Pop. (0-6yrs)		Pop. (7Yrs & above)	
		2001	2011	1991-2001	2001-2011		1991-2001	2001-2011	'01	'11	'01	'11	'01	'11
1.	AR	1097968	1382611	27	25.92	-1.08	2.42	2.33	893	920	964	960	878	913
2.	AS	26655528	31169272	18.92	16.93	-1.99	1.75	1.58	935	954	965	957	929	953
3.	MN	2293896	2721756	24.86	18.65	-6.21	2.25	1.72	974	987	957	934	977	995
4.	ML	2318822	2964007	30.65	27.82	-2.83	2.71	2.49	972	986	973	970	971	989
5.	MZ	888573	1091014	28.82	22.78	-6.04	2.57	2.07	935	975	964	971	930	976
6.	NL	1990036	1980602	64.53	-0.47	-65.0	5.11	-0.05	900	931	964	944	890	929
7.	SK	540851	607688	33.06	12.36	-20.7	2.9	1.17	875	889	963	944	861	883
8.	TR	3199203	3671032	16.03	14.75	-1.28	1.5	1.39	948	961	966	953	945	962
9.	IND	1028737436	1210193422	21.54	17.64	-3.9	1.97	1.64	933	940	927	914	934	944

Note: AS-Assam; MN—Manipur; ML—Meghalaya; MZ—Mizoram; NL—Nagaland; SK—Sikkim; TR—Tripura; AR—Arunachal Pradesh; IND—India)

Source: Census of India, 2011.

The same Table 27.1 shows that the distribution of sex ratios (females per 1000 males) among all the north-eastern states with reference to the total population, for child population (0-6 years) and population (7 years and above) of the respective states. The highest and the lowest sex ratios being 974 and 875 are observed in the states of Manipur and Sikkim respectively among all the North-eastern States, respectively; while in 2001 Census the only state with 'matriarchy' – Meghalaya is found to have the sex ratio being 972 after the state of Manipur. But during the period of 2011 all the North-eastern States exhibit higher sex ratios in comparison to the period of 2001. The highest sex ratio in terms of children (0-6 years) being 973 is observed in the state of Meghalaya; while the lowest sex ratio (927) is found in the state of Manipur during 2001. The sex ratios in the cluster of children aged 0-6 years of all the North-eastern States show lower values barring Mizoram (971) for the period of 2011 in comparison to the period of 2001. On the other hand, the highest sex ratio in the population of children aged 7 years and above being 977 is found in the state of Manipur and the lowest value of the same being 861 is found in the state of Sikkim during the period of 2001; The sex ratios among all the North-eastern States are observed to be higher in this category during the period of 2011 in comparison to the period of 2001.

Expectation of Life at Birth

Expectation of life at birth is one of the most important indices of mortality which reflects the overall health standards of a given population. It is generally estimated by constructing life Tables, for which age-specific death rates or the probabilities of surviving by age are the basic data required. Age specific death rates are commonly obtained from the vital registration of data while the probabilities of surviving by age can be estimated through indirect means (Gubhaju and Navunisaravi, 1989).

Table 27.2. Projected Levels of the Expectation of Life at Birth (e^o_0), 2001-2026

Sl. No.	*States*	*Male*					*Female*				
		2001 -05	*2006 -10*	*2011 -15*	*2016 -20*	*2021 -25*	*2001 -05*	*2006 -10*	*2011 -15*	*2016 -20*	*2021 -25*
1.	Assam	59.6	61.6	63.6	65.6	67.1	60.8	62.8	64.8	66.8	68.8
2.	NE States	66.6	68.1	69.1	70.1	70.9	70.6	71.8	73.0	74.0	75.0
3.	India	63.8	65.8	67.3	68.8	69.8	66.1	68.1	69.6	71.1	72.3

Source: Report of the Technical Group on Population Projections, 2001-2026: M/O Health & Family Welfare.

Table 27.2 describes expectation of life at birth of the males and females of the state of Assam, North-eastern States (combination of Meghalaya, Manipur, Nagaland, Arunachal Pradesh, Mizoram, Tripura and Sikkim), and India. This being one of the most important indices of mortality reflects the overall health standards of a given population. The values of expectation of life at birth of the males exhibit the range between 59.6 in 2001-2005 and 67.1 in 2021-25 and the same values of the females exhibit the range between 60.8 in 2001-2005 and 68.8 in 2021-25 in the state of Assam; while in the North-eastern States (combination of Meghalaya, Manipur, Nagaland, Arunachal Pradesh, Mizoram, Tripura and Sikkim) the same values of the males exhibit the range between 66.6 in 2001-2005 and 70.9 in 2021-25 and the range between 66.6 in 2001-2005 and 70.9 in 2021-25 of the expectation of life at birth of the females is observed. The trends of the values of the same in all Assam, North-eastern States and India show consistent increase for both the males and females between the periods of 2001-2005 and 2021-25.

Estimated Birth and Death Rates

Table 27.3: Estimated Birth Rates in Different North-eastern States, 1981, 1991, 2001, 2004 to 2009

Sl. No.	States	Birth Rate								
		1981	1991	2001	2004	2005	2006	2007	2008	2009
1.	Arunachal Pradesh	NA	30.9	22.2	21.2	23.3	22.5	22.2	21.8	21.1
2.	Assam	33.0	30.9	27.0	25.1	25.0	24.6	24.3	23.9	23.6
3.	Manipur	26.6	20.1	18.3	13.9	14.7	13.4	14.6	15.8	15.4
4.	Meghalaya	32.6	32.4	28.3	25.2	25.1	24.7	24.4	25.2	24.4
5.	Mizoram	NA	NA	15.7	19.1	18.8	17.8	18.2	17.8	17.6
6.	Nagaland	NA	18.5	NA	13.9	16.4	17.3	17.4	17.5	17.2
7.	Sikkim	31.0	22.5	21.6	19.5	19.9	19.2	18.1	18.4	18.1
8.	Tripura	26.4	24.4	16.1	15.0	16.0	16.6	17.1	15.4	14.8
9.	India	33.9	29.5	25.4	24.1	23.8	23.5	23.1	22.8	22.5

NA = Not Available.

Source: Sample Registration System - Registrar General, India.

Table 27.3 describes the distribution of estimated birth rates in north-eastern states of India for the years of 1981, 1991, 2001, and 2004 to 2009. Among all the northeastern states of India the highest birthrate is observed to be 33.0 in the state of Assam in comparison to the All India figure which is being 33.9, and the lowest value of the same being

26.4 is observed in the state of Tripura in 1981. From Table 27.3 it also indicates that the birthrate in all the North-eastern States keeps on decreasing as the year advances till 2009. During 2009 the highest birthrate is observed to be 24.4 in the state of Meghalaya in comparison to the All India figure (27.5), while the lowest value of the same being 14.8 is observed in the state of Tripura in 2009. It is interesting to note that the Tripura state remains the only state to have recorded a declining trend of birthrate among all the North-eastern States.

Table 27.4: Estimated Death Rates in North-eastern States, 1981, 1991, 2001, 2004 to 2009

Sl. No.	*States*	*Death Rate*								
		1981	*1991*	*2001*	*2004*	*2005*	*2006*	*2007*	*2008*	*2009*
1.	Arunachal Pradesh	2.4	4.6	3.6	2.9	4.5	4.1	4.0	4.4	3.9
2.	Assam	12.6	11.5	9.6	8.8	8.7	8.7	8.6	8.6	8.4
3.	Manipur	6.6	5.4	5.2	4.3	4.1	4.5	4.4	5.0	4.7
4.	Meghalaya	8.2	8.8	9.0	7.3	7.5	8.0	7.5	7.9	8.1
5.	Mizoram	NA	NA	4.4	5.2	5.1	5.5	5.2	5.1	4.5
6.	Nagaland	NA	3.3	NA	3.7	3.8	4.8	5.0	4.6	3.6
7.	Sikkim	8.9	7.5	5.1	4.9	5.1	5.6	5.3	5.2	5.7
8.	Tripura	8.0	7.6	5.6	5.5	5.7	6.3	6.5	5.9	5.1
9.	INDIA	12.5	9.8	8.4	7.5	7.6	7.5	7.4	7.4	7.3

Source: Family Welfare Statistics in India, 2011.

Table 27.4 describes the estimated death rates in different North-eastern States during 1981, 1991, 2001, 2004 to 2009. Among the North-eastern States barring Mizoram and Nagaland the highest death rate is observed to be 12.6 in the state of Assam in comparison to the All India figure which is 12.5, and the lowest value of the same being 2.4 is observed in the state of Arunachal Pradesh in 1981 as compared to the all India figure being 12.5. In those states the death rates over the years as mentioned above do slightly decline while a comparatively little better results are observed in the two states like Assam and Sikkim, but not at par with the development in national level where from death rate varies from 12.5 in 1981 to 7.3 in 2009. In spite of the development, i.e. decline of death rate from 12.6 in 1981 to 8.4 in 2009, Assam among the North-eastern States, still ranks the top.

Neonatal, Infant, and Child Mortality Rates

A quarter of world's neonatal deaths (one million each year) take place in India, mostly at home (65.4% of all births and 75.3% of births in rural areas occur at home) (UNICEF, 2008). Between the mid 1980s and early 1990s significant progress was made towards reducing the child mortality levels in India, but recent data indicate that there has been stagnation in child mortality rate at an unexpectedly higher level (Claeson *et al.*, 2000).

Table 27.5: Infant Mortality Rates (Total) in North-eastern States during: 2005 to 2009

Sl. No.	States	Infant Mortality Rate				
		2005	2006	2007	2008	2009
1.	Arunachal Pradesh	37	40	37	32	32
2.	Assam	68	67	66	64	61
3.	Manipur	13	11	12	14	16
4.	Meghalaya	49	53	56	58	59
5.	Mizoram	20	25	23	37	36
6.	Nagaland	18	20	21	26	26
7.	Sikkim	30	33	34	33	34
8.	Tripura	31	36	39	34	31
9.	India	58	57	55	53	50

Note : Infant Mortality Rates for smaller States and Union Territories are based on three-year period.

Source: Sample Registration System, Registrar General, India.

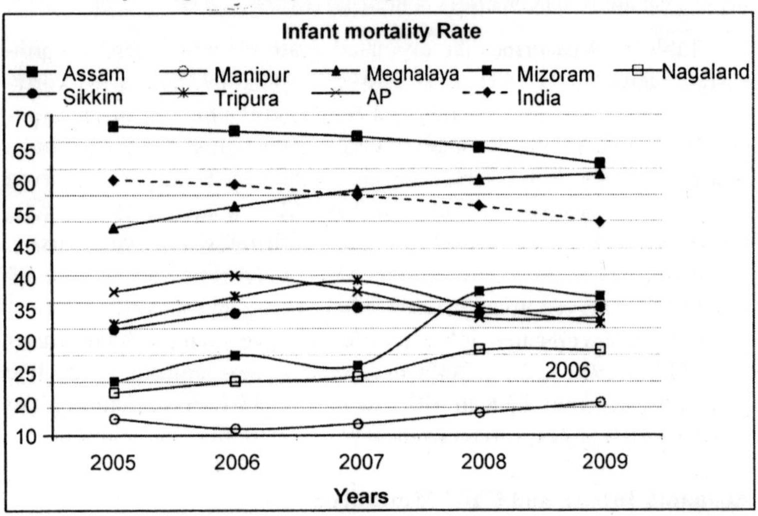

Fig. 27.1: Infant Mortality Rates in the North East India and India during – 2005 to 2009

In Table 27.5 the values of infant mortality rates in North-eastern States during 2005 to 2009 have been described and same values are graphically presented in Fig. 27.1. Among all the North-eastern States, the Assam ranks on top in terms of infant mortality rate which is being 68 and the lowest value of the same being 13 is observed in the state of Manipur during 2005 as compared to the all India Fig. 27.1 being 58. During the period between 2005 and 2009 the infant mortality rates in the states of Mizoram and Meghalaya are observed to be on the rise and the same trend is also observed in the state of Manipur but with comparatively a little rise. The same values of Infant mortality rates as shown in Table 27.4 and Fig. 27.1, decline over the years from 2005 to 2009 at the national level. Among all the North-eastern States during 2005 to 2009 only the state of Manipur is reported to have lower infant mortality rate as compared to all other states in North-eastern India. It is worthwhile to mention that among the states of North-eastern India the infant mortality rate in the state of Mizoram observes sudden increase from 23 in 2007 to 37 in 2008 and it continues till 2009.

Table 27.6: Child mortality rate by residence in the North-eastern States during – 2005 to 2009

Sl.No.	*States*	*Child Mortality Rate (0-4)*				
		2005	*2006*	*2007*	*2008*	*2009*
1.	Arunachal Pradesh	37	40	37	32	32
2.	Assam	19.7	19.7	18.2	20.4	19.0
3.	Manipur	13	11	12	14	16
4.	Meghalaya	49	53	56	58	59
5.	Mizoram	20	25	23	37	36
6.	Nagaland	18	20	21	26	26
7.	Sikkim	30	33	34	33	34
8.	Tripura	31	36	39	34	31
9.	INDIA	17.3	17.0	16.0	15.2	14.1

Source: Fam.ly Welfare Statistics in India-2011.

In Table 27.6 Child Mortality Rates (0-4 years) in the North-eastern India and at the national level from the 2005 to 2009 years are described and the same are graphically reflected in Fig. 27.2. Among all the North-eastern States Meghalaya ranks on top in terms of child mortality rate which is 49, while child mortality rate being 13 is reported by the state of Manipur in comparison of National level (17.3) in 2005. The child mortality rates from 2005 to 2009 decline at national level whereas the trend observed at national level is not the same as observed in other

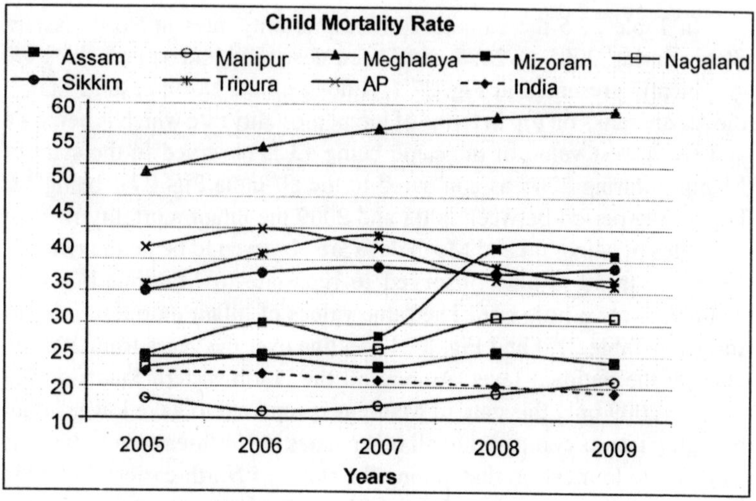

Fig. 27.2: Child Mortality Rates in the Northeast India and at the national level during – 2005 to 2009

North-Eastern States. Sometimes the child mortality rates over the years from 2005 to 2009 are either of the same values in the states of Assam and Tripura with little variations in between the years, or are on the rise like in the rest of the states in North-eastern India. Overall the most striking

Table 27.7: Neonatal, infant, child and under-five mortality rates and states-wise per capita net domestic product (NSDP), 2005-2006

States/India	*Neonatal mortality*[a]	*Infant mortality*[a]	*Child mortality*[a]	*Under-five mortality*[a]	*Per capita income (in Rs.)*[b]
Arunachal Pradesh	34.0	60.7	28.8	87.7	20037
Assam	45.5	66.1	20.2	85.0	14786
Manipur	18.7	29.7	12.6	41.9	17950
Meghalaya	23.6	44.6	27.1	70.5	18274
Mizoram	16.3	37.1	19.5	52.9	19691
Nagaland	19.8	38.3	27.5	64.7	NA
Sikkim	19.4	33.7	6.7	40.1	20609
Tripura	33.1	51.5	8.2	59.2	21231
India	39.0	57.0	18.4	74.3	20858

a National Family Health Survey, 2007 (Survey 2005-2006); IIPS.NFHS-3, 2007 (2005-2006).

b Central Statistical Organization, 2008;

NA: Not available.

feature of the child mortality rates in the North-eastern India is that the state of Meghalaya with higher child mortality rate in 2005 is observed to have increasing trend over the years from 2005 to 2009, and at the same time the state of Manipur in comparison to other states in North-eastern India and national level too is reported to have lower child mortality rate in 2005 and continues to have the same trend till 2009 excepting a little rise in 2009 while compared to the same value at national level in 2009.

Table 27.7 describes the values of neonatal, infant, child and under-five mortality rates and statewise per capita net domestic product (NSDP), 2005-06 in the North-eastern States based on the data available from National Family Health Survey, 2007 (Survey 2005-06); IIPS.NFHS-3 (2005-06), 2007 Central Statistical Organization, 2008. Assam among all the North-eastern states exhibits the higher neonatal mortality rate being 45.5 and the lower rate of the same being 16.3 is shown by the state of Mizoram in comparison to national level (39.0). In the same Table 27.7 infant mortality rate among the North-eastern States during 2005-06 remains higher in the state of Assam (66.1) and the lower value of the same being 29.7 is found in the state of Manipur. Child mortality rate during 2005-06 is higher in the state of Arunachal Pradesh (28.8) and is lower in the state of Sikkim (6.7). Under-five mortality rate in the North-eastern States during 2005-06, is higher in the state of Arunachal Pradesh (87.7) and the lower value of the same (40.1) being found in the state of Sikkim. The highest per capita income Rs. 21,231 is found in the state of Tripura and the lower per capita income Rs. 14,786 is found in the state of Assam.

Total Fertility Rate (TFR)

The total fertility rate is the most practical measure of current fertility. This rate is readily obtained from the information on live births which occurred during the year preceding the census.

In Table 27.8 description of total fertility rate (TFR) in the North-eastern States during 2005 to 2009 is presented. Whole North-eastern states are divided in to two clusters, viz. Major states and Smaller states respectively. The state of Assam falls under the jurisdiction of Major states' category and the other rest of the states in North-eastern India come under the jurisdiction of Smaller states category. The Total Fertility Rate (TFR) in the state of Assam declines during the period between 2005 and 2009, the same trend is also observed at the national

Table 27.8: Total Fertility Rate (TFR) in the Northeastern States during 2005 to 2009

Sl. No.	*States/India*	*Total Fertility Rate (TFR)*				
		2005	*2006*	*2007*	*2008*	*2009*
1.	Assam	2.9	2.7	2.7	2.6	2.6
2.	India	2.9	2.8	2.7	2.6	2.6

		Total Fertility Rate (TFR) for smaller states		
		2003-2005	*2004-2006*	*2005-2007*
3.	Arunachal Pradesh	2.5	2.7	2.7
4.	Manipur	1.7	1.6	1.6
5.	Meghalaya	3.2	3.2	3.1
6.	Mizoram	2.0	2.1	2.0
7.	Nagaland	1.7	1.9	2.0
8.	Sikkim	2.2	2.1	NA
9.	Tripura	1.6	1.7	1.7

Note: TFR for Smaller States/UTs are based on three years moving average.

Source: Sample Registration System, Registrar General India.

level. In all the North-eastern States the higher Total Fertility Rate (TFR) (3.2) is observed in the state of Meghalaya in 2003-2005, while the state of Tripura is reported to have lower Total Fertility Rate (TFR) (1.6). It is interesting to note that the values of the same TFR over the periods between 2004-2006 and 2005-2007 remain almost same in all the North-eastern States falling under the jurisdiction of Smaller states category.

Conclusion

In this chapter the demographical indicators influencing population in North-eastern India with reference to the National population perspectives have been dealt. Among all the demographical indicators that usually describe population in extensive manner, some like population size, sex ratio, estimated birth rates, estimated death rates, infant mortality rate, child mortality, neonatal mortality, and total fertility rate (TFR), have been discussed. The data used in this paper were collected from secondary sources like Census of India, 2011, Sample Registration System, Registrar General, India, Family Welfare Statistics in India, 2011, National Family Health Survey, 2007 (Survey 2005-06); IIPS.NFHS-3, 2007 (2005-06), Central Statistical Organization, 2008 etc. So far the population of India, 2011 is concerned the Assam ranks on top in population being 68.37 per cent (Table 27.1) and the state of Sikkim is found to have lower population size being 1.33 per cent of total population of North-eastern India. So far the percentage decadal growth in North-eastern India in 1991-2001 is concerned, the state of Nagaland is seen to have recorded highest decadal growth rate being 64.53 which is three folds more than the same at the national level. During 2001-2011 period the same state is found to have -0.47—the deviation which may indicate that some striking factors including some social/socio-economic aspects along with regular demographic phenomenon are responsible for the same. This phenomenon of percentage decadal growth in negative dimension during the period of 1991-2001 in the state of Nagaland is sufficiently enough to provoke to the demographers or the social scientists to go further exploration of the negative deviation for decadal growth rate. So far the sex ratio in the North-eastern States is concerned it is observed that all the states are found to have higher sex ratios in 2011 in comparison to 2001, which indicates the increase of female children as compared to their male children counterpart, and this may be a silver lining to the movement against negligence of the female. The relevant factors attributed to the increase of girl child may be of socio-economic or socio-cultural perspectives, which may enlighten the other parts of India particularly suffering from the social evil of female infanticide.

Expectation of life at birth is one of the most important indices of mortality which reflects the overall health standards of a given population. The trends of the values of the same in all Assam, other North-eastern States and India show consistent increase for both the males and females between the periods of 2001-2005 and 2021-25.Taking the values of expectation of life at birth being generally estimated by constructing life Tables resorted to age-specific death rates of the males and females into consideration, it is clear that the health standards of North-eastern India in particular and India in general, as measured by the expectations of life at birth, has improved significantly between 2001-2005 and will be so by 2021-25. The birth rate over the periods between 1981 and 2009 is hereby reported to have modest declining trend with little exception of the states of Nagaland and Mizoram which recorded almost stagnation in birth rate particularly during later years of 2004 to 2009. The declining trend in the same indicates the improvement in social awareness. The estimated death rates (Table 27.4) over the periods between 1981 and 2009 is hereby reported to have modest declining trend in the North-eastern States excepting the states of Meghalaya, Mizoram and Nagaland which recorded almost stagnation in death rate particularly during later years of 1981 and 2009. The declining trend of the estimated death rates in the same indicates the improvement in awareness and more access to the modern medicine system. The stagnation in the estimated death rates among these three states Meghalaya, Mizoram and Nagaland, call for special attention particularly, of social scientists and demographers.

The infant mortality rates over the period between 2005 and 2009 in the state of Assam shows very high in comparison to the other states but the trend remains to be declining; on the other hand the scenario of infant mortality rates in almost other North-eastern States barring Tripura is on the rise which invites special attention of the state, social scientists, and demographers to be more concerned. So far the mortality of the children under –5 per 1000 live births in India is concerned, in a few states of North-eastern India like Meghalaya and Assam the rate of the same is higher which indicates that the pace of the under-five mortality rate decline is not sufficient to hit the bulls-eye of achieving Millennium Development Goal (MDG) that targets minimizing under-five mortality to 39 per 1000 live births by 2015 (UNCF, 2010). Moseley and Chen's (1984) report based on a framework about causing childhood illnesses affecting survival of the children, indicates that the education and income being socio-economic factors, affect disease incidence and its consequences are attributed by "proximal determinants" like maternal factors, nutrient deficiency, environmental contamination, injury and personal illness etc. Since the whole North-eastern India mainly dominated by the tribal communities both in hilly and terrain locations, and of course on the plains too, followed with non-tribal populations the areas are marked with variations in cultural practices and beliefs reflecting inequalities in the proximate determinants of health that have influençes on the different demographic indicators like child birth, antenatal and post natal care, etc. A good number of studies at macro-level stressed the issues of education, female autonomy, women's work status and economic condition of the household (Kishor & Parasuraman, 1998; Bloom *et al.*, 2001; Basu & Stephenson, 2005; Bhattacharya, 2006) along with clean drinking water, nutritional status of mothers and infants including gender biased distribution of food, poor access to primary health care and education (Bardhan, 1998; IIPS.NFHS, 2007; UNICEF, 2008; Varma *et al.*, 2011) associated with child mortality.

REFERENCES

Ahmad, O.B., Lopez, A.D., Inoue, M. (2000). The decline in child mortality: A reappraisal. *Bulletin of the World Health Organization*, 78 (10), 1175-1191.

Anderson B.A., Romani JH, Phillips HE, van Zyl JA. (2002), Environment, Access to Health Care, and Other Factors Affecting Infant and Child Survival Among the African and Colored Populations of South Africa, 1989–94. *Population and Environment*, 23 (4), 349-364.

Bardhan P.K. (1998), Sex disparity in child survival in rural India. In: Srinivasan, T.N., Bardhan P.K., (eds.) *Rural poverty in South Asia*. New York: Columbia University Press, 473-480.

Basu, A.M., Stephenson, R. (2011), Low levels of maternal education and the proximate determinants of childhood mortality: a little learning is not a dangerous thing. *Soc Sci Med;* 2005; 60: 2023.

Becker, G. (1960), "An Economic Analysis of Fertility" in A.J. Coale, (ed.), *Demographic and Economic Change in Developed Countries,* Princeton, NJ: Princeton University Press, pp. 209-231.

Becker, G.S. Lewis H.G. (1973), On the interaction between the quantity and quality of children. *The Journal of Political Economy*, 1973 (81), 2:2.

Bhattacharya, P.C. (2006). Economic development, gender inequality, and demographic outcomes: evidence from India. *Popul Dev Rev*; 32:263-292.

Bloom, D.E., Canning, D. (2003). "How Demographic Change Can Bolster Economic Performance in Developing Countries", *World Economics*, Vol. 4, No. 4, October-December, pp. 1-14.

Bloom, S.S., Wypij, D., Gupta, M.D. (2001). Dimensions of women's autonomy and the influence on maternal health care utilization in a north Indian City. *Demography*; 38:67-78.

Bongaarts, J. (1978). A framework for analyzing the proximate determinants of fertility. *Population and Development Review*, 4 (1), 105-132.

Chowdhury, A.R. (1988). The infant mortality-fertility debate: some international evidence. *Southern Economic Journal*, 54, 666-674.

Claeson, M., Bos, E.R., Mawji, T., Pathmanathan, I. (2000). Reducing child mortality in India in the new millennium. *Bull. World Health Organ*; 78:1192-1199.

Galor, O. (2004), "The Demographic Transition and the Emergence of Sustained Economic Growth", CEPR Discussion Paper No. 4714, October.

Gubhaju, B.B., Navunisaravi, N. (1989). Trends in Fertility and Mortality in Fizi Based on the 1986.

Census. *Asia Pasic Population*.

Hill, K. (2003). Frameworks for studying the determinants of child survival. *Bulletin of the World Health Organization*, 81 (2), 138-139.

International Institute of Population Sciences and Macro International. (2007). National Family Health Survey (NFHS-3), 2005-06: India;. Volume 1, Mumbai, IIPS.

Kishor, S., Parasuraman, S. (1998). Mother's employment and infant and child mortality in India. Family Health Survey Subject Reports, Number 8, April 1998, International Institute for Population Sciences.

Kumar, C.; Singh, P.K.; Rai, R.K. (2012). Under-Five Mortality in High Focus States in India: A District Level Geospatial Analysis. *PLoS ONE* 7 (5): e37515. doi:10.1371/journal.pone.0037515.

Lee, R. (2003), "The Demographic Transition: Three Centuries of Fundamental Change", *Journal of Economic Perspectives*, Vol. 17, No. 4, fall, pp. 167-190.

Marmot, M. (2002). The influence of income on health: views of an epidemiologist: Does money really matter? or is it a marker for something else? *Health Affairs*, 21 (2), 31-46.

Mosley, W.H.; Chen, L.C. (1984) An analytical framework for the study of child survival in developing countries. Population and Development Review 10 (Supplement): 25–45.

Preston, S.H. (1975). The changing relation between mortality and level of economic development. *Population Studies*, 29 (2), 231-248.

Pritchett, L.; Summers L. (1996). Wealthier is Healthier. *Journal of Human Resources*, 31 (4), 844-868.

Rodgers, G.B. (1979). Income and inequality as determinants of mortality: an international cross-section analysis. *Population Studies*, 33 (2), 343-351.

Schultz, T.P. (1978). Fertility and child mortality over the life cycle: Aggregate and individual evidence. *The American Economic Review*, 68 (2), 208-215.

Sen, A. (1998). Mortality as an Indicator of Economic Success and Failure. *The Economic Journal*, 108 (446), 1-25.

UNICEF (2008). *The state of Asia—Pacific's children: Child survival.* UNICEF.

United Nation Children's Fund (UNICEF). (2008), *The State of the World's Children 2008*. Child Survival. UNICEF,.

United Nations Children's Fund. (2010), *Levels & Trends in Child Mortality. Estimates Developed by the UN Inter-agency Group for Child Mortality Estimation*. New York, USA: UNICEF.

Varma, G.R.; Kusuma, Y.S.; Babu, B.V. (2011), Antenatal care service utilization in tribal and rural areas in a South Indian district: an evaluation through mixed methods approach. *J. Egypt Public Health Assoc*; 86:11-15.

Wilkinson, R.G (1996), *Unhealthy Societies: The affliction of inequality*. London: Routledge.

Wilkinson, R.G. (1997), Socio-economic determinants of health: Health inequalities: relative or absolute material standards. *BMJ*, 314, 591-595.

28

Socio-Demographic Study Among the Sema Nagas of Assam

Indira Barua and *Deepanjana Dutta Das*

Introduction

In the present study, an effort has been made to discuss the socio-demographic aspects of the Sema Nagas of Assam. There are a few Sema Naga villages in Assam, and the present study is conducted in the village Lalpahar, under Margherita subdivision of Tinsukia district of Assam. One of the ideas is to project the socio-demographic aspects of the Semas, who are living in the midst of diverse communities of Assam, e.g. the Assamese, Nepalese and the Tangsas. Demography is the study of human population primarily with respect to their size. The term demography comes from two Greek words "demos" means people and "graphia" means to draw or write. Thus, literally speaking, demography is concerned with writing about people. Its relation is so close to Anthropology that it is mentioned in the Oxford dictionary as "Demography is a part of Anthropology which treats of the statistics of birth, death, and diseases etc." Demographic study is based on biological factors like fertility, fecundity and mortality etc. The social aspects like migration, marriage, divorce, pregnancy, restriction during pregnancy and child birth, child care, child mortality and overall hygienic condition, nutrition etc. also affect demography. It is hoped that a study of the Sema Naga population who have migrated to Assam long back, may give certain significant information about their social life.

The Sema Nagas is one of the major sub-tribes of the Nagas of Nagaland, the others being the Aos, the Angamis, the Rengmas, the Lotha, and the Konyaks. The Semas are located to the north-east of the Angami country and at present inhabit the valleys of three large rivers, the Dayang, the Chindwin and the Irawadi together with the mountainous ranges and plateaus separating their waters from the homeland proper of the Semas. They are of Mongoloid origin and primarily inhabitants of Zuhnabato in the state of Nagaland. The word "Sema" originates from "Sumi". This martial race has a political system of an autocratic secular character, having a chieftain being characterized by benevolent disposition. The Semas are to some extent, the Irishman of the Naga tribes—generous, hospitable and frequently improvident.

It has been noted by Hutton that due to their specific settlement and customary laws, they are prone to a migratory life. "The Sema polity is particularly suited to colonization, for it is customary for the eldest son of a Sema chief to take, when he is old enough to manage it, a colony from his father's village and found a new village at a convenient distance in which his authority is paramount. If the parent village is large enough, other sons will take other colonies in other directions, leaving a younger brother to succeed their father in the original village" (Hutton, 1968:8). Alemchiba (1970) states, "the Sema tribe lacks for the most part of the sentiment which ties most Naga villages so strongly to some particular site, or at least to stone, earth or water brought from that site ...Moreover, as little as thirty years ago, it was still at a migratory stage, throwing off new villages whenever it got a chance to do so". This tendency to a certain extent may be considered as one of the reasons why the Semas are not afraid of migrating to a new area.

II

The Area of Study

The present study has been conducted among the Sema Nagas of the village Lalpahar, under Margherita subdivision of Tinsukia district of Assam. Regarding the settlement of the Nagas in this area, it is reported by the villagers that they have made their permanent settlement during the year 1923-1930. So far the information goes in 1904 it was the British rulers who brought 300-400 young people of this tribe to Upper Assam to work either in the oilfield in Digboi or different coalfields in and around Margherita. Later on, when their number increased, they started to settle permanently in the area and now there are four Sema Naga villages in Margherita subdivision. According to the elderly villagers at present, approximately there are 6000 Sema Naga population in this area. Among the four villages, Longtong and Lalpahar are considered as the oldest Sema settlements. The village Longtong came to be established in 1923 for habitation by a group of 5 Sema families comprising 24 immigrants who belonged originally to the Nagaland. Intermittent waves of migration from the Naga Hills continued till 1934, when the last group of 15 Semas settled in the village. Most of the later groups of immigrants, besides being the kinsmen of the original settlers, were motivated by various considerations besides a search for fresh land. While about Lalpahar, it is found that the village was established in the year, 1936, when a few Sema families started to settle in this area. Gradually, the number of families increased because of the immigration of the new Sema families from their original homeland, i.e. Nagaland. The two other settlements of the Sema Nagas came in the later stages, when the number of families increased in their original settlement. This is in brief about the appearance of the Sema Nagas in the Margherita Subdivision of Tinsukia district of Assam.

The present village is situated in the eastern direction of Dibrugarh district. The Tipong River is flowing by the outskirts of the village. The whole area is rich in mineral resources and the Tipong coal field of eastern Assam is very close to the village. The village is situated in the foothills of the Patkai hills, which surrounds the village in the northern part. The communication system in Lalpahar may be considered suitable. Tipong Colliery road is joined at *Tirap gate tiniali*. The road is pitched one and the village road is joined with this road and a number of public buses, government buses run on the road. The communication system is mostly by bi-cycle and now-a-days many have their own cars.

Regarding the origin of the name of the village Lalpahar, it is revealed that the present village does not reflect its original shape. All agree that the village was situated on a rocky base, several metre above the bed of the river Tirap flowing by the outskirts of the village. It was originally a hilly area, but gradually earth is levelled for various purposes. Etimologically, the word "Lalpahar" means a village having red coloured soil (*Lal* means 'red' and *pahar* means "hills"). Thus, from the colour of the soil, the village is named as 'Lalpahar'. The village is situated in an undulating area. The surface area is not plain; there are some hills like structure on which a few houses are constructed. The village is mostly concentrated by the Sema Nagas. A few Nepali and Assami families are also found in the village. The houses are constructed on both sides of the road in a linear fashion. The Tipong colliery road passes along the village and the village road is connected with the main road on two places. There is a church in the middle of the village, which was established in the year 1986-87. The village cemetery is situated at the end of the village. With regards to the village boundary, it is found that the Patkai hills and the Tipong river are on the east, Lekhapani and Ledo on the west. In the north, there are Tipong Colliery and the Patkai hills; while in the South, there are Tirap gate *gaon* (village) and Lekhapani.

There are no natural sources of water except the Tipong river and the river has a great significance for the villagers. Those families, who are living by the side of the river, use river water for drinking and washing purposes. The Sẽma used to practice fishing in the river, they get the blasting materials from Coal India in a low price and use it for catching fishes. There are families, who have their own *Katcha* well, a few of them have ring well and tube well in their compound. Government water supply is not available in the village. There is no irrigation system inside the village, and so they have to depend solely on rain water for cultivation. Some of the villagers use water pump, when it is needed. The Tipong River flows by the side of the village, but it flows in a level lower than the earth level, so there is no scope of getting benefit for cultivation from river water. At the same time there is no chance of flood.

Demographic Profile

Table 28.1 shows that there are altogether 302 individuals in the village; the number of males and females are equal. Table 28.1 reveals that the highest frequency of males falls within the age group of (11-15) years, i.e. 22 (7.28%) and the lowest frequency falls within the age group of 86-90 and 96-100, i.e. 1 (0.33%). While the highest frequency of female falls in the age group of 16-20 years, i.e. 44 (14.57%) and the lowest frequency falls in the 86-90 and 101-105 years, i.e. 1 (0.33%). However, from the table we can say that the life span of Lalpahar village is very long.

Table 28.2 shows the distribution of the population age, sex and marital status of the Lalpahar village. Out of the total population of 302, 80 male and 72 females are unmarried and their percentages being 26.49 per cent and 23.84 per cent, respectively. On the other hand, 68 (22.52%) males and 75 (24.83%) females are married. The table also shows that there are 2 (0.66%) widowers and 5 (1.66%) widows reported from the village.

Table 28.1: Distribution of population by age and sex

Age group	*Male*	*%*	*female*	*%*	*Total*	*Total %*
0-5	10	3.31	9	2.98	19	6.29
6-10	11	3.64	15	4.97	26	8.61
11-15	22	7.28	14	4.64	36	11.92
16-20	20	6.62	24	7.95	44	14.57
21-25	16	5.30	20	6.62	36	11.92
26-30	13	4.30	9	2.98	22	7.28
31-35	4	1.32	13	4.30	17	5.63
36-40	11	3.64	15	4.97	26	8.61
41-45	9	2.98	7	2.32	16	5.30
46-50	10	3.31	9	2.98	19	6.29
51-55	9	2.98	—	—	9	2.98
56-60	4	1.32	6	1.99	10	3.31
61-65	5	1.66	2	0.66	7	2.32
66-70	3	0.99	2	0.66	6	1.99
71-75	—	0.00	2	0.66	2	0.66
76-80	2	0.66	2	0.66	4	1.32
81-85	—	0.00	—	0.00	—	—
86-90	1	0.33	1	0.33	2	0.66
91-95	—	0.00	—	0.00	—	—
96-100	1	0.33	—	0.00	1	0.33
101-105	—	—	1	0.33	1	0.33
Total	151	50.00	151	50.00	302	100.32

Table 28.3 shows the distribution of population by sex and education. From the table it is clear that 74 (24.50%) illiterate people are present in the village out of which 25 (8.28%) are males and 49 (16.23%) are females. The maximum number of literate people are found in the category of Middle (V-VII) level, i.e. 82 out of which 42 are males, 40 females. It is followed by a total literate population of 73 in H.S (IX-X) level out of which 43 (14.24%) are males and 30 (9.93%) females. In the H.S.S. Standard 23 literate individuals are recorded. Out of which 12 (3.97%) are males and 11 (3.64%) females. In the graduate category 3 individuals are there, out of which 1 (0.33%) is male and 2 (0.66%) females. No one is found in the Post graduate and Doctor Category.

Table 28.4 highlights the family size and it is revealed that there are 65 households in the village. The family size has been divided into 5 groups according to the number of individuals present in the family. Out of 65 households 45 households are of the medium family size whose percentage is 69.23 per cent in which number of individuals ranges between 4-6. It is followed by large family size with 10 (15.38%) number have number of individuals ranging from 7-9 which is followed by small

Table 28.2: Distribution of population by Age, Sex, and Marital status

Sl. No	Age group	Unmarried (M-Male; F-Female)				Married (M-Male; F-Female)				Widower	%	Widow	%	Total	%
		M	%	F	%	M	%	F	%						
1.	0-4	7	2.32	9	2.98	–	–	–	–	–	–	–	–	16	5.30
2.	5-9	12	3.97	7	2.32	–	–	–	–	–	–	–	–	19	6.29
3.	10-14	16	5.30	15	4.97	–	–	–	–	–	–	–	–	31	10.26
4.	15-19	26	8.61	18	5.96	–	–	1	0.33	–	–	–	–	44	14.57
5.	20-24	10	3.31	16	5.30	2	0.66	6	1.99	–		–	–	34	11.26
6.	25–29	7	2.32	7	2.32	7	2.32	4	1.32	–	–	–	–	25	8.28
7.	30-34	2	0.66	–	–	1	0.33	5	1.66	–	–	–	–	8	2.65
8.	35-39	–	–	–	–	11	3.64	15	4.97	–	–	1	0.33	27	8.94
9.	40-44	–	–	–	–	6	1.99	19	6.29	–	–	–	–	25	8.28
10.	45-49	–	–	–	–	18	5.96	11	3.64	–	–	–	–	29	9.60
11.	50-54	–	–	–	–	8	2.65	7	2.32	1	0.33	1	0.33	17	5.63
12.	55-59	–	–	–	–	4	1.32	1	0.33	1	0.33	–	–	6	1.99
13.	60-64	–	–	–	–	2	0.66	2	0.66	–	–	–	–	4	1.32
14.	65-69	–	–	–	–	5	1.66	1	0.33	–	–	2	0.66	8	2.65
15.	70-74	–	–	–	–	–	–	1	0.33	–	–	–	–	1	0.33
16.	75-79	–	–	–	–	1	0.33	1	0.33	–	–	–	–	2	0.66
17.	80-84	–	–	–	–	1	0.33	–	0.00	–	–	–	–	1	0.33
18.	85-89	–	–	–	–	–	–	–	0.00	–	–	–	–	–	–
19.	90-94	–	–	–	–	1	0.33	1	0.33	–	–	–	–	2	0.66
20.	95-99	–	–	–	–	–	–	–	0.00	–	–	–	–	–	–
21.	100-104	–	–	–	–	1	0.33	–	–	–	–	–	–	1	0.33
22.	105-109	–	–	–	–	–	–	–	–	–	–	–	–	–	
23.	110 and above	–	–	–	–	–	–		–	–	–	1	0.33	–	–
	Total	80	26.49	72	23.84	68	22.52	75	24.83	2	0.66	5	1.66	302	100.33

Table 28.3: Distribution of population by Sex and Education

Sl. No.	*Standard of education*	*Male*	*%*	*Female*	*%*	*Total*	*%*
1.	Illiterate	25	8.28	49	16.23	74	24.50
2.	Primary (I-IV)	28	9.27	20	6.62	48	15.89
3.	Middle (V-VIII)	42	13.91	40	13.25	82	27.15
4.	H.S. (IX X)	43	14.24	30	9.93	73	24.17
5.	H.S.S (XI-XII)	12	3.97	11	3.64	23	7.62
6.	Graduate	1	0.33	2	0.66	3	0.99

Table 28.4: Distribution of population by Family size

Sl. No.	*Family Size*		*Number*	*%*
1.	Single person	(1)	1	1.54
2.	Small	(2-3)	9	13.85
3.	Medium	(4-6)	45	69.23
4.	Large	(7-9)	10	15.38
5.	Very Large	(10 and above)	—	—
Total			65	100

Table 28.5: Distribution of Family Type and Composition

Family type	*No. of households*	*Percentage*
Nuclear	46	68.66
Joint	19	28.36
Broken	2	2.98
Total	67	100.00

family size and single family and their number is 9 (13.85%) and 1 (1.54%), respectively.

Table 28.5 reveals that out of the total 67 households/families 46 (68.66%) families are the nuclear family type bearing the highest frequency. The second position is occupied by the joint family type, i.e. 19 (28.36%), 2 (2.98%) families are found in the broken family type and it is composed of a widow and a widower.

Regarding the occupational pattern it is recoded that though they are mostly agriculturists yet the number of service holders is also significant. 10 (3.31%) individuals are service holders of which 7 (2.32%) are male and 3 (0.99%) are female. 10 (3.31%) individuals are dependent on business of which all are males.

III

Livelihood Pattern

The Sema Nagas mainly depend on agriculture and it may be considered as the main source of their livelihood. *Jhuming* was practiced as the universal traditional cultivation by the Semas in the Naga Hills. The original Sema method of cultivation is pure and simple *jhuming*. The land is cleared and cultivated for two successive seasons, after which it is allowed to go back to jungle again for a cycle of years which varies according to amount of land available (Hutton, 1968). Traditionally in their original habitat, the Sema practiced a type of *jhuming* which is slightly different from others. The Sema do not first burn and then clear like other tribes, but they clear the land, cutting down many of the trees, and then burn. Afterwards they cut down the burnt trunks of the remaining trees, then clear up the fields and dig the ashes into the soil (Hutton, 1968:60).

The Sema Nagas of Longtong initially practiced *jhuming* but slowly they have gone for terraced irrigated cultivation. As reported by Hutton (1968) a few Sema villages on the edge of the Eastern Angami country have adopted terraced and irrigated cultivation. An effort was made to spread the process but it could not succeed in other areas except occasional practiced by some. The Semas used to produce rice (*aghi*), of various kinds, job's tears (*akiti*,coix lachrymal), maize (*kolakiti*), green millet (*juar atsunakhi*) as their staple crops, besides some vegetables and vines in the *jhuming* fields.

As reported by the villagers, earlier most of the Sema practiced *Jhum* cultivation. They were to go to the *Jhum* field after walking 2 to $2^1/_2$ hours, which was very tiresome. They cultivated *Ahu,* corn, areca, chilly, red gourd, brinjal etc. in the *Jhum* field. But now they have opted for wet paddy cultivation. Unavailability of *Jhum* land and low outcome are probably two main reasons for which the Semas left their traditional system of cultivation. Moreover, wild elephants, monkeys, birds destroy or eat up the products. As reported by the villagers, during the last 3 years, there was not a single family, who was entirely depended in *Jhum* cultivation. Of course, there are few families, who along with wet paddy cultivation also continue their traditional *Jhum* cultivation. Those who were earlier entirely dependant on *Jhum*, now-a-days are to work as day labour or in other wage earning occupation. They do not have sufficient money to purchase wet land for cultivation. As a result their occupation has changed entirely. The Sema Naga had their own methods of cultivation and sowing. The sowing is done not by broadcasting the seeds, but sprinkling it carefully into little hollows made usually by the men with a blow of the small digging hoe (*akupu*) and scraped over by the women following with the horse hoe-like scraping hoe of bamboo or bamboo and iron (*akuwo*)." (Hutton, 1968). The grains are reaped from the stalks by hand and put straight into the pointed basket in which it is carried to the field-house.

In the present study also it is found that threshing is done in the field itself. Sometimes it is also winnowed in the field. The winnowed grains are brought to the house by various available means. In the village, the grains are stored in granaries with raised platform. Traditionally granary is built usually far enough from the village to give security from the fire. That tradition is still maintained by the Sema Nagas in their new settlement. Both the male and female members extend their helping hand in cultivation. But the implements used in agriculture have changed. Many of them started to use tractor both for cultivation and carrying paddy from the field. The livelihood pattern has changed sufficiently and those who have large land area and are in a position to utilize it effectively, have started tea-cultivation in the hill slopes.

The following two cases indicate the process of tea plantation among the Sema Nagas.

1. Shri G. S. (34 yrs) started tea cultivation in 16 bighas of land. The area is nearly 1 km away from the village. He started tea plantation 3 years back. He engaged two labour families to look after the plantation. He is to pay Rs. 1300.00 to each family on monthly basis. Besides all the family members extend their helping hand in plantation. Green leaves are supplied to the near by Lekhapani T.E. The rate varies from Rs 9.00 to Rs 17.00 per kg. He engaged labour for plucking the tea leaves. The rate is Rs. 50.00 per day. In the year 2010 L.S. (Light skip) was done on contact basis at the rate of Rs. 4000.
2. H.S. (65yrs) started tea plantation five years back in 3-4 bighas of land. In the year 2010 he got 14000 kg of green leaves. By and large family members are involved in various works relating to plantation. When leaves increase, he engaged labourers from nearby tea garden for plucking. In such cases the laboures do the job in the evening. In the initial stage, the rate of plucking per kg is Re.1 and in later stage they charged Rs. 2.00. In the year 2010, D.S. was done on contact basis at the rate of Rs. 3000.00.

IV

Marriage Pattern

The Sema Nagas are endogamous; having a number of exogamous clans. Hutton reported that clan feelings existed among the Nagas, as did tribal feeling. The predominant position, however, was of the chief, and of his relatives on the male sides (Hutton, 1968:122). This does not indicate that clan is unimportant among the Semas, but it plays a pivotal role in the life cycle rituals, his choice of food, marriage, and ritual function. The word for clan is *ayeh* or *aya* and the same word serves for custom, an indication, perhaps of an original differentiation between clans according to the customs they followed. Some of the food taboos may no doubt suggest the possibility of totemism but in reality except one clan, i.e. Wotzami, there is not a single clan which could pinpoint clans relation with animal and plant. Even Hutton has raised his doubt while mentioning about the clan system among the Semas in Nagaland. Twenty two clans given in the list are exogamous.

In the present study, it has been found that though they try to confine their marriage within their own tribe, yet there are significant numbers of cases where marriage took place outside the tribe itself. However, originally marriage with mother's brother's daughter or father's sister's son was preferred. It is said that such marriages conduce to domestic concord owing to the relationship between the parents of the couple, who see that their children behave well to one another.

Table 28.6: Marriage within and outside Sema population

Marriage	*Number*	*Percentage*
Within the Sema population	50	75.76
Outside the Sema Population	16	24.24

Table 28.6 reveals that 75.76 per cent of marriages took place within the Sema population. There are only 24.24 per cent of marriages which took place outside the Sema population.

Table 28.7 reveals that marital alliances took place with different tribes and communities. It is also reported that there are instances where individuals belonging to different tribes and communities came to the village and after marrying Sema girls, started to settle in the village. The table also reveals that 3 Tangsa males of Arunachal Pradesh married Sema girls and settle down in the village. One caste Hindu male of Lekhapani

Table 28.7: Distribution of marriages outside and within the Sema population

Marital alliance with population	*Sema boys*	*Sema girls*
Tangsa	2	3
Nepali	4	–
Manipuri	1	1
Nocte	–	1
Kalita	–	1
Ahom	–	1
Loma	1	–
Garo	–	1
Sema	50	50

married Sema girl. There are cases where a Garo male and a Manipuri male married Sema girls. Such instances indicate the prevalence of *Ghar Jawai* system exists among the Semas. Because of their new settlement such instances are bound to occur.

Age at marriage plays a significant role in the socio-demographic study. Table 28.8 shows the distribution of the Sema Naga women of the village.

Table 28.8: Distribution of women according to Age at Marriage in village Lalpahar

Sl. No.	*Age at Marriage*	*Number of women*	*Percentage*	*Mean*	*S.D.*	*S.E.*
1.	16	8	10.67			
2.	17	10	13.33			
3.	18	8	10.67			
4.	19	7	9.33			
5.	20	20	26.67			
6.	21	6	8.00			
7.	22	5	6.67			
8.	23	4	5.33			
9.	24	2	2.67			
10.	25	–	–	19.99	2.16	±0.24
11.	26	2	2.67			
12.	27	–	–			
13.	28	2	2.67			
14.	29	–	–			
15.	30	–	–			
16.	31	1	1.33			
Total	75	100.01				

Age at first marriage of women significantly influences the fertility because in every society fertility is permitted only after marriage. Age at marriage determines the duration of reproductive period of the women. If the age at marriage is low, it increases the mean duration of marriage life and also the reproductive span. Among the Sema Nagas marriage age varies from 16 to 31 years. There are total 75 married women in the village. The highest number of women, i.e. 20 (26.67%) got married at the age of 20 years. The next higher number of women (10 or 13.33%) got married at the age of 17 years. 2 (2.67%) each got married at the age of 24, 28 and 26 years. 8 (10.67%) woman each got married at the age of 16 and 18 years, 7 (9.33%), 6 (8.00%), 5 (6.67%), 4 (5.33%), and 1 (1.33%) got married at the age of 19, 21, 22, 23 and 31 years, respectively. Their mean age at marriage is 19.99 ± 0.24 which is found to have significant impact on their fertility.

From Table 28.9 it is clear that the mean age at marriage among the Sema Naga population is 19.99 ± 0.24 which is followed by the Garo (19.63 ± 0.30). It is highest among the Deori (23.57 ± 0.21) and the Tai Phake population (23.34 ± 0.28). The lowest mean age at marriage is observed among the Lalung (14.59 ± 0.18).

Table 28.9: Mean age at marriage: Sema Naga and some other population of Assam

Population	*No. of women*	*Mean ± E*	*Reference*
Sema Naga	75	19.99 ± 0.24	Present study
Sonowal	90	18.44 ± 0.61	Dad &Barman 1995
Tai Turung	101	21.47	Barua 2001
Tai Phake	130	23.34 ± 0.28	Das & Gogoi 2002
Ahom	66	17.98 ± 0.29	Das et al 1980a
Chutiya	62	18.06 ± 0.16	-do-
Mishing	82	18.43	-do-
Lalung	51	14.59 ± 0.18	-do-
Garo	95	19.63 ± 0.30	Das & Saikia 1999
Deori	204	23.57 ± 0.21	Deori 2006

Arranged Marriage

A study of the arranged marriage among the Sema Nagas reveals that the clan plays an important role in the marriage system. The role of mediator has a very important place in the formal negotiation. The boy or his parents normally do not negotiate directly with the girls' parents, and it is the mediator who fulfils this formal part.

H.S. narrated that in his case, his father requested his cousin brother (*Apuaitue*) to visit the girl's family and discuss about the prospective marriage. Accordingly, his uncle went to visit the girl's family at Longtong and offered the proposal of marriage from the boy's side. They received a positive response from girl's side after one month. After two months, the relatives/members of both the families gathered at girl's house. They initiated the discussion with a prayer to almighty. After that they showed due respect to their elders. Finally, formally, they sought formal consent from the boy and the girl. While getting consent from both, they finalized the matter (*Atsaita*). Thereafter, they started negotiation for bride price. It was decided that the boy's family would give Rs. 7000.00 and a pair of bullocks as bride price. At the same time, they also discussed the items to be given to the girl's uncle/untie, cousin etc. and the amount agreed upon. It was finalized that the boy's family had to give Rs.1000.00 each to those relatives. After finalizing, the boy's family entertained the girl's by killing a pig, which was brought by the boy's family and extended formal invitation for the marriage ceremony.

It is a custom among the Sema Nagas that on the day of marriage, the bride's family are to return the gift twice in number to the boy's family. Accordingly, the place and way of presentation is decided. Moreover, they are to give with the girl, the paddy required for 1 year, 4 numbers of pigs, 10-15 number of fowls and chicken. Along with these, they also give all the necessary items required for kitchen and other day-to-day requirements with the girls on the day of marriage. Besides providing these items, they also give 10 kg of rice and the hind portion of pig to the girl. The sentiment of giving the item is that the newly married bride girl should not face any difficulty immediately after entering her new household. Normally these items are cooked by the girl and entertain the family members.

The bride and the bridegrooms after offering prayer at the church enter into their new house.

As the arrange marriage is elaborate and costly, so they now prefer elopement marriage. In case of elopement, parents of both the parties should inform the village council immediately. The council after holding a meeting decides a date and invites the members of both sides. The meeting is normally attended by the members of both the families. Some elderly persons of the village also attend the meeting.

In such type of marriage, the council fixes the fine which varies from Rs. 2000.00 to Rs. 5000.00. In the meeting itself the members of both the parties are to give assurance that in future the boy and the girl will not separate from each other. The council notifies the responsibilities to the family members, and they are to sign an agreement to the council. It is also decided that in case of violation, they are to give Rs. 15,000.00 to Rs. 50,000.00 to the council. In case of such marriage, they are not getting holy water from the church till the couple is getting final approval from the council.

The fine is deposited in the joint account of the council and it is spent only for development and improvement of village road, school and other common facilities.

V

An effort has also been made to project the fertility status among the Sema Nagas.

Table 28.10: Distribution of Females on the basis of different Age Groups among the Sema Nagas

Sl. No.	*Age Group (in years)*	*Number of Females*	*Percentage*
1.	9 – 13	14	11.11
2.	14 – 18	17	13.49
3.	19 – 23	18	14.29
4.	24 – 28	15	11.90
5.	29 – 33	5	3.97
6.	34 – 38	15	11.90
7.	39 – 43	13	10.32
8.	44 – 48	9	7.14
9.	49 – 53	8	6.35
10.	54 – 58	2	1.59
11.	59 – 63	1	0.79
12.	64 – 68	4	3.17
13.	69 – 73	1	0.79
14.	74 – 78	1	0.79
15.	79 – 83	1	0.79
16.	84 – 88		0.00
17.	89 – 93	1	0.79
18.	94 – 99	–	0.00
19.	104 – 108	–	0.00
20.	109 – 113	1	0.79
Total		126	99.97

Note: In this table females below 9 years of age are not included.

Table 28.10 shows the distribution of the Sema Naga females on the basis of different age groups of Lalpahar village. The table reveals that the maximum number of females falls in the age group of 19-23 years with 18 females (14.29%) out of the total 126 females. This is followed by 17 (13.49%) females who fall in the age group of 14-18 years. It is followed by 15 (11.90%) females in 24-28 and 34-38 age-groups respectively, 14 (11.11) females in the 9-13 years, 13 (10.32%), 9 (7.14%), 8 (6.35%), 4 (3.17%) and 2 (1.59%) females in the 39-43,44-48, 49-53, 64-68 and 54-58 years accordingly. 1 (0.79%) female falls in each of the age group 59-63 years, 69-73 years, 74-78 years, 79-83 years, 99-93 years and 109-113 years, respectively.

The table also reveals that the life span of Sema Naga females of Lalpahar village is long.

Table 28.11: Distribution of Sema Naga girls according to Age at Menarche in village Lalpahar

Sl. No.	Age at Menarche	Number of Girls	%	Mean	S.D.	S.E.
1.	9	–	–			
2.	10	–	–			
3.	11	1	1.85			
4.	12	5	9.26	13.38	0.74	±0.10
5.	13	13	24.07			
6.	14	32	59.26			
7.	15	3	5.56			
8.	16	–	–			
Total		54	100			

Table 28.11 shows the distribution of women menstruating at different ages. It is observed from the table that the age at menarche varies from 11-15 years. The table also reveals that the maximum number of girls attains menarche at the age of 14 years, which they are 32 (59.26%) in number. However, concentration of women in 13 years is also appreciably high, i.e. 13 (24.07%) in number. It is followed by 5 (9.26%) women in 12 years and 3 (5.56%) women in 15 years and 1 (1.85%), respectively. The mean menarcheal age is calculated as 13.38. S.D is 0.74 and S.E. is ± 0.10.

From Table 28.12 it is clear that the mean age at menarche among the Sema Naga is 13.38 ± 0.10, which is followed by the Turung, i.e. 13.06 ± 0.20 and the Ahom 13.06, respectively. The lowest mean age at menarche among the Tai Phake is 11.52 ± 0.10.

Regarding the age at marriage among the Sema Naga women it has already been mentioned in Table 28.9 that their mean age at marriage is 19.99 ± 0.24.

Table 28.12: Mean Age at Menarche: Sema Naga and some other Mongoloid Population of Assam

Population	*Number of Women*	*Mean ± SE*	*Reference*
Sema Naga	54	13.38 ± 0.10	Present study
Turung	32	13.06 ± 0.20	Das 1985
Tai Turung	101	12.43	Barua 1992
Khamyang	40	12.80 ± 0.13	Das 1985
Mikir	52	12,75 ± 0.18	Khatoniar 1972
Lalung	51	12.36 ± 0.06	Das *et al.*, 1980
Mishing	67	12.68	Das *et al.*, 1980
Ahom	77	13.06	Das *et al.*, 1980
Garo	95	12.55 ± 0.10	Das and Saikia 1999
Sonowal Kachari	200	12.77 ± 0.12	Deka 1976
Tai Phake	130	11.52 ± 0.10	Das and Gogoi 2002
Deori	204	12.69 ± 0.05	Deori 2006

Table 28.13: Distribution of women according to number of conception in village Lalpahar

Sl. No.	*No. of conception*	*Up to 30 years*		*31–44 years*		*45+ years*		*Total*	
		No. of women	*%*	*No. of women*	*%*	*No. of women*	*%*	*No. of women*	*%*
1.	1	5	8.20	–	–	–	–	5	8.20
2.	2	2	3.28	9	14.75	4	6.45	15	24.59
3.	3	3	4.92	9	14.75	5	8.06	17	27.87
4.	4	–	–	2	3.28	3	4.84	5	8.20
5.	5	–	–	5	8.20	3	4.84	8	13.11
6.	6	–	–	1	1.64	3	4.84	4	6.56
7.	7	–	–	–	–	3	4.84	3	4.92
8.	8	–	–	–	–	3	4.84	3	4.92
9.	9	–	–	–	–	–	–	–	–
10.	10	–	–	–		1	1.61	1	1.64
Total		10	16.40	26	42.62	25	40.32	61	100.01

Table 28.13 shows the distribution of women according to number of conception. Out of 75 married women, 61 had experienced conception. The table also reveals that the number of conception ranges from 1 to 10.

Out of 10 (16.39%) women in the age group up to 30 years, 5 (8.20%) women had 1 conception. 2 (3.28%) had conceived twice. 3 (4.92%) woman had 3 conceptions, respectively.

In the age group 31-44 years, recording 26 (42.62%) women, their conception ranges from 2 to 10. Here, maximum of 9 (14.75%) women each had experienced 2 and 3, conceptions. 5 (8.20%) women had conceived 5 times. 1 (1.64%) woman had 6 conceptions.

In the age group 45 years and above, 25 (40.62%) women, their conceptions range from 2 to 10. Here, maximum of 5 (8.06%) women each had experienced 3 conceptions, 4 women had experienced 2 conceptions and 3 women had experienced 4, 5, 6, 7 and 8 conceptions, respectively.

Table 28.14: Distribution of women according to age at first childbirth in village Lalpahar

Sl. No.	*Age group (in years)*	*No. of women*	*%*	*Mean*	*S.D.*	*S.E.*
1.	17 – 19	18	29.51			
2.	20 – 22	19	31.15			
3.	23 – 25	15	24.59			
4.	26 – 28	5	8.20	21.93	2.4	±0.30
5.	29 – 31	4	6.56			
Total		61	100.04			

Table 28.14 shows the distribution of mothers according to their age at first childbirth. From the table it is evident that the age of mothers at the time of first childbirth varies from 17 to 31 years. The highest number of women, i.e. 19 (31.15%) have reported to have their first child birth in the age group of 20-22 years. It is followed by 18 (29.51%) women in the age group of 17-19 years. 15 (24.59%) women in the age group of 23-25 years and 5 (8.20%) and 4 (6.56%) women in the age group of 26-28, 29-31 years had their first childbirth. The frequency decreases as the age group increases. The mean age at first childbirth is 21.93±0.30 with the S.D. of 2.4.

Table 28.15 shows the pregnant and pregnancy outcome of mothers according to their present age. The table shows that there are total 68 mothers with all totals of 220 numbers of pregnancies with an average of 3.24. The table reveals that the average number of live birth is 0.93. Reproductive wastage, which includes abortion and still birth, totals at 15 with an average of 0.07 for all ever married women. The highest number of mothers falls in the age group 35-44 years, i.e. 19 mothers with the pregnancies, i.e. 60. The number of live births is also recorded in this category with 56 (25.45%) numbers. The second highest number of mothers falls in the category of 45-54 years, i.e. 16 mothers with the

Table 28.15: Distribution of Pregnant and Pregnancy Outcome of Mother's according to their presentage

Sl. No.	*Present age in years*	*No. of mothers*	*No. of pregnancies*	*Carrying child*	*Pregnant outcome*							
					L-B		*S-B*		*Spontaneous Abortion*		*Total No. of Foetal wastage*	
					No.	*%*	*No.*	*%*	*No.*	*%*	*No.*	*%*
1.	15–24	7	10	1	9	4.09	–	–	–	–	–	–
2.	25–34	14	31	–	28	12.73	3	1.36	–	–	–	–
3.	35–44	19	60	–	56	25.45	4	1.82	1	–	–	–
4.	45–54	16	63	–	60	27.27	3	1.36	–	–	–	–
5.	55–64	6	25	–	22	10.00	3	1.36	–	–	–	–
6.	65–74	5	23	–	22	10.00	1	0.45	–	–	–	–
7.	75–84	1	8	–	8	3.64	–	–	–	–	–	–
Total		68	220	1	205	93.48	14	6.35	1	0.45	15	6.81

number of pregnancies, i.e. 63 with 60 (27.27%) live births. 14 mothers fall in the age groups 25-34 years with 31 numbers of pregnancies respectively, with 28 (12.73%) live births accordingly. 7 mothers with 10 numbers of pregnancies and 9 (4.09%) live births in the age group 15-24 years. 6 mothers with 25 pregnancies and 22 live births. 5 mother with 23 pregnancies and 22 (10.00%) live birth in the age group of 65-74 years.

Out of 14, 4 and 1 numbers of stillbirths are recorded in the age group 35-44 and 65-74 years and 3 each in 25-34, 45-54 and 55-64. 1 case of foetal wastage are recorded which is due to spontaneous abortion falls in the 35-44 years of age group.

The table also reflects that 1 woman is pregnant in the village which falls in the 15-24 years.

Table 28.16: Mother's age at marriage and mortality experience in village Lalpahar

Sl. No.	*Age Group*	*No. of Mothers*	*Total Live Birth*	*Infant Mortality (0 – 1 yrs.)*	*Child Mortality (1.1-5 yrs.)*	*Juvenile Mortality (5.1-14 yrs)*	*14.1 + yrs.*
1.	Up to 14	—	—	—	—	—	—
2.	15 – 19	16	19	3	—	—	—
3.	20 – 24	20	28	2	—	—	—
4.	25 and above	26	158	3	4	—	—
	Total	62	205	8	4	—	—

Table 28.16 shows the distribution of mother's age at marriage and mortality experience of the Lalpahar village. The highest number of mothers, i.e. 26 out of the 75 mothers got married at the age group of 25 and above years and also experienced highest number of live births, i.e. 158 in number. It is followed by 20 mothers who got married in the age group of 20-24 years and the number of live births is 28. 16 mothers got married at the age of 15-19 years with 19 numbers of live births.

The table also reflects that mortality in the village is categorized in 3 categories, viz. infant mortality, child mortality and juvenile mortality. 8 infant mortalities are recorded in the village, out of which 3 falls each in the age of 25 and above years and 15-19 years of age group, and, 2 fall in 20-24 age group. 4 child mortalities are found in the village, where 4 fall in the 25 and above years of age group.

Table 28.17: Distribution of Sema Naga women according to age at menopause in village Lalpahar

Sl. No.	Age at Menopause	Number of Women	%	Mean	S.D.	S.E.
1	Up to 40	—	—			
2	41 – 43	—	—			
3	44 – 46	10	58.82	46.23	1.5	±0.36
4	47 – 49	7	41.18			
	Total	17	100.00			

Table 28.17 shows the distribution of women according to their age at menopause. The table shows that the range of the age at menopause of the Sema Naga women of Lalpahar village varies between 44 to 49 years. The highest number of women, i.e10 (58.82%) attained their menopause in the age group of 44-46 years. It is followed by 7 (41.18%) women who attained their menopause in the age group of 47-49 years. Their mean age at menopause is 46.23 years, standard error being ±0.43 with the S.D. of 1.5.

The present study among the Sema Nagas reveals a picture of continuity and change. Though marital alliances took place with different tribes and communities, yet they are able to maintain their distinct identity. The acceptance of Christianity has brought changes in their religious life but traditional values and sentiments are reflected in their socio-cultural life. The frequent visit to their kin members and relatives help in maintaining the solidarity which Durkheim referred to as mechanical solidarity. The very basis of mechanical solidarity rests on similar tasks which developed similar values and emotions. At the same time the organic solidarity where individual gets priority has brought tremendous changes in their socio-economic life. But this does not hamper their total social integration. In case of marriage, it is found that the number of negotiated marriage is not high but when it occurs they follow their traditional procedure in details. Clan still plays an important role in marriage. The mean age at marriage in the present sample is 19.99±0.24. The mean menarcheal age observed is 13.38±0.10 years. The range is 9-15 years, and majority of women having their first menstruation at the age of 14 years. The percentage is 59.20. This value falls well within the North- east Indian range. Regarding reproductive performance a total of 68 ever married women reported a total of 220 pregnancies with an average of 3.24 which is slightly lower in comparison to North-East Indian tribes. Overall the changes that emerged among the Sema Nagas are not unwelcomed to the people at large.

ACKNOWLEDGEMENTS

The present paper is a part of the project financed by ICSSR, New Delhi. The authors are thankful to ICSSR for financial assistance.

REFERENCES

Alemchiba, (1970), *A Brief Historical Account of Nagaland.* Kohima, Nagaland. Naga Institution of Culture.

Barua, I. (1992), The Tai Turungs of Assam: A Study of Socio-Demographic Profile. *Man In India.* 72.

Barua, I. (2001), The *Tai Turungs of Assam.* Allahabad, K.K. Publications.

Das, B. (1985), Fertility and Mortality Differentials among the Khamyang and Turung Population of Jorhat district, Assam *Assam Science Society*, 28.

Das, B.M. P.B., Das & R. Das. (1980 b.) *Biological Profile of Five Mongoloid Populations.* Study No 8. Department of Anthropology, Gauhati University.

Das, B.M., P.B. Das & R. Das (1980 a), *Lalungs: their Physical features & Biological Profiles.* Monographs: U.G.C. Report. Department of Anthropology. Gauhati University.

Das, F.A. & J.R.Saikia. (1999), Some aspects of Fertility of the Garo women of Paschim Basti Garo village in Sibsagar District, Assam. *Delhi Human Ecology 10 (4).*

Deka, R. (1976), Menarcheal Age among the Kachari Women of Upper Assam. *Bulletin, Department of Anthropology. Dibrugarh University.*

Gogoi, D. (1972), Menarche & Menopause among Women of an Ahom village of Upper Assam. *Bulletin Department of Anthropology, Dibrugarh University.*[1]

Hutton, J.H. (1968), *The Sema Nagas*, Second Editions, Oxford University Press.

29

Effect of Migration on Some Demographic Parameters Among Three Immigrant Tea Garden Labour Population Groups of Assam

Arundhati Phukan Gogoi and *Sarthak Sengupta*

Introduction

Demographic study of small population groups is an important area of research in physical anthropology. From an evolutionary point of view, demographic parameters like fertility and mortality are important to understand the genetic structure of a population. Natural selection, one of the major evolutionary forces, is operating on human population through differential fertility and mortality. A large number of biosocial factors, like maternal age, parity, education, religion, economic conditions, etc., influence most of the demographic parameters. The negative effect of age at marriage on fertility has also been reported in many studies. Studies conducted in different parts of India have revealed that fertility rate declines with the increasing mean age at marriage.

There were consistent relationships between fertility and education level. The effect of economic condition on fertility has also been revealed in many studies. Studies revealed that there is an inverse relationship between fertility and occupation and/or economic condition. Several researchers have also recorded close relation between fertility and religion. As such, demographic parameters are vital for understanding not only the genetic structure, but also the socio-economic condition of a population.

In the present study, we shall look into the variation that exists with regard to few reproductive characteristic features associated with fertility and mortality amongst three numerically dominant tea garden labour population groups, namely the Munda, the Oraon and the Savar in the tea gardens of Dibrugarh district, Assam.

In North East India, information on fertility and mortality from among the immigrant populations of region is very limited. Among relatively un-explored group of peoples, the tea-garden labour populations, a relatively late addition to the population of Brahmaputra valley, Assam, constitute an important component. In this chapter, thus, an attempt has been made to deal at a micro-level with the fertility and mortality patterns among the above mentioned three immigrant population groups from the tea gardens of Assam.

The recorded history of tea industry in Assam is nearly 170 years old. The first experimental tea estate was established in Chabua (*Cha* – tea, *bua* – to grow) in Dibrugarh district of Assam in 1837. At present, the tea garden labour population is about 20 per cent of the total population in the State of Assam. They are recognized as 'Other Backward Communities' in Assam, though their counterparts in their place of origin enjoy the status of either Scheduled Castes or Scheduled Tribes. There are around 760 major tea plantations in Assam covering an area of approximately 185,000 hectares of land. This area constitutes more than 51 per cent of the total area under tea in the whole of India.

In the early 19th century, during the formative stage of Assam plantation, the authorities of tea plantations of Assam were compelled to employ intermediaries (*arkathi*) to procure labourers from other provinces of India, since the required labourer could not be obtained from local people within the province. These tea labourers are overwhelmingly composed of various tribes and few low caste populations. They are either originally brought or migrated to Assam in between 1840 to 1961 from various cultural, linguistic and ethnic heritages and from many provinces of India, mainly from West Bengal, Bihar, Orissa, Madhya Pradesh, Andhra Pradesh and Madras. The first attempt to import labour from Chotanagpur was made by the 'Assam Company' (founded in 1839) in 1841. After 1836, when the system of recruitment was properly organized, Assam received a steady flow of labour from these provinces and it continued uninterruptedly until mid-twentieth century. The tribal communities like the Santhal, Oraon, Munda, Kharia, Gond, Khond, Kisan, Nagesia, Savar, Godava, Porja, and the Pankha, were mainly recruited. Some Hindu low caste groups were also recruited and they belong mostly to groups like the Kurmi, Tanti, Pan-Tanti, Gowala and others. (Roy Burman, 1968; cited from Karotemprel and Dutta Roy, 1990;

Sengupta, 2009). Besides, there are a good number of other ethnic groups also, those have contributed to the formation of total tea labour population in Assam. There is no reliable statistics about the tea garden labour population, however, the most numerous groups are the Oraon, Munda, Santhal, Savar, Kharia, and the Ho etc.

The plantation in Assam compelled these varied groups of people to come together and share the common working and living condition. These labourers were accommodated within the plantation boundary, but they were kept isolated from the neighbouring indigenous population. Due to migration in a new habitat, they had to give up many of their traditional beliefs and customs. Their original cultural identity rarely remained intact in new geo-demographic environment. A new society emerged after complex interaction that underwent among different sections of tea garden labour population belonging to various tribes and castes. However, notwithstanding the fact of having socio-cultural affinity (Kar, 1981), their bent of mind is generally towards establishing nuptial relationship primarily within their own ethnic groups (Sengupta and Sharma, 1990).

The Dibrugarh district, situated on the Southern bank and upper reaches of the river Brahmaputra lies on the North-eastern corner of Assam. Formerly, it was a part of undivided Lakhimpur district since 1842 until the bifurcation of the district was made on October 1971. It is bounded by the river Brahmaputra on the North, Tinsukia district on the East, and Tirap district of Arunachal Pradesh on the South-east. The South-western boundary of the district runs along the Eastern boundary of Sibsagar district.

The tea garden labour population groups have settled in Assam more than one and half century ago, and are far remote from their native land for a prolonged period. They mainly earn their livelihood as tea garden labourers. Both the males and the females work in the garden as permanent or temporary (*Faltu*) workers. The males involve in plantation, preparation of seedlings, maintaining nursery, transplanting seedlings from one place to another and work generally in factory. However, the females mostly work in collection of tea leaves etc. Due to migration to a new habitat, settling down within the plantation as multi-ethnic community, and change of occupation from agriculture to industrial labour etc., it is expected that in course of time some changes in biological sphere from the native (sedente) population might have been taken place.

In Assam, the Munda is a numerically dominant immigrant groups working mostly in the tea plantations. Ethnically they are proto-Australoids and the language spoken by them has been known as Kolarian, which is a sub-family of the Austro-Asiatic (*Kherwari*) group of languages (Grierson, 1906; Crawford, 1924; Fuchs, 1982). It is believed that their Hindu neighbours gave the name Munda to them although they prefer to call themselves the *Horoko*, *Horo* being the word for a 'Man' (*ko* is the sign of the plural). They are mainly concentrated in Ranchi district of Jharkhand and exhibit relatively lesser concentration in some districts of West Bengal, Bihar and Orissa.

The Oraon is the Dravidian speaking community who migrated to tea plantations of Assam mainly from Ranchi and its adjacent districts (Dalton, 1872; Hunter, 1877; Risley, 1891; Roy, 1915). Linguistically they belong to Khurukh, which is intermediate group of Dravidian language family (Risley, 1891). Guha (1931) considers that the Oraons are related to the proto-Australoid racial stock. On the other hand, Gates (1960) finds Mongoloid and Negrito ethnic strain in them.

The Savar on the other hand, is a cultivating population group of Kolarian linguistic family, who are widely scattered all over the Central India. They inhabit in the States of Orissa, Bihar, West Bengal, Assam, Madhya Pradesh, Andhra Pradesh, and in Maharashtra. They belong to the proto-Australoid racial stock and on linguistic ground placed amongst the Dravidian group in general (Risley, 1891; Dalton, 1872) and Kolarian family in particular (Cunningham, 1884).

Material and Method

For the present analysis, the data on pregnancy outcome of 526 married women [Hindu Munda (MH) - 100, Christian Munda (MC) - 100; Hindu Oraon (OH) - 124, Christian Oraon (OC) - 101; Savar (SV) - 101] aged 40 years and above and on the wastage (death of their embryonic as well as live-born offspring) have been considered. In view of relatively earlier menopausal age and decline of fertility in women of North East India, mothers over 40 years of age are considered to have completed their fertility. In many earlier studies conducted in North East India, it is observed that fertility declines drastically when the mothers reach 40 years of age. In the present study, we had to estimate the age of individual in certain cases, consequently some amount of error might have occurred in estimating the age of persons. However, these data were crosschecked from a number of sources in any case.

The tea gardens selected for the present study are Basmotia Tea Estate; Nandanban Tea Estate; Bamunbari Tea Estate; Moran Tea Estate; Bijulibari Tea Estate; Hatiali Tea Estate; Kailashpur Tea Estate, Lengrai

Table 29.1. Demographic parameters among the tea labourers of Assam

Population	*No*	*Mean age Menarche*	*Age at First Marriage*	*Age at First Child-birth*	*Mean of live-births*	*Surviving children*	*Mean age at Menopause*
Munda (Hindu)	100	13.09 ± 0.09	19.70 ± 0.17	21.18±0.18	5.78±0.21	5.08±0.18	42.78±0.14
Munda (Christian)	100	12.80 ± 0.07	19.71 ± 0.15	21.00±0.26	5.05±0.19	4.33±0.15	42.89±0.15
Munda	200	12.94 ± 0.06	19.70 ± 0.11	21.09±0.16	5.42±0.18	4.71±0.12	42.83±0.13
Oraon (Hindu)	124	13.42 ± 0.11	19.34 ± 0.18	20.75±0.22	6.12±0.18	5.18±0.16	42.33±0.14
Oraon (Christian)	101	13.19 ± 0.08	19.16 ± 0.20	20.49±0.22	5.45±0.21	4.66±0.18	42.50±0.13
Oraon	225	13.31 ± 0.07	19.26 ± 0.13	20.63±0.16	5.82±0.17	4.95±0.12	42.41±0.12
Savar	101	13.15 ± 0.07	19.19 ± 0.12	20.21±0.10	4.91±0.15	4.35±0.12	42.39±0.08

Tea Estate; and Teamakpho Tea Estate—all from Dibrugarh district of Assam.

In Assam, although the majority of the Oraon, Munda and the Savar people identify themselves as Hindu, while individuals from the Oraon and the Munda groups subscribing to Christian faith, are also considerable in number. The interaction between these two segments of the Oraon and the Munda seem to be very limited in their day-to-day life as well as in religious celebrations. The Hindu section of both the populations has been reported to avoid inter-dining and matrimonial alliances with their Christian counterparts. Therefore, data have been collected from two populations, i.e. the Munda and the Oraon based on religion.

Results and Discussion

Studies conducted earlier reveal that the onset of menarche vary from population to population because of multitude of factors like heredity, nutrition, ethnic, rural-urban living, latitude of the place, chronic disease etc. In the present study, the Munda women (12.94 ± 0.06 years) experience menarche at a relatively early age than the Oraon (13.31 ± 0.07 years) and the Savar (13.15 ± 0.07 years) women (Table 29.1). The Munda population stands statistically significantly apart from the Oraon and the Savar populations whereas variation observed in between the Oraon and the Savar is not statistically significant. The two sub-samples of the Oraon based on religion also show close statistical affinity to each other, but the Christian Munda having the lowest mean menarcheal age (12.80 ± 0.07 years) not only differ significantly from the Hindu Munda (13.09 ± 0.09 years) but also stand significantly apart from the other samples taken into consideration. The Hindu Oraon (13.42 ± 0.11 years) on the other hand, showing the highest mean menarcheal age, differ significantly from each of the Hindu Munda and the Savar populations.

Information on the menarcheal age from among the tea garden labour populations like the Munda, Oraon, and the Savar of Assam, as well as data on these population groups from their original homeland like Ranchi, Chotanagpur, Khunti area etc. are nearly absent. From the tea gardens of Assam, until date we have information on the Oraon (13.19 ± 0.17 years; Ahmed Das and Konwar, 2002); Santhal (13.24 ± 0.12 years; Buzarbarua, 1983); and the Munda (12.42 ± 0.10 years; Buzarbarua, 1983) population only. Studies reveal that the Munda of Ranchi has the mean age at menarche at 12.49 ± 0.06 years, whereas among the Oraon it is 12.54 ± 0.06 years (Ratnawali and Roy, 2000). Age at menarche for the Munda

Table 29.2: Reproductive wastage and mortality rates among the tea labourers of Assam

Population	*No.*	*Mean conception*	*Mean live-birth*	*Abortion %*	*Still birth %*	*Mortality (%)*			
						Neonatal	*Infant*	*Child*	*Juvenile*
Munda (Hindu)	100	6.35	5.78	5.66	3.31	4.32	2.25	3.63	1.90
Munda (Christian)	100	5.73	5.05	7.16	4.71	5.15	2.77	4.55	1.78
Munda	200	6.04	5.42	6.37	3.97	4.71	2.49	4.06	1.85
Oraon (Hindu)	124	6.69	6.12	4.22	4.33	4.87	3.29	5.53	1.71
Oraon (Christian)	101	6.13	5.45	5.82	5.33	6.00	1.64	4.54	2.18
Oraon	225	6.44	5.82	4.90	4.76	5.35	2.60	5.12	1.91
Savar	101	5.36	4.91	4.62	3.70	4.23	2.01	3.23	2.02

of Khunti region, Bihar was found to be 12.64 + 0.10 years (Buzarbarua, 1983). All these values are significantly lower than that of their counterparts from Assam.

Statistical analysis reveals that the mean age at menarche of the present Munda sample is not in agreement with that obtained on the same population by Buzarbarua (1983, 12.42 + 0.10 years; *t* value = 4.46). It is to be mentioned here that the later sample was collected from the Sibsagar district (Sonari), which is adjacent to Dibrugarh district of Assam. The present Munda sample are also very different and deviate significantly from the Santhal of Assam (Buzarbarua, 1983; 13.24 + 0.12 years; *t* value = 2.24), as well as from their sedente counterpart from Khunti (Buzarbarua, 1983; 12.64 + 0.10 years; *t* value = 2.57) and Ranchi (Ratnawali and Roy, 2000; 12.49 + 06 years, *t* value = 5.31) of Jharkhand. However, no such marked variation could be detected when they are compared with the Oraon of Assam (Ahmed Das and Konwar, 2002; 13.19 + 0.17 years; *t* value = 1.39).

The difference in menarchaeal age between the present Oraon sample and the Santhal of Assam (Buzarbarua, 1983) is not well marked (*t* value = 0.50). One more Oraon sample reported by Ahmed Das and Konwar (2002) from Assam also shows close statistical affinity (*t* value = 0.65) in this regard. However, the present Oraon sample stands significantly apart from the Munda sample reported by Buzarbarua (1983; *t* value = 7.30) from Assam and their sedente counterparts from Ranchi (Ratnawali and Roy, 2000; 12.54 + 0.06 years; *t* value = 8.36).

The present Savar sample deviate significantly from the Munda of Assam (Buzarbarua, 1983; *t* value = 5.98), but significance of test fails to record any marked variation when they are compared with the Oraon (Ahmed Das and Konwar, 2002; *t* value = 0.21) and the Santhal (Buzarbarua, 1983; *t* value = 0.64) of Assam with regard to mean menarcheal age.

It merits to be mentioned here that the well-off girls experience earlier menarche than those belonging to the lower socio-economic strata of the society (Eveleth and Tanner, 1990). It is suggested that the earlier menarche and maturation are mainly due to improved environmental conditions, especially in nutritional status. Satyanarayana and Naidu (1979) have also suggested, "...Shortness and late menarche are both attributed to under-nutrition". Likewise, Malhotra and Singh (1988) have shown that the mean age at menarche is significantly higher in the lower social classes than that in the higher ones. The relatively higher mean menarcheal age in the immigrant populations like the present one than their sedente counterparts is noteworthy in this context.

The mean age at marriage (Table 29.1) among the Hindu and Christian sub-samples of both Munda and Oraon shows close statistical affinity (Table 29.3). Compared to other, among the Munda (19.70 + 0.11 years), the mean age at marriage is relatively higher than the Oraon (19.26 + 0.13 years) and the Savar (19.19 + 0.12 years). Test of significance reveals that both the sub-samples of the Oraon are statistically close to the Savar having smaller mean values in all of them, but they all stand far apart from the Munda population (Table 29.3).

The mean age at marriage of the present Munda sample deviate significantly from the Oraon (Ahmed Das and Konwar, 2002; 20.50 + 0.23 years, *t* value = 3.14); Santhal (Buzarbarua, 1983; 18.26 + 0.27 years; *t* value = 4.94); and the Munda (Buzarbarua, 1983; 18.50 + 0.21 years; *t* value = 5.06) sample of Assam (Table 29.1). Marriage also takes place at significantly earlier ages among the Mundas of Khunti, Bihar (Buzarbarua, 1983; 19.18 + 0.18 years; *t* value = 2.46). The present Oraon sample also stand significantly apart from the Santhal (*t* value = 3.33), Munda (t value = 3.07) and the Oraon (t value = 4.69) of Assam. The females of the present Savar sample also record significantly higher mean marital age than that of the Santhal (*t* value = 3.14), Munda (t value = 2.85) and the Oraon (t value = 4.96) population of Assam.

The mean age at first childbirth is given in Table 29.1. Like the case of mean age at marriage, the differences in mean age at first childbirth between the different population groups under study with their sub-samples are found to exhibit almost similar pictures (Table 29.3). The Savar (20.21 + 0.10 years) have the lowest mean age at first childbirth, which rises through the Christian Oraon (20.49 + 0.22 years), Hindu Oraon (20.75 + 0.22 years), Christian Munda (21.00 + 0.26 years) and the Hindu Munda (21.18 + 0.18 years). Hence, the Savar having the lowest mean age at first childbirth differ significantly from the Hindu as well as the Christian Munda and the Hindu Oraon (Table 29.3). The difference between the Hindu Munda and the Christian Oraon is also found to be significant. Ignoring the religious affiliation, the three population groups under present investigation when compared, exhibit statistically significant heterogeneity among them with regard to the trait.

The number of mean live births to all married women considered in the present study, is incorporated in Table 29.1. It is found that mean live births per married women are 5.42 + 0.18; 5.82 + 0.17; 4.91 + 0.15 in the Munda, Oraon and the Savar population, respectively. The Hindu sub-samples of the Munda and the Oraon population records relatively higher mean live births than their Christian counterparts. These differences in mean number of live births of mothers in the sub-samples of the Munda and the Oraon population based on religion are statistically significant (Table 29.3). The mean live birth is much lower in the Savar when compared with the others. The test of significance (Table 29.3) indicates that the Savar population stands statistically significantly apart from others with regard to mean live births per mother.

The mean number of live births per married woman of these tea garden labour population groups shows almost similar consistency with the Santhal (6.20; Buzarbarua, 1983); Munda (5.92; Buzarbarua, 1983) and the Oraon (4.70; Ahmed Das and Konwar, 2002) population of Assam. However, the present sample on the Munda (5.42) shows markedly high mean live births per mother than the Munda sample reported from Khunti, Bihar (3.94; Buzarbarua, 1983). Unfortunately, no attempt could be made to statistically evaluate the variation in this regard due to lack of relevant statistical derivatives.

The reproductive wastage (abortion and stillbirths) for the populations under consideration is given in Table 29.2. It is observed that the reproductive wastage is relatively high in these populations. The reproductive wastages as a whole in the Munda (10.34%) are markedly higher than that of the Oraon (9.66%) and the Savar (8.32%) populations. The abortion rates in these populations are much higher than the still birth rate. The table also reveals that the incidence of abortion and stillbirth is relatively higher in the Christian sub-samples of both the Munda and the Oraon populations than that of their Hindu counterparts.

The incidence of reproductive wastages in the population groups under present study, is markedly higher than that of the Santhal (5.32%) and the Munda (5.12%) as reported by Buzarbarua (1983); and the Oraon (6.53%; Ahmed Das and Konwar, 2002) of Assam, but exhibit a close degree of approximation with the sedente Munda of Khunti, Bihar (8.37 per cent, Buzarbarua, 1983).

The mortality rate in the populations covered under present study is low. It is found that the neonatal mortality rate is slightly higher in the Oraon (5.35%) than the Munda (4.71%) and the Savar (4.23%). Similar higher incidence in the Oraon is recorded with regard to infant, child and juvenile mortality rate also. Infant mortality rates are low especially between the Christian Oraon (1.64%) and the Savar (2.01%). In conformity with the neonatal and infant mortality rates, the child mortality rate is also found to be little higher among the Oraon (5.12%) than the

Table 29.3: Test of significance

Population Compared	*Mean age Menarche*	*Age at First Marriage*	*Age at First Child-birth*	*Mean of live-births*	*Surviving children*	*Mean age at Menopause*
MH X MC	2.54*	0.04	0.57	2.58*	3.20*	0.53
MH X OH	2.32*	1.45	1.51	1.23	0.42	2.27*
MH X OC	0.83	2.06*	2.43*	1.11	1.65	1.46
MH X SV	0.53	2.45*	4.71*	3.37*	3.37*	2.41*
MC X OH	4.75*	1.60	0.73	4.09*	3.88*	2.73*
MC X OC	3.67*	2.20*	1.49	1.41	1.41	1.98*
MC X SV	3.54*	2.71*	2.84*	0.58	0.10	2.94*
OH X OC	1.69	0.67	0.84	2.42*	2.16*	0.89
OH X SV	2.07*	0.69	2.24*	5.16*	4.15*	0.37
OC X SV	0.38	0.13	1.16	2.09*	1.43	0.72
Munda X Oraon	4.02*	2.59*	2.03*	1.62	1.41	2.37*
Munda x Savar	2.28*	3.13*	4.67*	2.18*	2.12*	2.88*
Oraon x Savar	1.62	0.40	2.23*	4.02*	3.53*	0.14

d.f. = 8

* indicates statistically significant at 5.0 per cent level of probability

Munda (4.06%) and the Savar (3.23%) populations. Incidence of juvenile mortality rate is found to be very low in all the populations under present study.

Incidence of death below 4 years of age (neonatal + infant mortality) in the present Munda (7.20%); Oraon (7.95%); and the Savar (6.24%) populations of Assam is much higher than those found in the Santhal (4.54 per cent, Buzarbarua, 1983), Oraon (4.56%, Ahmed Das and Konwar, 2002) and the Munda (5.49%, Buzarbarua, 1983) populations of Assam. However, they show close affinity with those reported for the Munda of Khunti, Bihar (7.87%, Buzarbarua, 1983).

The child mortality rate is also found to be little higher among the Oraon (5.12%) than that of the Munda (4.06%) and the Savar (3.23%); and there is not much variation with those reported from the Munda (5.46%; Buzarbarua, 1983) of Assam as well as the Munda from Khunti, Bihar (4.06%, Buzarbarua, 1983). Child mortality rate among the Santhal of Assam is conspicuously lower (1.64%, Buzarbarua, 1983) than that of the others.

Incidence of juvenile mortality rate is found to be consistently low in the Munda (1.85%), Oraon (1.91%), and the Savar (2.02%) population of present study, and they show close degree of approximation with the Santhal (0.96%, Buzarbarua, 1983); and the Munda (2.03%, Buzarbarua, 1983) of Assam. The sedente Munda of Bihar (1.78%, Buzarbarua, 1983) also stand close to the range displayed in this regard.

It is found that the mean number of surviving children per mother is 4.95 ± 0.12; 4.71 ± 0.12; and 4.35 ± 0.12 among the Oraon, Munda and the Savar populations respectively. The differences between the Oraon, the Munda and the Savar populations in respect of surviving children are found to be statistically significant (Table 29.3). The number of surviving children in the Hindu sub-samples of both the Munda and the Oraon populations shows significantly higher mean values than that of the Christian sub-samples. The Hindu Oraon (5.18 ± 0.16) having the highest number of surviving children, stands significantly apart from the Christian Munda (4.33 ± 0.15) and the Savar (4.35 ± 0.12) populations. The difference between the Savar and the Hindu Munda (5.08 ± 0.18) is also found to be statistically significant.

The mean menopausal age among the Munda (42.83 + 0.13 years) of Assam exhibit significant differences with that of the Oraon (42.41 ± 0.12 years) and the Savar (42.39 ± 0.08 years). The Christian Munda (42.89 ± 0.15 years) having the higher mean menopausal age is statistically not in agreement with that obtained from the Hindu Oraon (42.33 ± 0.14

years), Christian Oraon (42.50 ± 0.13 years) and the Savar. The mean menopausal age of the Hindu Munda (42.78 ± 0.14 years), also deviate significantly from the Hindu Oraon and the Savar, who shows significantly lower mean age at menopause than the former.

Mean age at menopause in the present Munda sample is somewhat early and is significantly lower than that of the Santhal (43.98 ± 0.24 years, Buzarbarua, 1983; *t* value = 4.21), Munda (43.99 ± 0.17 years, Buzarbarua, 1983; *t* value = 5.42) and the Oraon (45.52 ± 0.56 years; Ahmed Das and Konwar, 2002; *t* value 4.67) of Assam. The sedente Munda (44.25 ± 0.18 years; Buzarbarua, 1983; *t* value = 6.39) also stand apart from them. With regard to mean menopausal age, the Oraon women markedly distinct from the Munda (*t* value = 7.59); Santhal (*t* value = 5.85) and the Oraon (*t* value = 5.43) of Assam. The Savar also deviate significantly from the Munda (*t* value = 8.51), Santhal (*t* value = 6.28) and the Oraon (*t* value = 5.53) of Assam in this regard.

The study reveals that the populations under present investigation are unique in their demographic characteristics and are quite different from the other neighbouring tea garden labour populations of Assam. There is considerable difference between the Hindu and the Christian segments of the population under study. Comparatively late menarche in the immigrant tea garden labour populations than that of their sedente counterparts of original homeland, reflects the under nutritional status of the former. In a number of demographic characters, information obtained from the present populations is also not in agreement with their sedente counterparts of original homeland.

Acknowledgements

Authors are indebted to all women participants of Basmotia Tea Estate; Nandanban Tea Estate; Bamunbari Tea Estate; Moran Tea Estate; Bijulibari Tea Estate; Hatiali Tea Estate; Kailashpur Tea Estate; Lengrai Tea Estate; and Teamakpho Tea Estate from Dibrugarh district of upper Assam for their sincere help and co-operation during data collection.

REFERENCES

Ahmed Das, F. and J. Konwar, (2002), 'A note on some Demographic features of the Oraon of Tingkhong Tea Estate of Tingkhong, Dibrugarh, Assam', *Bulletin of the Department of Anthropology, Dibrugarh University,* 30: 113-122.

Buzarbarua, P.M. (1983), *Effect of Migration and Environment on Physical and Genetic Characters of some Santal and Munda Population of Assam*, Unpublished Ph.D. Thesis, Dibrugarh University.

Crawford, T. C. (1924), *Hand Book of Castes and Tribes Employed on the Tea Estates in North East India*. Calcutta, Indian Tea Association.

Cunningham, A. (1884), *Report of a Tour in the Central Provinces and Lower Gangetic Doab*. Volume 17. Calcutta, Archaeological Survey of India.

Dalton, E.T. (1872), *Descriptive Ethnology of Bengal*. Calcutta, Indian Studies Past and Present.

Eveleth, P.B. and J. M. Tanner, (1990), *Worldwide Variation in Human Growth*. Cambridge, Cambridge University Press.

Fuchs, S. (1982), *The Aboriginal Tribes of India*. Delhi, McMillan and Co.

Gates, R.R. (1960), 'Australoid Tribes in India'. *Mankind Quarterly*, 1: 83-88.

Grierson, G.A. (1906), *The Linguistic Survey of India*, Volume IV.

Guha, B.S. (1931), 'The racial affinities of the peoples of India'. Census of India. Volume I, Part III.

Hunter, W. W. (1877), *Statistical Accounts of Assam*. Volume II, London.

Kar, R.K. (1981), *The Savaras of Mancotta*. New Delhi, Cosmo Publications.

Karotemprel, S. and B. Dutta Roy. (1990), *Tea Garden Labourers of North East India*. Shillong, Vendrame Institute.

Malhotra, P. and S.P. Singh, (1988), 'Sexual maturation and physical growth of Patiala girls'. *Journal of Indian Anthropological Society*. 23: 63-68.

Ratnawali and K. Roy, (2000), 'Age at menarche among the tribal and non-tribal girls of Ranchi, Bihar'. In K. Khongsdier (Ed.): *Contemporary Research in Anthropology*, pp 180-187, New Delhi, Commonwealth Publishers.

Risley, H.H. (1891), *Tribes and Castes of Bengal: Ethnographic Glossary*. Volumes I and II. Calcutta, Bengal Secretariat Press.

Roy, S.C. (1915), *The Oraon of Chotonagpur*. Ranchi, Man in India Office.

Satnarayana, K. and A.N. Naidu, (1979), 'Nutrition and menarche in rural Hyderabad'. *Annals of Human Biology*. 6: 163-165.

Sengupta, S. and J.L. Sharma. (1990), 'Jhuman: Folk songs and dances of tea garden labourers of Assam'. In S. Karotemprel and B. Dutta Roy (Eds.): *Tea Garden Labourers of North East India*. Shillong, Vendrame Institute.

Sengupta, S. (2009), *The Tea Labourers of North East India – An Anthropo-historical Perspective*. New Delhi, Mittal Publications, New Delhi.

30

Prevalence of Tuberculosis in Some Population Groups of Upper Assam: A Preliminary Appraisal on Biological and Social Aspects

Debolina Biswas and *Sarthak Sengupta*

The health and diseases are related to cultural as well as biological factors and this in turn brings about the convergence of medical and cultural anthropological interests. Diseases are caused not only of biological factors but also of certain socio-cultural factors like cleanliness, hygiene, sanitation, certain rites and rituals, family condition etc. that have influence on the occurrence of diseases in a particular society. Diseases immensely deter the health of a person and thereby the health of a population or nation.

North East India, with such a diverse population and varied biome, many communicable diseases are prevalent in this remote part of our country. One of them is tuberculosis. It is considered not only a medical problem, but also social and economic problem as well. However, in spite of applying huge measures to eradicate this disease, it is still prevalent in North East Indian population groups and running at a high risk causing innumerable deaths annually. In North East India, particularly in Assam, the incidences of it are growing year by year but till remain low priority. Social scientists have been trying to know the biological, socio-economic and cultural factors (Narzary and Narzary, 2005; Tungdim *et al.*, 2008; Tungdim and Kapoor, 2008, 2010a, 2010b), which are supporting this disease to remain at a dormant state in human society.

Tuberculosis is an ancient chronic infectious disease known to be endemic in animals from the Paleolithic period. However, in man, the disease is followed by the development of agriculture and group living. The infection is germ caused and severely running a rapid and fatal course when the population is susceptible. Although, tuberculosis is not a hereditary disease, however, twin studies indicate that inherited susceptibility is an important risk factor (Comstock, 1978). Certain characteristics, which predispose one to tuberculosis and render the body usually vulnerable to attack by *tubercle bacilli*, may be inborn.

In Assam, there are no separate epidemiological surveys of tuberculosis conducted till date. During 1998-99, tuberculosis prevalence rate was 710 per lakh population. The DOTS strategy was first introduced on 16 November, 1998 in two places; one in Dibrugarh in Assam and the other in Imphal in Manipur. In Assam, Revised National Tuberculosis Control Programme (RNTCP) started at Dibrugarh District on 16 November, 1998 and in 2002 all the districts of Assam implemented RNTCP where 'DOTS' is widely used. The programme is integrated with general health services. Therefore, facilities for free examination and full course of treatment are available in health centres.

Tuberculosis may occur at any age but mostly it occurs in people above 5 years of age and mainly affect the economically productive age group. There are many social and biological factors, which support the spread of this deadly disease. Factors like illiteracy, unawareness of the disease, unhygienic and thickly populated living condition, lack of knowledge about the disease and proper treatment of it, food habits, occupation, presence of other disease, attitude towards the improvement etc. influence a lot in the treatment of this disease. Recently, there has been an increase in the tuberculosis cases globally, especially with the increase in the incidence of HIV infected cases.

In the present chapter, an attempt has been made to highlight some of the factors, which might be supporting this deadly disease to remain in an active state in two districts of upper Assam and bring miseries to thousands of families.

Material and Methods

The present investigation aims at endeavouring an investigation concerning with the collection of biological and social aspects as causative factors for the incidence of tuberculosis. The data have been collected mainly from diagnosed and registered patients attending Assam Medical College and Hospital, Dibrugarh; besides District Tuberculosis Centre, Tinsukia and Lankashi Tea Estate Hospital, Makum, Assam.

A cross-sectional study among 170 tuberculosis patients (Male = 104, Female = 66) was conducted in 2004 (Biswas, 2004). The patients

Table 30.1: Basic data of the tuberculosis patients

Characters of T.B. Patients		*Male*	*Female*	*M + F*
Patient by Age and Sex	1 yr – 10 yrs	3.85	4.55	4.11
	11 yrs – 20 yrs	12.50	28.79	18.82
	21 yrs – 30 yrs	39.42	42.42	40.58
	31 yrs – 40 yrs	26.92	16.67	22.94
	41 yrs – 50 yrs	11.54	4.55	8.82
	51 yrs – 60 yrs	3.85	1.52	2.94
	61 yrs – 70 yrs	0.96	1.52	1.17
	71 yrs – 80 yrs	0.96	—	0.58
Birth Order	1	47.11	40.91	15.88
	2	24.04	24.24	9.41
	3	8.65	13.64	5.29
	4-5	14.42	16.67	6.46
	6+	5.77	4.55	2.33
Educational Status	Literate	58.65	54.55	57.05
	Illiterate	41.35	45.45	42.95
Level of Education (N = 97)	Up to Middle School	19.67	36.11	25.77
	Up to High School	57.38	36.11	49.48
	Above High School	22.95	27.78	27.74
Marital Status	Married	69.23	62.12	66.47
	Unmarried	30.77	37.88	33.52
Age at Marriage (N = 113)	11 yrs – 15 yrs	5.56	9.76	7.07
	16 yrs – 20 yrs	27.78	58.54	38.93
	21 yrs – 25 yrs	33.33	19.51	28.31
	26 yrs – 30 yrs	22.22	12.20	18.58
	31 yrs – 35 yrs	6.94	—	4.42
	36 yrs – 40 yrs	4.17	—	2.65
Monthly Income	Below Rs.1000	24.03	22.72	23.52
	Rs.1001 – Rs.2000	32.69	34.85	33.52
	Rs.2001 – Rs.3000	22.11	16.67	20.00
	Rs.3001 – Rs. 4000	5.77	6.06	5.88
	Rs.4001 – Rs.5000	4.81	6.06	5.29
	Above 5000	10.58	13.64	11.76
Place of Residence	Rural	40.38	22.73	33.52
	Urban	50.96	56.06	13.52
	Semi-Urban	8.65	21.21	52.94
Type of Locality	Thickly Populated	62.50	74.24	67.05
	Sparsely Populated	37.50	25.76	32.94
Type of Residence	Thatched	73.08	57.58	67.05
	Assam Type	21.15	28.79	24.11
	RCC	4.81	9.09	6.47
	Semi RCC	0.96	4.54	2.35
Ventilation Facility in House	Having Ventilation	77.88	72.73	75.88
	No Ventilation	22.11	27.27	24.11
Age at Detection	1 yr – 10 yrs	5.77	6.06	5.88
	10 yrs – 20 yrs	14.42	33.33	21.76
	21 yrs – 30 yrs	42.31	37.88	40.58
	31 yrs – 40 yrs	21.15	15.15	18.82

(*Contd.*)

Table 30.1 *(Contd.)*

Characters of T.B Patients		*Male*	*Female*	*M + F*
	41 yrs – 50 yrs	11.54	4.55	8.82
	51 yrs – 60 yrs	2.88	1.52	2.35
	61 yrs – 70 yrs	0.96	1.52	1.17
	71 yrs – 80 yrs	0.96	—	0.58
Knowledge of Symptoms	Not Aware of Symptoms Initially	14.42	21.21	17.05
	Aware but Not Worried	14.42	15.15	14.70
	Worried but Not Attended Hospital	23.08	13.64	19.41
	Worried and Attended Hospital	48.08	50.00	48.82
Classification of the Disease	Pulmonary	72.11	75.76	73.52
	Sputum Positive	45.19	57.58	50.00
	Sputum Negative but X-ray Positive	26.92	18.18	23.52
	Extra Pulmonary	27.88	24.24	26.47
	Pleural Effusion	13.46	4.55	10.00
	Abdominal	3.85	4.55	4.11
	Lymphatic Gland	5.77	10.61	7.64
	Tubercular-Meningitis	2.88	3.03	2.94
	Cold Abscess	0.96	—	0.58
	Spinal	0.96	1.52	1.17
Knowledge of Disease	Aware	77.88	78.78	78.23
	Unaware	22.11	21.21	21.76
Knowledge of Treatment	Aware	39.42	43.93	41.18
	Unaware	60.58	56.06	58.82
Type of Diet	Vegetarian	3.85	1.52	2.94
	Non-vegetarian	96.15	98.48	97.05
Sleeping Habit of Pulmonary TB Patients Before Detection	Patients Sharing Their Beds	78.66	84.00	80.80
	Patients Not Sharing Their Beds	21.33	16.00	19.20
Sleeping Habit of Pulmonary TB Patients After Detection	Patients Sharing Their Beds	18.66	30.00	23.20
	Patients Not Sharing Their Beds	81.33	70.00	76.80
Sleeping Habit of Extra Pulmonary TB Patients Before Detection	Patients Sharing Their Beds	89.66	93.75	91.11
	Patients Not Sharing Their Beds	10.34	6.25	8.89
Sleeping Habit of Extra Pulmonary TB Patients After Detection	Patients Sharing Their Beds	44.83	62.50	51.11
	Patients Not Sharing Their Beds	55.17	37.50	48.89

(Contd.)

Table 30.1 *(Contd.)*

Characters of T.B Patients		*Male*	*Female*	*M + F*
Use of Utensils by Pulmonary TB Patients Before Detection	Patients Sharing Their Utensils	81.33	92.00	85.60
	Patients Not Sharing Their Utensils	18.67	8.00	14.40
Use of Utensils by Pulmonary TB Patients After Detection	Patients Sharing Their Utensils	9.33	22.00	14.40
	Patients Not Sharing Their Utensils	90.67	78.00	85.60
Use of Utensils by Extra Pulmonary TB Patients Before Detection	Patients Sharing Their Utensils	96.65	93.76	95.55
	Patients Not Sharing Their Utensils	3.45	6.25	4.44
Use of Utensils by Extra Pulmonary TB Patients After Detection	Patients Sharing Their Utensils	44.83	37.50	42.22
	Patients Not Sharing Their Utensils	55.17	62.50	57.78
Spitting Habits by Pulmonary TB Patients	Spits on Spittoon	22.67	28.00	24.80
	Does Not Spit on Spittoon	77.33	72.00	75.20
Spitting Habits by Extra Pulmonary TB Patients	Spits on Spittoon		6.25	2.22
	Does Not Spit on Spittoon	100.00	93.75	97.78
Believe in Witchcraft	Believe in Witchcraft	40.38	34.85	38.23
	Do Not Believe in Witchcraft	59.62	65.15	61.76
Use of Local Medicine	Taken Local Medicines	38.46	24.24	32.94
	Not Taken Any Local Medicines	61.54	75.76	67.05
Patients Having Past History of TB	Having Past History of TB	34.61	18.18	28.23
	Not Having Past History of TB	65.38	81.82	71.76
Patients Having TB Patients in Family	Family Having TB Patients	32.69	39.39	35.29
	Not Having TB Patients in Family	67.31	60.61	64.71
Patients Having TB Patients in the Neighbourhood	Having TB Patients in the Neighbourhood	36.53	40.91	38.23
	Not Having TB Patients in the Neighbourhood	63.46	59.09	61.76
Attitude Towards Treatment	Taking Medicines Regularly	80.64	81.82	80.95
	Irregular in Taking Medicines	19.35	18.18	19.05
Patients by Level of Improvement	Improved	80.43	82.46	81.20
	No Improvement	19.57	17.54	18.79

(*Contd.*)

Table 30.1 *(Contd.)*

Characters of T.B Patients		Male	Female	M + F
Distance from Dispensary	0 km – 5 km	81.76		
	6 km – 9 km	13.52		
	10+ km	4.71		
Distance from Hospital	0 km – 5 km	50.00		
	6 km – 9 km	20.00		
	10+ km	30.00		

selected were those who had been taking regular medicines as confirmed tuberculosis patients (Pulmonary TB patients – Male = 75, Female = 50; 45 Extra Pulmonary tuberculosis patients – Male = 29, Female = 16) from Doctors at their respective tuberculosis centre. Subjects were unrelated to each other by birth or marriage. Patients willing to cooperate in the present study only selected. A well-informed written consent from the subjects for their willingness to participate in the study was taken.

Results and Discussion

The prevalence of tuberculosis was found to be effected by socio-economic status, nutrition, and family size, use of medical facilities, poverty, overcrowding, customs and beliefs. In the present study, altogether 170 patients have been studied. The number of male patients (104; 61.18%) is more compared to female patients (66; 38.82%). The maximum number of patients (69; 40.58%) is of the age group 21-30 years.

The present study reveals that the frequency of the tuberculosis patients decreases with the increasing birth order. Irrespective of sex, maximum number of patients belongs to the first birth order. Out of 104 male patients, 49 (47.11%) belong to first birth order. Similarly, out of 66 female patients, 27 (40.91%) belong to the first birth order.

Most of the patients (97; 57.05%) are literate while the incidence of illiterates (73; 42.94%) also quite high. A great majority of the subjects (113; 66.47%) are married and 57 (33.52%) are unmarried. Among the married patients, 72 (69.23%) are males and 41 (62.12%) are females while among the unmarried patients, 32 (30.77%) are males and 25 (37.88%) are females.

Certain occupation acts as a contributing factor for the spread of the disease. The subjects of the present study are from different occupational background and mostly from poor economic bracket (Table 30.2). Out

Table 30.2: Distribution of tuberculosis patients by occupation

Occupation	Male	%	Female	%	M + F	%
Labourer	34	32.69	17	25.76	51	30.10
Tea Garden Labourer	19	18.27	11	16.66	30	17.64
Daily Wage Labourer	2	1.92	2	3.03	4	2.35
Painter	2	1.92	—	—	2	1.17
Carpenter	6	5.77	—	—	6	3.52
Rickshaw Puller	2	1.92	—	—	2	1.17
Mason	2	1.92	—	—	2	1.17
Maid Servant	—	—	4	6.06	4	2.35
Barber	1	0.96	—	—	1	0.58
Service	34	32.69	2	3.03	36	21.17
Government Service	16	15.36	2	3.03	18	0.58
Private Service	1	0.96	—	—	1	0.58
Works in Tyre Rethreading Shop	2	1.92	—	—	2	1.17
Works in Private Pharmacy	1	0.96	—	—	1	0.58
Welder	1	0.96	—	—	1	0.58
Works in Factory	1	0.96	—	—	1	0.58
Hotel Accountant	1	0.96	—	—	1	0.58
Mechanics	2	1.92	—	—	2	1.17
Security Guard	1	0.96	—	—	1	0.58
Driver	8	7.69	—	—	8	4.70
Petty Businessman	14	13.46	—	—	14	8.23
Vegetable Vendor	1	0.96	—	—	1	0.58
Business	12	11.54	—	—	12	7.05
Shop Owner	1	0.96	—	—	1	0.58
Agriculturists	9	8.65	2	3.03	11	6.47
Student	7	6.73	9	13.64	16	9.41
Tutor	—	—	1	1.52	1	0.58
Tailor	1	0.96	—	—	1	0.58
Butcher	1	0.96	—	—	1	0.58
Housewife	—	—	22	33.33	22	12.94
Dependant	4	3.85	13	19.69	17	10.00

of 170 patients, 51 (30.10%) are labourers and of them 30 (17.64%) subjects work in tea garden, four (2.35%) earn livelihood as daily wage labourers, others include two (1.17%) rickshaw pullers, 2 (1.17%) are masons, 4 (6.06%) are maidservants and the remaining one (0.96%) is a barber. Again, 36 (21.17%) patients in the present study are service holders who include 18 (10.58%) government service holders, 2 (1.92%) working as mechanics and 1 (0.96%) working in private sector, 8 (7.69%) drivers and 14 (13.46%) earn livelihood as petty businessmen, 1 (0.96%) vegetable vendor, 12 (11.54%) of them are businessmen and 1 (0.96%)

is a shop owner, 11 (6.47%) are agriculturists, 16 (9.41%) are students, 22 (33.33%) are housewives, and 17 (10.00%) are dependents, 1 (1.52%) is private tutor and 1 (0.96%) is tailor and butcher respectively.

The incidence of tuberculosis patients decreases along with the increase in monthly income. Majority of the patients belong to the category where the monthly income ranges from Rs.1001.00 to Rs.2000.00. In the present study, relatively higher number of patients is reported from urban areas (90; 52.94%) which is closely followed by the subjects reside in rural area (57; 33.52%) while only 23 (13.52%) of them reside in semi-urban areas.

Patients reported from thickly populated and having unhygienic living condition is overwhelmingly high (114; 67.05%). On the other hand, patients living in sparsely populated and hygienic living condition are 56 (32.94%) in number. Patient living in thatched houses (114; 67.05%) surpass the patient living in Assam type houses (41; 24.11%). Only a few of them live in R.C.C. building (11; 6.47%) and only four (2.35%) subjects live in semi R.C.C. building. Most of the patients (129; 75.88%) have reported to have ventilation in their residences against 41 (24.11%) patients who lack proper ventilation.

The symptoms of tuberculosis do not usually appear at an early age because although the germ may enter the body at an early age, these remain in a dormant stage for a long period and start multiplying causing infection in the body mainly in the lungs. When the immunity power of the body totally fails to fight with the germ, it becomes active and then all the symptoms of the disease start to appear. Tuberculosis is often found to be detected within the age group 21 to 40 years.

In the present study, the disease has been detected in 69 (40.58%) subjects at the age group of 21-30 years, followed by the age group at 11-20 years (37; 21.76%), 31-40 years (32; 18.82%), 41-50 years (15; 8.82%), 1-10 years (10; 5.88%), 51-60 years (4; 2.35%), and 61-70 years (2; 1.17%). Only 1 (0.58%) male patient who was detected, belongs to the age group of 71-80 years.

Patients mostly reported the symptoms of fever and cough for a prolonged period accompanied with chest pain, swelling in chest, spitting of blood, weakness and loss of appetite, fever and swelling in neck glands, headache, pain and swelling in abdomen, backache, pain in spinal cord and leg pain etc.

It is seen that the subjects, more particularly the female subjects, do not take the symptoms seriously and so do not pay proper attention to these (Table 30.3). When they have fever and cough for more than 3-4 weeks, they usually ignore to go to the doctor for a thorough medical check up and sometimes have medicines of their own. However, when the condition worsens, then only they approach to the doctor. It is evident from the present study that only half of the subjects (83; 48.82%) were worried when symptoms appeared and attended nearby hospitals or health centre, 33 (19.41%) of them were worried but not attended hospital, 29 (17.05%) of them were not at all aware of symptoms initially. Moreover, 25 (14.70%) of them were aware but not worried of the symptoms.

Table 30.3: Distribution of tuberculosis patients by symptoms of detection

Symptoms at detection	*Male*	*%*	*Female*	*%*	*M+F*	*%*
Fever and Cough for three weeks or more	33	31.73	24	36.36	24	33.52
Fever, Cough and Chest pain	25	24.04	15	22.73	15	23.52
Fever, Cough, Chest Pain, Spitting of Blood, Weakness and Loss of Appetite	26	25.00	8	12.12	8	20.00
Fever and Swelling Neck Glands	4	3.85	7	10.61	7	6.47
Fever, Cough, Chest pain, and Swelling in Neck glands	2	1.92	—	—	—	1.17
Fever, Headache and Faint	—	—	3	4.55	3	1.76
Fever, Headache and Pain in Abdomen	5	4.81	4	6.06	4	5.29
Fever, Cough, Backache, Pain in Spinal Cord, and Leg Pain	3	2.88	—	—	—	1.76
Cough for three weeks or more	5	4.81	2	3.03	2	4.11
Swelling in Abdomen	—	—	3	4.55	3	1.76
Swelling in Chest	1	0.96	—	—	—	0.58

Pulmonary tuberculosis occurs more frequently (125; 73.52%) than the extra-pulmonary tuberculosis (45; 26.47%). Out of 125 pulmonary tuberculosis patients, 85 (50.00%) are sputum positive pulmonary tuberculosis patients and 40 (23.52%) are sputum negative but X-ray positive pulmonary tuberculosis patients. Similarly out of forty-five extra-pulmonary tuberculosis patients, 17 (10.0%) are pleural effusion patients, 7 (4.11%) are having abdominal tuberculosis, 13 (7.64%) are suffering from lymphatic gland tuberculosis, 5 (2.94%) are meningitis tuberculosis patients, 2 (1.17%) are spinal tuberculosis patients and one (0.58%) male is cold abscess tuberculosis patients.

It has been noticed that most of the patients (both literate and illiterate) have the knowledge of the disease but are not fully aware of treatment. They know that tuberculosis is a deadly disease but they do not know that today tuberculosis is curable. Some people even do not know that the costly medicines for treatment of tuberculosis is given free of cost at the nearby District Tuberculosis Centre (DTC), State Dispensaries, Public Health Centre (PHC) etc.

Majority of them (133; 78.23%) although are aware of the disease but not many of them (70; 41.76%) are aware of the proper treatment. Due to space problem, the patients usually share rooms with other family

Table 30.4: Distribution of tuberculosis patients by sex and incidence of different habits

Different Habits	*Male*		*Female*		*Total*
	Before detection	*After detection*	*Before detection*	*After detection*	
Chewing Habits					126 (74.11%)
Pan and Beetle	86 (68.25%)	23 (18.25%)	38 (30.15%)	16 (12.69%)	
Tobacco	72 (57.14%)	12 (16.66%)	22 (17.46%)	8 (6.34%)	
Pan and Tobacco	68 (53.96%)	15 (11.90%)	23 (18.25%	5 (3.96%)	
Smoking Habits					39 (22.94%)
Beedi	22 (56.41%)	1 (2.56%)			
Cigarettes	25 (64.10%)	5 (12.82%)			
Beedi and Cigarrate	9 (23.07%)				
Drinking Habits					65 (38.23%)
Alcohol	60 (92.30%)	6 (9.23%)	5 (7.69%)	2 (3.07%)	
Local	8 (12.30%)	6 (9.23%)	5 (7.69%)	2 (3.07%)	
Branded	9 (13.84%)				
Local and Branded	43 (66.15%)				

members. In most of the cases, the pulmonary tuberculosis patients (101; 80.80%) share their bed and sleep together with other family members. However, after detection of the disease many of them (96; 76.80%) do not sleep together following the instruction of the medical practitioner. Out of 170 patients, 126 (74.11%) have chewing habits, 39 (22.94%) have smoking habits and 65 (38.23%) have drinking habits (Table 30.4). However, quite a large number of patients discontinue this ill habit after the detection of the disease.

It is also observed that far-reaching changes occur in the diet and food habits of the patients after detection of the disease. The patients become more conscious about their diet and takes meals regularly with essential nutrients according to their financial capacity. Patients, who can afford, take non-vegetarian items like chicken, egg, fish etc. Usually people take all vegetables and fruits which are available in the season. However, some of them have certain restrictions and religious taboos with regard to certain vegetables like lady's finger, brinjal, tomato, pumpkin, bottle gourd, arum etc. and among citrus fruits like lemon are not taken by some patients in different circumstances. They also do not take certain non-vegetarian food items like *Goroi* fish (*Channa punctatus*), duck's meat, pork and small fishes. The patients also avoid pulses like '*mati dal'* (black gram/*Vigna mungo*).

Tuberculosis is a communicable disease. If proper prevention is not taken, the disease can easily spread from the patients to family members, relatives, friends, neighbourhood etc. Therefore, the items used by the patients for example – the utensils, should be kept away from the others. The doctors also, advice tuberculosis patients (especially the sputum positive patients) to stay in complete isolation and not allow others to use the utensils and other items used by them till their sputum is detected negative.

Before detection of the disease, sharing of utensils with others is a usual practice among the pulmonary tuberculosis patients (107; 85.60%). The situation is same with regard to extra pulmonary tuberculosis patients also. However, such habits have radically changed after detection of the disease.

The germs responsible for tuberculosis usually spread though air by coughing and sneezing by the patient. When a patient coughs, lakhs of tubercle germs come out of the body through patient's sputum, which if not discharged in a proper place, may turn out to be a causative factor for spread of the disease. It is often seen that tuberculosis patients knowingly or unknowingly spit anywhere and as a result, the germs get into the body of a normal person and make her/him a victim. Out of 125 pulmonary tuberculosis patients, only 31 (24.80%) patients use spittoon during discharge of sputum. On the other hand among the extra pulmonary patients 44 patients (97.78%) do not spit in a spittoon, which is considered as a dangerous habit causing the spread of the disease.

In the present sample many patients have strong belief in witchcraft and believe that by the practice of witchcraft they could get rid of the diseases. They have strong belief in indigenous medicines also. Some patients, instead of approaching to the doctor, go for treatment through local medicine.

History of tuberculosis among the patients refers to the occurrence of the disease earlier but not cured completely and the disease relapsed again. Most of the patients do not take the medicines regularly. Many of them have past history of tuberculosis. More than one third of the subjects have family members who were or are victim of tuberculosis. Some of them (65; 38.23%) have in their neighbourhood, person victims of tuberculosis.

Certain diseases like diabetes, cancer and AIDS etc. have a great influence on tuberculosis. These diseases reduce the immunity power of the body and the person easily becomes victim of tuberculosis. These also decrease the rate of recovery of the patients. The present study reveals that many tuberculosis patients suffer from several other diseases also (Table 30.5).

Distance of dispensary and hospital has an important role in the treatment of the disease. In the study area, most of the patients (139; 81.76%) have access to the dispensary, which is located within a radius of 0-5 km. the District Hospital is also located in their close proximity.

Tuberculosis patients who are aware of the fact that DOTS treatment can cure them completely, are very sincere towards the treatment and takes medicines regularly. Also at times due to community and social influence, the patients are misguided and due to one's own insincerity, a patient becomes irregular in his treatment.

Level of improvement is closely related with attitude toward treatment. Tuberculosis requires prolonged treatment. Some patients who had a bit of improvement in their health condition after taking medicines for a few days, become irregular in their treatment. Continuation of certain habits like chewing of pan and beetle nut, drinking etc. greatly affects the patient's health. In addition, lack of proper balanced diet and presence of various other diseases like diabetes etc., also have great impact on the disease. Sign of improvement is reported in majority of the cases (121; 81.21%).

Table 30.5: Distribution of tuberculosis patients suffering from other diseases

Diseases	*Male (N=46)*	*%*	*Female (N=19)*	*%*	*M + F (N=65)*	*%*
Diabetes	4	8.70	—	—	4	6.15
Asthma	1	2.17	—	—	1	1.53
Liver Problem	1	2.17	—	—	1	1.53
Cardiac Disease	1	2.17	1	5.26	2	3.07
Kidney Problem	—	—	1	5.26	1	1.53
Kidney Stone	—	—	1	5.26	1	1.53
Gall Bladder Stone	—	—	2	10.52	2	3.07
Appendicitis	1	2.17	2	10.52	3	4.61
Mentally Retarded	—	—	1	5.26	1	1.53
Malaria	16	34.78	2	10.52	18	27.69
Jaundice	16	34.78	—	—	16	24.61
Pneumonia	1	2.17	—	—	1	1.53
Typhoid	—	—	1	5.26	1	1.53
Cholera	1	2.17	—	—	1	1.53
Stomach Ulcer	1	2.17	—	—	1	1.53
Epilepsy	1	2.17	—	—	1	1.53
Sinus Problem	—		1	5.26	1	1.53
Gastric Problem	1	2.17	6	31.58	7	10.76
Influenza	—	—	1	5.26	1	1.53
Cysticercosis of Brain	1	2.17	—	—	1	1.53

Conclusion

The present study corroborates the earlier findings that tuberculosis afflicts a person in active period of life. The study reveals absence of sex difference in the prevalence of tuberculosis before sixteen years of age; thereafter it is prevalent more in males. This gender difference in reporting and diagnosis of tuberculosis may be due to social stigma attached to tuberculosis. Tuberculosis decreases the women's marriage prospects and increases the married woman's exposure to divorce, increases feeling of insecurity, fear of isolation, which depresses them from acknowledging symptoms and proper care. On the other hand, Folstad and Karter (1992) suggest that a higher level of testosterone in males could have an immunosuppressive effect thereby making males more susceptible to infectious disease. Tuberculosis is also found to occur in patients belonging to the first birth order.

The disease is reported to occur more in married patients than unmarried patients. Since the disease is found to be detected within the age group 21-30 years, it is the period when people are mostly married. In addition, it might have happened that due to lack of care and attention, the single unmarried patients must have died. An enquiry among Indian Army Personnel showed that the married men had a significantly higher incidence of pulmonary tuberculosis than unmarried men. Infection transmitted from family members in their congested room and their precarious nutritional status arising from economic conditions may be the reasons.

The symptoms by which the disease is detected are fever and cough for prolonged period along with chest pain and spitting of blood, weakness and loss of appetite; swelling in neck gland etc. People although are well aware of the symptoms but do not give much importance to these. However, when its severity increases, then only they become worried and visit health centre for checkup by the doctors. Many of them do not have proper information about the treatment also.

It is also found that pulmonary tuberculosis (especially sputum positive pulmonary tuberculosis) occurs in maximum. The sputum positive patients are responsible to spread the germ in a population. There are a number of other factors like locality of a person; ventilation facilities in the house, economic condition etc. which are found to be responsible for the occurrence of the disease. It is observed that people living in unhygienic and thickly populated areas, are caught with the disease in maximum. In such locality, the houses are compactly build and even though they have proper ventilation, still, the air in the surroundings always remain polluted and also the houses are devoid of sufficient amount of sunlight.

The victims of the diseases are reported from different occupational groups, especially more number of patients are found from the labour class. In addition, the disease is also reported among subjects who have very low monthly income. Obviously, in such economic condition, the standard of living will also be low. They pay less importance to health and hygiene. Lower socio-economic condition, less education and lack of hygienic practices and lesser awareness level are found to be responsible for the spread and prevalence of the disease. The living condition of most of these subjects is not very healthy, with many family members staying in small houses with inadequate number of rooms; thus, they are compelled to share rooms, beds and utensils with the other inmates. With regard to sanitation facilities, very few patients had proper toilets and most of them have habits to defecate in the open fields. After detection of the disease, when patients are advised by the doctor about the necessary precaution, majority of them do not follow the advice seriously and thus call for an open invitation to several contagious and infectious diseases.

It is noted that most of the tuberculosis patients rarely use spittoon. Many patients have either smoking, chewing or drinking habits. Maximum patients are found to be non-vegetarian. However, some patients are found to have stopped taking certain non-vegetarian items like pork, duck's meat, small fishes etc. and some vegetables like brinjal, pumpkin, bottle gourd, lady's finger, tomato, arum, lemon etc. following their respective traditional customs.

Some patients have past history of tuberculosis while some have tuberculosis victims in their family or in the neighbourhood. Many patients have access to District Hospital, Public Health Centre close to their residence, which enhance the regular intake of medicines by the patients. There is lack of awareness among the people, however.

It is now urgent that we find ways to combat tuberculosis, one of the fatal infectious diseases worldwide. In this regard mass awareness campaign with the help of media, NGO etc. should be given priority. World Health Organization already declared tuberculosis as a global emergency in 1993. Proper health education should be provided in all sections of the society. Discussions and seminars in schools, colleges, and universities etc. to educate the children and youth about tuberculosis, its evil effects and most necessarily about its treatment, should be undertaken. Only then, we can hope of winning the age-old battle against tuberculosis.

Acknowledgements

All subjects who participated in the study are gratefully acknowledged. Special thanks are due to Prof. (Mrs) N. Choudhury, former Principal Assam Medical College and Hospital, Dibrugarh; Dr. D.K. Bhattacharjee and Dr. B. Hazarika, Tuberculosis and Other Chest Diseases, AMCH, Dibrugarh; Dr. U.N. Bora and Dr. S. Dutta Bhuyan, District Tuberculosis Officer; Dr. M. Barua, Tuberculosis Centre, Dibrugarh; Dr. S. Medhi, Lankashi Tea Estate Hospital, Tinsukia; and Dr. J. Biswas, Dibrugarh for their active support in the present study.

REFERENCES

Biswas, D. (2004), *A Biosocial Study of Tuberculosis Patients*, Unpublished M.Sc. Dissertation, Anthropology Department, Dibrugarh University.

Comstock, G. W. (1978), Tuberculosis in twins: A reanalysis of the Prophit survey. *Am.Rev.Respair.Dis*. 117 : 621-624.

Folstad, I. and A.J. Karter. (1992), Parasites, Bright Males and the Immunocompetance Handicap. *American Naturalist*. 139 : 603-622.

Guidelines for Revised National Tuberculosis Control Programme. (1997), Central TB Division, Directorate General of Health Services, Ministry of Health and Family Welfare, Nirman Bhavan, New Delhi.

Narzary, P.K. and B. Narzary, (2005), Treatment seeking behaviour of the tuberculosis among Bodo tribe in India, *Studies on Tribes and Tribals*. 3, 2: 129-132.

Tungdim, M.G. and S. Kapoor (2008) Tuberculosis treatment and nutritional status among the tribals of North East India, *Acta Biol. Szeged*. 52, 2 : 323–327.

Tungdim, M.G.; S. Kapoor and A.K. Kapoor (2008), Tribes, tuberculosis and treatment: A study in North East India. In R.K. Pathak, A.K. Sinha, B.G. Banerjee, R.N. Vashisth, and C.J. Edwin (Eds): *Biosocial Issues in Health*, pp 520-528. North Book Centre, New Delhi.

Tungdim, M.G. and A.K. Kapoor (2010a), Nutritional status and chronic disease among the adult tribal population of North East India. *The Open Anthropology Journal*. 3: 188–191.

Tungdim, M.G. and S. Kapoor (2010b), Gender differentials in Tuberculosis: Impact of socio-economic and cultural factors among the tribals of North East India. *The Open Social Science Journal*. 3 : 68–74.

14 Index